SIR NICHOLAS HARRIS NICOLAS was born in 1799, and served in the Royal Navy in the Mediterranean from 1808 to 1816 under Admiral Duckworth and Lord Exmouth. Retired on half-pay at the end of the Napoleonic Wars, he turned to antiquarian and literary pursuits after a brief legal career, compiling and editing a large number of scholarly works. This seven-volume annotated compilation of Nelson's correspondence was originally published by Henry Colburn between 1844 and 1847, and was to be followed by his ambitious *A History of the British Navy, from the Earliest Times to the Wars of the French Revolution*, but when he died in France in 1848, only the first two volumes, covering up to the year 1422, had been completed.

THE

DISPATCHES AND LETTERS

OF

VICE ADMIRAL

LORD VISCOUNT NELSON

WITH NOTES BY

SIR NICHOLAS HARRIS NICOLAS, G.C.M.G.

" The Nation expected, and was entitled to expect, that while Cities vied with each other in consecrating Statues in marble and brass to the memory of our NELSON, a Literary Monument would be erected, which should record his deeds for the immortal honour of his own Country, and the admiration of the rest of the World." — QUARTERLY REVIEW.

THE FOURTH VOLUME.

SEPTEMBER 1799 TO DECEMBER 1801.

CHATHAM PUBLISHING

LONDON

Published in 1998 by
Chatham Publishing,
1 & 2 Faulkner's Alley, Cowcross Street,
London EC1M 6DD

Chatham Publishing is an imprint of
Gerald Duckworth an Co Ltd

First Published in 1845
by Henry Colburn

ISBN 1 86176 051 5

A catalogue record for this book is available
from the British Library

Printed and bound in Great Britain by
Redwood Books, Trowbridge, Wiltshire

PREFACE.

The Letters of Lord Nelson in this Volume commence while he was still acting as Commander-in-Chief in the Mediterranean, and extend from September 1799, to December 1801, a period of two years and four months. His Correspondence, until the arrival of Lord Keith in that command, related principally to the blockade of La Valetta in Malta; to the business of his Squadron; and to the affairs of Sicily, Turkey, Egypt, and the Roman States.

The appointment of Lord Keith so deeply mortified his feelings, (for he did not expect that any Officer would be placed over him in the Mediterranean, after the retirement of Earl St. Vincent,) that he determined to return to England, as soon as he had obtained the permission of the Admiralty. In the meantime, he joined Lord Keith at Leghorn, accompanied him to Palermo, and thence to Malta. On the 18th of February 1800, Lord Nelson, in the Foudroyant, with other Ships, captured " Le Généreux," of seventy-four guns, a prize of the greatest value in his opinion, because she was one of the only two Ships of the Line that had escaped at the Nile; and, to his infinite satisfaction, the other, "Le Guillaume Tell," was also taken by the Foudroyant and a small Squadron, in the following month; when the whole of the French Fleet present in that Battle, were thus either captured or destroyed.

LORD NELSON was left by Lord Keith in command of the blockade of Malta in February 1800, but his health obliged him to return to Palermo, where he remained until June; and then, having the Queen of Naples and her children, and Sir William and Lady Hamilton on board, he proceeded in the Foudroyant to Leghorn. He struck his Flag on the 13th of July, and set out for England, by way of Ancona, Trieste, Vienna, and Hamburgh, being everywhere received on his journey with marks of veneration and respect. He arrived in England on the 6th of November, and instantly reported himself to the Admiralty as ready to serve. The offer was accepted; and having, on the 1st of January 1801, been promoted to the rank of VICE-ADMIRAL OF THE BLUE, he was directed to hoist his Flag in the San Josef, under the Earl of St. Vincent, in the Channel Fleet.

A formidable Coalition having been formed against this Country, by Russia, Denmark, and Sweden, it became expedient, in March 1801, to send an Armament to the Baltic, when a large Fleet was placed under Admiral Sir Hyde Parker, of which LORD NELSON was appointed Second in Command, with his Flag in the Saint George.

Hence ensued, on the 2nd of April 1801, the memorable BATTLE OF COPENHAGEN, in which NELSON was the
real Chief, and, as the inevitable consequence, another
great Naval Victory. A few weeks after that event,
he succeeded to the Command of the Baltic Fleet,
but he retained it only until the 19th of June, when
the state of his health compelled him to return to
England.

No part of NELSON'S Correspondence is more remarkable or characteristic than his Letters after the
Battle of Copenhagen—his well-known Note " To the
Brothers of Englishmen, the Danes"—the account of
his interview with the Prince Royal of Denmark—his
spirited remonstrance against the official report of the
Danish Commodore—his indignant complaints that the
gallantry of his Captains had not, as after other great
Battles, been rewarded with Medals, and that the City
of London had withheld its Thanks from those who had
fought on that occasion. " I long to have the Medal for
Copenhagen," he said, " which I would not give up to be
made an English Duke;" and the refusal to bestow that
simple distinction, was the more severely felt by him, because there can be no doubt that it had been promised;
and still more, because no reward whatever was bestowed
on the Captains who had signalized themselves, with
whom NELSON always identified himself. "I am," he said,
" fixed never to abandon the fair fame of my Companions
in dangers. I may offend, and suffer ; but I had rather
suffer from that, than my own feelings." His Corre-

spondence with the Danish, Swedish, and Russian Authorities, is no less interesting; but few will share
NELSON'S surprise, that his arrival in the Bay of Revel,
with eleven Sail of the Line, at a most critical state of
affairs, was not deemed a *compliment* by the Emperor
of Russia; or think that, because he had not actually
brought the *whole* of his Squadron, nor a Bomb, nor a
Fire-ship, his intentions ought not to have created any
uneasiness !

Buonaparte's threat of Invasion, and the appearance of
a large Army and Flotilla at Boulogne, in the summer of
1801, rendered it necessary to prepare a Squadron speci-
ally for the defence of the English Coast, and to entrust
it to an Officer who enjoyed the confidence of the Nation.
Public opinion pointed unanimously to NELSON ; and he
was, accordingly, on the 24th of July, made Commander-
in-Chief, from Orfordness to Beachy Head.   From that
time to nearly the end of 1801, his Correspondence
relates principally to the duties of his Command, and the
proceedings of his Squadron.   It proves that his zeal,
abilities, and energy were unabated ; and he had the
happiness of knowing that, so long as the defence of the
Coast was in his hands, not even a single Boat had been
captured by the Enemy.   But it was a sense of duty
alone which induced him to accept that Service.   Its
nature and details were new and disagreeable to him;
and his health was unequal to the labour it required.
To these causes, added to the disappointment about the
Medals for Copenhagen, to the neglect of the City of

London, and to pecuniary inconvenience, (for having settled half his income upon Lady Nelson, and con- tributed largely out of the remainder to the support or assistance of his relations, he was scarcely able to maintain his rank,) the irritability and discontent shown in some of his Letters, may fairly be attributed. His pri- vate Letters, and particularly those in which he speaks of his protégé, Captain Parker, while that gallant Officer was lingering from the fatal wound he received in the attack on Boulogne, are additional and affecting evidence of the warmth and goodness of his heart.

The Government had not been altogether unmind- ful of NELSON'S merits. Besides a VISCOUNTCY, he obtained the grant of a new BARONY OF NELSON to the descendants of his Father, in case he should die without heirs male of his own body ; and he was, doubtless, informed by his friend Mr. Addington, the Prime Minister, of the gracious manner in which the King had signified his consent to that measure.[1]

After the Preliminaries of Peace were ratified, LORD NELSON obtained leave of absence ; and, though he was not actually relieved from his Command until April 1802, he lived mostly at Merton in Surrey, (where he had purchased a small estate,) from November 1801, until he was appointed Commander-in-Chief in the Mediterranean, in May 1803.

A few words are required respecting the additional Letters with which the Editor has been favoured since

[1] Vide p. 424, post.

the publication of the last Volume. In the Preface to
the Second Volume, it was said that Vice-Admiral Sir
William Parker, the possessor of LORD NELSON's Correspondence with the Earl of St. Vincent, had expressed
his desire to afford him any assistance, as soon as he
had had an opportunity of examining those papers.
Sir William Parker has lately been so good as to fulfil
that intention, by sending him, through Mr. Jedediah
Stephens Tucker, a great number of Letters of LORD
NELSON, from the year 1797 to 1804, being the *originals*
of some that have been partly printed in this Work, from
Drs. Clarke and M'Arthur's " Life of Nelson," together
with others that had never been published. The Editor
regrets, however, to find that several important Letters
to Earl St. Vincent, which Drs. Clarke and M'Arthur
seem to have obtained from his Lordship, are no longer
in that collection. Mr. Tucker informs him that " he
has forwarded all the Letters in his custody, except some
which he had sent to Sir William Parker for his consideration, among which may be part of the Letters in question; but he had heard that many Letters which Lord
St. Vincent had himself lent to Authors, were never
returned."

One of the most valuable contributions with which
the Editor has been favoured, is from Colonel Hugh
Percy Davison, consisting of nearly one hundred Original
Letters from LORD NELSON to his confidential friend, the
late Alexander Davison, Esq., from the year 1797 until
within a week of the Battle of Trafalgar, and relating

to almost every circumstance, public or private, in which LORD NELSON was interested. So much of the present Volume had, unfortunately, been printed before these valuable Papers reached the Editor's hands, that the earliest of the Letters to Mr. Davison which he could insert, from the autograph, is dated in May 1801.

The Letters to the late Admiral Skeffington Lutwidge, which occur in this Volume, remind the Editor that he accidentally omitted, in his former acknowledgments to Contributors, to include the name of the Admiral's nephew, Major Lutwidge: he begs leave now, however, to offer that gentleman his best thanks, and to apologize for the omission.

1st September, 1845.

CONTENTS.

LETTERS.

1799.

1799, *continued.*

1799, *continued.*

1799, *continued.*

1799, *continued.*

1800, *continued.*

1800, *continued.*

1800, *continued.*

1801, *continued.*

1801, *continued.*

1801, *continued.*

1801, *continued.*

1801, *continued.*

1801, *continued.*

1801, *continued.*

APPENDIX.

ERRATUM.

P. 176, l. 16, *for* " Tuesday, 14th June," *read* " Tuesday, 14th January, 1800."

ANALYSIS

OF THE

LIFE OF NELSON,

FROM SEPTEMBER 1799 TO DECEMBER 1801.

YEAR.	MONTH.		FACTS.

1799.

— September 1st to — October 4th { REAR-ADMIRAL OF THE RED, acting as Commander-in-Chief in the Mediterranean, with his Flag in the *Samuel and Jane* Transport, at Palermo, until the 4th of October, when it was re-hoisted in the *Foudroyant.*

— — 5th ....Sailed from Palermo.

— — 12th ....Off Mahon.

— — 13th ....Anchored in Mahon Harbour.

— — 18th ....Sailed from Mahon.

— — 22nd ....Arrived at Palermo.

— — 23rd to
1800. January 15th { At Palermo. On the 29th of October he shifted his Flag to the *Perseus* Bomb: on the return of the *Foudroyant* on the 17th of November, it was re-hoisted on board of her; but it was removed to the *Atty* Transport on the 25th of that month. On the 30th of November, LORD NELSON was directed to place himself under the command of Vice-Admiral Lord Keith, which orders he received on the 6th of January 1800; and on the 14th of that month, he re-hoisted his Flag in the *Foudroyant.*

— — 16th ....Sailed in the Foudroyant from Palermo.

— — 20th ....Arrived in Leghorn Roads and joined Vice-Admiral Lord Keith.

— — 25th ....Sailed from Leghorn in company with Lord Keith.

YEAR.	MONTH.		FACTS.

1800, *continued* .. ..REAR-ADMIRAL OF THE RED, in the Mediterranean.

— February 1st ......Off Monte Christi.

— — 3rd ......Arrived at Palermo.

— — 12th ......Sailed from Palermo in company with Lord Keith, and passed through the Faro of Messina for Malta.

— — 18th ......Off Cape Passaro, in Sicily. The *Foudroyant*, *Northumberland*, *Audacious*, *Success* Frigate, and *El Corso* Brig, fell in with a French Squadron under Rear-Admiral Perrée in *Le Généreux*, and captured that Ship and a Frigate.

— — 19th ⎫
      to ⎬ Off Malta. On the 24th of February, Lord Keith left him in command of the Squadron blockading La Valetta.
— March 10th ⎭

— — 16th ....Arrived in the Foudroyant at Palermo.

⎛ At Palermo. On the 24th of March, he shifted his Flag to a Transport, the *Foudroyant* having returned to the blockade of Malta, off which Island, under the command of Captain Sir Edward Berry, in company with the *Lion* and *Penelope*, she captured *Le Guillaume Tell* on the 30th of March. Removed his Flag from the Transport to the *Peterel* on the 19th, and to the *Foudroyant* on the 21st of April.
      to ⎨
— April 23rd ⎝

— — 24th ....Sailed from Palermo in the Foudroyant, having Sir William and Lady Hamilton on board.

— — 30th ....Arrived at Syracuse.

— May 3rd ....Sailed from Syracuse.

— — 4th ....Anchored in St. Paul's Bay, Malta.

— — 11th .. ..Anchored in Marsa Sirocco Bay, Malta.

— — 20th ....Under sail, off Malta.

— June 1st ....Arrived in the *Foudroyant* at Palermo.

      to ⎰ At Palermo. On the 2nd of June he was appointed a Knight Grand Cross of the Order of St. Ferdinand and Merit of the Two Sicilies.
— — 9th ⎱

— — 10th...............Sailed in the *Foudroyant* for Leghorn, having on board the Queen of Naples, three Princesses, and Prince Leopold, and Sir William and Lady Hamilton.

— — 14th...............Arrived at Leghorn.

      to ⎛ At Leghorn, on the 28th of June, he shifted his Flag to the *Alexander*; and on the 9th of July, the Queen of Sicily, with her children, took refuge on board that Ship, but landed the next day.
— July 12th ⎝

YEAR.   MONTH.   FACTS.

1800, *continued* .... REAR-ADMIRAL OF THE RED.

—   July 13th ....Struck his Flag.

—   — 17th...............Left Leghorn, on his way to England, with Sir William and Lady Hamilton.

—   — 19th...............Arrival at Florence.

—   — 24th...............At Ancona, embarked on board a Russian Frigate for Trieste.

— August 9th...............At Trieste.

— September 25th   ...At Vienna.
to

—   —   26th ......Left Vienna.

—   —   29th ......At Prague, and thence proceeded to Magde-burg and Hamburgh.

— November 6th   ......Landed at Yarmouth.

In London. On the 10th, (Lord Mayor's Day,)

—   —   8th   he dined with the Lord Mayor, and received
to   the Sword voted to him by the City of Lon-

— December 15th   don. On the 20th, he took his Seat in the House of Lords.

—   —   20th ......Visited Salisbury, Fonthill, &c.

—   —   29th ......Returned to London.

1801. January 1st............Promoted to be VICE-ADMIRAL OF THE BLUE, and was soon after ordered to hoist his Flag in the *San Josef* at Plymouth, in the Chan-nel Fleet, under Earl St. Vincent.

—   —   13th ....Finally separated from Lady Nelson, and left London for Plymouth.

—   —   17th ....Hoisted his Flag in the *San Josef* at Ply-mouth.

—   —   21st ....At Exeter, when he received the Freedom of that City.

—   —   23rd   At Plymouth, and was admitted a Freeman of
to   that Borough on the 24th.

—   —   30th

In Torbay. On the 12th of February, he shifted his Flag to the *Saint George;* and

— February 2nd   on the 17th of that month, was ordered
to   to place himself under the command of

19th   Admiral Sir Hyde Parker, in the Fleet destined for the Baltic; on the following day was directed to proceed to Spithead.

—   —   21st.........Arrived in the *Saint George* at Spithead, and on the 23rd, proceeded, on leave for three days, to London.

— March 2nd ....Sailed from Spithead for Yarmouth

YEAR.	MONTH.	FACTS.

1801, *continued* ... .VICE-ADMIRAL OF THE BLUE, Second in Command in the Baltic.

— March 6th
   to
— — 11th } At Yarmouth, where he joined Admiral Sir Hyde Parker.

— — 12th ....Sailed with the Fleet, under Admiral Sir Hyde Parker for the Baltic.

— — 18th ....Reached the Naze.

— — 19th ....Off the Scaw.

— — 24th ....Off Elsineur.

— — 26th ....Sailed for the Great Belt; but returned in the evening to the anchorage off Elsineur.

— — 29th ....Shifted his Flag from the *Saint George* to the *Elephant.*

— — 30th ....Proceeded with the Fleet through the Sound, and about noon, anchored between the Island of Huen and Copenhagen.

— April 1st ....The Fleet removed to an anchorage within two miles of Copenhagen; and at one P.M. the Division of Ships placed under his command weighed, and in the evening anchored off Draco.

— — 2nd ....BATTLE OF COPENHAGEN.

— — 3rd...............Rehoisted his Flag on board the *Saint George.*

— — 9th...............Signed an Armistice with Denmark.

— — 19th ....Went in a Boat from the *Saint George* in Copenhagen Roads to the Fleet under Sir Hyde Parker, which had sailed in pursuit of the Swedish Squadron; was soon after followed by his own Ship, the *Saint George*, and proceeded in her, with the Fleet, to Carlscrona.

— — 27th
   to
— May 6th } In Kioge Bay. On the 5th of May, he received his appointment as COMMANDER-IN-CHIEF in the Baltic, dated on the 21st of April.

— — 7th ....Sailed from Kioge Bay.

— — 11th ....At the entrance of the Gulf of Finland.

— — 12th
   to
— — 16th } ....In Revel Roads.

— — 17th ....Sailed from Revel, and applied to be superseded in the command, in consequence of ill health.

— — 19th ....Off Gothland.

— — 22nd ....Created VISCOUNT NELSON OF THE NILE AND OF BURNHAM THORPE in the County of Norfolk.

| YEAR. | MONTH. | FACTS. |

1801, *continued* ....VICE-ADMIRAL OF THE BLUE.

— May 24th
    to   }...Off Rostock.
— June 1st

— — 4th
    to   In Kioge Bay. On the 14th of June he Invested Rear-Admiral Graves with the Ensigns of the Order of the Bath, on board the *St. George.*
— — 18th

— — 19th ....Resigned the command of the Baltic Fleet, and sailed in the *Kite* Brig for England.

— July 1st ....Arrived at Yarmouth.

— — 2nd
    to   In London. On the 24th of July he was appointed COMMANDER-IN-CHIEF of a Squadron employed between Orfordness and Beachy Head, to prevent an Invasion.
— — 28th

— — 27th..............Hoisted his Flag on board *L'Unité* at Sheerness.

— — 29th..............Hoisted his Flag on board the *Leyden* in the Downs.

— August 2nd

    to

— December 31st

At divers places on his Station, with his Flag in the *Medusa*, Captain John Gore. On the 16th of August, he made an attack on the Enemy's Flotilla at Boulogne, without success. On the 18th of August was created BARON NELSON OF THE NILE AND OF HILBOROUGH IN THE COUNTY OF NORFOLK, with special remainders. About the 27th of August he shifted his Flag to the *Amazon*, Captain Samuel Sutton. On the 22nd of October he proceeded to Merton on leave of absence, and on the 29th of that month, took his Seat in the House of Lords as a Viscount.

LETTERS.

1799—ÆT. 40.

TO CAPTAIN COCKBURN, H.M. SHIP LA MINERVE.

[Order-Book.]

The Samuel and Jane Transport, at Palermo, 3rd September,[1] 1799.

You are hereby required and directed to proceed in His Majesty's Ship, under your command, to Gibraltar, and put yourself under the command of Rear-Admiral Duckworth, or the senior Officer at that place, following his orders for your further proceedings. But should it so happen that you are the senior Officer at that place, you will use your endeavours to succour the Garrison, and yield them every assistance in your power to procure supplies and keep the Ports on the coast of Barbary open, and protect the trade in the Gut from the Enemy's gun-boats, &c.

NELSON.

TO THE COMMANDING OFFICER OF HIS MAJESTY'S SHIPS AT GIBRALTAR AND OFF CADIZ.

[Letter-Book.]

Palermo, 4th September, 1799.

The Minerve I consider as such an active Ship, and most particularly her Captain, that I must desire that on no account you will send her off the limits of the Mediterranean station: no one is more equal to watch Cadiz, until an equal force may get there, than Captain Cockburn. I am, &c.

NELSON.

[1] On this day, being the anniversary of that on which the news of the Battle of the Nile reached Naples, a magnificent entertainment was given at Palermo, in honour of Nelson and his companions, in the name of the young Prince Leopold.

TO EVAN NEPEAN, ESQ., ADMIRALTY.

[Original, in the Admiralty.]

Samuel and Jane Transport, Palermo, 4th September, 1799.

Sir,

I beg leave to enclose you a letter I have received from Commodore Troubridge, respecting Mr. Daniel Butler Dawes, Purser of His Majesty's Ship Culloden, whom I appointed to act as Commissary to the English and Portuguese Marines, landed from the Squadron under my command at Naples, for reduction of St. Elmo and Capua. As his appointment did not make mention of any salary or emoluments, his accounts have been made up without his even being reimbursed some necessary expenses he has been at; but as no salary can be adequate to his zeal and services, and the fatigue he has gone through on this occasion, and the great satisfaction he has given to all, I must beg leave to recommend him to the notice of their Lordships, as highly deserving promotion. I have the honour to be, &c.

NELSON.

TO CAPTAIN HARDY, H. M. SHIP FOUDROYANT.

[Order-Book.]

The Samuel and Jane Transport, Palermo, 4th September, 1799.

You are hereby required and directed to proceed in His Majesty's Ship, under your command, to Cagliari in Sardinia, and receive on board their Sardinian Majesties and Family, with such other persons as he may think proper to take with him, and proceed without loss of time to Genoa or Leghorn, as His Majesty may think proper, when, having landed them, you will return and join me at this place. But should His Majesty not be ready to embark when you arrive at Cagliari, you will immediately return here, previously informing yourself of the probable time he may be ready; or request him to appoint some period, when a Ship shall be ready to attend him as near the time he may appoint as possible.

NELSON.

TO THE RIGHT HONOURABLE EARL SPENCER, K.G.

[Letter-Book.]

My dear Lord,　　　　　　Palermo, September 4th, 1799.

The courier by which I wrote my letter fourteen days since, is still at Palermo, and the time of his departure so uncertain that I am determined to tell you briefly our situation. The Turkish and Russian Squadron, now united with Vice-Admiral Kartzow, are eleven Sail of the Line, Frigates, &c. The object of the Russian Admiral is Malta solely; as to the idea of going to Naples to land troops, in order to go into the Roman State, or to prevent anarchy in the Kingdom, those are to him secondary operations. It is my intention to have six or seven Sail of the Line at Gibraltar, and four at Minorca, but at present I cannot send all this force down, as Commodore Troubridge is at Naples, which he cannot leave, until the Russian Admiral sends Ships to supply the place of these Ships. The Russian Admiral makes no secret that his Ships cannot keep the sea during the winter, and the Turks we know cannot, therefore if the Coast of Naples requires a Naval Force during that season, His Sicilian Majesty is likely to be in a worse state than before the arrival of this United Squadron. The Portuguese Squadron must return home, and the Alexander, Audacious, and Lion are in a truly wretched state; therefore the Foudroyant will be the only Ship of the present force, this side Minorca, fit for service. I have just heard accounts that the Spaniards have not four Sail of the Line at Carthagena—therefore I shall detain the Minotaur, and send Troubridge to arrange a proper Naval protection for the security of Minorca, which I have never yet considered in the *smallest* danger, but it has been a misfortune that others have thought differently from me on that point.[2] I send you a letter from General Acton. It will convey to your Lordship an idea of my situation here. It is indeed an uncomfortable one; for plain common sense points out that the King should return to Naples, but nothing can move him. Believe me I shall do my best in all circumstances, but I am almost blind, and truly very unwell; and, which does not mend matters, I see no King in Europe really assisting these good Monarchs, but our gracious Sovereign. I am, &c.,　　　　NELSON.

[2] Vide vol. iii. p. 410.

TO CAPTAIN BALL.

[Letter-Book.]

Palermo, September 5th, 1799.

My dear Ball,

Mr. Alos is, doubtless, a scoundrel. He had persuaded some here that he had an interview with Vaubois,[2] which I believe is a lie; and as to his conduct with the Maltese, it was probably to show his consequence. I am sure the good Queen never had a thought of any underhand work against us; therefore I would recommend sending him here with a kick in the breech, and let all the matter drop. The Russians are anxious to get to Malta, and care for nothing else—therefore I hope you will get it before their arrival. The Strombolo carries a mortar, and I think from the number of men which can be landed from the Squadron, that we shall very soon call it ours. There is a great scarcity of corn in this Island—therefore I fear the supplies for Malta will be very small. You must not expect any troops from Messina. I thank you, my dear Ball, for all your goodness to me, and be assured I retain the full impression of it. I have letters from Suwarrow,[3] detailing the glorious battle of Novi, in which the French lost 20,000 men, by their own account. I am, &c.,

NELSON.

TO COMMODORE TROUBRIDGE, H. M. SHIP CULLODEN.

[Letter-Book.]

Palermo, September 5th, 1799.

My dear Troubridge,

I send you the Transfer, that you may employ her till the Turks and Russians go to Naples; but the thoughts of the latter is only Malta. I agree in all you say of the state of Naples, and of the necessity of his Majesty's return to Naples; but I am afraid our preaching is really spending our breath for no good purpose. I see the misfortune of our Naval force being withdrawn at this moment from the Coast of Italy, but

---

[2] The French Commandant at Valetta.
[3] Printed by Clarke and M'Arthur, vol. ii. p. 216.

what can I do? I dare say the account from Cadiz is as erroneous as that from Carthagena; but we bear all this, and more. Foley did not join Hallowell in time to send in the Summons; for the Peterel joined at the same moment, and they properly immediately sailed for this place, and depart for Gibraltar this evening. I am, &c.,

NELSON.

TO THE MARQUIS DE NIZA.

[Letter-Book.]

My dear Marquis,   September 5th, 1799.

I send the Strombolo, and a large mortar; and I hope, from the number of people you will be able to land, that La Valetta will fall to your efforts. The Russians are very anxious to go there—therefore I am doubly interested for your success. May God Almighty crown your efforts with success, is the prayer of your affectionate,

NELSON.

TO REAR-ADMIRAL DUCKWORTH.

[Letter-Book.]

My dear Admiral,   Palermo, September 5th, 1799.

Should the force sent down to Gibraltar be more than is necessary for guarding Cadiz, you will send me the North-umberland, or such other Ship as may be able to keep the sea during the winter; for the Russian Admiral has already told me that his Ships cannot. In short, for active operations, none but English Ships are of use. Marquis de Niza is off Malta, where also the Russian Admiral wishes to go; for he thinks the Port of Malta the most pleasing station. I am, &c.

NELSON.

TO EARL SPENCER, K.G.

[Letter-Book.]

My dear Lord,   September 6th, 1799.

I send you a copy of the Queen's letter to Lady Hamilton, as a postscript to that of General Acton. The King has

prevailed on the Russian Admiral to go to Naples, but the
more I see, the more I am satisfied they can do no good for
active operations, and that they will be a dead weight on
their Sicilian Majesties. The Russian Admiral has a polished
outside, but the bear is close to the skin. He is jealous of
our influence, and thinks whatever is proposed, that we are at
the bottom. The Turk, who is by no means a fool—on the
contrary, has more natural sense than the other—is our brother;
and I am sure there is not a thing that we could desire him
to do that he would not instantly comply with. I make use of
the word 'we,' as both Sir William and Lady Hamilton have
more merit in gaining the affection and implicit confidence
of Cadir Bey and his Officers, than I have. The Austrians
are only ten miles from Rome. Ever, my dear Lord, &c.,

                                                    NELSON.

TO CAPTAIN TROUBRIDGE, H.M. SHIP CULLODEN.

[Letter-Book.]

Most secret.

                                      Palermo, September 7th, 1799.
My dear Troubridge,
    Having secured the free access of the Straits by the force
detached to Gibraltar, and, from your account and Hood's,
being perfectly at my ease about Minorca, you have my full
permission to either immediately send Louis to Città Vecchia,
with what Vessels you can give him, Perseus—or to keep
under sail when you think the Russians and Turks are approaching, and go direct to Città Vecchia, and try what can
be done; and if you can get possession, then to land not
only your Marines, but such other force as you can spare, and
not to move till further orders from me; for, as I have before
said, I am perfectly easy about Minorca. Now you know my
sentiments, you will act and arrange accordingly; but this
must be kept secret, or we shall give jealousy to the Russians.
As for the Turks, we can do anything with them. They are
good people, but perfectly useless. I think if you go, you
had better keep Captain Dunn, although I believe he has
stock on board for Duckworth. Do you manage this; for he

sails with Secret orders. Your Boatswain's mate shall have an Acting order, and Harriman will, of course, travel with you. All here join in regard. I am, &c.,

NELSON.

TO CAPTAIN TROUBRIDGE.

[Letter-Book.]

Most secret.

September 7th, 1799.

My dear Troubridge,

The Perseus is this moment arrived. I am not surprised at what you tell me about Procida, but never mind it. If the Russian frigates will tell you that they are to stay at Naples, and you think the Capital will remain quiet, I would have you go immediately to Cività Vecchia—not telling any person where you are going. The Perseus stays to take her anchor and a new cable. She shall follow you to Cività Vecchia, if she misses you at Naples. I am, &c.,

NELSON.

TO J. SPENCER SMITH, ESQ.

[From a Copy in the Nelson Papers.]

Palermo, 10th September, 1799.

My dear Sir,

As Sir William Hamilton has told your Excellency the whole of the very unpleasant affair which happened on Sunday last,[4] I shall only say, that no fault attaches itself in the least to *Cadir Bey*; for a man of more conciliating manners does not exist, and he has gained all our hearts in this house, in which he is considered as a brother. Poor fellow! he is full of affliction, fearing that his enemies, if it is possible he can

---

[4] Miss Knight says in her *Journal*—"Unfortunately, in the town an affray happened between the Palermitans and some of the Turkish sailors. Some of the first, and many of the latter were killed; and the Turks were so much irritated with the cruelty of the Sicilians, that they rose against their Admiral, and obliged him to return with his Squadron to Corfu." Lord Nelson went on board of the Turkish Admiral's Ship, and subdued the disturbance. The subject is again noticed by Lord Nelson, in pp. 11, 17.

have any, may do him an injury with the Sultan. That
nothing of that kind may happen, I beg your kindness. I
have examined his Ship with much attention, and could not
but admire her extreme good order and remarkable cleanli-
ness.   Your exertion of good offices for Cadir Bey, will much
oblige us all.   Since I wrote you a line, about fourteen days
back, I have not had a Vessel from the westward.   Although
it is now six weeks since Lord Keith passed the Straits, I
have heard nothing of his movements.   If he can but meet the
Combined fleet, I shall be happy.   In Italy all goes on well,
although the Austrian Eagle appears to wish to cover with his
wings more than I think the other Powers will allow him.

By desire of Cadir Bey, I have presumed to write a line to
the Grand Signior, of which I send your Excellency a copy.
I sincerely hope your brother has returned to Constantinople,
having finished his hard expedition : if so, you will make my
kindest regards to him, and believe me, my dear Sir, your
obliged and faithful servant,

NELSON.[5]

TO HIS IMPERIAL MAJESTY THE GRAND SIGNIOR.

[Letter-Book. This letter was enclosed to the Capitan Pasha.]

Palermo, 10th September, 1799.

Sire,
I trust that your Imperial Majesty will permit the servant
of your most faithful Ally to bear his testimony to the good
conduct of your Admiral, Cadir Bey.   I can assure your
Majesty that Ships in higher order cannot be than those under
his command, and the little disturbance which arose in this
place has not been owing to any want of attention from your
Majesty's Admiral.   Cadir Bey is with me every day, and a
better man does not live in the world, or a better Officer : he
is my brother.   And I am, in the truest sense of the words,
your Majesty's attached and faithful servant.

BRONTE NELSON.

[5] On this Paper is written—"N.B. Received at Constantinople, on 7th October,
and the needful done to save the Ottoman Admiral harmless. J. S. S."

TO ADMIRAL OUSCHAKOFF.

[Letter-Book.]

Palermo, September 11th, 1799.

Dear Sir,

As you have been so obliging as to furnish me with the disposition of the Squadron under your Excellency's command, I here enclose, for your information, the disposition of those under mine ; and be assured that I shall always be happy to co-operate with you by every means in my power for the good of the Common cause. I have the honour, &c.

NELSON.

DISPOSITION OF THE SQUADRON UNDER THE COMMAND OF REAR-ADMIRAL LORD NELSON—VIZ.,

[September 11th, 1799.]

Off Alexandria and coast of Egypt, under Sir Sidney Smith :
Le Tigre, 80 guns.
Theseus, 74.
Cameleon, 18.

Off Malta, under Rear-Admiral the Marquis de Niza :

Principe Real, 92, ⎫
Rainha, 74, ⎪
Affonço, 70, ⎬ Portuguese.
Benjamin, 18, ⎪
El Corso, 16, ⎭

Alexander, 74.
Audacious, 74.
Lion, 64.
Success, 32.
Bonne Citoyenne, 20.
Strombolo, Bomb, 16.

At Palermo :
St. Sebastian, 64.
Balloon, 16.
Fulminante Cutter, 4.

On the coast of Naples, and Roman coast, under Commodore Troubridge :

Culloden, 74.
Minotaur, 74.
La Mutine, 18.

Transfer, 16.
Perseus Bomb, 20.

On the North coast of Italy, and to go down to Gibraltar as
soon as relieved by a Russian Squadron:

Northumberland, 74.	Seahorse, 38.
Thalia, 36.	Santa Teresa, 36.
Peterel, 18.	San Leon, 14.

To blockade Cadiz, and protect the Straits of Gibraltar,
Minorca, &c.:

Leviathan, 74.	La Minerve, 40.
Majestic, 74.	Emerald, 36.
Vanguard, 74.	L'Alceste, 36.
Powerful, 74.	Mermaid, 32.
Bellerophon, 74.	Santa Dorothea, 36.
Zealous, 74.	Incendiary Fire Ship, 18.
Goliath, 74.	Salamine, 18.
Swiftsure, 74.	St. Vincent Cutter, 16.

Enemy's Force as reported.

At Cadiz—7 Sail of the Line,⎫
Carthagena—4 ditto,   ⎪ Besides Frigates, Cor-
Toulon—2 ditto,   ⎬   vettes, &c.
Ancona,   ⎭
Alexandria—2 Ships, late Venetians.

TO REAR-ADMIRAL DUCKWORTH.

[Letter-Book.]

Palermo, September 12th, 1799.

My dear Admiral,

I approve very much of your first plan of visiting Gibraltar,
after looking into Carthagena; but I wish you had fixed to
send some of the best Ships immediately back to Minorca, and
as Goliath and Swiftsure go from hence direct to Gibraltar,
you will send two Ships of the Line, and, if they are to be
found, some small Ships; for at present I know not the names
of the Frigates left by Lord Keith, or how they are disposed
of. When winter gets a little more advanced, all the present
Ships off Malta must go down the Mediterranean, and some
part to England; therefore, keep no more Ships below Minorca than you think the service requires; for I had plenty of

reasons lately to write to the Admiralty, that if a Naval force should be wanted for the Coast of Italy, that England must find it; for the Russian Admiral has told me, his Ships *cannot* keep the sea in the winter; and I see *no desire* to go to sea in the summer. The Turks are returned to Constantinople, having had a fray with the Sicilians, in which many lives were lost. I have nothing new since my letters by the Bulldog, and Incendiary. In case Lord Keith is not in the Mediterranean, I send you an Acting order for Captain Buchanan;[6] but as I am ignorant of the intention of the Commander-in-Chief, respecting the fitting her for sea, and whether any Officers are to be appointed to her, I leave the making use of the order to your judgment.

If I am left in the command even for a few months, I shall send those French frigates[7] which cannot be manned to England, and for that purpose fifty good men shall be left by those Ships going to England. The Alceste may serve for a convoy for Leghorn, or Sardinia for provisions; but Junon and Courageux cannot be made useful, at least I am told so; and to keep them lying at Mahon appears to me a waste of public money. My mind is fixed that I will not keep one Ship in the Mediterranean which is not fit for *any* service. During the winter those half-fit, drain us of all the stores, and render us all useless. You have acted on this principle in sending the Aurora and Dolphin, and it is my *particular* desire that you continue it. Therefore, if the Seahorse, whose state requires docking and a thorough re-fit, cannot, without robbing us of all our stores, be put in order at Gibraltar or Minorca, she must, and sorry I shall be to part with her, go to England; and I beg you will write to the Admiralty of my intentions to keep no Ships but what are fit for service in the Mediterranean; and I am sure the King will save by the measure being adopted on stations so near England. I am aware of the argument which may be used

---

[6] Captain William Buchanan, who was posted in October 1809, and died in April 1833.

[7] La Junon (afterwards called the Princess Charlotte), L'Alceste, Courageux, and two brigs, La Salamine and L'Alerte, afterwards called Minorca, which were taken off Cape Sicie, by a detachment of Lord Keith's Squadron, on the 18th of June, 1799.

against my plan—viz., our seamen get no good by going to England, to which I perfectly agree ; but the Ships left here with me are beyond all common refit, nor can they be furnished with stores, not having any foundation to be kept up ; and what would be an ample supply to keep up a Squadron, is really nothing in our situation. Lord Keith will, be the event what it may, with the combined Fleet, probably be at Gibraltar ; but I hope he will make allowances that I am acting in the same way as if I knew nothing of his [being there.] If Captain Buchanan goes to Port Mahon, it is your wish, I understand, to have Captain Dunn ; if so, I will send an order, and you will have the goodness to direct the Lieutenant of the Incendiary to bring her to me, that I may put an Acting Commander into her. We are longing for news of the Fleet—therefore, trust you will not keep us longer in suspense than you can help. Make our best regards to General O'Hara. I am, &c.,

NELSON.

Do you know what was the intention of the Commander-in-Chief respecting the French prizes at Mahon? for it is my wish to follow up his plan.

TO REAR-ADMIRAL DUCKWORTH.

[From Clarke and M'Arthur, vol. ii. p. 218.]

[Apparently about 12th September, 1799.]

I am venturing certainly out of my line of duty, but as the Commander-in-Chief may not even be on the station, I must do the best which my judgment points out during his temporary absence. If Sir James would have allowed the troops from Lisbon to have proceeded to Malta, I would have forfeited my life if, in three days, it had not surrendered. I am far from being in good health, and the infamous politics of the Austrian Minister Thugut, who ought to be hanged if half what is said be true, do not serve to give me comfort. I am, &c.,

NELSON.

TO HIS HIGHNESS THE BASHAW OF TRIPOLI.

[Autograph, in the possession of William Upcott, Esq.]

Palermo, September 13th, 1799.

Sir,

I am told that your Highness thinks that I should have shown you greater friendship in sending a Ship of War to pay you a compliment, than in the way I have employed them; but your Highness will not think so, when I tell you how the British Fleet has been employed.

You will have heard that a French Fleet ventured itself into the Mediterranean, and how the British Fleet has chased it into the Ocean, where I hope they will meet; and if so, I venture to assure you that the Naval power of France will be totally annihilated. You will have heard of the total defeat of that vain fool Buonaparte by the English and the brave Inhabitants of St. Jean D'Acre: you will have heard of a part of my Squadron taking all the French Frigates and Corvettes from Egypt: you will have heard of the glorious successes of Field-Marshal Suwarrow, and that an English Squadron was on the Coast of Tuscany and Genoa to support him: you will have heard that I went into the Bay of Naples, landed the people from my Fleet, took the Castles of St. Elmo, Capua, and Gaeta, and had upwards of 6000 French prisoners at my feet, besides rebels; and that, having placed his Neapolitan Majesty again on his throne, a part of my Royal Master's fleet is gone to carry the King of Sardinia and his family to his Kingdom. This is the glorious work I have been engaged in, and which I should have the greatest pleasure in giving your Highness, did you want, the assistance of the Ships of your most faithful Ally.

I am now pressing Malta very hard, and it shall soon surrender. Your Highness will not now think I have either been neglectful of your friendship, or been idle. Never, I entreat your Highness, think so of your attached and faithful servant,

NELSON.

TO B. M'DONOUGH, ESQ., CONSUL AT TRIPOLI.

[Autograph, in the possession of William Upcott, Esq.]

Palermo, September 13th, 1799.

Sir,

As I send you a copy of my letter to his Highness the Bashaw, you will be able to answer all the points which appear to have given him discontent. He is right that if he had behaved ill, I would have brought the whole Squadron to Tripoli; but as His Highness is come to a proper way of thinking, I have sent nothing. You will explain it, that I had not the smallest cause for complaint. He will see the Ships under my orders have not been paying compliments, but rendering most important services, to him as well as all the rest of the world. Make His Highness understand this, and his good sense will approve of my conduct. I have sent every paper to England, and in due time he will, I dare say, have an answer, as Mr. Lucas tells me of his intention of returning to Tripoli. I shall only trouble you with telling Mr. Horneman[8] that his letter for Sir Joseph Banks is gone to England, and to say that I am sensible of the care you have taken to maintain a good understanding with his Highness, which I shall not fail to mention in my letter to England. I am, Sir, with great esteem, your most obedient servant,

NELSON.

TO LIEUT.-GENERAL SIR JAMES ST. CLAIR ERSKINE, BART., MAHON.

[Letter-Book.]

Palermo, September 13th, 1799.

My dear Sir James,

Many thanks for your very kind and flattering letter of September 1st. It is true, and I see with pleasure, that you do not envy me my good fortune. The field of glory is a large one, and was never more open to any one than at this moment to you. Rome would throw open her gates and

---

[8] Frederick Horneman, author of " Travels from Cairo to Mourzouk, the capital of the Kingdom of Ferran, in 1797-8." London, 4to, 1802.

receive you as a deliverer; and the Pope would owe his
restoration to the Papal Chair to an *heretic*. This is the first
great object, as it would not only be the complete deliverance
of Italy, but restore peace and tranquillity to the torn-to-pieces
Kingdom of Naples. For such an occasion, a part of the
garrison of Messina might be taken. The next great object
is the reduction of Malta, and in any other moment than the
present, it would be a most important one. Vaubois only
wanted a pretence to give up. His only hope is, that in the
next month he may escape with the Ships. To return to the
first object, I can take upon me to say, that our King would
be much gratified that *Britain* not *Austria* should re-instate
the Pope. You are at perfect liberty to say this from me;
for the world sees the ambition of Austria, and her eagle
wants to extend her wings from the Adriatic to the Mediterranean. I will not say more, but that I will support you to
the utmost of my abilities. We are not officially informed, but
have every reason to believe, that a revolution is on the point
of breaking out in France for the restoration of Louis XVIII.
The accounts are also arrived of the Archduke Charles's
complete defeat of Massena, who, having lost his arm, is dead.[9]
Lucerne, and all Switzerland is now free. The Cutter goes
on direct for Gibraltar, to get us news of the Fleet: the
anxiety respecting them half kills me. But ever believe me,
my dear Sir James, yours, &c.,

　　　　　　　　　　　　　　　　　　　NELSON.

TO CAPTAIN DARBY.

[Letter-Book.]

Palermo, September 13th, 1799.

My dear Darby,

I am sure Duckworth could not have left any one who will take
better care of Minorca than yourself, if you *have* the means; but
it was not quite my intention to have stripped Minorca so bare
of Ships. Duckworth has directed you to stop Northumberland,
and to use her actively. This, Martin will like. Respecting Fri-

---

[9] The Archduke Charles defeated Massena, near Klotten, on the 5th of June; but
the account of that battle must have reached Lord Nelson before the middle of September: the report of Massena's wound and death was untrue.

gates and smaller Vessels, I am totally ignorant of what Lord Keith has left me. If the Seahorse cannot be refitted without draining us of all our stores, send her to Admiral Duckworth who has my directions, if Gibraltar does not afford the means of refitting her, to send her to England. I wish you would send me the state of the French frigates, whether they are appropriated for any particular service in Mahon, or whether they are fitting for a voyage to England? for being left completely in the dark, I am obliged to feel my way. I trust Sir James will make application to you for assistance to bring troops to the Continent, where, at this moment, they would render the greatest service. All our news from the Continent is good. Archduke Charles has completely defeated and killed Massena : a revolution in favour of Louis XVIII. has probably, by this time, taken place. Ignorant as I am of the Ships left with you, I can only say, take care of Minorca; and if, in any way, I can do you a pleasure—if I am left in the command—tell me, and it shall, as soon as possible, be complied with, for believe me, my dear Darby, your obliged and affectionate friend,

NELSON.

TO HIS EXCELLENCY REAR-ADMIRAL THE MARQUIS DE NIZA.

[Letter-Book.]

Palermo, September 13th, 1799.

My dear Marquis,

I know not what to say to the state of the Affonço. If, on a survey of three good carpenters, it is absolutely necessary that she should go to Lisbon, keep her as long as it is prudent, and then send her home. Respecting the state of the poor inhabitants of Malta, nothing has been wanting on my part to give them every relief. I send Ball, who is now regularly appointed to the command of the Maltese people, a paper of the corn sent since this time last year. I wish I could do more. If Mr. Vaubois puts his garrison afloat, I have no doubt but some of your Ships will catch him. If such an event should happen, push immediately part of your Ships on the west side of Sardinia, and part on the east side. The latter, in my opinion, will be his route, and he will be taken; but no time must be lost in the pursuit.

I approve very much of your directing guns to be landed from the Alexander. I would have *every exertion* used, and *every nerve* strained, to finish this tedious blockade. As Mr. Lucas, the Consul, must return to Tripoli, I beg you will order either the El Corso or Bonne Citoyenne to carry him; you can also write to the Bashaw a compliment. As I think all my public answers are finished, I can only most heartily wish you a speedy termination of your labours. The Russian Squadron is still here, nor can I guess when they sail. The Turks have had a quarrel with the Sicilians, and are gone towards Constantinople in *disgust* and *mutiny*. News since you left us is, Archduke Charles defeated Massena, completely taken Lucerne, and not a French scoundrel in Switzerland; Massena, having lost his arm, *dead*, and d——d, of course; the King of the French expected in Switzerland, as probably a revolution in his favour is now broke out in France; Russia and Sweden attack Holland; England, the Low Countries, under the Duke of York; I hope all will succeed, and gain us an honourable peace. Forty-four days since, Lord Keith passed the Straits, since which I have never heard from him, nor any report of him. I fear it is a bad omen, but we will hope the best. I am, &c.,

NELSON.

TO CAPTAIN FOOTE.

[Letter Book, and Captain Foote's "Vindication," p. 148.]

Palermo, September 14th, 1799.

My dear Sir,

I did not send your Box by the Goliath as I thought it probable that some event might bring you to Palermo, and, to say the truth, I did not like to trust it in a four-gun Cutter; therefore I fear it must remain in my possession a little longer. I can assure you, my dear Sir, that it affords me infinite pleasure to convey to you the distinguished mark of his Sicilian Majesty's approbation. The dispatch expresses ' for most important services, when left with the command in the Bay of Naples, when Lord Nelson was obliged to order

Commodore Troubridge to join him, and for taking Castel del Mare."

I am this day again requested by his Sicilian Majesty to interest myself with you, and all others who have any of the carronades belonging to his little Yacht, and given his Majesty by the King our Master, and His Sicilian Majesty attaches great value to them on that account. I think I spoke to you before on this subject, therefore I beg you will have the goodness to send them to his Majesty, who will feel very much obliged. If money has been paid for them, I will, with the greatest pleasure, repay it. If Hallowell or any of my friends are in possession of any of them, pray say this for me. I hope that what I have wrote to Darby and Duckworth will please you; for believe me with the very greatest esteem, your obliged humble servant,

NELSON.

TO CAPTAIN BALL, MALTA.

[Letter-Book.]

Palermo, September 14th, 1799.

My dear Ball,

As the Deputies will tell you, nothing has been wanting on my part to get provisions, and, indeed, every necessary for the Maltese; but, alas, this Country is not like ours! and until it is in hand we never know whether we have succeeded or not. As far as relates to myself, I wish to strain every nerve to get Malta before the bad weather sets in, therefore land guns and use what the Ships afford for taking it. The Alexander is in a wretched state. Would it not be better to send her to Mahon? not that there is a fathom of rope there, more than at this place. If you are fortunate to get La Valetta, she will serve for a guard-ship, till the spring. Take care the French ships are not plundered, if you are so fortunate as to get into possession. I send you General Acton's dispatch, naming you as Head of the Maltese people—therefore, let who will come, you will still hold that post. The Russians are very much disposed to pay you a visit. If so, you will, I am sure, heartily co-operate with them, but in that case none but his Sicilian Majesty's colours are to fly in the *whole* Island. *All*

the Ships are to remain without colours, in the care of the
Governor, and to be disposed of as the Allied Courts shall
agree, but I hope you and Niza will take them, which will
save me much trouble.

16th : Noon.—I have been with General Acton this
morning, and I hope to get the King to give up to me the two
Polaccas loaded with corn ; then I shall be sure it will go to
Malta. I have an order for wood, and Tyson shall have a
Transport to send for it. He intends buying for other Ships,
as it will come cheap, I am told. The Turks are returned to
Constantinople, the Russians gone to Naples, and not a word
of the two Fleets. Captain Gore[1] left the Combined fleets
round Cape St. Vincent's, arrived on the morning of the 6th
in London, and has put the whole Kingdom in alarm. Every
small Vessel is ordered to sea to collect our scattered Ships,
and prepare Ireland. Sir James St. Clair Erskine will not
send a soldier at this moment. Duckworth is gone to Gibraltar. God bless you, my dear Ball, and be assured of every
support, both public and private, from your obliged and
affectionate

NELSON.

TO COMMODORE TROUBRIDGE, H. M. SHIP CULLODEN.

[Letter-Book.]

Palermo, September 16th, 1799.

My dear Troubridge,

I have now only to say, How are you? Since I wrote last,
not the least thing has occurred. Two vessels from Mahon,
where they know nothing of the two Fleets. It has been ru-
moured at Barcelona that the Combined fleets are arrived at
Brest ; but I do not believe they can have any such . . . vant,
although I fear it will be so, and overturn our secret expedition to Flanders, under the Duke of York. Duckworth
sailed the 4th from Mahon, with five Sail of the Line—more
than I intended to leave that Island, but I have directed two
to be returned. Northumberland he has left orders with Darby
to keep, and send to the Coast of Spain. They have more troops

---

[1] Of the Triton: afterwards Vice-Admiral Sir John Gore, K.C.B.

c 2

in Minorca than they know what to do with. I wished Sir James St. Clair Erskine to let me have 1200 for either the Roman State, or for Malta; but I have not been able to succeed at this moment—under pretence that General Fox is hourly expected, and it would not be proper to lessen the garrison under these circumstances; and then Sir James enters upon the difficulty of the undertaking in a true soldier way. I can only say, my dear Troubridge, that I am perfectly easy about Minorca, and I see no immediate use of sending more Ships off Malta—therefore, you need not hurry, if it is of any importance, or probability of success attending your labours, by remaining at Città Vecchia. If not, I shall rejoice to see you soon.

The Court has just got an account of Captain Gore, and you know he carried the news of the Combined fleets sailing, and of their being past Cape St. Vincent. As Gore left them the 24th, and arrived in London on the 6th, in the morning—although a Frigate moved as fast again as the Fleet—yet, as the probability is that Lord Keith was not much, if anything, to the westward of Cape St. Vincent, when Gore arrived in London, there is but little hopes of his overtaking them, for they must have had a good wind. In England it has created a general consternation. Every small Vessel is sent forth to collect our scattered Ships, and to prepare Ireland for this damned event. God bless you. I am, &c.,

NELSON.

Lieutenant Parkinson landed at Yarmouth on the 9th. The Courier spoke to him and Sylvester.

TO LIEUTENANT-GENERAL SIR JAMES ST. CLAIR ERSKINE, MAHON.

[Letter-Book.]

Palermo, 17th September, 1799.

My dear Sir James,

The Salamine[2] brought me your letter of September 5th, and the original, by a Polacca, came yesterday. I was sorry to find that, under your present circumstances, it was not in

[2] Commanded by Captain, now Vice-Admiral Sir Thomas Briggs, G.C.M.G.

your power to make such a detachment as I so earnestly requested, and which I am convinced would have so much
assisted the King of Naples in restoring peace and quietness
to his Kingdoms, by first driving the French out of the
Roman State. Whenever, my dear Sir James, you can
with propriety send these troops, it will be my business to
take care they be properly conveyed; and nothing you will
believe will be wanting on my part to afford them every support, either in the attack of Cività Vecchia, in landing them
in the City of Naples, or in sending them to finish this very
tedious business of Malta. Certainly some small articles necessary for a siege would be desirable to be brought—if on
the Continent, particularly entrenching tools; gunpowder, &c.,
we can get from Gaeta. If Malta may be judged more
eligible, mortars and shells are the principal things wanted.
Guns can be landed from our Ships, but shot of 32 pounds
and downwards may be wanted. I know if we could get an
outwork, Vaubois would be forced to give up.

I was sorry Duckworth took so many Ships from Minorca.
It was not my intention, as I had sent Ships direct from the
Coast of Naples for Gibraltar. I am sure you will agree with
me in the necessity of keeping the door of the Mediterranean
open. Northumberland will be with you and some Frigates,
and I have desired Duckworth to send up two Sail of the Line
to Mahon, which shall always be an object of my attention.

A Neapolitan courier is just arrived—left London the 6th,
on which day arrived Captain Gore of the Triton, who left
the Combined fleet, on the 24th July, to the northward of
Cape St. Vincent. The news has created much surprise. I
have now my fears that this Fleet will safely enter Brest.

Pardon what I am going to repeat, that either in Malta or
on the Continent, a field of glory is open; and I can take upon
myself to say, that every support of His Sicilian Majesty will
be a most acceptable service to our good King. I need not
say how anxious I am to support the good Cause, and to get
an honourable peace, but which can only be hoped for by
activity and vigour of all the Allies. Ever believe me, my
dear Sir James, &c.,　　　　　　　　　　　　Nelson.

P.S.—His Sicilian Majesty has 2000 men raised, regular
troops, at Veletri, and about 6000 Calabrese, and troops *en
masse.*

TO CAPTAIN DARBY, H.M. SHIP BELLEROPHON.

[Letter-Book.]

Palermo, 18th September, 1799.

My dear Darby,

I return the Salamine to you, with my answer to Sir James St. Clair, and I am sure you will make every arrangement in your power should Sir James St. Clair wish to embark any troops. I am ignorant of what Transports are at Mahon, but the Princess Charlotte, if a hundred men from four different Ships could be lent to her, would carry a great number of troops. Troubridge and Louis are off Cività Vecchia, and I hope to force that garrison to evacuate that place. They are trembling for fear of an exasperated populace. Totally ignorant as I am of the Frigates and Sloops left me by Lord Keith, I cannot fix what shall be in my power to give to Minorca. But take care of it I will, but not a Ship more than is necessary. The object is to prevent troops passing from the Continent to the Island. I send you a line for Admiral Duckworth, which you will send when opportunity offers. Captain Gore arrived in London on August 6th, and all are surprised at his news. Small craft are sent everywhere to call in our detached Ships, but I fear the Combined fleet will reach its destination safely.

I am, &c.,

NELSON.

TO THE MARQUIS DE NIZA.

[Letter-Book.]

Palermo, 18th September, 1799.

My dear Marquis,

Should the Affonço be found in so bad a condition as to make it necessary to send her down the Mediterranean, I must request of you to order the Marines, or Soldiers, landed from her, to the number of a hundred, to be left behind on shore, to strengthen the force there. With my best wishes for a speedy reduction of the place, I am, my dear Marquis, &c.,

NELSON.

TO EVAN NEPEAN, ESQ., ADMIRALTY.

[Autograph, in the Admiralty.]

Palermo, September 20th, 1799.

Sir,

I am honoured with your letter[3] of August 20th, conveying to me their Lordships' approbation of my conduct in having gone into the Bay of Naples, for the purpose of endeavouring to bring His Sicilian Majesty's affairs in that City to a happy conclusion, and of my having landed a large body of men to reduce the Castle of St. Elmo. I have also received their Lordships' disapprobation of my conduct in having sent a part of the crews of the Squadron against Capua, and their direction not to employ them in like manner in future. And I also observe, and with great pain, that their Lordships see no cause which could justify my disobeying the orders of my Commanding Officer, Lord Keith, or for leaving Minorca exposed to the risk of being attacked.

I have to request that you will have the goodness to assure their Lordships that I knew when I decided on those important points, that perhaps my life, certainly my commission, was at stake by my decision ; but, being firmly of opinion that the honour of my King and Country, the dearest object of my heart [were involved], and that to have deserted the cause and person of His Majesty's faithful Ally, His Sicilian Majesty, would have been unworthy my name and their Lordships' former opinion of me, I determined at all risks to support the honour of my gracious Sovereign and Country, and not to shelter myself under the letter of the law, which I shall never do when put in competition with the Public Service.

I only wish to appeal to His Sicilian Majesty, Sir John Acton, Bart., and His Excellency Sir William Hamilton, whether they are not clearly of opinion, that if I had drawn any part of the force landed from the Squadron from the shore, that Capua and Gaeta would at this moment have been in the hands of the French ; and who can say what evil consequences might not have ensued from it?

[3] Vide vol. iii. p. 410.

I beg to thank their Lordships for the promotion of Lieutenant Parkinson to the rank of Commander; and am with great truth, your most obedient servant,

NELSON.[4]

TO EVAN NEPEAN, ESQ., ADMIRALTY.

[Original, in the Admiralty.]

Samuel and Jane Transport, Palermo, 20th September, 1799.

Sir,

The enclosed is the Medal intended by His Majesty to have been presented to Captain Ralph Willet Miller, to commemorate the Battle of the Nile. As that Officer has been unfortunately killed by the bursting of some shells on board the Theseus, I now return it to be disposed of as His Majesty or their Lordships may think proper. I have the honour, &c.

NELSON.

---

[4] About this time Lord Nelson received the following letter from His Royal Highness the Duke of Clarence :—

" Bushy House, August 4th, 1799.

" Dear Nelson,

" It is a long time since I wrote last, and, besides, I owe you two letters, in answer to yours of April and May. I was earnestly engaged in Parliament upon the Slave Trade for several weeks, when I received your first; and Davison assuring me you was shortly to return home, I did not think of acknowledging the second ; however, as maritime affairs have taken so strange a turn in the Mediterranean, I think this letter must reach you.

" Your first letter, I perceived, was wrote in ill spirits ; however, thank God, the Arch-Duke and Suwarrow have brightened up our prospects, and by this time, Italy is delivered from French freedom. Had the same good fortune attended our Fleets, as has the Austrian and Russian Arms, I believe the war would have been over. I trust it is only protracted, and that another Naval victory will seal the fate of France. I lament on every account the illness of Earl St. Vincent, and particularly in the present moment ; for I believe the enemy's Combined Fleet would not have escaped from his Lordship's vigilance and abilities.

" Your friend Buonaparte and his Army are no more. I am in great hopes that the formidable expedition from this country, together with the Russians and Swedes, will recover Holland and the Netherlands, and drive the French into their own country. Sure France cannot withstand all these attacks and misfortunes, and tranquillity must at length be restored to Europe. Adieu for the present ; write as circumstances arise, and ever believe me, yours sincerely,—WILLIAM."

TO EVAN NEPEAN, ESQ., ADMIRALTY.

[Autograph, in the Admiralty.]

Sir, Palermo, September 21st, 1799.

I have received their Lordships' secret orders, of the 11th July, respecting the re-establishment of the Order of Malta, should we be so happy as to force it to surrender. I am glad I can assure their Lordships that Captain Ball who is named by His Sicilian Majesty (who is the undoubted Sovereign of that Island) at my request, and by the unanimous desire of the Maltese people, Chief of the Island of Malta, has had since last March my secret orders and instructions for a cordial co-operation with the Russians, should they arrive. The better sort of people of Malta know that the Emperor of Russia is named Grand-Master, yet the lower order have not an idea that the Island is to be under the Order again, or bad consequences might be expected, from the dread of, as they say, their former oppressors: the better sort hope, from the character of the Emperor Paul, to have their condition meliorated. I am, Sir, &c.,

NELSON.

DISPOSITION OF THE SQUADRON UNDER THE COMMAND OF LORD NELSON, THE 21ST SEPTEMBER, 1799.

[Original in the Admiralty.]

Le Tigre, 74,
Theseus, 74, } On the Coast of Egypt, bad state.
Cameleon, 18,
Alexander, 74, very bad state,
Audacious, 74, bad state,
Lion, 64, very bad state,
Success, 32, } Blockading Malta.
La Bonne Citoyenne, 20, bad state,
El Corso, 16,
Strombolo bomb, 10, bad state,
Culloden, 74,
Minotaur, 74, } Off Città Vecchia, and if they do not suc-
Mutine, 18, ceed, to return to Palermo.
Transfer, 14,
Perseus bomb, 20,

Bellerophon, 74, bad state,
Northumberland, 74,
Seahorse, 38, to heave down, or go to England,
Princess Charlotte, 36, not manned,   } at Mahon,
Peterel, 16,
San Leon, 14, bad state,

Alceste, 36, { Not to be considered in force as a Frigate : gone with Convoy from hence to Mahon ; half-manned.

Santa Dorotea, 34—not known, very bad.
Santa Teresa, 34—cruizing off Genoa, to return to Mahon.
Courageux, 20—not manned, at Mahon.

Leviathan, 74,
Powerful, 74,
Zealous, 74, must go to England,
Majestic, 74,   do.   do.
Vanguard, 74,
Goliath, 74,   do.   do.
Swiftsure, 74,   } At Gibraltar and off Cadiz.
La Minerve, 40,
Emerald, 38, not known,
Thalia, 36, represented as very bad,
Mermaid, 32,
Bulldog, 14, represented as very bad,
Earl St. Vincent Cutter,
Fulminante   do.

Foudroyant, 84, { Gone to Sardinia to convey His Sardinian Majesty and Family to Leghorn, or some part of the Continent.

Alliance, half-manned—at Palermo, to proceed to England.

Portuguese Squadron :

Principe Real, 92,
Affonço, 74,
Rainha, 74,   } Off Malta, blockading that Island—all very bad state.
St. Sebastian, 64,
Benjamin, 18,

Balloon, 14—gone to join Commodore Troubridge.
Any other Ships on the Station not known.

NELSON.

TO EVAN NEPEAN, ESQ., ADMIRALTY.

[Original, in the Admiralty.]

Palermo, September 21st, 1799.

Sir,

I was yesterday honoured with your letter of August 20th, covering to me their Lordships' directions to the particular services it would be my duty to attend to; and I beg you will assure their Lordships that I shall pay the strictest attention to all the directions pointed out, and shall endeavour to deserve the good opinion their Lordships are pleased to have of my zeal and exertions. Many of the Ships of the Line on this station, having been several years from England, are in that state that it is absolutely necessary they should return to England before the winter; therefore I shall endeavour to get those Ships to Gibraltar and off Cadiz, that they may go home the moment Ships arrive to relieve them; the worst are those mentioned in the within list.

Their Lordships will not, I hope, depend on anything at sea from the Russians, as the Admiral has notified to me that his Ships cannot keep the sea during the winter. It is therefore naturally my wish not to have a Ship but what is fit to keep at sea the whole winter, the number and force must be left to their Lordships' judgment. I can only promise that not one shall be idle. I am, &c.,

NELSON.

P.S.—I herewith enclose the Disposition of the Squadron under my command :—

Zealous,
Goliath,
Majestic,
Sea-Horse, } Now at Gibraltar.
Thalia,
Bulldog,
San Leon, at Mahon.
Alexander,
Lion,
Audacious, } Off Malta.
Bonne Citoyenne.

And the Portuguese Squadron are in a wretched condition.

[Added, in Lord Nelson's own hand.]

Santa Dorothea, is in the Mediterranean, but I have no
list of what Ships are left on the station.   Theseus very bad.

NELSON.

TO EVAN NEPEAN, ESQ., ADMIRALTY.

[Original, in the Admiralty.]

Palermo, 24th September, 1799.

Sir,

I herewith enclose you the copy of a letter from Sir John
Acton to Sir William Hamilton, His Majesty's Minister at
this Court, and have to acquaint their Lordships that His
Sicilian Majesty has been graciously pleased to bestow on each
of the Captains mentioned in the enclosed schedule, serving
under my command, a very valuable Gold Box, set round
with diamonds.   In the centre of that given Commodore
Troubridge was His Majesty's portrait, and to him he gave
also an elegant diamond ring.

In the centre of the others was His Majesty's cipher of
F.R., neatly set in diamonds, and he has been pleased to par-
ticularize the services for which they were given; and to Captain George Hope he has presented a diamond ring for embarking His Majesty and the Prince Royal in his barge on the night
of the evacuation of Naples, in December last.   His Majesty
has also presented Captain T. M. Hardy, my Captain in the
Foudroyant, with an elegant Box, set round with a double
row of diamonds, and his portrait in the centre, and an elegant
diamond ring; and to Mr. Tyson, my Secretary, he has also
presented a diamond ring of great value.

I have the honour to be, with great respect, &c.,

NELSON.

TO ADMIRAL OUSCHAKOFF.

[Letter Book.]

Palermo, 25th September, 1799.

Dear Sir,

By my letters from England of August the 20th, I find
that the Combined Fleets entered the Port of Brest on the

13th of that month, and the British Fleet arrived off that harbour the same day. Being now, from these circumstances, left with the temporary command of the British Fleet in the Mediterranean, I am more at liberty to act from myself; therefore I again take the opportunity of assuring your Excellency that it is my wish and desire that we should co-operate and join most cordially together for the benefit of the common Cause, and, as is my duty, I shall be as open to you as our two Sovereigns are to each other. I shall rejoice most cordially when we can go against Malta; for I am satisfied it is not to be taken without more force against it. When the Culloden and Minotaur return, I shall go to Minorca for a few days, to look at its Naval protection, and to endeavour to induce the Commanding General to lend us a few troops, mortars, stores, &c., against Malta, or Cività Vecchia. I beg my sincere regards to the Chevalier Italinsky, and that you will believe me ever your Excellency's obedient servant,

BRONTE NELSON.

TO EARL SPENCER, K.G.

[Letter-Book.]

Palermo, September 26th, 1799.

My dear Lord,

As the Courier is not yet gone, I have the opportunity of sending you the translation of a letter I received yesterday from Cardinal Albani.[5] Although I dare say his Eminence has sent similar letters to England, yet I feel it right for me to send it to your Lordship. The immeasurable ambition of Austria is seen by the lowest, as well as the highest understanding.

Our dear Queen is most exceedingly angry with Gallo, for his folly at Petersburg. Her language has ever been the same as before the first war of Austria. She has a wise head and a great soul. I have also certain information from Toulon, of the 15th September, that five Vessels are loading salt

---

[5] The original letter, dated Venice, 20th August, 1799, is in the Nelson Papers. Cardinal Albani requested Lord Nelson to induce the King of England, and the other Sovereigns of Europe, especially the Emperor Francis, to obtain the release of Pope Pius the Sixth, and to restore him to his Dominions.

provisions for Malta; also that the two old Venetian ships were
loading stores for the above destination. One Frigate and two
Corvettes are also ready for sea. A Ship of the Line which I
suppose to be the Généreux, is heaving down, and another old
Ship is repairing. I shall keep an eye to that quarter—not
by blocking Toulon; for, the first N. W. wind, they would
get out in spite of us. I shall place Ships in the track from
Toulon to Ajaccio, for on that coast I think they will go, and
also off the Island of Lampedosa, stretching to Cape Bon, in
Africa. I may be wrong, but I feel confident I am right; for
if I cannot get troops, starving is our only hopes; but I hope
General Fox[6] will help me. I have not yet heard whether we
have been able to get hold of Città Vecchia. I know I am
a bad hand at describing my operations;—I only beg your
indulgence, that my works may speak for themselves. With
every sentiment of regard, believe me, my dear Lord,

Your obliged

NELSON.

I thank you for your intention about the St. Joseph. I wish
Troubridge to have the Foudroyant, the finest two-decker
in the world.

TO JOHN UDNEY, ESQ., CONSUL, LEGHORN.

[Letter-Book.]

Palermo, 26th September, 1799.

Sir,

I have to request you will give information to the British
merchants at Leghorn, and all others concerned in Ships at
that place, that such of His Majesty's Ships as may touch at
Leghorn, in future, will be directed to take under their protection all Trade bound down the Mediterranean, and will
convoy them to Minorca, which will hereafter be the general
rendezvous for all Convoys. I am, &c.,

NELSON.

---

[6] Major General, the Honourable Henry Edward Fox, fourth son of Henry first
Lord Holland, who had been appointed Commander of the Forces in Minorca, and
in the Mediterranean: he died a full General in 1811.

TO CAPTAIN BALL, CHIEF OF THE ISLAND OF MALTA.

[Autograph, in the possession of Sir William Keith Ball, Bart.]

Palermo, 27th September, 1799.

My dear Ball,

I sent your letter with all the arguments I could use for provisions, which I hope to get; as to any more money, I believe it will be impossible to get a farthing. General Acton tells me that he will endeavour to send to me two or three ship-loads of corn, and with them a person to go to Malta, to receive cotton in payment. I am using every effort to get troops from Minorca to assist you, and I also hope, now some Russian troops are expected at Naples, that the Fleet will come to your assistance. I need not urge the most sincere and cordial co-operation with the Russian Admiral, which also my late instructions from the Admiralty enjoin in the most positive manner. The Rear-Admiral tells me he thinks he can land 2000 men, and he has ladders, &c. No language is to be held that any of the three Powers mean to keep it; when taken the three Courts are to arrange what is to be done. I have here two 13-inch mortars, and 12,000 shells, carcases, &c., if you, with your present force, want any. I wish you may be able to hold your intended new post, but I have my doubts; you will see that the letter from Tunis, which I know to be true, accounts for Vaubois' determined resistance. If Niza can send any Ships to Lampedosa, I have no doubt but he will get hold of them, for probably the five ready will not sail at the same time. We are all very unwell; the air of Palermo is very bad; Sir Thomas Troubridge, Baronet, gone to try if the French can be talked out of Cività Vecchia, but I expect him and the Minotaur, and Foudroyant, every moment. Inglefield writes me, he is sending the Chichester with some stores for Minorca—a part shall directly go to Malta for your disposition. May God bless your endeavours with a speedy success is the fervent wish of your obliged and affectionate friend,

NELSON.

TO HIS EXCELLENCY THE MARQUIS DE NIZA.

[Letter-Book.]

Palermo, September 27th, 1799.

My dear Marquis,

Your meeting with Vaubois has this good effect—that we must take Malta, if we mean to have it: therefore, all our exertions must be used. I have applied earnestly to Minorca for some troops, and I hope also, that the Russian Admiral will soon be able to leave Naples and to join you off Malta, when, he tells me, he can land 2000 men. You will, I am sure, co-operate with the Russian Admiral in the most cordial and friendly manner, and give directions to all under your orders to do the same. I have got two 13-inch mortars and 1200 shells, if any more are wanted, with carcases, &c., but the Maltese do not like to have the Town destroyed. That would not be minded, if we had a regular force. I send you an extract of a letter from Tunis. I know it to be true from other quarters, therefore I think if you can, to have some Vessels off Lampedosa, and a look-out kept on the top of it. I shall send also to Minorca for our Ships to keep a look-out towards Sardinia. It is these succours which make Vaubois so determined to hold out, therefore our intercepting them is of the very greatest consequence.

I am truly sorry to see all our Ships in such a bad state, but I yet hope we shall have it before the winter. I have sent bread and wood by a Transport. Duckworth arrived at Gibraltar the 13th. In England not a word is said against Lord Keith: all minds are taken up with the secret expedition—therefore, I think it very probable, we may see the French Fleet once more in the Mediterranean: therefore, be on your guard by a good look-out. We are all ill and uncomfortable, but ever regard you and believe me, my dear Marquis, &c.,

NELSON.

TO EVAN NEPEAN, ESQ., ADMIRALTY.

[Original, in the Admiralty.]

Palermo, 28th September, 1799.

Sir,

I have received your letter of the 11th June, and observe with great surprise the premature complaint laid before their Lordships by a Messrs. Patterson, Lie, and Iselim, previous to their knowing whether any injustice had been done them, respecting the 400 pigs of lead landed at Palermo by my order from on board the Oporto, Plofield, Master, which His Sicilian Majesty was in absolute want of for the War; and consequently, I desired Mr. James Tough,[7] His Majesty's Consul here, to value the lead at the price it would fetch at Leghorn, the place of its destination.

This was strictly attended to, and I am informed that the produce has been remitted long since to Messrs. James Sutton and Company, of London, to be distributed to the just proprietors, who at the period of landing the lead were not known, by the bills of lading appearing to order.

Mr. Tough assures me that the nett produce deducting freight, average, aggio, and charges, which Patterson has entirely forgot in demanding the sum of 1663*l.* 11*s.* sterling, will be about 1350*l.* sterling, which exceeds what it would have rendered at Leghorn at the price of 70 ducats, exchange 48, the above charges deducted, and gives a very considerable profit to Patterson and Co. ; and I beg you will assure their Lordships that I took care, in the present indispensable case, that every justice was done to all parties. I have the honour to be, with great respect, &c.,

NELSON.[8]

---

[7] Vide vol. iii. p. 265.

[8] On the following day, the 29th of September, Lord Nelson completed his fortieth year, on which occasion the Queen of Naples wrote to congratulate him :—

"Palerme, le 29 Septembre, 1799.

"Mon digne et estimable Lord Nelson, recevez mes vœux biens sincéres, pour votre jour de naissance, dans cette année, qui vous venez de terminer. Combien d'innombrables motifs de réconnoissance n'avons nous point pour vous être attachés et éternellement dévoués ! Nous vous devons tout, et croyez que le souvenir en est ineffaçablement gravé dans nos cœurs, car je ne suis que l'interprète des sentimens du Roi, et de toute ma chère Famille, qui unis avec moi vous assurent de leur éternelle réconnoissance, et des vœux qu'ils font au Ciel, pour votre parfait bonheur

TO EVAN NEPEAN, ESQ., ADMIRALTY.

[Autograph in the Admiralty, and published in the "London Gazette" of November 16th, 1799.]

Palermo, 1st October, 1799.

Sir,

I have desired Commodore Troubridge to send you for the information of their Lordships extracts of all his letters to me with the terms entered into with the French for the evacuation of the City of Rome and Città Vecchia,[9] on which event I sincerely congratulate their Lordships, and am, Sir, with great respect, &c.,

NELSON.

TO COMMODORE SIR THOMAS TROUBRIDGE, BART.

[Letter-Book.]

October 1st, 1799.

My dear Troubridge,

Most affectionately do I rejoice in the honour the King has conferred upon you;[1] and you may depend that if the Marines can be got at, they will be at your service. General Acton sent me a letter this morning detailing what you have done at Città Vecchia, but as no dates are stated I can only hope that you have done the job. If it is necessary to leave a few of your and Louis's Marines, do it, and one or two of the Small craft, for the protection of the trade. I want certainly all the Line of Battle Ships, and such of the Small craft, as are not absolutely wanted there. My intention is, to go almost directly to Minorca, and arrange a proper Naval defence for that Island, and to try to get troops to finish the business of

---

et longue conservation. Recevez donc les souhaits d'une famille, d'une nation entière, qui sent toute l'obligation qu'elle vous doit, et croyez moi pour la vie, avec la plus profonde estime et véritable reconnoissance, votre très attachée et affectionée, CHARLOTTE."—*Autograph*, in the Nelson Papers.

[9] Captain Troubridge's official Letter, Terms of Capitulation, &c., were published in the London Gazette of the 16th of November, 1799. On the same day, Lord Nelson wrote to Earl Spencer, to precisely the same effect, adding, "I sincerely congratulate your Lordship on this event, so honourable to our Country, for the French would treat with no Country but Britain."—Letter-Book.

[1] A Baronetcy.

Malta, which the French intend to relieve. Five polacres and the two Venetian Ships are loading provisions and stores: therefore, I want to fix our Ships on the spot most likely to intercept them: at Lampedosa, and Cape Bon, and in the track from Toulon to Ajaccio. These are my ideas; for as to blocking Toulon for so few Ships, they would escape, the first north-west wind, if the whole Fleet was there. I need only say to you these are my objects, for you to support me, which it is my pleasure always to acknowledge.

I send you an order respecting the re-establishing the Sovereign Pontiff, as far as my power extends. Great Britain only (I hope) wishes to see all things as they were before the war. I send you a little bread. To say the truth I have been expecting you so long that it has been deferred from time to time. If the place has not fallen and you think it useful to keep the blockade, I leave it to you. Captain Mundy[2] is this moment arrived. I am confident, my dear friend, that you have acted in the best manner for all parties. I have only to repeat that you have my ideas of what is necessary to be done, and you will come as soon as you can; for our business is never done. I have sent to General Acton, as the Pope is dead, whether the Pope's colours ought to be hoisted. At this moment therefore be guided by Acton's order; but always hold out that our Country has no object but the good of all Europe. I desire you will say to Mr. Nepean, that in obedience to orders from me, that you send extracts of your letter to me, and the Capitulations, &c.; for I am the temporary Commander-in-Chief in the Mediterranean. May God bless you, and remember me to Louis and all with you. Believe me, your affectionate,

NELSON.

How happy you have made us! my pen will not say what I feel.

---

[2] Of the Transfer, now Vice-Admiral Sir George Mundy, K.C.B.

TO HIS EXCELLENCY THE HONOURABLE WILLIAM F. WYNDHAM.

[Autograph, in the possession of the Honourable Mrs. Wyndham.]

Palermo, October 1st, 1799.

Sir,

Although His Majesty's Ships are in duty bound to protect the trade of His Allies when bound the course of the respective Ships, I am afraid it will be impossible for our country to keep Convoys for all the trade of Tuscany, but my endeavours shall not be wanting to afford them all the protection consistent with the utmost stretch of my duty, and therefore it was needless for your Excellency to lay such a stress to remind me of what, I dare say, you thought the duty of a British Admiral. I am not accustomed to be wanting in the service of our King, of which, I trust, you will bear witness.[3] I am, with great respect, your Excellency's most obedient servant,

NELSON.

TO COMMODORE SIR THOMAS TROUBRIDGE, BART.

[Letter-Book.]

Secret.

Palermo, October 1st, 1799.

My dear Troubridge,

Mr. Parker[4] is just gone home by desire of the King of Sardinia—therefore it is matter for consideration whether Lord Spencer would take it well, sending one on every occasion; but if you think it will answer a good purpose, send your First Lieutenant, and write Lord Spencer and Mr. Nepean, that it is my directions, as a mark of entire approbation of

---

[3] The letter of Mr. Wyndham's here alluded to, has not been found, nor does the Letter-Book contain a copy of any part of it.

[4] Lieutenant William Parker, now Vice-Admiral Sir William Parker, Bart., G.C.B., who is mentioned in the Preface to the second Volume. Lady Nelson writing to her husband from Roundwood, on the 21st of October 1799, said—

"Lieutenant Parker called last night at ten o'clock, just to tell me you were well on the 8th of September. Thank God for it; and may you enjoy health, and every other blessing this world affords. This young man's extreme gratitude and modesty will never be obliterated from your good father's and my memory. He stayed a very few minutes, as the express from Vienna was in the chaise at the door."

your conduct.   If Mr. Schomberg[5] is the Officer of your choice, send him.   I have got the King's order for hoisting the Pope's colours, but since hearing of the Pope's death, I have sent for a confirmation.   God bless you.   I send you an extract of Mr. Wyndham's unhandsome mode of expressing himself towards me.   Appoint a Vessel for that service— either Mutine or Transfer; the Cutter shall come to you to-morrow.   Ever faithfully,

NELSON.

TO HIS EXCELLENCY SIR JOHN ACTON, BART.

[Letter-Book.]

Palermo, October 2nd, 1799.

My dear Sir,

The Portuguese brig shall be ready, or some other, by one o'clock, to carry General Naselli to Cività Vecchia.   I send your Excellency a letter from Lisbon, by which you will see that the Portuguese Squadron is ordered to return.   This under our present circumstances is a very serious thing, as the 500 Marines landed from them will be re-embarked; and I am sorry to tell you that I have the most positive information from Toulon of 15th September, that two Venetian Ships of the Line and five other Vessels are loaded with provisions and stores for Malta, of which I have given notice to the Marquis de Niza, that Ships might be stationed at proper places to intercept them, which will, I fear, be frustrated, if I cannot, not only get a Squadron, but troops, to land in Malta.   I therefore beg leave to propose to your Excellency, whether under our present circumstances, it would not be right for his Sicilian Majesty to desire that the English garrison at Messina should instantly go to Malta, and also that Admiral Ouschakoff should be instantly wrote to, desiring he would send a part of his Squadron and troops to Malta, for I am clear, that if Malta is relieved, that our forces got together could not take it, and the commencement of a new blockade

---

[5] Lieutenant Charles Marsh Schomberg, Lieutenant of the Minotaur, from whom, and from her Captain, Louis, Sir Thomas Troubridge said, in his dispatches announcing the surrender of Rome, " he had received the greatest assistance." Mr. Schomberg was soon after made a Commander, and obtained the rank of Post-Captain in 1803. He died in January 1835, being then a Companion of the Bath, and a Knight Commander of the Order of the Guelphs.

[would be] useless; and this would not be the worst consequence, for all the Barbary cruizers would there have their
rendezvous, and not a Vessel of his Sicilian Majesty's could
put to sea, and Great Britain and Russia not being at war
with those Powers, the case would be dreadful, and ruinous to
the subjects of his Sicilian Majesty. I have stated the situation under mature reflection, and have only to request it may
be taken into immediate consideration.

Ever your Excellency's obedient Servant,
Bronte Nelson.

TO COMMODORE SIR THOMAS TROUBRIDGE, BART.

[Letter-Book.]

Palermo, October 2nd, 1799.

My dear Troubridge,
    I send you General Naselli, your old Leghorn friend, who
is going Governor to Rome. The Court has nobody better—
you may think they can have nobody worse. The Portuguese
Squadron, by letter received this day, are ordered to Lisbon.
I am more than ever anxious for your arrival, that, at least,
we may lay wait for the Ships from Toulon. I have wrote
again and again to Mahon for troops, but without effect. I
have this day given my opinion in writing, that his Sicilian
Majesty should desire the garrison of Messina to go to Malta,
and also to Admiral Ouschakoff to be wrote to, for Ships and
troops from Naples. Nothing shall be wanting on my part,
but I am almost mad with the manner of going on here.
Captain Bayley [6] will tell you the Minorca news, and I have
only to say how happy I shall be to see you; for believe me
ever your affectionate friend,

Nelson.

    As there is no Pope, it should be only the Cross Keys
without the Tiara. General Acton says it is of no consequence
whether the Tiara is in the Colours or no. His Sicilian
Majesty only wishes to show the world that his views are disinterested. Zealous, Majestic, and Seahorse, are sailed for
England.

---

[6] Apparently Captain Thomas Bayley, who was made a Post-Captain on the 15th
of March, 1800, and died between 1816 and 1820.

TO THE COMMANDING OFFICER OF HIS MAJESTY'S SHIPS AT MAHON.

[Letter-Book.]

Sir,　　　　　　　　　　　　　Palermo, 2nd October, 1799.

As Captain Bayley, of His Majesty's Ship L'Alceste, has been constantly employed in the conducting of Convoys up and down the Mediterranean to Mahon since he has been in the command of that Ship, I request that he may be allowed to put my orders of this date in execution, on his arrival with the Convoy from Messina at Mahon, relating to his cruizing on the Coast of Spain, for three weeks, if His Majesty's service will admit thereof. I am, &c.,

NELSON.

TO THE MARQUIS DE NIZA.

[Letter-Book.]

My dear Marquis,　　　　　　Palermo, 3rd October, 1799.

I have received a letter from Don Roderigo de Souza, saying, that as the Squadron under your orders were not now necessary in the Mediterranean, his Royal Highness had directed their return. Upon this belief your orders are founded; but as the contrary is the fact—for your services were never more wanted than at this moment, when every exertion is wanting to get more troops of English and Russians to Malta—I must, therefore, most positively desire that your Excellency will not on any consideration withdraw one man from the shore, or detach any Ship down the Mediterranean. On the contrary, keep this fine Brig, and I will in two days send you the Balloon; and I send you an order to justify your Excellency's not complying with his Royal Highness's orders, and I am confident he will approve of my conduct.

Should the Russian Admiral come to Malta, I am sure you will act like brothers. I am going to Minorca to get ten Sail of the Line together, in order, should the Squadron of thirteen Sail of the Line and one Three-decker, seen off Cape Finisterre on the 18th of September, be bound into the Mediterranean, which I am satisfied they are not, but trying for our outward bound Convoy. Ever yours affectionately,

NELSON.

TO HIS EXCELLENCY THE MARQUIS DE NIZA, REAR-ADMIRAL
COMMANDING THE BLOCKADE OF MALTA.

[Order-Book.]

Palermo, 3rd October, 1799.

As the reduction of the Island of Malta is of the greatest
consequence to the interests of the Allied Powers at war with
France, and the withdrawing the Squadron of His Most
Faithful Majesty under your command, at this time, from the
blockade of that Island, will be of the most ruinous consequences to their interests, particularly when an Enemy's fleet
of thirteen Sail of the Line are daily expected in those seas, and
two Sail of the Line and several other Ships with provisions
and stores, for the relief of Malta, are now lading at Toulon;
you are hereby required and directed, in consideration of
the above circumstances, and notwithstanding the orders you
may have received from your Court to return to Lisbon, not
on any consideration whatsoever to withdraw one man from
that Island, which may have been landed from the Squadron
from under your Excellency's command, or detach one Ship
down the Mediterranean, until further orders from me for that
purpose; and you are also required to keep the Brig which
will bring you these dispatches, and employ her for the good
of the service; and the Balloon shall be sent to you in a few
days, which you may, if you think proper, send to Lisbon
with your dispatches.

NELSON.

TO CAPTAIN BALL, CHIEF OF THE MALTESE.

[Autograph, in the possession of Sir William Keith Ball, Bart.]

Palermo, October 3rd, 1799.

My dear Ball,

I hope Brigadier-General Graham[7] will soon be with you and
some Russians. I have strained every nerve to get you
troops. With respect to rank and command, General Graham
will command his, and, if you like, some of yours. You are
Chief of the Maltese people, and in all matters will have an

---

[7] Afterwards General Lord Lynedoch, G.C.B.

important voice, with a most undoubted right to sign the Capitulation. I only touch on the subject, but I well know your conciliating manners will make everything go on smooth. Niza was ordered to Lisbon, but I have directed his stay off Malta. You may depend, in October, I will get 2000 men on shore at Malta. I have but two mortars and 700 shells in the Alliance for your use; she goes to Messina to take Graham on board. I am going to Mahon to get together ten Sail of the Line to meet the thirteen, should they come our way. They were seen on the 18th September off Cape Finisterre and Ortegal. Our secret expedition is thought to go on well; our troops are all landed in the Texel. God bless you, and send you a speedy finish of your hard and long labour. Ever yours faithfully,

NELSON.

TO BRIGADIER-GENERAL GRAHAM, MESSINA.

[Letter-Book.]

My dear Sir,   Palermo, October 3rd, 1799.
You will most likely have an application from His Sicilian Majesty to go with part of your garrison to Malta, which is an object now of the very greatest importance to the Two Sicilies, and also what our Government has much at heart to finish.[8] The Russian Admiral will be wrote to in the same manner to go to Malta with what troops it is thought proper to withdraw from Naples. Some Russians are also expected at Leghorn, destined for the service of Malta.

---

[8] General Graham did not consider himself authorized to quit his post at Messina; and his Commander-in-Chief, Sir James St. Clair Erskine, writing to Lord Nelson, on the 31st of October, said: "The probability of General Fox being able to form and detach such a corps as may be adequate to undertake the siege of Malta, becomes now much more doubtful: a few days, however, must clear up all these points. I find that the Marquis de Niza, Captain Ball, and General Acton, have all written, to try to induce Colonel Graham to embark with a part of his corps for Malta: in answer to which he has acted in strict obedience to his instructions, and in my opinion with the most perfect propriety; for no Officer would have been justified, even if left to his discretion, in forming a project for besieging 5000 men, and proceeding on active operations, with a corps of 500 men only. I mention this, because I collect from Graham's letter that the last application was pressed, even after his answer that he could not take any step without orders from Minorca."— *Clarke and M'Arthur*, vol. ii. p. 224.

I know what a jumble all this is, but the very great importance of getting immediate possession of Malta makes me
recommend it to you in the strongest manner. We have 500
men landed from our Ships, and I send you a letter and plan
of Lord Blayney's.[8] The French intend trying to relieve it.
Let us try and get it in any way. My orders are to co-operate most cordially with the Russians in the reduction of it,
and, when taken, the Order is to be restored. It is the hobby-
horse of the Emperor of Russia; and England wishes of all
things to please him. I shall send you the Alliance, with
some shells, carcases, &c., and they can carry all your troops
for such a short voyage ; but the Alceste will be with you in
a few days, and her Captain will have orders to attend to your
desires on that head.

I must now tell you, to complete the glorious jumble, that
except the Russian troops before-mentioned, no one is in
Italy. Suwarrow, in consequence of the Arch-Duke's going
to the Rhine, is gone into Switzerland; and as a finish to all
this, thirteen Sail of the Line, French and Spaniards, were, on
the 18th September, laying-to off Cape Ortegal. Whether they
are bound this way, time will show; in the meantime I am
getting ten Sail of the Line together, and, if they venture
into the Mediterranean, I will endeavour to get hold of
them. All these events will but rouse us to greater exertions. Not a sail shall be drawn from Malta, and, respecting
commands on shore, there can be no difficulty. Ball is Chief
of the Maltese; you will command all the British; and the
Russians I hope will soon be on shore, and two Admirals will
be afloat. I can only recommend acting as brothers. I sail
to-morrow for Mahon, and General Fox I hope is arrived. I
shall try him hard ; for nothing at this moment is equal to
our getting the French out of Malta. Lord Elgin[9] has just
arrived on his way to Constantinople,—left London September 3rd. Our troops had made good their landing[1] with
some loss, and it was thought all would go well. Pray God
it may. Ever believe me, &c.,

                                                NELSON.

    [8] Colonel Andrew Thomas, 11th Lord Blayney in the Peerage of Ireland. He
died a Lieutenant-General, in April 1834.

    [9] Thomas, 11th Earl of Kincardine and 7th Earl of Elgin, who was many years
Ambassador to the Porte, and a General in the Army. He died in November 1841.

    [1] In Holland, under the command of H. R. H. the Duke of York.

TO CAPTAIN BAYLEY, H. M. SHIP ALCESTE.

[Letter-Book.]

3rd October, 1799.

Sir,

Notwithstanding my orders to you of yesterday, on your arrival at Messina, should Colonel Graham want your assistance to carry any part of the garrison of Messina to Malta, you will embark as many of them as you can conveniently carry, with such stores, baggage, ammunition, and other implements of war as he may send on board, and proceed with them to that Island, and having landed them there, will then proceed to Messina, and put the former order in execution.

I am, &c.,

NELSON.

TO COMMODORE SIR THOMAS TROUBRIDGE, BART.

[Letter-Book. The Foudroyant arrived at Palermo on the 1st of October from Leghorn, where she landed the King of Sardinia; and on the 4th, Lord Nelson rehoisted his Flag on board of her. On the 5th, "dressed Ship in colours in honour of the birthday of the Hereditary Prince, and saluted with seventeen guns. Weighed and made sail."—*Journal.*]

Palermo, October 4th, 1799.

My dear Troubridge,

For these two days I cannot get the Balloon to move, although of such importance. Thirteen Sail of the Line, French and Spaniards, are on the Coast of Portugal. I sail for Mahon to-morrow, probably to Gibraltar, and if I can but get a force to fight these fellows, it shall be done quickly. I am in dread for our outward-bound Convoys—700 Sail under a few Frigates, in England thinking all the force was at Brest. I need only say, get to Mahon as quick as possible, that we may join. If you are so much distressed for bread that you must call here, I shall be sorry, but the blame is mine for not keeping you better supplied. All the Small craft which are not wanted, particularly the Cutter, send to me.

Ever yours affectionately,

NELSON.

TO CAPTAIN SIR WILLIAM SIDNEY SMITH.

[Letter-Book.]

Palermo, October 4th, 1799.

My dear Sir,

The Admiralty hope, with all the civilized world, from the consequences of your great exertions and bravery at St. Jean d'Acre, that all the French are destroyed in Egypt, together with their Shipping, &c. I am therefore particularly instructed to direct you, that if this has happily taken place, that all the English ships are to join me. You will, therefore, should that be the case, join me immediately, with the Tigre, and all the English ships; and as the Enemy have a large force on the Coast of Portugal, it is of the utmost importance that the junction should be made as soon as possible. At all events the Theseus cannot be wanted. The frigate carrying Earl Elgin to Constantinople has my orders to return immediately here. You will not therefore on any account detain Captain Morris one moment. The Turks having no object to attend to but their own Coast, I should think are equal to that service. Ever, my dear Sir, your faithful humble servant,

NELSON.

TO CAPTAIN SIR WILLIAM SIDNEY SMITH, H.M. SHIP LE TIGRE.

[Order-Book.]

Palermo, 4th October, 1799.

In consequence of instructions from the Lords Commissioners of the Admiralty, you are hereby required and directed, should the French shipping be destroyed in Egypt, and the English ships be no longer necessary on that Coast, to join me with the whole as fast as possible, as the Enemy have a large force on the coast of Portugal; and it is of the utmost importance, that a junction should be formed without delay. But should the French shipping not be destroyed, and you can spare the Theseus, I request you will send her down to Mahon. And you are further required not, on any account whatsoever, to detain the Phaëton[2] one moment, who is carrying the Earl of Elgin to Constantinople.

NELSON.

---

[2] Captain James Nicoll Morris, who commanded the Colossus at Trafalgar, and died a Vice-Admiral and a Knight Commander of the Bath in April 1830.

TO CAPTAIN BALL, CHIEF OF THE MALTESE.

[Letter-Book.]

At Sea, 5th October, 1799.

My dear Ball,

I fervently hope that Niza has got hold of the French ships from Toulon. As that business is over, I have only to hope the best. This day, by his Sicilian Majesty's orders, a letter is wrote to Messina to request General Graham to go to Malta with five hundred men. The Russian Admiral is wrote to, to go with at least seven hundred. A corps of Russian grenadiers are also expected at Leghorn for Malta. If Niza has been successful, all will end well. Ever yours most faithfully,   NELSON.

I am not well, and left our dear friends Sir William and Lady Hamilton very unwell.

TO LIEUTENANT BLOW, ACTING COMMANDER OF THE ALLIANCE.

[Order-Book.]

5th October, 1799.

Ordered Lieutenant Blow,[3] Acting Commander of the Alliance, to proceed with the mortars, &c., he has on board to Messina, and there wait the final decision of Brigadier-General Graham, whether he will send part of that garrison to Malta. If he determines in the affirmative, to take on board the troops, and carry them to Malta, land them there, delivering the mortar, shells, &c., to Captain Ball, Chief of the Maltese, and then to proceed without delay to Mahon.

TO HIS EXCELLENCY THE MARQUIS DE NIZA.

[Letter-Book.]

Foudroyant, at Sea, October 5th, 1799.

My dear Marquis,

Having this day received information that the French ships from Toulon are at sea, with Transports, bound to Malta, I

---

[3] Lieutenant John Aitkin Blow : he was not promoted until 1826, and was made a Post Captain in 1842.

am anxious in the extreme to know the result of their approach. I pray God it may have been glorious to you, by the destruction of all the scoundrels; therefore I beg your Excellency will send me the account by the Salamine, who is ordered to join me at Mahon. I hope the Benjamin had joined you before their approach. Ever, my dear Marquis, your faithful servant,   NELSON.

TO COMMODORE SIR THOMAS TROUBRIDGE, BART., OR SENIOR OFFICER AT MAHON.

[Letter-Book.]

Dear Sir,   Foudroyant, at Sea, 10th October, 1799.

In case the wind will not admit of my calling at Mahon in my passage down to Gibraltar, and as in all probability the Enemy's Squadron seen on the Coast of Portugal may attempt to come through the Straits, you will immediately, on receipt hereof, proceed down and join me at that place, with the Northumberland, and either Minotaur or Bellerophon, leaving the other behind at Mahon, with such a sufficient number of Frigates and Sloops as you may think necessary, for the protection of that Island; but should Minorca be threatened by a superior force, and you think it not safe to quit it, you will send some Vessel down to me immediately [with a notice] of such event. I am, &c.,

NELSON.

TO COMMODORE SIR THOMAS TROUBRIDGE, BART., CAPTAIN DARBY, OR THE COMMANDING OFFICER OF HIS MAJESTY'S SHIPS AT MAHON.

[Letter-Book.]

Sir,   Foudroyant, at Sea, October 11th, 1799.

As I am on my way to Gibraltar, to look after a Squadron of the Enemy of thirteen Sail of the Line which has been seen towards Cape Finisterre, for which purpose it is necessary I should collect as large a force together as the service will admit,

Commodore Troubridge is ordered with the Culloden and Minotaur to join me at Mahon ; but it is my intention that one Ship of the Line should remain, with a proper number of Frigates and Sloops, for the protection of the Island of Minorca, and to give Convoys to Victuallers, &c. It is therefore my wish that Captain Darby should be left with the command, unless the wants of any other Ship makes it more eligible to send the Bellerophon to Gibraltar, and to direct the Ship wanting a re-fit to remain. If the Northumberland is at sea, it is my directions that a Vessel be dispatched to direct Captain Martin to join me at Gibraltar, or wherever I may be, upon intelligence gained there from the Commanding Sea-Officer, or the Commissioner.

It is also my directions that the Thalia is sent directly to Gibraltar, with similar orders, and the Earl St. Vincent Cutter. I also have to desire that you, as soon as convenient, send a Vessel with my letter to his Excellency the Right Honourable Sir William Hamilton, at Palermo. The Alceste is ordered to take the Convoy of Victuallers from Messina, Palermo, and Cagliari, for Mahon. The Salamine I have sent to put the Ships off Malta on their guard, although I believe the Vessels seen by the Fly schooner were the Alceste and her convoy. I send you a copy of my directions [5] to the Masterbuilder relative to the Ships. For your further instructions, I have only to refer you to the general directions of the Earl of St. Vincent, the orders left you by Rear-Admiral Duckworth, and your own judgment. I have received the report of the Naval Hospital, and also of the Princess Charlotte and Courageux. I am, &c.,

NELSON.

---

[5] These directions merely referred to the refitting of some inefficient Ships.

TO CAPTAIN DARBY, H.M. SHIP BELLEROPHON.

Letter-Book. "October 12th, (11th,) Port Mahon, N.N.E. 4 miles; made the Bellerophon's signal for a Captain. Sunday 13th, spoke H. M. Sloop Bulldog; anchored in Port Mahon; found at anchor here, H. M. Ships Bellerophon, Santa Dorotea, Princess Charlotte, [late Junon,] Courageux, Vincejo, and Entreprenant Cutter."—*Journal.*]

Foudroyant, 11th October, 1799.

My dear Darby,

I wish to see you for ten minutes, or if you are not able, send a boat and an Officer, for I wish to know the state of Minorca in as short a space of time as possible, that I may not lose this very fine wind.   Ever faithfully,

NELSON.

P.S.—You will hurry the Chichester to execute my orders for carrying stores to the Ships off Malta, immediately on the return of the Salamine, depending on the information she may bring.   If the Dover is a Store-ship, and not wanted at Minorca, send her down when Troubridge sails, for those Ships are much wanted in England.

TO LIEUTENANT-GENERAL SIR JAMES ST. CLAIR ERSKINE, BART.

[Letter-Book.]

Foudroyant, at Sea, 11th October, 1799.

My dear Sir James,

I wrote you a line last night to tell you, in case I had not been able to reach Minorca, that the Phaëton brought me an account that thirteen Sail of the Line, French and Spaniards, were seen off Cape Finisterre.   This of course has made me call together some of my Squadron, except from Malta—that I shall never take away, I hope, till we have reduced it.   I am endeavouring to make up nine Sail of the Line, that, if they come this way, (but which I do not think,) I may be able to meet them—therefore, for the moment I shall only leave you one Ship of the Line; but of Frigates, except the Thalia, I take nothing from you, and I have no doubt but in fourteen days from this day I shall be in Mahon harbour, consulting with you and General Fox on the best mode of taking Malta— an object which I know our Ministry are very anxious to accomplish, as it is not only of the greatest importance to us, but will be highly pleasing to our Ally, the Emperor of Russia, whose mind, as Grand Master, is set upon getting full possession of his new Dignity. Rome and Città Vecchia being now evacuated by the French, on an agreement entered into between Commodore Troubridge and General Grénier, Malta and Ancona are the only remaining posts of the Enemy, from Genoa.

I have with great difficulty induced His Sicilian Majesty to permit Sir John Acton to write to Colonel Graham, that he might take 500 men from the Citadel of Messina, for the important service of Malta; and Sir John has wrote in the same strong manner to the Russian Admiral at Naples, for 700 troops. I have 500 English and Portuguese Marines on shore on the Island; and if I am so happy as for you and General Fox to agree to the sending 1000 or 1200 men, I am sure we shall have it; and without their assistance I fear we shall miscarry in spite of all our exertions. I trust that you will, my dear Sir James, represent me to General Fox as I am, for I am entirely unknown to him. If I did not feel confident of our success, I would not urge it so strongly, although I attach so much importance to driving the French villains from Malta, that there is scarcely any proper risk that I would not run to obtain it. In fourteen days, I hope to be with you. Ever believe me, my dear Sir, your obliged and faithful servant,

NELSON.

TO THE COMMANDING OFFICER OF HIS MAJESTY'S SHIPS AT MAHON.

[Letter-Book.]

Foudroyant, at Sea, 11th October, 1799.

Sir,

I send you herewith nine books of the New Signals, to be distributed to the Ships of the Line as they may arrive at Minorca, and to the Thalia and Mermaid one each,[6] but not to the Ships that are employed about the Island of Minorca, or going

------

[6] In the margin, Lord Nelson put the names of the Ships: "Culloden, Bellerophon, Minotaur, Northumberland, Thalia, Mermaid."

to the eastward, as the Ships off Malta are not yet in possession of them, not having received as yet a sufficient number for the whole Squadron. You will therefore be guarded in the distribution, and only give them to such Ships as absolutely stand in need. They are to be considered as in force from the 1st of September, although they have only come to my hands a few days ago. I am, &c.,

NELSON.

TO REAR-ADMIRAL DUCKWORTH.

[Letter-Book.]

Port Mahon, 14th October, 1799.

My dear Admiral,

I send you down the Bellerophon, who, Darby says, and I believe truly is, in exceeding good order, and fit to stand fair winter's service. The Thalia also goes with him. I wish I could say anything in her praise, inside or out. You will receive an order for holding a Court-Martial on the Lieutenant of Marines. Perhaps you may be able to make something of Captain Nisbet; he has by his conduct almost broke my heart. The Ship I believe wants some little matter doing to her. If so, I wish Inglefield[7] would bring her out of the Mole as soon as possible, and if, after all our pains, no good can be got out of either Ship or Captain, send the Thalia to England with some of the Convoys, or send her anywhere out to try. I wished to have placed him with my friend Cockburn, but, alas, he will not let me do for him what my heart wishes. I am sorry I cannot put Captain Buchanan into the Princess Charlotte, as Hardy[8] is named by me for her; but it is of the less consequence to Captain Buchanan, as the Port Mahon will be launched on the 31st. I shall, I assure you, be happy in always paying attention to your wishes; and as I hear you have a young man who you wish to place with Captain

---

[7] Captain John Nicholson Inglefield, Commissioner at Gibraltar. Vide vol. i. p. 312.

[8] Captain Hardy had acted as Lord Nelson's Captain in the Foudroyant during the absence of Captain Sir Edward Berry, who was detained in England for some months by severe illness. He came from Gibraltar in the Bulldog, and rejoined the Foudroyant on the 13th of October.

Buchanan as Lieutenant, send him to Mahon as soon as you can, to assist in fitting her out. The Powerful I cannot think of sending home, when so many others are on this station in such a bad state—viz., Alexander, Lion, and Audacious, Culloden, &c., &c., &c. I send you orders for the Ships on the Coast of Portugal to put themselves under your command, and you will be so good as to have an eye that way, and get a particular return of all Vessels taken from the 1st of August. Lord Keith arrived in Torbay the 17th. Whether we are to be considered as the only two Flag-officers in the Mediterranean, custom will point out; and freights of money, by Lord St. Vincent's acting, belong to the Commander-in-Chief. Whether that is so or no, we shall never differ about. My only wish is, to do as I would be done by.

Respecting the Squadron seen off Cape Ortegal, I am still of opinion they were there, although certainly they did not remain. Yet I do not blame Captain Faulknor[9] for using a degree of caution, especially, as it appears by Captain Blackwood's[1] orders, that the Admiralty are exceedingly on their

---

[9] Captain Jonathan Faulknor, of the Terrible 74. He died a Flag Officer between 1809 and 1814.

[1] Captain the Honourable Henry Blackwood, of the Penelope, fifth son of Sir John Blackwood, Bart , by Dorcas Baroness Dufferin. This distinguished Officer, whose zeal and ability were eminently conspicuous in watching the combined Fleets before the Battle of Trafalgar, and who possessed a large share of his Chief's esteem and regard, as will appear from his letters to him in a subsequent Volume, was introduced to Lord Nelson by the following letter from Commissioner Isaac Coffin:—

"Portsmouth, 24th August, 1799.
" My dear Lord,
"Whenever I recommend to your notice and protection a friend, you may always conclude I have the best opinion of him. Receive, therefore, into the list of your firm support rs, Penelope and her gallant Captain; and credit me, when I assure you, that neither one or the other will ever omit to act up to the expectation you may form of them. Blackwood will tell how I am to be disposed of. Present my best love to your heroes, particularly Troubridge and Hallowell, being ever, my dear Lord, your obliged friend,
"ISAAC COFFIN.

" If an opportunity offers, let me [hear] at Halifax how my young friend Colquite goes on."—Autograph, in the Nelson Papers.

Captain Blackwood obtained his Flag in June 1814, was created a Baronet the same year, and was made a Knight Commander of the Bath in 1819. He was also a Knight Grand Cross of the Order of the Guelphs, and died, a Vice-Admiral of the White, in December 1832.

E 2

guard. I was on my way to join you at Gibraltar, having directed Culloden and Minotaur to join me here, and I was between this Island and Majorca, when I fell in with the Bulldog, which removed the necessity of my going further down. I am very anxious about a report that the Ships from Toulon have been seen on their passage to Malta. Although Niza has under his orders seven Sail of the Line, a Frigate, and three Sloops, they are, I fear, so carelessly thrown about, that some of these Vessels will get into La Valetta, which will give us much trouble. I will take care and give you the best Frigates, and everything in my power to make your situation easy; and for the employment of them from Cape Finisterre to Gibraltar and upwards, if necessary I leave to your excellent judgment. I want, if Malta is not effectually relieved, to get troops from home to assist in reducing it; for my friend Ball now acknowledges he was too sanguine in his expectations. Niza and Company are ordered to Lisbon—therefore I shall be truly distressed for Ships for the various services wanted. Having lately received a letter from the Russian Admiral, saying he had orders for the giving up of the Leander to us, I shall send the Chichester with all the appointment of Officers, to bring her to this Port. Sir James St. Clair has begged me not to send away the Dover, as troops will either move to Malta, if General Fox approves the measure, or, what I am more afraid of, that two regiments will be ordered to England.

Captain Buchanan has just told me that you wish to put two young men into the Port Mahon, and that Lord St. Vincent had intended you should name all the Officers for her. Believe me, I would not on any consideration do less than was intended by the Earl—therefore I beg you will send up all Officers you like, and I will leave Acting orders for them with Captain Buchanan. I am, &c.,

NELSON.

TO JOHN M'ARTHUR, ESQ.

[Fac-simile in Clarke and M'Arthur, vol. i. p. 2.]

October 15th, 1799, Port Mahon.

My dear Sir,

I send you a Sketch of my Life,[2] which I am sensible wants
your pruning-knife, before it is fit to meet the public eye,
therefore, I trust you and your friend will do that, and turn
it into much better language. I have been, and am, very unwell, therefore you must ·excuse my short letter. I did not
even know that such a Book[3] as yours was printed, therefore I beg you will send me the two volumes, and consider
me as a sincere friend to the undertaking. That every success
may attend you, is the sincere wish of your obliged friend,

NELSON.

TO EVAN NEPEAN, ESQ., ADMIRALTY.

[Autograph, in the Admiralty.]

Port Mahon, October 15th, 1799.

Sir,

In consequence of information received by the Phaëton (by
the arrival of the Speedy Brig at Gibraltar, the night of the
24th) that a Squadron of large Ships supposed to be French
and Spaniards to the number of thirteen, had been seen on
the 8th and 9th of September, laying-to, off Cape Ortegal, I
detached a Vessel to direct the Culloden and Minotaur to
proceed directly and join me off Mahon. The day I sailed
from Palermo I fell in with the Salamine Brig, bringing me a
letter from Captain Darby at Mahon, that a Vessel had
arrived there on the 1st, which two days before had fallen
in with a Fleet of twenty vessels of various description, and
amongst which were two Sail of the Line and several Frigates,
steering to the S.E. If this is true they can only be the two
Venetian Ships from Toulon with a convoy for Malta, but as
the Marquis de Niza has under his command seven Sail of the
Line, one Frigate and three Sloops, I have a fair right to

---

[2] Vide vol. i. p. 1.
[3] Apparently the "Naval Chronicle" which first appeared in 1799, and was continued until 1818.

hope that the greater part of them will be taken. I have sent
the Salamine to know the event and anxiously expect her
arrival.

I arrived off here the 12th, and leaving orders for Commodore Troubridge with some other ships to follow me, I proceeded on my route for Gibraltar; between this place and
Májorca I fell in with the Bulldog, ten days from Rear-
Admiral Duckworth at Gibraltar, who giving little or no
credit to the report of the Ships seen off Cape Ortegal, and
Sir Edward Berry from Lisbon assuring me that the information was entirely disbelieved there, I returned to this Port:
where, if Malta is not effectually relieved, I wish to arrange a
plan with General Sir James St. Clair for forcing its surrender, as that Island will, if allowed to remain in the hands
of the Enemy this winter, call for more Ships to attend to it
than I may have the power of placing there. It will necessarily
cramp other services required of us, for not only our Levant
trade will be exposed, but the trade of His Majesty's Allies
will be ruined if we are forced to draw our Squadron from
that service. However, their Lordships may depend I will do
my best as circumstances may arise, but it is of the very
greatest importance to us and our Allies, that a land-force
should be assisting our labours for its reduction.

The Chichester Store Ship, Captain Stevens, sails in a few
days with the Officers of the Leander, for Corfu, I having
now got the Russian Admiral's order for her delivery; and I
have no doubt but Captain Stevens,[4] who appears an excellent
seaman, will very soon get her to this Port. From what the
General tells me, this Island is in such a state of security as
to bid defiance to any force Spain can send against it: and if
General Fox was not hourly expected, Sir James would go
with me to the attack of Malta with 1500 good troops, which
with the Garrison of Messina about 1000, as many Russian
Marines, and as many as we could spare from our Ships' would
in all probability ensure its reduction.

I am sending the Bellerophon to Gibraltar, as she has been
well refitted here, and is fit to stand a fair winter service off

---

[4] Captain, or, more properly, Commander John Stevens. He and his son, several
Officers, and fifty-eight of the crew of the Chichester, died of a malignant fever on
her passage from Jamaica to Halifax, in October 1802.

Cadiz. I have sent directions to Rear-Admiral Duckworth to arrange all the Ships on the Coast of Portugal, and to correspond with you during my absence. I have the honour to be, &c.,   NELSON.

TO CAPTAIN RICHARDS,[5] H.M. SHIP COURAGEUX.

[Order-Book.]

Foudroyant, Port Mahon, 15th October, 1799.

Whereas, William White, Boatswain's mate of His Majesty's Ship Gibraltar, but serving on board His Majesty's Ship Courageux, hath been tried by a Court-Martial on charges exhibited against him by Lieutenant John Glover, of the said Ship, for having seized him by the collar, and wishing he had the said Lieutenant Glover on shore, he would then do his business, and other mutinous expressions; and the Court having found him guilty of the twenty-second Article of the Articles of War, hath adjudged the said William White to suffer death by being hanged by the neck at the yard-arm of such Ship, as the Commanding officer for the time being might direct; and, whereas, I think it proper that the said sentence should be carried into execution,

You are hereby required and directed to see the said sentence of death carried into execution upon the body of the said William White, in the usual manner, on Thursday next, the 18th instant, at nine o'clock in the morning, by causing him to be hanged at the fore yard-arm of His Majesty's Ship Courageux under your command, according to the sentence, a copy of which you have enclosed.

NELSON.

TO EARL SPENCER, K.G.

[Letter-Book.]

My dear Lord,   Port Mahon, October 15th, 1799.

I have little to add to my letter to Mr. Nepean, except to assure you that all my exertions shall be used to meet your

---

[5] Captain John Richards : he was not made a Post Captain until June 1809, and died in 1830 or 1831.

wishes. You will believe I have but one object in view—that of faithfully serving my Country, in which I have considered the security of his Sicilian Majesty's Dominions as very near the heart of the King. This makes the reduction of Malta of the very utmost importance, and to accomplish which, is now, in Italy, the dearest object I have in view. If Niza has stopped their supplies I shall be happy; and I hope General Fox will spare us a part of this garrison to complete that good work, which has cost us so much labour in the blockade, and in keeping the poor Islanders in tolerable humour. I wish General Fox had arrived here, that the business might have been settled. I thank you for promoting Lieutenant Compton to the rank of Commander, and I shall always endeavour to merit your kindness, for believe me, my dear Lord, with the greatest regard, your obliged and affectionate,

NELSON.

Sir Edward Berry joined the Foudroyant by the Bulldog. I have put Captain Hardy into the Princess Charlotte, and, mustering a few men, I shall take her to sea with me. My friend Hardy will make a Man-of-War of her very soon, and I make it my earnest request, that if Captain Stephenson is not sent out to her, that Captain Hardy may be allowed to remain in her, and receive an Admiralty commission.

I have given my brother[6] belonging to the Navy Office a strong letter of recommendation to your Lordship, that he may be appointed a Commissioner of the Navy. I mention the circumstance that you may be aware such a letter is coming, and prepared, I most earnestly hope, to meet my wishes.

TO THE COMMANDING OFFICER OF HIS MAJESTY'S SHIPS WHICH MAY BE IN MAHON HARBOUR.

[Order-Book.]

ORDERS LEFT WITH THE COMMANDING OFFICER FOR THE REGULATION OF THE SQUADRON AT MAHON.

Foudroyant, Port Mahon, October 16th, 1799.

The following Ships are to be considered as belonging to the Mahon station, and to be employed in cruizing for the

------

[6] His eldest brother, Maurice Nelson.

protection of the Island, going with Convoys, and for annoying
the trade of the Enemy, when it can be done consistent with
the other two objects:—

Mermaid, 32.	Dorotea, 32.
Santa Teresa, 32.	L'Alceste, 32.
Vincejo, 20.	Salamine, 18.
Peterel, 20.	Bulldog, 18.

There will also be the Entreprenant Cutter, and Fulminante, to carry letters, or employed as the service may require. The Dover, while she remains, is a proper Ship for
going with Convoys to Sardinia for bullocks; but she is never
to be sent far from the Island, as she may be wanted to carry
troops. The Ships are to be kept as constantly at sea as possible; and none of the above Ships, on pretence of being Commanding Officer, is to lay in Port when his Ship is ready for
sea, and the cruize of no one is to be directed to extend
more than fourteen or sixteen days without coming off the
harbour. But she is not to enter the Port without permission
of the Commanding Officer, as orders will most probably be
immediately [sent] for her proceeding where the service may
require her. All desires of his Excellency, the Commanding
General or Governor, are to be paid the strictest attention to,
and complied with as far as is possible. The Cutters are to
be sent to me frequently with information necessary for me to
be acquainted with.

No Ship, under pretence of its being the Commanding Officer's Ship, is to take more stores from the Naval Yard than
her fair proportion. In all other respects I must leave the
service to be regulated according to the judgment of the
Senior Officer, they being answerable to me for their conduct.

NELSON.

There are eight empty Transports to go down to Gibraltar,
and from thence to be seen clear off the Gut by a proper
force, and the Alliance is to take them on to England—therefore, when the Alliance comes, she and some other Ship is to
see them safe to Gibraltar, and such of the Troop ships as the
General does not wish to keep here.

Between the 1st and 10th of every month, a Ship or Sloop
of War is to go to Leghorn with such Vessels under convoy
as may be bound to that place, and return with them when

laden to this place. But, as it may be a week, ten days, or
more, that the Convoy may be preparing, the Ship is at liberty
to cruize during that time, or afford any assistance which may
be required by His Majesty's Allies; and as there will be
generally money to be brought from Leghorn for the use of
the Army, it is advised that the Ships should, as nearly as the
service will admit, take their turn.

NELSON.

N.B.—These directions to be delivered from one Commanding Officer to another, as they may arrive in port, or
sail.

TO COMMODORE SIR THOMAS TROUBRIDGE, BART.

[Letter-Book.]

Port Mahon, October 17th, 1799.

My dear Troubridge,

Nothing having arrived here, from either Palermo or Malta
since my arrival, I am a little puzzled to know how to direct
your, the Minotaur, and the Northumberland's further proceedings. You must be guided by the accounts brought me by
the Salamine. All my letters from the Marquis de Niza and
Ball you will open, but not those from Sir William Hamilton or
Palermo, as there may be many things in them which I do not
wish any one to be acquainted with. Should the French
Ships, reported to have been seen on the 28th September,
have actually got into Malta, the Ships on that service must
be increased; and as the Marquis de Niza's Squadron is
ordered to Lisbon, you must proceed off there, and prevent the
French Squadron from doing any mischief; for, in that case, I
suppose we shall have no footing on the Island; but you must
judge of this when you see the letters. If Niza will not remain
there, but obey his orders from Lisbon—even if the accounts
of the French Ships should be false—still I must increase our
force there, and keep a good look-out that they do not relieve
it; therefore, at all events, we must look sharp towards
Malta.

Sir James St. Clair has a wish to send over to Algiers, and if
you had arrived before my sailing, I intended getting you
to go on the mission, for these pirates are getting saucy. They

have taken many Vessels with passports signed by me, in
which I cannot blame them; for every body knows, that when
I signed any passports at Naples, it was against my inclination,
and telling the people that brought them, my opinion of their
inutility. If the Dey had respected them, we should have
been obliged to him; but as he has not, we can only try if he
will liberate the poor devils from slavery; and he ought to
be sensible how kind I have been, in keeping the Portuguese
Squadron hitherto from molesting him. This is what, my
dear Troubridge, I would talk to you about, was you by my
side, which I earnestly wish you were; and your going to
Algiers must depend on what you hear from other quarters,
and what you know. As General Fox is very soon expected
here, not a troop can be moved, be the exigency of the service
what it may; therefore I can only say, whether one, two, or
three Ships come to me at Palermo, or go off Malta, that I leave
with implicit confidence to your judgment. You will see the
orders I have left for regulating the Ships named for the
Minorca station; and ever believe me your affectionate friend,

NELSON.

TO CAPTAIN LONG,[7] COMMANDING H. M. SLOOP VINCEJO.

[Order Book.]

Foudroyant, Port Mahon, 17th October, 1799.

You are hereby required and directed to proceed, in the
Sloop you command, off the Port of Toulon, and reconnoitre
that harbour as near as you are able, consistently with the
safety of your Ship, and to cruize in the vicinity of that place
for fourteen days, looking into the harbour occasionally, as
also into the Hieres Islands. And should you gain any
intelligence which you think of consequence for me to know,
you will either return and communicate the same to the Commanding Officer here, (but without coming into Port with
your Sloop,) or to me at Palermo. And should you fall in
with the French convoy, which are said to be fitting out at

---

[7] Captain George Long, who was made a Commander in that year. He was
killed while commanding the Vincejo, in September 1801, in an attack on the enemy
at Elba. Vide "London Gazette" of the 14th of November, 1801.

Toulon for the relief of Malta, you will act to the best of your judgment to frustrate their design, either by informing the Commanding Officer off Malta of their approach, or in any other manner, that they may be intercepted. But not falling in with anything to oblige you to quit your station, you will, at the expiration of fourteen days, return to this place, sending in a boat to the Commanding Officer for further orders.

NELSON.

TO CAPTAIN THOMAS BERTIE, H.M. SHIP ARDENT.[8]

[From the " Naval Chronicle," vol. xxvi. p. 12.]

Port Mahon, October 17th, 1799.

My dear Bertie,
I feel very much gratified by your kind and affectionate letter of August 1st, and most heartily rejoice on all your unexampled success in Holland; and I most fervently hope, that, by all our joint exertions, peace will very soon come amongst us. To say the truth, I am most heartily tired of the war; for our Allies have, in so many instances, played us foul, that they are not to be trusted. Austria, I fear, in particular. I am glad Mitchell is amongst you. Pray remember me kindly to him, and Lord Duncan, and to all my friends about you. I expect Troubridge here every moment. He is as excellent as ever. Berry joined a few days ago, and desires his kind remembrances; and believe me, dear Bertie, with the greatest affection, your old and attached friend,

NELSON.

TO H. R. H. THE DUKE OF CLARENCE.

[From Clarke and M'Arthur, vol. ii. p. 225.]

Sir,   Port Mahon, 17th October, 1799.
Although I have really but a moment, yet I am sure I cannot better bestow it than in assuring your Royal Highness

---

[8] Afterwards Admiral Sir Thomas Bertie, Knight Commander of the Order of the Sword, of Sweden. He then commanded the Ardent, 64, one of Vice-Admiral Mitchell's Squadron off the Texel. At the moment this letter reached Captain Bertie, Lord Duncan and Admiral Mitchell happened to be dining with him. He died in June 1825. In Vol. ii. p. 458, and in Vol. iii. p. 1, Sir *Thomas* Bertie is erroneously called " *Albemarle*."

of my respectful attachment; and I shall retrace our late occurrences as fast as my pen and head will allow me.

Having on the 1st of October received the terms on which the French were to evacuate the City of Rome and Cività Vecchia, on the 2nd, the Phaëton arrived, bringing me an account, that, on the 8th and 9th of September, thirteen large Ships, supposed to be of the Line, had been seen off Cape Ortegal. On this information, in case they should be bound into the Mediterranean, I directed the Culloden and Minotaur, with some small Vessels that were off Cività Vecchia, to proceed immediately, and join me off Mahon harbour; the Foudroyant arriving the same day, I sailed from Palermo on the morning of the 5th. I had hardly got clear of the Gulf, when I met the Salamine with information from Mahon, that on the 28th of September, a Vessel from Tunis to Minorca had fallen in with two strange Sail of the Line, Frigates, and other Vessels, to the amount of twenty, steering towards Malta. As I have seven Sail of the Line, one Frigate, and three Sloops on the service there, I had to send the Brig to ascertain the event. This news, which I still hope is false, did not tend to make me easy, as in truth I required, being very unwell: however, the more difficulty, the more exertion is called for.

On the 12th, I got off Mahon, and, having given all necessary directions for the Ships on that Station, I made sail for Gibraltar. In the evening, between this Island and Majorca, I fell in with the Bull-dog, having on board Sir Edward Berry, who brought me letters from Rear-Admiral Duckworth, discrediting the account of the Enemy's ships being off the Coast of Portugal; with this knowledge I instantly returned to Mahon, where so much has required doing, that, except to pay my visit to the General, and to the Naval Yard, I have not been out of the Ship. General Fox being hourly expected, it has not been in my power to arrange a plan of operations for the immediate reduction of Malta, should it not be effectually relieved by these Ships; which is an object of very great importance to us and his Majesty's Allies: but as neither the Brig nor any Vessel is arrived, I am in total darkness; nor are the Ships from Cività Vecchia come in. However, I sail to-morrow for Palermo, to see what is going on, and prepare all the force I can for Malta. I beg that your Royal Highness will believe me, with the truest attachment, your faithful servant,

NELSON.

TO THE COMMISSIONERS OF THE TRANSPORT BOARD.

[Original, in the Record Office, in the Tower.]

Port Mahon, 17th October, 1799.

Gentlemen,

I earnestly beg to recommend to your notice, as a fit person for your interesting yourselves with the Admiralty for promotion, Lieutenant Philip Lamb,[9] your Resident Agent at this port. Mr. Lamb has been employed under my eye for more than a year, and I say that a more able, sober, and zealous Officer, does not exist in any service. His situation with me has been on many and trying occasions. Believe me, Gentlemen, with great respect, &c.,

NELSON.

TO HIS EXCELLENCY THE MARQUIS DE NIZA.

[Letter-Book. Lord Nelson sailed from Mahon in the Foudroyant on the 18th, and arrived at Palermo on the 22nd of October.]

Palermo, October 24th, 1799.

My dear Marquis,

I earnestly desire that your Excellency will not think of quitting Malta till I have a proper force to relieve you. We shall soon have an Army against it, and I am yet in hopes that you will be there, with the Ships of Her Most Faithful Majesty, when it surrenders. You was the first at the blockade, and I hope will be at its surrender. Your Excellency's conduct has gained you the love and esteem of Governor Ball, all the British officers and men, and the whole Maltese people; and give me leave to add the name of Nelson as one of your warmest admirers, as an Officer and a friend. I write to Ball on the subject of land operations; he will show

---

[9] Notwithstanding this strong testimony to his merits, Mr. Lamb was not promoted until April 1802, and he died, a Commander, in 1837.

you the letter, for I cannot write two letters on the same subject. Sir William and Lady Hamilton desire their warmest regards; and believe me ever your obliged and affectionate friend,

NELSON.

TO THE RIGHT HONOURABLE LORD MINTO.

[Letter-Book.]

Palermo, October 24th, 1799.

My dear Lord,

On my return here two days past from the westward, last from Mahon, (where I had been on information of an Enemy's Squadron having been seen on the Coast of Portugal, now gone into Ferrol, and allowed our outward-bound Convoy to pass unmolested; ten days after they returned to Port.) I received your kind and friendly letter of August 31st, which gave equal pleasure to Sir William, Lady Hamilton, and myself. We are the real *Tria juncta in uno*.

Yesterday, your whole letter was read to the Queen. I am charged to say everything which is grateful and thankful, on Her Majesty's behalf. But I know I need not say much, as she intends, I believe, to write you herself. We all have the most affectionate regard for your public and private character, and I should do injustice to my friends, was I to attempt to say my regard exceeded theirs. My conduct, as yours, is to go straight and upright. Such is, thank God, the present plan of Great Britain!—at least, as far as I know; for if I thought otherwise, I am afraid I should not be so faithful a servant to my Country as I know I am at present. As I shall send you my letters to Mr. Nepean and Lord Spencer, they will speak for themselves; therefore, I will only say, believe I am the same Nelson as you knew Captain of the Agamemnon; and more than ever your attached and faithful friend,

NELSON.

TO CAPTAIN SIR WILLIAM SIDNEY SMITH, H.M. SHIP TIGRE.

[Letter Book.]

Palermo, October 24th, 1799.

My dear Sir,

When I arrived here yesterday from Mahon, (having been down the Mediterranean to look out for a French and Spanish Squadron which had been on the Coast of Portugal, but returned to Ferrol,) I received all your letters by the Turkish corvette, which is arrived at Messina. The details you have given me, although unsuccessful at Aboukir, will, by all military men, ever reflect upon you and your brave companions the highest honour; and I beg you will tell all those whose conduct you have so highly approved, that their merits (even of the lowest) will be duly appreciated by us, and for which reason I have given all the promotion, and shall continue to do it, if they deserve it, amongst them. All the arrangements for your young men are filled up as you desired, and, my dear Sir, you shall ever find, that although I am jealous of having a particle of my honour abridged, yet that no Commanding officer will be so ready to do everything you can wish. We have but little here of stores; but I have stripped the Foudroyant of everything. At Mahon there is nothing; but your demands, with a bare proportion for the Theseus, go to-morrow for Gibraltar; and although I am pretty sure you will not receive half what your Ships want, I shall urge Inglefield to send you everything he can.

You will have heard, probably, that Lord St. Vincent still retains the Mediterranean command, and that I am, by order, acting till his return—therefore, I have not the power of giving Commissions, or anything more than Acting orders. As to getting Neapolitan Gun-boats to you, there are many reasons against it. In the first, they have none for such a voyage : this is enough ; but, was not this sufficient, it would be a thing impossible. I believe we are as bad a set to deal with, for real service, as your Turks. Mr. Harding has sent me word he does not choose to return to Egypt, for which he is a fool. Your brother will, of course, tell you all our good news from Holland and Germany, and I hope the King of Prussia has joined the Coalition. May peace, with a Monarchy in France, be soon given to us. I have just got a report that appears to have some foundation, that Buonaparte has passed Corsica in a Bombard, steering for France.[1] No Crusader ever returned with more humility—contrast his going in L'Orient, &c. &c. Again, be assured, that I place the greatest confidence in all you do; and no Commanding officer shall ever have more attention to all your wants and wishes, than will your, &c.

NELSON.

Should it so happen, after all which I can do, that Mr. Penny still wishes to give up the Tigre—if you have any young man that you wish provided for in that line, send him to me, and I will give him a good Sloop to begin, and advance a Purser of a smaller Ship than yours to the Tigre.

TO CHEVALIER ITALINSKY.

[Letter-Book.]

Palermo, 24th October, 1799.

My dear Sir,

I am just returned from Minorca, having found that the Enemy's Squadron have put into Ferrol, and allowed our valuable Convoy to pass unmolested. Malta, my dear Sir, is in my thoughts, sleeping and waking. I have talked fully to Sir John Acton on the subject, and his Excellency will write to you fully upon it. The object is dear to my Royal Master, and, of course, it is my duty [for it] to be so to me—in particular, as it will be pleasing to the *Grand Master*, the faithful Ally of my Sovereign. Could I order British troops from Minorca, they should have been at Malta, ready to co-operate most cordially with the Russian troops; but, alas, they are under the orders of General Fox, who is not yet arrived from England. General Sir James St. Clair, the present Commanding Officer, has prepared 1500 excellent troops, besides the garrison of Messina, with stores of every description, should General Fox approve of the plan we have made; but they will not move without knowing when, and how many Russian troops will be there to co-operate with them. No time should be lost. The

---

[1] Buonaparte arrived at Toulon from Egypt early in October, on board La Muiron, of 28 guns, bearing the Flag of Rear-Admiral Ganteaume.

Portuguese Squadron is ordered home, and I have no Ships to relieve them at present. I wish I could be with you and the Admiral for a few minutes to fix all matters. Believe me, there is not a thing that the Admiral could propose, that I would not meet him half-way. The honour and glory of the Emperor Paul is as dear to me, both from my duty and inclination, as that of my own Sovereign; and I am sure that we shall disoblige our Royal Masters, if we do not as cordially unite together for the destruction of the French villains, as they are happily doing in the North Seas, both at sea and on shore. I beg the Admiral will consider this letter as jointly wrote to him and you, as it is more pleasant to me for your upright and honourable heart to interpret for me than a stranger. Our news from Egypt has not been pleasant; but I trust will be of no consequence beyond the moment. With my sincerest regards to Admiral Ouschakoff and Admiral Kartzow, believe me, with the sincerest regard and esteem, your obliged and faithful friend,

BRONTE NELSON.

TO MR. JOHN PENNY, PURSER, H. M. SHIP LE TIGRE.

[Letter-Book.]

Foudroyant, Palermo, 25th October, 1799.

Sir,

I have received your letter of the 7th July last, addressed to the Earl St. Vincent, complaining that the provisions under your charge, as Purser of Le Tigre, have been repeatedly thrown overboard without survey, and some collusively expended by the Master's interference, to cover his neglect, and that large quantities of necessaries have been sent out of the Ship, which you think ought not to have been at your expense, and, in consequence thereof, the necessary money is vastly inadequate to supply the Ship, and requesting to be superseded, as there was no likelihood of these complaints being investigated at an early period; and also your letter of the 1st September, addressed to Lord Keith, requesting to be superseded as Purser of the Tigre, having affairs to transact in England, which require your personal attendance;

In answer to which, I have to inform you that I have written
to Captain Sir Sidney Smith, desiring him to investigate those
complaints, that justice may be done you; and at the same
time you will reflect more maturely on the request you have
made to be superseded from such a Ship as Le Tigre. I
am, &c.,

NELSON.

TO LIEUTENANT THOMAS ENGLAND,[2] ON BOARD THE TURKISH CORVETTE, AT MESSINA.

[Letter-Book.]

Foudroyant, Palermo, 25th October, 1799.

Sir,

I have sent the Valiant transport, laden with provisions,
powder, shot, &c., to supply the Ships under the command of
Sir Sidney Smith for the present, and I desire you will immediately take her under convoy with the Turkish corvette, and
proceed to join Sir Sidney with all possible expedition; but
should the Turkish corvette not be ready to sail in the space
of six hours after the arrival of the said Transport at Messina,
you will leave her and repair on board the Transport, and conduct her to Sir Sidney without delay. I am, &c.,

NELSON.

TO CAPTAIN SIR WILLIAM SIDNEY SMITH, H.M. SHIP LE TIGRE.

[From a Copy in the Admiralty.]

Foudroyant, Palermo, 26th October, 1799.

Whereas you have represented to me that it is absolutely
necessary for the service on which you are employed on the
Coast of Egypt to have Gun-boats to act against the Enemy
in the Lakes and Bays near Aboukir, and on the Nile, and
that four of those you captured from the Enemy are well
adapted to the service for which they are wanted:—

You are, therefore, hereby required and directed to cause
the hulls of the said four Gun-boats, with the boatswain's,
gunner's, and carpenter's stores that are on board them to be

---

[2] He was promoted to the rank of Commander in 1813, and died between 1816
and 1820.

F 2

regularly surveyed, and a valuation put on each of them, delivering into the charge of the Lieutenants appointed to command them, all the stores they may respectively contain, that a regular account may be kept of their expenditure, as they will be answerable to Government for any misapplication of them or the provisions, the same as Lieutenants commanding Gun-boats in England are; and you will transmit to the Commissioners of His Majesty's Navy the account of their several valuations, with the abstract of the Stores of each at the time it was taken, in order to have the same charged against their Commanders, and that they may be paid for.

NELSON.

TO CAPTAIN BALL, CHIEF OF THE MALTESE.

[Letter-Book.]

[Apparently about 26th October, 1799.]

My dear Ball,

General Acton has your letter, and I have begged, almost on my knees, for money, for the present subsistence of the Maltese who bear arms. We shall hear soon to a certainty of at least 5000 Russian troops for the service of Malta. As far as I can, the arrangement is made with General Sir James St. Clair at Minorca; but unfortunately General Fox is hourly expected, and all must be submitted to him. I trust that Niza will not go till I can get not only a proper force to relieve his Ships, but those of his people who are on shore; for if the Marquis should withdraw his people, I do not see how you can hold your ground under La Valetta, and therefore Malta may be lost beyond all our efforts even to land. Under all these circumstances, and those you have pointed out, can it be of real importance to urge the French to a sortie, which, by your account, must succeed, and of course must be highly detrimental to our taking such advantageous positions? therefore, from all I hear, and particularly from yourself, ought the intended battery to be shown? for within a month I hope to see 10,000 men in arms against La Valetta. But I leave all this to your consideration, and only offer my opinion with deference.

I have sent for Troubridge and Martin, that I may get a

force to relieve the Marquis. I trust to his loyalty and attachment to the cause of the world, against French villany, that he will not abandon you. May God bless you, my dear Ball, and believe me ever your obliged and affectionate friend,

BRONTE NELSON.

The Chichester store-ship is bringing you wine and some stores, in her way to Corfu, for the Leander.

TO LIEUTENANT-GENERAL SIR JAMES ST. CLAIR ERSKINE, MINORCA.

[From a Copy in the Admiralty.]

Palermo, October 26th, 1799.

My dear Sir James,

I am in desperation about Malta—we shall lose it, I am afraid, past redemption. I send you copies of Niza's and Ball's letters, also General Acton's, so that you will see I have not been idle. If Ball can hardly keep the inhabitants in hopes of relief by the 500 men landed from our Ships, what must be expected when 400 of them, and four Sail of the Line, will be withdrawn? and if the Islanders are forced again to join the French, we may not find even landing a very easy task, much less to get again our present advantageous position. I therefore entreat for the honour of our King, and for the advantage of the common Cause, that, whether General Fox is arrived or not, at least the garrison of Messina may be ordered to hold post in Malta until a sufficient force can be collected to attack it, which I flatter myself will in time be got together; but while that is effecting, I fear our being obliged to quit the Island; therefore, I am forced to make this representation. I know well enough of what Officers in your situation can do ; the delicacy of your feelings on the near approach of General Fox I can readily conceive ; but the time you know nothing about ; this is a great and important moment, and the only thing to be considered, *is His Majesty's Service to stand still for an instant?* I have no scruple in declaring what I should do, knowing the importance of possessing Malta to England and her Allies, that if even two regiments were ordered from Minorca, yet it must be considered, (for which the Officers certainly must be responsible,) was the call for these troops known at home, would they not order them to proceed where the Service near at hand loudly calls for them? *this is the only thing in my opinion for consideration.* If we lose this opportunity it will be impossible to recall it. If possible, I wish to take all the responsibility.

I know, my dear Sir James, your zeal and ability, and that delicacy to General Fox has been your sole motive for not altering the disposition of the troops; but I hope General Fox is with you, and I am sure, from his character, he will approve of my feelings on the subject. If he is not, I must again earnestly entreat that, at least, you will give directions for Colonel Graham to hold Malta till we can get troops to attack La Valetta. May God direct your counsels for the honour of our King and his Allies, and to the destruction of the French, is the fervent prayer of yours, &c.,

NELSON.

TO COMMODORE SIR THOMAS TROUBRIDGE, BART.

[From a Copy in the Admiralty.]

Palermo, October 26th, 1799.

My dear Troubridge,

My letter to Sir James St. Clair, if this finds you at Mahon will show you what I feel about Malta. I hope the General will give troops to at least hold possession till we can get a force to attack La Valetta in a regular way. I have entreated and ordered Niza not to quit his post, or withdraw a man from the shore till I can get troops to relieve them. If he does, and I fear he will be persuaded by the Commodores, we shall lose all hold on the Island, and it would perhaps be more difficult to regain our present position than to take La Valetta at this moment. I hope General Fox is arrived, and I know Sir James will lay all circumstances before him. From experience I know Sir James to be a most fair, honourable, and zealous Officer, and I earnestly hope that you will have the carrying him and 1500 troops to Malta. If, alas! all my arguments are in vain against *orders* (*not knowing our situation here*) or the delicacy of the approach of General Fox, then it is only for me to grieve, and entreat of you to

come here, and bring the Northumberland, that at least I may
prevent supplies getting in; and for this purpose I shall be
under the distressing necessity of taking as many Ships as
possible from Minorca, which I assure you would hurt me
very much. Ask the General to give me, on proper receipts,
3000 or 2000, 32-pound shot. I have sent most of mine to
the Tigre and Theseus, and Minotaur's is very short. We
have nothing new here. Send or bring me all my letters which
came from Palermo in the St. Vincent Cutter, and Entreprenant will sail in two days. Bring what stores you can for
Louis, and in particular a boat. Ever yours, &c.,

NELSON.

TO HIS EXCELLENCY THE MARQUIS DE NIZA.

[Letter-Book.]

October 27th, 1799.

My dear Marquis,
This moment, on the departure of the Transfer, I received
your letters relative to your going down the Mediterranean.
By every tie of honour to your Court, the Ally of my gracious
Sovereign, do not quit the blockade of Malta, or withdraw a
man from the Island, until I can get troops and Ships to
relieve them, for which purpose I have sent an express both
to Naples and Minorca, pressing for orders for the garrison
of Messina to go directly to Malta. If you quit your most
important station till I can get these things, depend upon it,
your illustrious Prince will disapprove of (in this instance) your
punctilious execution of orders. I shall send El Corso in a
few days. Ever believe me your obliged and affectionate
friend,

BRONTE NELSON.

TO CAPTAIN BALL, CHIEF OF THE MALTESE.

[Letter-Book.]

27th October, 1799.

My dear Ball,
Sir William has sent your letter to General Acton. The
Order of Malta is to be restored—therefore the King of

Naples is only the Founder-Lord, for which he receives an acknowledgment from the Order, but I believe he has no more power when the Order is restored—which is the moment the French flag is struck. I have wrote to Naples, to Minorca, and Messina, for troops and Ships to relieve Niza. It would grieve me to think of our losing possession for a moment. I will write to Commodore Campbell by El Corso; for the Transfer is on the eve of sailing. Acton I hope will send an answer to the purpose by El Corso. The Court have all the inclination, but to my knowledge they have not cash enough for the common purposes of the Government. Ever believe me, yours most faithfully,

NELSON.

TO CAPTAIN BALL, CHIEF OF THE MALTESE PEOPLE.

[Autograph, in the possession of Sir William Keith Ball, Bart.]

Palermo, October 28th, 1799.

My dear Ball,

This night a Cutter goes off for Minorca with duplicates of my letters for assistance; I hope the Fleet seen are the Russians. I am sure you will co-operate cordially with both Admiral and General; at the same time, you will take care of the honour of our King and Country, and also of His Sicilian Majesty; and recollect that Russia, England, and Naples, are the Allies of the Great Master, that although one Power may have a few men more in the Island than the other, yet they are not to have a preponderance. The moment the French flag is struck, the colours of the Order must be hoisted and no other, when it was settled otherwise the orders from England were not so strong. The King of Naples sends 4000 ounces to assist the poor Islanders who bear arms; this will do for the present; the large sum required must come from the three Allied Courts, who now compose the three *langues*. I shall come to you on the return of the Foudroyant. The Portuguese are faithful Allies of the Grand Master of Malta, therefore in every situation must be treated with great respect. Ever yours faithfully,

BRONTE NELSON.

TO CAPTAIN SIR EDWARD BERRY.

[From a Copy, in the Nelson Papers. Tuesday 29th, "Hoisted the Flag on board the Perseus bomb; sailed His Majesty's Ships Minotaur, Foudroyant, and El Corso Brig for Malta."—*Journal.*]

October 28th, 1799.

My dear Sir,

Make the signal and have the Foudroyant and Minotaur ready to sail; I mean to be at single anchor, for it is possible it may be necessary before noon. Whether I go to sea in the Ship or not you will always consider that my table is kept on board, and I desire you will without ceremony use all my stores. Ever yours faithfully,

BRONTE NELSON.

Send the Steward on shore for stock, &c.

TO THE MARQUIS DE NIZA.

[Letter-Book.]

Palermo, October 28th, 1799.

My dear Marquis,

In case the Ships seen should be French, I send you the Minotaur and Foudroyant. Louis will tell you my sentiments respecting withdrawing a man from the Island, even should the Fleet seen be the happy arrival of the Russians. We shall soon get more troops from Messina and Minorca; and I am not a little anxious for the honour of Portugal and your Excellency, that you should be present at the surrender. Do not detain the Foudroyant, even should Admiral Ouschakoff be arrived, as I wish very much to meet him, and now only wait here to be ready to expedite the garrison of Messina, the moment the order arrives from the General commanding at Minorca.

Again and again I desire—for which you may be certain I hold myself responsible—that you will not on any consideration withdraw a single man belonging to your Squadron from the Island. Ever, my dear Marquis, believe me your obliged, faithful, and affectionate friend,

BRONTE NELSON.

I need not repeat the recommendation of your cordial cooperation with the Russian Admiral and General.

TO SPIRIDION FORESTI, ESQ., CORFU.

[Letter-Book.]

Palermo, October 29th, 1799.

My dear Sir,

I thank you sincerely for all your letters, and I can assure you that Lord Elgin is gone to Constantinople with the most favourable opinion of your character. The situation of the Ottoman Squadron was very unpleasant. With the English they would have been happy, but the bigotry of the Sicilians was the first cause of the disturbance at Palermo. I love Cadir Bey, and respect all the other Officers. I wish you could use my name to restore harmony amongst them. Our successes in Holland still continue. The Duke of York has taken the command, and is at the head of a victorious army of 70,000 men. Our successes in the East Indies are great beyond example, and, thank God, all is happiness in old England! The serious attack of Malta will commence in a few days, as troops are collecting for that purpose.

If you think the kind present of the Island of Zante[4] is ready for me, Captain Compton will, on your telling him so, go for it, and bring it to me. Pray forward the letters for Constantinople. They are not of that great consequence that any very extraordinary means need be used to hasten their arrival, although I wish them to get to their place of destination in reasonable time. A Ship is sailed from Mahon in order to bring the Leander down. You will find Captain Stevens of the Chichester ordered for this service, a very good and valuable man. Believe me, dear Sir, with great regard, your obliged servant,

BRONTE NELSON.

A Sword and gold-headed Cane. Vide infra.

October 29th, 2 P.M.—Your letter of October 3rd is this moment received. The more I hear of you, the more I am impressed with your extraordinary attention to the business of your office. Never have I seen anything to equal it, and I shall feel an honour to be called upon to bear my testimony of your worth. Captain Compton will receive the acknowledgment of my services, as the inhabitants of Zante, and you, are pleased to call their handsome present; but I consider the honour done me by Zante as equal, and, I believe I may say, superior, to what has been done by any Country for any Officer. The Emperor of Russia only comes near it. I beg you will always say everything for me to those good people. If possible I will one day pay them a visit, with every wish for their prosperity.

TO THE RIGHT HON. THE EARL OF ELGIN, CONSTANTINOPLE.

[Letter-Book.]

Palermo, October 29th, 1799.

My Lord,

You will recollect I went from Palermo towards Gibraltar, thinking it possible the Enemy's squadron, (who we now know to have been all Spanish, and that they went into Ferrol the 14th September), might have come into the Mediterranean. Off Majorca I met the Bulldog, with letters from Rear-Admiral Duckworth, telling me of the happy arrival of the outward-bound Convoy, and that he was just, on the 3rd October, passing the Straits' mouth, with the homeward-bound one. My business downwards being settled, I returned to Minorca, and arranged with General Sir James St. Clair a plan of attack for Malta, which should have a fair prospect of forcing its speedy reduction. This plan is subject to the approval of General Fox, who is daily expected, and to any particular orders he may bring. But the getting the French out of the Island of Malta is now a great object, and particularly interesting to our Levant trade, as well as the trade of His Sicilian Majesty, who does not return to Naples, to my regret, this some time. Prince Caparo, a Secretary of State, is appointed Lieutenant General of the Kingdom, in the room of the Cardinal,[5] who is going to Venice, to try, I have no doubt, and be made Pope; and, as fame says, he has *laid in a good stock of wealth*, and the other Cardinals nothing to give but *promises*, I think he stands a fair chance. Those at Venice are already squabbling, and protests are made by some of them against holding the Conclave at Venice.

May I venture to tell you news from the Armies? Lord William writes me that Suwarrow would attack the French on St. Gothard as soon after the 19th September as possible, and reports are got here that they have been attacked and defeated—twenty-six pieces of cannon taken. I will not say more.

The conduct of Admiral Ouschakoff is so very high, that it has given disgust. On every occasion where things do not go to his mind, he says, 'I will go away to Corfu,' holding this language as a kind of threat. Not to trouble your Lordship with uninteresting events, I can only assure you, that in common occurrences I shall write by Vienna; but that in any event of consequence I shall send directly to Mr. Spiridion Foresti, who I can recommend to your Lordship as a most zealous and good Consul.

Sir Sidney Smith having wrote me word that the services of the Theseus 74, were still wanted in Egypt, I have sent up stores, &c. for the Ships. The Squadron is Le Tigre, 80, Theseus, 74, and Cameleon Brig; and you may assure the Porte, that if the service in Egypt required it, from England, I would add a Frigate, but when I consider the whole Turkish Marine as having no employment out of the Levant, it cannot be necessary. With every sentiment of respect, believe me, your Lordship's obliged and obedient servant,

BRONTE NELSON.

TO ADMIRAL CADIR BEY.

[Letter-Book.]

Palermo, October 29th, 1799.

My dear Friend,

Sir William, Lady Hamilton, and myself, all love you like our brother; and I sincerely hope that the Sublime Porte, so

[5] Cardinal Ruffo.

far from laying any blame on you, will applaud and reward
your great zeal for the service of the Common Cause against
the French villains. I shall be proud at all times to bear my
testimony of your great worth as an Officer, and of your real
goodness of heart as a man, and believe me, Sir, ever your
affectionate friend,   BRONTE NELSON.

TO HIS EXCELLENCY J. SPENCER SMITH, ESQ.

[From a Fac-simile in Orme's " Graphic Memoirs of Lord Nelson," and Letter-
Book.]

                                    Palermo, October 30th, 1799.
My dear Sir,

The arrival of Lord Elgin will necessarily draw my official
communication to his Lordship, but be assured that I shall
ever entertain the warmest regard for all your kind and flattering, and interesting letters; and, from my heart, I most sincerely
thank you. Being now the Commanding Officer of the Mediterranean Fleet, your brother has already experienced, and will
continue so to do, every mark of my affectionate regard, both
as an Officer and a friend. Lord St. Vincent did not give
Sidney the disposal of poor Wilmot's[6] vacancy, the first act of
my command, without having had an opportunity of making
one Captain. I gave your brother the disposal of poor dear
Miller's[7] vacancy, and have promoted all his young men, as he
desired, besides authorizing him to declare that all vacancies
in his Squadron should be given to those serving with him.
You know me not, if you ever believed me capable of wishing
to hurt Sidney's feelings for a moment. I feel too much myself
on such occasions, and I cannot want to crop any man's
laurels: the world has been over-bountiful to me. I rejoice
with you that our dear friend Cooke[8] is likely to recover. No
one knows his worth to his Country more than myself. Whenever an opportunity may offer, I shall have much pleasure in
making your personal acquaintance, and in assuring you how
much I feel myself your obliged,

                                    BRONTE NELSON.

    [6] Captain Wilmot, of the Alliance. This gallant officer, one of " the best and
bravest," was killed by a rifleman, as he was mounting a howitzer on the breach at
Acre, on the 8th of April, 1799. *Vide* Sir Sidney Smith's dispatch, of the 2nd of
May, 1799, in the " London Gazette."
    [7] Captain Miller, of the Theseus. *Vide* vol. ii. p. 465.
    [8] *Vide* vol. i. p. 409.

TO HIS IMPERIAL MAJESTY THE EMPEROR OF RUSSIA.

[Letter-Book.]

Palermo, October 31st, 1799.

Sire,

As Grand Master of the Order of Malta, I presume to
detail to your Majesty what has been done to prevent the
French from re-possessing themselves of the Island, blockading
them closely in La Valetta, and what means are now pursuing
to force them to surrender.

On the 2nd of September 1798, the inhabitants of Malta
rose against the French robbers, who, having taken all the
money in the Island, levied contributions; and Vaubois, as a
last act of villany, said, as baptism was of no use, he had sent
for all the Church plate. On the 9th, I received a letter
from the Deputies of the Island, praying assistance to drive
the French from La Valetta. I immediately directed the
Marquis de Niza, with four Sail of the Line, to support
the Islanders. At this time, the crippled Ships from Egypt
were passing near it, and 2000 stand of arms, complete,
with all the musket-ball cartridges, were landed from them,
and 200 barrels of powder. On the 24th of October, I
relieved the Marquis from the station, and took the Island
of Gozo—a measure absolutely necessary, in order to form
the complete blockade of La Valetta, the garrison of which,
at this time, was composed of 7000 French, including the
seamen, and some few Maltese; the Inhabitants in the
Town, about 30,000; the Maltese in arms, volunteers, never
exceeded 3000. I entrusted the blockade to Captain Alexander John Ball, of the Alexander, 74, an Officer not only of
the greatest merit, but of the most conciliating manners.
From that period to this time, it has fell to my lot to arrange
for the feeding of 60,000 people, the population of Malta and
Gozo, the arming the peasantry, and, the most difficult task, that
of keeping up harmony between the Deputies of the Island.
Hunger, fatigue, and corruption appeared several times in the
Island, and amongst the Deputies. The situation of Italy, in
particular this Kingdom, oftentimes reduced me to the greatest
difficulties where to find food. Their Sicilian Majesties, at
different times, have given more, I believe, than £40,000 in

money and corn. The blockade has, in the expense of keeping the Ships destined alone for this service, [cost] full £180,000 sterling. It has pleased God hitherto to bless our endeavours to prevent supplies getting to the French except one Frigate and two small Vessels, with a small portion of salt provisions. Your Majesty will have the goodness to observe, that, until it was known that you were elected Grand Master, and that the Order was to be restored in Malta, I never allowed an idea to go abroad that Great Britain had any wish to keep it. I therefore directed his Sicilian Majesty's flag to be hoisted, as, I am told, had the Order not been restored, that he is the legitimate Sovereign of the Island. Never less than 500 men have been landed from the Squadron, which, although with the volunteers, not sufficient to commence a siege, have yet kept posts and battery not more than 400 yards from the works. The quarrels of the Nobles, and misconduct of the Chiefs, rendered it absolutely necessary that some proper person should be placed at the head of the Island. His Sicilian Majesty, therefore, by the united request of the whole Island, named Captain Ball for their Chief Director, and he will hold it till your Majesty, as Grand Master, appoints a person to the Office. Now the French are nearly expelled from Italy by the valour and skill of your Generals and Army, all my thoughts are turned towards the placing the Grand Master and the Order of Malta in security in La Valetta, for which purpose, I have just been at Minorca, and arranged with the English General a force of 2500 British troops, cannon, bombs, &c., &c., for the siege. I have wrote to your Majesty's Admiral, and his Sicilian Majesty joins cordially in the good work of endeavouring to drive the French from Malta. The laborious task of keeping the Maltese quiet in Malta, through difficulties which your Majesty will perfectly understand, has been principally brought about—[*imperfect.*]

TO EVAN NEPEAN, ADMIRALTY.

[Original, in the Admiralty. The Perseus Bomb sailed on the 1st of November, and (the Foudroyant being still absent) Lord Nelson's flag was transferred to the Samuel and Jane transport.]

Perseus Bomb, Palermo, 1st November, 1799.

Sir,

I herewith enclose you, for the information of their Lordships, a copy of Sir Sidney Smith's letter to me of the 22nd August, detailing the defeat of the first division of the Ottoman Army at Aboukir, under Mustapha Pacha Seraskier, with a copy of the probable causes of that defeat, as sent to me. I also, from Sir Sidney's representation of his want of Gunboats to act against the Enemy, have given him an order to purchase four into the Service, which have been employed for some time on the Coast and at Acre (a copy of which is also enclosed) which I hope their Lordships will approve. I have the honour to be, &c.,

NELSON.

TO CAPTAIN HENRY COMPTON, H. M. BOMB-VESSEL PERSEUS.

[Order-Book.]

Perseus Bomb, Palermo, 1st November, 1799.

You are hereby required and directed to proceed in the Bomb-vessel under your command, through the Faro of Messina, to the Island of Corfu, and as his Sicilian Majesty has requested a passage to Catania for a Signor Graffer, his wife, and family, you will receive them on board, and victual them at whole allowance during their stay; and having landed them at Catania, you will proceed on your route to Corfu, delivering the letter you will receive herewith to Spiridion Foresti, Esq., his Majesty's Consul there, and having waited a reasonable time for his answers, you will return and join me at this place. But should Mr. Foresti request you to call at Zante on your return, to settle any matters at that Island, you will comply with his wish.

NELSON.

TO SIR ISAAC HEARD, GARTER KING OF ARMS.

[Autograph, in the possession of James Pulman, Esq., Richmond Herald.]

Palermo, November 1st, 1799.

My dear Sir,

I am not certain that I answered your kind congratulatory letter on my elevation to the Peerage—if not, I beg your pardon, and probably deferred it at the moment, in expectation of receiving the plan of the Arms you sent to Lord Grenville, but which has never reached me. I should be much obliged to you for them, but now I suppose the Ducal Arms of Bronté must have a place. If His Majesty approves of my taking the Title of Bronté, I must have your opinion how I am to sign my name. At present I describe myself ' Lord Nelson, Duke of Bronté in Sicily.' As the Pelises given to me and Sir Sidney Smith are novel, I must beg you will turn in your mind how I am to wear it when I first go to the King ; and, as the Aigrette is directed to be worn, where am I to put it ? In my hat, having only one arm, is impossible, as I must have my hand at liberty ; therefore, I think, on my outward garment. I shall have much pleasure in putting myself into your management, for, believe me, dear Sir, your most obliged servant,

BRONTE NELSON.

I have just received the Imperial Order of the Crescent from the Grand Signior,[9] a diamond Star ; in the centre, the Crescent and a small Star.

[9] The following Letters from Mr. Spencer Smith, the British Minister at Constantinople, dated on the 8th and 9th of September, 1799, show the history of the institution of the Order of the Crescent, which was afterwards conferred on many British and other European Officers :

" Your Lordship will find the Vizir's dispatch accompanied by a translation carefully done under my eye ; also, by an answer to a letter from Vice Admiral Lord Keith upon a part of the same subject ; and last, though not least, by a rich diamond ornament, which, as a mark of unprecedented distinction, and attention to our usages, has been adapted to the form and purposes of a Badge of Knighthood ; and as such I comprehend your Lordship is expected to employ it. I have suggested that it may be entitled the Order of the Crescent."

" Constantinople, 9th September, 1799.

" Cramped as I am for the time necessary even to obey the Sultan's command by means of the annexed dispatches, I cannot let this communication pass without addressing my very cordial congratulations upon the occasion.

" It is, indeed, matter of flattering recollection to me, after having it fall to my lot

TO EARL SPENCER, K.G.

[Letter-Book.]

Palermo, November 1st, 1799.

My dear Lord,

My letter to Mr. Nepean will tell you of my arrival here, and also that the Marquis de Niza intended to leave Malta. In my public letter, for ' *King,* except a few pounds,' read *Queen.* She has a noble generous disposition. Unfortunately the [King and] her Majesty do not at this moment draw exactly the same way; therefore, His Majesty will not go at this moment to Naples, where his presence is much wanted; but sends Prince Caparo, a Secretary of State, as Lieutenant of the Kingdom. But in a few weeks I yet hope the King will go. I need not tell you, my dear Lord, the Queen's sentiments about you. Not a day passes but she expresses her feelings—not that the King is unmindful of your attention to him, but from the other it flows warm from the heart. In every way and in everything, believe me, I will do my best. You have placed an unbounded confidence in me, and you shall not have reason to repent it. The first act of my command was to name Sidney Smith's First Lieutenant to the death-vacancy of Captain Miller. I have placed two of his young men in Gun-boats, and have authorized him to declare that all services performed by his Squadron should be rewarded by Officers in it. I own I am jealous of being trampled upon, but my disposition, as a Public man, is to reward merit, find it where I may. In this I only follow your example, and in all points I should be proud to do it, for, believe me, my dear Lord, your attached and faithful

NELSON.

to be the first to convey to a Countryman that decoration (the Chelengk, or Plume of Triumph) which Ottoman grandeur had hitherto exclusively reserved for conquerors of their own race, that I should be charged to present the same Hero with a Civic crown—for such may be considered the Emperor's gift, which accompanies this. I hope you will long live to display, with honest pride, these genuine Badges of Merit, and that after the one and the other have successively passed through my hands, I may again see them united upon the person of the first *Knight of the Crescent.*"—Copies in the Nelson Papers.

TO VICE-ADMIRAL OUSCHAKOFF.

[Letter-Book.]

Palermo, November 1st, 1799.

My dear Admiral,

My pride and pleasure will ever be to act with you as a brother—to be open and sincere to you, as we should be close to every one else. This is my duty, this is my inclination ; and if any person should attempt to disturb the harmony which ought to subsist between Officers of such faithful Allies as our Sovereigns, he should be exposed. But, thank God, that can never happen to us, who have such a good man as Italinsky between us. Everything which my brave friend Troubridge has done, has been by my orders. You have only to know him; and love, honour, and respect, will follow, united with admiration for the qualities of his head and heart. Nothing which he has done in the Papal State, but what had the approbation of His Sicilian Majesty, perfectly, I believe, known to the Cardinal, and, as I thought, fully explained by me at Sir William Hamilton's, to my friend Italinsky ; so much so, that I think I told him that I did not expect you would find Commodore Troubridge at Naples, but that he would be gone to join the Ships off Cività Vecchia—an object of the greatest importance, and on which I conceived the future happiness of Italy depended. Secrecy was everything, and Troubridge, under those orders, would not have been justified in revealing a tittle of them, especially as your Excellency had just left me. Success was beyond my most sanguine expectation. Had two hours been lost, Rome would have been in other hands than those of His Sicilian Majesty. It was an object so dear to me, that I begged Italinsky to urge it to you, as soon after your arrival at Naples as possible ; for I did not expect such a happy event, on which I most cordially, and from my heart, rejoice with your Excellency. Let us go together to Malta. Let us unite all our means to place the Grand Master in La Valetta. Russia, England, and Naples, are pledged to do it ; let it be our business to redeem that pledge ; and ever believe me, with all the openness of heart, your Excellency's most faithful Brother-in-Arms,

BRONTE NELSON.

G 2

TO CHEVALIER ITALINSKY.

[Letter-Book.]

Palermo, November 1st, 1799.

My dear Sir,

From what I have heard, there must have been some mistake relative to the orders of the excellent Commodore Troubridge. I thought, and so did Sir William, that I had fully explained the orders of the Commodore—approved on the 1st of August by His Sicilian Majesty, and perfectly, as I believed, understood by the Cardinal. The troops under Bouchard, marching into the then (but now, thank God, Papal State!) Roman State, was a part of the plan. How fortunate that they did not wait! What a happy combination of circumstances! By less than two hours, and the Roman State would have been in the hands of another Power; and Russia, England, and Naples, would have had nothing to do with it. Nothing but God's Providence ordained it, on which I rejoice with you, with all my soul. I look upon Troubridge's activity as a happy event for Italy. May God continue to prosper us! Assure Admiral Ouschakoff, from your knowledge of me, that I have only in view to finish the war, and to see every Prince in possession of his Government; and the time is now arrived that every nerve must be strained for the speedy restoration of the Grand Master of Malta in La Valetta. Nothing shall be wanting on my part. I long to see you, and have much to say, but I have not one hour given me to write my letters to Naples. Sir William and Lady Hamilton join me in kindest respects and good wishes, and I beg you will believe me ever your attached and obliged friend, BRONTE NELSON.

I have mislaid the copy of my last letter; pray send me a copy of it.

TO THE HONOURABLE WILLIAM WYNDHAM.

[Letter Book.]

Palermo, November 1st, 1799.

Sir,

We have nothing new here from any quarter. Troops are preparing for the siege of Malta, which, by vigorous exertions,

I hope will soon fall to the Allies. Should any public event occur, your Excellency may rest assured that I shall inform you of it as expeditiously as possible.

I have the honour to be, &c.,

BRONTE NELSON.

TO COMMISSIONER INGLEFIELD, GIBRALTAR.

[Letter-Book.]

Palermo, November 2nd, 1799.

My dear Sir,

You will send such stores as may be a fair proportion for the Tigre and Theseus; but we are all stripped to the skin. We are preparing for the siege of Malta, and are anxiously waiting the arrival of General Fox, without whose assistance all our hopes would fail. Sir William and Lady Hamilton are better than they have been, and always speak of you with the most affectionate regard. Make my best respects to the General, and believe me, dear Sir, your obliged and sincere friend,

BRONTE NELSON.

TO EVAN NEPEAN, ESQ., ADMIRALTY.

[Original, in the Admiralty.]

Palermo, November 3rd, 1799.

Sir,

Having arranged a proper force for the protection and comfort of Minorca, and given such directions as were necessary for the refitting of the Ships at the Arsenal, &c., I sailed from Mahon on the 17th, and, in my route falling in with the Minotaur, I arrived here with her on the 21st, where I found letters from Captain Ball, who acts as Governor of the Island of Malta, and from the Marquis de Niza, who commands the blockade, giving me an account of the deplorable state of the inhabitants, particularly of those who have borne arms, having no pay to support themselves, or clothes, &c. And fearing that the French should make a sortie in their present state, and from the Marquis saying that his orders were so strong from his Court for the return of the Portuguese Squadron to

Lisbon, that he could not much longer justify the disobedience,
and of course he must withdraw the 400 men landed at Malta
from that Island. If this was to take place, and we consequently obliged to keep afloat, it would take more time and
loss of men (if possible to effect it) to regain our present
advantageous positions for the attack of La Valetta, than it
would at this moment to take the Town. I have been with
General Acton to advance some money for the support of the
people bearing arms, to my knowledge, because it has been by
my application alone that His Sicilian Majesty has granted the
money, (taken, for it was nowhere else to be had, from his
children,) and it was, and is I hope, to be replaced by the
money promised by Lord Grenville to the Marquis de Circello. The enormous expenses incurred within the last eight
months have drawn the King's chest very low; but His Majesty has never failed giving everything I could ask. I hope
General Fox will agree to the arrangement made by General
Sir James St. Clair and myself, for a cordial co-operation with
the Russian Admiral and General, to effect this important object.
Malta has not yet been relieved, and I have sent the Foudroyant and Minotaur to assist in the blockade. I have again
requested General Sir James St. Clair to order the garrison
of Messina to Malta, in order to hold our present advantageous
positions until a proper force can be collected to attack it. I
have wrote to the Russian Admiral, urging the measure with
all my power, and I hope he will see the force of my reasoning,
as he ought to be satisfied I can have no object in view but
the speedy restoration of the Grand Master and the Order.
Nothing shall be wanting, I can assure you, on my part, to
conciliate the affections of the Officers of His Majesty's Allies,
and if any difficulties arise, to leave the matter open for the
amicable settlement of the Courts. Ever believe me, Sir, &c.,

NELSON.

TO HIS EXCELLENCY THE GRAND VIZIR.

[Letter-Book.]

Palermo, November 4th, 1799.

Sir,

I was yesterday honoured with your Excellency's letter [1] of September 9th, in which you announce to me that his Imperial Majesty had been pleased to order me a Medallion, which his Majesty desired I would wear, as a mark of his pleasure for my conduct to Osman Hadji, and for the interest which I take in the prosperity of the Sublime Porte. I entreat that your Excellency will present, with the most profound gratitude, my thanks to the Emperor for this new and distinguished honour conferred upon me. I have placed it on my coat, on the left side, over my heart. I cannot say, however flattering this mark of favour is to me, that I can in any manner serve the Sublime Porte more than I have done, for it has ever been with all my soul; but this mark of favour shows, in the strongest light, that the smallest services are watched, and most magnificently rewarded, by his Imperial Majesty, whose life may God prolong, with health and every other earthly happiness; and may he give me opportunities of showing my gratitude, by risking my life for the preservation of the smallest grain of sand belonging to the Ottoman Empire, and may the enemies of his Imperial Majesty fall into dust by the wise councils of your Excellency.

Respecting the force employed in Egypt, it is now far superior to all the Naval force of the Enemy, it consisting of two Sail of the Line and a fine Corvette; but Lord Elgin will join me in assuring your Excellency, that if more force is necessary in those seas, it shall instantly be sent. But to keep a large Naval force there would be useless, and, indeed, do harm to the Common Cause, by preventing so complete a blockade of the French and Spanish ports. I have just ordered four Gun-boats, taken by that excellent Officer Sir Sidney Smith, to be purchased, as it has been represented to me they may be useful in the Nile. I am just going to the siege of La Valetta, and to satisfy the Sublime Porte of my wishes to com-

---

[1] A translation of that Letter is in Clarke and M'Arthur.

ply with its desires, the moment the French are driven out of Malta, I will send to Egypt two more Corvettes. May Almighty God prosper all your Excellency's councils, is, and shall ever be, the fervent prayer of your obliged and faithful servant,   BRONTE NELSON.

Abdur Ahmed has executed his commission in a manner highly honourable to the dignity of his Imperial Majesty and your Excellency, and most pleasing to me; and I beg leave to recommend him to your notice.

TO HIS EXCELLENCY THE CAPITAN PACHA.

[Letter Book.]

Palermo, November 4th, 1799.

Sir,

I was honoured yesterday by your Excellency's letter, by the gentleman who brought the magnificent present of his Imperial Majesty. Could anything increase my desire of showing my attachment to the Sublime Porte, the goodness of the Emperor would insure it, but that is impossible.

I long for the time when I may make a personal acquaintance with your Excellency; and I assure you till then I shall be happy in uniting my councils and services for the benefit of the Common Cause, and for the destruction of the French. I congratulate your Excellency on the total defeat of the French Army in Switzerland: 35,000 men are killed and prisoners to General Suwarrow. I am collecting a force of troops to besiege La Valetta, and hope soon to drive the French out of Malta, when more Ships, if necessary, shall be sent to Egypt. I again beg leave to recommend Admiral Cadir Bey to your notice. He is a good Officer, and appears a truly good man. His Ship was in particularly fine order. All the Admirals and Captains were my friends; and did the service of our two Sovereigns call upon us to act together, I am sure we should be like brothers.

I am much pleased with, and was highly gratified by, the manner in which he spoke of your Excellency's head, and goodness of heart. With every sentiment of regard and affection, believe me your Excellency's Brother-in-Arms.

BRONTE NELSON.

TO THE RIGHT HON. THE EARL OF ELGIN.

[Letter-Book.]

Palermo, November 4th, 1799.

My Lord,

Having yesterday received such a mark of the Grand Signior's favour, I have been puzzled how to express myself properly. I must, therefore, trust to your Excellency's goodness in supplying my deficiency of language. The Vizir wishes for more force in Egypt: it is natural for him to do so, as none but our countrymen render the Porte any service. Your Lordship knows I have not Frigates or Corvettes enough for the common service of the Mediterranean ; at the same time, to second your endeavours for the success of your important mission, a Corvette shall be found, and after the fall of La Valetta, two ; but the French ought to be out of Egypt before that time, or even this. We have nothing new here since I wrote you a few days ago. In any manner in which I can be useful, pray tell me, and I shall be happy in assuring your Lordship with what respect I am, &c.,

BRONTE NELSON.

TO HIS EXCELLENCY J. SPENCER SMITH, ESQ., CONSTANTINOPLE.

[Letter-Book.]

Palermo, November 4th, 1799.

My dear Sir,

I am penetrated by your kindness, and can truly assure you how much I wish to make your acquaintance. Accept again and again my thanks for all your goodness to me, both public and private. What a voyage—from September 9th to November 3rd ! I have not got a force, even was it necessary, to send at this moment into Egypt ; for Lord Keith carried off all he could lay his hands upon. Your excellent brother will find me everything he can wish his Commanding Officer to be, and should the French not be extirpated in Egypt before they are in Malta, I will send him two more Corvettes. The Turkish Corvette has only reached Messina, being leaky ; but I hope she will be able to carry this gentleman back to Constantinople. As he leaves this place to-morrow, I have

sent to get some Sherry wine and sugar; but as to Madeira,
or Claret, there is not a drop of such even in this Island, or in
all Italy. Only tell me in what I can be useful to you, and I
shall have great pleasure in assuring you, by fact, that I feel
myself your most obliged friend,

BRONTE NELSON.

Remember me affectionately to your brother, when you
write. I have just sent him a large cargo of good things.

TO THE RIGHT HON. EARL SPENCER, K.G.

[Letter-Book.]

My dear Lord,   Palermo, November 6th, 1799.

I had entertained sanguine hopes that troops would have
been obtained from Minorca to join the Russians in the
attack of Malta; but that hope is much diminished by a letter
from General Sir James St. Clair, writing me word that the
28th Regiment was ordered for England, and that he expected
General Fox every moment, and that [till] he was here, the
General would not, on any consideration, break his orders for
any object.

Much as I approve of strict obedience to orders—even to a
Court-Martial to inquire whether the object justified the
measure—yet to say that an Officer is never, for any object,
to alter his orders, is what I cannot comprehend. The circumstances of this war so often vary, that an Officer has
almost every moment to consider—What would my superiors
direct, did they know what is passing under my nose? The
great object of the war is—*Down, down with the French!* To
accomplish this, every nerve, and by both Services, ought to
be strained. My heart is, I assure you, almost broke with
that and other things. The moment I get General Fox's
answer . . . . . .[1] for General St. Clair cannot lend me even
the garrison of Messina, to hold the posts occupied by our and
the Portuguese Marines, till a force can be collected to attack
it properly. If I am obliged to withdraw from the shore of
the Island, what a thorn it will remain to our trade and to our
Allies! It will require a constant succession of good Ships,

[1] Sic.

which are very scarce with me, to cruize off it; and if the Enemy get supplies in, we may bid adieu to Malta. This would complete my misery; for I am afraid I take all services too much to heart. The accomplishing of them is my study, night and day.

The services of Captain Ball will not, I am confident, be forgot by you, but I feel sensible that my pen is far unequal to do justice to the merit of my friends; for could I have described the wonderful merit of Sir Thomas Troubridge and his gallant party in the Kingdom of Naples—how he placed his battery, as he would his Ship, close alongside the Enemy —how the French Commander said, 'This man fancies he is on board Ship—this is not the mode a General would adopt;' in what a few days this band went to the siege of Capua, where, whatever was done, was done by the English and Portuguese, for the Russians would *fight*, but *not* work. The Neapolitan corps were in air, and 600 Swiss were all who Troubridge could depend upon. If I had, as their Chief, a looker-on, a pen to describe their extraordinary merits, they would not be diminished by the comparison of our success in Holland, or by the gallant exertions of my friend, Sidney Smith—of whose zeal, judgment, and gallantry, no man is more sensible than myself—and been equally entitled to the thanks of their Country, by its representatives in Parliament. A few days ago, a gentleman from the Grand Signior came here with letters for me, and also a magnificent diamond Star, in the centre of which, on a blue enamel, is the Crescent and a Star. It is desired by the Grand Signior, that I will wear it on my breast. I have, therefore, attached it to my coat, over the Star of the Order of the Bath. This is sent simply as a mark of his—[*imperfect.*]

TO HIS EXCELLENCY J. SPENCER SMITH, ESQ.

[From a Copy in the Nelson Papers.]

Palermo, 6th November, 1799.

My dear Sir,

I send you a cask of sugar, such as I think you mean by saying prize-sugar: I would also have sent loaf-sugar, but it

is not to be had any more than Sherry. Had the Foudroyant
been here, I should have sent you a cask, which I will not
omit the first opportunity, as it always gives me pleasure to
execute your commissions. I send you a paper of 27th
September, which may not have reached you. In it you will
see the honourable and deserving manner in which your
gallant brother is mentioned. I hope Cadir Bey will be
perfectly satisfied with his reception; he appears a good man.
I am thinned of Ships: seven Sail of the Line since I wrote
last, besides Frigates and Sloops. Believe me, my dear Sir,
your obliged friend,

BRONTE NELSON.

TO LADY NELSON.

[From Clarke and M'Arthur, vol. ii. p. 234.]

7th November, 1799.

Since my arrival from Minorca, my task here has still continued arduous; for I cannot get the General at Minorca to
give me some troops for the service of Malta, and I have not
force enough to attack it. One day or other I shall rest
from all my labours. I still find it good to serve near home,
there a man's fag and services are easily seen; next to that,
is writing a famous account of your own actions. Yours, &c.

BRONTE NELSON.

TO CAPTAIN BALL, CHIEF OF THE ISLAND OF MALTA.

[Autograph, in the possession of Sir William Keith Ball, Bart.]

Palermo, November 7th, 1799.

My dear Ball,

I am anxiously waiting the answer from Minorca to my last
very strong application, at least for the Garrison of Messina,
till we can get troops to attack the place. The moment the
                which, I own, I expect will be unfavourable to
our wishes, I intend to go to Naples, to see what the Austrians
will do, and his Sicilian Majesty will send some men; and if,
after all our exertions, we should be forced to give up the idea
of anything beyond the blockade, it is none of our fault. I

trust that Niza will not take a man from the shore till I can get my answers, and communicate them. Lord Spencer, in a late letter, says, 'and that Malta has also fallen before the meritorious and unparalleled vigilance and exertion of Captain Ball, who has, indeed, shown himself worthy of the friendship with which you have honoured him.' I only send this, my dear Ball, to show I do not forget my friends. As to honouring you, that is not in my power; but to render you justice is my duty. I have this day wrote to the Emperor of Russia, Grand Master of Malta, requesting for you the Order of Malta; for I have never had any answer from Sir Charles Whitworth to the former application, therefore I have now gone to the fountain head. The Grand Signior has again manifested his friendship for me by sending a diamond Star, in the centre of which, on blue enamel, is a Crescent and Star; and I have called myself 'First Knight of the Order of the Crescent.' I know, my dear Sir, that no jealousy reigns in your breast, and that whatever honours are heaped on me, give you pleasure. Captain Stephenson is just come out to the Princess Charlotte—poor Hardy, consequently, turned adrift! You will have the Frigate off Malta. I send you some papers; and believe me ever your obliged and affectionate friend,

BRONTE NELSON.

TO HIS EXCELLENCY THE MARQUIS DE NIZA.

[Letter-Book.]

Palermo, November 7th, 1799.

My dear Marquis,

I every moment expect the answers from Minorca. Ball will show you my letter to him of my intentions. I only beg that you will not take a man from the Island till my directions can get to you of the future measures necessary to be taken. But if your Ship wants to come here before that time, leave the command with Captain Louis, giving all your Ships orders for that purpose; but again I desire you will not draw one person from the shore. The Grand Signior has just created me first Knight of the Imperial Order of the Crescent, and sent me a diamond Star.

We have reports of our check in Holland, September 19th,

and of our complete victory on the 24th;[2] also of Suwarrow's success on the 10th and 11th October—8000 killed, 20,000 prisoners, 15,000 of which laid down their arms in a body—Massena carried off in a car, wounded. The loss of the Russians 9000, of which 1000 were Officers—Suwarrow wounded.[3] But we have no official accounts. From Spain we know that the Spanish Ambassador is fled from Paris, and that an insurrection had taken place in Paris. All will end well. Adieu, my dear Marquis, and believe me ever your obliged friend,

BRONTE NELSON.

TO EVAN NEPEAN, ESQ., ADMIRALTY.

[Original, in the Admiralty.]

Palermo, November 9th, 1799.

Sir,

This letter, with all my dispatches, will be delivered to you by Captain Thomas Masterman Hardy, who has been my Captain from the Battle of the Nile till October 13th, when he was superseded by Sir Edward Berry. I beg leave to recommend him to their Lordships in the strongest manner, as one of the best Officers in His Majesty's Service, and to refer to him for the particular state of the Ships under my command, and of my own situation in this Country, certainly a very extraordinary one; for if I move they think the Country in danger, and that they are abandoned. If my Flag is in a Transport, they seem contented. Believe me, Sir, &c.,

NELSON.

TO HIS ROYAL HIGHNESS THE DUKE OF CLARENCE.

[Letter Book.]

Palermo, 9th November, 1799.

Sir,

I beg leave to present to your Royal Highness, Captain Hardy, late of the Foudroyant, an Officer of the most dis-

---

[2] The success of the army in Holland here alluded to, occurred on the 2nd of October. Vide "London Gazette" of the 8th and 13th of October, 1799.

[3] This report was without any foundation.

tinguished merit, and therefore highly worthy of your notice.
He will tell you of all my arduous work in this Country, and
that all my anxiety is at present taken up with the desire of
possessing Malta. But I fear, notwithstanding all my exertions, that I shall not get any British troops from Minorca,
without which the business will be prolonged, perhaps
till it is relieved, when all the force we can collect would be
of little use against the strongest place in Europe. I am
anxiously waiting the arrival of General Fox, and hope he will
not consider the order for the removal of one or two Regiments, of such great consequence as the reduction of Malta,
by keeping them for two months longer in the Mediterranean.
On the one hand, they must, in England, or on the Continent,
be like a drop of water in the ocean. By staying here, and
employed, they would liberate us from our Enemy close to our
door, gratify the Emperor of Russia, protect our Levant trade,
and relieve a Squadron of our Ships from this service; besides
giving us one 80-gun Ship, two 40-gun Frigates, a Maltese
new Ship of the Line ready for sea, and two Frigates. With
these in the scale, I cannot comprehend that a moment can be
lost in deciding; but, Sir, I find few think as I do—but to
obey orders is all perfection! To serve my King, and to destroy
the French, I consider as the great order of all, from which
little ones spring; and if one of these little ones militate
against it, (for, who can tell exactly at a distance?) I go back
to obey the great order and object, to *down, down* with the
damned French villains. Excuse my warmth; but my blood
boils at the name of a Frenchman. I hate them all—Royalists
and Republicans.

My late letters from Egypt are, that Sir Sidney Smith is
hurt at the notorious cowardice and want of discipline in the
Turkish army, and I find that General Koehler[4] does *not
approve* of such irregular proceedings as Naval Officers attacking and defending Fortifications. We have but one idea
—to get close alongside. None but a sailor would have placed
a battery only a hundred and eighty yards from the Castle of
St. Elmo; a soldier must have gone according to art, and the
ZZ way; my brave Sir Thomas Troubridge went straight, for

---

[4] Vide vol. i. p. 375.

we had no time to spare. Your Royal Highness will not believe that I mean to lessen the conduct of the Army; I have the highest respect for them all; but General Koehler should not have wrote such a paragraph in his letter: it conveyed a jealousy, which I dare say is not in his disposition.

May health and every blessing attend your Royal Highness is the constant prayer of your attached and obliged servant,

BRONTE NELSON.

TO EVAN NEPEAN, ESQ., ADMIRALTY.

[Original, in the Admiralty.]

Palermo, November 10th, 1799.

Sir,

Yesterday the Vincejo Brig, who I had sent to look into Toulon on the 16th, joined me with an account that the two Venetian Ships armée en flute, two Frigates and two Corvettes sailed from Toulon on the 16th, in the evening, loaded with provisions; and that the Généreux and three Frigates, one the Ettiani [?] of 56 guns, were ready for sea. As Captain Long judged Malta their object, he made sail for that Island and gave the Marquis de Niza that information. As I have placed for the moment nine Sail of the Line, one Frigate, and three Corvettes in the track to that Island, I hope they cannot relieve it; for if they do, we shall have all to begin again, and I believe worse, for we shall be drove off the Island; but it has been no fault of the Navy that it has not been attacked by land, but we have neither the means ourselves, or the influence with others who have the power.

Reports say the Ships are put into Ville Franche. I have sent the Penelope to look after them, for she is the only Frigate I have really fit to go to sea (besides the Phaeton at Constantinople.) The Russians are supposed to have a Squadron on the Coast of Genoa, but I cannot depend, nor would I have their Lordships, on any operations but by English Ships. Marquis de Niza will be forced to quit his station in a week, for his Squadron cannot keep the sea like ours. I assure their Lordships nothing shall be wanting on my part to get hold of these gentry, and I am sure of the exertion of all under my command. I am, &c.,

NELSON.

TO SIR THOMAS TROUBRIDGE, BART., OR THE COMMANDING
OFFICER OF HIS MAJESTY'S SHIPS AT MINORCA.

[Letter-Book.]

Palermo, November 10th, 1799.

My dear Troubridge,

The miserable situation of the Minotaur makes it absolutely
necessary for her to go to Minorca to re-fit, and it must be
done in the best manner we are able, but should it be impossible to re-fit her there, she must go to Gibraltar without loss
of time ; and when re-fitted, join me as soon as possible, unless Admiral Duckworth should require her services down the
Mediterranean. I am almost in desperation about Malta. If
our General cannot help us nor the Russians, I see only that
we must abandon the Island, and confine ourselves to a sea-
blockade. I am anxious to see you here, that you may relieve
Niza and the Portuguese, for they must come away. Ever
yours faithfully,

BRONTE NELSON.

TO THE MARQUIS DE NIZA.

[Letter-Book.]

Palermo, 11th November, 1799.

My dear Marquis,

I am afraid the French Ships are put into Ville Franche,
and will not as yet come to pay you a visit. If they do, I have
no doubt but you will take them all. I send you the Princess
Charlotte ; she may be of some use, although not to be calculated as an English-manned Frigate. I am wanting the Foudroyant very much, therefore, if she has not left you before
this letter gets to you, pray send her to me. I expect the
Russian Admiral's answer every moment, but I beg you will
not draw a man from the Island till you have my directions.
Ever believe me, my dear Marquis, your sincere and faithful
friend,

BRONTE NELSON.

TO THE RIGHT HON. LORD MINTO.

[Autograph, in the Minto Papers.]

Palermo, November 11th, 1799.

My dear Lord,

I beg leave to introduce my friend Captain Hardy to your notice; he was Lieutenant with Cockburn in the Meleager and Minerve. He will tell you precisely our state here. When you have read the letters, be so good as to direct their being sealed and delivered to Captain Hardy. I am all anxiety about Malta; I want the Army to help me, but I cannot yet succeed. Pray tell me if I can do anything for you here; if so, you have only to command, for believe me, as ever, your attached and affectionate friend,

BRONTE NELSON.

You will know the Goliath is sailed for England; George,[5] a thorough seaman, and perfectly well.

TO MAJOR-GENERAL SIR JAMES ST. CLAIR ERSKINE, BART.[6]

[From a Copy in the Admiralty.]

Palermo, November 12th, 1799.

My dear Sir James,

I am uneasy at not having yet had answers to my last letter of October 26th by the Salamine; therefore I must in duty again state the very great importance of driving the French out of Malta, and endeavour to impress my opinion by such arguments as offer themselves to my mind. I consider the great order of all (implied by the commencement of the war) is to destroy the power of the French: to accomplish this in the quietest and easiest way, is the object of all lesser orders; and if it can be proved that a breach of the lesser order is a more strict compliance with the former, then there can be no doubt of the duty of the breach of the lesser order.

----

[5] The present Honourable Rear-Admiral George Eliott, C.B.

[6] Addressed to Sir James St. Clair Erskine, but it came to the hands of General the Hon. Henry Fox, who had arrived at Minorca in the interim, and taken the command of the troops.

I will suppose two Regiments ordered to England from Minorca,—certainly they not knowing of the important object of possessing Malta to us and our Allies, and probably believing, from reports, that La Valetta would fall to the present force employed against it,—the detaining these two Regiments for two months would probably, with the assistance of the Russians, give us Malta, liberate us from an Enemy close to our door, gratify the Emperor of Russia, protect our Levant trade, relieve a large Squadron of Ships from this service, and enable me the better to afford Naval protection to the Island of Minorca, and assist our Allies on the Northern coast of Italy, and to annoy the Enemy on the Coast of France. It would give us one 80-gun Ship, two 40-gun Frigates, French, besides a new Maltese 70-gun Ship and two Frigates, all ready for sea. With these in the scale against sending away the two Regiments, can there be a doubt as to the propriety of keeping them a little longer? In England or on the Continent, they would be like a drop of water in the ocean, and here they would be of the importance I have pointed out. I earnestly hope that you and General Fox will see the object in the same way as I do; if unhappily you do not, nor can allow the garrison of Messina to hold post in Malta till a force can be got to attack it, the worst consequences may be apprehended to our trade and that of our Allies. I have not yet received answers from the Russian Admiral and General at Naples. The weather has been so very bad. God forbid we should be obliged to give up the idea of taking La Valetta, only the thought of it almost breaks my heart.

I have so many Ships looking out for the Ships which sailed from Toulon the 16th October, that I do not think they can easily get to Malta. I beg that this letter, if General Fox is with you, may be considered as addressed to him as yourself; and ever believe me, with great truth and regard, your obliged friend,

NELSON.

TO THE COMMISSIONERS OF THE VICTUALLING BOARD.

[Letter-Book.]

Palermo, November 14th, 1799.

Gentlemen,

I have received by post your answer to my letter from the Bay of Naples, in which you beg me to accept your acknowledgments for the trouble I had taken in investigating the report made by Mr. Lock, on the subject of the purchase of fresh beef. I must own, that I conceived your letter couched in terms of such coldness, as a little surprised me; but it was not till this moment of the departure of Captain Hardy, that I have heard a report, circulated by Mr. Lock, that you had received a letter from him on this subject, and that you had thanked him for having saved Government 40 per cent. If it is true, which I cannot believe, that you have wrote Mr. Lock any letters on this subject, I desire to say, and not to be misunderstood, that the conduct of the Board is very reprehensible, and scandalous in its treatment to me, the Commanding Officer of his Majesty's Fleet in the Mediterranean. I hope you will send these expressions to our superiors, the Board of Admiralty; for if it is true, which I cannot believe, it would make it more scandalous not to have sent me copies of these letters. I will never, for any power on earth, retract a syllable of what I have wrote in this letter. I defy any insinuations against my honour. Nelson is as far from doing a scandalous or mean action as the heavens are above the earth. I will now tell you the result of the inquiry of an honest man, a faithful servant of his King and Country, was, (from the papers I sent to your Board,) that the accusation of Mr. Lock was malicious and scandalous; and if any Board or individual apply any softer terms to the papers sent you by me, I desire to apply the same terms to them.

I have ever treated all Boards, and every individual, with the greatest respect and consideration; but when my honour, or that of my brave friends is concerned, I will never stop till the examination is made; for Mr. Lock would not, or could not, (which I believe,) but both are equally criminal, bring forward any single point of accusation. I therefore demand that you will direct (subject to my inspection) a strict and impartial inquiry to be made into this saving of 40 per cent. I have only to observe, that Mr. Lock never made any complaint of the price, until I wrote a Note to say that I should not interfere in the purchase—that he that sold the best and cheapest, would, of course, be the seller.[7] I have desired Captain Hardy to call on your Board on this subject, as he was Captain of the Foudroyant at this time, and knows perfectly my opinion of Mr. Lock. I had every inclination to serve him, but *never* at the expense of the State, by giving a monopoly against a competition. I am, Gentlemen, your most obedient servant,

BRONTE NELSON.[8]

TO CHARLES LOCK, ESQ., CONSUL, NAPLES.

[Letter Book.]

Palermo, November 15th, 1799.

Sir,

You having told Sir William Hamilton that your conduct respecting the purchase of fresh beef had not been disapproved of at home, and, as Captain Hardy understood you, that you had been thanked for saving Government 40 per cent., I do, therefore, in consequence of these reports circulated by you, demand in my situation as Commanding his Majesty's Fleet in the Mediterranean, from you, as his Majesty's Consul for the Kingdom of Naples, copies of all Public letters[9] which you have wrote respecting the Fleet under my command, and of all the answers which you have received to those letters, in order that I may know what steps it may be proper for me to take. I am, &c.,

BRONTE NELSON.

---

[7] Vide vol. iii. p. 420.

[8] The Commissioner of the Victualling Board, in reply to this letter, on the 20th of December, said, " After declaring to your Lordship that we never had any correspondence with Mr. Lock on the subject to which it relates, we submit to your Lordship's own reflection the manner in which you have thought proper to arraign the conduct of this Board merely upon a rumour, the authenticity of which you twice profess yourself to disbelieve."—*Original* in the Nelson Papers.

[9] Mr. Lock complied with this demand. Vide p. 129, infra.

TO COMMISSIONER INGLEFIELD, GIBRALTAR.

[Letter-Book.]

Palermo, November 15th, 1799.

My dear Sir,

I have sent everything from the Foudroyant to the Ships in
Egypt, for no other Ship has any stores; therefore you will be
so good as to ship the proportion of stores demanded in such
Ship as the Commanding Sea-officer may appoint. I can
only say, my dear Commissioner, that we are all in distress,
and I know not who is in the best state. I am in desperation
about Malta, and know not which way to turn. I look
anxiously towards Minorca, and the Russians, at Naples; for
you know the importance of getting Malta from the French.
As this is what I call a flying letter, I have only to say what
is truth and comes from the heart, is, that I am your sincere
and affectionate friend,

BRONTE NELSON.

I must beg your assistance in getting the ordnance stores
forwarded also.

TO HIS EXCELLENCY THE MARQUIS DE NIZA.

[Letter-Book.]

Palermo, 15th November, 1799.

My dear Marquis,

I have this moment received your letters by the Foudroyant,
of the 6th and 7th, which I have sent to General Acton, and
I hope the mast will be immediately ordered for the Principe
Real. I trust that Commodore Troubridge will be soon
here, when I shall send him to relieve you; for I am, I can
assure you, perfectly sensible of your exertion, and *loyal* and
proper disobedience of the orders of his Royal Highness, who,
I am sure, as a faithful and attached Ally of my most gracious
Sovereign, will highly approve [of it.] I hope that the
General at Minorca, and also the Russian Admiral and
General at Naples, will soon send you sufficient force for the
reduction of La Valetta, and place the Grand Master firmly
in his seat. A brig is said to be in sight.

November 17th.—The brig is from Naples: 3000 Russians would sail for Malta on the 17th, therefore, for Heaven's sake, do not take a man from the Island till their arrival. I expect also the troops from Minorca; and I should wish, for your sake, that your Marines could be left. It would, I am sure, flatter the Prince of Brazil, to have an opportunity of assisting in placing the Grand Master in Malta. I would not have this matter of the Russians being so near, talked of, as it is possible, as a last effort, the garrison may not only make a *sortie* and destroy our battery, but drive us from the Island; therefore the more private this account is kept the better. I expect every moment Commodore Troubridge, who shall instantly come to your relief. Your Excellency's conduct as an Officer and as a man, in every situation, has been most grateful to my feelings; but your conduct since you have been off Malta, will stamp your character as a Sea-officer, second to none in Europe. If it is of any value, you have my warmest gratitude for your support of me on every occasion; and believe me, for ever, my dear Marquis, your affectionate friend,

BRONTE NELSON.

TO HIS EXCELLENCY LE CHEVALIER LIZAKOVITZ.

[Letter-Book. The Foudroyant having returned to Palermo on the 17th of November, Lord Nelson's Flag was rehoisted on board of her.]

Palermo, 17th November, 1799.

Dear Sir,

I know not how to sufficiently thank your Excellency for all your kindness towards me, for I never receive any details from Tuscany but from you. I earnestly hope that Prince Suwarrow will be completely successful in Switzerland, and that we shall be the same in Holland. I then think the war must be brought to a happy issue. My great object now is to see the French drove out of La Valetta, and the illustrious Grand Master in quiet possession. For this purpose I have been to Minorca, to arrange with our Generals a plan of operations with the Russian Admiral and General at Naples. As yet I have had no answer from Naples, but I look for it every moment. All our affairs in this Island are exactly as you left us. The King has been a little unwell, but is now perfectly recovered. Sir William and Lady Hamilton feel equally obliged as myself for all your most interesting letters. We beg our best respects to Madame Lizakovitz, and believe me, dear Sir, your Excellency's most obliged

Bronte Nelson.

TO HIS EXCELLENCY SIR JOHN ACTON, BART.

[Letter-Book.]

Palermo, November 18th, 1799.

The moment I can get a Corvette she shall carry the Consul to Tunis; therefore be so good as to keep him ready at a moment's warning. Your Excellency's last observation, about a new disposition when Malta is taken, that the Flag of the Order is to be hoisted instead of the three Flags, appears to convey that my sentiments of respect for his Sicilian Majesty's flag were lessened. I send you two papers, on which my order to good Captain Ball was founded. If I have erred, it is not too late to call back my order, and if you think so, I shall be happy to meet your Excellency, and the Ministers of England and Russia, on this subject. There is not, I can assure you, that man on earth, who would so strongly unite the two Monarchs whom we serve as myself, and may perdition seize the wretch who would do the least thing towards lessening that harmony! And could it ever happen that any English Minister wanted to make me an instrument of hurting the feelings of his Sicilian Majesty, I would give up my commission sooner than do it. I am open to your Excellency, and I think you are so to me. The interest of our Sovereigns requires it, and I am sure that we both only think of uniting the Courts of London and Naples still closer together. I am placed in such a situation—a Subject of one King by birth, and, as far as is consistent with my allegiance to that King, a voluntary Subject of his Sicilian Majesty—that if any man attempted to separate my two Kings, by all that is sacred, I should consider even putting that man to death as a meritorious act. Therefore, my dear Sir John, never, never for a

moment think that I am capable of doing anything but endeavouring to exalt the glory of their Sicilian Majesties; and
believe me, my dear Sir, with the sincerest esteem and
affection, your obliged,

BRONTE NELSON.

TO CAPTAIN BALL, CHIEF OF THE MALTESE.

[Letter-Book.]

Palermo, November 19th, 1799.

My dear Ball,

The Chevalier Italinsky will be with you in a few days—
probably before the arrival of the Russian troops. He is the
second Minister from the Emperor of Russia to this Court,
or Corresponding Minister, through whom everything relative
to the Fleet and Army passes. He has a proclamation to pub-
lish at a proper time. You knew him, I believe, at Naples.
He is an old acquaintance of Sir William's, and a worthy,
good, and able Minister; and you will ever, I am confident,
experience his friendship and just way of thinking.

The troops going against Malta, will, of course, be maintained at the expense of their respective Sovereigns; but the
Maltese, till the restoration of the Order (at least) by the
three Powers of Russia, England, and Naples. I shall give
the Chevalier Italinsky a letter to you when he goes, and he
will explain to you our conferences with General Acton.
Ever, my dear Ball, your affectionate,

BRONTE NELSON.

TO SIR JAMES ST. CLAIR ERSKINE, BART.

[Letter-Book.]

Palermo, 20th November, 1799.

My dear Sir James,

The movement of the Russians towards Malta only acts as
an additional reason for the troops from Minorca going
straight to Malta, instead of coming to Palermo, that the
business may be soon settled; and does not take away from
me my argument respecting the two Regiments. Ever, my
dear Sir James, your obliged,

BRONTE NELSON.

TO THE RIGHT HONOURABLE LORD WILLIAM BENTINCK.

[Letter-Book.]

Palermo, November 22nd, 1799.

My dear Lord,

By your last letter from Trieste, I take for granted you are with the Austrian army, under the command of the Baron Melas. We are anxious to hear of the success of our friend Suwarrow. Although I never had the pleasure of seeing him, yet, as an individual of Europe, I love, honour, and respect him. Others may love the great hero—Nelson loves the man, for I hear that he despises wealth, if it stands in the road to fame. The corps of Russians is just about sailing for Malta, and I hope that our Generals at Minorca will give a part of that garrison to assist in the capture of Malta. Our Squadron have had a blockade by sea and land, for more than a year past; but we have never had a force to commence a regular siege. But I now hope to see an end put to our truly hard service. The Royal Family do not return to Naples till after the capture of Ancona, which I am looking for every day, when both Sir William Hamilton and myself, think they will go to Naples as soon as possible. At home the Admiralty think, and naturally, that the Russian Squadron, eleven Sail of the Line, besides Frigates and Corvettes, would look out on the Coast of Genoa; but in truth their Ships have not the ability of keeping on that Coast in the winter season, and I regret that at present I have not Ships enough for that service. I beg you will assure Baron Melas, that whenever he approaches the Coast, I will endeavour, at the expense of cramping other services, to have a small Squadron at the Coast of Genoa, to support his communication with the sea. I rest confident of your kindness in expressing [my sentiments], and to do everything that is possible for the finishing the war, and I beg that your Lordship will believe me truly your obliged humble servant,

BRONTE NELSON.

TO HIS EXCELLENCY THE MARQUIS DE NIZA.

[Letter-Book.]

Palermo, November 24th, 1799.

My dear Marquis,

Your Officer who brought your letter yesterday noon, did not wait my arrival from Court, and I did not know where to send to him. This moment he gives me hopes that you will wait my answer before you leave Malta, which has relieved my anxious mind from the deepest affliction, which your letter of the 19th had plunged me into. The moment I can get Ships, you shall be relieved; but, for all our sakes, do not draw, in this critical moment, one man from the Island. Do not, my dear Marquis, let any man draw your excellent judgment from doing what is for the good of our respective Sovereigns, and their Allies. They are not your true friends, or faithful servants of their Sovereigns; therefore, again, and ten times again, I direct you, I entreat you, not to abandon Malta. Stay till the Russians, or English troops, arrive; it cannot be many days. You have, my friend, gained more honour by obeying my order against that of your Prince, and for which His Royal Highness will thank you, than ever can be done by obedience, if it is to injure the good Cause. You are a seaman, and we never wish to find shelter, when the public service requires our being exposed; and as we risk our lives, so we willingly risk our commissions, to serve the public. Ever your faithful friend,

BRONTE NELSON.

TO CAPTAIN BALL, CHIEF OF THE ISLAND OF MALTA.

[Autograph, in the possession of Sir William Keith Ball, Bart.]

Palermo, November 24th, 1799.

My dear Ball,

I love, honour, and respect you, and no persons ever have, nor could they, if they were so disposed, lessen you in my esteem, both as a public Officer and a private man: therefore never let such a thought come into your head, which was never more wanted to be clear from embroils than at this moment. I trust the Marquis will stay till the Russians arrive, or that he is relieved by Troubridge, who I expect every moment; and, from the delay, I think the Troops may come with him. The Foudroyant is in momentary readiness to go to Messina to fetch Colonel Graham. But, my dear friend, your holding your post so long as you have, is matter of the greatest credit to you. But, alas, I am neither able to do justice to my friends by telling a good story, like Sir Sidney Smith, nor are we so near home as Holland. If you are forced to even quit the Island, it cannot lessen your exertion or abilities, and do not let such an event, should it unfortunately happen, depress your spirits for a moment; and believe me, as ever, your obliged and affectionate friend,

BRONTE NELSON,

TO BRIGADIER-GENERAL GRAHAM.

[Letter-Book. Lord Nelson's Flag was shifted on the 25th of November to the Atty Transport, as the Foudroyant sailed on that day with the Culloden for Malta.]

Palermo, November 25th, 1799.

My dear Sir,

Commodore Sir Thomas Troubridge is the Officer destined by me to co-operate with you for the reduction of Malta. One more able and active could not be selected from our service; and as the Commodore is in full possession of my sentiments on every point, there can no doubt arise on any subject, which he cannot immediately clear up. Ball has been, by his Sicilian Majesty, the legitimate Sovereign of the Island, placed at the head of the Maltese, in both a civil, and, as I understand, military capacity. His conciliating manners will overcome all difficulty with the inhabitants. They adore him; therefore, I think in any Capitulation he should sign. I will not state the necessity of a most cordial co-operation with the Russian General. It is the desire of our Government to gratify the Emperor in every wish about the Order of Malta. The Chevalier Italinsky, the Minister at War for the Navy and Army in Italy, is just going to Malta, to concert measures with the Allied forces for the government of the Order, whenever La Valetta shall fall to our exertions. He is a very amiable good man, and a perfect man of business. The inhabitants of Malta may, till the Order has got back its wealth, want some little help in corn. It has been agreed on, in that case, by the Ministers of Russia, Naples, and England, that the expense should be defrayed by the three Courts. Wishing you, from my soul, a speedy termination of this tedious business, and assuring you of my firm and cordial support, in every respect, I have only to beg that you will believe me, with the truest regard, &c.

BRONTE NELSON.

TO COMMODORE SIR THOMAS TROUBRIDGE, BART., CAPTAIN OF H. M. SHIP CULLODEN.

Foudroyant, Palermo, 25th November, 1799.

You are hereby required and directed to take under your command the Ships named in the margin,[1] whose Captains have my instructions to follow your orders, and proceed to Messina, and embark on board the said Ships, or any British Transports that may be there, such part of the garrison of that place, as Brigadier-General Graham may think proper, with such stores, guns, ammunition, baggage, provisions, &c. as he may wish to have embarked, and proceed with them to the Island of Malta; and having landed them there, you will take upon you the command of the blockade of La Valetta, whenever the Marquis de Niza quits the Island, and co-operate with Captain Ball, who is appointed by his Sicilian Majesty, Chief of the Maltese people, as well as with Brigadier-General Graham, or the Officer commanding the British troops. And on the arrival of the Russian Ships and troops, which may be daily expected, you will also most cordially co-operate with their Admiral and General, and preserve the good understanding which at present so happily exists between us, rendering them any service or assistance in your power. And in the event of the surrender of La Valetta, the colours of the Order of Malta are to be hoisted, and the Government restored according to the plan sent to me, a copy of which is here enclosed for your guidance. And with respect to the

---

[1] Northumberland, Foudroyant.

public property found in the place, my wish is that it should be valued; and as to the Ships of War, they are to remain for the disposal of the three Allied Courts of London, Petersburg, and the Two Sicilies.

BRONTE NELSON.

TO EVAN NEPEAN, ESQ., ADMIRALTY.

[Original, in the Admiralty.]

Palermo, November 26th, 1799.

Sir,

It was with extreme concern that I read your letter of October 11th, being perfectly conscious that want of communicating where and when it is necessary, cannot be laid to my charge. I find on looking at my Letter-book that I did write to Admiral Duckworth to correspond with you on such points as might be necessary,[2] and which it was impossible I could detail. I also find that by a Neapolitan courier which left Palermo, the same day, that I wrote, not only to you, but to Lord Spencer. I own I do not feel that if Cutters and Couriers go off the same day, that it is necessary to write by a Convoy. I know the absolute necessity of the Board's being exactly acquainted with everything which passes, and they, I beg, will give me credit for attention to my duty.

As a Junior Flag Officer, of course without those about me, as Secretaries, Interpreters, &c., I have been thrown into a more extensive correspondence than ever, perhaps, fell to the lot of any Admiral, and into a political situation I own out of my sphere. It is a fact which it would not become me to boast of, but on the present occasion, that I have never but three times put my feet on the ground, since December, 1798, and, except to the Court, that till after eight o'clock at night I never relax from business.

I have had hitherto, the Board knows, no one emolument— no one advantage of a Commander-in-Chief.

I have the honour to be, &c.,

BRONTE NELSON.

---

[2] Vide vol. iii. p. 453, and p. 11, ante.

TO HIS EXCELLENCY THE HONOURABLE WILLIAM WYNDHAM.

[Letter-Book.]

Palermo, 26th November, 1799.

Sir,

I have to request that your Excellency will have the goodness to forward the two letters sent herewith. Yesterday, an order came from General Fox for the garrison of Messina to proceed to Malta, and as the Russians are destined for the same object, I hope we shall very soon be in possession of it. But, from the slowness of the movements, I have great fears that the French may have made a sortie, and that our batteries will, at least, be destroyed, if nothing worse happens. His Sicilian Majesty, I am sorry to say, [will not,] at this moment, return to Naples; but as Ancona is, we hear, taken, we hope it will expedite his Majesty's departure. I have nothing from Egypt for some months. Believe me, with great respect, &c.,

BRONTE NELSON.

TO HIS HIGHNESS THE BEY OF TUNIS.

[Letter-Book.]

Palermo, November 26th, 1799.

Sir,

I cannot permit an English Cutter to go even into the Bay of Tunis, without expressing to your Highness my most sincere respect, which, on all occasions, I shall feel happy in showing, not only as an obedience to the great King, my Master, but also from my own inclination. It would have given me much pleasure, could I have interfered in the capture of a Vessel, belonging to one of your Subjects, taken by a Portuguese corvette; but as peace had not then taken place between your Highness and the Court of Portugal, it was impossible for me to be of any use. Your Highness well knows that not one Portuguese ship has been cruizing on your Coast. This is such a mark of my attention, as no time can efface from your Highness's head. The number of Vessels taken, having certificates from me, and the English

Commander off Malta, that they were actually employed in carrying provisions for those who were fighting against the common Enemy, I own, hurt me. To a mere trader, I never have, nor ever will give a certificate; but as people cannot fight without food, I did hope that those Vessels would have been considered as the Vessels of true friends. But at Algiers, I find other sentiments prevail. If your Highness has any Vessels taken by your Cruisers of this description, I trust that you will order their restoration, and, in particular, the poor people carried into slavery. This will be considered as a great act of friendship and esteem shown by your Highness to your most faithful and attached,

Bronte Nelson.

TO HIS EXCELLENCY SIR JOHN ACTON, BART.

[Letter-Book.]

Palermo, November 26th, 1799.

My dear Sir,

As I hear your Corvette goes off for Malta this evening, would it not be a good opportunity to send, as your Excellency told us you have, some of the money belonging to the Order, for the use of the poor Maltese? The Inhabitants and Troops under arms, are by this time, again in want, and I hope that the Ministers of the Allied Powers will immediately fix some mode of keeping distress from the Island till the Order is restored.

I have talked much with Sir Thomas Troubridge and Captain Louis on what they think would satisfy the Captains, Officers, and Men, for their renouncing all claim to the French property, and all salvages; and they are clearly of opinion, that to the Navy no sum less than £60,000 could be offered; and that, from our own Sovereign, three times as much would be paid; for that the stores and cannon, even at Città Vecchia, would, if sold by his Sicilian Majesty, exceed three times this amount. The antiques found packed up at Città Vecchia, and in the Custom-House at Rome, and which would have been in France but for the blockade by the English, are undoubtedly objects for a large salvage. This sum will only

give the Captains employed on this service £3000 each,
and Commodore Troubridge can receive no more prize-
money than the Commander of the smallest Vessel of War.
The Perseus came from Corfu last night. I find the 3500
Russians are arrived at Constantinople. I hope the Russians
from Holland will come by sea into Italy, and make head
against any attack of the French, next spring. Ever, my
dear Sir, your Excellency's most obliged,

BRONTE NELSON.

TO REAR-ADMIRAL DUCKWORTH.

[Letter-Book.]

Palermo, 27th November, 1799.

My dear Admiral,
Many thanks for your letter of November 12th, and I approve very much of your calling at Algiers. I do not consider
what are called my passports as anything more than a certificate
that the Vessel carrying, was employed in fetching provisions
for people fighting against the common Enemy. I am aware
that the first moment any insult is offered to the British flag [the
best plan] is to get as large a force as possible off Algiers and
seize all his Cruizers; but if, in such a contest, any English
vessel is taken, I know what will be said against me, and how
little support I shall experience. But, my dear Admiral, when
the object of the actor is only to serve faithfully, I feel superior
to the smiles or frowns of any Board. Apropos, I have received
a severe set-down from the Admiralty, for not having wrote
by the Charon, attached to a Convoy, although I wrote both by
a Cutter and Courier the same day. But I see clearly that
they wish to show I am unfit for this command. I will readily
acknowledge it, and therefore they need have no scruples
about sending out a Commander-in-Chief. Troubridge did
not anchor. The Foudroyant weighed, and joined, and they
both proceeded for Messina, as expeditiously as possible, in
order to take on board the garrison of Messina. I hope
they may arrive at Malta in time, but I have my strong fears
that the garrison may have made a sortie, and destroyed our
batteries. The Russians are slow, but by this time, I hope, are

before Malta. They were to sail from Naples the 20th. The Perseus, who is just come in from Corfu, and is in want of everything, goes straight to Gibraltar, to refit, and with orders to come up again immediately, and the Russians and Turks, with the Neapolitans excluded from the Capitulation, which has given great offence. I believe Austria will make her peace with France, and that Russia and Prussia will be at war with the Emperor of Germany. Sir William and Lady Hamilton desire their kindest regards. I am nearly blind, but things go so contrary to my mind *out* of our profession, that truly I care not how soon I am off the stage. Your Surgeon's mate is appointed to the Mahon, and all your other wishes are, as far as I am able, complied with; and I assure you that I shall always be glad of occasions of proving to you with what regard and esteem I am your obliged,

Bronte Nelson.

Pray don't let the Admiralty want for letters of every occurrence.

TO EVAN NEPEAN, ESQ., ADMIRALTY.

[Original, in the Admiralty.]

Palermo, November 28th, 1799.

Sir,

I wrote to you by the post (now open) yesterday, but as the Perseus is going direct to Gibraltar to refit, I write a line just to say that General Fox's permission for the Garrison of Messina going to Malta was brought me by Commodore Sir Thomas Troubridge, the day before yesterday. I directed, in the moment, the Foudroyant to weigh, and both are gone to Messina for the troops. I earnestly hope they will arrive in time at Malta to hold our present advantageous positions, but I have my fears; nothing but the prudence, judgment, and bravery of my friend Captain Ball could have kept us on the Island for many months past. The Russians, I hope, sailed from Naples on the 20th, their Lordships may be assured of our cordial co-operation with them, and of my earnest endeavours to merit their Lordships' approbation.

Last night I received from the inhabitants of the Island of Zante a letter of which I enclose a copy, and also a very massy and elegant gold-hilted Sword, and a beautiful Cane, enriched with diamonds; these flattering marks of approbation from all Religions cannot but afford me the greatest pleasure, and be a stimulus for the greatest exertions, not only from myself, but also to the Officers in our Service growing up to the superior ranks.

I have the honour to be, &c.,
BRONTE NELSON.

I send a letter from Mr. Spiridion Foresti, and I must beg leave earnestly to recommend him to their Lordships' notice, and I also desire to do the same to Major Magra, the Consul at Tunis. These two gentlemen are the *only* ones I have found who really and truly do their duty, and merit every encouragement and protection.   B. N.

TO THE RIGHT HONOURABLE EARL SPENCER, K.G.[3]

[Letter-Book.]

Palermo, 28th November, 1799.

My dear Lord,

I am writing a letter to you on the subject of our situation with the Barbary States, but I shall not keep the Perseus, by detaining her a moment with this fine levanter. I hope Ball

---

[3] It must have been about this time that Lord Nelson received the following letter from Earl Spencer, the importance of which has been pointed out. Vide vol. iii. p. 509.

"Admiralty, 7th October, 1799.

"My dear Lord,

"In answer to your Letter of the 23rd of July, which did not reach me till the 26th of last month, I can only now repeat what I believe I have before said on the subject—namely, that the intentions and motives by which all your measures have been governed, have been as pure and good as their success has been complete.

The arrival of the Squadron detached under Admiral Duckworth to Minorca, was a very satisfactory event to us, as it put that Island in a more perfect state of security, though I do not apprehend that in the present state of things there is much danger of its being attacked, and we are now looking forward in the expectation of hearing

I 2

will be able to hold fast a little longer. All the Marines from
the Foudroyant are on shore at Malta, and nothing has been
wanting on my part to second his truly meritorious exertions.
The Marquis de Niza has the greatest merit in obeying my
orders, in direct disobedience to those of his Court, but by his
letter of the 19th—I fear by the advice of some of his English
Commodores—he may be induced to quit Malta, which would
be ruin to us in that Island. He has quoted Sir James St.
Clair Erskine and Colonel Graham as a justification of his
obedience of orders; for they would not, he says, disobey their
orders, to save Malta—therefore, why should he? But as he
would, about that time, receive from me, a stronger order and
requisition if possible, than ever, holding out the certain
displeasure instead of approbation of his Royal Highness the
Prince of Brazil, should he obey, in this critical moment, the
order to proceed to Lisbon, I trust he will remain. Commodore
Sir Thomas Troubridge will relieve him, and all will then be
well.

In General Fox's orders to Colonel Graham, he says, ' you
will not incur any expense for stores, or any article but provisions.' What can this mean? But I have told Troubridge
that the Cause cannot stand still for want of a little money.
This would be what we call 'penny-wise and pound foolish.'
If nobody will pay it, I shall sell Bronté and the Emperor of
Russia's box; for I feel myself above every consideration but

either from you or from Captain Ball, of the surrender of Malta, which, I hope, cannot hold out much longer, as the approach of the bad weather may much increase
the difficulty of the blockade. You will receive a copy of a communication on the
subject of this Island from the Secretary of State, which was left with Lord Keith
by Lord St. Vincent, and from the circumstances under which the former quitted the
Mediterranean, had not been transmitted to your Lordship. I have only to add to
what you will collect from that paper, that the utmost importance is attached by his
Majesty's Government to the object of carefully avoiding to do anything which may
raise any jealousies in the mind of the Emperor of Russia, who is particularly bent
on the point of restoring, under some new regulations, the Order of Malta, and whose
conduct ever on this subject, though one on which he may perhaps have been sus ·
pected by the world of entertaining more ambitious views, has been, as far as we are
enabled to judge of it, of the most disinterested and honourable kind.

" I trust this letter will find you in good health and spirits, and shall conclude
with assuring you, that I am, very faithfully, your obedient humble servant,
SPENCER."—*Autograph*, lately in the possession of Mr. Evans, of Maddox Street,
Hanover Square.

that of serving faithfully. Do not, my dear Lord, let ₁the
Admiralty write harshly to me—my generous soul cannot
bear it, being conscious it is entirely unmerited; and ever
believe me your obliged,

BRONTE NELSON.

TO THE RIGHT HONOURABLE LORD GRENVILLE, SECRETARY OF
STATE FOR FOREIGN AFFAIRS.

[Autograph, in the State Paper Office.]

Palermo, November 28th, 1799.

My Lord,

I send you a letter sent me by Mr. Spiridion Foresti from
Corfu, addressed to your Lordship, also one I received a few
days ago, which Mr. Foresti thinks of some consequence. I
cannot let this opportunity slip of recommending this gentleman to your Lordship's notice; and as I am on this subject,
give me leave to recommend another Consul to the notice of
Government, Major Magra, residing at Tunis. It is strict
justice only in me to say that these two Consuls are the ONLY
ones I have found in the Mediterranean who have really attended to their duty. I have the honour to be your Lordship's
most obedient servant,

BRONTE NELSON.

TO CAPTAIN BALL, CHIEF OF THE ISLAND OF MALTA.

[Autograph, in the possession of Sir William Keith Ball, Bart.]

Palermo, November 28th, 1799.

My dear Ball,

This will be delivered to you by the Chevalier Italinsky,
who I beg leave strongly to recommend to your kind notice;
he is fully sensible of your merits, and will I trust do full
justice to them at Petersburg. He knows of my application
for the Cross for you, I have opened fully to him on all the
points which I think can occur about Malta, and in particular of
your situation there. I trust, and indeed have no doubt, but
that all will be harmony with the Russian Commander, which

is most strongly recommended to me by my letters of October. I have only to wish you, which I do from my heart, a speedy termination of your labours, and a proper reward for them, to obtain which nothing shall be wanting on the part of your faithful and obliged friend,

BRONTE NELSON.

TO COMMISSIONER INGLEFIELD.

[Letter-Book.]

November 28th, 1799.

My dear Inglefield,

Many thanks for your letter of the 9th, and I shall only say, and desire you will bear it in mind, that I shall always be glad of opportunities of proving my sincere regard and esteem for you. But you must make allowances for a worn-out, blind, left-handed man; therefore, to business. If the Hulk is to be commanded by a Boatswain, I hope it will be given to my old and valuable friend, King;[3] and request your influence that no other should stand in his way. The Perseus wants re-fitting. Pray do it as expeditiously as you can, that she may return to me. I am glad stores are going in the Gorgon to Minorca; for our Ships off Malta, when that long and tedious business is brought to a finish, will want a complete equipping.

Troubridge, who brought me General Fox's permission for the garrison of Messina to go to Malta, did not anchor the Foudroyant, and joined him, for I keep her always ready to weigh, without any notice. If we are not turned out of Malta before Colonel Graham arrives there, we shall do well; but I have very great fears the garrison will make a sortie, and drive us to the Devil. But I hope our usual good fortune will attend us through this enterprise. Ball's perseverance has been wonderful. Sir William and Lady Hamilton desire their kindest wishes. I am, &c.,

BRONTE NELSON.

[4] Vide vol. i. p. 257.

TO COMMODORE SIR THOMAS TROUBRIDGE, BART.

[Letter-Book.]

Palermo, November 28th, 1799.

My dear Troubridge,

This will be delivered to you by the Chevalier Italinsky, to whom I have communicated my sentiments fully on all the points about Malta; and in all your communication of any consequence with Admiral Ouschakoff, I would strongly recommend to have Italinsky present, and not trust to any other representation at Petersburg. You will find this gentleman one of the best Foreigners you ever dealt with; and he sees the absolute necessity of the Allies drawing together as strongly as we do. There is nothing in reason I would not give into rather than a shade of difference should arise. I need only say, be kind and civil to the Chevalier, and I know that your goodness will do all that is necessary. Should any particular stores be wanting, I desire you will send to Minorca, and ask them of General Fox in my name. The Perseus is arrived, and if the Corvette does not sail very early this morning, the Artillerymen shall be put on board her. No appearance of Martin[5] or the Transport. For the present, adieu; but ever believe me your affectionate friend,

BRONTE NELSON.

TO THE RIGHT HONOURABLE EARL SPENCER, K.G.

[Letter-Book.]

Palermo, November 29th, 1799.

My dear Lord,

The situation of our affairs with the Barbary States calls for serious attention;[6] for, from the circumstances of the war, it has been impossible to make them fear us as they ought, particu-

---

[5] Captain Martin, of the Northumberland, so often mentioned.

[6] Mr. Lucas, the English Consul at Tripoli, informed Lord Nelson, in a letter dated on the 14th October, 1799, that " The Bashaw is not averse to the peace with his Sicilian Majesty, but wishes to know what sum he is to receive for it, particularly as he has Neapolitan slaves; and should he make peace with Naples, he must declare war with some other nation, or lay up his cruizers." On the envelope of that letter Lord Nelson wrote—" *Very good reasons for being at war*—well said, Bashaw!"

larly Algiers; and that State is now getting to such a pitch of insolence, that cannot much longer go unchastised. But I well know in England how an Officer would be reprobated, was he to permit this, and in the contest, which could not be long, any English vessels be taken. These States have taken many Maltese vessels and Neapolitans, having a pass, as they call it, from me. As no Vessel, either at Malta or Naples, on our first going there, would go to sea, without a paper signed by me, His Sicilian Majesty desired me many times under his own hand, to sign the passport, which was a recommendation to the Allies of Great Britain to the Vessel described, she being employed to carry provisions for the use of those fighting the common Enemy. I never signed one of those papers that I did not declare that it could be of no use for protection, and that I thought it was consigning seamen, poor creatures, to slavery. The answer always was, we are not worse for your signing, may be better, and our seamen will not go to sea without it. Many of these passes were respected by Tripoli and Tunis; but the Algerine cruizers paid not the smallest attention, and several Vessels loaded with salt, for the supply of the Capital, have been taken, and their crews, sixty-five in number, are now in slavery.

As the greatest number of their papers were signed on board the Foudroyant at Naples, by desire of General Acton, and the Government of the City, at whose head was Cardinal Ruffo, it was not known under what circumstances the papers were signed—therefore, Prince Luzzi, Secretary of State, addressed a dispatch to Sir William Hamilton, a copy of which, and his Excellency's answer, I send you. I also send some papers sent me by Major Magra, also an account of an Algerine firing, in the Bay of Tunis, at an English vessel. I do not say, or think that the papers signed by me, ought, by the laws of Nations, to protect traders, but under all circumstances the Barbary States ought to be made sensible of the attention which is due to the signature of an English Admiral, and that, at least, the poor people ought to be liberated.

The Dey of Algiers has been several times very impertinent about giving supplies for Minorca, and is getting from one insolence to another, which if not checked by vigorous measures, will end in a quarrel. My idea is for me to go to him and settle the business, and if I find that he will be insolent, to show him in the moment that he cannot go robbing in the Mediterranean without the consent of Britain. I think the greatest part of his Cruizers would be seized in a month, and then bring him to reason. Terror is the only weapon to wield against these people. To talk kindly to them is only to encourage them. Demand nothing that is not just, and never recede, and settle the whole in half-an-hour. I should say to him that ' I expected that, being embarked in the same Cause, you would not have taken Vessels only carrying provisions for people fighting against the French, but you had not humanity enough to do this. However, I insist that you shall not keep the poor people in slavery. It was by my having too good an opinion of you that they fell into your hands. With respect to the presuming to fire at any Vessel in a neutral Port bearing the English flag, the most ample satisfaction must be made.' I hope we shall soon be rid of Malta, and then our Ships for a little time cannot be so well employed. If this letter ought to be addressed to the Board, I beg of you to lay it before them; but I consider it, and its enclosure, as a letter for the Cabinet Minister. I am anxious to know the sentiments of Government relative to these people. Believe me, my dear Lord, with the sincerest respect, your obliged and faithful

BRONTE NELSON.

TO CAPTAIN BALL, CHIEF OF THE MALTESE.

[Autograph, in the possession of Sir William Keith Ball, Bart.]

Palermo, November 29th, 1799.

My dear Ball,

I have before told you that the Ministers of England, Russia, and Naples, had, a few days ago, agreed that for the future (it being impossible for His Sicilian Majesty to give all that was wanted for the relief of the poor Maltese) the three Powers should each find a sum of money for this purpose. His Sicilian Majesty has this day sent me 8000 ounces, to be sent to you for this purpose. You must now look to both Russia and England for an equal sum, before I can presume to solicit again from by far the poorest of the three Powers.

You know what great things His Sicilian Majesty has done for the poor Maltese, and I can assure you and them, that he never has been able to afford anything. What gratitude ought to be shown for such unparalleled goodness! Pray send an account of the expenditure to be laid before the King. I trust Sir Thomas Troubridge will be with you. God bless you, and send you completely triumphant, is the fervent prayer of your attached and affectionate friend,

BRONTE NELSON.

TO BRIGADIER-GENERAL GRAHAM.

[Letter-Book.]

Palermo, Dec. 1st, 8 o'clock in the morning.

My dear Sir,

Your letter of the 28th did not get to me till several hours after its arrival at Palermo, as it was directed to Mr. Tyson. In fact it was laying in my Secretary's office unheeded. I only mention this to guard the future. Whatever you do about the leaving Major Lockart,[7] I am sure His Sicilian Majesty will approve, if Prince Cuto does not like that arrangement,—at all events, you are right to leave all your baggage, convalescents, &c., but I am sure it is better to have the name of a British garrison. I have this moment General Acton's order to Prince Cuto. There will also be orders for Augusta and Syracuse. I observe what General Fox says, in his orders, about expense. I wonder not a little at it. How can you get stores, without paying for them? and pray will it not be necessary to have many people to work at the batteries? Everything we receive from Sicily must one day be accounted for. Who is to pay? It cannot be expected that the poorest of the three Powers is to pay what is jointly undertaken. I shall, my dear Sir, afford you every support and assistance in money, as well as all other things. Could General Fox, or any other General, carry on a siege without money? Two days ago I sent you twenty-two fine English artillerymen from the Perseus, and to Ball, 8000 ounces for the poor Maltese. England and Russia are now to do the same, and when Malta

---

[7] Afterwards Major-General William Lockhart. Vide " Military Calendar," vol. ii. p. 110.

is taken, the three Powers must balance the accounts. The Northumberland is not yet arrived, nor the Transports, with tents and blankets. If the wind is westerly she shall come by Messina, but if easterly, as I shall be sure you are gone, she will go round Maritimo, for I want you to have your blankets.

I have only again to say you are sure of my exertions in every way which can bring our Maltese matters to a close; and wishing you from my heart every success, believe me, with the truest regard, your most faithful and obliged,

BRONTE NELSON.

MARGINAL NOTE MADE BY LORD NELSON, IN THE COPY OF GENERAL ACTON'S LETTER, SENT TO SIR THOMAS TROUBRIDGE, PER EXPRESS, TO MESSINA.

[Letter-Book.]

[About 1st December, 1799.]

Not desired, nor will be, from his Sicilian Majesty. Our Government must find money: I should feel it derogatory to the British character to strip his Sicilian Majesty. If we want money, we must find it.

BRONTE NELSON.

TO COMMODORE SIR THOMAS TROUBRIDGE, BART.

[Letter-Book.]

Palermo, December 1st [1799], 8 o'clock in the morning.

My dear Troubridge,

Many, many thanks for your two letters of the 28th: the last was particularly pleasant. Whatever you can assist General Graham in, must meet my approbation. Money must be had, or money's worth. What are all the Stores asked for, but so much money? The order of General Fox I am surprised at. It appears it is to throw difficulties in the way. Could he besiege a place without expense? I can get money on my estate—therefore there shall be no want, if you are not paid the 15,000 cobs. If General Graham sends here, it can be had. At this moment it[8] is favourable; but if the least

---

[8] Query, the rate of Exchange?

hint is given, Mr. Gibbs says it will, as it did when the Fleet is here, turn much against us. I see nothing of the Northumberland or Transports: the east winds keep her back. If the wind is westerly when she is ready, she shall pass by Messina, and ask Major Lockhart if he has anything to send to Malta; but if easterly, or very fine weather, she shall go round Maritimo, for the soldiers may want the tents and blankets. The Perseus is gone with 8000 ounces to Ball for the Maltese, and I have sent, by another conveyance, twenty-two fine Artillerymen. The Russians, I hope, are passed the Faro by this time. Your other letters I shall answer by the Northumberland. I think it most probable she will not go by Messina —therefore you must send something from Malta. May success attend, &c.,

BRONTE NELSON.

TO HIS EXCELLENCY THOMAS JACKSON, ESQ., MINISTER AT TURIN.

[Letter-Book.]

My dear Sir,   Palermo, December 1st, 1799.
Pity the sorrows of a blind, and (in constitution) old man; make due allowances for my wants, and then I shall be happy. I will do all in my power to cultivate your friendship, and to deserve your good opinion. Pray make his Sardinian Majesty sensible how much I feel all his kindness towards me, and assure him of my eternal gratitude, which I shall be happy in showing both in my public and private conduct. All news will be most interesting to us in our situation. Malta, I hope, will soon fall to the efforts now going to be made against it; and I beg you, my dear Sir, to believe me, with the greatest esteem, your obliged Servant,

BRONTE NELSON.

TO MR. JOSEPH CASTELLS.

[Letter-Book.]

Sir,   Palermo, December 1st, 1799.
I certainly have received letters from you on the subject of a Prize purchased by you, and which had been taken from

you by those acting for her former owners—enemies of Great
Britain. I regret that you who are so much attached to the
good Cause, should suffer; but all villains are our enemies,
and no power on earth could have a right to touch your legal
purchase. I am truly sorry that it does not depend upon me
to get you back the Vessel and cargo. If I am not mistaken,
you ought to look to your own Government for the non-
protection of your property. I am, &c.,

BRONTE NELSON.

TO HIS EXCELLENCY THE HONOURABLE WILLIAM WYNDHAM.

[Letter-Book.]

Palermo, 2nd December, 1799.

Dear Sir,

I am this moment favoured with your letter of November
21st; and my blood boils that I cannot chastise these Pirates.
They could not show themselves in the Mediterranean, did
not our Country permit. Never let us talk of the cruelty of
the African Slave Trade, while we permit such a horrid war.
But on the other hand, was I present with the Fleet of
England, I could not prevent it, without plunging our Country
in a war which our Merchants would reprobate, and Ministers
not support me in. The Germans having entire possession of
the Tuscan State, can by the help of the Russian ships send
troops for the protection of those Islands. My heart bleeds.
Let Government send me the necessary orders, and I will
answer for chastising these Pirates. Your Excellency will
see my letter to Lord Spencer on the subject of Algiers, and
if you will state the melancholy history of Giglio, it may
rouse up a strong resentment at home. I wonder how the
French privateers can be so annoying, as the Russian squadron
relieved ours on that Coast, and it was but reasonable to
expect would do the duty of ours. If I had the means I
assure your Excellency that I would always keep Cruizers
about Leghorn, &c.; but at home they calculate that the
Russian fleet is to do something. The Mutine is stationed
off Cape Corse, and in case she puts into Leghorn, or the
Vincejo, I send orders for them. I feel it my duty to protect
Tuscany, and Tuscan property, from the French; and it is

truly my inclination. The merchants of Leghorn may rest
sure of my attention to their interest. Alas! I wish I could
do the same against the Algerines. I have no Vessel to send
to Giglio: probably the Portuguese may fall in with them. I
shall write to Niza off Malta directly. I thank your Excellency for the good Italian news, and I hope that from Switzerland is likewise true. I am not surprised at our evacuation
of Holland. Who can make war in such a Country, where
every canal is a fortification? Our garrison from Messina, I
hope, sail this day for Malta; and from what I hear the
Russians will pass about this day, and if my friend Ball can
hold his own till their arrival, the affair will soon finish. I
have the honour to be, &c.,

BRONTE NELSON.

P.S.—The only reason I have ever heard given to justify
our peace with the Barbary States, is to throw all the trade
into British bottoms—therefore, the English merchants trading
in any [other] bottoms, is very wrong and prejudical to us.

TO EVAN NEPEAN, ESQ., ADMIRALTY.

[Original, in the Admiralty.]

Palermo, December 2nd, 1799.

Sir,

Herewith I have the honour to send you a copy of General
Fox's letter to me, and of the instructions sent to Colonel
Graham. I dare say they appear to the General perfectly
proper, but as the troops going to a siege cannot act without
stores of all kinds, it is tying their hands. The first thing
done has been an application for a great value of stores from
His Sicilian Majesty, which, as we have desired them, I
suppose we must be answerable for. I have wrote to Colonel
Graham, and instructed Sir Thomas Troubridge not to let
the Colonel be in distress, in consequence of his instructions.
Money must be had from somewhere; I leave the letter and
orders to speak for themselves. The Foudroyant in going
through the Faro, was thrown on shore, but got off without
any damage. The troops I expect will sail this day for
Messina. I am, &c.,

BRONTE NELSON.

TO EVAN NEPEAN, ESQ., ADMIRALTY.

[Letter Book.]

Sir,   Palermo, 4th December, 1799.

Having had occasion to communicate with the Victualling
Board respecting the improper interference of Mr.
Lock, the Consul at Naples, in supplying the Squadron in that Bay, I
beg leave to enclose you, for their Lordships' information,
copies of the letters which have passed on this occasion
between us.[8] No. 1, being my first letter to him, and No.
2, his answer, in consequence of which, I ordered my Secretary

---

[8] These letters respecting Mr. Lock require, in justice to that gentleman, some
explanation, and the insertion of extracts from his letters to Lord Nelson on the subject,
the originals of which are in the Nelson Papers. The letter No. 1, is not extant.
Mr. Tyson's reply to it, dated on the 1st December, stated that it was unsatisfactory;
that Lord Nelson insisted upon knowing whether he told Sir William Hamilton that
his conduct at Naples about fresh beef, had been approved; and also whether he
had not informed Captain Hardy that he had been thanked for saving government
forty per cent. on the purchases; and Mr. Tyson enclosed to him a copy of Lord
Nelson's letter to the Victualling Board, in p. 100, ante. Mr. Lock's answer has
not been found, but its purport is shown by the following extract from his letter of
the 3rd of December, which gave Lord Nelson so much offence:

                                        "Palermo, 3rd December, 1799.
"My Lord,
"Understanding from his Excellency Sir William Hamilton, that your Lordship
excepts to that part of my letter of yesterday, in which I declare that I consider
myself, in my civil capacity of Consul, independent of military authority, it is
necessary that I should explain what I mean by such a declaration. "The
right which your Lordship's situation gives you of demanding the inspection of
all public documents relative to the Service at the head of which you are, I
have incontestibly proved that I acknowledge, by answering the demand which your
Lordship made me, of copies of all public letters which I had written respecting the
Fleet under your command. Upon what ground you extend the right of inquisition
into my private conversations, I confess I cannot so clearly discover. As Consul-
General for the Kingdom of Naples, I consider myself independent in the exercise of
my functions, answerable to Lord Grenville for the due discharge of them, and not
subject to your Lordship's control, as you must have conceived I was, when you
insisted that I should pass accounts, for which I alone was to be responsible. I yesterday offered, through the channel of Sir William Hamilton, to put your Lordship in
possession of the contents of the private letters I had received, touching the victualling of the Fleet. You rejected the proposal. However, that your Lordship may
be convinced that it was not without foundation I concluded my conduct had not
been disapproved by the Victualling Board, I have transcribed for your perusal
those parts of them which make mention of it."
The extracts alluded to were from a letter from Mr. Lock's father and sister, in which

to write him No. 3, and a copy of his answer is No. 4: and I have to request that their Lordships will be pleased to take such steps as may be necessary, for the support of my dignity as the Commanding-Officer of His Majesty's Ships in the Mediterranean. I have the honour to be, &c.,

BRONTE NELSON.

TO CHARLES LOCK, ESQ., HIS MAJESTY'S CONSUL AT NAPLES.

[Letter-Book.]

Sir,   Palermo, 4th December, 1799.

Your letter to me of yesterday's date is incomprehensible, except the highly improper language in which it is couched. I shall send it to the Board of Admiralty, that they may either support the dignity of the Admiral they have entrusted with

---

the former informed him that Mr. Marsh, one of the Commissioners of the Victualling Board, had said that the Board "felt very much obliged to Mr. Lock's interference, being persuaded it has occasioned the Fleet's being victualled forty per cent. lower than it would otherwise have been." His sister wrote on the 8th of September, that Sir William Bellingham (the Chairman of the Board) who had dined with them on the preceding day, had repeated the same statement, and said that " they are greatly obliged to you, and feel themselves so ;" and there was another similar private remark. Mr. Lock, therefore, concluded his letter by saying "As your Lordship has demanded of the Victualling Board their public opinion of this affair, I hope I may with reason flatter myself that it will be an echo of their private sentiments ;" adding in a postscript, " As I have already informed your Lordship that I have neither written nor received any letter from the Victualling Board, and do now deny ever having said that I obtained a letter of thanks from them, I demand it of your justice to undeceive the Victualling Board, on the false statements of that part of my conduct forwarded to them by your Lordship."

Lord Nelson's letter to the Victualling Board of the 5th of December, in the text, was caused by an apologetical letter to him from Mr. Lock, of the 4th of December, in which he said " It was far from my intention to assail your Lordship's integrity by any expression which may have fallen from me ; and as every purpose of justification [of the Officers of the Fleet] is clearly answered, which a further investigation could produce, I trust your Lordship will deem it unnecessary to press the matter further." Though the Victualling Board's declaration to Lord Nelson, of the 20th of December, that they never had any *correspondence* with Mr. Lock on the subject, [vide p. 101, ante,] may have been literally true, it is evident that the Board had received Mr. Lock's written statements, and that the Chairman, and some of the Commissioners, had expressed their approbation of his conduct—facts scarcely to be reconciled with the impression which their official letter to Lord Nelson was intended to convey, and which was certainly most uncandid to him. Mr. Lock died at Malta, on the 11th of September, 1804.

the command of the Mediterranean fleet, or remove him. Your never mentioning the extraordinary price paid for fresh beef, for the several days you were soliciting to have the exclusive privilege of supplying the Fleet, and your refusal afterwards to bring forward any proof of fraud, warrants every expression in my letter to the Victualling Board. If you could bring proof of what you asserted, you are in the highest degree, as a public Officer, criminal; and if you could not, your conduct is highly reprehensible. My letters to you are all directed ' On His Majesty's Service,' and I desire yours may be so to me. I am, &c.

BRONTE NELSON.

TO THE COMMISSIONERS FOR VICTUALLING HIS MAJESTY'S NAVY.

[Letter-Book.]

Gentlemen,　　　　　　Palermo, December 5th, 1799.

Letters which had passed between Mr. Lock and myself, brought forward yesterday, in the presence of Sir William Hamilton, a meeting between us, and as it turns out that false friends in this Country, and nonsensical ones in England, have been the cause of Mr. Lock's highly improper conduct, and as any inquiry can only end in the ruin of Mr. Lock's character, I consent not to desire the inquiry demanded in my letter of the 14th November, by Captain Hardy. It was justice to the public and a vindication of my own honour, that I sought, and not ruin to a young man setting off in life with a family of children. This lesson will, I trust, and believe, be of more use to Mr. Lock than the approbation of ignorant people. I do not mean to withdraw a syllable of my last letter to the Board, for they will see that I did not believe them capable of such conduct; only to that part which gives up the demand for inquiry. If there are those residing in Somerset Place, who merit the full force of some of my words, let them have it. One of my greatest boasts is, that no man can ever say I have told a lie. With every sentiment of proper respect to the Board, I am, Gentlemen, your most obedient Servant,

BRONTE NELSON.

TO CAPTAIN BALL, CHIEF OF THE ISLAND OF MALTA.

[Letter-Book.]

My dear Ball,   Palermo, 7th December, 1799.

I trust that in a short time, all your truly hard service, both of body and mind, will be over. How you are to be rewarded, time must discover, but a more fatiguing service never fell to the lot of human being. I am ignorant, my dear friend, how the Island is to be governed till the Grand Master's Representative arrives; or whether the Military Commanders will manage the affairs. Talk to Chevalier Italinsky on this subject. Let it be decided as it may, the truth will always stand, that La Valetta could not have been taken, but by the patience, ability, gallantry, conciliating manners, and goodness of Captain Alexander John Ball. This, I believe, is known to all Europe, and shall be repeated. If the Allies ask you as a great favour to govern Malta till the orders of the Grand Master [arrive], I shall not object. They cannot get your equal for that service. I have given it as my opinion that on the fall of La Valetta, all public property should be valued separately, and then, that our Governments should decide who is to have particular things, be they Ships or other articles. Each Power to draw up the expense they have been put to *at Malta;* and it must always be admitted, that but for the blockade, all the Ships would at this moment have been part of the French fleet. I am almost blind, therefore, can only say God bless you, in which joins cordially Sir William and Lady Hamilton, and believe me ever your affectionate friend,

BRONTE NELSON.

TO EVAN NEPEAN, ESQ., ADMIRALTY.

[Original, in the Admiralty.]

Sir,   Palermo, December 7th, 1799.

Captain Brenton,[9] of his Majesty's Sloop the Speedy, having, on the 6th of November, with a Convoy from the Coast of

---

[9] Afterwards Rear Admiral Sir Jahleel Brenton, Bart., K.C.B., whose celebrated action in the Bay of Naples, is so well known. He died in April 1844.

Portugal, when attacked in the Straits by twelve Spanish Gun-Boats, displayed uncommon skill and gallantry in saving the Sloop under his command, and all his Convoy, I beg leave to recommend him to their Lordships' notice; and if the merits of a brother[1] may be allowed to have any weight, I have the sorrow to tell you, that he lost his life, then [Lieutenant] of the Peterel attempting, with great bravery, to bring off a Vessel which the Sloop had run on shore : he died of his wounds a few days ago at Minorca hospital. I have the honour to be, Sir,

Your most obedient servant,

BRONTE NELSON.

TO CAPTAIN SIR WILLIAM SIDNEY SMITH.

[From Clarke and M'Arthur, vol. ii. p. 237.]

Palermo, 8th December, 1799.

All our Mediterranean operations are pretty nearly at a stand-still; for the Enemy have no Fleet at this moment to make us keep a good look-out, although I should not be surprised if the whole combined Fleet should again pay us a visit this winter. They were perfectly ready for sea the latter end of October, forty-eight Sail of the Line. Admiral Duckworth, with all the Ships, Frigates, &c., is ordered by the Admiralty from Gibraltar, to go off Ferrol; and I think from thence will be called to the Channel; therefore, at this moment I have only two Sail of the Line, and not more than two Frigates, in a condition to go to sea. Our Government naturally look to the Russians for aid here, but they will find their mistake : the Russian Ships are not able to keep the sea. I am now trying to bring our long blockade of Malta to a close; the Garrison of Messina has been permitted to embark for that service, and 2500 Russians are, I hope, at this moment at Malta. The French Ships destined for the relief of Malta went to Ville Franche, and landed their provisions and stores for the Army, which has since been defeated by General Melas, and 11,000 are said, in the report, to be killed and taken. This must put Coni into the hands of the Austrians, and secure Italy from that quarter; but, alas! we have reports that the Emperor is

---

[1] Lieutenant James Wallace Brenton; he was killed when commanding the Boats of the Peterel, in an attack on an armed Vessel, near Barcelona.

going to make a truce with the French, and wishes to keep all
Italy himself. We are anxious to hear from you, for I have
my fears that your personal bravery will one day end in some
accident. You have gained credit enough in that way, and
you must now take care of yourself for other occasions. I
am, &c.,

BRONTE NELSON.

TO CAPTAIN SIR WILLIAM SIDNEY SMITH, K.S.

[Letter-Book.]

Palermo, 8th December, 1799.

My dear Sir,

The Lords of the Admiralty have directed me, in their
letter of October the 22nd, to signify to you, and the Officers
and Men under your command, the very high sense they
entertain of your very meritorious services on the several
important occasions to which your letters relate, as also of the
several Officers and Men whose conduct you have particularly
mentioned. And their Lordships also inform me, that a
Commission is prepared for promoting Lieutenant Canes[2] to
the rank of Commander.

It gives me real pleasure to communicate these orders of
the Board, and nothing shall be wanting on my part to reward
the merits of those who distinguish themselves; for believe
me, dear Sir, your faithful friend,

BRONTE NELSON.

TO ALEXANDER DAVISON, ESQ.

[Letter-Book.]

Palermo, December 9th, 1799.

My dear Davison,

Reports are here prevalent that the Ethalion, Alcmene,
and Naiad have taken some very valuable Prizes off Cape
Finisterre. The two former belonging to the Mediterranean
command, devolved upon me by the return to England of all
my Senior Officers, some of whom have struck their Flags, and
others gone under the command of other Admirals, I there-

[2] Vide vol. iii. p. 450.

fore, although the orders for those Ships cruising may have been given by my Seniors at that time in the Mediterranean, yet consider myself from the time (I think, of their quitting the Station, but most assuredly from either their Flags being struck, or having passed under the command of other Officers,) entitled to the emoluments arising from Prizes taken by Mediterranean Ships, as much as if I had a Commission as Commander-in-Chief. I therefore desire, in case any difficulty arises from improper claims, that you will lay in my claim as Commander-in-Chief for all Prizes taken; and if this is not authority enough for you to act, pray beg Messrs. Marsh and Creed to do it. I am cut short enough by having no other emoluments. I, as the King gives me this, am determined no power shall take it from me. I consider my right for the Ethalion and Alcmene, as two-thirds of one-eighth, and Duckworth for the other. Ever, my dear friend, believe me your obliged,

BRONTE NELSON.

TO LIEUTENANT PHILIP LAMB.

[Letter-Book.]

Palermo, 11th December, 1799.

Dear Sir,

I have received your letter of November 21st, relative to the propriety of Admirals sharing prize-money for a Ship under the circumstances of the Dover. Although it is not in my power to give up without the consent of Admiral Duckworth, yet from the circumstances as stated by you, and the accompanying paper, I have no scruple of declaring that, in my opinion, the Admirals have no right to share for the Vessel taken by the Dover. Having given this as my opinion, I cannot but highly reprobate the measure of granting a Letter of Marque to the Transport-Board, as an act highly detrimental to the King's service, by holding out a reward for the searching for Prizes, instead, probably, of pursuing the voyage, and of giving to the Board a part of the profit arising from the cruizing of the Store-ships. Here let me be clearly understood, that although I reprobate the idea of prize-money for the Board in all cases, yet it should be held out to

the Commander and crews of such Store-Ships, that if
they are attacked by any armed Vessel of the Enemy, in
case of capture, they should not only be entitled to whole
profit, but also, that if they beat off any armed Vessel, they
should be entitled to a reward equal to the magnitude of the
service. I would recommend your keeping back the claimed
one-eighth, but of sharing the other, and also that you send a
copy of my letter to the Transport Board. Believe me, dear
Sir, with real regard, your sincere friend,

BRONTE NELSON.

TO HIS EXCELLENCY LIEUTENANT-GENERAL THE HONOURABLE
EDWARD HENRY FOX.

[Letter-Book. From Sir Thomas Hanmer's Correspondence, p. 424.]

Dear Sir,   Palermo, December 13th, 1799.

I have received a letter from the Transport Board, of which
I send you a copy ; and I am of opinion that a strong letter
should be wrote to the Governor of Barcelona, or whom else
it may concern, our determination to comply with the orders
of our Government. I venture to send your Excellency a
letter signed by me, if you approve of it—if not, I beg you
will either send a letter without my name, or put my name to
it, as you please. I send orders to the senior Naval Officer at
Mahon, not on any account to send a Cartel, without your
concurrence. I think, Sir, you will agree with me, that his
Majesty's declaration to Europe had better never be made,
unless they are carried rigidly into effect.

Believe me, dear Sir, with every sentiment of esteem,

Your Excellency's most obedient servant,

BRONTE NELSON.

TO THE GOVERNOR OF BARCELONA.

[Letter-Book. Inclosed in the preceding. This letter was not sent—General Fox
having written another instead of it.]

Mahon.

Sir,

We demand from your Excellency the exchange of all his
Britannic Majesty's Subjects, our Royal Master, in which we

not only include all Minorquins, but also all those who may have been captured under the British flag, and carried into the Ports of Spain: in particular, we claim the exchange, by this Flag of Truce, of Mr. Jeremiah Motter, an inhabitant of Minorca. In making these just demands, we expect an instant compliance. We announce to your Excellency, that the severest retaliation shall take place; thus your Government will open such a dreadful scene of warfare as has never yet disgraced Europe, for which they will receive the execration of all good men in this world, and eternal damnation in that which is to come. We reserve to ourselves the right of thinking Mr. Jeremiah Motter has been murdered, if he is not returned by this Flag of Truce; the consequences must be dreadful to every feeling heart: therefore, we again warn you not to touch a hair of his head. It has, we assure your Excellency, given us great pain to have occasion to write this letter to a Spaniard whose honour has hitherto been untarnished, and we only hope that it will ever remain so, and are your Excellency's most obedient servants,

BRONTE NELSON.

TO HIS EXCELLENCY THE HONOURABLE WILLIAM WYNDHAM.

[Letter-Book.]

Palermo, December 13th, 1799.

Sir,

I was yesterday honoured with your Excellency's letter of November 30th, sending me two letters from Austrian Generals, calling for a Naval co-operation from Great Britain, as they say the Russian Ships do not approach the Coast, and that they cannot get supplies of provisions and ammunition to take Genoa, without our assistance. There is not that Officer in Europe that knows the necessity of our co-operation better than myself, and you will do me the justice to say that I kept a Squadron for that service, till regularly relieved by the Russians, who it was naturally expected would perform all the necessary services; and our Admiralty at home expect it, as eight Sail of the Line are taken out of the Mediterranean, with a proportion of Frigates and Corvettes; in fact, there are at this moment only two Sail of the Line really fit for service.

However, at this moment all our Ships and Troops are employed at Malta, yet I will try on this application of General
Klenau, and the other General, to send a small Squadron sufficient to ensure the convoys of provisions and ammunition.
In joining in this co-operation, it shall be formally declared by
the Austrian General, that no Capitulation, or any terms,
shall be entered into with the Enemy, in which the Commanding Officer of the Squadron so employed, shall not be
consulted, and his signature made as a necessary measure.   If
our assistance is necessary, we have an undoubted right to be
concerned in every measure, and to give an opinion; and it
shall not be considered that if the Squadron is either blown
off the Coast, or absent for Convoys of provisions, but in the
same manner as if they were actually present, and in all terms
entered into with the Enemy, it shall be expressly stated, that
the Squadron of his Britannic Majesty acting with the Austrian Army, and in as strong terms as your Excellency can
draw it up.   This measure, so necessary to his Majesty's
honour, I leave in the hands of your Excellency to settle, and
the Ships shall call at Leghorn for the determination.   The
Austrians either *want* us or *not:* this is the plain fact.   If they
do, we have a full right to a share of the honour and profit
for our labour: if they do not, the call for our Ships is very
great in other parts of the Mediterranean.   As to Small craft,
if I have not been misinformed, Baron d'Espard fitted out
several Privateers for the express purpose of securing the small
Vessels from the depredation of Privateers.   The garrison of
Messina is gone to Malta, and I am in hopes when joined
with the Russians, that I shall be able to send a Ship of the
Line.   We have nothing from England later than October
the 24th; of course are very anxious.   With every sentiment
of respect, I have the honour to be, &c.

Bronte Nelson.

P.S.—I am sensible of General Palffy's flattering compliments, but as I cannot be a judge of the movements of an
Army, so he cannot of that of a Fleet.   He either is ignorant,
or appears so, that the greatest Naval force of the Enemy is
blocked up in Malta by our Ships; and also that we are trying all our efforts to get possession of that important place, in
order for the restoration of the Order of Malta.

TO HIS EXCELLENCY THE HON. LIEUTENANT-GENERAL FOX.

[Letter-Book.]

Palermo, 14th December, 1799.

Dear Sir,

I send your Excellency Colonel Graham's letters, both from Messina and Malta, where, thank God, he landed on the 10th. We shall now be able to hold our own, till a sufficient force can be collected to attack La Valetta. Graham wants many stores, as, I dare say, he tells you, and I am sure your Excellency will afford every assistance to get this very long business to a close. The Austrians are calling out for a Naval co-operation on the Coast of Genoa. It is my wish; for no man knows more the necessity than myself—having this war served with the Austrians, when they were on that Coast. They complain that the Russian Ships never come near them. Our Government think, naturally, that eleven Sail of the Line, Frigates, &c., should do something: I find they do nothing. On the 17th of November—at latest, the 19th, the Admiral was to sail from Naples with the troops for Malta; but, alas! on the 9th of December, it was said it would be five or six days. The troops are represented by those who have seen them as a very fine body of men; and as I feel confident that you will have orders to send more troops to Malta, we shall soon find our Squadron liberated, and on other service; for at this moment I have not a Ship to send on the North Coast of Italy.

I send you Mr. Wyndham's letter and enclosures. I have directed the Convoy for England to sail the moment the Speedy appears off Mahon, with the trade from Messina. Captain Louis is directed to proceed to Malta, with stores for our Ships, which are in a truly miserable state. In every-thing I shall be truly happy in meeting your wishes: my only desire is to know them; for believe me, with the greatest respect, your Excellency's most obedient servant,

BRONTE NELSON.

TO CAPTAIN LOUIS, H. M. SHIP MINOTAUR.

[Letter-Book.]

My dear Sir,   Palermo, December 14th, 1799.

You will receive the orders for the sailing of the Convoy
for England, which you will give the necessary direction for
being carried into execution.   You must load your Ship with
stores for our Ships off Malta.   Cables, sails, [they are] in
very great distress for, particularly the Lion.   If you cannot
carry all which the Yard can give, take one of the Frigates
to assist.   You know from experience the want of cables
and sails, with every other store—therefore you will have a
fellow-feeling.   In case the Princess Charlotte should not be
arrived in time for the Convoy, I would not have them kept
one moment for her.   We must take care that they are seen
in safety past Cape de Gatte, and not left but with a levanter.
I am called on for a Naval force on the Coast of Genoa, but,
at this moment, I have not the means in my power; for I
wish to leave General Fox every means to keep up a constant
communication with Leghorn.   If you want to send this
Cutter to Gibraltar with the letters of the General, do so,
directing her not to stay more than forty-eight hours, and to
return with the Garrison letters for Minorca and for ours.   If
the St. Vincent Cutter is gone on that service, I wish L'Entreprenant returned to me.   Trusting to your activity, believe
me ever your obliged humble servant,

BRONTE NELSON.

If this letter should find you at sea, if not far advanced, I
would have you return for the stores; but if well on your
way, to proceed direct for Malta, and Troubridge will send
either Audacious or Lion to Mahon.

TO THE OFFICERS OF HIS MAJESTY'S DOCK-YARD, PORT MAHON.

[Letter-Book.]

Atty Transport, Palermo, 14th December, 1799.

Gentlemen,

I have received your letter of 26th November, enclosing a
list of stores wanting for re-fitting his Majesty's Ships at

Mahon, and the necessity of purchasing them, if no supplies were expected from England ; and as his Majesty's Ships now cruizing off Malta must all, or the greatest part of them, shortly go down to Mahon to refit, and they being in want of stores of every kind, you will, therefore, cause to be purchased at Leghorn, or wherever else they may be procured, such stores as are absolutely necessary for refitting the Ship that may be sent to you, as there are no stores at present expected from England; and it is my positive direction that no Captain whatsoever, who may occasionally become senior Officer in the Port of Mahon, do in future attempt to order the purchase of stores of any kind, and that you do not purchase them by such order. I am, &c.,

BRONTE NELSON.

TO HIS EXCELLENCY COMTE MUSCHIN P. BRUCE, RUSSIAN
AMBASSADOR.

[Letter-Book.]

Palermo, 14th December, 1799.

Sir,

I am this moment honoured with your Excellency's letter, putting to me several questions from Admiral Ouschakoff, which, I am happy to say, it is in my power to answer in a very few words—viz., that, by order of my Royal Master, every exertion in my power is to be made, (which is done,) and I hope that also every exertion from the Officers of his Imperial Majesty will be made, to place the Flag of the Order of Jerusalem in La Valetta. I have the honour to be, &c.

BRONTE NELSON.

I request that your Excellency will, if possible, send off this night to the Emperor of Russia's Admiral a copy of my answer, as the service of the Grand Master of Malta will be seriously affected by any delays; and I have further to observe, that if the Russian troops are ready to go to Malta, and that if Admiral Ouschakoff does not think it right to convoy them, and [will] permit me to embark them, I will make the necessary arrangement as expeditiously as possible.

B. N.

TO EVAN NEPEAN, ESQ., ADMIRALTY.

[Original, in the Admiralty.]

Atty Transport, Palermo, 14th December, 1799.

Sir,

I have received a letter from the Transport Board, enclosing copies of their Lordships' letters to that Board, of the 8th and 11th October last, respecting the exchange of prisoners of war with Spain, and the natives of Minorca in particular; and I beg you will be pleased to inform their Lordships, that all proper steps shall be taken to get exchanged all his Majesty's Minorcan subjects that are prisoners of war in that Kingdom. I have the honour to be, &c.,

BRONTE NELSON.

TO EVAN NEPEAN, ESQ., ADMIRALTY.

[Original, in the Admiralty.]

Palermo, December 14th, 1799.

Sir,

I have this moment a letter from Commodore Troubridge, telling me that the Culloden and Foudroyant arrived with the two British regiments from Messina on the 10th. I trust this force will, at least, hold our present advantageous post till a proper force can be got together to attack La Valetta. The Russians had not left Naples on the 9th, and it was thought it would be five or six days before they sailed for Messina. On every account, I am anxious for this business being finished. Our Ships are torn to pieces; the Audacious has the knee of her head loose, and in a wretched state; the Lion as bad, and the Alexander at present absolutely unable to keep the sea; the Culloden, although my brave friend never complains, is in such a state, that, for the world, I would not send her to sea by herself. I have had yesterday a very strong call for a British Squadron on the Coast of Genoa. I see the necessity of one as strong as any man in Europe, for the Russians do nothing by sea; therefore, if their Lordships expect any active sea operations from them, they will find their mistake. Captain Martin was relieved by an Admiral, two Sail of the Line, Frigates, &c.: they have never yet been on the Coast since last September; but I will try and get a small Squadron for that service. I was anxious to get more Ships off Cadiz since the departure of Admiral Duckworth; but at this moment it is not possible, from the circumstance of General Fox's orders to Colonel Graham. In addition to my other occupations, I am a Commissary for our Troops. I have pledged Bronté for 12,000 ounces, if any difficulties arise in the payment; and I am obliged to beg, as an individual, of this Government, for those necessary stores, without which, our Troops would stand still, and which are not sent from Minorca, or allowed to be purchased. The Emperor of Russia's magnificent Box is ready to go to market, in order to assist in placing the Grand Master of Malta in his seat of Government. As to myself, I can see, and that is all I can say; therefore, having not been placed in a situation of those who are Commanders-in-Chief, I want many of those helps which they possess, and this must plead my excuse with their Lordships, if I appear wanting in attention. I have the honour to be, &c.

BRONTE NELSON.

TO HIS EXCELLENCY THE IMPERIAL AMBASSADOR.

[Letter-Book.]

Palermo, 16th December, 1799.

Lord Nelson, Duke de Bronté, has the honour to inform his Excellency, the Imperial Ambassador, that no Imperial Vessel has been seized by any of the Ships of the Squadron under his command.

The Vessel alluded to, in his Excellency's letter of the 14th instant, was taken under Neapolitan colours, and the cargo shipped in Tunis, by French Agents, for the relief of La Valetta. All the papers and documents respecting her are lodged in the British Court of Vice-Admiralty at Gibraltar for adjudication, therefore Lord Nelson cannot interfere.

TO COMMODORE SIR THOMAS TROUBRIDGE, BART.

[Letter-Book.]

My dear Troubridge,   Palermo, 16th December, 1799.

When the Minotaur arrives, if you think you can spare me
the Northumberland, I want to send Captain Martin to act
with the Austrians, on the Coast of Genoa; for they complain
bitterly of the Russian Ships, and that all their Convoys of
provisions and ammunition have been prevented passing
on the Coast, which has delayed the fall of Genoa. The
Penelope arrived here yesterday, but as it is not improbable
that the Enemy's fleet may again make us a visit, I have determined on sending her to the westward, that we may not be
surprised. I am totally ignorant of what Duckworth has left,
and except the Line of Battle Ships, of what he has taken. I
would recommend a good look-out, but not to be unnecessarily
alarmed. We must in our situation trust to the look-out of
Lord Bridport's fleet. The two Transports which I have
been obliged to fit out, you had better keep for your service.
The Cutter sailed yesterday morning for Minorca, and as the
wind is easterly, she may make a good passage. Our news
from France is, that the Directory and Councils are abolished,
that Buonaparte, Sièyes, and Roger Ducos have called themselves Consuls, are removed to St. Cloud, and hold out that
peace for the Republic is their only object; and peace it
must bring us; for either it is a plan to restore the King, or
such a firm Government will be fixed, as will force us to make
peace. Your patent for the Baronetage, Lord Spencer writes
me, was in the Office in September, and he wonders has not
appeared in the Gazette.[2] The business of Holland has, I dare
say, kept it back, as they wish to do something for Mitchell[3]
and the soldiers.

I send you the answer of Prince Cuto about the artillerymen. If the Russians do not bring them, perhaps you may
send the Lion for them. I am blind—therefore both Graham

---

[2] The dignity was not notified in the London Gazette until the 30th of November
1799.

[3] Vice Admiral Andrew Mitchell, who received the Order of the Bath, in January
following.

and Ball must forgive me not writing them. May speedy
success attend you is the sincere wish of your affectionate
friend,

BRONTE NELSON.

Remember us to Italinsky. General Acton's answer does
not say a word about Syracuse or Augusta, but I will try and
get the order. Harriman wishes to go to you—therefore I
send him, and we must try and get him something as In-
terpreter, or if the place is taken, he might be useful in
making inventories. The 28th Regiment is said to be gone
to   [*sic*] where they will die. Flora is reported to be
gone with them.

TO CAPTAIN HENRY BLACKWOOD, H. M. SHIP PENELOPE.

The Atty Transport, Palermo, 16th December, 1799.

Whereas I have received information that the Combined
fleets of the Enemy are destined for the Mediterranean, and
as I think such an event very probable, if they elude the
vigilance of our Channel fleet, you are hereby required and
directed to proceed down the Mediterranean, without calling at any place on your route, and on your arrival at
Gibraltar, you will, *in confidence*, communicate this order,
and the circumstances you know respecting this information,
to his Excellency the Governor, to Commissioner Inglefield,
and the Officer commanding his Majesty's Ships there. Which
having done, you will proceed immediately through the
Gut, and station the Penelope in what you think the most
eligible position for falling in with the Fleet of the Enemy,
between Cape Spartel and Cape St. Vincent, keeping a
very good look-out. And in case of your seeing them,
or having intelligence that you can depend on, of their actual
approach off Cape St. Vincent, you will directly return through
the Gut, and make the same known to the Governor and
Senior Officer of his Majesty's Ships at Gibraltar, by sending your Boat on shore, proceeding in the Ship you command up the Mediterranean, giving information to any of
his Majesty's Ships you may fall in with, of the Enemy's
approach, that they may make it known to the Com-

manding Officer at Mahon, proceeding yourself to Malta, to give them information also, and to put them on their guard. But in case you do not fall in with any of his Majesty's Ships in your passage up the Mediterranean, you will, in that case, call at Mahon, and communicate the intelligence you have received, and proceed to Malta. Not meeting with the Enemy's fleet, or gaining such intelligence as may cause you to leave your station between Cape Spartel and Cape St. Vincent, you will continue to cruize there, for the space of six weeks, when you will return to Gibraltar, putting yourself under the command of the Senior Officer at that place, and following his orders for your further proceedings.

BRONTE NELSON.

TO HIS EXCELLENCY THE MARQUIS DE NIZA.

[Letter-Book.]

Palermo, 18th December, 1799.

My Lord,

I cannot allow you to pass from under my command without assuring you of my sincere and cordial thanks for your constant and ready obedience to every order and wish I have directed to your Lordship for the Public service ; and allow me to say, that it is impossible for any Officer to have executed them with [more] alertness and judgment than yourself. I have, in particular, to express to your Lordship my approbation of your judgment in continuing to obey my orders for the Public service in remaining at Malta till I could get Ships to relieve you, instead of an immediate obedience to your orders from the Court of Portugal, which, had you obeyed, the French would, most probably, [have] been in possession of the whole Island, and the Allies might not have been able to even effect a landing. Your orders, which it would be no longer proper to disobey, forces me with regret to part from you. I have, therefore, again to thank you for all your kindness towards me, and to assure [you] with what respect and esteem I feel myself your most obliged, humble servant,

BRONTE NELSON.

TO HIS EXCELLENCY THE MARQUIS DE NIZA.

[Letter-Book.]

Palermo, 18th December, 1799.

Sir,

I beg leave to acquaint your Excellency that I no longer consider you, or the Ships of your Squadron, under my command: I therefore again beg you will accept of my sincere thanks for your prompt obedience and execution of all my orders for the public service, and [wishes] that you may meet with a just reward for your meritorious conduct on your return to Lisbon. I am, with the greatest respect and esteem, &c.,

BRONTE NELSON.

TO THE RIGHT HONOURABLE EARL SPENCER, K.G.

[Letter-Book.]

Palermo, December 18th, 1799.

My dear Lord,

I cannot get the Russian Admiral to come from Naples— therefore, our troops are at a stand still at Malta, and seem preparing to resist an attack from the French, [rather] than to make one. I think the Emperor of Russia will not be pleased with his Admiral, but nothing shall be wanting on my part to finish this business, consistent with the other services entrusted to me. The Phaeton arrived yesterday from Constantinople; and Lord Elgin presses me, if it can be done, to send a larger Squadron into the Levant Seas. But your Lordship knows that is not possible, and, indeed, except to gratify the Turks is there any service for a large Squadron, Malta having kept everything not wanted for other particular services. If I could have any Cruisers, as was my plan, off Cape Bon, in Africa, and between Corsica and Toulon, Mr. Buonaparte could not probably have got to France; but if it bring on a confusion at Paris, I hope it will be for the best. As the Board have called Admiral Duckworth to watch Ferrol, and I have no Ships of the Line, (Foudroyant excepted,) except the Northumberland, which is fit to go out of the Mediterranean, I have detached the Phaeton and Pene-

lope to cruize between Cape Spartel and St. Vincent, in case
the Enemy's fleet should be coming this road, and elude the
vigilance of Lord Bridport, that I may have timely notice of
their approach; and this station will also be favourable for intercepting any outward-bound Ships from Cadiz. The Grand
Signior has sent me, with a very elegant letter, a drawing of
the Battle of the Nile, together with a drawing of myself—a
curious present, but highly flattering to me, as it marks I
am not in the least forgotten. I am almost blind—therefore,
my dear Lord, excuse my writing more at this moment, and
only believe me ever your obliged,

BRONTE NELSON.

TO HIS HIGHNESS THE DEY OF ALGIERS.

[Letter-Book.]

Palermo, 18th December, 1799.

Sir,

His Imperial Majesty Sultan Selim, having sent an Officer
with dispatches for your Highness, I have directed an English
frigate to carry him to Algiers; and I take this early opportunity of acquainting you that the Portuguese Squadron are
no longer under my command since yesterday. It having
ever been my study to prove his Britannic Majesty, my
gracious Master, your Highness's best friend, you will receive
this extraordinary mark of my duty as an incontestible proof
of it. Your Highness must be sensible how steadily my
attention must have been employed to keep such a Squadron
from your Coast. In return for this kindness, the Ships of
your Highness have taken Vessels having my recommendation, in consequence of which, they have many of them
gone to your Ships, where they were captured and carried
into slavery; and these Vessels having certificates were not
carrying merchandize, (for to such I never gave certificates,)
but provisions, for those who were fighting against the
common Enemy. You might as well have taken their arms
as their bread. I look forward, from your Highness's character
for humanity, for the immediate release of poor people, who,
in consequence of my paper, put themselves in your power,
[and] for the restitution of the Vessels. I only look for

justice, and I pray you to have the goodness to think for a
moment that it was Nelson who put them in the power of
your Cruisers, and not their activity. There cannot, your
Highness will allow, be a stronger proof of my attention,
than in my communication of this day, which puts you in the
way to avoid your enemies, the Portuguese, now no longer
restrained by me, gives you an opportunity of showing to
the world your humanity and justice, and of highly gratifying
your Excellency's most faithful friend and servant,

BRONTE NELSON.

TO EVAN NEPEAN, ESQ., ADMIRALTY.

[Original, in the Admiralty.]

Atty Transport, Palermo, the 18th December, 1799.

Sir,
I beg leave to acquaint you that his Majesty's Ship Phaeton
arrived here yesterday from Constantinople, having, by desire
of the Ottoman Ministry, brought two Turks from thence—
the one to be landed at Tunis, the other at Algiers, which
Captain Morris will do on his way down the Mediterranean.

Not knowing whether Rear-Admiral Duckworth hath left
any Ship to cruize between Cape Spartel and Cape St.
Vincent, I have put the Penelope under Captain Morris's
orders, and directed him to cruize in such a position between
those Capes as he may think most eligible for annoying the
Enemy, as well as to keep a good look out for the approach
of the Combined fleets, whom I have reason to suppose, from
the information I have received, are destined for the Mediterranean; and, in case of their approach, to run for Minorca
and Malta, to put them on their guard.

Captain Blackwood having sprung his fore-yard, calls at
Minorca in his way down, to take either the fore or main-
yard of the Courageux to replace it, as there are no spars at
Mahon to make one. The Russian Squadron, which should
have sailed from Naples Bay for Malta, with their Troops, on
the 17th of last month, are still laying there, and the Troops
not yet embarked, although the necessity for using dispatch
has been strongly urged to their Admiral. Those delays on

their part, very much retard the operation against Malta, but nothing has been wanting on ours.

The Marquis de Niza arrived here two days ago from Malta to refit and victual, having left the command of the blockade to Commodore Sir Thomas Troubridge, Bart., from whence he proceeds immediately, by order of his Court, to Lisbon, with the Squadron under his command.

I have the honour to be, &c.,
BRONTE NELSON.

TO THE HONOURABLE LIEUTENANT-GENERAL FOX.

[Autograph, in the possession of Dawson Turner, Esq., F.R.S.]

Palermo, 18th December, 1799.

Sir,

I have received your Excellency's letter of the 6th inst., requesting my assistance for his Majesty's Ships to convey from Sardinia, Elba, or Leghorn, such Corsican recruits as may be raised at those places, from time to time, to Mahon; and I beg leave to assure your Excellency, that I shall at all times be ready to meet your wishes, and render you all the assistance in my power; and whenever you may have occasion for any Ship for this service, you will be pleased to make application to the senior Officer of his Majesty's Ships at Mahon, who will send such Ship as may be necessary to take them to Mahon. I have the honour to be your Excellency's most obedient and faithful servant,

BRONTE NELSON.

TO J. FAGAN, ESQ., ROME.

[From Harrison's Life of Nelson, vol. ii. p. 202. It is also printed, with some trifling variations, in the " Naval Chronicle," vol. iii. p. 145.]

Palermo, December 19th, 1799.

Dear Sir,

Sir William Hamilton has been so kind as to communicate to me the distinguished honour intended me by the inhabitants, by you, and other Professors and Admirers of the Fine Arts, at Rome, to erect a Monument. I have not words sufficient to express my feelings, on hearing that my actions have contributed to preserve the works which form the School of Fine Arts in Italy, which the modern Goths wanted to carry off and destroy. That they may always remain in the only place worthy of them, Rome, are and will be my fervent wishes, together with the esteem of, dear Sir,

Your most obliged servant,
BRONTE NELSON.

TO COMMODORE SIR THOMAS TROUBRIDGE, BART.

[Letter-Book.]

Palermo, 19th December, 1799.

My dear Troubridge,

If I rightly remember, I mentioned in one of my letters to you, that I intended the Princess Charlotte as the Ship to take charge of the present Convoy to England, and the Alliance to go under her command; therefore, if you have not already dispatched those two Ships to Mahon for that purpose, I beg they may be sent down immediately, as the Convoy will wait for their arrival, there being only the Gorgon there, which is not of force sufficient. By the Boyne Transport I have sent you bread and wine, with an assortment of provisions; and by the Arab tender I have sent also thirty pipes of wine; and a Transport sails this evening to load wood at Coronea, which I hope will be with you soon. General Acton has informed me that four cargoes of wood have already been ordered for the troops at Malta, on the demand of Chevalier Italinsky. Wishing you every success, believe me, &c.,

BRONTE NELSON.

TO CAPTAIN MORRIS, H.M. SHIP PHAETON.

[Letter-Book.]

Atty Transport, Palermo, 19th December, 1799.

Sir,

On your return to Gibraltar from carrying my orders into execution, you will, in all probability, find yourself the senior Officer: in that case, you will render every assistance to

General O'Hara and the Garrison of Gibraltar, and use your endeavours to keep the Ports of the Barbary States open, as well as the Gut of Gibraltar, to protect the trade, and keep a good look out on Cadiz, or of the approach of the Enemy's fleet, that timely information may be given to the different stations of Mahon and Malta, either by dispatching such Ships as you have at Gibraltar, or running up yourself for that purpose. I am, &c.,

BRONTE NELSON.

TO HIS EXCELLENCY THE MARQUIS DE NIZA.

[Letter-Book.]

Palermo, 19th December, 1799.

My Lord,

I have to request you will be pleased to communicate to the Commodores of the Squadron of her Most Faithful Majesty under your Excellency's orders, my sincere thanks and approbation of their services whilst under my command, as well as to the Captains and Officers serving under them, on board their respective Ships; and also to the Officers and Men serving on shore in the Kingdom of Naples, and at the Island of Malta, for their very exemplary, brave, and meritorious conduct, and strict obedience to command.

And I have further to request that you will be pleased to communicate my entire approbation, and sincere thanks, to the Captains, Thomson and Welch, for the activity and alacrity with which they have performed the various services in which they have been employed, and that your Excellency will be pleased to recommend them, and the Captain of the Fleet, Don Rodrigo de Pinto, to his Royal Highness the Prince of Brazil for promotion. Believe me, with the sincerest regard and esteem, your Excellency's most obedient and most faithful servant,

BRONTE NELSON.

TO THE PRESIDI OF ZANTE.

[Letter-Book.]

Palermo, December 21st, 1799.

Gentlemen,

I have received, through the hands of Mr. Spiridion Foresti, your very elegant and highly flattering present of a Sword and Cane, with a letter,[4] valuable ten thousand times more than any gold and diamonds; and I shall preserve them for my descendants, who, I trust, never will forget for a moment

[4] The following is a translation of the Letter alluded to, which, with the original, is in the Nelson Papers:

"To the Most Honourable Lord Nelson, Knight of the Bath, Rear-Admiral of the Red, and Commander of His Majesty's Fleets in the Mediterranean.

"Most Honourable Sir,

"Magnanimous Hero!—your astonishing Victories have liberated this part of Greece, which had fallen an involuntary victim to French rage. Harassed by so many misfortunes, surrounded on all sides by the horrors of anarchy, destruction was not far removed from us. In the midst of this so great affliction of our hearts, who could have foreseen that a man of such talents, sprung from the great nation of Britain, would have flown to have altered the face of our destiny? Your appearance in the Seas of Egypt was a prodigy, but a still greater prodigy was your immortal Victory. These Seas were rendered free; the Imperial combined Fleets descended, and, from that moment, the august voices of Religion, of Nature, of Justice, and of Humanity were, without terror, heard amongst us; our hearts, kindled by the sacred flame of gratitude, consecrate to you a Sword and a Truncheon; accept of them, generous hero, as a small testimony of our veneration, and preserve it as a faithful emblem of that eternal gratitude and remembrance, in which your immortal name will ever be held by this City, ever an admirer of your mighty deeds. May they accelerate that brilliant day, in which, with the glory and peace of thrones, the miseries of the human race may cease! We remain, with the most respectful veneration, your most humble, devoted, and obliged Servants,

"ANASTASIO LOGOTATI.
". : . : GAITA.
"BASILIO MACRI.
"NICCOLO FOSCARDI.
"ANDREA COCCHINI.
"GIOVANNI SICURO.

Presidi.

"Zante, 25th October, 1799."

These presents are thus mentioned in Miss Knight's MS. *Journal:*—

"Arrived the Perseus, Captain Compton, from Corfu. Brought a gold-hilted Sword and Cane, as a present from the inhabitants of Zante to Lord Nelson. On the Sword are trophies, and this inscription—*Phario Victori Zacynthus.* Round the Cane is a row of diamonds, and a button. It was intended that it should have been richly ornamented with jewels; but though the ladies gave what they had, enough was not to be found. They are warmly attached to the English name."

the honour conferred upon me by the Inhabitants of the Island of Zante. To be considered by you, Gentlemen, as the first cause of your liberation from French tyranny, is, although true, yet such an example of gratitude, as will ever do you the highest honour. I only wish for an opportunity to mark the sense I entertain of your goodness to me, by doing something more to increase the prosperity of your Island. That all the Inhabitants of Zante may increase in happiness is the sincere prayer, and shall be the exertion of, Gentlemen, your most faithful and obliged,

BRONTE NELSON.

TO SPIRIDION FORESTI, ESQ., CORFU.

[Letter-Book.]

Palermo, December 21st, 1799.

Dear Sir,

I beg leave to transmit you a letter of thanks for the high and flattering honour conferred upon me by the inhabitants of Zante; and I beg that you will have the goodness to express in fuller terms than any words I can find, my sense of their kindness, and of my wish to prove myself further useful to them.

I have sent by a Neapolitan messenger a packet of great importance, and the Minister of his Sicilian Majesty tells me he has a Tartan waiting at Corfu; but I beg you will take care that it is expedited as expeditiously as possible. Our news here is of a civil war in France—Buonaparte against Barras. May God increase their confusion. You must excuse this short letter: [it] will only allow me to thank you sincerely for all your kindness to me, and be assured that I shall ever feel myself your obliged

BRONTE NELSON.

If General Villettes is at Corfu, I beg my sincerest regards to him.

TO THE RIGHT HONOURABLE THE EARL OF ELGIN.

[Letter-Book.]

Palermo, 21st December, 1799.

My Lord,

I was honoured with your letter of November 28th, by Captain Morris, and I did not fail to pay immediate attention to your good wishes for him, by sending him directly off Cadiz, calling in his way down the Mediterranean, at Tunis and Algiers, to land two Officers sent by the Capitan Pacha, with the dispatches. They were lodged in this house during their very short stay here; and your Lordship will be so good as to inform the Ottoman Minister, that by this day I hope the person for Tunis is arrived at his destination; and they do me but justice in believing that I am always alert to do them every kindness, for as no man ever received greater favour from the Sublime Porte, so no one shall be more grateful.

I have regretted sincerely the escape of Buonaparte; but those Ships which were destined by me for the two places where he would certainly have been intercepted, were, from the Admiralty thinking, doubtless, that the Russians would do something at sea, obliged to be at Malta, and other services which I thought the Russian Admiral would have assisted me in—therefore, no blame lays at my door. The Vincejo, a few days ago, took a Vessel from Egypt with General Voix and seventy-five Officers, mostly of Buonaparte's staff; and also Captain Long was happy enough to save the dispatches, which were thrown overboard, but with an insufficient weight to instantly sink them. I send you copies of all those which you have not got. (Apropos, your dispatches went for Gibraltar the day of the Phaeton's arrival, 17th December.) I hope that your recommendation for the Vizir's pushing on in Egypt will be duly attended to, and I have no doubt that the campaign will end in the destruction of the French.

I shall endeavour to get some Ships on the Coast of Africa, to watch for any small Vessels going with supplies to Egypt; but the Porte may rest assured that the Enemy have no Ships in Toulon, able to carry any useful reinforcement of men. I

own my hope yet is, that the Sublime Porte will never permit
a single Frenchman to quit Egypt; and I own myself wicked
enough to wish them all to die in that Country they chose to
invade. We have scoundrels of French enough in Europe
without them. We have nothing from England since October 24th: being in a corner, we are forgot. I cannot get the
Russian Admiral to move from Naples. He was to have
sailed the 17th November. I hear the General Prince W.
is very much displeased. Our troops landed there the 10th,
and are waiting impatiently their arrival. The fall of Malta
would enable me instantly to attend to all the services required
of me. The Austrian Generals in the Riviera of Genoa call
loudly for a Naval co-operation from me, although the Russians
have an Admiral and Squadron on that Coast. I do not think
the application to the Court of Portugal, for the release of
Algerines can be listened to ; for I should be very sorry to
see the doctrine established that free Ships make free goods.
Last war, the circumstances of our situation forced us to
acquiesce ; but this war we take Enemy's property, wherever
we find it. I again take the liberty of repeating that it is
contrary to my opinion, allowing a single Frenchman from
Egypt to return during the war to France. It would [be a]
paper I never would subscribe to; but I submit to the better
judgment of men. Ever, my Lord, believe me, &c.

                              NELSON AND BRONTE.

TO BRIGADIER-GENERAL GRAHAM.

[Letter-Book.]

Palermo, December 22nd, 1799.

My dear Sir,

I thank you sincerely for your letter of the 15th, which I
have sent to General Acton, and as he has told Sir William
that a carte-blanche is gone to Syracuse and Augusta, I hope
you will get everything those places can supply, but we cannot expect them to lay out money for us. If they give us
money worth, it is all we can have a right to expect. The
Transports, which go from here with provisions, and one for
wood, shall have my directions to call at Messina for the

artillerymen. If they are ready, they will soon be with you as
the Vessels are only kept here by bad weather. The Russian
Admiral is very slow in his movements, and I hear the General
Prince W. is very angry at his not carrying him to Malta. I
am very anxious for the business of Malta being speedily
finished. I am, &c.,

NELSON AND BRONTE.

TO COMMODORE SIR THOMAS TROUBRIDGE, BART.

[Letter-Book.]

Palermo, 22nd December, 1799.

My dear Troubridge,
    Your letters of December 15th are at this moment arrived,
by express, from Messina. Everything we have here I have
ordered to be shipped on board a Transport, and she shall
sail as expeditiously as possible. The other two are detained
here by very bad weather. I have wrote to you by them.
Never mind the Culloden's getting on shore. She has done
enough, and I shall write to Lord Spencer by post, that if he
does not send you or me another Ship, that your services will
be lost for a short time, and even that our Country cannot
afford. At all events do not fret yourself. As to the Russians,
I doubt their being in a hurry—at least, the Admiral. A
Frigate is just coming in : I fancy the Pearl—if so, she shall
join you to-morrow.

    The Frigate is the Phaeton, put back by bad weather. Do
not send the Foudroyant, but use her ; and when you can
get Ships enough, send one or two off Cape Bon, or on the
Coast most likely to meet Vessels going to Egypt, but the
Captains must be cautioned of the shoals off Lampedosa and
towards Tripoli. The [Esquerques?] they all know. The
Vincejo a few days ago took a Vessel from Alexandria with
General Voix and a number of Officers—also the dispatches,
which are of the greatest importance. By the Pearl I will send
them for your and Graham's perusal. In short, either more
money and ammunition must be sent to Egypt, or that Army
will fall. In my opinion, the combined Fleets are destined
for that service, and the relief of Malta, if the commotions at

Paris do not alter their intentions. I hope the Strombolo will
carry the artillerymen from Messina ; for I dare not order the
Transport with provisions to call there, as he is an old trader
and wishes of all things to go there. We have nothing from
England since October 22nd. The Peterel has left two
cases for you, but I will not trust them but by a Vessel of
War. I have wrote by Harriman. I am undergoing a course
of electricity, which I begin to think will give sight to my
blind eye. May God bless you.

BRONTE NELSON.

Remember me kindly to Ball. I would write, but I am
dispatching the Peterel to Corfu, with letters for Constanti-
nople ; and for England by the Phaeton. The wood Vessel,
I am sorry to say, must be kept another day to take in the
Phaeton's powder, as her magazine has overflowed. If the
Princess Charlotte is not sailed for Mahon, send her directly.
The vessels at Messina were not in the least ready for a
Convoy. They have now sent an express, which Government
pays for, to ask for the Speedy to stay till they can load their
Ships. The Alliance I ordered from Trapani, and she is
ready to sail from Mahon. I send a letter for Mahon, if
the Princess Charlotte is not gone, in consequence of my
former letter.

TO HIS EXCELLENCY THE GRAND VIZIR.

[Letter-Book.]

Palermo, 22nd December, 1799.

Sir,
    Was I to attempt by words to express what I felt on receiv-
ing the Imperial present of the drawing of the Battle of Aboukir, and the highly flattering letter wrote by your Excellency,
in obedience to the Imperial command, I should feel myself
unequal to the task ; therefore, I can only beg your Excellency to express, in words most adapted to convey my gratitude
to his Imperial Majesty, my sense of the extraordinary high
honour conferred upon me, by a Present more valuable than
gold or jewels, as they may come only from the hand of a great
Monarch, while this can only flow from the benevolent heart
of a good Man. That the Almighty may pour down his

choicest blessings on the Imperial head, and ever give his arms
victory over all his enemies, is the fervent prayer, and shall
ever be, as far as my abilities will allow me, the constant exertion, of your Excellency's obliged servant,

BRONTE NELSON.

TO HIS EXCELLENCY J. SPENCER SMITH, ESQ., SECRETARY OF
EMBASSY, CONSTANTINOPLE.

[Letter-Book.]

Palermo, 22nd December, 1799.

(Look at my seal.)
My dear Sir,

I have not only to thank you for your letters of October 20th,
27th, and November 18th, but for all your kind attention to
me, and I assure you it will give me real pleasure to have an
opportunity of cultivating your personal acquaintance.

The present from the Grand Signior is certainly curious,
and particularly in this point, that it assures me of the goodness of his heart; and, a rare qualification for Monarchs,
that he does not forget services rendered him. A handful of
diamonds comes naturally from the hand of a great Monarch,
but this drawing, made probably for the occasion, could only
come from an affectionate, amiable disposition; and I beg
you will have the goodness to express my sensations, when
you deliver the letter sent herewith. I feel perfectly unable
to tell my feelings on this, to me, gratifying occasion.

Except Sir Thomas Troubridge, all your Levant friends are
gone to England, as is the ———; and I fancy I have no
more reason to be satisfied with her Captain's kindness than
yourself. He was angry that I could not get him pratique,
and I fancy said some things not perfectly correct when he
got to England. I have read with pleasure all that has passed
in Egypt between Buonaparte, Kleber, and the Grand Vizir;
and I send Lord Elgin some very important papers, which
will show their very deplorable situation. But I cannot bring
myself to believe they would entirely quit Egypt; and, if
they would, I never would consent to one of them returning
to the Continent of Europe during the war. I wish them to
perish in Egypt, and give a great lesson to the world of the jus-

tice of the ALMIGHTY. I wish if the Russian troops you mention were at Malta, as also those from Naples; but Admiral
Ouschakoff cannot be got to move ; and by his carelessness,
the fall of Malta is not only retarded, but the Island may be
lost. The Ships in the harbour are ready for sea, and will try
to escape. Four days ago three shells fell into the Guillaume
Tell, and her poop is blown up. When you write to your
brother, remember me kindly to him. I regret I have not a
Vessel to send with these letters to Egypt, but I have nothing
equal to the service imposed upon me. Adieu, my dear Sir,
and believe me ever your obliged

BRONTE NELSON.

<hr />

TO THE RIGHT HONOURABLE EARL SPENCER, K.G.

[Letter-Book.]

Palermo, 23rd December, 1799.

My dear Lord,
    You will see with some sorrow the accident which has befell
the Culloden, and now it only remains for you to decide
whether the services of Troubridge are to be lost in the
Mediterranean : he must evidently have another Ship, or
be an established Commodore. You will have received the
important papers from Egypt, copies of those which Lord
Elgin has not, go off this day for Corfu, and from thence
by land to Constantinople. I wish to have a Squadron
of two or three Vessels off Cape Bon, in Africa, and
another to assist the Austrians in the Riviera of Genoa ;
but I absolutely want more than I have for the blockade of
Malta. The Ships are ready to sail, and will probably try to
escape as a last effort. The Russians, even if at sea, of which
I see no prospect, cannot sail, or be of the least service. I have
wrote very plainly to the Russian Minister, that in my opinion
the Emperor will not be well pleased with Admiral Ouschakoff.
Culloden, Alexander, and Lion cannot go to sea, and all I
hope for is to get them to England a few months hence. I
am here, in addition to my other employments, a Commissary
for our troops at Malta. I get no help from Minorca, and I
am obliged to go begging from this Government, who scarcely
have it to give. All these things fret me a little. Was I

merely to do my duty at sea, it would be nothing; but to want the means of doing all which is naturally expected of me hurts me. I know it was expected that the large Russian Squadron would have been of some use. To this moment, to my knowledge, they have been of none; but all shall end well, and I have only to beg that you will, my dear Lord, ever believe me your obliged and affectionate,

BRONTE NELSON.

TO BRIGADIER-GENERAL GRAHAM.

[From Clarke and M'Arthur, vol. ii. p. 241.]

[About 23rd December, 1799.]

I only wish that I could always do all you ask me. It is certain that you cannot go on at Malta without money; therefore I declare, sooner than you should want, I would sell Bronté. But, I trust, from General Fox's letter to me, that you will have his consent for ordering what money may be necessary. I send you all the Egyptian papers, for yourself, Ball, and Troubridge; and, if you like, in confidence, Italinsky. Suwarrow is at Prague with his whole Army, ready to act with the Austrians, if they come to their senses—or perhaps against them. Moreau is at Vienna, treating for peace. What a state the Allies bring us into! but it is in vain to cry out. I am, &c.,

BRONTE NELSON.

TO CAPTAIN SIR EDWARD BERRY, H. M. SHIP FOUDROYANT.

[Autograph, in the possession of Lady Berry.]

Palermo, December 23rd, 1799.

My dear Sir,

I thank you very much for your kind letter. All our Ships are so much torn to pieces that I look for (where I am sure of finding them) very active services from the Foudroyant. The Russian Admiral is very lazy. I wish the troops were in Malta. I have nothing from England since October 22nd, and then only a miserable letter from the Admiralty. With best regards to all about you, believe me, my dear Sir Edward, your sincere and obliged friend,

BRONTE NELSON.

As a death vacancy is to be filled in the Peterel,[5] I would
have you choose the best young man in the Foudroyant. You
will see that I move the Lieutenant of the Courageux. If
any Captains wish to have young men promoted, they must
go into the Flag Ship, unless by some extraordinary conduct.

TO EVAN NEPEAN, ESQ., ADMIRALTY.

[Original, in the Admiralty.]

Sir,   Palermo, 23rd December, 1799.

I beg leave to inform you, for the information of their
Lordships, that His Majesty's Ship Culloden, on going into
the Bay of Marsa Sirocco, in the Island of Malta, to land
the cannon, ammunition, &c., taken on board that Ship at
Messina for the siege, struck on a rock, and Commodore Sir
Thomas Troubridge, Bart., her Commander, has informed
me that the rudder and greatest part of the false keel are
carried away, and the rudder would have been lost but for the
timely exertion in getting a hawser secured through it, the
pintles are all broke, and the Ship was steered to the anchorage
with her sails, where she is now in safety, but very leaky.
If I can get her, the Alexander, and Lion, to England a few
months hence, it is all that I can expect from them, as they
are not fit to keep the sea.

I have not as yet had the least co-operation or assistance
from Admiral Ouschakoff or the Russian Fleet; they are, I
believe, still in Naples Bay, and not any of their troops yet
arrived at Malta, where their presence is so absolutely necessary. I have the honour to be, Sir, &c.,

BRONTE NELSON.

TO HIS HIGHNESS THE BEY OF TUNIS.

[Letter-Book.]

Sir,   Palermo, 23rd December, 1799.

I cannot permit a Frigate to proceed to Tunis, without
writing a letter to your Highness, to acquaint you that, from

[5] Vide p. 131, ante.

your well-known justice and goodness of heart, I have been long
looking for the release of those poor men who were taken by
your Cruizers, when carrying provisions to the Island of Malta.
Their Vessel, also, I have no doubt but your Highness will
release, as they were through my recommendations pursuing
their voyage, and relying on them as a protection against your
Cruizers. I have already informed your Highness that I have
never granted a passport to any Vessel for trade, but only
for the purpose of carrying provisions to our Ships of War
and soldiers at Malta. Your Highness is also well aware that
I have never suffered the Portuguese Squadron, since they
have been under my command, to approach your Coast, which
I might have done, if it was not out of respect to your Highness, being the Ally of my Royal Master.

These considerations will, I hope, on due reflection, induce
your Highness to release these poor men and their Vessels,
and show to the world your justice and benevolence of heart.
I beg your Highness to believe that I am, with the sincerest
respect, your most obedient and faithful servant,

BRONTE NELSON.

TO EVAN NEPEAN, ESQ., ADMIRALTY.

[Letter-Book.]

Palermo, 23rd December, 1799.

Sir,

I beg leave to inform you, for the information of their
Lordships, that his Majesty's Ship Culloden, on going into
the Bay of Marsa Scirocco, in the Island of Malta, to land the
cannon, ammunition, &c. taken on board that Ship at Messina,
for the siege, struck on a rock, and Commodore Sir Thomas
Troubridge, Bart., has informed me that the rudder and great
part of the false keel are carried away, and the rudder would
have been lost, but for their timely exertion in getting a
hawser reeved through it. The pintles are all broke, and
the Ship was steered to the anchorage with her sails, where
she is now in safety, but very leaky. If I can get her, the
Alexander, and Lion to England, a few months hence, it is
all that I can expect from them, as they are not fit to keep
the sea. I have not as yet the least co-operation or assistance

from Admiral Ouschakoff or the Russian fleet. They are, I believe, still in Naples Bay, and not any of their troops yet arrived at Malta, where their presence is so absolutely necessary. I have the honour to be, &c.

BRONTE NELSON.

TO COMMODORE SIR THOMAS TROUBRIDGE, BART.

[Letter-Book.]

Palermo, 29th December, 1799.

My dear Troubridge,

I have this moment received your letters of December 19th, 20th, 21st, 22nd, and 23rd, by express from Syracuse, five days on his journey. I went with Sir William directly to General Acton, and I had the pleasure of finding that three Vessels loaded with corn from Naples for Malta, were in this Port, under convoy of the Sirena Frigate, that another was at Messina, and a fourth, with flour, was daily expected from Naples. The General assures me that there is a great scarcity of corn in this Island, and that the granaries at Girgenti are not full of corn, and I must believe the want, when so large a bounty is given for the importation. The spars, if any, at this place, shall go in the Frigate. I find in the General a disposition to give us all in his power. It has been settled by the Ministers of England, Russia, and Naples, that from the day of the meeting, seven weeks past, that each Power should bear a share of the expense. The King of Naples instantly sent 8000 ounces, and has ever since been giving stores, &c. I will not, I assure you, ask for any more, till England and Russia perform their part. A general order for supplying our troops and Ships will be repeated, but not for the supply of Malta, for General Acton declares they have it not to give; but that everything shall be done to give us content. If we can take the Recazzoli, it will put all our minds at ease, and part of our crippled Ships can be sent to Minorca to refit, as no supplies can then get into the harbour; but in that case I think Vaubois would be glad to give up.

It is my intention at present, when I hear that the Russian

Admiral is really determined to sail from Naples, to go to Malta, and to give him, the Russian General, Graham, yourself, and Ball, a meeting, and to fix things for Malta, either for siege or otherwise, on a permanent footing; therefore, send me the Foudroyant as soon as you can spare her. I have sent for more provisions to Minorca, and by every opportunity you shall have supplies. I send an order for Captain Mundy to purchase what you want at Syracuse, if he can get it from the Governor; and Mr. Tough assures me that he never has wrote or desired his Consuls not to take Government bills, but not to think that bills drawn by all Officers were for account of Government. This is his history. Captain Weir[6] shall have the brevet rank of Major, as General Graham desires; and I only wish, for Captain W.'s sake, it may be permanent, for no man deserves promotion more than himself. I have wrote very strongly to Lord Spencer about you, and you are sure that nothing will be wanting on my part to serve you, both as a public and private man. Your resources never fail, and you would contrive something, I dare say, if the Ship's bottom was knocked out.

You will, of course, communicate this letter to Graham and Ball, as far as relates to provisions, that the latter may know who to apply to, when the Island again wants. If Italinsky is with you, remember me kindly to him. General Barusden arrived at Corfu, December 1st, with about 2000 men. We have not a syllable from the Continent, when we are so anxious to hear of what is passing in France. Something must turn up; however, no Power can make a peace till some Government is established. We have nothing from England but a newspaper of November 2nd, which tells us nothing but that the Enemy's fleet, were ready to sail. You will have received my order to send the Princess Charlotte to Minorca, in order to go home with the Convoy. God bless you, &c.

BRONTE NELSON.

I have only heard that this Government is selling property

---

[6] Captain James Weir, of the Royal Marines : he obtained a brevet Majority December 1799, retired on full pay before 1809, and died about 1821.

at Città Vecchia and Rome, for paying the captors. General Acton, I am confident, intends uprightness, and so does the Queen.

TO HIS EXCELLENCY THE MARQUIS SPINOLA.

[Letter-Book.]

Palermo, 29th December, 1799.

Sir,

Since my arrival at this place, now twelve months ago, there has been many men belonging to the Ships under my command murdered by some of the crews of the Ships under your Excellency's command; and three nights ago there was an Englishman murdered by two men which are known to belong to your Ships, and which men can be pointed out. I must, therefore insist upon your Excellency's securing those men, that they may be punished for the murder they have committed. I am, &c.

BRONTE NELSON.

TO LIEUTENANT-GENERAL THE HONOURABLE EDWARD FOX, MINORCA.

[From " Sir Thomas Hanmer's Correspondence," p. 426.]

Palermo, January 1st, 1800.

Dear Sir,

We have not had a letter of what is passing on the Continent, since the 10th December, from Florence : therefore, I cannot pretend to give you any news from that quarter. I hope this wind will induce the Russian Admiral to sail from Naples : the General I hear is much dissatisfied at being kept back. 2000 Russian troops arrived December 1st at Corfu. General Villettes arrived there also the 27th November. He has found some difficulties about raising the men for such a regular service as ours, but he expects to get over them all without much trouble. As I send your Excellency a letter from Graham, I shall give no opinion about Malta, but I hope, if the Fort at the entrance of the Port can be carried, that General Vaubois will be induced to capitulate without further trouble. Every Ship which I can get hold of is sent to prevent supplies getting in: therefore, what a release it will be to me when it falls! Wishing your Excellency many happy returns of the season, believe me, with great respect, your most obedient Servant,

BRONTE NELSON.

TO HIS EXCELLENCY DON RODRIGO DE SOUZA COUTINHO, MINISTER OF MARINE, LISBON.

[Letter-Book.]

Palermo, January 2nd, 1800.

Sir,

I cannot allow Captain Thompson to present himself to your Excellency without a testimony from me of his great worth, and of his abilities as an Officer; and I can assure your Excellency that he is highly deserving of promotion. And I shall also give Captain Welch, of the Balloon, a similar letter to your Excellency; and, if I may be permitted, to Don Rodrigo de Pinto, who is an Officer of the greatest merit, and strongly attached to the English. When I mention my brother and friend, Niza, I must say that I never knew so indefatigable an Officer. During the whole time I have had the happiness of having him under my command, I have never expressed a wish that Niza did not fly to execute, and I can say the same of all the Commodores; and all the Officers and men under their command have at all times shown bravery, good conduct, and strict obedience to orders. I can assure your Excellency that this letter but very faintly expresses my feelings, in endeavouring to do a small act of justice to so many deserving Officers, and good men.

Believe me, with every sentiment of respect, your Excellency's most obedient, humble Servant,

BRONTE NELSON.

TO COMMODORE SIR THOMAS TROUBRIDGE, BART.

[Letter-Book.]

Palermo, January 2nd, 1800.

My dear Troubridge,

I cannot get the Frigate out of the Mole—therefore, I must learn to be a hard-hearted wretch, and fancy the cries of hunger in my ears.[7] I send you orders for the different Governors. You will see they are for the supply of the Army

---

[7] The deplorable condition of the Maltese, is shown by the following extracts from the letters of Sir Thomas Troubridge to Lord Nelson:—

" Malta, 1st January, 1800.

"We are dying off fast, for want. I learn, by letters from Messina, that Sir William Hamilton says, Prince Luzzi refused corn some time ago, and Sir William does not think it worth while making another application. If that be the case, I wish he commanded at this distressing scene instead of me. Puglia had an immense harvest, near thirty sail left Messina before I did, to load corn;— will they let us have any? If not, a short time will decide the business. The German interest prevails. I wish I was at your Lordship's elbow for an hour—all, all will be thrown on you, rely on it. I will parry the blow as much as is in my power; I foresee much mischief brewing. God bless your Lordship—I am miserable, I cannot assist your operations more. Many happy returns of this day to you—I never spent so miserable a one. I am not very tender-hearted; but really the distress here would even move a Neapolitan."—*Clarke and M'Arthur*, vol. ii. p. 243.

" January 5th, 1800.

" I have this day saved 30,000 people from dying; but with this day my ability ceases. As the King of Naples, or rather the Queen and her party, are bent on starving us, I see no alternative, but to leave these poor unhappy people to starve, without our being witnesses to their distress. I curse the day I ever served the King of Naples. I, who know your Lordship so well, can pity the distress you must suffer; what must be our situation on the spot? If the Neapolitan government will not supply corn, I pray your Lordship to recall us. We are of no use. The Maltese soldiers must call on the French in Valetta, who have the *ability* to relieve them. The consequence will be, General Graham and his troops will be cut up to a man, if I do not withdraw them. I hourly expect him to apply to me for that purpose. All we brought, I shall leave—I mean the guns, &c. belonging to his Sicilian Majesty. I never expected to be treated in this manner by General Acton, who certainly influences the King's council : he complains he cannot get his orders put in force ; how can he expect it, when he never punishes any of the traitors ? On the contrary, is he not daily promoting the traitors we exposed to him ? We have characters, my Lord, to lose ; these people have none. Do not suffer their infamous conduct to fall on us. Our Country is just, but severe. I foresee we shall forfeit the little we have gained. Before supplies can possibly come, many thousands must perish, even if these supplies arrive in two days. The situation is worse than ever ; there are not even locusts. Such is the fever of my brain

and Navy—therefore, whatever Graham and you send for, will, if possible, be granted. I hope the Russians will sail this N.E. wind, and it is my intention to give you all a meeting the moment the Foudroyant arrives. We have nothing very late from the Continent. The return of the Russian Army is countermanded, but Suwarrow is gone to Petersburg. At Vienna I know they will be happy to make peace with Buonaparte, who will, if he gains his point, be declared Protector of the Liberty of the French Republic. If this happens, England can do nothing but make peace. Remember me kindly to General Graham, Ball, Martin, Gould, &c., &c. : and I wish you all, from my heart, many happy returns of the season. I

this minute, that I *assure you, on my honour*, if the Palermo traitors were here, I would shoot them first, and then myself. Girgenti, I beg to inform you, is full of corn—the money is ready to pay for it—we do not ask it as a gift. The moment the Transfer arrives I shall send her, with Italinsky, to Palermo, who, I suppose, will tell the government the Russian troops cannot go to Malta to be starved, and I hope influence the Generals to withdraw their men from the Country. I know well how things will then go. God bless your Lordship, is the prayer of the most unhappy being existing at present, your ever faithful and sincere, T. TROUBRIDGE. Oh, could you see the horrid distress I daily experience, something would be done. I wrote you long letters, via Messina, by the Strombolo, who is gone to seize corn, if any can be got hold of; money first to be offered. I have called on the Governor of Girgenti to fulfil the Treaty, and not shut their Ports against us."— *Autograph*, in the Nelson Papers.

" January 7th.

" Your Lordship will perceive that some engine is at work against us at Naples, and I believe in my former letters I hit on the proper person. If you complain, he will be immediately promoted, agreeably to the Neapolitan custom: my friend Yauch is in high favour, and at present intriguing deeply. All I write to you is known at the Queen's: I suspect my letters are opened before they reach you. For my own part, I look on the Neapolitans as the worst of intriguing enemies; every hour shows me their infamy and duplicity. It may be necessary to caution General Acton respecting what is going on: as that can be done in English, you may be sure of what is said. I pray your Lordship be cautious ; your honest, open manner of acting will be made a handle of. It is necessary to be very vigilant over the deceitful set you have to deal with : every nerve of mine shall be exerted to forward your Lordship's views and the service. I cannot assist you so fast as I could wish, so little depends upon me: that little you shall find well done." — *Clarke and M'Arthur*, vol. ii. p. 244.

" January 8th.

" From the Russians not arriving by the contrivance of these Ministers, is to be attributed our inactivity, which creates discontent. In short, my Lord, when I see you, and tell of their infamous tricks, you will be as much surprised as I am with them: the whole will fall on you, which hurts me much. The Foudroyant shall go as complete to your Lordship as I can possibly let her."—*Ibid.*

am told that we are in the old century. Be that as it may,
I hope you will all live all the days of your lives; and, whilst
I live, believe me your truly affectionate friend,

BRONTE NELSON.

TO COMMODORE SIR THOMAS TROUBRIDGE, BART.

[Letter-Book.]

Palermo, January 7th, 1800.

My dear Troubridge,

I know all your wants, and it is always my sorrow, when I
cannot relieve the wants of my friends. The Vessels with
corn cannot be got out from hence—indeed, the Benjamin
arrived this morning, having had a hard gale off Maritimo.
Sir William is just come from General Acton, and has the
promise that the corn bought by the Senate of Palermo, at
Girgenti, shall go to Malta, and the corn here be landed for
Palermo; and that an express shall be sent this day to Girgenti.
I cannot do more than get these orders. I wish for the Frigate
to go for them, as she has spars for ladders and planks on
board; but I do not expect to succeed: therefore, you had
better send a Vessel to Girgenti; and as it is very possible,
after all, that no orders sent may be obeyed, I wish you
would, if that should be the case, direct an express to be sent
to me. I still hold my intention of making you a visit if any
Ship comes soon here, although I expect Lord Keith very
soon at Palermo. I hope the Gorgon is nearly at this moment
with you, and if the Victuallers are not met with on their
passage, one shall sail in ten minutes after her arrival. I send
you a number of letters from England, but I own my surprise
to see one directed by Lord Spencer to ' Captain Troubridge';[8]
but I hope the inside will be more pleasant to you, than the
outside is to me.

Suwarrow is retreated to the Prague with his whole Army,
ready to act in the spring with the Emperor, or, perhaps,
against him. *Moreau is at* Vienna, treating for peace. What
a history! I send you the letters from Egypt. For the moment,

---

[8] It seems that Lord Spencer did not address Sir Thomas Troubridge as a
Baronet, and the Admiralty had ordered his Broad Pendant to be struck. Vide
p. 142, ante, and p. 178, infra.

adieu! Do not keep the Vincejo, but let her go to Minorca.
For ever believe me your obliged and affectionate,

BRONTE NELSON.

Louis is certainly sailed by this time. No account of the
Pearl.

TO HIS EXCELLENCY LIEUTENANT-GENERAL THE HONOURABLE
EDWARD FOX, MINORCA.

[Letter-Book.]

Dear Sir,   Palermo, January 7th, 1800.

I am honoured with your Excellency's two letters of December 28th, and return you the letter for the Captain
General of Catalonia : I have no doubt but your letter is a
most proper one. I hope that you will have permission
to assist in getting rid of this long—very long business of
Malta. The Russians I hope are there by this time : they
arrived at Messina the 4th. As Graham wrote fully, he tells
me, to you, by the Princess Charlotte, I shall not trouble
you with any opinion of mine. All, I trust, will end well.
This Country has great calls upon it and unfortunately
has nothing to give. You may depend that Graham shall
share the fate of our Ships—I shall never suffer him to want,
if I can beg, borrow, or steal, to supply him. Lord Keith is,
I dare say, with you at this moment, and I am sure all matters
will be much better arranged with him than I have the ability
of doing : I have only the disposition to do what is right and
the desire of meriting your esteem, for believe me, with great
respect, your Excellency's most obedient servant,

BRONTE NELSON.

TO BRIGADIER-GENERAL GRAHAM, MALTA.

[Letter-Book.]

Palermo, 7th January, 1800.

My dear Sir,

I can assure you it is as grievous to me, as it can be to you,
to hear of the distress of the Maltese; but I pray and beg,
alas! in vain. Corn is here for Malta, but the Vessels will
not go to sea. Sir William and myself are trying to get the

corn here exchanged for corn at Girgenti. I have wrote Troubridge about it. Nothing is well done in this Country. I hope to soon pay you a visit, and I only wish that I could always do all you ask me. It is certain that you cannot go on at Malta without money: therefore I declare sooner than you should want, I would sell Bronté. But I trust, from General Fox's letter to me, that you will have his consent for ordering what money may be necessary. I send you all the Egyptian papers for you, Ball, and Troubridge, and, if you like, in confidence, Italinsky. Suwarrow is at the Prague with his whole Army—ready to act with the Austrians if they come to their senses, or perhaps against them. *Moreau* is at Vienna, treating for peace. What a state the *Allies* bring us into! But it is in vain to cry out. John Bull was always ill-treated. May a speedy success attend you, is the sincere wish of, my dear Sir, your obliged and faithful servant,

BRONTE NELSON.

I beg my best respects to Italinsky.

TO VICE-ADMIRAL LORD KEITH, K.B.

[Letter-Book. On the 30th of November, Lord Keith, then off Vigo, issued an order to Lord Nelson, which stated that the Admiralty had directed him to proceed forthwith to the Mediterranean, and take under his command such Flag Officers, Ships, and Vessels as he might find on that station, applying to the Senior Officer for such orders as might remain in his hands unexecuted ; and Lord Nelson was desired to put himself under Lord Keith's command accordingly.]

Palermo, 7th January, 1800.

My dear Lord,

Last night I received your letters and orders to December 14th from November 30th, all of which I shall endeavour to obey, and with the greatest pleasure to give you the state of the Squadron, and of affairs on this side of Minorca. I shall begin in the East. My last accounts from thence were by the Phaeton, Captain Morris ; and as your Lordship will probably see him, I shall only say that I have not heard immediately from Sir Sidney Smith since 7th September. At Constantinople, they heard he was communicating with the Grand Vizir at Gaza respecting the French army. The Ships with him are Theseus and Cameleon, but the Bulldog

is directed to go to him till the Smyrna convoy is ready to
return.   I have lately sent provisions and some few stores—
all we had, for those Ships; and I have wrote to Duckworth
and Inglefield to send particularly for those Ships.   What
Turkish Ships of War Sir Sidney has under him, I know not;
but I am told there are several.   The Turkish Admiral, Captain
Morris tells me, who served under him, had his head taken
off for leaving the Port of Alexandria open, and permitting the
escape of Buonaparte.   I would have kept up a more constant
communication with Egypt; but I have never had the benefit
of small Vessels.

At Corfu, General Villettes is arrived, and raising two
Regiments of Albanians.   Our Consul there, Mr. Spiridion Foresti, is a very able man, and from thence the passage of an express by land to Constantinople is twelve days.
To get to Malta—which has kept for sixteen months every
Ship I could lay my hands on fully employed, and has,
in truth, almost broke my spirits for ever—I have been
begging of his Sicilian Majesty small supplies of money and
corn to keep the Maltese in arms, and barely to keep from
starving the poor inhabitants.   Sicily has this year a very
bad crop, and the exportation of corn is prohibited.   Both
Graham and Troubridge are in desperation at the prospect of
a famine.   Vessels are here loading with corn for Malta; but
I can neither get the Neapolitan Men-of-War or Merchant-
Vessels to move.   You will see by the report of the disposition of the Ships, what a wretched state we are in.   In truth,
only the Foudroyant and Northumberland are fit to keep the
sea.   The Russians are on the 4th arrived at Messina; six
Sail of the Line, Frigates, &c., with two thousand five hundred
troops.   It is not to be expected that any one Russian Man-
of-War can or will keep the sea : therefore, the blockade by
sea can only be kept up by our Ships; and it is my intention,
if the Foudroyant, or even a Frigate, comes soon, to go for
two days to Malta, to give the Russian Admiral and General,
Graham, Troubridge, and Governor Ball, a meeting—not
only on the most probable means of getting the French out,
but also of arranging various matters, if it should fall to our
exertions.   The Maltese have, Graham says, two thousand
excellent troops; we have, soldiers and sailors, fifteen hundred;
the Russians will land full three thousand.   I hope the

Recazzoli may be carried; and if it is, I think the French General will no longer hold out. What a relief this would be to us.

If I cannot get to Malta very soon, I shall, from your letter, remain here, to give you a meeting and receive your orders. It is impossible to send from Mahon too many supplies of stores to Malta—sails, rope, plank, nails, &c. You can form no idea of our deplorable state for the last year. In Sicily we are all quiet. I have been trying, with Sir William Hamilton, in which the Queen joins, to induce the King to return to Naples, but hitherto without effect. I must suppose his Majesty has reasons which I am unacquainted with. It has long been my wish to send a small Squadron on the Coast of Genoa (for the Russian Ships are of no use) to co-operate with the Germans; but I have them not to send. Mutine I have directed to protect our trade about Leghorn, and to assist, as far as she is able, in giving convoy to Vessels carrying provisions to the Austrian Army. The report of the Combined Fleets being ready for sea, induced me to direct the Phaeton and Penelope to cruize between Cape Spartel and Cape St. Vincent, that I may have timely notice of their approach if bound this way, *which I believe.* I have run over our present state, perhaps, too hastily; but I am anxious not to keep the Brig one moment longer than my writing this letter. With every sentiment of respect, believe me, my dear Lord, your most obedient servant,

BRONTE NELSON.

TO COMMODORE SIR THOMAS TROUBRIDGE, BART.

[Letter-Book.]

Palermo, January 8th, 1800, 9 A.M.

My dear Troubridge,

This moment has brought me your and Ball's letters of the 4th and 5th. I have sent to General Acton for an order for an immediate supply, and I hope to send it by the express. The Frigate was to sail last night alone for Girgenti for some Vessels loaded with corn, and to carry them to Malta; but she is not yet out of the Mole. Nothing has been neglected on my part to get supplies for Malta, and by the greatest exertions, for this Country is in absolute want. Mr. Noble, two days ago, went to Termini, twenty-four miles from Palermo, the greatest corn country in this Island. The granaries here are really empty, and what was in them, of a very bad quality. The Kingdom of Naples is full of corn, but, as we know, the Neapolitan seamen will not go to sea in the winter. The Vincejo sails this morning for Malta, with all your letters from England, and a great many from me; but as it is uncertain who may get first, I have not, nor has Tyson, taken anything out of the Frigate or Vincejo. Your glasses are in the Frigate, with hat-box, &c. I send you Acton's letter to Sir William. If such lies can be told under my nose, what must be expected at a distance. We have had five days, from January 1st, of the very finest weather.

I expect Lord Keith here in a few days; but if the Foudroyant comes, it will not alter my intention of going to Malta. You must, in the last extremity seize Vessels loaded with corn : the inhabitants cannot starve. If, unfortunately, you are forced to this measure, I am confident it will be exercised with great discretion; but I hope all will yet end well, and that it may be soon, is the fervent prayer of your affectionate friend,

BRONTE NELSON.

TO CAPTAIN BALL, MALTA.

[Letter-Book.]

Palermo, January 8th, 1800.

My dear Ball,

As I have wrote to Troubridge on the subject of corn, I shall refer you to him, for writing to me is worse than ever. With respect to money for the payment of the Maltese troops. England and Russia are, by agreement between the three Ministers, to bear an equal expense. His Sicilian Majesty immediately paid his money—8000 ounces. In common justice, if the services of these men are wanted, Russia and England must find the most money. If we are alone to do it, and General Graham does not feel himself fully authorized, I am ready to join him in the responsibility, in any way he pleases; but I never will ask his Sicilian Majesty for another ounce till our part is fulfilled. May a speedy finish be put to your labours by the surrender of La Valetta; and ever believe me, your obliged and faithful servant,

BRONTE NELSON.

TO JAMES TOUGH, ESQ., CONSUL-GENERAL, PALERMO.

[Letter-Book.]

9th January, 1800.

Sir,

In consequence of the loss of his Majesty's hired Transport Susannah, at Melazzo, in this Island, through the obstinacy of the Health Office, in not permitting assistance to go on board her in time, and preventing her having *pratique*, although she went from this Port under my orders, I desire you will give directions to all your Vice-Consuls throughout this Island to inform the Officers of the Health Offices, in the different places in which they reside, that those Transports shall be considered as King's Ships, and that they are not, nor shall not be, subject to the Doganas, by clearances, or Bills of health, and that my signature, or the signature of any Captain under my command, shall be a sufficient Bill of health, and respected as such by all the Officers of Health in this Island. I am, &c.,

BRONTE NELSON.

TO VICE-ADMIRAL LORD KEITH, K.B.

[Letter-Book.]

Palermo, 10th January, 1800.

My Lord,

I beg leave to acquaint your Lordship that the Portuguese Squadron, under the command of the Marquis de Niza, has not been considered as under my orders since the 18th of December. Three Ships of the Line are at this place, fitting for their return to Lisbon, and one is at Syracuse for the same purpose.

I am sorry to inform your Lordship of the loss of the Susannah Transport, at Melazzo, in this Island, having on board a quantity of bread and shells, and going to Caronia, to take in wood for the use of the troops at Malta. Part of the bread and shells are saved, and the Ship's materials will be saved, but the hull will be entirely lost. This, from the report to me, was occasioned by gales of wind, and bad weather, which occasioned him to cut from his anchors at Caronia, and run for Melazzo, where he was lost on the 31st ultimo. I have the honour to be, &c.

BRONTE NELSON.

TO COMMODORE SIR THOMAS TROUBRIDGE, BART.

[Order-Book.]

Palermo, 10th January, 1800.

Rear-Admiral Lord Nelson, Duke of Bronté, &c., has the satisfaction of communicating to Commodore Sir Thomas Troubridge, Bart., and the Officers and men under his command at the Siege of Capua, &c. the high sense entertained by the Lords Commissioners of the Admiralty of their meritorious services. Their Lordships cannot too highly applaud the good conduct of Commodore Sir Thomas Troubridge, Bart., and the zealous exertions of Captains Hallowell and Oswald, and the Officers and men employed under his orders on those important occasions, and are pleased to direct that the same should be made known to them accordingly. Lord Nelson therefore desires that Commodore Sir Thomas Troubridge, Bart., would make the same known to those Officers and men serving under his command at Malta.

BRONTE NELSON.

TO THE RIGHT HONOURABLE SIR WILLIAM HAMILTON, K.B.

[Letter-Book.]

Palermo, January 10th, 1800.

Sir,

Your Excellency having had the goodness to communicate to me a dispatch from General Acton, together with several letters from Girgenti, giving an account that a violence had been committed, in that Port, by the seizing, and carrying off to Malta, two Vessels loaded with corn,[9] I beg leave to express to your Excellency my real concern that even the

---

[9] Apparently by the Strombolo, Captain Broughton. Vide p. 167, note, *ante*.

appearance of the slightest disrespect should be offered, by
any Officers under my command, to the Flag of his Sicilian
Majesty; and I must request your Excellency to state fully
to General Acton, that the act ought not to be considered as
any intended disrespect to his Sicilian Majesty, but as an
act of the most absolute and imperious necessity, either that
the Island of Malta should have been delivered up to the
French, or that the King's orders should be anticipated for
these Vessels carrying their cargoes of corn to Malta.

I trust, that the Government of this Country will never
again force any of our Royal Master's servants to so unpleasant an alternative.   I have the honour to be, &c.

                                        BRONTE NELSON.

TO COMMODORE SIR THOMAS TROUBRIDGE, BART.

[Letter-Book. " Tuesday, 14th June. Arrived H. M. Ship Foudroyant from
Malta, and Thalia from Leghorn; hoisted the Flag on board the Foudroyant."—
Journal.]

                                    Palermo, January 14th, 1800.
My dear Troubridge,
I have received all your letters to January 7th, and you
will now see that England has only to rely on herself for any
exertion.   The Russians are all ordered to Corfu.   The
King has wrote to Messina, to endeavour to prevail on
Ouschakoff to go to Malta; but I am sure he cannot disobey
the orders of his Court, therefore now it only remains for me
to hope that General Graham will consent to hold his post
till General Fox receives his orders from England.   I have
been this morning with General Acton, and I have spoke
fully to him—plainer than I have always done is impossible.
He has prepared a paper to lay before the King, respecting
sending 2600 troops from Sicily to Malta.   This will, we
know, be a work of some time; but if Graham thinks it will
ease his soldiers, he might get 500 at a time.   I told him fairly
whatever troops were sent, they must only look to this [Go-
vernment?] for supplies, for that we should never ask what
they had to eat.   I trust Graham will not think of giving the
Island to the French by withdrawing, till he receives orders
from General Fox.   The object to France will be accomplished
without an effort.

Lord Keith is gone to see what the Austrians are after on the Coast of Genoa, and from thence comes here; then I have nothing to do but obey. I send you the Gorgon and three Victuallers: when the latter are cleared, I would have all which are not necessary sent to Mahon. I have little apprehension of any Privateers. I am sensible of the necessity you were under of getting provisions, but you will now know that no blame attaches itself to the King of Naples, or to Acton. The measure of sending into a Port was strong; but at sea there could be no difficulty. I hope the urgency of the case will not happen again. Lord Keith believes the Ferrol Squadron is destined for the Mediterranean, and also the Combined fleet, therefore, has desired me to be on the alert; and, from the disgust given by the Court of Vienna to Russia, it is impossible for me to foresee the evil consequences.

2, P.M.—The Foudroyant is just arrived; many thanks for your sending her. It is my present intention to endeavour to find Lord Keith directly, and to state to him our situation in this Country, and now he must give such orders and advice as he may judge necessary; but I trust he will not think of abandoning the Island of Malta, without most positive orders from home. I write a line to Graham and Ball. Ever, my dear Troubridge, believe me your obliged and affectionate

BRONTE NELSON.

TO JAMES TOUGH, ESQ., CONSUL-GENERAL, PALERMO.

[Letter-Book.]

Sir,   Palermo, 14th January, 1800.

The Right Honourable Lord Keith having declared the Port of Genoa, and the Coast thereof, in a state of blockade, and stationed a Squadron there to prevent any supplies being carried into the Genoese State, it is my request that you give information thereof to the Consuls of all Neutral Powers residing within this Island, that in case any Ship or Vessel, of what Nation soever, be found entering, or attempting to enter, any of the Ports of the Genoese Territory, they will be seized and treated as Enemies to the Allied Powers at war against France. I am, &c.

BRONTE NELSON.

TO COMMODORE SIR THOMAS TROUBRIDGE, BART.

[Letter-Book.]

Palermo, January 14th, 1800.

My dear Troubridge,

When the Gorgon is cleared of her stores, I would have three months' provisions of all species, except bread, of that only six weeks, (as Sir Sidney Smith, in some of his former letters, said bread he could procure) [put in her.] Lord Keith has destined the Gorgon for other services; but as he directed me to send to Egypt dispatches and provisions, I know of no way so eligible. Part of the dispatches are secret, but relate to the French army, which is not to be allowed to return to Europe, but to a prison in some of the States at war with France :[a] therefore, if such an event should have happened, the French troops are to be seized and conducted to either Mahon, some of the States of the Allies, or even to England ; and you will, therefore, if they should fall in your way, cause them to be seized, even if they are embarked in any Turkish, or any other Nations' Ships of War, or escorted by them. I have not six weeks' provisions at Palermo, for one Ship of the Line. May God bless you, and believe me ever your affectionate friend,

BRONTE NELSON.

TO COMMODORE SIR THOMAS TROUBRIDGE, BART.

[Letter-Book.]

Palermo, 14th January, 1800.

Sir,

I herewith enclose you the copy of a letter I have received from the Admiralty, respecting the hoisting your Broad Pendant; and, notwithstanding the intimation therein contained about striking it, I have to desire that you will continue to wear the said Distinguishing Pendant, until you have orders to the contrary from the Right Honourable Lord Keith, the Commander in Chief, as the necessity for your wearing it is as great as ever, in order for the better carrying on of the service, and co-operation with the Russians going to the blockade of Malta. I am, &c.

BRONTE NELSON.

a Vide p. 210, infra.

TO CAPTAIN SIR SIDNEY SMITH.

[Letter-Book.]

My dear Sir,   Palermo, January 15th, 1800.
I send you dispatches from the Commander-in-Chief, and
you will be so good as to detain the Vessel which carries
them as short a time as possible, as Lord Keith is anxious to
know your state and condition, with an account of what is
going on in Egypt. I have wrote to Lord Keith, and home,
that I did not give credit that it was possible for you to give
any passport for a single Frenchman, much less the Army,
after my positive order[9] of March 18th, 1799. All the
Transports which may not be absolutely necessary—which
cannot exceed one, you will direct to repair to Mahon, in
order that they may get to England. Wishing you every
success, believe me, my dear Sir Sidney, your faithful
Servant,

BRONTE NELSON.

TO BRIGADIER-GENERAL GRAHAM.

[Letter-Book.]

My dear Sir,   Palermo, January 15th, 1800.
Notwithstanding the very unpleasant circumstance of the
Russians not coming at this moment to your help, I hope
that you will not think of quitting the Island, till you may
receive either positive orders from General Fox, or from
England. I believe, and we have it strong in report from
Tuscany, that the two Imperial Courts have settled matters,
and that the Russians are again marching to the Rhine. If
so, these Troops will again be with you; but even should
this not be the case, I attach so much importance to the Island
not being entirely in the hands of the French, that I never
would consent to leave it. The troops from this Country are
not good, but it is probable they would save the fatigue of
ours. General Acton is preparing 2600 to go from Sicily.
They will, of course, be under your command; and I have
told the General that all provisions, &c., they must carry

9 Vide vol. iii. p. 296.

N 2

with them, for all that you would do was to order them on service. If you would like to begin by getting these men to the Island, you had better write a line to General Acton, and 500 can be sent at a time. To-morrow, I sail to Leghorn, in order to talk all matters over with Lord Keith; and I am sure he will either come to you immediately, or allow me. General Fox has now 7000 healthy troops, at Minorca, but will not part with a man, without orders from home.

Secret.—The French troops from Egypt are not to be allowed to return to France under any Capitulation. Excuse this short letter, as I am pressed for time; but ever believe me, my dear Sir, your obliged and faithful,

BRONTE NELSON.

TO COMMODORE SIR THOMAS TROUBRIDGE, BART.

[Letter-Book.]

Palermo, 15th January, 1800.

My dear Troubridge,

As the Gorgon may be detained by the Victuallers, perhaps it will be better to send the Transfer, or El Corso, with the dispatches for Sir Sidney Smith; and an assortment of provisions can be sent, I think, with perfect safety, in one of the Transports. I do not much like to begin by interfering with the Commander-in-Chief's arrangements of Ships; but if you think the Transport is not fit for the voyage, send the provisions in the Gorgon, with the most precise orders for her immediate return; but this must not stop the dispatches more than twenty-four hours. I send the news from Carthagena, to be forwarded, by Lord Keith's orders to Egypt; and I wish you would put the last French letters of M. Poussielgue in it; for that is one that was found secreted, after the others were sent off, and is not gone to Constantinople. Lord Keith supposes I may send some of these stores to Egypt —therefore, if the Ships off Malta are likely to find more than they want, send some. Do not, my dear Troubridge, send the Gorgon to the East, if you think a Transport will perform the service; but we must take care the provisions get in safely. I shall see you very soon, and, in all situations, believe me, your affectionate friend,

BRONTE NELSON.

TO EVAN NEPEAN, ESQ., ADMIRALTY.

[Original, in the Admiralty. "Tuesday, 16th January. At 4, unmoored Ship; at 6, weighed, and made sail" [for Leghorn.]—*Journal.*]

Palermo, 16th January, 1800.

Sir,

I beg leave to acquaint you for the information of their Lordships, that two days ago I received from the Russian Admiral a letter stating that he was proceeding with his Ships and Troops to Corfu, and that he could not go to Malta. This is the more distressing to us at this moment when their arrival was so anxiously looked for to proceed on more active operations against the Enemy.

I have also received a letter from Brigadier-General Graham stating, that the force he has at present is totally inadequate to any serious attack on the Enemy's works. I have written to inform him that his Sicilian Majesty hath promised to send 2400 men from Sicily, which will be ready in a short time. I proceed this day in His Majesty's Ship Foudroyant to the Coast of Genoa to join the Commander-in-Chief, to concert measures with him and to receive his orders for my further proceedings. I have the honour to be, &c.,

BRONTE NELSON.

TO ALEXANDER DAVISON, ESQ.

[Letter-Book. "20th January. At 2 P.M. anchored in Leghorn Roads; found Lord Keith here, in the Queen Charlotte; saluted with 17 guns."—*Journal.*]

Leghorn, 23rd January, 1800.

My dear Davison,

Notwithstanding Dr. Lawrence's opinion, I do not believe I have any right to exclude the junior Flag-Officers of the Fleet; and, if I have, I desire that no such claim may be made:[1] No, not if it was sixty times the sum, and, poor as I

---

[1] Doubts then existed as to the right of the Junior Flag Officers of a Fleet to a share of the Freight and Prize money due to a Commander-in-Chief. Lord St. Vincent's resistance to those claims, was the subject of two Law-suits—one in June, 1800, with Vice-Admiral Sir William Parker, respecting Freight money; and another, in the same year, (which will be again noticed,) with Lord Nelson, respecting Prize-money, in both of which suits Lord St. Vincent was unsuccessful.

am, [were] I never to see prize-money. Lord Keith is now here, and I have only to obey. Make my best respects acceptable to Mrs. Davison, and ever believe me your most obliged friend,

BRONTE NELSON.

TO THE RIGHT HONOURABLE EARL SPENCER, K.G.

[Letter-Book.]

Leghorn, 23rd January, 1800.

My dear Lord,

I came here in order to meet Lord Keith, and we are going together to Palermo and Malta. If Sir James St. Clair or General Fox had felt themselves authorized to have given us two thousand troops, I think Malta by this time would have fallen, and our poor Ships released from the hardest service I have ever seen. The going away of the Russians has almost done me up, but the King of Naples has ordered two thousand six hundred troops from Sicily to assist Graham, and they are to be under our command. It is true they are not good soldiers, but they will ease ours in the fatigues of duty. The feeding the inhabitants of Malta and paying two thousand of the people who bear arms, has been a continued source of uneasiness to my mind. His Sicilian Majesty has done more than it was possible to expect he had the ability of performing; for the revenues of his Kingdom are hardly yet come round, and his demands are excessive from all quarters of his Dominions. Lord Keith will now be able to judge with his own eyes and ears, and your Lordship will see his report.

The loyalty and attachment of their Sicilian Majesties to our King and Country is such, that I would venture to lay down my head to be cut off, if they would not rather lose their Kingdom of Naples than hold it on terms from Austria and the French, by a separation from their alliance with England. There is not a thing which his Majesty can desire, that their Majesties of the Two Sicilies will not have the greatest pleasure in complying with. I have before ventured an opinion on the character of their Sicilian Majesties. The King is a real good man but inclined to be

positive in his opinion : the Queen is certainly a great
Monarch and a true daughter of Maria Theresa. I am just
favoured with your letter of December 12th, which, although
so entirely contrary to my expectations, cannot alter my
respect for all your kindness.[2] I am in debt, from my situation ;
but time and care will get me out of it. Since May 1798, I
have had all the expense of a Commander-in-Chief, without
even the smallest advantage. Lord Keith shall find in me an
Officer ever ready to anticipate his wishes, so long as my health
will permit. With every sentiment of regard, believe me, my
dear Lord, your obliged,

BRONTE NELSON.

TO VICE-ADMIRAL LORD KEITH, K.B.

[Letter-Book. " Sunday, 25th January. At ½ past 12, weighed and made sail,
Queen Charlotte, Thalia, and Minorca brig in company."—*Journal.* They arrived
at Palermo in the afternoon of the 3rd of February.]

My dear Lord,   At Sea, January 26th, 1800.
I send you my last orders respecting Malta, with my letter
to Ball in consequence—at that time he being Commanding

---

[2] Lord Spencer's letter of the 12th of December, 1799, has not been found. The
conveyance which brought it, probably brought also the annexed letter from his
Father :—

" My dear Hor.,—You are too prudent to judge either of things or persons by
appearances, and too good to believe that the few letters you receive from me can
happen from any cause except the insecure conveyances which offer, or that indo-
lence, which I find is in the train of infirmities, which accompany those years when
we shall say in the morn, would the even was come, that I may rest; and at night
we are weary before the twilight returns. This is too often my case, even in the
midst of blessings; and allow me to say, that yourself, under Providence, are the
cause of many of these. Your public merit every mouth proclaims : your private
virtues every day are experienced. A recent generous act has made your family
happy by so handsome a present of £500 each, Bolton's more especially; he has
occasion for all. The boy George is got so gay—I hope a happy omen. There is
another boy, whom I have desired to be kept at school two years longer, and then
brought forward. I have hoped he may be got to the East Indies. This was
intended for a very long letter, but [I] must curtail it : the courier is going off
directly. Our hopes of seeing you are one day revived, another destroyed : all I
can say, you know best, and, in the end, will do what is right. If honour is your
object, all men say you have enough; if riches, you are too generous to heap up
many; if the *amor patriæ*, you have shown it. If your dearest friends are to be
gratified, they are, no doubt, very much so, by hearing of your health and prosperity,
which pleasure can be increased only by seeing you. Memento, your father is
seventy-seven years of age, December 15th, 1799. God bless you!—EDM. NELSON."
—*Autograph,* in the Nelson Papers.

Officer—for the hoisting, when the French flag should be struck, the flag of the Order. At present, circumstances are changed, as the Grand Master appears to reject the *Rock* of Malta. His Sicilian Majesty's colours are flying at present on the Island. I send you Graham's last letter to me, which had been mislaid; but since then, sufficient corn for the present has gone to the Island. Ever yours faithfully,

BRONTE NELSON.

TO ADMIRAL THE EARL OF ST. VINCENT, K.B.

[From " Memoirs of Earl St. Vincent," vol. ii. p. 50.]

H. M. Ship Foudroyant, off Monte Christi, February 1st, 1800.

My dear Lord,

I thank you very much for your kind letter of December 15th, and order. My heart rejoices to hear you are so well recovered, and that there are hopes of your being employed in the Home Fleet, when our gentlemen will not find it so necessary, as it has been, to go into harbour to be refitted. But you will have an Herculean labour to make them what you had brought the Mediterranean Fleet to.[3] Peers and Members of Parliament *must* attend their duty in London; but the Nation will be better taken care of by their being off Brest. You taught *us* to keep the seamen healthy without going into Port, and to stay at sea for years without a refit. We know not the meaning of the word. The Audacious, Alexander, and others, have never seen an Arsenal since they have been under my command. Louis, to his great comfort, has had a treat of shifting his masts, and stayed six weeks in harbour; but he sees not a Port again, if I had the command, for the next year. Our friend Troubridge is as full of resources as his Culloden is full of accidents; but I am now satisfied, that if his Ship's bottom were entirely out, he would find means to make her swim. He must go home this summer, for he

---

[3] Lord St. Vincent succeeded Lord Bridport as Commander in-Chief of the Channel Fleet, in April 1800, and appointed Sir Thomas Troubridge Captain of the Fleet. His Lordship's attempt to introduce the discipline of the Mediterranean Fleet, was strongly resisted by the Captains of some of the Ships under his command. See Tucker's *Memoirs*, vol. ii. pp. 70, 74.

never can now go to sea, except for a fine passage, without
being hove down. He is now at Malta, which place, I hope,
time and perseverance, will put into our hands. Lord Keith
is now going with me from Leghorn (where I went to meet
him) to Palermo and Malta.

February 6th.—Lord Keith has just got accounts, that
General Fox is to send some Troops for Malta. The King
of Naples sends twelve hundred in our Ships; therefore I
hope this terrible long business will be brought to a close. I
sincerely thank you, my dear Lord, for your good wishes for
my return to England : that event hangs on those things
which are not in my power to command; but at present I
see no prospect of my return. I did not fail to present your
kindest regards to Sir William and Lady Hamilton, and they
rejoice with me at your recovery. May the heavens ever
bless you, my dear friend; and believe me, for life, your affectionate and obliged,

NELSON AND BRONTE.

TO LADY HAMILTON.

[From the " Letters of Lord Nelson to Lady Hamilton," vol. i. p. 13.]

February 3rd, 1800.

My dear Lady Hamilton,

Having a Commander-in-Chief,[4] I cannot come on shore
till I have made *my manners* to him. Times are changed ;
but if he does not come on shore directly, I will not wait. In
the meantime, I send Allen to inquire how you are. Send

---

[4] Lord Nelson felt deeply mortified at a Commander-in-Chief being sent to the
Mediterranean; and his friends Sir William and Lady Hamilton, as well as some
of his Captains, frequently expressed themselves very unfavourably towards
Lord Keith. Soon after Lord Keith arrived in the Mediterranean, Sir William
Hamilton was superseded as Minister to the King of the Two Sicilies, by the
Honourable Arthur Paget, (the late Right Honourable Sir Arthur Paget, G.C.B.,)
and in a letter to Lord Nelson, written on the 7th of February 1800, Sir William
Hamilton, after speaking slightingly of Lord Keith, and eulogizing all Nelson's
measures, said, " As I now find that Lord Keith is really in the place of Lord St.
Vincent, established Commander-in-Chief in the Mediterranean, I have now not a
doubt but we shall have the extreme satisfaction of returning home with our dearest
friend Lord Nelson; for your Lordship will have known from Emma, that I have
either (after thirty-six years service at this Court,) been either kicked up or down out
of my post; and Mr. Paget, Lord Uxbridge's son, is named Envoy Extraordinary and

me word, for I am anxious to hear of you. It has been no fault of mine, that I have been so long absent. I cannot command, and now only obey. Mr. Tyson and the Consul have not been able to find out the betrothed wife of the Priore, although they were three days in their inquiries, and desired the Neapolitan Consul to send to Pisa. I also desired the Russian Admiral, as he was going to Pisa, to inquire if the Countess Pouschkin had any letters to send to Palermo; but as I received none, I take for granted she had none to send.

May God bless you, my dear Lady; and be assured, I ever am, and shall be, your obliged and affectionate,

BRONTE NELSON.

TO THE REVEREND MR. NELSON.

[Autograph, in the Nelson Papers.]

My dear Father,   Palermo, February 7th, 1800.

I can assure you that one of the greatest rewards in this world is your approbation of my conduct; and in having done my duty in life so fortunately, I have always recollected what pleasure this will give my father. Although few things in this world could give me so much pleasure as seeing you, yet I see but little prospect of my going to England at this moment of the war; but we shall meet when and where it pleases God, and my only prayer is that your life may be prolonged, and that every moment I may be able to increase your felicity: but whether I am higher or lower in the world, or whatever fate awaits me, I shall always be your dutiful son,

BRONTE NELSON.

Plenipotentiary to the King of the Two Sicilies, and is on his way here in a Frigate. I have not had the least hint of such an intention from England, public or private; but Lord Grenville has a letter of mine, the beginning of the year 1798, authorizing his Lordship to dispose of my place to whom he pleased, if he would ensure me an annuity for life, of clear *two thousand pounds* sterling—not a *nominal pension*, as I would rather continue all my life at Naples than retire for less. So that, as the Marquis Circello's letter to Acton says that my retreat is at my own desire, and that the King reserves for me what will always give me the pleasing satisfaction of having gained the esteem and approbation of their Sicilian Majesties, my request must have been fully granted. I suppose it is a Cabinet job, wishing to provide for Paget, and they could do it no other way than by satisfying me. I see it gives much uneasiness at this Court, and poor Emma is in the greatest distress. But let me get home, and settle my affairs, and she and the Queen may dispose of my old carcass as they please."—*Autograph*, in the Nelson Papers.

TO CAPTAIN SIR EDWARD BERRY, H. M. SHIP FOUDROYANT.

[From a Copy in the Nelson Papers. On the 9th of February, his Sicilian Majesty went on board the Queen Charlotte, and on the following day he visited the Foudroyant. She received some Sicilian troops for Malta, and sailed for that Island on the 12th, in company with the Queen Charlotte, bearing Lord Keith's flag. Passing through the Faro of Messina, they made the Island of Malta on the 15th, and early in the morning of the 18th, fell in with a small French Squadron, under Rear-Admiral Perrée, in Le Généreux, 74, bound from Toulon to Malta with troops. The fate of those Ships is described in Lord Nelson's official letter to Lord Keith, of the 18th of February.]

Palermo, February 7th, 1800.

My dear Sir Edward,

You shall rally—you shall be well: young men will be young men, and we must make allowances. If you expect to find anything like perfection in this world you will be mistaken: therefore do not think of little nonsenses too much. Such strictness as you show to your duty falls to the lot of few, and no person in this world is more sensible of your worth and goodness in every way than myself. Let all pass over, and come and dine here. As you are ready to execute my orders, take this of coming to this house as a *positive* and *lawful* one. When I see a Ship better ordered than the Foudroyant, I will allow you to confine yourself on board. Ever, my dear Sir Edward, believe me your truly sincere friend,

BRONTE NELSON.

Lady Hamilton humbly insists that you come on shore.

TO VICE-ADMIRAL LORD KEITH, K.B.

[From the Letter-Book, and the "London Gazette" of the 29th of March 1800. Lord Keith wrote to the Admiralty, on the 20th of February, the following dispatch, transmitting Lord Nelson's letter:—

"Sir,—My letter of the 15th acquainted you, for the information of their Lordships, that I had received intelligence of the reported approach of an Enemy's Squadron towards this Island; and although I had considerable difficulty in persuading myself that they would hazard the attempt in the face of so superior a force, I nevertheless considered it incumbent upon me to take the necessary precautions of reconnoitring the quarter in which they were to be expected, and, at the same time, guarding most particularly the entrance of the harbour of Valetta, as the only point in which they could secure themselves, and debark their troops and stores. The wind being strong from the S.E., and accompanied with rain, I could only communicate by signal. I accordingly denoted the bearing and reputed force of the Enemy, and directed the Foudroyant, Audacious, and Northumberland to chase to windward, and the Lion to look out off the passage between Gozo and Malta, while the Queen Charlotte was kept as close in with the mouth of the harbour as the batteries would admit of; the Alexander, at the same time, was under weigh on the South-East side of the Island. On the 16th, I was joined by the Phaeton, from Palermo; and the wind having shifted to the N.W., which afforded a favourable opportunity for landing the Neapolitan troops at Marsa Sirocco, I accordingly embraced it, and in the afternoon returned off the harbour of Valetta. Signals were made from various parts of the Island, of an Enemy's being in sight, and with the Queen Charlotte, Phaeton, Sirena Neapolitan Frigate, and Minorca Sloop, I anxiously continued to maintain a position near the shore, to prevent the Enemy from passing within us, and to expose them to the attack of his Majesty's Ships that were in pursuit of them. On the morning of the 19th, El Corso joined with a large French armed Store Ship, which she took possession of at four o'clock in the afternoon of the 18th, by signal from Lord Nelson, whose Squadron was then engaged with the French. Captain Ricketts reported this Ship to be the Ville de Marseilles, loaded with salt meat, brandy, wine, clothing, stores, &c., &c. She sailed from Toulon on the 7th instant, in company with the Généreux, seventy-four, Admiral Perrée, Badine, twenty-four, and two Corvettes, having near four thousand troops on board for the relief of Malta. At four, P.M., the Foudroyant and Audacious joined me, and I was acquainted by Rear-Admiral Lord Nelson, that the Généreux had surrendered without any action, and that the three Corvettes had escaped, from all the Line-of-Battle Ships having anxiously pressed after the French Admiral. I have the honour to enclose a copy of Lord Nelson's letter. His Lordship has on this occasion, as on all others, conducted himself with skill, and great address, in comprehending my signals, which the state of the weather led me greatly to suspect. Captain Peard has evinced excellent management from the moment he first discovered the Enemy off the South-West end of Sicily, until the period of the capture; and Lieutenant William Harrington, commanding the Alexander in the absence of Captain Ball, has shown great merit in so ably conducting that Ship in presence of so superior a force, previously to the appearance of Lord Nelson. I beg leave to recommend him to their Lordships' consideration. I have detached Ships in all directions to endeavour to pick up the stragglers. I have the honour to be, &c., KEITH."—*London Gazette* 29th of March, 1800.]

Foudroyant, at Sea, off Cape di Corvo, eight Leagues West of Cape Passaro, off Shore four miles, 18th February, 1800.

My Lord,

This morning at daylight, being in company with the Ships named in the margin,[5] I saw the Alexander in chase of a Line of Battle Ship, three Frigates, and a Corvette. At about eight o'clock she fired several shot at one of the Enemy's frigates, which struck her colours, and leaving her to be secured by the Ships astern, continued the chase. I directed Captain Gould of the Audacious, and the El Corso brig, to take charge of this prize. At half-past one P.M., the Frigates and

---

[5] Northumberland, Audacious, and El Corso Brig.

Corvette tacked to the westward; but the Line of Battle Ship not being able to tack without coming to action with the Alexander, bore up. The Success being to leeward, Captain Peard,[6] with great judgment and gallantry, lay across his hawse, and raked him with several broadsides. In passing the French Ship's broadside, several shot struck the Success, by which one man was killed, and the Master and seven men wounded. At half-past four, the Foudroyant and Northumberland coming up, the former fired two shot, when the French Ship fired her broadside, and struck her colours. She proved to be the Généreux, of seventy-four guns, bearing the Flag of Rear-Admiral Perrée,[7] Commander in Chief of the French Naval force in the Mediterranean, having a number of troops on board from Toulon, bound for the relief of Malta.

I attribute our success this day to be principally owing to the extreme good management of Lieutenant William Harrington,[8] who commanded the Alexander in the absence of Captain Ball, and I am much pleased with the gallant behaviour of Captain Peard, of the Success, as also with the alacrity and good conduct of Captain Martin and Sir Edward Berry. I have sent Lieutenant Andrew Thomson,[9] First Lieutenant of the Foudroyant, to take charge of the Généreux, whom I beg leave to recommend to your Lordship for promotion, and [have] sent her under care of the Northumberland and Alexander to Syracuse, to wait your Lordship's orders. I have the honour to be, &c.

BRONTE NELSON.

[6] Captain Shuldham Peard, of the Success, was made a Superannuated Rear-Admiral in 1814, but was placed on the Active List in 1827, and died a Vice-Admiral of the White, in December 1832.

[7] Rear-Admiral Perrée was struck by a shot from the Success, and died of his wounds on the following day; and on the 19th, the Major of Division, Poulain, wrote to Lord Nelson, requesting him to order that funeral and military honours should be rendered to the deceased, adding—" Veuillez ne point me refuser cette faveur, que je regarderai comme un hommage rendu aux manes d'un brave homme, qui emporte avec lui les regrets et l'estime de tous ses camarades."—*Autograph*, in the Nelson Papers.

[8] Lieutenant William Harrington, who obtained that rank in 1796. In 1802, he commanded the hired armed Brig La Védette, and appears to have died a Lieutenant before 1809.

[9] Lieutenant Andrew Thomson was not promoted until October 1801, and died a Commander in 1828.

TO LADY HAMILTON.

[From the " Letters of Lord Nelson to Lady Hamilton," vol. i. p. 15.]

Off La Valetta, February 20th, 1800.

My dear Lady Hamilton,

Had you seen the Peer[1] receive me, I know not what you would have done; but I can guess. But never mind! I told him, that I had made a vow, if I took the Généreux by myself, it was my intention to strike my Flag. To which he made no answer.

If I am well enough, I intend to write a letter to Prince Leopold, and to send him the French Admiral's flag; which I hope you will approve of, as it was taken on the Coast of his Father's Kingdom, and by as faithful a Subject as any in his Dominions. I have had no communication with the shore; therefore, have seen neither Ball, Troubridge, nor Graham: nor with the Lion; but when I have, I shall not forget all your messages, and little Jack. I only want to know your wishes, that I may, at least, appear grateful, by attending to them.

My head aches dreadfully, and I have none here to give me a moment's comfort. I send the packet to General Acton,[2] as I think it may go quicker, and he will be flattered by presenting the Flag and letter to the Prince. Malta, I think, will fall very soon, if these other Corvettes do not get in. Pray make my best regards acceptable to Mrs. Cadogan, Miss Knight, little Mary Ré Giovanni, Gibbs, &c., and ever believe me your truly faithful and affectionate,

BRONTE NELSON.

[1] Lord Keith.

[2] Sir John Acton wrote to Lord Nelson on the 27th of February, and after congratulating him on the capture of Le Généreux, which Ship, he said, "was certainly to belong to the Hero of the Nile," and conveying "their Sicilian Majesties thanks and most sensible congratulations," he added, "What can I express in the name of his Royal Highness Prince Leopold, to present his gratitude? I went immediately to his Royal Highness's apartments with your Lordship's letters, and the fine present of the French Admiral's flag. The young Prince was in raptures, and continues to be so. He answers himself to your Lordship, either with this occasion, or with a courier to Sorrenza. You have made happy all the Royal Family, and it is not certainly the first occasion of the many and most essential feelings which they have been beneficated with, from your loyalty and attachment."—*Autograph*, in the Nelson Papers.

TO MAURICE NELSON, ESQ., NAVY OFFICE.

[From Clarke and M'Arthur, vol. ii. p. 246.]

[About the 20th February, 1800.]

I have written to Lord Spencer, and sent him my Journal, to prove that the Généreux was taken by me, and owing to my plan ; that my quitting Lord Keith was at my own risk, and for which, if I had not succeeded, I might have been broke. If I had not, the Généreux would never have been taken. I am, &c.   BRONTE NELSON.

TO VICE-ADMIRAL LORD KEITH, K.B.

[Letter-Book. On the 24th of February, Lord Keith issued an Order to Lord Nelson, which stated that he was " called from the Blockade of Malta, to attend to other services of public importance," and directed Lord Nelson to take the command of the Ships therein named, " and to adopt and prosecute the necessary measures for contributing to the complete reduction of Malta." Full and explicit directions were given for his conduct in the event of the surrender of La Valetta, and for the disposition of the Squadron, &c. As the remoteness of Palermo from Malta, rendered it an inconvenient place of rendezvous, Lord Keith directed it to be discontinued, and substituted Syracuse instead of it; but if Lord Nelson preferred Messina or Augusta, he was at liberty to use one of them, provided he made Lord Keith acquainted therewith. The Order concluded in these words—" During the progress of this complicated and important service, and on the eventual surrender of Valetta, many circumstances will naturally occur, and a variety of objects present themselves, for which it is impossible to provide. But impressed as I am with every conviction of your Lordship's ability, zeal, firmness, discretion, justice, and humanity, I rely, with all confidence, on your being prepared to act, on every exigency, for the honour of the nation, the advantage of the public, and the interest of the forces employed under your direction : and also, whenever it may depend upon you, for the protection of individuals, the security of private property, and the distribution of public justice."—*Original*, in the Nelson Papers.

On the reception of this Order Lord Nelson wrote the following public and private letters :]

Foudroyant, off Malta, 24th February, 1800.

My Lord,

My state of health is such, that it is impossible I can much longer remain here. Without some rest, I am gone. I must therefore, whenever I find the service will admit of it, request your permission to go to my friends, at Palermo, for a few weeks, and leave the command here to Commodore Troubridge. Nothing but absolute necessity obliges me to write this letter, being, with the greatest respect, &c.

BRONTE NELSON.

TO VICE-ADMIRAL LORD KEITH, K.B.

[Letter-Book.]

Off Malta, February 24th, 1800.

My dear Lord,

I could no more stay fourteen days longer here, than fourteen years. I am absolutely exhausted, therefore I have been obliged to write you a Public letter. As to the state of the Foudroyant, nothing but the exigencies of the service has prevented her being refitted months ago. This very day is a sufficient proof to me that she cannot keep the sea, even if the main topmast stands, which I doubt, in a severe gale. But her rigging, both standing and running, must be overhauled; everything gives way. But I send Sir Edward Berry, and submit to your decision as to the Ship; to myself you will not, I am sure, object. The Northumberland and El Corso would have been an acquisition, instead of the Audacious, Lion, or Alexander, or Strombolo, who is useless as a cruiser. But I wish not to complain; but my incapacity as to health I feel; and, as a Seaman, I think the Foudroyant must be refitted. Ever, my dear Lord, &c.

BRONTE NELSON.

TO GOVERNOR BALL.

[Autograph, in the possession of Sir William Keith Ball, Bart.]

February 25th, 1800.

My dear Ball,

I have the pleasure to announce to you that I am directed by His Imperial Majesty, the Emperor of all the Russias, and Grand Master of the Order of St. John of Jerusalem, to present you with His letter and the Grand Cross of the Order, and that you have an Honorary Commanderie.[3] This mark of

---

[3] The success of Lord Nelson's application to the Emperor of Russia for the Cross of the Order of St. John of Jerusalem (commonly called the Cross of Malta) for Captain Ball and Lady Hamilton, was thus announced to him by Sir Charles Whitworth, K.B., Envoy at St. Petersburg:

"St. Petersburg, 4th January, 1800.

"My Lord,

"I have the honour to acknowledge the receipt of your Lordship's letter of the first of November, by a Neapolitan Courier, and I have now the satisfaction to ac-

the Grand Master's sense of your zeal and ability, in the conducting of the affairs in the Island of Malta, cannot but give
me the very highest satisfaction, who so well know your gallantry and excellent judgment. Whenever you do me the
honour of coming afloat, I shall present you with this distinguished mark of honour. Believe me, my dear Ball, your
most obliged and affectionate,

BRONTE NELSON.

TO THE RIGHT HONOURABLE LORD MINTO.

[Autograph, in the Minto Papers.]

Foudroyant, off Malta, February 26th, 1800.

My dear Lord,

Not that person in this world values your friendship more than
myself, and so I ought, because no one has taken more pains
to make me noticed in the world than yourself. You, my dear
friend, [will] rejoice to hear that it has been my extraordinary
good fortune to capture the Généreux, 74, bearing the Flag of
Rear-Admiral Perrée, and a very large Storeship, with 2000
troops and provisions and stores for the relief of La Valette.
I came off Malta with *my Commander-in-Chief*, Lord Keith;
we parted company in bad weather the same day. Having information that such a Squadron had sailed from Toulon, Lord
K. remained off Malta; but my knowledge of their track
(rather my knowledge of this Country from seven years' experience) I went towards the Coast of Barbary, where three
days afterwards I fell in with the gentlemen; those Ships which
fell in with me after our separation from the Commander-in-
Chief attached themselves to my fortune. We took them after a
long chase, four miles only from Sicily, and a few leagues from

quaint your Lordship that his Imperial Majesty has been graciously pleased to accede to your recommendation of Lady Hamilton, and of Captain Ball. Her Lady-
ship is named *Dame* Petite Croix de l'Ordre de St. Jean de Jerusalem, and Captain
Ball, Commandeur Honoraire. I have, according to his Imperial Majesty's desire,
made his Majesty acquainted with such his intention, requesting that his Majesty
would be pleased to allow Lady Hamilton and Captain Ball to accept and wear the
same. I should feel extremely happy could I flatter myself with having been
the least instrumental in furthering the object of your Lordship's wishes; and
have the honour to be, &c., CHARLES WHITWORTH."—*Autograph*, in the Nelson
Papers.

Cape Passaro. Perrée was killed by a shot from the Success Frigate, Captain Peard. His ship struck when the Foudroyant fired only two shot; this, my dear Lord, makes nineteen Sail of the Line and four Admirals I have been present at the capture of, this war. Ought I to trust Dame Fortune any more? her daughter may wish to step in and tear the mother from me. I have in truth serious thoughts of giving up active service—Greenwich Hospital seems a fit retreat for me after being *evidently* thought unfit to command in the Mediterranean. The Emperor of Russia has just granted my request for a Cross of Malta to our dear and invaluable Lady Hamilton, also, of an Honorary Commandery to Captain Ball of the Alexander, who has with so much ability governed Malta for these last sixteen months. This fortunate capture I consider so much for the interest of the Grand Master, that I have presumed to send Admiral Perrée's sword to be laid at his feet.

Being here, I am deprived of the pleasure of seeing your letters to Palermo. The Queen, my dear Lord, has a thorough and implicit confidence in your friendship, and my Lady and myself assure her of your real concern for her interest. We have been, and are, trying everything to induce the King to go to Naples, but hitherto in vain. I almost doubt Acton's sincerity as to wishing him, yet he appears as anxious as any of us: the Junto of State are as bad as the Cardinal—all are open to the foulest corruption, and the presence of a Monarch was never more necessary to heal the disorders of a Kingdom. For some cause, which I do not understand, the pardon and act of oblivion is not yet issued, although I know it has been signed near three months; the heads of a whole Kingdom cannot be cut off, be they ever such rascals. I hope that all matters are arranged between the two Emperors, for the Emperor Paul says, in his letter, that the Prince Volkonsky with three battalions of grenadiers shall come here. If Lady Minto is with you,[4] I beg my very best respects, and whatever fate awaits me, or however much I may be forgot by others, yet believe this as true, that I shall ever feel myself your obliged and affectionate,

BRONTE NELSON.

---

[4] Lord Minto was then Envoy Extraordinary to the Court of Vienna.

TO GOVERNOR BALL, MALTA.

[Autograph, in the possession of Sir William Keith Ball, Bart.]

February 27th, 1800.

My dear Ball,

Your letter relative to the movements of the French Ships has put me a little on the alarm for fear they should escape, therefore, I wish to know precisely whether I may depend on information by guns, signals, &c., if the French Ships make any movements, for instance, this night. I only wish to have an opportunity of getting our lost anchor, to proceed and anchor off La Valetta; my heart would surely break if they escape; therefore, either tell me to go directly off Valetta, or say you may stay safely and trust to our vigilance. The Vincejo brig, the only Vessel with me, shall go off the Town, —communicate to General Graham. Would not false attacks and firing down the harbour prevent their waiting? for if the Enemy are serious in getting out their Ships, the game is up in La Valetta: write to me this night if it is possible. If we are here to-morrow, I shall rejoice to see you and Captain Vivian; I rely on Captain Vivian not to let these fellows steal their Ships from us. I rejoice to hear Troubridge is better: I wrote him a line this morning.[5] Ever, my dear Ball, believe me, your obliged and affectionate friend,

BRONTE NELSON.

[5] A very interesting and warm-hearted letter from Sir Thomas Troubridge to Lord Nelson, of the 24th of February, shows that his Lordship had taken slight offence at a supposed want of attention towards him : "My Lord,—The trip of yesterday, and the efforts made the day before, though really more an object for an hospital, than one to pay a friendly visit, General Graham and Ball will tell your Lordship how ill I was, and did not reach my Ship till ten o'clock, much tired, &c., &c. All this will, I trust, cause your Lordship to acquit me of the smallest want of respect and attention, which your letter of the 22nd, which I found on my return last night, accuses me of. . . . . . It has really so unhinged me, that I am quite unmanned and crying. I would sooner forfeit my life—my everything, han be deemed ungrateful to an Officer, and friend, I feel I owe so much to. Pray, pray, acquit me; for 1 really do not merit it. There is not a man on earth I love, honour, and esteem more than your Lordship. Please God I recover, and get from my bed, which I am now confined to, I will be again on board the Foudroyant. Yesterday I had not received your letter; 1 had only heard, in a friendly note, that you were surprised at not hearing from me. At that very time two letters of mine were, and had been for days, on their way. . . . By what Lord Keith said yesterday to the General, you will be left here. Remember, my Lord, the prospects are rather good at present of

TO MRS. SUCKLING.

[From " The Athenæum."]

February 27th [1800], off Malta.

My dear Madam,
　I am only this day favoured with your letter of November, and have immediately signed the powers of attorney, which, I trust, will satisfy all parties; nothing, believe me, will ever give me greater pleasure than fulfilling the will of my dear Uncle. I can say little good of myself: I am far from well; but ever believe me, your most affectionate friend,

BRONTE NELSON.

TO VICE-ADMIRAL LORD KEITH, K.B.

[Letter-Book.]

28th February, 1800.

My dear Lord,
　The Entreprenant is this moment arrived from Corfu, and I send her directly to your Lordship, only directing her to call at Marsa Sirocco, to carry seventy Maltese to the Généreux. The French Ships are perfectly ready to put to sea: six hundred Maltese have been raised to complete their complements, and Ball thinks they will assuredly attempt it the first fair wind. With the Alexander, who is just arrived, I shall anchor off La Valetta, and prevent their escape, if possible. The intended movements of their Ships is a convincing proof to me that the Garrison has lost all hopes of a successful resistance, and I wish that General Graham would make false attacks; but I am no soldier, therefore ought not to hazard

reducing this place, and that William Tell, Diane, and Justice, are the only three ships left from the Nile Fleet. I beseech you hear the entreaties of a sincere friend, and do not go to Sicily for the present. Cruizing may be unpleasant. Leave the Foudroyant out, and hoist your Flag in the Culloden, to carry on the operations with the General. Everything shall be done to make it comfortable and pleasing to you: a month will do all. If you comply with my request, I shall be happy, as I shall then be convinced I have not forfeited your friendship. The strong fever I labour under at present must plead my excuse for this jumble: I am unable at present to correct it; I therefore conclude, praying your Lordship not to harbour the smallest idea that I am not the same Troubridge you have known me."—*Autograph*, in the Nelson Papers,

an opinion. But if I commanded, I would torment the scoundrels night and day. Lion was said to be seen last night, and, except Vincejo, all have been blown to leeward. I send your Lordship my letters from Corfu and Constantinople. The Russian plan for those Islands is pretty evident. My state of health is very precarious. Two days ago I dropped with a pain in my heart, and I am always in a fever; but the hopes of these gentry coming out shall support me for a few days longer. I ardently desire to see this Malta business finished. With every sentiment of respect, believe me, my dear Lord, your most obedient servant,

BRONTE NELSON.

TO BRIGADIER-GENERAL GRAHAM.

[Letter-Book.]

March 3rd, 1800.

My dear General,

I send you a copy of Lord Keith's letter to me, by which you will see (what I never doubted) that the French Corvettes will certainly endeavour to get into La Valetta; and as, from the weather we have lately had, there is the greatest probability that, in time, one of them may escape our vigilance—for instance, last night laying-to, under reefed mainsail, and from my having orders to keep the Squadron as closely collected as possible, as a French Fleet may be expected, I have not the power to send Ships of the Line to cruize to the westward. I beg leave, therefore, with all due deference to your superior judgment, to submit whether it would not be possible, by false attacks at night, and by a constant firing of guns and mortars, so to harass a half-starved Garrison, as to induce them to give in, before some one of the Vessels may arrive; for if the French Government persevere in their endeavours, at all risk of capture, to relieve by small Vessels the distresses of the Garrison, they must in time succeed.

It will not be long, from my very ill state of health, that I can be with you, when the command will devolve on my brave and dear friend Troubridge, or be resumed by Lord

Keith, both of whom I am ready to allow, with more judgment to effect, but not with more ardent desire to finish this long and tedious blockade, than, my dear General, your affectionate

BRONTE NELSON.

Martin has a letter for you from Lord Keith.

TO THE BASHA OF TRIPOLI.

[Letter-Book.]

Foudroyant, off Malta, March 4th, 1800.

Sir,

I have the pleasure to send you, in his Britannic Majesty's Ship Strombolo, all your Subjects who I had the happiness to retake in the French Ship, Le Généreux, of 74 guns, on the 18th February. Lord Keith, the Commander in Chief of the British Fleet in the Mediterranean, has I am told wrote to your Highness, but I cannot deprive myself of the pleasure of addressing one line to you, in order to assure your Excellency of my happiness in having had an opportunity of rescuing so many of your Subjects from a French prison, and begging you to believe that I am your Highness's obedient servant,

BRONTE NELSON.

TO SIMON LUCAS, ESQ., CONSUL AT TRIPOLI.

[Letter-Book.]

Foudroyant, off Malta, 4th March, 1800.

Dear Sir,

As Lord Keith, the Commander in Chief of the Mediterranean Fleet, has doubtless wrote to you, it is not necessary for me to trouble you much at length. The Bashaw will, of course, receive my great attention, in sending over his subjects taken by the French, as it deserves; and you will not fail to impress on his mind, that Nelson is never unmindful of his friends, and what pleasure it gives me to mark my attention to him. The Bashaw was very good in supplying

the El Corso with some rope, which was duly reported
to me, and for which I beg you will thank his Excellency
in my name. The French in Egypt were to enter into
a treaty with the Turks for the evacuation of Egypt, and
some progress is reported to be made in it, but Europe
can never suffer those robbers to return but as prisoners of
war. The three French Corvettes who escaped, when the
Généreux and Store-ship were taken, I think, may have put
into some of the Ports in Tripoli; if they have, I trust the
Bashaw will give a good account of them. You will have
heard that Buonaparte has had the impudence to ask a peace
with England; which, of course, has been refused, unless it
was a general one for all the world. The campaign in Italy
was to open February 25th; therefore I expect daily to hear
of the taking of Genoa, and of the march of the Imperial army
to Nice. This place will very soon fall, I have no doubt, as
I daily expect 2000 more troops from Minorca, and the
French are in great distress for provisions. I hope your
health has been long re-established, and I beg you to believe
that I am, dear Sir, your obedient servant,

BRONTE NELSON.

TO VICE-ADMIRAL LORD KEITH, K.B.

[Letter-Book.]

March 8th, 1800.

My dear Lord,

You will see, by my Journal, what terrible weather we have
had, and all our movements. The fever still increases in the
Northumberland, although every man is sent on shore the
moment he is seized. The French prisoners are put into the
Fame transport, and I shall soon try and remove them to the
Island of Comino. I dread to hear of the Ships with you;
the disorder is, as you said, a jail fever, and of the worst kind.
I expect General Graham on board, and shall detain the
Penelope till he comes. I have directed Captain Blackwood
to call and deliver a letter from me to Sir William Hamilton,
requesting his urging General Acton for four Gun-boats. I
know you have made a similar requisition; but I hope very
soon that the weather will become so moderate, that they can

be employed to watch off the harbour, a measure very necessary, as on the night of the 4th, a fast-sailing Polacca, of about
seventy tons, did get out, but was chased in again by our
Ships. I think Vaubois wants to get information of his deplorable situation to France.

We have no tidings of the French Corvettes, and I begin
to think that they are either gone to Egypt or Corsica; for if
they have stayed at sea twenty-nine days, the time they have
left Toulon, they must have the plague. We have got the
Prize Ship afloat, and Troubridge intends to have her
round to Marsa Sirocco; he has sent her by the Sirene
Tender, to offer her for sale to the Bashaw of Tripoli; but of
course she will not be delivered without your permission.
Troubridge thinks the brass guns might be sold with her,
for we do not want them. I do not believe, from what I hear,
that except the Ship, there is £500 of property in her. All
the Tripolines are sailed in the Sirene, with a fair wind, and
tolerable weather. The Success is watering in St. Paul's,
but goes to the westward this evening.

I am sorry to tell you that my health continues to be so
very indifferent, that I am obliged, in justice to myself, to
retire to Palermo for a few weeks, and to direct Troubridge
to carry on the service during my necessary absence. I shall
quit this station when matters are all put in a right way. I
am, &c.

NELSON AND BRONTE.

JOURNAL FROM THE 26TH OF FEBRUARY TO THE 10TH OF
MARCH, 1800.

[Autograph, in the Nelson Papers.]

February 26th, at 2 P.M.—Ordered the Foudroyant to be
anchored on St. Paul's bank—she having split her main-
topsail and foresail, parted the cable, let go another anchor.
The Commander-in-Chief weighed and stood to the North
East, leaving in sight the Lion, Minorca, and Perseus, and
under my command Culloden, Lion, Success, Bonne Citoyenne. All night, hard gales. A.M. Hard gales, no communi-

cation with the shore—two Sail in sight, under main-topsails and foresails.

27th.—Strong gales till evening, when it moderated. Governor Ball sent me word that he was sure the French Ships would attempt to put to sea the first favourable moment. No Ship near us, blowing very fresh all night. A.M. In the morning, more moderate : attempted to get our anchor; but the wind freshening, was obliged to give up, leaving a stream cable on it.

28th.—The Entreprenant Cutter joined from Corfu : read her dispatches, and directed her to the Commander-in-Chief; but having received seventy Maltese for the Genéréux, I directed her to call off Marsa Sirocco, as Commodore Troubridge had them all ready, and the way the wind blew, it could not make a difference of two hours. At nine, the Cameleon joined from Sir Sidney Smith with dispatches. At half-past ten, sent to Lord Keith to Syracuse, or to follow him to Leghorn.

1st March.—Governor Ball came on board to tell me of the state of the Ships in La Valetta, and that, in his opinion, the wind coming round to the S.W., they would endeavour to put out in the night : directed the Lion to anchor off Marsa Scala, the Alexander off St. Julian's, Foudroyant off La Valetta, the Success to keep near us, as also the Vincejo, the Minorca, and . . . . In the night it came on a sudden squall at N.E., by which, I believe, the Ship was drove in shore; for at daylight she was within reach of shot, which the French fired at her till ten o'clock, when she was warped out of gun-shot without any damage except wounding the fore top-mast.

2nd.—At four, weighed with a light breeze, southerly. In the night, variable winds and squally. Strong gales to the N.W. all day.

3rd.—At four, joined the Northumberland; received Lord Keith's letters and orders of the 27th February; heavy gales all night; laying to under a reefed mainsail. A.M. More moderate ; directed Captain Martin to carry the powder into Marsa Sirocco, and to desire Commodore Troubridge to dispose of the French prisoners in a Transport, as they have a bad fever.

4th.—The wind coming to W.S.W., got the Foudroyant to

an anchor on St. Paul's bank; Bonne Citoyenne showed his
pendants; all night fresh breezes to the southward. At daylight, employed shifting the fore-topmast; found two of the
main-shrouds on the larboard side carried away, the sails all
split and none to replace them, all, except one fore-sail, being
unfit for a gale of wind, all the ropes very bad, and continually
breaking. The Alexander and Lion at anchor, as by order
of the 1st; Vincejo off La Valetta; Success near the Strombolo, preparing to go to Tripoli; Minorca not in sight; Bonne
Citoyenne never joined. Wind, southerly.

5th.—The Governor[6] came on board to dinner: at sunset,
the wind west; the station of the Ships—Foudroyant on St.
Paul's bank; Alexander off St. Julian's; Lion off Marsa
Scala; Success, Minorca, and Vincejo, off La Valetta; Bonne
Citoyenne supposed to be west of Goza, as ordered; Strom-
bolo standing to the N. N. West, being bound to Girgenti.
All night fresh breezes. A.M. At daylight, increasing to a
heavy gale of wind, which lasted till noon.

6th.—Heavy gales till sunset, when it moderated a little.
A.M. At 10, a boat came from the Governor to say a Cor-
vette had got into La Valetta the night of the 5th, which I
cannot believe from the position of the Ships. At noon, the
Governor came on board to say he began to think it was a
Vessel attempting to get out.

7th.—It is ascertained the Polacca was attempting to get
out. All these twenty-four hours, strong breezes to the N.W.

8th.—Strong breezes and variable from S. to N.W. The
report from the Northumberland very unfavourable. The
Penelope joined, but brought no dispatches from England.

9th.—Strong gales from the N.W. all these twenty-four
hours.

10th.—Hard gales the whole twenty-four hours, from
W.S.W. to N.N.E. Only Alexander and Penelope in sight.
A.M. At 8 the Speedy joining.

<hr/>

[6] Captain Ball.

TO THE RIGHT HONOURABLE SIR WILLIAM HAMILTON, K.B.

[From "Letters of Lord Nelson to Lady Hamilton," vol. ii. p. 256.]

March 8th, 1800.

My dear Sir William,

I thank you kindly for all your letters and good wishes. It is my determination, *my health requiring it*, to come to Palermo, and to stay two weeks with you. I must again urge, that four Gun-boats may be ordered for the service at Malta; they will most essentially assist in the reduction of the place, by preventing small Vessels from getting in or out. I think, from the Enemy, on the night of the 4th, trying and getting out for a short distance a very fast sailing Polacca, that Vaubois is extremely anxious to send dispatches to France, to say he cannot much longer hold out; and if our troops, as Captain Blackwood thinks, are coming from Gibraltar and Minorca, I have no idea the Enemy will hold out a week. I beg General Acton will order the Gun-boats. Troubridge has got the jaundice, and is very ill. As I shall so very soon see you, I shall only say, that I am ever, your obliged and affectionate,

BRONTE NELSON.

TO COMMODORE SIR THOMAS TROUBRIDGE, BART., CAPTAIN
OF H. M. SHIP CULLODEN.

[Order-Book. Lord Nelson left Malta in the Foudroyant, on the 10th, and arrived at Palermo on the 16th of March.]

Foudroyant, off Malta, 10th March, 1800.

You are hereby required and directed, during my illness and temporary absence, to take under your command the Ships named in the margin,[7] whose Captains have instructions from me to follow your directions, and to obey the orders of the Commander-in-Chief, copies of which I have already sent you. You will once a-week send me, *viâ* Girgenti, by express to Palermo, an account of your proceedings. I send you the situation of the Ships as they are at present disposed

[7] Northumberland, Alexander, Lion, Success, Strombolo, Bonne Citoyenne, Minorca, Penelope, Vincejo.

of by me, and you will keep the Foudroyant, when she returns, in a situation to be ready to sail for me at a moment's notice.

BRONTE NELSON.

TO GOVERNOR BALL.

[Autograph, in the possession of Sir William Keith Ball, Bart.]

March 10th, 1800.

My dear Ball,

I request you will have the goodness to always inquire and collect any letters which may arrive for me from Palermo. One of *great* consequence to me was sent by the Maltese Consul's relation, Matei. Pray make inquiries, whenever he may arrive, if such a letter is received by Matei at Malta; and all letters, as well as this, to be sent over by you to Girgenti, and forwarded to me by express; and I will thank you to write our Vice-Consul there a letter of thanks, in my name, for his attention; for I have received several very civil letters from him, and, having nobody to write Italian, cannot answer them. The weather is so bad, and the wind so far to the northward, that we must weigh or slip after breakfast. I am, &c.,   BRONTE NELSON.

The Speedy brings nothing later than the Penelope, except a report from Cadiz that the combined Fleets are expected there, as is supposed from the Merchant Ships being ordered up the harbour.

TO ADMIRAL GOODALL.

[Autograph, in the possession of John Dillon, Esq.]

March 11th [1800], at Sea, off Malta.

My dear Admiral,

It was only two days past that I received your letter of November 15th,[8] the day Lord Keith sailed from Spithead, to

---

[8] Admiral Goodall's letter was a very amusing one: Lord Nelson does not notice his allusion to the "Enchantress:"

"London, No. 34, South Audley-street,
"My good Lord,   November 15th, 1799.

"I hope, as the sailor says, 'this will find you well, as I am at this present.' I have wrote at different times three letters to you in favour of my protégé, Captain

take from me all opportunity of my rewarding merit and obliging my friends.　Captain Broughton, from his merit, was to be
amongst the first for being made Post, and I told Lord Keith
so.　I was happy to find that, as an Admiralty man, Captain
Broughton stands very high in the long list they have given
Lord Keith.　I can assure you, my dear Admiral, that a
more modest, excellent Officer does not exist; and it has been
a hard case to be kept so long in a d——d *Collier* Bomb
Vessel.[9]　We have been so long in hopes of the speedy fall of
Malta, and, consequently, of my Ships,[1] the William Tell, and
the Diane and Justice Frigates, that I doubt you will but little
more than believe that I think we are nearer obtaining them
than a year past, and then Captain Broughton had my promise of the Justice.　Don't say I am selling the skin before I
have killed the bear; but the bear shall be killed.

As to my health, I believe I am almost finished.　Many
things, [some] of which YOU have felt in your time,[2] contribute
towards it.　I am now on my route to my friends at Palermo.
I shall there rest quiet for two weeks, and then judge by my
feelings whether I am *able* to serve well, and with comfort to
myself.　It is said the Combined fleet is coming this road,
confiding it can escape as it did last year; but the pitcher
never goes often to the well, but it comes home broke at last.
They had better be d——d than come here, for Lord Keith
owes them a grudge, which I trust, if that happens, I shall
assist him in paying.　Our dear friends, Sir William and Lady
Hamilton, are as hospitable, as kind, and as good as ever, and

Broughton of the Strombolo Bomb, and flattered myself that I should have heard
you had had an opportunity of giving him Post.　Keep him in your mind's eye, and
let it be so.

" They say here you are Rinaldo in the arms of Armida, and that it requires the
firmness of an Ubaldo, and his brother Knight, to draw you from the Enchantress.
To be sure 'tis a very pleasant attraction, to which I am very sensible myself.　But
my maxim has always been—*Cupidus voluptatum, cupidior gloriæ.*　Be it as it will,
health and happiness attend you, and believe me always yours, J. GOODALL.　Remember me to Lady Hamilton and Sir William, and all my friends."—*Autograph*, in
the Nelson Papers.

[9] The Strombolo.

[1] Because they had formed part of the French Squadron at the Nile.

[2] Alluding to the mortification felt by Admiral Goodall at not being entrusted
with the Mediterranean command, on the retirement of Admiral Hotham, in 1795.
Vide vol. ii. p. 18.

you will join with me, they are nonpareils. I shall rejoice to
see you, and it is possible it may be very soon. Be that as
it may, ever believe me your obliged and affectionate friend,

BRONTE NELSON.

Acton is married to his niece, not fourteen years of age;[3] so
you hear it is never too late to do well. He is only sixty-
seven.

TO COMMODORE SIR THOMAS TROUBRIDGE, BART.

[Letter-Book.]

Palermo, March 20th, 1800.

My dear Troubridge,

We arrived here on the 16th, having had a very tedious
passage. As yet it is too soon to form an opinion whether I
ever can be cured of my complaint, which appears to me
growing something like Oakes's. At present, I see but glim-
mering hopes, and probably my career of service is at an end,
unless the French fleet shall come into the Mediterranean,
when nothing shall prevent my dying at my post. I hope,
my dear friend, that your complaints are better. Pray do not
fret at anything. I wish I never had, but my return to
Syracuse in 1798, broke my heart, which on any extraordinary anxiety now shows itself, be that feeling *pain* or *pleasure*.
I have agreed with Mr. Woodhouse, at Marsala, for 500 pipes
of wine ; and as I have fixed the price, no person has any occasion to think whether it is dear or cheap. I have wrote to Mr.
Aldridge in answer to his letter about supplying beef at Malta,
and have told him, that if his present price is not sufficient, for
the Governor and other respectable inhabitants to fix a price,
and I will agree to it; for fresh beef we must have, and Lord
Keith does not seem to wish a constant competition—therefore it must be made worth some person's interest to supply
us well : who that person is I care not.

We have newspapers to January 28th, and I have a letter
of February 17th from Bristol ; but they contain nothing
interesting. The Brest fleet were perfectly quiet : in short,

----

[3] Sir John Acton had by this marriage three children; and, dying in 1811, was
succeeded by his eldest son, Sir Ferdinand Richard Edward Acton, Bart., born in
1801, father of the present Sir John Emerich Edward Dalberg Acton, Bart.

I am an infidel about their trusting themselves again in the Mediterranean. The Russians are certainly coming to Malta : the Squadron under Vice-Admiral K——, a good sort of man ; the Troops, under Prince Volkonsky. You have so much my implicit confidence, that I need not say a word about them. All will be harmony with these Russians. You will have heard that Mr. Arthur Paget is daily expected, to replace, for the present, Sir William : Count Pouschkin is also superseded by Italinsky. In short, great changes are going on, and none that I see for the better. I have not yet seen General Acton ; but I am led to believe that the King's not returning to Naples has been entirely owing to the General. At present, perhaps he has so much frightened him, that the act appears his own. *We of the Nile* are not equal to Lord Keith in his estimation, and ought to think it an honour to serve under such a *clever* man. I wish you would send me an account of what money you have laid out for the King of Naples's service, and if they do not pay you, I will give an order for you to draw bills for it. I shall also, the first time I see this man, talk to him about the Roman prize-money, and of the King's intentions towards you. But Acton has, I am almost convinced, played us *false.* May God bless you, my dear Troubridge, and believe me ever your affectionate,

BRONTE NELSON.

TO VICE-ADMIRAL LORD KEITH, K.B.

[Letter-Book.]

Palermo, 20th March, 1800.

My dear Lord,

You will know, by the Speedy, of my coming to this place, where I arrived on the 16th. It is too soon to form any judgment of what effect it may have on my health ; but on the 18th, I had near died, with the swelling of some of the vessels of the heart. I know the anxiety of my mind, on coming back to Syracuse in 1798, was the first cause ; and more people, perhaps, die of broken hearts, than we are aware of. The Foudroyant sails to-morrow, and will return here in about a fortnight, by which time I hope some decisive turn will take place in my complaint. The weekly report from Malta, which I directed to be sent by Girgenti, is not yet arrived, but probably it may before this letter can go; for I have no conveyance to you but by post. The Valiant transport is arrived with Lieutenant England from Larnica, in Cyprus; but sailing one day later than the Cameleon. I shall, of course, send Lieutenant England to you as soon as his quarantine is performed, and send the Transport to Mahon. I have agreed with Mr. Woodhouse, at Marsala, for 500 pipes of wine, to be delivered to our Ships at Malta, at 1s. 5d. per gallon; and as Mr. Woodhouse runs all risks, pays all freights, &c., I don't think it a bad bargain. The wine is so good that any gentleman's table might receive it, and it will be of real use to our seamen.

I hope from the reports by the Penelope, that Sir Charles Stuart is coming to Malta, which will relieve our Ships from a very tedious, and has been hard, service. I put into this, Sir Sidney Smith's letter to me. I cannot exactly approve of his interference as an English Officer with the disputes between the Ottoman Government and the Pacha of Acre, and without much farther communication with Lord Elgin, I should never consent to *our attacking* Acre; but I have formed an opinion on this subject, and I dare say it will agree with yours. Our friends, Sir William and Lady Hamilton, are tolerable; and I am ever, my dear Lord, your faithful and obedient,   BRONTE NELSON.

TO CAPTAIN SIR EDWARD BERRY, H. M. SHIP FOUDROYANT.

[Order-Book. The Foudroyant sailed from Palermo on the 24th of March, when Lord Nelson's flag was removed to a Transport.]

Foudroyant, Palermo, 21st March, 1800.

You are hereby required and directed to proceed with His Majesty's Ship Foudroyant, under your command, to the Island of Malta, taking your route by Maritimo; from thence, towards Cape Bon, and, if the wind will permit, to pass between the Island of Pantaleria and Linosa; and, on your arrival at Malta, you will put yourself under the orders of Commodore Sir Thomas Troubridge, Bart. On Sunday, 6th of April, you are to sail from Malta for Palermo, in order to receive me: and, for so doing, this shall be your order.

BRONTE NELSON.

MEMORANDUM.

[Order-Book.]

By my Patent of Creation, I find that my Family name of Nelson has been lengthened by the words, ' of the Nile.' Therefore, in future my signature will be,

' Bronté Nelson of the Nile.'

Given on board the Foudroyant, at Palermo, 21st March, 1800.

BRONTE NELSON OF THE NILE.

To the respective Captains, &c.

TO HIS HIGHNESS THE DEY OF ALGIERS.

[Letter-Book.]

Palermo, March 24th, 1800.

Sir,

I must again call to your Highness's recollection the very particular case of the Brigantine Nostra Signora della Grazia, Semetre Cesare, Master; for although I have no doubt but that all the Vessels furnished with my passports will be given up, yet this Vessel sailed from this place expressly at my desire, and with a cargo of corn for Malta, absolutely under the powerful protection of his Britannic Majesty—therefore, the Vessel and cargo is absolutely the property of the English Government, and of course the seizure is not only censurable, but almost an act of hostility. Therefore, Nelson of the Nile, who has always endeavoured to prove himself the sincere friend of your Highness, hopes that this Vessel, or her value, with the Cargo, will be immediately given up. This act will mark the justice of your Highness. That health may ever attend your Highness is the sincere prayer of your most obedient servant,

BRONTE NELSON OF THE NILE.

TO HIS HIGHNESS THE BEY OF TUNIS.

[Letter-Book.]

Palermo, March 28th, 1800.

Sir,

By the return of Major Magra to Tunis, who is much attached to the true interest of your Highness, and in full possession of my sentiments respecting the seizure of Vessels carrying provisions for those who were fighting the common Enemy, the *infamous* FRENCH; and that they were so employed was attested under my hand and seal, I expect daily orders from England to regulate my proceedings; but at this moment I must call your Highness's attention to the case of the Nostra Signora della Grazia, a brigantine—the Master's name, Semetre Cesare; for although I have no doubt but that all the Vessels and the poor men will be given up, yet this Vessel sailed from this place at my desire, with a cargo of corn, for Malta, which is under the powerful protection of my Royal Master; therefore, this Vessel and cargo is, *bonâ fide*, the property of the British Government, who must pay the value to the proprietors, and the crew of this Vessel can be considered only as under Great Britain's protection ; and, of course, the seizure was not only highly censurable, but almost an act of hostility. Therefore, Bronté Nelson of the Nile, who has always endeavoured to prove himself the sincere friend of your Highness, hopes that the crew of this Vessel, together with the Vessel and cargo, or her value, will be immediately restored to his Majesty's Consul and Agent, Major Magra. This act will mark the justice of your Highness. That health may ever attend your Highness is the sincere prayer of your Highness's most obedient servant,

BRONTE NELSON OF THE NILE.

TO COMMODORE SIR THOMAS TROUBRIDGE, BART.

[Letter-Book.]

March 28th, 1800.

My dear Troubridge,

I received your letters of the 12th and 16th, on the 25th— the day after the Foudroyant sailed. You have had an

arduous task, I well know, to keep our Ships in tolerable
order, and all my wonder is, where you have found the
means.   But all will soon end, for if the Ships get out,
the Garrison intends not to hold out; this I am certain of.
You know, my dear friend, that I highly approve and admire
your public conduct; but for you to fret yourself to death,
because you believe that all the world are not so honest as
yourself, is useless—for you cannot reform it, were you an
angel; and makes all people sorry to see you torment yourself.   It is my present intention to pay you a visit, before I
return from this station, which I think must happen.

I have this moment a courier from Constantinople stating,
that the French treaty[4] for quitting Egypt is ratified by the
Porte, and that the Ministers of England and Russia have
acquainted the Porte of the determination of the Allies not to
suffer the French Army to return to Europe, which the Turks
have notified by a courier to General Kleber.   The Russian
Squadron is on its way to cruize off Cape Bon for that purpose, and I again direct you to repeat the orders already
given, for making the French from Egypt, under whatever
protection they may be, of passports, or Ships of War, come
into some of the Ports of the Allies; for on no consideration
must they be allowed to return to France, either in mass, or
in separate Ships.

I now come to the most painful part of this letter—the loss
of the Queen Charlotte by fire.[5]   Lord Keith is safe, and,

4 The Treaty of El Arish.   Vide p. 215, infra.

5 The following account of the loss of the Queen Charlotte, Lord Keith's Flag-
ship, is taken from Schomberg's "Naval Chronology," vol. iii. p. 430, slightly
abridged from the "Naval Chronicle," vol. iii. p. 299:

"On the 17th of March, Vice-Admiral Lord Keith ordered Captain Todd to proceed with the Queen Charlotte of 110 guns, to reconnoitre the Island of Cabrera,
about thirty miles from Leghorn, in the possession of the French, and which it was
his Lordship's intention to attack.   On the morning of that day, when the Queen
Charlotte was about three or four leagues from Leghorn, she was discovered to be
on fire.   Every possible assistance was immediately forwarded from the shore; but
a number of boats, it seems, were deterred from approaching the Ship, in consequence
of the firing of the guns, which were shotted, and when heated by the fire, discharged
their contents in all directions.

"Mr. John Baird, the Carpenter, who was one of those saved, gives the following
statement of this melancholy and calamitous disaster.

"He reports, that about twenty minutes after six o'clock in the morning, as he
was dressing himself, he heard throughout the ship a general cry of 'fire!' on

I hope, most of the Officers and crew.   She sailed from
Leghorn at daylight of the 17th, with a strong land wind.
She was, when five miles distant, discovered to be on fire,
and at noon she blew up, about twelve miles from the Light-
house.   This is the whole we know.   Vessels were fearful,
after some time, to approach her—therefore many poor fellows
must be gone.

Buonaparte has made another offer of peace, which has
been rejected, to the great dissatisfaction of many in England.
I am, &c.,

BRONTE NELSON OF THE NILE.

which, he immediately ran up the fore-ladder to get upon deck, and found the whole
half-deck, the front bulk-head of the Admiral's cabin, the main-mast's coat and
boat's covering on the booms all in flames, which, from every report and probability,
he apprehends was occasioned by some hay, which was lying under the half-deck,
having been set on fire by a match in a tub, which was usually kept there for signal-
guns.   The main-sail at this time was set, and almost instantly caught fire ; the
people not being able to come to the clue-garnets on account of the flames.   He
immediately went to the forecastle, and found Lieutenant Dundas and the Boatswain encouraging the people to get water to extinguish the fire.   He applied to
Mr. Dundas, seeing no other Officer in the fore part of the Ship, (and being unable
to see any on the quarter-deck, from the flames and smoke between them,) to give
him assistance to drown the lower decks, and secure the hatches, to prevent the
fire falling down.   Lieutenant Dundas accordingly went down himself, with as many
people as he could prevail upon to follow him ; and the lower-deck ports were
opened, the scuppers plugged, the main and fore hatches secured, the cocks turned,
and water drawn in at the ports, and the pumps kept going by the people who came
down, as long as they could stand at them.   He thinks, from these exertions, the
lower deck was kept free from fire, and the magazines preserved for a long time
from danger : nor did Lieutenant Dundas or he quit this station, but remained with
all the people who could be prevailed upon to stay, till several of the middle-deck
guns came through the deck.   About nine o'clock, Lieutenant Dundas and he, finding it impossible to remain any longer below, went out at the foremost lower-deck
port, and got upon the forecastle, on which he apprehends there were then about
150 of the people drawing water, and throwing it as far aft as possible upon the
fire.   He continued about an hour on the forecastle ; and finding all efforts to
extinguish the flames unavailing, he jumped from the jib-boom, and swam to an
American boat approaching the Ship, by which he was picked up and put into a
Tartan, then in the charge of Lieutenant Stewart, who had come off to the assistance
of the Ship.

" Leghorn, March 18th, 1800."   " JOHN BAIRD.

" Captain Todd remained upon deck, with his First Lieutenant, Mr. Bainbridge,
to the last moment, giving orders for the saving of the crew, without thinking of
their own safety.   Before he fell a sacrifice to the flames, he had time and courage
to write down the particulars of this melancholy event, for the information of Lord
Keith, of which he gave copies to different sailors, entreating them, that whoever
should escape might deliver it to the Admiral.   Out of the Ship's company, which
consisted of upwards of 840 persons, about 167 only were saved."

TO SPIRIDION FORESTI, ESQ., CORFU.

[From Clarke and M'Arthur, vol. ii. p. 247.]

28th March, 1800.

All your letters are highly interesting, and continue to prove your unabated zeal in the cause of your King and Country. Be assured that there is not any man in Europe that estimates your services higher than myself. Most probably my health will force me to retire in April, for I am worn out with fatigue of body and mind. Yesterday we had the melancholy account of the loss of the Queen Charlotte, by fire, on the 17th, off Leghorn. Lord Keith was on shore, but many lives were lost. Buonaparte has again offered terms of peace, which have been rejected. The Ships at Malta are preparing to get out of the harbour, and whenever that event happens, the Garrison will, of course, surrender. I wish the Prince Volkonsky was there, with his 3000 troops. The Grand Master wrote to me himself, that he had named him as Commander of the troops ordered for Malta, and his letter was dated January 4th, New Style. I am, &c.

BRONTE NELSON OF THE NILE.

P.S. A friend of mine has heard, and read in a French book, that your Islands have an infallible remedy for the gout, I therefore beg that you will either send the receipt or ingredients.

TO THE RIGHT HONOURABLE SIR WILLIAM HAMILTON, K.B.

[Letter-Book.]

Palermo, March 30th, 1800.

My dear Sir William,

As, from the orders I have given to all the Ships under my command, to arrest and bring into Port all Vessels and troops returning, by convention with the Porte, to France, and as the Russian Ships have similar orders, I must request that your Excellency will endeavour to arrange with the Government of this Country, how in the first instance they are to be treated and received in the Ports of the Two Sicilies; for it is obvious I can do nothing more than bring them into Port; and, if they are kept on board Ship, the fever will make such ravages as to be little short of the plague.

It is a very serious consideration for this Country, either to receive them, or let them pass; when they would invade, probably, these Kingdoms. In my present situation in the King's fleet, I have only to obey; had I been, as before, in the command, I should have gone one short and direct road to avert this great evil—viz., to have sent a letter to the French, and the Grand Vizir, in Egypt, that I would not, on any consideration, permit a single Frenchman to leave Egypt; and I would do it at the risk of even creating a coldness, for the moment, with the Turks. Of two evils, choose the least; and nothing can be so horrid as permitting that horde of thieves to return to Europe.

If all the wise heads had left them to God Almighty, after the bridge was broke, all would have ended well. For I differ entirely with my Commander in Chief, in wishing they were permitted to return to France; and, likewise, with Lord Elgin on the great importance of removing them from Egypt. No; there they should perish, has ever been the firm determination of your Excellency's most obedient and faithful servant,

BRONTE NELSON OF THE NILE.

TO HIS EXCELLENCY THE EARL OF ELGIN.

[Letter-Book.]

Palermo, March 31st, 1800.

My Lord,

By the Neapolitan courier, and the courier of the Captain Pacha, I am honoured with your Excellency's letters from February 18th to March 1st, all of which, by the very first opportunity, I shall forward to the Commander-in-Chief, who is at Leghorn; and he, of course, will answer your Excellency fully on the subject. But I cannot help most sincerely regretting that ever any countenance was given to the Turks to enter into such a treaty with the French; for I ever held it to be impossible to permit that Army to return to Europe, but as prisoners of war, and in that case, not to France. And

was I Commander-in-Chief, even when the thing was done,
I should have refused to ratify any consent or approbation of
Sir Sidney Smith, and have wrote to both the Grand Vizir
and the French General, the impossibility of permitting a
vanquished Army to be placed by one Ally in a position
to attack another Ally. In doing this, I should have taken
all means to have made the Sublime Porte sensible of the
necessity of the conduct Great Britain was forced to, but I
never should for a moment have forgot my text—that at all
risks of giving offence, *not one Frenchman should be allowed
to quit Egypt.*

I have sent all your Lordship's private letters to Lord
Keith, who will, I am sure, make a proper use of them. I
write by this occasion a letter to the Capitan Pacha, in answer
to his, and I am sending them all to the Commander-in-
Chief. With every sentiment of respect, believe me, my dear
Lord, your most obedient and faithful servant,

BRONTE NELSON OF THE NILE.

TO HIS EXCELLENCY THE CAPITAN PACHA.

[Letter-Book.]

Palermo, 31st March, 1800.

Sir,

By the arrival of your Excellency's courier, I have been
honoured with two letters, both of which I have transmitted
to Lord Keith, who at present commands the British fleet in
the Mediterranean ; and I can assure your Excellency that
there is not the smallest cause of alarm, even should the whole
combined Fleets of the Enemy venture into the Mediterranean;
but, in my opinion, they will not again come inside the Straits.
Respecting the second part of your letter, the sending Ships
to Egypt to escort the French army to France, I have left my
Commander-in-Chief to answer that part of your Excellency's
letter. But I cannot help regretting, and with the deepest
sorrow, that any such Treaty[6] should have been entered into

---

[6] The Treaty, or rather Convention of El Arish, concluded by Sir Sidney Smith
and General Kleber, on the 24th of January, 1800, by which it was agreed that the
French Army should evacuate Egypt, with all its stores, artillery, baggage, &c.,

with the French invaders and despoilers of the fairest Provinces in the Ottoman Empire, more especially as I own I
see not how it is possible to fulfil the Treaty; for one Ally
cannot have the power of getting rid of an Enemy's vanquished
Army, by sending them with arms in their hands to fight
against a friend. Could I have been fortunate enough to
have been either at the Camp of the Grand Vizir, or with
your Excellency, it would have been easy to convince [you]
that no Ally could consent to receive 16,000 troops to fight
against them. I regret in the extreme that the Foreign
Ministers at the Sublime Porte did not make proper representations of the impossibility of permitting the return of such
an Army, but as *prisoners of war*, [as] must be obvious to
every capacity. But, situated as I am at this moment in the
Mediterranean fleet, my station is only to obey the orders of

together with the Ships of War and Transports in Alexandria, and return to France,
unmolested by the Allied Powers. As soon as Lord Keith was informed of the
transaction, he wrote a letter to General Kleber, dated on the 8th of February 1800,
in which he informed him, that he had received positive orders from his Majesty to
consent to no Capitulation with the French Army in Egypt, except as prisoners of
war, abandoning all the Ships and the stores in the Port and Citadel of Alexandria
to the Allied Powers; and that in case of such Capitulation, he was not at liberty to
allow any troops to return to France before they were exchanged. " I think it also
proper," Lord Keith said, " to inform you that all Ships having French troops on
board, and sailing from that country furnished with passports signed by others than
those that have a right to grant them, will be forced by the Officers of the Ships
which I command, to remain at Alexandria. In short, the Vessels which shall be
met returning to Europe with passports, granted in consequence of a separate
Treaty with any of the Allied Powers, shall be detained as prizes, and all persons
on board considered as prisoners of war." On receiving this letter, General
Kleber published it to the French Army, with the following remark—' Soldiers!
we know how to reply to such insolence—prepare for battle!'

   The British Government, however, consented to the Convention being carried into
effect, though it highly disapproved of its conditions; and on the 29th of March, 1800,
the Admiralty issued an order to Lord Keith, stating that " his Majesty had been
pleased to signify his command that instructions should be transmitted to your Lordship, expressing his Majesty's disapprobation of the terms entered into by the said
Capitulation—those terms appearing to his Majesty to be more advantageous to the
Enemy than their situation entitled them to expect, and being likely to prejudice the
interests of the Allies, by restoring to the French Government the services of a considerable and disciplined body of troops. That, besides this objection to the terms,
his Majesty does not consider Captain Sir Sidney Smith as having been authorized
either to enter into, or to sanction any such agreement in his Majesty's name—that
Officer having had no special authority for that purpose, and the case not being one
in which the Captain commanding his Majesty's Ships on the Coast of Egypt
ought to have taken upon himself to enter into an agreement of this nature, without
the sanction of his commanding Officer; but that, as the General commanding the

my Commander-in-Chief. I rejoice to hear that your Excellency enjoys good health, and I trust the time will come
when I can assure you in person with what respect and
attachment I feel myself your faithful friend,

BRONTE NELSON OF THE NILE.

TO JOHN TYSON,[7] ESQ.

[Autograph, in the possession of Edwin Beedell, Esq.]

My dear Tyson,   April 1st, 1800.
The Foudroyant will be here about the 9th, and I think of
returning to Malta about the 11th, for a few days, till I can get

Enemy's troops appears to have treated him as a person whom he, *bonâ fide*, conceived to possess such authority, and as a part of the Treaty was to be immediately
executed by the Enemy, so that by annulling this transaction, (in as far as his
Majesty's Officer was a party thereto,) the Enemy could not be replaced in the
same situation in which he before stood, his Majesty, from a scrupulous regard to
the public faith, has judged it proper that his Officers should abstain from any act
inconsistent with the engagements to which Captain Sir Sidney Smith has erroneously given the sanction of his Majesty's name. And whereas Lord Grenville has
at the same time acquainted us, that with this view he shall transmit to the Earl of
Elgin his Majesty's commands to settle with the Porte the form of a passport to be
given in the name of his Majesty, not as a party to the Capitulation, but as an Ally
of the Porte ; and that it is his Majesty's further pleasure the said passports, as well
as those which may have been in the interval (however informally) granted by Sir
Sidney Smith, are to be respected by his Majesty's Officers : but that, although, from
the considerations above mentioned, his Majesty does not think proper to obstruct
the execution of this Treaty by the Porte, in the manner therein stipulated, he does
not feel himself bound to authorize his Officers to take any active part in it, or to
furnish any Convoy or Transports for its execution, or to take any other share in
carrying it into effect ; yet if any application should be made to your Lordship for
liberty to send Cartel Ships from France to Egypt for the transport of the Army
under the Capitulation, your Lordship is to grant such passports accordingly, under
such restrictions and precautions as you may judge necessary, according to circumstances, to prevent this liberty being abused to any other purpose. . . . . . In case
your Lordship should see any ground to apprehend any intention on the part of the
Turks, or of the Russians to prevent the execution of the Capitulation, or to commit
any act of hostility against the French Army, either before or after its embarkation,
we do further direct your Lordship, in such case, to use your utmost endeavours to
persuade them to all such measures as may be most consistent with the faithful observance of the engagement contracted with the Enemy. Given under our hands,
the 29th day of March, 1800.—SPENCER, J. GAMBIER, W. YOUNG."—*Copy*, in the
Nelson Papers. Before, however, this Order arrived, the state of affairs had become
totally changed in consequence of the renewal of hostilities by General Kléber, and
the Convention was never executed.

[7] His Secretary.

Lord Keith's permission to go home for the benefit of my health, which is very indifferent; therefore you will regulate your coming to me accordingly.　Till the 20th of April, I may be at Malta, after that, for ten days, at Palermo; but ever, in all situations, I am your faithful and affectionate friend,

BRONTE NELSON OF THE NILE.

Our dear Lady Hamilton, Sir William, Mrs. Cadogan, and Miss Knight, all long for your speedy arrival.

TO EVAN NEPEAN, ESQ., ADMIRALTY.

[Original, in the Admiralty.]

Sir,　　　　　　　　　　　　　　Palermo, April 4th, 1800.

I have received no official reports; but I have letters from Commodore Troubridge, Captain Dixon, and Sir Edward Berry,[8] telling me of the capture of the William Tell[9] on the morn of

----

[8] The following is Sir Edward Berry's Note:—

"In great haste.　　　　　　　　　　"Foudroyant, 30th March, 1800.

"My dear Lord,

"I had but one wish this morning—it was for you. After a most gallant defence, Le Guillaume Tell surrendered. She is completely dismasted. The Foudroyant's lower masts and main topmast are standing, but every roll I expect them to go over the side, they are so much shattered. I was slightly hurt in the foot, and I fear about 40 men are badly wounded, besides the killed, which you shall know hereafter.

"All hands behaved as you could have wished. How we prayed for you, God knows, and your sincere and faithful friend,　　　　　E. BERRY.

"Love to all. Pray send this to my wife, or write Admiralty. .

"Within hail before I fired."

[9] As the Généreux, the only other Ship of the Line which escaped at the Nile, was taken in January of this year, the *whole* of the French Fleet, present at that Battle, (except two Frigates, one of which soon after fell into our hands,) was, by the capture of Le Guillaume Tell, either taken or destroyed. The name of Le Guillaume Tell (whose gallant defence against a very superior force reflected honour upon her Commander) was changed to " Malta," and she was long one of the finest ships in our Navy. Captain Manley Dixon's (afterwards Admiral Sir Manley Dixon, K.C.B., who died in February 1837) official report of the Action was published in the " London Gazette" of the 3rd of June, 1800. He said, that " the termination of the battle must be attributed to the spirited fire of the Foudroyant, whose Captain, Sir Edward Berry, has justly added another laurel to the many he has gained during the war." The following account of the event is from the Foudroyant's Journal:—

" Sunday, 30th March.—At 12, saw a number of guns fired on shore, with

the 30th of March, after a gallant defence of three hours. The Lion and Foudroyant lost each about forty killed and wounded; the French Ship is dismasted; the French Admiral Decrès wounded; the Foudroyant much shattered. I send Sir Edward Berry's hasty note.

Thus, owing to my brave friends, is the entire capture and destruction of the French Mediterranean Fleet to be attributed, and my orders from the great Earl of St. Vincent fulfilled. Captain Blackwood of the Penelope, and Captain Long of the Vincejo, have the greatest merit. My task is done, my health is finished, and, probably, my retreat for ever fixed, unless another French Fleet should be placed for me to look after. Ever, Sir, your most obedient humble servant,

BRONTE NELSON OF THE NILE.

TO CAPTAIN SIR EDWARD BERRY.

[Autograph, in the possession of Lady Berry.]

Palermo, [April] 5th, 1800.

My dear Berry,

I am sensible of your kindness in wishing my presence at the finish of the Egyptian Fleet, but I have no cause for sorrow. The thing could not be better done, and I would

---

signals. A.M. at 12, slipped the cable, set all sail, saw and heard the report of several guns to the eastward, with signals. Made all sail, and stood for it. At day-break, having all sail set, saw his Majesty's Ships, Lion and Penelope, engaging a French Line-of-Battle Ship, with her main and mizen-topmasts gone. At 6, came up with her, when Sir Edward Berry hailed her, and desired him to strike, but received no answer. An Officer shook his sword at him, and a broadside was fired from her, which was immediately returned within half pistol-shot. Her first broadside cut our rigging very much, and second carried away our fore-topmast and main-topsail-yard. Half past 6, shot away the main and mizen-masts : saw a man nail the French ensign to the stump of the mizen-mast. At 7, Penelope fired at the enemy in passing under her stern. Half past 7, spoke the Penelope. 5 minutes past 8, shot away the enemy's fore-mast. 10 minutes past 8, all her masts being gone by the board, the enemy struck his colours, and ceased firing. Sent a boat on board her. She proved to be the Guillaume Tell, of 84 Guns, a Ship that came out of the harbour of Valetta, having on board Rear-Admiral Decrès, Captain Saumier, Adjutant-General Brouard, and 1200 men. Performed divine service, and returned thanks to Almighty God for the victory. At 11, our mizen-mast fell, and wounded five men. Mustered Ship's company, found eight men killed, and sixty-one wounded."—*Copy*, in the Nelson Papers.

not for all the world rob you of one particle of your well-
earned laurels. Thank kindly for me all my brave friends in
the Foudroyant; and whatever fate awaits me, my attachment
to them will never cease but with my life. I am very anxious
to get the official account, and I keep the Perseus to send it
off to Lord Keith. But your letter with Dixon's to Troubridge, and Troubridge's, I sent by post to the Admiralty in
two hours after my reception. I hope the Foudroyant will be
able to come here to carry us first to Malta, and from thence,
taking the Queen of Naples to Leghorn, proceed with us at
least to Gibraltar, if not to England. My task is done, my
health is lost, and the orders of the great Earl of St. Vincent are
completely fulfilled—thanks, ten thousand thanks, to my brave
friends! Ever, my dear Berry, your sincere and affectionate
friend,

BRONTE NELSON OF THE NILE.

TO VICE-ADMIRAL LORD KEITH, K.B.

[Letter-Book.]

Palermo, 6th April, 1800.

My Lord,
    I had the honour of receiving your Lordship's letter of 2nd,
20th, 23rd, 25th, 28th, and 29th of March, by the Speedy,
who arrived here last night, which I beg leave to answer
according to their dates.
    The secret orders of the Admiralty have long since been
furnished to the Ships of the Squadron under my command.
By my application to your Lordship for leave to go to
England, you will perceive that my health is very indifferent.
The Northumberland has got men from the Culloden, and is
now off Valetta. I will take care to distribute the notifica-
tions, accompanying your Lordship's letter of the 23rd March.
I enclose your Lordship copies of the Admiralty orders
respecting Egypt and Malta, which are the only orders respecting the command in my possession. The Signal-books are
on board the Foudroyant. As soon as I can get them, they
shall be sent to your Lordship by the first opportunity. I
received with the deepest sorrow your Lordship's list of those

who were lost in the Queen Charlotte, and condole with your Lordship, and our Country, on that melancholy accident, and the loss of so many good and brave Officers and Men. The secret order accompanying your Lordship's letter of 29th March, I will take care to distribute to the Squadron without loss of time. I received Captain Beaver's[1] letter of 27th March, and shall circulate the Memorandum accompanying it. I have the honour to be, &c.,

BRONTE NELSON OF THE NILE.

TO HIS EXCELLENCY THE HON. LIEUTENANT-GENERAL FOX.

[Letter-Book.]

Palermo, 6th April, 1800.

Sir,

Andrea Perandello of this place, who has, on many occasions, been very useful to such of our Ships as resorted here, having acquainted me that his son, Pietro Perandello, is going to Mahon for the purpose of purchasing a Vessel, and is desirous of obtaining a Minorcan Pass to prevent his being seized by the Algerines, I beg leave to recommend him as a person deserving the protection of the English Government. I have the honour to be, &c.,

BRONTE NELSON OF THE NILE.

TO THE RIGHT HONOURABLE LORD MINTO.

[Autograph, in the Minto Papers.]

Palermo, April 6th, 1800.

My dear Lord and Friend,

A ten times better title, and to me invaluable—I find *Lords* who are not my friends. Our dear great Earl of St. Vincent's orders to me were to follow the French Mediterranean fleet,

---

[1] Captain Philip Beaver, of the Aurora. This gallant Officer, who was distinguished alike for his professional and literary attainments, died at the Cape of Good Hope, in command of H.M. Ship Nisus, on the 10th of April, 1813. His Life has been written by Captain William Henry Smyth, R.N.

and to annihilate them: it has been done, thanks to the zeal and bravery of my gallant friends! My task is done, my health lost, and I have wrote to Lord Keith for my retreat. May all orders be as punctually obeyed, but never again an Officer at the close, of what I must, without being thought vain, (for such I am represented by my enemies,) call a glorious career, be so treated! I go with our dear friends Sir William and Lady Hamilton; but whether by water or land depends on the will of Lord Keith. May God bless you, in which joins Sir William and Lady Hamilton with your affectionate friend,

BRONTE NELSON OF THE NILE.

TO HIS EXCELLENCY THE CAPITAN PACHA.

[Letter-Book.]

Palermo, April 6th, 1800.

Having answered your Excellency's letters, as far as is in my power, I have only to again assure you of my earnest desire on all occasions to prove myself deserving of the favour of the Sublime Porte, and the friendship of your Excellency. The happy capture of the William Tell is the finish to the whole French fleet, which my Royal Master desired me to destroy. Having, by the bravery of the Officers and Men under my command, accomplished my task, I am going to England for the benefit of my health; but I can assure you, and beg of your Excellency to assure the Grand Signior of the same, that should the Enemy again send a Naval force to attack his Dominions, I shall hold myself ready to come forth again for their destruction.

Wishing your Excellency the blessing of health, and that success may ever crown your services against all the enemies of his Imperial Majesty, I remain, with the greatest attachment, your faithful friend,

BRONTE NELSON OF THE NILE.

TO HIS EXCELLENCY THE CAIMAKAN PACHA.

[Letter-Book.]

Palermo, 7th April, 1800.

Sir,

I was honoured, four days past, with your Excellency's letter, dated January the 30th, and feel most sincerely your kind expressions towards me, and must be highly flattered at the opinion the Sublime Porte has testified of my zeal in the execution of my Royal Master's orders.

It was my orders, in May 1798, to destroy the French Mediterranean fleet. By the happy capture of the Généreux and William Tell, (the last on the 30th March,) thanks to the Almighty, and the bravery of the Officers and Men under my command, all, all, are taken, burnt, or sunk. Of the thirteen Sail of the Line, not one remains ; and I trust that very soon the same may be told of their Army, who dared to land on the Territory of the Sublime Porte. Perish all the enemies of his Imperial Majesty the Grand Signior ! Having completely obeyed my orders, with great injury to my health, I am going to England for the benefit of it ; but should the Enemy (which I do not believe) dare to send another Fleet to menace the Dominions of his Imperial Majesty, I shall hold myself ready, if I am thought fit for such a service, to come forth, and be the instrument of God's vengeance on such miscreant infernal scoundrels.

That the Almighty may prosper all your endeavours for the honour and glory of the Sublime Porte, is the constant prayer of your Excellency's most obliged Servant,

BRONTE NELSON OF THE NILE.

TO COMMODORE SIR THOMAS TROUBRIDGE, BART.

[Letter-Book.]

7th April, 1800.

My dear Troubridge,

The two Venetian Ships, with the Egyptian, and another Frigate, are sailed from Toulon ; therefore till we know something about them, would it be eligible to trust the William

Tell to Minorca, with any force we could send with her?
Therefore would it not be well to get her into Marsa Sirocco,
for she will be plundered at Syracuse, till we can send a
proper force to insure her safe arrival? I am still very unwell,
but mean to come to take my farewell. I am anxiously waiting for the official account of the capture of the William Tell.
God bless you, my dear Troubridge, and believe me ever
your affectionate friend,

                                   BRONTE NELSON OF THE NILE.

TO THE RIGHT HONOURABLE EARL SPENCER, K.G.

[Letter-Book.]

                                        Palermo, 8th April, 1800.
My dear Lord,
    I send you Sir Edward Berry's letter,[2] and am sure your
Lordship will not be sparing of promotion to the deserving.
My friends wished me to be present. I have no such wish;
for a something might have been given me, which now cannot.
Not for all the world would I rob any man of a sprig of laurel
—much less my children of the Foudroyant! I love her as a
fond father, a darling child, and glory in her deeds. I am
vain enough to feel the effects of my school. Lord Keith
sending me nothing, I have not, of course, a free communication. I have wrote to him for permission to return to England,
when you will see a broken-hearted man. My spirit cannot
submit patiently.[3] My complaint, which is principally a

----

[2] Describing the capture of the Guillaume Tell, now in the Nelson Papers.

[3] On the 25th of April, 1800, Lord Spencer wrote to Lord Nelson, acknowledging
the receipt of his letters of the 14th of December, 1799, and of the 20th of February
and 10th of March, 1800, none of which have been found. Their contents may,
however, be understood from Lord Spencer's answer:—" To the first [of those
letters] it does not occur to me that I have anything to say at present, the circumstances having very materially changed since the date of it. To the second, I
think I should feel disposed to say a great deal, if I were not, at the same time, so
strongly impressed with a conviction that, on mature reflection, you will see in a very
different light the circumstances of your situation from that in which you seemed
then disposed to represent them, that any observation I might think it necessary to
make, might perhaps appear very much displaced at the moment when it reached
you.

" With respect to Lieutenant Bolton, it will be impossible to give him promotion
immediately, because if the circumstance of the capture of the Généreux had been

swelling of the heart, is at times alarming to my friends, but not to, my dear Lord, your obliged and faithful,

BRONTE NELSON OF THE NILE.

If I may again say it, what would I feel if my brother[4] was a Commissioner of the Navy—for ever grateful!

TO CAPTAIN SIR EDWARD BERRY, H.M. SHIP FOUDROYANT.

[From a Copy in the Nelson Papers.]

My dear Sir Edward,   April 8th, 1800.

I rejoice that you think you will be able to carry us to Malta, and, I hope, afterwards, to Gibraltar or England. I have wrote to you at Malta, and, therefore, only now acknowledge the receipt of your letter from Syracuse, as I believe this will not find you there. My mind is fixed for retreat at this moment. Assure all the Foudroyants of my sincere regard and affection for them. *They may depend upon me;* and do you believe that I am, as ever, your truly sincere and affectionate friend,

BRONTE NELSON OF THE NILE.

I have sent for Tyson.

thought one on which an Officer should be promoted—which, however well performed and useful a service it may have been, (as it certainly was,) from the great superiority of the capturing Squadron, does not appear to be, by any means, a case on which promotion of that kind should be given, it would undoubtedly have been the First Lieutenant of your Ship, and not one of the junior ones, who would have been selected; and I am very happy to hear that Lieutenant Thompson, whom I had recommended to the Commander-in-Chief, has been found worthy to bear so distinguished a situation on board the Foudroyant. I cannot with propriety quit this subject, without observing that after the marked attention which I have ever shown to your *élèves* and followers, an attention which I am most happy to show them, both on your account and theirs, I do not think I had any reason to expect the kind of hint you throw out on the subject of *interest,* in what you say of this Officer

" To your letter of the 20th of March, all I shall say is, to express my extreme regret that your health should be such as to oblige you to quit your station off Malta, at a time when I should suppose there must be the finest prospect of its reduction. I should be very sorry that you did not accomplish that business in person, as the Guillaume Tell is your due, and that ship ought not to strike to any other. If the Enemy should come into the Mediterranean, and whenever they do, it will be suddenly, I should be much concerned to hear that you learnt of their arrival in that Sea, either on Shore or in a Transport at Palermo. Believe me, my dear Lord, ever sincerely and faithfully yours, SPENCER."—*Autograph,* in the Nelson Papers.

[4] Mr. Maurice Nelson.

TO VICE-ADMIRAL LORD KEITH, K.B.

[Original, in the Admiralty.]

My Lord,   Palermo, 8th April, 1800.

I have the happiness to send you a copy of Captain Dixon's letter to Commodore Sir Thomas Troubridge, informing him of the capture of the William Tell; the circumstances attending this glorious finish to the whole French Mediterranean Fleet, are such as must ever reflect the highest honour to all concerned in it. The attention of the Commodore in placing Officers and Men to attend the movements of the French Ships, and the exactness with which his orders were executed, are a proof that the same vigour of mind remains, although the body, I am truly sorry to say, is almost worn away. Then came the alacrity of the Vincejo, Captain Long, and other Sloops of War; the gallantry and excellent management of Captain Blackwood of the Penelope frigate, who, by carrying away the Enemy's main and mizen topmasts, enabled the Lion to get up, when Captain Dixon showed the greatest courage and Officer-like conduct in placing his Ship on the Enemy's bow, as she had only 300 men on board, and the Enemy 1220. The conduct of these excellent Officers enabled Sir Edward Berry to place the Foudroyant where she ought, and is the fittest Ship in the world to be, close alongside the William Tell—one of the largest and finest two decked Ships in the world—where he showed that matchless intrepidity and able conduct, as a Seaman and Officer, which I have often had the happiness to experience in many trying situations. I thank God I was not present, for it would finish me could I have taken a sprig of these brave men's laurels: they are, and I glory in them, my darling children, served in my school, and all of us caught our professional zeal and fire from the great and good Earl of St. Vincent.

I am confident your Lordship will bestow the promotions in the properest manner, therefore I have done nothing in that respect; and on this occasion I only beg leave to mention, that Governor Ball would be much flattered by the command of the William Tell, and Captain Ormsby,[5] a volun-

---

[5] Captain George Ormsby died at Plymouth Dock, early in 1801 being then Commander of the Scout sloop.

teer in the Penelope, would be happy in fitting her for him during his very necessary attendance at Malta; and in complying with their request, your Lordship will highly oblige, your most obedient servant,

BRONTE NELSON OF THE NILE.

TO THE RIGHT HONOURABLE SIR WILLIAM HAMILTON, K.B.

[Letter-Book.]

Palermo, 9th April, 1800.

My dear Sir William,

I send your Excellency an extract of a letter from Sir Thomas Troubridge, which I request you will have the goodness to communicate to his Excellency Sir John Acton. I have also had several, and very serious, applications made to me, to know when the £60,000 sterling is to be paid for the captures of Città Vecchia and Rome. By the British laws, the whole of the Public property became the immediate property of the Captors; and they had a right to it, if they chose to exert that right. But situated as his Sicilian Majesty's affairs were in the Roman State, they thought it better to submit the matter to me, and to give up everything—the rich Museums, the Ships in the Port of Città Vecchia, &c. &c.— to his Sicilian Majesty's Officers. The abovementioned sum was arranged and agreed to, I understood, by General Acton; for although certainly not a quarter of what was right, yet the exertions to get that right, would have forced the Romans to call in the Austrians, and to expel the Neapolitan troops by insurrections of the people. I own I am anxious, and feel my credit with the Captains, Officers, and Men committed, that this sum of money should be paid before I quit my present situation, which my health forces me to.

I am confident your Excellency will do everything which is right and just for the brave Officers and men under my command, and who look up for protection to, my dear Sir William, your faithful and obliged friend,

BRONTE NELSON OF THE NILE.

TO THEIR EXCELLENCIES SIR WILLIAM HAMILTON, CHEVALIER
ITALINSKY, AND SIR JOHN ACTON.

[Letter-Book.]

Palermo, April 10th, 1800.

Sir,

I have the honour to transmit to your Excellency, a copy
of a letter I have received from Governor Ball, with two enclosures. In having done this, I have only to observe, that if
Governor Ball is not allowed what must appear to your
Excellency as just, that this good and valuable Officer must be
ruined in his pecuniary affairs, and I shall have been the
innocent cause of it. But when it is reflected that without
the abilities, bravery, and conciliating manners of my friend
Ball, all Malta would long ago have been in full possession
of the French, I submit with confidence his case; and have
the honour to be, with the greatest respect, your Excellency's
most obedient servant,

BRONTE NELSON OF THE NILE.

TO THE RIGHT HONOURABLE SIR WILLIAM HAMILTON, K.B.

[Letter-Book.]

Palermo, 10th April, 1800.

My dear Sir William,

Reports are brought to me, that the Spanish Ships of War
in this Port are preparing to put to sea—a circumstance which
must be productive of very unpleasant consequences, to both
England and this Country. It is fully known, with what
exactness I have adhered to the neutrality of this Port; for,
upon our arrival here, from Naples, in December 1798, from
the conduct of his Catholic Majesty's Minister, I should have
been fully justified in seizing these Ships. We know that one
object of the Spanish fleet, combined with the French, was
to wrest entirely from the hands of his Sicilian Majesty his
Kingdoms of the Two Sicilies. The Spaniards are, by bad
councils, the tools of the French; and, of course, the bitter
enemy of his Sicilian Majesty and Family. The conduct I
have pursued towards these Ships, circumstanced as they are,

has been moderate, and truly considerate towards his Sicilian Majesty.

The time is now come, that, profiting by my forbearance, the Spanish Ships are fitting for sea. It is not possible, if they persist in their preparations, that I can avoid attacking them, even in the Port of Palermo; for they never can, or shall be suffered to go to sea, and placed in a situation of assisting the French, against not only Great Britain, but also the Two Sicilies. I have, therefore, to request, that your Excellency will convey my sentiments on this very delicate subject, to his Sicilian Majesty's Ministers, that they may take measures to prevent such a truly unpleasant event happening, which would be as much against my wish as it can be against theirs; and I request that your Excellency will, through the proper channel, assure his Sicilian Majesty that his safety and honour are as dear to me as that of our Royal Master. I have the honour to be, with the greatest respect, my dear Sir William, your Excellency's most affectionate, humble servant,

BRONTE NELSON OF THE NILE.

TO LIEUTENANT INGLIS,[6] ON BOARD THE GUILLAUME TELL, AT SYRACUSE.

[From Clarke and M'Arthur, vol. ii. p. 252.]

16th April, 1800.

My dear Sir,

How fortunate I did not permit you to quit the Penelope, to be a junior Lieutenant in the Foudroyant! You will now get your promotion in the pleasantest of all ways, by the gallant exertions of yourself and those brave friends who surrounded you on that glorious night. What a triumph for you— what a pleasure to me—what happiness to have the Nile Fleet all taken under my orders and regulations! Blackwood's coming to me at Malta, and my keeping him there, were something more than chance. Ever, my dear Sir, believe me your truly sincere friend,

BRONTE NELSON OF THE NILE.

---

[6] Lieutenant Charles Inglis: he was made a Commander in October 1800, was promoted to Post Captain in April 1802, and died in February 1833.

TO THE COMMANDING OFFICER OF HIS MAJESTY'S SHIPS AT MAHON.

[Letter-Book. The Peterel having arrived at Palermo on the 19th of April, Lord Nelson's Flag was removed to her from the Transport; but on the arrival of the Foudroyant, on the 21st, it was shifted to that Ship.]

Sir,   Palermo, 21st April, 1800.

As I understand that the Spanish Ships are preparing to quit the Port of Palermo, and take their route along the Barbary coast, as far as Algiers, I think it right to acquaint you therewith, that you may cause a strict look-out to be kept for them. I am, &c.

BRONTE NELSON OF THE NILE.

TO HIS EXCELLENCY SIR JOHN ACTON, BART.

[Letter Book.]

My dear Sir,   Palermo, April 21st, 1800.

When I was last at Malta, it was my intention to have selected all the receipts for stores, received from his Sicilian Majesty's Arsenals and Ships, and, together with the expenses for repairing the Culloden,[7] to have drawn bills upon the British Government for the value; but the capture of the French Ship, and my Secretary being obliged to go to Mahon, have prevented this affair being arranged. I entreat that your Excellency will not attribute this apparent neglect to any fault of mine. I hope to find Mr. Tyson at Malta, and all shall be prepared against my return.

In Commodore Troubridge's letter to me, sent to your Excellency by Sir William Hamilton, you will see the Commodore has laid out, when at Naples and at Cività Vecchia, for information, rewards, &c., the sum of £500 sterling. Should, my dear Sir, there be the least difficulty in repaying the Commodore this money, I will direct its being done, but it is a just thing that Troubridge should be repaid. Respecting the affairs of Cività Vecchia, and the Roman State, I rely on the known justice of your Excellency, and the liberality of his Sicilian Majesty. I mention this circumstance at this moment, as I understand that Sir William Hamilton, with whom we

---

[7] The Culloden was repaired at Castel-à-Mare, after the Battle of the Nile.

have so long, and so honourably and beneficially, for the
benefit of both Monarchs, acted, has sent to desire his audi-
ence of leave, and it gives a finish to all my public affairs.
Believe me, with every sentiment of respect, your Excellency's
most obliged and faithful

BRONTE NELSON OF THE NILE.

If Sir William Hamilton has finished his affairs, it is my
intention to sail to-morrow night, or Wednesday morning, for
Malta, and to return here the first week in May.

TO ALL WHOM IT MAY CONCERN.

[Order-Book. On the 24th of April, Lord Nelson proceeded in the Foudroyant
from Palermo to Syracuse, at which place he arrived on the 30th of that month.]

Foudroyant, at Syracuse, 1st May, 1800.

Whereas, I have every reason to be satisfied with the conduct of Mr. John B. Reymondi, His Majesty's Vice-Consul at
Syracuse, during the time I commanded His Majesty's Ships,
&c., in these seas, I do hereby give permission to the said
Mr. John B. Reymondi to wear an Epaulette[8] on his left
shoulder with the Consular uniform.

BRONTE NELSON OF THE NILE.

TO THOMAS LEMPRIERE, ESQ., COMMISSARY FOR PRISONERS OF
WAR, MAHON.

[Letter-Book. On the 3rd of May, Lord Nelson sailed from Syracuse, and
anchored the next day in St. Paul's Bay, Malta, whence the Foudroyant went, on the
11th, to Marsa Sirocco Bay, in that Island: he was accompanied in the Foudroyant
by Sir William and Lady Hamilton.]

Foudroyant, Malta, 5th May, 1800.

Sir,

As the French Admiral and Officers taken in Le Guillaume
Tell, and sent down to Mahon, will without doubt have in-

---

[8] To wear an Epaulette appears to have been a great object of Sicilian ambition.
Speaking of Lord Nelson's visit to Termini, in December 1799, Miss Knight says,
" Dr. Sigismondo Gallegra, who is one of the principal families of this place, and
acts as Vice-Consul for the English, came, with one of his sisters, out to meet
Lord N., &c., and conducted us to his house, when petards were fired, &c., where
he was decorated with an Epaulette, which it seems was all his ambition."

telligence of the greatest importance to communicate to the
French Government, respecting the distressed state of La
Valetta, and which it is necessary, as far as it can be prevented, from being made known in France, it is my desire
that you do not permit any of the said Officers to be exchanged, or sent to France, on any account, until you receive
orders for their exchange from the Commander-in-Chief. I
am, &c.,

BRONTE NELSON OF THE NILE.

TO ALEXANDER DAVISON, ESQ.

[Letter-Book. This letter is particularly referred to in vol. iii. p. 510.]

My dear Sir,   Malta, 9th May, 1800.

Mr. Fox having, in the House of Commons, in February,
made an accusation against somebody, for what he calls a breach
of a treaty with Rebels, which had been entered into with a
British Officer; and having used language unbecoming either
the wisdom of a Senator, or the politeness of a Gentleman,
or an Englishman, who ought ever to suppose that His
Majesty's Officers would always act with honour and openness in all their transactions; and as the whole affairs of the
Kingdom of Naples were, at the time alluded to, absolutely
placed in my hands, it is I who am called upon to explain my
conduct and therefore send you my Observations, on the
infamous Armistice entered into by the Cardinal; and on his
refusal to send in a joint declaration to the French and Rebels,
I sent in my Note, and on which the Rebels came out of the
Castles, *as they ought*, and as I hope all those who are false
to their King and Country will, *to be hanged*, or otherwise
disposed of, as their Sovereign thought proper. The terms
granted by Captain Foote of the Seahorse, at Castel-del-mare,
were all strictly complied with, the Rebels having surrendered
before my arrival. There has been nothing promised by a
British Officer, that His Sicilian Majesty has not complied
with, even in disobedience to his orders to the Cardinal. I
am, &c.,   BRONTE NELSON OF THE NILE.

Show these papers to Mr. Rose, or some other; and, if
thought right, you will put them in the papers.

TO ALEXANDER DAVISON, ESQ.

[Letter-Book.]

Malta, 9th May, 1800.

My dear Davison,

When I laid claim to my right of Prize-money, as Commanding Admiral of the Mediterranean Fleet, I had not an idea of Lord St. Vincent attempting to lay in any claim, for I have ever considered him as far from attempting, notwithstanding any law opinion, to take away my undoubted property. I am confident it will be given up, the moment you show his Lordship my manner of thinking respecting the Nile prize-money. No lawyer in Europe can, I am confident, make either the Earl or myself do a dishonourable act, which this claim, if persisted in, would be ; let my Earl lay his hand on his heart, and say, whether his Nelson, subject to all the responsibility of this command, is not entitled to the pittance of Prize-money—be it £5, or £50,000, it makes no difference. No Admiral ever yet received Prize-money, going for the benefit of his health from a Foreign station, and Lord St. Vincent was certainly not eligible to have given me any order till his return to this station ; and so think the Board of Admiralty, by their directions to me of August 20th, and many subsequent ones, which would have passed through Lord St. Vincent, had they considered him eligible to give orders; but whether they did or not I could not have obeyed. I trust I shall hear no more of this business, which I blush to think should have been brought forward. I shall very soon see you in England, and ever believe me, my dear Davison, your obliged,

BRONTE NELSON OF THE NILE.

TO ALEXANDER DAVISON, ESQ.

[Letter-Book.]

Should any person dispute my right to share Prize-money as Commander-in-Chief from the 17th August, when all my Senior Admirals had either struck their Flags, or were under the orders of other Admirals, their superiors, to the 30th of November following, in the year 1799, when Lord Keith returned to the Mediterranean station, I empower you, jointly with my Agents, Messrs. Marsh, Page, and Creed, or separately, as you please, to support my just and undoubted claim by due course of law; but as any claim for such Prize-money is contrary to custom, I am confident no claim will be prosecuted by Lord St. Vincent.

Given on board the Foudroyant, at Malta, May 9th, 1800.

BRONTE NELSON OF THE NILE.

ANSWER TO MR. TUCKER'S STATEMENT, TRANSMITTED TO ALEXANDER DAVISON, ESQ., RESPECTING THE EARL OF ST. VINCENT'S SHARING PRIZE-MONEY, AS COMMANDER-IN-CHIEF ON THE MEDITERRANEAN STATION, WHILE HE WAS IN ENGLAND.

[Letter-Book.]

1st.—Mr. Tucker[9] says, the Earl St. Vincent had neither resigned or returned from the command of the Mediterranean station, but had come to England on leave from the Lords Commissioners of the Admiralty, for the benefit of his health only:

Answer.—Lord Nelson received a letter from Mr. Nepean, dated the 20th August 1799, stating, that as the Earl of St. Vincent had returned to England, and Lord Keith, with the other Flag-Officers, having quitted the Mediterranean station, in pursuit of the Enemy, Lord Nelson had become the Senior Officer of his Majesty's Ships there, and that he had all the important duties of the station to attend [to]; and proceeds to direct his Lordship's attention to the different points of the war, and of the operations to be carried on by the Squadron under his command. Lord Nelson considers this order alone to be sufficient to entitle him to share for all captures, as the Commander-in-Chief for the time being, as he had all the responsibility; and in no instance before, have Admirals

---

[9] Benjamin Tucker, Esq., for many years Private Secretary to Lord St. Vincent, afterwards Second Secretary to the Admiralty and Comptroller of the Treasurer's Accounts of the Navy, and father of Mr. Jedediah Tucker, mentioned in the Preface to the Second Volume.

claimed to share when they left the station where they commanded, on account of ill health, or otherwise; and, as an instance, Lord Hood's going home for his health, as well as Lord Nelson, who were both retained in pay, but were not allowed to share any Prize-money; and in the case of Lord Hood and Admiral Hotham, there was no claim whatever made by Lord Hood, because neither him nor any Sea-Officer thought he could have a shadow of claim for such.

2nd.—Mr. Tucker says, that after the arrival of the Earl of St. Vincent in England, he was borne and considered by the Admiralty, in every point of view, as the Commander-in-Chief, and corresponded with them as such until the 26th November, when he resigned the command:

Answer.—If the Earl of St. Vincent was considered as Commander-in-Chief, as Mr. Tucker states him to be, why were not all the Admiralty orders sent to Lord Nelson addressed to the Earl of St. Vincent, as is usual, and by him transmitted to Lord Nelson? On the contrary, all orders from the Admiralty were addressed to Lord Nelson, as the Commanding-Officer in the Mediterranean; and in no instance whatsoever did Lord Nelson receive any orders from the Earl of St. Vincent from the time he left the Mediterranean; and it is presumed that the Earl of St. Vincent did not interfere in the command, or give any orders or directions for the carrying on any service on the station.

Answer to 3rd.[1]—With respect to the Alcmene being cruizing under the orders of the Earl of St. Vincent, and had not received any directions from any other Officer, this proves nothing, as though the orders from Lord Nelson did not reach the Alcmene before the capture of those prizes, yet orders were transmitted from Lord Nelson to Rear-Admiral Duckworth, to be forwarded as well to the Alcmene as the other ships on the Station, to put themselves under his Lordship's command; and if Lord Nelson had thought it proper, he was fully authorized to give orders to the Alcmene to cruize on any part of the station he might point out. Lord Nelson had it in his power to give directions to any of His Majesty's Ships on the station, in contradiction to any

---

[1] The *Third* Statement does not occur in the Letter-Book.

orders given by the Earl of St. Vincent: on the contrary, the Earl of St. Vincent had it not in his power to give any orders in contradiction of those given by Lord Nelson, until his return within the limits of the Mediterranean Station.

BRONTE NELSON OF THE NILE.

TO VICE-ADMIRAL LORD KEITH, K.B.

[Letter Book.]

Foudroyant, Malta, 10th May, 1800.

My Lord,

I have received your Lordship's letter of the 3rd April, conveying intelligence from Mahon of the intended sailing of the Spanish ships, with quicksilver, from Palermo for Spain.[1] Your Lordship's information is perfectly correct; for the Spanish Admiral is arrived, and I have given directions, in case of their preparing to leave that Port, to send Express-boats in all directions, to give the necessary information for their being pursued, and have also written to Mahon on the subject. I have the honour to be, &c.,

BRONTE NELSON OF THE NILE.

TO EVAN NEPEAN, ESQ., ADMIRALTY.

[Letter-Book.]

Foudroyant, Malta, May 12th, 1800.

Sir,

I have the pleasure to send you, and to request you will present it to their Lordships, the Flag of the last of the French Squadron who fought at the Battle of the Nile, on the entire destruction of which I most cordially congratulate their Lordships. This Flag has been presented to me in the most flattering manner by the gallant Captors of the William Tell. I have the honour to be, &c.,

BRONTE NELSON OF THE NILE.

[1] These Ships succeeded in escaping from Palermo.

TO VICE-ADMIRAL LORD KEITH, K.B.

[Letter-Book.]

Foudroyant, Malta, 12th May, 1800.

My Lord,

Lieutenant Harrington of his Majesty's Ship Alexander, who commanded that Ship in the absence of Captain Ball, for some time past hath been in a bad state of health, and is now so ill that he hath been obliged to go to sick quarters; and Captain Ball not thinking the next senior Lieutenant capable of such a charge, I have, in consequence, appointed Captain George Ormsby, a Commander, serving as volunteer on board the Penelope, to command the Alexander for the present, as Captain Ball cannot, at this crisis, be absent from his duty on shore, which I hope your Lordship will approve.

I purpose going in the Foudroyant, in a few days, to Palermo, as I am under an old promise to her Sicilian Majesty, that whenever she returned to the Continent, I would escort her over. Her Majesty has now made application to me for that purpose; and, as it may be necessary to take another Ship for the escort, I purpose taking the Alexander with me. The Lion is perfectly refitted, and in as good a state as before the action, in every respect; and Lord William Stuart[2] hath joined her, a few days since, in the Champion, who brought up two Transports with powder, shot, mortars, &c., from Gibraltar; and in which Ship Captain Dixon goes to the Généreux at Mahon, having directed Captain Hamond[3] to convoy to that Island the three Transports having on board the crew of Le Guillaume Tell, the French Admiral and Officers being on board the Champion. I have the honour to be, &c.,

BRONTE NELSON OF THE NILE.

[2] Younger son of John, first Marquis of Bute: he died, a Post Captain, in July 1814.

[3] Now Vice-Admiral Sir Graham Eden Hamond, Bart., K.C.B., then Captain of the Champion.

TO THOMAS LEMPRIERE, ESQ., AGENT FOR PRISONERS OF WAR, MAHON.

[Letter-Book.]

Foudroyant, Malta, 12th May, 1800.

Sir,

In addition to my former directions to you of the 5th instant, respecting the French Admiral and Officers taken in Le Guillaume Tell, being kept at Minorca, and not exchanged until you receive orders from the Commander-in-Chief to that effect, I do further require and direct that not one of the Officers taken on board the French Ship Bellona, by the Success, and sent with the others, be exchanged or suffered to depart from Mahon, as they have pledged themselves to return to the relief of Malta, and perfectly know all our stations and posts. I am, &c.,

BRONTE NELSON OF THE NILE.

TO EVAN NEPEAN, ESQ., ADMIRALTY.

[Letter-Book.]

Foudroyant, Malta, 16th May, 1800.

Sir,

I herewith enclose you a list of the Captains and Officers of the Navy, as well as the Officers of the Marine Forces, who were landed from the Squadron under my command at Naples, and as the Officers of the Marine Corps have been ordered by the Lords of the Treasury to have bat and forage money paid them, I think it but justice that the Officers of the Navy should be paid also, according to their respective ranks.

I have, therefore, to request that you will be pleased to solicit their Lordships for an application to the Treasury, on behalf of the Sea-Officers landed at Naples from the Squadron under my command, that they may be allowed bat and forage money according to their several ranks, as they were at as much expense as the Officers of the Marines were, and the Marines were commanded by the Sea-Officers. I have the honour to be, &c.

BRONTE NELSON OF THE NILE.

TO COMMODORE SIR THOMAS TROUBRIDGE, BART.

[Letter-Book.]

Foudroyant, 22nd May, 1800.

My dear Troubridge,

I herewith enclose you Lord Keith's letters of the 29th, respecting the promotion of Captain Broughton[4] and Lieutenant Thompson;[5] of 6th May, respecting my taking Culloden to England; of the 9th of May, respecting the Pursers of the Princess Charlotte and Peterel, and of the 10th May, respecting the Northumberland and a Frigate being sent to Alexandria when Valetta falls; as also Lord Keith's Memoranda respecting the seizure of all French Ships coming from Egypt, with my remarks and memoranda thereon, which you will please to order to be carried into execution. At the same time, as the Transports are all gone to Sicily, I do not see the necessity of any Ship of War remaining in Marsa Sirocco Bay, but this you will judge of, and leave such directions as you think necessary. At the same time you will give the most positive directions, that the Northumberland, the only real effective Ship now before Valetta, do not on any account go into the Bay of Marsa Sirocco; but keep her, and all the force you have, off Valetta, except the look-out Ships. But if you think it is necessary for a Ship to remain there, let the Culloden keep that station, until she may be ordered to England, or receive other directions from the Commander-in-Chief.

On your passage to Leghorn in the Princess Charlotte, I should be glad if you would call at Palermo, in your route, if you do not find it inconvenient. I am, my dear Troubridge, your very faithful and obedient servant,

BRONTE NELSON OF THE NILE.

---

[4] Vide p. 205, ante.　　　　　[5] Vide pp. 189, 225, ante.

TO GENERAL DUGUA.[6]

[Letter-Book. The Foudroyant got under weigh on the 20th of May, and continued off Malta until the 1st of June, when she returned to Palermo.]

Foudroyant, at Sea, 22nd May, 1800.

Sir,

As you would certainly have been at this moment on your way to France, could I have prepared a Cartel for your reception, I do not think it fair to make you a sufferer by this accident; and, therefore, have directed the Commodore to send the Cartel, notwithstanding the new orders received in consequence of General Kleber's renewal of hostilities. Wishing you, Sir, a speedy passage, I remain your most obedient servant,

BRONTE NELSON OF THE NILE.

TO CAPTAIN ORMSBY, ACTING CAPTAIN OF HIS MAJESTY'S SHIP ALEXANDER.

[Letter-Book.]

Foudroyant, at Sea, 22nd May, 1800.

Sir,

I herewith enclose you a letter from the Commander-in-Chief, conveying his Majesty's most gracious pardon for John Jolly,[7] Private Marine, late belonging to the Ship you command, and desire that you will make the same known to him accordingly, and give him such admonitions for his future conduct as you shall judge necessary and proper on the occasion, and return the order from the Lords of the Admiralty to me the first opportunity, and enter the said John Jolly on the books of the Alexander, agreeable to the date of his discharge from the Foudroyant. I am, &c.,

BRONTE NELSON OF THE NILE.

---

[6] In the expedition into Syria, General Dugua commanded the province of Cairo. He afterwards (it is believed) served on the staff in St. Domingo, under General Leclerc; and in October, 1802, shocked at the cruelties perpetrated by his countrymen, he quitted the French army, and assisted the Blacks, but being discovered, he was sentenced to death, and became his own executioner.

[7] Vide vol. iii. pp. 401, 402.

TO HIS SACRED MAJESTY THE KING OF THE TWO SICILIES.

[Letter-Book.]

Palermo, 2nd June, 1800.

Sire,

Your Majesty's most gracious approbation of my conduct, so marked to the world by the most distinguished Honour[8] you have conferred upon me, fills me with sensations which no words I can find will in any manner express. I must, therefore, confine myself to simply assuring your Majesty, that there is not that man living who is more attached to your sacred person, the Queen, and your Majesty's whole Royal Family, than your faithful and devoted servant,

BRONTE NELSON OF THE NILE

TO HIS EXCELLENCY SIR JOHN ACTON, BART.

[Letter-Book.]

Palermo, 2nd June, 1800.

Sir,

I was this morning honoured with your Excellency's letter transmitting a letter from his Sicilian Majesty, also the Statutes of the Order of St. Ferdinand, and, also, such expressions of kindness that has made the most sensible impression on my mind, and filled my heart with affection, pleasure, and gratitude. I beg that your Excellency will lay me at the King's feet, assure him of my gratitude, and that, compatible with the duty I owe my legitimate Sovereign, I will lay down my life for his Majesty, and the Queen, and the whole Royal Family; and allow me to subscribe myself your Excellency's obedient and obliged servant,

BRONTE NELSON OF THE NILE.

---

[8] King Ferdinand wished to confer an Order upon Lord Nelson, and his Captains, Troubridge, Ball, Hood, Louis, and Hallowell, but as it was then considered that Protestants could not be admitted into the Order of St. Januarius, his Majesty instituted the Order of St. Ferdinand and Merit, on the 1st of April, 1800. It consisted originally of two Classes only, Knights Grand Cross, and Knights Commanders; but a third and inferior Class was added in 1810. The first three Knights Grand Cross were, Lord Nelson, Field-Marshal Suwarrow, and the Emperor Paul.

TO VICE-ADMIRAL LORD KEITH, K.B.

[Letter-Book.]

My dear Lord,   Palermo, 2nd June, 1800.

The day after I left Malta, I met the Princess Charlotte; but as all the arrangements were made for my coming to Palermo, in order to carry the Queen to Leghorn, I sent her to Troubridge, with directions for the execution of your orders, and then to carry him to Leghorn. The state of the Foudroyant is such, that I have hitherto avoided saying anything of it, wishing you to see the almost impossibility of fitting her in this Country; and I therefore hope she will be the Ship, when a little refitted, to carry all my party to England.[9] We sail on the 5th, and hope for a quick passage.

Ever, my dear Lord, your obliged servant,

BRONTE NELSON OF THE NILE.

[9] On the 9th of May, the Admiralty sent orders to Lord Keith, that if Lord Nelson's health rendered him incapable of doing his duty, and that he should be desirous of returning to England, he was to be permitted to do so, and to take his passage in the first Ship Lord Keith might have occasion to send home, unless he should prefer returning by land, in which case he was to be at liberty to strike his Flag in the Mediterranean, and come on shore. On the same day, Lord Spencer wrote to Nelson the following private letter:—

" Private.

" My dear Lord,

" I have only time to write you a line by the Messenger, who is just going, which I am desirous of doing, in order that the eventual permission, which we now send out for you to come home, in case your health should make it necessary, may not be misunderstood. It is by no means my wish or intention to call you away from service, but having observed that you have been under the necessity of quitting your station off Malta, on account of the state of your health, which I am persuaded you could not have thought of doing without such necessity, it appeared to me much more advisable for you to come home at once, than to be obliged to remain inactive at Palermo, while active service was going on in other parts of the station. I should still much prefer your remaining to complete the reduction of Malta, which I flatter myself cannot be very far distant, and I still look with anxious expectation to the Guillaume Tell striking to your Flag. But if, unfortunately, these agreeable events are to be prevented by your having too much exhausted yourself in the service to be equal to follow them up, I am quite clear, and I believe I am joined in opinion by all your friends here, that you will be more likely to recover your health and strength in England than in an inactive situation at a Foreign Court, however pleasing the respect and gratitude shown to you for your services may be, and no testimonies of respect and gratitude from that Court to you can be, I am convinced, too great for the very essential services you have rendered it.

" I trust that you will take in good part what I have taken the liberty to write to you as a friend, and believe me, when I assure you that you have none who is more sincerely and faithfully so than your obedient humble servant, SPENCER."—*Autograph*, in the Nelson Papers.

TO HIS EXCELLENCY SIR JOHN ACTON, BART.

[Letter-Book.]

Sir,   Palermo, 2nd June, 1800.

My object at Bronté is to make the people happy, by not suffering them to be oppressed, [and] to enrich the country by the improvement of agriculture. For these reasons I selected Mr. Graffer, as a proper person for Governor, as his character for honesty is unimpeachable, and his abilities as an agriculturist undeniable; and yet it would appear that there are persons who wish, for certain reasons, to lessen the King's most magnificent gift to me, and also to make the inhabitants of that country more miserable than they were before the estate came into my possession. Several people who have hired farms, on the contract of not letting them to what we, in England, call ' middle-men,' have already done so; and I am told that I either have been, or am to be, induced to consent that a superior, or rather that all Bronté causes shall be tried at Palermo. Now as this is a measure so repugnant to justice, and which must heap ruin on those it is my wish to render happy, I entreat, that except such causes as the present laws of Sicily oblige to resort to some superior Court, that it may never be imagined that I will consent to do an unjust act.

It is possible, from my not reading Italian, that I may sign a very improper paper, (which God forbid !) if men in whom I place confidence lay it before me for my signature. In his Majesty's most gracious gift of Bronté has been omitted the word ' Fragila,' a farm belonging to me. The reasons of this omission are, I fear, too clear; and, at a future day, I may lose it, and his Majesty not retain it. These are, in brief, the letters of Mr. Graffer. I have, therefore, by his desire, to request his Majesty to grant me the following favours :—First, that the farm of ' Fragila' may be inserted in the Patent; secondly, that a Billet-Royal, may be granted to annul the present Contract of the Feuds of St. Andrea and Porticello. I send your Excellency copies and extracts of Mr. Graffer's letters, which prove him an honest and upright man. In arranging these matters for me, it will be an additional obligation conferred upon your Excellency's most obedient and obliged,   BRONTE NELSON OF THE NILE.

TO HIS SACRED MAJESTY THE KING OF THE TWO SICILIES.

[Letter-Book.]

Palermo, 2nd June, 1800.

Sire,

The Almighty, who granted to my legitimate Sovereign's arms the Battle of the Nile, impressed your Majesty with a favourable opinion of me, which has led your Royal heart to grant me the most distinguished honours, and a fortune which I never had an idea of expecting. I presume, therefore, to request that your Majesty will permit me to lay on your table a gold Medal,[1] highly flattering to your Majesty's devoted and faithful,

BRONTE NELSON OF THE NILE.

TO GOVERNOR BALL, MALTA.

[Autograph, in the possession of Sir William Keith Ball, Bart.]

Palermo, June 2nd, 1800.

My dear Ball,

We had a terrible long passage, and only arrived the 31st at night. We are to sail on Thursday the 5th. It has afforded me real pleasure to find that his Sicilian Majesty has given you one of the Commanderies of the Order of St. Ferdinand, and a present with it of 1000 ounces.[2] You merit everything, and this Court is not ungrateful: this is for your services at Naples; and Malta is quite another thing. You may rely you will not be forgotten. I wish circumstances had been so ordered that we could have remained; but it was impossible. Six thousand fresh troops are arrived at Minorca; and as Sir Charles Stuart[3] is momentarily expected at· Leghorn, some orders must soon be given for your having troops at Malta. Lord St. Vincent sailed in the Namur, April 20th, to join the Fleet, and was then to take the command. Savona was taken the 15th; but the Austrians, who are now obliged to go to Piedmont to meet Berthier, seem to me to divide their forces

---

[1] Query, if one of the Medals struck by Mr. Davison. Vide vol. iii. p. 321.
[2] Vide p. 250, infra.   [3] Vide vol. i.. p 401.

too much. Make my best respects to General Graham and
all our Sea friends; and I have only to say, God bless you,
and believe me ever your affectionate and obliged friend,

BRONTE NELSON OF THE NILE.

TO VICE-ADMIRAL LORD KEITH, K.B.

[Letter-Book.]

Palermo, 3rd June, 1800.

My dear Lord,

I wish you could have promoted Mr. Ronicet, as he has
now served our Country seven years, next August, Surgeon's
Mate with me, in the Agamemnon, Captain, and Theseus,
has been Acting-Surgeon of the Thalia, and Lord St. Vincent
would have given him a Ship of the Line, for a better Surgeon,
or one who has served more faithfully, does not exist; and Lord
Hood promised those particular young men who served in our
hospital at Toulon promotion, if they entered into our service.
I have besides, whenever I part for England, to recommend
several persons to your notice—in particular, my Clerk and
Surgeon's Mate. The Clerk, Mr. M'Donough, came to me
from Martin—also, a good Carpenter's Mate and some Mids;
but, as I hope to have the pleasure of seeing you at Leghorn,
I shall then be able to tell you all my wishes, which I hope
you will be able to comply with. Ever, my dear Lord, believe
me your obliged,

BRONTE NELSON OF THE NILE.

TO VICE-ADMIRAL LORD KEITH, K.B.

[Letter-Book.]

Palermo, 5th June, 1800.

My dear Lord,

The bad news from Vienna stopped the Queen's departure;
but it is now fixed for the 8th. The Princess Charlotte
arrived yesterday, and no Troubridge. I send you his letters.
Had I been near him, I should have directed his taking the
Guillaume Tell down with him; but, poor fellow, he is very
ill, and, I believe, fully unequal to the laborious office of

Captain of the Channel Fleet! The Ships will be overflowing
with the Queen's retinue. The Alexander shall not be ten
hours at Leghorn, and the Foudroyant shall be sent for your
inspection. Ever, my dear Lord, believe me your obliged,

BRONTE NELSON OF THE NILE.

I congratulate you on Duckworth's success.

TO HIS EXCELLENCY THE EARL OF ELGIN, CONSTANTINOPLE.

[Letter Book.]

Palermo, 6th June, 1800.

My dear Lord,

Your letter by the Turkish Messenger of April 21st, I have
just received and read, and I will forward the letter and box
to Lord Keith. My health is such, that repose probably is
necessary, especially as by the appointment of that excellent
Officer and good man, Lord Keith, my presence cannot be
necessary. Had I retained the command, not even death
should have prevented my trying to give the Capitan Pacha
a meeting, and assisting most cordially in the good work of
extirpating those infamous robbers from off the face of the
earth. I assure you, my dear Lord, I rejoice in whatever
may give you comfort, and I hope both Lady Elgin and your
daughter[4] will do well. With every sentiment of respect,
believe me your obedient servant,

BRONTE NELSON OF THE NILE.

The Queen, three Princesses, and Prince Leopold proceed
to Leghorn on the 8th, in the Foudroyant, as do Sir William
and Lady Hamilton. Prince Castelcicala goes to England, on
a special mission.

TO VICE-ADMIRAL LORD KEITH, K.B.

[Letter-Book.]

Palermo, 6th June, 1800.

My dear Lord,

As General Acton does not go to England, but the Prince
Castelcicala, as Ambassador, I have directed the Dorotea,

---

[4] Lady Elgin gave birth to her eldest *son* at Pera, on the 5th of April, 1800, who
died unmarried in April, 1840. Her eldest *daughter* was born in August, 1801.

when she has landed Mr. Wyndham at Naples, to proceed to Leghorn, and there receive on board the Prince and his family, (for they go to Leghorn with the Queen;) and to proceed with them to England, as in your orders respecting General Acton.

The dispatches from Constantinople I am sure you have, by way of Corfu; but I shall leave it to the Messenger, in a very bad Vessel, to come to you or not.   At all events, I shall take care of the very handsome Box sent you, in the Foudroyant. We have thirty gentlemen and ladies, besides Sir William's family: Alexander has twenty-four.   We cannot stir.   Ever, my dear Lord, yours faithfully,

BRONTE NELSON OF THE NILE.

TO VICE-ADMIRAL LORD KEITH, K.B.

[Letter-Book.]

[About 6th June, 1800.]

My dear Lord,

By the Teresa, I was favoured with your letters of April 17th, 19th, and 20th.   Every order and wish of yours, as far as our circumstances would admit, have been complied with; and I feel sensibly your kind intentions of accommodating us to England.   The state of the Foudroyant renders it, I believe you will think it right, for her to go to England, when she has had some refit; for in her present state she should not be trusted at sea, except for a passage of a few leagues.   Where she put into Port, if it blew fresh, I should have cut down her Main and Fore-masts; but we have neither spars or cordage for to fit her.   The situation of Malta at present is critical— that is, if no Vessels get in, it must very soon fall; and for the blockade, we have as few Ships as is possible; and when I feel obliged to take the Alexander for an assistant in carrying the Queen of Naples to Leghorn, I hope you will approve of my ordering the return of the Champion.   The Minorca is gone with a convoy of Cotton-ships off Barcelona, for the Maltese cannot exist without this trade to Spain.   I know, for I have felt, what few Ships we have for such an extent of service, from Cape Finisterre to Constantinople.   If troops come to Malta, I am sure a week will finish it; for mortar-batteries are erected within, I am told, pistol-shot of the walls of the   ; but General Graham does not think it right to open them without more force to protect them against a sortie, which, he says, would assuredly happen; for they could not exist in La Valetta. The fall of this place would leave you at ease, and enable you to get your force, now so necessarily scattered, more collected.

From circumstances, I have not been able to man the William Tell to Minorca, nor, till 300 or 250 men are found for her, do I see how it can be effected. Troubridge says the Culloden is able to go to England. I say she ought not to be trusted. Fourteen days would heave her down at Mahon, and stop her leaks: 100 men from her, for she is full-manned, and good men, would greatly assist in navigating the William Tell to England; for she is well fitted with Jury-masts.

Most sincerely do we congratulate you on the success of the Navy, I may say, in the Riviere of Genoa;[5] and you will now bear me out in my assertion, when I say that the British Fleet could have prevented the invasion of Italy, and at that time we had nothing to do; and if our friend Hotham had kept his Fleet on that Coast, I assert, and you will agree with me, no Army from France could have been furnished with stores, or provisions; even men could not have marched. I hope our next account from you will be the surrender of Genoa. Wishing you every success, and hoping to meet you at Leghorn, believe me your most faithful,

BRONTE NELSON OF THE NILE.

TO HIS EXCELLENCY THE AMBASSADOR OF HIS IMPERIAL MAJESTY.

[Letter-Book.]

Foudroyant, Palermo, 6th June, 1800.

Sir,

I have received your Excellency's letter desiring informa-tion respecting the Ragusan Brig taken by an armed Ottoman

---

[5] See Lord Keith's Dispatch of the 21st of May, in the "London Gazette," of the 28th of June, 1800.

Polacca, with Austrian property on board, bound to Genoa:
and in answer thereto, I beg leave to assure your Excellency
that I have not the least knowledge of the capture in question,
nor can I give you the least information concerning it. I
have the honour to be, &c.,

BRONTE NELSON OF THE NILE.

TO HIS EXCELLENCY THE CAPITAN PACHA.

[Letter-Book.]

Palermo, 6th June, 1800.

Sir,

There was a time when I could have done what I thought
best; but at present, for reasons, Lord Keith is appointed
Commander-in-Chief, and I have only to obey, and my health
is seriously impaired. From the very bottom of my soul, I
wish your Excellency every success which your distinguished
merit entitles you to expect; and I fervently pray that you
may speedily exterminate that den of thieves from the face of
Egypt. May the Almighty bless and protect you, is the
sincere wish of your Excellency's obliged friend,

BRONTE NELSON OF THE NILE.

TO HIS HIGHNESS THE DEY OF ALGIERS.

[Letter-Book.]

Foudroyant, Palermo, 7th June, 1800.

Sir,

I have been informed that one of your Highness's cruizers
hath captured a Neapolitan vessel called San Francisco de
Paula, laden with oak pipe staves from the Port d'Anze, in
the Roman State, bound to Marsala, in Sicily; and that the
said staves are the property of Mr. John Woodhouse, a
respectable British merchant, as appears by the bill of lading,
and the said staves were intended to make casks for the use
of his Britannic Majesty's Navy, and the Ships forming the
blockade of Malta; I must, therefore, request of your Highness, that you will be pleased to order the restitution of the
said cargo of staves, otherwise to pay the amount of the

value thereof, at the invoice price, to the Consul General of Great Britain resident at Algiers, which from the well-known justice and humanity of your Highness, I can entertain no doubt will be done. I have the honour to be, &c.,

BRONTE NELSON OF THE NILE.

TO HIS EXCELLENCY SIR JOHN ACTON, BART.

[Letter-Book.]

Palermo, June 7th, 1800.

My dear Sir,

In sending the enclosed, your Excellency will, I am confident feel I am only doing my duty to the brave Officers and men who served the cause so well in the Roman State ; and any arrangements your Excellency makes, I am sure, will give satisfaction to all parties ;[6] therefore, I shall not presume to say a word on the subject, but only to assure your Excellency, I am your obliged,

BRONTE NELSON OF THE NILE.

---

[6] Sir John Acton replied to this letter on the following day :—

"Palermo, June 8th, 1800.

" My dear Lord,

" I return you my thanks for your kind letter of yesterday. Your Lordship may be assured that I shall take every possible measure to obtain and satisfy the just expectation of the Officers and Ships' Companies on board of the Ships who so bravely acted for the recovery of the Roman State. I shall not be easy till this arrangement has been entirely settled : therefore, if Mr. Tyson is not present at the time of the payments, I shall direct to apply to Mr. Gibbs for the receiving that money, according to what you advise me in your letter of yesterday. Enclosed, I present you the three letters for Sir Thomas Troubridge, Captains Hood and Hallowell, for advising them of their nomination to the Order of the *Merit*, or *St. Ferdinand*, as *Commandeurs*. The Medals, unluckily, are not quite terminated : therefore I shall either send them to your Lordship at Leghorn, or direct them, with Mr. Campbell, to London. With the Medals I shall send the King's formal letters to each of the brave *Commandeurs*. In Sir Thomas Troubridge's letter, the pension of a thousand ounces a year is mentioned for his life's time ; and I ordered yesterday that a thousand ounces, already granted to Sir Thomas, should be paid for him to your Lordship, as a reimbursement for the expenses he has been suffering, in his useful expeditions for the common cause, and benefit to his Sicilian Majesty.

" I have wrote to Captain Ball for the *Order* likewise granted to him, and a gratification of 1000 ounces for his expenses in Malta.

" If I have got a Medal made to-day, I shall send it for Commodore Troubridge, as I hear, in this moment, that it might be finished in this day or to-morrow. Every obligation due to these brave Officers are certainly due to your Lordship, who selected them, and they have most honourably answered your choice. His Sicilian

TO HIS EXCELLENCY SIR JOHN ACTON, BART.

[Letter-Book. Early in the morning of the 10th of June, the Queen of Naples, three Princesses, and the young Prince Leopold, embarked, with all her attendants, on board the Foudroyant, together with Sir William and Lady Hamilton, and Miss Knight. The Foudroyant immediately sailed, in company with the Alexander, Princess Charlotte, and a Neapolitan Packet, for Leghorn, and they arrived there on the 14th. This disposition of the Ships was inconsistent with Lord Keith's wishes, and on the 5th of June he issued an order, (but which had not reached Lord Nelson,) directing him to send the Foudroyant and Alexander immediately to Malta, and forbidding the King's Ships to be employed on any other service than such as he had appointed.]

Leghorn Roads, Sunday, Noon, June 15th, 1800.

My dear Sir,

After a very good passage as to time, we arrived here last evening in a fresh gale from the west—so much, that the Ship went eleven miles an hour, at times more. We have with difficulty got a boat on shore, and returned, which is the only communication we have been able to hold with the shore : and the weather still is so bad, that I see no prospect this day of a boat getting from the shore to us. The contradictory news has a little agitated the Queen ; but when particulars, on examination of different persons, are placed before her Majesty, she will be able to form a proper judgment as to the measures to be taken. I have therefore only to request that your Excellency will assure his Majesty, in which join Sir William and Lady Hamilton, that nothing shall make us quit the Queen and Royal Family until *all is safe*, and their future plans *perfectly* and securely settled. On every occasion, I only wish for opportunities of proving to their Majesties my desire [to show] my gratitude for the numerous favours, honours, and magnificent presents they have heaped upon me; and I beg, my dear Sir, that you will believe me your Excellency's most obliged,

BRONTE NELSON OF THE NILE.

If the Queen wishes to send any of the Neapolitan vessels under Lord Keith's command, to Palermo, I shall take upon me to give them orders for that purpose.

Majesty shall be most sensible to what you will be so good to mention to our excellent *Commandeurs*, in presenting them with his Majesty's thanks and acknowledgments. I beg to be believed, with faithful and friendly regard, your Lordship's most obedient and most obliged humble servant, J. ACTON."—*Autograph*, in the Nelson Papers.

TO VICE-ADMIRAL LORD KEITH, K.B.

[Letter-Book. On the 15th of June, Lord Keith ordered Lord Nelson, in case he arrived at Leghorn with the Foudroyant, or any other Ship of the Squadron, to proceed with them, without a moment's loss of time, to join him at Genoa.]

Leghorn, 16th June, 1800.

My dear Lord,

Having wrote to you my intentions of leaving Palermo on the 8th June, I have now only to say, that we sailed on the 9th, full of passengers, and arrived here on the 14th; but from bad weather, it was this morning before the Queen could land.

I send the Princess Charlotte to you this night, with two Couriers from Constantinople. The Foudroyant shall be with you the moment some little matters are got for her safety. I send you Sir Edward Berry's letter to me of this morning, and when you see the Ship, I think you will allow us to carry her to England, as she cannot, I believe, be re-fitted in this Country. But should I be mistaken, I have then to request that the Foudroyant may take us to Gibraltar, and from thence the Hindostan carry us to England. Neither Culloden nor Princess Charlotte are, in my opinion, to be trusted by themselves. The Alexander will return to Malta to-morrow evening. I was obliged to bring her, or the party never could have been accommodated : I therefore trust you will approve of it.

I most sincerely congratulate you on the fortunate moment of getting into Genoa. The release of that part of the Austrian army will, I trust, have the happiest effects, in driving the French out of Italy. It is possible we may see you here before our final departure ; for the Queen does not leave Florence before her road is perfectly clear and secure. The Dorotea carries Prince Castelcicala to England instead of General Acton. The Queen is not perfectly content with the news of this day, but we hope for better to-morrow. Ever, my dear Lord, your faithful and obliged,

BRONTE NELSON OF THE NILE.

TO LADY HAMILTON.

[From the " Letters of Lord Nelson to Lady Hamilton," vol. i. p. 18.]

June 16, [1800.]　Seven o'clock.

My dear Lady Hamilton,

What a difference—but it was to be—from your house to a boat! Fresh breeze of wind, the Ship four or five leagues from the Mole; getting on board into truly a hog-stye of a cabin, leaking like a sieve, consequently floating with water. What a change! Not a Felucca near us. I saw them come out this morning, but they think there is too much wind and swell. Pray, do not keep the Cutter, as I have not a thing, if anything important should arrive, to send you. Only think of Tyson's being left! May God bless you, my dear Lady ; and believe me, ever, your truly affectionate and sincere friend,

NELSON.

Lady Hamilton—put the candle-stick on *my* writing-table.

TO THE RIGHT HONOURABLE EARL SPENCER, K.G.

[Letter-Book.]

Leghorn, 17th June, 1800.

My dear Lord,

We arrived here on the 14th, after a passage of five days ; but it was the 16th before the weather would permit her Majesty to land. All the honours which his Majesty's Ships could show to the Queen have, I trust, been shown her—and too much to so great and good a Monarch could not be done. The situation of the two Armies renders the Queen a little anxious; but her great mind is superior to all difficulties. I am waiting the orders of Lord Keith, and expect he will order the Foudroyant to carry me to England ; for in this Country she cannot be refitted. Four days out of seven I am confined to my bed, but I hope for better times; and ever feel myself your Lordship's obedient servant,

BRONTE NELSON OF THE NILE.

TO HIS EXCELLENCY THOMAS JACKSON, ESQ., TURIN.

[Letter-Book.]

Leghorn, 18th June, 1800.

My dear Sir,

The King's messenger going to Turin, I have the pleasure of writing a line—probably the last during my present stay in Italy, as I am going to England for the recovery of my health. I arrived here on the 14th, with the Queen· of Naples on board, three Princesses, and Prince Leopold—also Sir William and Lady Hamilton, who desire to be kindly remembered to you. The Queen is detained here, by the state of the Armies; and [if] I heard the French beat the Austrians, I have only to carry her and the Royal Family to Naples; but I fervently pray that the French may be beat. But they are active, and the Austrians *very* slow.

I cannot attempt to give you much news. I have just sent a messenger from Constantinople to Lord Keith. The Porte wish my being sent to Egypt to act with the Capitan Pacha; but my state of health will not allow me. Although General Kléber beat, by treachery, and inattention of Sir Sidney Smith, the Grand Vizir's Army, yet a part of the Turkish Army, joined with the inhabitants of Cairo, who flew to arms, have and keep Grand Cairo; and the French now only possess Damietta, Rosetta, and Alexandria: and the plague, thank God, has got amongst them! Malta will fall in a very short time by famine; and it would long since have been ours, if some of the 15,000 troops now at Minorca had been sent to that Island. Adieu, my dear Sir, and believe me ever your obliged and obedient servant,

BRONTE NELSON OF THE NILE.

TO VICE-ADMIRAL LORD KEITH, K.B.

[Letter-Book.]

Leghorn, 18th June, 1800.

My dear Lord,

I was half inclined to send you the Pallas, as I thought you might want to fill her with troops or prisoners; but the arrival of the messenger has determined me on sending her directly.

The Queen waits here, with impatience, news from the Armies; for if the French beat, I have only to return with my sacred charge; but a very few days must decide the question. What a sad thing the attempt on our good King's life![7] But from what I hear, it was not a plan of any Jacobin party, but the affair of a madman. With every sentiment of respect, believe me your obedient servant,

BRONTE NELSON OF THE NILE.

TO VICE-ADMIRAL LORD KEITH, K.B.

[Letter-Book.]

Leghorn, June 19th, 1800.

Your order of the 17th reached me at twelve last night;[8] and as it is the only intimation we have to this moment of anything less than a complete victory by the Austrians, it

---

[7] By the maniac Hadfield, in Drury Lane Theatre, on the 15th of May, 1800.

[8] This Order stated that a Capitulation had been entered into between the Commanders of the Imperial and French Armies, by which all the forts and garrisons in the Genoese territories were to be evacuated, without any stipulation for their inviolability by the British forces, and Lord Nelson was directed to repair, with all the Ships at Leghorn, to the Gulf of Especia, and to adopt every measure for obtaining possession of St. Maria, and other garrisons in the Bay; and on their evacuation by the Austrians, to bring off or destroy the guns. The Order also stated that the French were to march into Genoa on the 24th of June, and that Leghorn, as well as Tuscany, remained with the Emperor's troops. On the 19th of June, Lord Keith sent Lord Nelson peremptory Orders not to employ the Line-of-Battle Ships in conveying back the Queen of Naples to Palermo, (in case her Majesty did not proceed to Vienna,) and authorizing him to strike his Flag, and proceed to England by land, or in the Princess Charlotte, or in any Troop Ship at Mahon, or in the Seahorse; but if, on his arrival at Mahon, he determined to remain on the station, he was to take upon him the duties of Senior Officer there. These instructions were accompanied by the following private letters:—

"My dear Lord,   "Genoa, 19th June, 1800.

"It is not matter of caprice, but of actual duty and necessity, which has obliged me to send the order, which I must desire to be final. Her Majesty is too just, and too well-informed, to place anything like neglect to me. With her good understanding I am sure to stand acquitted. So, my dear friend, let me insist that the Ships instantly follow my public orders. A Frigate and all the Neapolitans may attend the Queen, if you think proper, and that, perhaps, may be at the expense of Sardinia. With every real respect, I am most affectionately yours, &c.—KEITH."

"My dear Lord,   "Genoa, 19th June, 1800.

"The wretched situation to which we are reduced distracts me. I am told from England there is not a Ship to be sent out. I am directed to undertake many and

very much surprised us.   Baron Fenzell is clear there must
be some mistake in the date, as your letter to him of the 16th
announces a victory.   However it may be, I have directed
the Santa Dorotea and Alexander, (which last I stopped from
sailing for Malta till the event of this battle was known,) to
repair immediately to the Gulf of Especia, and to carry, as
far as is possible, your orders into execution.   But I own,
from what I guess must have been the terms of the Treaty
between the two Armies, that no Austrian Officer will allow
us to destroy any of the works, or to bring off the guns ; for
it would be a manifest breach of the Treaty—which is, I
suppose, permission for the Austrians to retire unmolested
into Tuscany, on the conditions mentioned in your order.
What is to become of Piedmont ?

distant important services, which renders it impossible to let the Foudroyant go to
England : her masts are made at Mahon.   It is likewise impossible I should permit
the Teresa to leave this station, if Acton does not go thither ; and I could not
consent to yielding a Frigate to a lesser application than that of the King.   I
am surprised to hear that the Princess Charlotte is in a bad condition.   I had
understood otherwise.   Now, my dear Lord, I think for the accommodation of those
I love, who are with you, they should get to Mahon instantly, (where I shall
soon be going,) and there the Seahorse is hourly expected with Sir R. Bickerton.
The Ship is instantly to return, and, of course, at their command.   Besides this,
there are many excellent Troop-ships, and two Store-ships, at the same place, now
under orders.   Any of them shall be directed to take in what may be required.   As
to yourself, the Princess Charlotte will take you, provided you persist in going
home, of which I hope your health does not stand in need.   Troubridge was at
Mahon, came here, and is returned to that Port.   He is quite content with the
Culloden.   If the Alexander is not gone to St. Especia, she may return to Malta
immediately until Theseus can get there.   Tell Madame Castelcicala and the Prince,
if they go to Mahon I will direct a Troop or Store-ship for them.   God knows, I
wish more was in my power for you all ; but really the late unfortunate events
make me tremble for all Italy.   You know there is a great force at Mahon, but no
General ; and I have been refused a single man, as usual.   I am, with my duty to
the Queen, and sincere regard to our friends, most assuredly yours,—KEITH."—
Autograph, in the Nelson Papers.

Two days afterwards, Lord Keith again wrote to Lord Nelson :

"Genoa, June 21st, 18 10.

" Most confidential,

" I have seen a man who has come from Buonaparte.   He, *Buonaparte*, said,
publicly, there's one Power still in Italy to be reduced, before I can give *it Peace*.
Pignatelli, &c., are with him.   Let the Queen go to Vienna as fast as she can.   If
the Fleet gets the start of ours a day, Sicily cannot hold out even that one day.
Yours, &c.,

" KEITH."

I keep the Foudroyant here, and some Neapolitan Vessels, ready to receive the Queen and Royal Family, should such an event be necessary. We shall, of course, soon see you here, which will give real pleasure to, my dear Lord, your faithful,

BRONTE NELSON OF THE NILE.

I send a copy of my order to Captain Downman.

TO CAPTAIN HUGH DOWNMAN, OF H. M. SHIP SANTA DOROTEA.

[Order-Book.]

Leghorn Roads, 19th June, 1800.

You are hereby required and directed to take under your command Captain Ormsby, with His Majesty's Ship the Alexander, and proceed with all possible dispatch to the Gulf of Especia, and carry into execution, as far as you are able, the orders of the Commander-in-Chief respecting the Fortifications there; a copy of which you have herewith. And you are to endeavour by all the means in your power, to induce the Austrian Commander to give you possession of the Fort St. Maria and other Garrisons in the Bay; the works of which you will destroy as far as you are able, and bring off the guns.

But, in the event of the Austrians refusing to deliver up the Forts to you, and persisting in delivering them up to the Enemy, you are, on their evacuation of them, or having performed the service of destroying the Forts, to return to Leghorn Roads, unless otherwise directed by the Commander-in-Chief,

BRONTE NELSON OF THE NILE.

TO THE RIGHT HONOURABLE LORD MINTO, VIENNA.

[Autograph, in the Minto Papers.]

My dear Lord,   Leghorn, June 21st, 1800.

Poor Frediani[9] has just been with me, and requested my
writing to you on the subject of his pension. I own he appears
to me to merit one as well as many others. He quitted Tuscany when the French entered it last time, and resided at
Palermo till their expulsion. If you, therefore, my dear Lord,
would assist this old gentleman, it would be most serviceable
to him : I therefore send you his letter to me. The shameful
scandalous terms entered into with Buonaparte, must ever
reflect disgrace on the Austrian arms, unless the signer and
adviser are *shot*, for nothing can justify a General, at the
head of 20,000 brave men for signing such a paper.[1] *I am mad.*
Our dear Queen of Naples is to-day very unwell, agitated by
these events. As soon as we can see her safely off, Sir
William, Lady Hamilton, and myself, pursue our route to
England, if Lord Keith pleases, in the Foudroyant. They
join me cordially in every kind and good wish to yourself,
Lady Minto, and family; and I beg you to believe me, my
dear Lord, ever your affectionate friend,

BRONTE NELSON OF THE NILE.

TO CAPTAIN SIR EDWARD BERRY, H.M. SHIP FOUDROYANT.

[From a Copy in the Nelson Papers.]

My dear Sir,   Leghorn, June 21st, 1800.

The Foudroyant must be kept ready for sea, and is to
proceed to Mahon : at present, it is very uncertain whether I

---

[9] Who had been Governor of the Province of Balagne, in Corsica, when Lord
Minto was Viceroy. Vide vol. i. p. 368.

[1] Apparently General Melas' Convention of the 16th of June, two days after the
battle of Marengo, with Buonaparte, by which a truce was agreed upon until the
return of a messenger from Vienna; and, in the meantime, the fortresses of Tor-
tona, Alexandria, Milan, Turin, Pizzighitone, Arona, and Placenza, with those of
Coni, Ceva, Savona, Urbino, and the city of Genoa, were to be delivered up to the
French. To ensure the fulfilment of those conditions, the Austrian Army was
permitted to march only by divisions, and at different times.

can go in her. Perhaps the Ship in sight may be Lord Keith. His Lordship believes reports of the Brest Fleet, which I give not the smallest credit to. Ever, my dear Sir, yours faithfully,

BRONTE NELSON OF THE NILE.

TO HIS HOLINESS THE POPE.

[Autograph draft, in the Nelson Papers.]

Holy Father, Leghorn, 24th June, 1800.

As an individual, who from his public situation has had an opportunity of using his utmost exertions to assist in bringing about the happy event of your Holiness's return to Rome, I presume to offer my most sincere congratulations on this occasion; and with my most fervent wishes and prayers that your residence may be blessed with health, and every comfort this world can afford.

Your Holiness will, I am sure, forgive my mentioning a circumstance which, although at the time it was spoken appeared impossible, yet the fact did happen. Father M'Cormick, a Friar, coming to the House of Sir William Hamilton, in September 1798, to congratulate me on the Battle of the Nile, said, (as can be testified,) ' What you have done is great, but you will do a greater thing—you will take Rome with your Ships.' And although I do not believe that the Father had the gift of prophecy, yet his guess was so extraordinary, and has turned out so exactly, that I could not in my conscience avoid telling your Holiness of it. I will now only trespass on your time, by assuring your Holiness with what respect I am your most obedient servant,

BRONTE NELSON OF THE NILE.

TO CAPTAIN LORD COCHRANE,[2] H. M. SLOOP SPEEDY.

[Letter-Book.]

Foudroyant, Leghorn Roads, 24th June, 1800.

My Lord,

I have received your letter, inclosing the orders you are under from the Right Honourable Lord Keith, the Com-

[2] Now Vice-Admiral the Earl of Dundonald.

mander-in-Chief, and in answer thereto, I beg to inform you
that I will not in any manner interfere with the orders you
have received from Lord Keith. Inclosed I return you the
order, and have the honour to be, &c.,

BRONTE NELSON OF THE NILE.

TO CAPTAIN DIODATO MICHEROUX, OF HIS SICILIAN MAJESTY'S SHIP MINERVA.

[Letter-Book.]

Foudroyant, Leghorn Roads, 24th June, 1800.

Sir,

I beg you will not consider that I, in the smallest manner,
interfere to prevent your carrying into execution any orders
you may be under from Lord Keith. I am, &c.,

BRONTE NELSON OF THE NILE.

TO VICE-ADMIRAL LORD KEITH, K.B.

[Letter-Book. On the 24th of June, Lord Keith arrived at Leghorn with the
Squadron.]

Leghorn, 24th June, 1800.

My dear Lord,

The idea of removing the Foudroyant has created an
alarm at the Palace, and I send you a letter from thence. If
Sir William and Lady Hamilton go home by land, it is my
intention to go with them; if by water, we shall be happy in
taking the best Ship we can get; but we are all pledged not
to quit the Royal Family till they are in perfect security. If
the Prince Castelcicala had not been wanted to attend the
Queen to this place, the Dorotea would certainly have, in
obedience, as I conceived, to your orders, gone direct to
England, as I understood the King of Naples had asked for a
Frigate to carry his Minister to England, and had sent one of
his Frigates in her room. To say the truth, I never thought
General Acton was to be the Minister, but the present person.
Near 300 packages are on board the Dorotea; but you will
now arrange all matters as you please. Both she and the
Alexander are still at Especia, and probably I shall see you
before then. I own I do not believe the Brest fleet will return

to sea; and if they do, the Lord have mercy on them, for our Fleet will not, I am sure.

I shall enter [no] further on the various subjects of your order, only to assure you that as little as possible do I ever interfere with your orders. I do not recollect I ever did; for I should not like it myself, and I never wrote what could be called a Public letter to Mr. Nepean, since I have been under your command; but I authorized Duckworth, when under my orders, to correspond directly with the Admiralty, and we know that the Admiralty sends orders to Junior Admirals on the station to perform particular services, without even mentioning the circumstance to the Commanding Flag-Officer on this station; therefore, the Admiralty themselves set the example of this new mode of communication to and from the Board. Hoping to see you, my dear Lord, before twenty-four hours pass over, believe me your obliged,

BRONTE NELSON OF THE NILE.

I hear all is done as you wish at Port Especia.

TO COMMODORE SARAIVA, HER MOST FAITHFUL MAJESTY'S SHIP VASCO DA GAMA.

[Letter-Book.]

Foudroyant, Leghorn Roads, 25th June, 1800.

Sir,

As there are many British Ships now at this place, which are ready for sea, and would wish to avail themselves of your offer to take them under Convoy, I have to request that you will be pleased to send me an answer, in writing, for the satisfaction of all concerned, whether you will protect all such British trade as may sail under your Convoy, from the Spaniards, as well as all other the Enemies of Great Britain, until their arrival at the Port of Lisbon? I have the honour to be, &c.,

BRONTE NELSON OF THE NILE.

TO COMMODORE SARAIVA, HER MOST FAITHFUL MAJESTY'S SHIP VASCO DA GAMA.

[Letter-Book.]

Foudroyant, Leghorn Roads, 25th June, 1800.

Sir,

I have received a letter from the Right Honourable Lord Keith, K.B., Commander-in-Chief, expressing his belief that the Combined Fleets of the Enemy are at sea, I therefore think it necessary to give you this information that you may regulate yourself accordingly. I have the honour to be, &c.

BRONTE NELSON OF THE NILE.

TO CAPTAIN SIR EDWARD BERRY, H. M. SHIP FOUDROYANT.

[Autograph, in the possession of Lady Berry. On the 28th of June, Lord Nelson shifted his Flag to the Alexander, as the Foudroyant[3] sailed for Minorca, to be refitted; and on the 11th of July he struck his Flag, and proceeded to Vienna, on his way to England. Two days before he left Leghorn, he received an order from Lord Keith, directing him to authorize the Queen of Naples, her family, and suite, to be received on board the Alexander, that they might be immediately conveyed to Palermo, Messina, or such Port in the Adriatic as might be best suited for her Majesty's accommodation. In the event of the Queen's landing at any Port for the purpose of proceeding to Vienna, and if Lord Nelson determined to strike his Flag and accompany her Majesty, he was to leave the Alexander in charge of Lieutenant Cribb, and send her to Malta to re-embark her guns, and proceed to Mahon to be refitted. If Lord Nelson resolved on returning to England by sea, he was permitted to do so in the Seahorse, or from Malta in the Alkmaar, or any other Troop Ship.]

Alexander, Leghorn, July 9th, 1800.

My dear Sir Edward,

I will not ask your civilities to the Prince Castelcicala; for I am sure of all your kindness towards him and his family.

---

[3] On quitting the Foudroyant, Lord Nelson received this Letter from his Barge's crew:—

" Foudroyant, 26th June, 1800.

" My Lord,

" It is with extreme grief that we find you are about to leave us. We have been along with you (although not in the same Ship) in every Engagement your Lordship has been in, both by Sea and Land; and most humbly beg of your Lordship to permit us to go to England, as your Boat's crew, in any Ship or Vessel, or in any way that may seem most pleasing to your Lordship. My Lord, pardon the rude style of Seamen, who are but little acquainted with writing, and believe us to be, my Lord, your ever humble and obedient servants,

" BARGE'S CREW OF THE FOUDROYANT."—*Original*, in the Nelson Papers.

We are again afloat, bound to Trieste ; but in what a different
Ship to the dear Foudroyant ; and I have not the least thing
for comfort of any kind or sort.　In one of my table drawers
are some letters copied by Miss Knight in a book : pray look
for it, and send it safely to England.　Leghorn is in a little
alarm : the people are strongly against the French, and have
seized the arms in order to defend the Town; but it does not
appear to me they will be supported.　May God bless you,
and all the Foudroyants, in which all with me join ; and
believe me ever your affectionate,

BRONTE NELSON OF THE NILE.

TO THE RIGHT HONOURABLE LORD MINTO.

[Autograph, in the Minto Papers.　In consequence of an attempt made by the
populace of Leghorn to detain the Queen and Royal Family, her Majesty became
alarmed, and they went on board the Alexander, Lord Nelson's Flag Ship, on the 9th
of July, but landed again the next day, and set off for Florence, on their way to
Ancona.　Lord Nelson, Sir William and Lady Hamilton, and Miss Knight, followed
on the ensuing day.　Clarke and M'Arthur (vol. ii. p. 255) notice very briefly Lord
Nelson's journey to England.　Harrison (vol. ii. p. 249) has, however, supplied
many particulars ; but the most interesting account is in Miss Knight's letters to
Sir Edward Berry, now in the possession of Lady Berry, with whose permission the
following extracts are given :—

" Leghorn, July 2nd, 1800.

"Dear Sir,

" The very great, indeed, I may say, fraternal care you had the goodness to take of
me while I was on board the Foudroyant, and the very sincere esteem I shall
always have for Sir Edward Berry, induces me to trouble you with these few lines,
as you will be desirous to hear of Lord Nelson, and the plan proposed for the party.
The Queen wishes, if possible, to prosecute her journey.　Lady Hamilton cannot
bear the thought of going by sea; and, therefore, nothing but impracticability will
prevent our going to Vienna.　Lord Nelson is well, and keeps up his spirits
amazingly.　Sir William appears broken, distressed, and harassed.

" July 16th.—It is, at length, decided that we go by land ; and I feel all the
dangers and difficulties to which we shall be exposed.　Think of our embarking on
board small Austrian Vessels at Ancona, for Trieste, as part of a land journey ! to
avoid the danger of being on board an English Man-of-War, where everything is
commodious, and equally well arranged for defence and comfort; but the die is cast,
and go we must.　Lord Nelson is going on an expedition he disapproves, and
against his own convictions, because he has promised the Queen, and that others
advise her.　I pity the Queen.　Prince Belmonte directs the march; and Lady
Hamilton, though she does not like him, seconds his proposals, because she hates
the sea, and wishes to visit the different Courts of Germany.　Sir William says *he*
shall die by the way, and he looks so ill, that I should not be surprised if he did.
I am astonished that the Queen, who is a sensible woman, should consent to run so
great a risk ; but I can assure you, that neither she nor the Princesses forget their

great obligations to you. If I am not detained in a French prison, or do not die upon the road, you shall hear from me again."

"Ancona, 24th July, 1800.—As I find delays succeed each other, and England still recedes from us, I will not omit, at least, informing you of our adventures. We left Leghorn the day after I wrote to you by Mr. Tyson, and owing more to good fortune than to prudence, arrived in twenty-six hours at Florence, after passing within *two miles* of the French advanced posts. After a short stay, we proceeded on our way to this place. At Castel San Giovanni, the coach, in which were Lord Nelson, and Sir William and Lady Hamilton, was overturned; Sir William and Lady Hamilton were hurt, but not dangerously. The wheel was repaired, but broke again at Arezzo—the Queen two days' journey before them, and news of the French Army advancing rapidly, it was therefore decided that they should proceed, and Mrs. Cadogan and I remain with the broken carriage, as it was of less consequence we should be left behind, or taken, than they. We were obliged to stay three days, to get the coach repaired; and, providentially, Arezzo was the place, as it is the most loyal city in Tuscany; and every care, attention, and kindness that humanity can dictate, and cordiality and good manners practise, were employed in our favour." . . . . "Just as we were going to set off, we received accounts of the French being very near the road where we had to pass, and of its being also infested with Neapolitan deserters; but at the same moment arrived a party of Austrians, and the Officers gave us two soldiers as a guard. We travelled night and day; the roads are almost destroyed, and the misery of the inhabitants is beyond description. At length, however, we arrived at Ancona, and found that the Queen had given up the idea of going in the Bellona, an Austrian Frigate, fitted up with silk hangings, carpets, and eighty beds for her reception, and now meant to go with a Russian Squadron of three Frigates and a Brig. I believe she judged rightly; for there had been a mutiny on board the Bellona, and, for the sake of accommodation, she had reduced her guns to twenty-four, while the French, in possession of the Coast, arm Trabaccoli, and other light Vessels, that could easily surround and take her. This Russian Squadron is commanded by Count Voinovitsch, a Dalmatian, who having seen his people ill-treated, and their colours destroyed by the Germans last year at the Siege of Ancona, made a vow never to come ashore, and keeps it religiously, for he has not returned the Queen's visit. I fancy we shall sail to-morrow night or the next morning. Mrs. Cadogan and I are to be on board one of the Frigates, commanded by an old man named Messer, a native of England, who once served under Lord Howe, and has an excellent reputation. The rest of our party go with the Queen, and say they shall be very uncomfortable. Lord Nelson talks often of the Foudroyant, whatever is done to turn off the conversation; and last night he was talking with Captain Messer of the manœuvres he intended to make in case he accepted of another command. In short, I perceive that his thoughts turn towards England, and I hope, and believe he will be happy there. The Queen and her daughters have been very kind to me, especially when I was ill; and poor Sir William suffered much when he left me at Arezzo. The Queen speaks of you often, and always with the highest esteem. Our party is very helpless; and though it is their own fault that they have brought themselves into these difficulties, I cannot help pitying them, and have the comfort to be of some use to them. Lord Nelson has been received with acclamations in all the towns of the Pope's States. Success attend you. Where shall *we* be on the 1st of August? The Queen asked me for the Christian and Surname of all the Captains of the Nile. I am ashamed of the length of this letter, but it is pleasant to forget oneself for some moments, and renew a quarter-deck conversation. Our cots are ready, and the carriages on board, or I should not have had spirits to write so much."

" Trieste, 9th of August, 1800.—As I know you will be anxious to hear how Lord Nelson proceeds on his journey, and as new delays continually occur, I will not refuse an opportunity offered me by Mr. Anderson, the Vice-Consul. Perhaps I am a little interested in the affair; for, as I have small comfort in my present situation, my thoughts willingly recur to the Mediterranean, where there were always resources to be found. I told you we were become humble enough to rejoice at a Russian Squadron conveying us across the Adriatic; but had we sailed, as was first intended, in the Imperial Frigate, we should have been taken by eight Trabaccoli, which the French armed on purpose at Pisaro. Sir William and Lady Hamilton, and Lord Nelson, give a miserable account of their sufferings on board the Commodore's Ship, (Count Voinovitsch.) He was ill in his cot; but his First Lieutenant, a Neapolitan, named Capaci, was, it seems, the most insolent and ignorant of beings. Think what Lord Nelson must have felt! He says a gale of wind would have sunk the Ship. I, with Mrs. Cadogan, came in another Ship, commanded, as I believe I told you, by an Englishman, a Captain Messer, a plain, good man, who behaved with distinguished bravery last year at the siege of Ancona, and who was kind and attentive beyond description." . . . . " Poor Sir William Hamilton has been so ill, that the physicians had almost given him up: he is now better, and I hope we shall be able to set off to-morrow night for Vienna. The Queen and thirty-four of her suite have had fevers: you can form no idea of the *helplessness* of the party. How we shall proceed on our long journey, is to me a problem; but we shall certainly get on as fast as we can; for the very precarious state of Sir William's health has convinced everybody that it is necessary he should arrange his affairs." . . . . . " Poor Lord Nelson, whose only comfort was in talking of ships and harbours with Captain Messer, has had a bad cold; but is almost well, and, I think, anxious to be in England. He is followed by thousands when he goes out, and for the illumination that is to take place this evening, there are many *Viva Nelsons*, prepared. He seems affected whenever he speaks of *you*, and often sighs out, ' Where is the Foudroyant ?' "

From Trieste the party proceeded to Vienna, where the Queen of Naples had arrived two days before them. Lord Nelson, &c. quitted Vienna, according to Harrison, on the 26th of September, and passed his forty-second birthday, the 29th of September, at Prague, when a grand fête was given by the Archduke Charles. They came down the Elbe to Dresden, thence to Magdeburg and Hamburgh, where he became personally known to General Dumourrier, and they landed at Yarmouth on the 6th of November. During the journey Lord Nelson everywhere received the most gratifying attentions; and Harrison relates many anecdotes, showing the interest he created.]

Friday morning, Vienna, August 22nd, 1800.

My dear Lord,

Many thanks for your kind note of this morning. We will settle the place of our meeting when we meet at dinner: the time is not the best chosen for either of us. The Queen of Naples has desired anxiously Lady Hamilton to bring you to her this afternoon. The Empress would see us yesterday evening, and we had the noise of five fine healthy children for an hour. With all our best wishes to you and Lady Minto, believe me, my dear Lord, as ever, your truly obliged and affectionate,

BRONTE NELSON OF THE NILE.

TO THE RIGHT HONOURABLE LORD MINTO.

[Autograph, in the Minto Papers.]

September 6th, 1800.

My dear Lord,

Many thanks for your kind note ; and we must all approve of the conduct of Captain Ricketts:[3] it will teach the Cisalpines that it is dangerous to touch edged tools. We have seen the Queen this morning. The Emperor left Town at six o'clock; the Empress very melancholy, but the Queen, I think, reconciled to the propriety of the Emperor's going to the Army : but it will be very difficult to make her, in any degree, bear Thugut. She thinks he will in the end deceive us. I hope it is true that our troops are landed in Holland : it must create a powerful diversion in favour of the Austrian army. I long for a battle, and the sooner after the Armistice the better. We are all well, and wish for your company, and beg our best regards to Lady Minto, and all your family. Believe me for ever, your truly obliged and affectionate,

BRONTE NELSON OF THE NILE.

TO THE RIGHT HONOURABLE LORD MINTO.

[Autograph, in the Minto Papers.]

Friday Morning, [September 19th, 1800.]

My dear Lord,

We cannot dine with you to-day; but will, with much pleasure, on Saturday, the day before our departure. I wish, my

----

[3] Captain William Ricketts of the El Corso Sloop, with the Pigmy Cutter, was sent by Lord Keith to destroy some Vessels in the Port of Cesenatico on the 26th of August, which was fully accomplished by their boats, under Lieutenant James Lucas Yeo, (who died, a Post Captain, and a Knight Commander of the Bath, in August 1818.) Captain Ricketts then sent on shore the following Note:—

"TO THE INHABITANTS OF CESENATICO.

"The treachery of your Municipality, in causing to be arrested an Officer with dispatches, has been long known to the British Admiral in these seas. The Municipality may now sadly know that the severity of judgment long delayed is always exemplary. That the innocent suffer with the guilty, though much to be regretted, is the natural feature of war ; and the more terrible the infliction on this occasion, the more striking the example should prove to surrounding municipalities.

"W. RICKETTS."

dear friend, you would visit the neglected Queen of Naples : she will be glad to see and talk with you. She is scarcely ever out in the afternoon between five and six. Our best compliments to all in your house. Believe me ever, yours,

BRONTE NELSON OF THE NILE.[4]

TO EVAN NEPEAN, ESQ., ADMIRALTY.

[Original, in the Admiralty. Lord Nelson and his friends arrived at Yarmouth on the 6th of November ; and it being the first time he had landed in England since the Battle of the Nile, he was received with enthusiastic admiration. The instant he stepped on shore " the populace assembled in crowds to greet the gallant Hero of the Nile ; and, taking the horses from his carriage, drew him to the Wrestler's Inn amidst bursts of applause. The Mayor and Corporation immediately waited on his Lordship, and presented him with the Freedom of the Town, some time since voted to him for his eminent services. The infantry in the Town paraded before the inn where he lodged, with their regimental band, &c. &c., firing feux-de-joie of musketry and ordnance till midnight. The Corporation in procession, with the respectable Officers of the Navy, went to church with him, accompanied by Sir William and Lady Hamilton, to join in thanksgiving. On leaving the Town, the corps of cavalry unexpectedly drew up, saluted, and followed the carriage, not only to the Town's end, but to the boundary of the County. All the Ships in the harbour had their colours flying."—*Naval Chronicle*, vol. iv. p. 429.]

Sir,   Yarmouth, November 6th, 1800.

I beg you will acquaint their Lordships of my arrival here this day, and that my health being perfectly re-established, it is my wish to serve immediately; and I trust that my necessary journey by land from the Mediterranean will not be considered as a wish to be a moment out of active service. I have the honour to be, &c.,

BRONTE NELSON OF THE NILE.

TO MARSH AND CREED, NAVY AGENTS.

[Autograph, in the possession of J. Baas, Esq.

Yarmouth, Nov. 7th, 1800.

£50 for His Worship the Mayor, to be distributed by him.

5 Guineas for the Town Clerk.

1 Guinea for the Officer.

To be paid by Mr. Warmington for Lord Nelson of the Nile.

---

[4] To this Note Lady Hamilton added the following lines :—" Do, my dear Lord, go to the Queen. She told me yesterday she would be glad to see you. You need not send—go to her apartment.—E. H."

TO THE REVEREND DIXON HOSTE.

[Autograph, in the possession of Captain Sir William Hoste, Bart. Lord Nelson arrived at Nerot's Hotel, in St. James-street, on Saturday the 8th of November, where he found Lady Nelson and his venerable father; and in the evening went to the Admiralty to see Lord Spencer. His reception by Lady Nelson is said to have been extremely cold and mortifying to his feelings; but the little that need be said on this painful subject will be found in a subsequent page.

The next day being Sunday, the Lord Mayor's Feast was kept on Monday the 10th of November, to which Lord Nelson was invited. At Ludgate-hill, the mob took the horses from his carriage, and drew him to Guildhall amidst repeated huzzas. All the way he passed along Cheapside, he was greeted by the Ladies from the windows with their handkerchiefs, and the loudest acclamations. After the usual toasts had been drunk, he was requested to come forward, that he might receive the Sword lately voted to him. Lord Nelson then presented himself, taking his station, as requested, under a triumphal arch, when he was addressed by the Chamberlain of the City; to which he replied—

" Sir, it is with the greatest pride and satisfaction that I receive from the Honourable Court this testimony of their approbation of my conduct; and, with this very Sword, [holding it up] I hope soon to aid in reducing our implacable and inveterate Enemy to proper and due limits ; without which, this Country can neither hope for, nor expect a solid, honourable, and permanent Peace."]

Dover Street, November 18th, 1800.

My dear Sir,

Many thanks for your kind letter. Your son deserved more than I could give him : he ought to have been Post, and would long since, had I retained the command. He will do me and the [Service] credit in whatever situation he is placed. Excuse this short line, and with my best compliments to Mrs. Hoste, believe me, your most obedient servant,

NELSON OF THE NILE.

TO MRS. SUCKLING.

[From " The Athenæum."]

My dear Madam,   November 18th, 1800.

It is my full intention to come to you some morning very soon, of which I will give you notice. I regret exceedingly not having had the pleasure of seeing you ; but my time hitherto has not been my own. I beg my best respects to Miss Rumsey ; and believe me ever, your obliged,

NELSON OF THE NILE.

I congratulate you and the family on the good sale of the Suffolk estate.

TO HERCULES ROSS, ESQ., ROSSIE CASTLE, NORTH BRITAIN.

[Copy, in the Nelson Papers. On the 20th of November, Lord Nelson took his Seat in the House of Lords. He was introduced in his Robes between Lords Grenville and Romney, with the usual formalities, and " was placed in his due place next below the Lord Seaforth."—*Journal of the House of Lords*, vol. xlii. p. 661.]

London, November 21st, 1800.

My dear Ross,

The remembrance of all your goodness to me is, perhaps, stronger engraved on my mind, at this moment, than at any former period, because I have seldom seen such true kindness, as you have for years shown me. I promise never to visit Scotland, without coming to you. Mrs. Parish and her sons were truly kind to us, and we regretted leaving our friends at Hamburgh. This place of London but ill suits my disposition. However, till the war is finished, I shall not be much from my proper element. The St. Josef[5] is to be my Flag-ship. You must excuse a short letter, but believe that I am, as ever, your obliged and affectionate friend,

NELSON.

I beg my best compliments to Mrs. Parish, and Lady N. joins me in the same to Mrs. Ross.

TO CAPTAIN SIR EDWARD BERRY.

[From a Copy in the Nelson Papers.]

December 5th, 1800.

My dear Sir Edward,

Many thanks for your letter : you know how I am fixed with Hardy, who could not get a Ship. I wrote immediately to Lord Spencer, who says, that if the Princess Charlotte[6] is good, you have a fair chance for her, and that he shall be happy to show his regard for you. Therefore, I write this

---

⁵ Which he had captured at the Battle of St. Vincent. He did not, however, hoist his Flag until the 17th of January, 1801.

⁶ Note by Sir Edward Berry:—" Lord Spencer ordered the Princess Charlotte to be repaired : when I had her nearly ready, I was superseded by F. Gardner (a senior Officer), and appointed to the Ruby by Lord St. Vincent or Sir Thomas Troubridge."

scrawl to say how you stand. I hope we shall serve together, and mine will not, I hope, be an *inactive* service. My dear Sir Edward, your faithful servant,

NELSON.

P.S.—The Duke of Clarence spoke much of you this day.

TO THE REV. ROBERT ROLFE,[6] SAHAM, WATTON, NORFOLK.

[Autograph in the possession of the Reverend Robert Rolfe. Lord Nelson, accompanied by Sir William and Lady Hamilton, visited Mr. Beckford, at Fonthill, on the 20th of December. An account of his reception by the Corporation of Salisbury, of the festivities to his honour, and of his interview with some sailors who had served under him at Teneriffe and the Nile, will be found in the *Gentleman's Magazine*, vol. lxxi. pp. 206, 297.]

December 16th, 1800.

My dear Sir,

Believe me it has not proceeded from inattention or want of regard that I have not answered your truly kind letter, on my first arrival; but the goodness of my friends has excused me, and amongst the foremost of them I hope you will ever stand. As I am preparing for new services, and under my loss of a hand, you must forgive my writing so short a letter, and with my best compliments to Mrs. Rolfe, your good mother and sister, believe me, as ever, your affectionate cousin,

NELSON.

TO JOHN LOCKER, ESQ.

[From a Copy in the possession of Edward Hawke Locker, Esq.]

27th December, 1800.

My dear John,

From my heart do I condole with you on the great and irreparable loss we have all sustained in the death of your dear, worthy Father[7]—a man whom to know was to love, and

---

[6] His first cousin, whom he appointed his Domestic Chaplain on the 6th of July, 1801—namely, son of the Reverend Robert Rolfe, Rector of Hilborough, by Alice Nelson, (vide vol. i. pp. 17, 18.) Mr. Rolfe is still living.

[7] His old friend and Commander, Commodore William Locker, Lieutenant-Governor of Greenwich Hospital, who died on the 26th of December, 1800, aged seventy, and was buried at Addington in Kent.

those who only heard of him honoured. The greatest consolation to us, his friends who remain, is, that he has left a character for honour and honesty which none can surpass, and very, very few attain. That the posterity of the righteous will prosper we are taught to believe; and on no occasion can it be more truly verified than from my dear much lamented friend; and that it may be realized in you, and your sister, and brothers, is the fervent prayer of, my dear John, your afflicted friend,

NELSON.

TO JOHN LOCKER, ESQ.

[From a Copy in the possession of Edward Hawke Locker, Esq.]

December 29th, 1800.

My dear John,
    I will most assuredly attend the remains of your dear Father in the way and time you may fix. I shall attend in my own carriage. Ever yours most faithfully,

NELSON.

TO LIEUTENANT-COLONEL SUCKLING.

[From the " Athenæum." The date is not given, but it was probably written towards the end of 1800, soon after Lord Nelson's return to England.]

My dear Suckling,
    I deferred answering your truly interesting letter, till I could see a little into my affairs, and, on your account, I am sorry to say, that I find myself in debt to my Agents; however, I can find money's worth to pay them, and I hope to be able soon to advance you 300l. As to getting a place, you must see I can neither do it for my father or brothers; but do you cheer up, and don't be cast down. Sensible men will not value you the less for not being at *this* moment rich; and you may, my dear Suckling, always rely on all the kindness in my power to show you, not only on your own account, but from my real affection to your dear good father, and believe me ever your affectionate,

NELSON.

Compliments to Mrs. Suckling.

TO MRS. SUCKLING.

[From " The Athenæum." On the 1st of January, 1801, in a general promotion of Admirals, Lord Nelson was made a Vice-Admiral of the Blue, and he hoisted his Flag in the St. Josef, at Plymouth, on the 17th of that month, having Captain Hardy as his Captain, in the Channel Fleet, under Admiral the Earl of St. Vincent. The " Naval Chronicle," (vol. v. p. 94,) states, that when Lord Nelson's Flag was hoisted, it was " cheered by the whole Fleet."]

[Post-mark, 7th January, 1801.]

My dear Madam,

I am truly concerned that it has not been in my power to come and see you at Hampstead ; but the days have been so short, and I have been so pressed for time, that this must plead my excuse; and I am just on the eve of going to Portsmouth, therefore I fear it will be the Spring before I can do myself that pleasure. I rejoice that the estates have sold so well, and as Mr. Hume[9] tells me that I have given him full authority to do the needful, it is not necessary for me to act beyond what I have done. Respecting the legacy left by my dear Uncle, I have to request you will pay it to Mrs. William Nelson, who is now with my brother, at No. 6, Stafford Street, Dover Street, and her receipt shall be a full discharge. I beg my compliments to Miss Rumsey, and that you will ever believe me your obliged servant,

NELSON.

TO LADY NELSON.

[From Clarke and M'Arthur, vol. ii. p. 256. After much uneasiness and recrimination on both sides, Lord Nelson took his final leave of Lady Nelson on the 13th of January, and soon after left London for Plymouth. On quitting her, he emphatically said, " I call God to witness there is nothing in you or your conduct I wish otherwise." He was accompanied to Southampton by his brother, the Reverend William Nelson, and from that place wrote the following Note :]

Southampton, 13th January, 1801.

My dear Fanny,

We are arrived, and heartily tired ; and with kindest regards to my father and all the family, believe me your affectionate

NELSON.

[9] Co-executor with himself to his uncle, Mr. Suckling. Vide vol. iii. p. 458.

TO EVAN NEPEAN, ESQ., ADMIRALTY.

[Letter-Book.]

San Josef, Plymouth, 17th January, 1801.

Sir,

I beg you will be pleased to acquaint the Lords Commissioners of the Admiralty, that I have this day hoisted my Flag on board his Majesty's Ship San Josef, in obedience to their order of the 9th instant.

I have to request that their Lordships will not consider my necessary coming from Italy as a dereliction of the service, but only a remove from the Mediterranean to the Channel Fleet, and that, therefore, they will be pleased to give directions for my being paid full pay up to the present day.[1] I am, &c.,

NELSON.

TO ADMIRAL THE EARL OF ST. VINCENT, K.B.

[Autograph, in the possession of Vice-Admiral Sir William Parker, Bart., G.C.B.]

January 17th, 1801.

My dear Lord,

My Flag is up on board the San Josef, and Wednesday next I have fixed for her going to Cawsand Bay, where, as she must be two days or three, she shall be finished by the joiners, who have not yet begun my cabin; but I shall live in Hardy's. I have to thank you for your note; and, as I had just finished our conversation about the Baltic, I enclosed [it] to him.[2] I beg my most respectful compliments to Lady St. Vincent, Mrs. Cary,[3] and all your happy party; and believe me, my dear Lord, your obliged and affectionate,

NELSON.

I have received the inclosed from a brother Freeman of Exeter. If the application is *true*, I am sure you will feel what is proper.

[1] He was informed that his request could not be complied with.
[2] Earl Spencer.
[3] Lord St. Vincent appears to have been then on a visit to George Cary, Esq., at Tor Abbey, near Dartmouth.

TO THE RIGHT HONOURABLE EARL SPENCER, K.G.

[From a Copy in the possession of the Right Honourable John Wilson Croker.]

Plymouth Dock, 17th January, 1801.

My dear Lord,

I was with Lord St. Vincent yesterday, when Sir Hyde Parker's letter arrived, announcing his appointment to the North Sea command. This naturally led to a confidential communication as to my views and present situation, and he gave me leave to tell you our conversation. Next to getting a command which I was a candidate for, whenever Lord Keith gave up his, of course my pleasure would have been to serve under him, but that circumstances had so altered since my arrival, that it was almost certain I should go to the Baltic ; and I related our communication on this subject. The Earl was very handsome to me, and hoped that, by a temporary absence of a few months, I should not lose my San Josef, the finest Ship in the world; and only one voice points out the Formidable as the Ship fittest for me, for real and active service. I told him the King's desire about Captain Grindall,[4] to which he desired me to say, as his opinion, that Captain G. could suffer no inconvenience in keeping the San Josef in order, till my return, or some new arrangement takes place. He mentioned several other Ships, degrees below the Formidable, but entreated I would not go in the Windsor Castle; that she was such a leewardly Ship, that he knew she would break my heart; for that I should often be forced to anchor on a lee shore, and never could lead a Division in a narrow Sea, like the Baltic. Having related this conversation, I shall leave the subject, as far as relates to myself. It naturally enlarged on the best means of destroying the Danes, &c., &c., and I found him clearly of opinion that 10,000 troops ought to be embarked, to get at the Danish Arsenal. I told him this matter had been canvassed with your Lordship, but the difficulty was, where to find such a General as was fit for the service, to which he, of course, was forced to acquiesce ; but General Simcoe seemed the only man.

---

[4] Afterwards Vice-Admiral Sir Richard Grindall, K.C.B., who commanded the Prince at Trafalgar, and died in May, 1820.

Having stated this conversation, I have only to add, what you, my dear Lord, are fully satisfied of, that the service of my King and Country is the object nearest my heart; and that a First-Rate, or Sloop of War, is a matter of perfect indifference to your most faithful and obliged

NELSON.

The San Josef, as far as relates to Captain Hardy, is ready for sea, but the Dock-yard have not done with her. My cabin is not yet finished, of course—nor even painted; but that I do not care about: I shall live in Captain Hardy's. My wish is to get her to Torbay, and, in seven days alongside the Ville de Paris. She will be perfection, and I leave myself to your friendship.

The note from Lord St. Vincent is this moment arrived.

TO ADMIRAL THE EARL OF ST. VINCENT, K.B.

[From Tucker's Memoirs of Earl St. Vincent, vol. ii. p. 172.]

Plymouth Dock, January 20th, 1801.

May this day, my dear Lord, which I am told is your birthday,[5] come round as often as life is comfortable, and may your days be comfortable for many, many years. Almost my only ungratified wish is, to see you alongside the French Admiral, and myself supporting you in the San Josef. We may be beat, but I am confident the world will believe we could not help it. I called on Troubridge's sister this day, and I find I have given great offence in not going to the Long Room last night; but my promise is solemnly made not to go to an Assembly till a Peace. The people in the Yard did not believe that I wished to get to sea till the winter was worn more away, and now all are bustle. I hope five cables will be on board this night, and I have borrowed the St. George's messenger and stern cable. My cabin was finished yesterday, but I shall get into Hardy's. There are no orders for completing the Ship, or for his movements. To-

---

[5] Lord St. Vincent was born on the *ninth* of January, 1734, old style, which became the *twentieth* on the alteration of the Calendar, in 1752.

T 2

morrow morning will produce them. With every kind wish to Lady St. Vincent, Mrs. Cary, and all your cheerful party, believe me ever, my dear Lord, your obliged and affectionate, NELSON.

_____

TO SIR EDWARD BERRY, KENSINGTON.

[Autograph, in the possession of Lady Berry. On the 21st of January, Lord Nelson arrived at Exeter from Plymouth, on his way to Tor Abbey, to meet Lord St. Vincent. He was received in that City with every mark of honour, and the Mayor and Corporation conferred upon him its Freedom, which appears (vide p. 273) to have been voted to him some time before. In reply to a complimentary address from the Recorder, Lord Nelson said, "Whatever merit may have been attributed to him in the Action of the Nile, it was only for having executed the orders intrusted to him; that those orders came to him from his Commander-in-Chief who had received them from the Lords of the Admiralty. They were very concise: it was to take, burn, sink, and destroy the French Fleet wherever he should meet them, and he had only been the instrument employed to effect this service." He assured those around him, from his own knowledge, "that to this war, however burdensome it may have been considered, we owed the blessings we now experienced, in the enjoyment of our liberties, laws, and religion; and, although we might at one day hope to be at peace with France, we must ever be at war with French principles."

On the 24th of January, the Corporation of Plymouth likewise voted Lord Nelson the Freedom of their Borough in a silver Box.]

San Josef, Cawsand Bay, January 26th, 1801.

My dear Sir Edward,

I yesterday received your kind letter of the 20th, and I beg, if you think the £200 is enough for poor dear Miller's[6] monument,[7] that you will direct Flaxman to instantly proceed about

---

[6] Captain Miller, who was blown up in the Theseus. Vide vol. ii. p. 465.

[7] Sir Edward Berry wrote, on the 28th of March, the following Note to Sir Thomas Troubridge on this subject:—

"Princess Charlotte, Woolwich, 28th March, 1801.

"Dear Sir Thomas,—Amongst the many reflections that can possibly occur, that of remembering our old and dear friend stands foremost; and truly happy I am to hear you and Lord St. Vincent approve of the monument for our late dear coadjutor Miller—a man whom we knew, and there was but one opinion of him. £500 will by no means be too much, if the Captains of the 14th of February subscribe, and those of Sir Sidney Smith; and my opinion is, they _ought to have that honour_, but none but brother officers; and _I_ would not even allow Davison to subscribe, but that you will be a better judge of. Sir James and Sir Thomas Thompson are the only subscribers I know of, though no doubt can be entertained of all hands, _nem. con._ I have corresponded with the Dean of St. Paul's on the subject, who is very polite, and will do what is proper on the occasion. Flaxman is the artist, and in him we may all trust. I want to get the precise date, and a few other documents, and then we can form an inscription. Of course our aim _must be simplicity_. Truth needs no ornament; Miller requires none, himself was all. . . . .—E. BERRY."

it, and as far as that sum, if no one subscribes, I will be answerable. If those of the 14th February[8] are to be allowed the honour of subscribing, I then think we ought to subscribe £500—a less sum would not be proper for such a body. Pray let me know the intended subscription, for we must take care not to say too much, or too little. The language must be plain, as if flowing from the heart of one of us Sailors who have fought with him. Whatever you arrange in this matter, I shall agree to. If our friend Davison will receive the subscription, and take the matter in hand, it can be nowhere so well placed. I am truly concerned about Mr. Fellowes,[9] but what can I do ? I have signed every paper for the victualling those men which he says stop his accounts, and have told him that as Lord Hood and myself were then in London, we could clear him of any blame for victualling men by our order. I will with pleasure do anything I am desired : I would lend him money, but in truth I have it not.

As far as we can judge of the San Josef, she will answer all our expectations. She is ready this moment to go alongside the finest Ship out of France ; and on such a happy occasion I can assure you that there is not that man in the service I would sooner select as my second than yourself. My brother is with me, and joins in best respects to Mrs. Godfrey, Lady Berry, and all your family, and believe me as ever, your most sincere friend,

NELSON AND BRONTE.

TO REAR-ADMIRAL COLLINGWOOD.

[Autograph, in the possession of the Hon. Mrs. Newnham Collingwood. Admiral Collingwood's Flag, as Rear-Admiral of the Red, was flying on board the Barfleur 98. He was hourly expecting Mrs. Collingwood at Plymouth, when orders arrived for him to proceed immediately to Torbay. They met, however, for a few hours, and in a letter to Mr. Blackett, his father-in-law, on the 6th of February, Admiral Colling-wood said :

" Sarah will have told you how and when we met. It was a joy to me that I can not describe, and repaid me, short as our interview was, for a world of woe which I was suffering on her account. I had been reckoning on the possibility of her arrival that Tuesday, when about two o'clock I received an express to go to sea im-

---

⁸ The Captains who were at the Battle of St. Vincent.

⁹ Mr. Thomas Fellowes, who was Purser of the Agamemnon in 1793. Vide vol. i. pp. 300, 483, and post.

mediately, with all the Ships that were ready; and had we not been then engaged at a Court-Martial, I might have got out that day; but this business delayed me till near night, and I determined to wait on shore until eight o'clock, for the chance of their arrival. I went to dine with Lord Nelson, and while we were at dinner their arrival was announced to me. I flew to the inn where I had desired my wife to come, and found her and little Sarah as well after their journey as if it had lasted only for the day. No greater happiness is human nature capable of than was mine that evening, but at dawn we parted, and I went to sea."—*Memoirs of Lord Collingwood*, vol. i. p. 111.

The following allusion to Lord Nelson, in a letter from Admiral Collingwood to Mr. Blackett, dated on the 25th of January, is remarkable:—"Lord Nelson is here, and I think he will probably come and live with me when the weather will allow him; but he does not get in and out of Ships well with one arm. He gave me an account of his reception at Court, which was not very flattering, after having been the adoration of that of Naples. His Majesty merely asked him if he had recovered his health; and then, without waiting for an answer, turned to General ——, and talked to him near half an hour in great good humour. It could not be about his successes."—*Memoirs of Lord Collingwood*, vol. i. p. 110.]

Tuesday, [27th January, 1801.]

My dear Friend,

I truly feel for you, and as much for dear Mrs. Collingwood. How sorry I am! For Heaven's sake do not think I had the gift of foresight; but something told me so it would be. Can't you contrive and stay to-night? it will be a comfort, if only to see your family one hour. Therefore had you not better stay on shore, and wait for her? Ever, my dear Collingwood, believe me, your affectionate and faithful friend,

NELSON AND BRONTE.

If they would have manned me, and sent me off, it would have been real pleasure to me. How cross are the fates!

TO EVAN NEPEAN, ESQ., ADMIRALTY.

[Letter-Book.]

San Josef, Plymouth, 28th January, 1801.

Sir,

I have to acknowledge the receipt of their Lordships' order of the 26th instant, directing me to put myself under the command of Admiral the Earl of St. Vincent. I am, &c.,

NELSON.

TO LADY HAMILTON.

[From " Lord Nelson's Letters to Lady Hamilton," vol. i. p. 20.]

January 28th, 1801.

What a fool I was, my dear Lady Hamilton, to direct that your cheering letters should be directed for Brixham! I feel, this day, truly miserable, in not having them; and, I fear, they will not come till to-morrow's post. What a blockhead, to believe any person is so active as myself! I have this day got my orders, to put myself under Lord St. Vincent's command; but, as no order is arrived to man the Ship, it must be Friday night, or Saturday morning, before she can sail for Torbay. Direct my letters, now, to Brixham. My eye is very bad.[1] I have had the Physician of the Fleet to examine it. He has directed me not to write, (and yet I am forced this day to write Lord Spencer, St. Vincent, Davison, about my law-suit, Troubridge, Mr. Locker, &c., but you are the only female I write to;) not to eat anything but the most simple food; not to touch wine or porter; to sit in a dark room; to have green shades for my eyes—(will you, my dear friend, make me one or two?—nobody else shall;)—and to bathe them in cold water every hour. I fear, it is the writing has brought on this complaint. My eye is like blood; and the film so extended, that I only see from the corner farthest from my nose. What a fuss about my complaints! But, being so far from my sincere friends, I have leisure to brood over them.

I have this moment seen Mrs. Thompson's friend. Poor fellow! he seems very uneasy and melancholy. He begs you to be kind to her! and I have assured him of your readiness to relieve the dear, good woman; and believe me, for ever, my dear Lady, your faithful, attached, and affectionate,

NELSON AND BRONTE.

I will try and write the Duke[2] a line. My brother intended to have gone off to-morrow afternoon: but this half order may stop him.

---

[1] While at Plymouth, Lord Nelson suffered severely from ophthalmia in his only remaining eye, with acute pain and want of sight. He was attended by Dr. Trotter, Physician of the Fleet, who soon effected his recovery.

[2] Apparently the Duke of Hamilton.

TO ADMIRAL THE EARL OF ST. VINCENT, K.B.
COMMANDER-IN-CHIEF.

[Original, in the possession of Vice-Admiral Sir William Parker, Bart., G.C.B., and Letter Book. On the 28th of January, Lord Nelson informed the Earl of St. Vincent that he had received the directions of the Admiralty to place himself under his command.]

San Josef, Plymouth, 29th January, 1801.

My Lord,

I have the honour to acknowledge the receipt of your Lordship's two orders of yesterday's date (together with the several documents which accompanied them) directing me to put myself under your command, and as soon as his Majesty's Ship San Josef shall be in all respects ready for sea, to proceed in her to Torbay. I have the honour to be, &c.,

NELSON.

[Added by Lord Nelson, in his own hand.]

P.S.—The San Josef is directed to be manned with ordinary and landsmen. If they can be got on board in this gale, and the weather will permit the Commissioner to pay them to-morrow, she shall sail on Saturday.   N.

TO HERCULES ROSS, ESQ., ROSSIE CASTLE, N.B.

[Autograph, in the possession of his son, Horatio Ross, Esq.]

San Josef, Plymouth, January 29th, 1801.

My dear Friend,

It was only yesterday I was favoured with your letter, enclosing one for your nephew, Captain Colquhoun. There is not the smallest foundation for the report of my going to the Mediterranean, nor of Lord Keith's coming home at present. I rather believe my destination is Northwards; but I will keep your letter, in case I should go to the Mediterranean, which is not impossible, after the affairs of the North are settled. In that case you may be sure of my attention to your relation.

We are now arrived at that period, what we have often heard of, but must now execute—that of fighting for our dear Country; and I trust that, although we may not be able to

subdue our host of Enemies, yet we may make them ashamed
of themselves, and prove that they cannot injure us. With
every good wish to yourself and Mrs. Ross, believe me, as
ever, your obliged and affectionate friend,

NELSON AND BRONTE.

TO ADMIRAL THE EARL OF ST. VINCENT, K.B.

[Autograph, in the possession of Vice-Admiral Sir William Parker, Bart., G.C.B.]

San Josef, January 30th, [1801,] 8 P.M.

My Lord,

The Thames is anchored with a French Corvette[3] from the
Mauritius, and Captain Lukin,[4] this evening, off the Ram-head,
found the dispatches sent herewith, concealed in the false
bottom of a trunk belonging to the Officer who was charged
with them, and I have thought them of so much consequence
that I have sent Captain Parker to your Lordship with them.
I opened the three noted, in order to ascertain their importance.

It was not Captain Lukin's intention, but the day was gone,
and having 157 prisoners on board, and blowing fresh, he
thought it proper to anchor, which I approved. The Ship
having been at sea a length of time, is in some want of sails
and provisions, and, also, her payment is due ; but Captain
Lukin says he is sure he can go to sea without any difficulty
the moment he receives your Lordship's orders. I do not
find that either Unicorn or Diamond are sailed, although Sir
C. Cotton[5] tells me he has urged them to move. The Thames
passed last evening, at dusk, our in-shore Squadron, and at
ten o'clock, Sir H. Harvey,[6] ten miles from Ushant, who
spoke the Canada three days ago. I have the honour to
be, &c.

NELSON.

[3] L'Huron, of 20 guns and 70 men, captured off Bordeaux.
[4] Captain William Lukin. He died a Rear-Admiral of the White, in 1823 or 1824.
[5] Rear, afterwards Admiral, Sir Charles Cotton, Bart.: he died in February 1812.
[6] Vice-Admiral Sir Henry Harvey, K.B., who died a full Admiral in December 1810.

TO THE RIGHT HONOURABLE HENRY ADDINGTON.[7]

[Autograph, in the Sidmouth Papers.]

San Josef, Torbay, February 2nd, 1801.

My dear Sir,

During my short stay at Plymouth, I had great pleasure in making the acquaintance of General Simcoe, who I consider as a very enterprising and able Officer. No man appears to have more zeal for the honour of his Country than the General, and I find that he has turned his thoughts very much to the Island of Zealand, and the fortifications of Copenhagen; but this was a subject I could not then enter upon with him, not feeling myself at liberty to say I was likely to be employed. I own I think much useful knowledge might be obtained from the General, were he properly consulted, but I beg my name may not escape you, as it may be thought it is no business of mine, and it is true, further than an anxiety for the success of our Expedition, which I shall hope will always be the nearest and dearest object to the heart of, my dear Sir, your most obliged and grateful

NELSON AND BRONTE.

TO ADMIRAL THE EARL OF ST. VINCENT, K.B.

[Autograph, in the possession of Vice-Admiral Sir William Parker, Bart., G.C.B.]

San Josef, February 4th, 1801.

My dear Lord,

I return you many thanks for your French news. I can only hope, but, as far as I know, I see no prospect of any of your Fleet falling in with them; for, on Friday, they certainly knew nothing about their having sailed. I wonder Captain Linzee did not try and give them some information. The

---

[7] Mr. Addington received the King's commands to form a new Administration, on the 31st of January 1801, and consented to do so on the 5th of February; but, owing to his Majesty's illness, the Ministers did not actually take Office until the 14th of March. Mr. Addington became First Lord of the Treasury and Chancellor of the Exchequer; and the Earl of St. Vincent succeeded Earl Spencer as First Lord of the Admiralty, the other Members of the Board being, Sir Philip Stephens, the Hon. William Eliot, Captain Sir Thomas Troubridge, James Adams, Esq., Captain John Markham, and William Garthshore, Esq.

first morning it moderates, I shall have pleasure in paying you my respects, and assuring you, in person, how much I am your attached,

NELSON.

TO LIEUTENANT M. W. SUCKLING, R. N.

[Autograph, in the possession of Samuel Simpson, Esq., of Lancaster.]

San Josef, Torbay, February 5th, 1801.

My dear Sir,

Although I am going from the San Josef into the St. George, yet I will take your friend's son, with much pleasure, whenever he is sent. You know, as well as I do, that it was LOVE made you leave me, and naturally others stepped in and supplied your place. Why the Tonnant[?] was not in Holland, or why she may not go to the Baltic with Sir Hyde Parker, I am unacquainted with; nor do I believe, if you were so inclined, that I have interest to get you there, for not one favour has to my knowledge been granted me since I came to England, and you may believe me, when I cannot get Nisbet [?] a Ship, or my elder brother removed from being a Clerk in the Navy Office. With my best respects to Mrs. Suckling, and all my friends about you, believe me, as ever, your sincere friend,

NELSON AND BRONTE.

TO MRS. COLLINGWOOD.

[Autograph, in the possession of the Hon. Mrs. Newnham Collingwood.]

San Josef, Torbay, February 8th, 1801.

My dear Madam,

Collingwood, I dare say, has found an opportunity to tell you that he is ordered to Cawsand Bay. If he has not, such are the orders at present, but you must never be sure of any orders continuing in force, for circumstances may, and often do, alter in one moment. I own I should have sent my friend after the French Squadron, because I think him much fitter than the one[8] sent, and I do not believe there are

---

[8] Rear-Admiral Calder, in the Prince of Wales, with seven Sail of the Line and two Frigates, was sent in quest of Rear-Admiral Gantheaume's Squadron, which had escaped from Brest.

two opinions on the subject. Hoping you may soon see my dear friend, believe me, my dear Madam, your very faithful servant,

NELSON AND BRONTE.

TO LADY HAMILTON.

[From " Lord Nelson's Letters to Lady Hamilton," vol. i. p. 23.]

San Josef, February 8th, 1801.

My dear Lady,

Mr. Davison demands the privilege of carrying back an answer to your kind letter; and, I am sure, he will be very punctual in the delivery. I am not in very good spirits; and, except that our Country demands all our services and abilities, to bring about an honourable Peace, nothing should prevent my being the bearer of my own letter. But, my dear friend, I know you are so true and loyal an Englishwoman, that you would hate those who would not stand forth in defence of our King, Laws, Religion, and all that is dear to us. It is your sex that make us go forth; and seem to tell us—' None but the brave deserve the fair !' and, if we fall, we still live in the hearts of those females, who are dear to us. It is your sex that rewards us ; it is your sex who cherish our memories; and you, my dear, honoured friend, are, believe me, the *first*, the best of your sex. I have been the world around, and in every corner of it, and never yet saw your equal, or even one which could be put in comparison with you. You know how to reward virtue, honour, and courage ; and never to ask if it is placed in a Prince, Duke, Lord, or Peasant: and I hope, one day, to see you in peace, before I set out for Bronté, which I am resolved to do.

Darby's is one of the Ships[9] sent out after the French Squadron; I shall,' therefore, give the print to Hardy. I think, they might come by the mail-coach, as a parcel, wrapped up round a stick; any print shop will give you one: and direct it as my letters. The coach stops, for parcels, at the White Bear, I believe, Piccadilly. Pray, have you got any picture from Mrs. Head's ? I hope Mr. Brydon has exe-

---

[9] Captain Henry D'Esterre Darby, who commanded the Bellerophon at the Nile; he was then Captain of the Spencer. Vide vol. iii. p. 90.

cuted the frames to your satisfaction ; the bill he is directed to send to me.　Only tell me, how I can be useful to you and Sir William ; and believe, nothing could give me more pleasure, being, with the greatest truth, my dear Lady, your most obliged and affectionate friend,

NELSON AND BRONTE.

I am told, the moment St. George arrives, that I am to be tumbled out of this Ship, as the Ville de Paris is going to Plymouth, to be paid, and the Earl will hoist his Flag here : and if I am as fortunate in getting a fresh painted cabin, (which is probable,) I shall be knocked up.　At all events, I shall be made very uncomfortable by this hurry.　It has been very good and friendly of Mr. Davison to travel upwards of two hundred miles to make me a visit.　I rather think the great Earl will not much like his not having called on him, but his manner of speaking of Mr. Davison, for his friendship to me, in the matter of the law-suit, Lord St. Vincent states to my solicitors as offensive to him.　Why should it? only that Mr. Davison wishes that I should have justice done me, and not to be overpowered by weight of interest and money. Once more, God bless you and Sir William.

N. & B.

Sir Isaac Heard has gazetted Troubridge's, Hood, &c.'s honours, but has not gazetted mine ;[1] and he has the King's orders for mine as much as the others.

TO REAR-ADMIRAL HOLLOWAY.

[Autograph, in the possession of his son-in-law, Admiral Sir Robert Otway Bart., G.C.B.]

San Josef, February 11th, 1801.

My dear Holloway,

This moment brought me your letter of the 9th, which is the only one I have received from you since my arrival, although if I had had the pleasure it is probable it would have been

---

[1] To accept and wear the Cross of Knight Commander of the Order of St. Ferdinand and Merit, conferred upon them by the King of the Two Sicilies. The King's permission to Lord Nelson to accept the Dukedom of Bronté, and to wear the Grand Cross of the Order of St. Ferdinand and Merit, was not gazetted until the 5th of September 1801, though the Royal Licence was granted in January of that year.

some days, perhaps weeks, unanswered, for I could not have
got through the congratulations of my friends, but I always
beg my friends to excuse my being so quick as those with two
hands in replying; but be assured, my dear Holloway, there is
not that man in the service who respects you more than
myself, or more grateful for the many kind favours *you* have
shown me on various occasions, and I assure you that if it
ever should be in my power to do you a kind turn that I shall
have real pleasure in doing it. You may depend on my notice
of Mr. Lyons,[2] and I can answer that if he is proper to be
rated, as I see he is, he will be continued; but you know our
Earl has taught us to be very particular in these respects. All
the Lieutenants of the St. George are now in San Josef. I
like the appearance of Mr. Parry very much, but I was, of
course, full, and should have been so if I had twenty vacancies.
I beg my best respects to Mrs. Holloway, and believe me ever,
your sincere and faithful friend,

                              NELSON AND BRONTE.

TO ADMIRAL THE EARL OF ST. VINCENT, K.B.

[From Clarke and M'Arthur, vol. ii. p. 257.]

12th February, 1801.

My Flag is on board the St. George, but my person, owing
to the heavy sea, cannot be conveyed from the St. Josef. You
may rely, my dear Lord, that all your directions and wishes,
if I can guess them, shall be complied with. Now you are on
the spot, I trust you will have full scope for giving your opinions, as to the most proper mode of humbling our Enemies.
You will never, I think, recommend an ignominious peace :
no, let us be conquered, and not submit tamely to the fetters
of the French Republic, or a wild Monarch of the North. I
am, &c.,

                              NELSON AND BRONTE.

---

[2] Mrs. Holloway's nephew, and apparently the present Captain John Lyons, who
was a Midshipman of the Victory at Trafalgar.

TO ADMIRAL THE EARL OF ST. VINCENT, K.B.

[From Clarke and M'Arthur, vol. ii. p. 258.]

16th February, 1801.

I feel all your kind expressions, and in return I have only to assure you, that I never will ask you for what my judgment may tell me is an improper thing. My sole object, and to which all my exertions and abilities tend, is to bring this long war to an honourable termination ; to accomplish which, we must all pull in the collar, and, as we have got such a driver who will make the lazy ones pull as much as the willing, I doubt not but we shall get safely, speedily, and honourably to our journey's end. With every kind wish, both as a friend and as an Englishman, for your Ministerial prosperity, believe me, as ever, my dear Lord, your obliged and affectionate,

NELSON AND BRONTE.

TO ADMIRAL THE EARL OF ST. VINCENT, K.B.

[Autograph, in the possession of Vice-Admiral Sir William Parker, Bart., G.C.B. In consequence of the Northern Coalition, it had for some time been determined to send a powerful Fleet into the Baltic, under Admiral Sir Hyde Parker, with Lord Nelson as Second in Command ; and on the 17th of February 1801, the Admiralty issued their orders to Lord Nelson "to put himself under the command of Sir Hyde Parker, Knight, Admiral of the Blue, and Commander-in-Chief of a Squadron of his Majesty's Ships and Vessels, to be employed on a particular service." On the 18th of February, he was directed to proceed in the St. George to Spithead, and remain there until further orders.]

St. George, February 20th, 1801.

My dear Lord,

Our friend Troubridge will tell you his opinion of the present Acting-Captain of the San Josef. I have no doubt but that he may be a clever young [man] for a small [Vessel;] but if he stays in the San Josef a week longer, I believe she will be ruined : therefore, if Wolseley[1] is obliged to go on shore to attend his dying wife, some proper person must be sent to the San Josef. In my life I never saw such an alteration : I

---

[3] Captain William Wolseley, afterwards an Admiral of the Red. Vide vol. i. p. 350, and *passim*.

should have been proud to have gone alongside anything in her a week ago, and now really I should hardly think her masts safe. This Ship has not been cleansed down below since last November, and Hardy cannot yet for two days have her fit for me to visit. I have been very ailing these two days—a violent cold, I fancy; and here I am neither wind or water-tight; but she has a Ship's Company which, Hardy tells me, will do, he is sure; and I take the *Ghost's* word. I have the order to put myself under Sir Hyde's command, but none from him yet to go to Portsmouth; but I take for granted I shall have them to-morrow, and we shall be ready to start at the moment. Before we go to the North, I shall have to request either public or private leave for three days, to settle some very important matters for myself. Whether the service will admit of that absence on my arrival at Portsmouth, or at a more convenient time during my stay, you must, my dear Lord, be the best judge; and believe me ever your obliged and affectionate,

NELSON AND BRONTE.

If your Lordship do not take your Musicians on shore, I should be very happy to have ten or twelve of them, and will with pleasure pay them the same as you do. There are twenty-six, Grey[4] tells me, on board.

TO THE PRINCIPAL OFFICERS AND COMMISSIONERS OF HIS MAJESTY'S NAVY.

[Letter-Book.]

St. George, Torbay, 20th February, 1801.

Gentlemen,

Having hoisted my Flag on board the St. George, and finding her not fitted for a Flag, I request you will be pleased to give the necessary directions for her being fitted as such on her arrival at Portsmouth, as she is now under weigh for that anchorage. The boats are not calculated for the service I am to be employed on. I have further to request they may be altered as I direct. I am, &c.,

NELSON AND BRONTE.

---

⁴ The Honourable Captain George Grey, afterwards Sir George Grey, Bart., K.C.B., who died in October 1828.

TO ADMIRAL THE EARL OF ST. VINCENT, K.B.

[Autograph, in the possession of Vice-Admiral Sir William Parker, Bart., G.C.B.]

St. George, February 23rd, 1801.

My dear Lord,

As I find that Sir James Saumarez has no orders but to proceed to Torbay, therefore, I have communicated to him the orders left with me, and have taken the liberty of recommending, after he has received his men from the San Josef, and finding no orders then for his proceedings, to execute the orders left with me—viz., to join Sir H. Harvey off Ushant, which I hope you will approve—to merit which is always the inclination of, my dear Lord, your most affectionate,

NELSON AND BRONTE.

A letter from Clerk's Waggon-office, desiring that the keys of your plate-chest might be sent, in order to examine the contents; and as no person here had the keys, I called on the Collector, who said they could not be sent without examination; for that, having permitted one of the King's Sons' baggage to go unexamined, he had been reprimanded. I offered to pass my word that you were sending up no smuggled goods; but my word would not pass current. I then asked to have the seal of the Custom-House put upon them, and that they might be directed to your house. *No*, they must go to the Custom-House: therefore, you must send to the Commissioners of the Customs, to have either a dispensing order for their coming from the Waggon-office to your house, or to have an Officer there to go through the form of an examination. I told Clerk's people to write to you what was done, and the things will go to night, and be in London Wednesday night.

Monday, Noon, St. George.

1 o'clock.—Have just received your leave of absence, and shall see you to-morrow.

TO THE REVEREND MR. NELSON, HILBOROUGH.

[Autograph, in the Nelson Papers.]

St. George, February 28th, 1801.

My dear Brother,

I have this moment your letter of February 25th, and have sent your letter, as it was, to Lord Eldon.[5] My stay in Town was so short, that you could not have arrived in time to see me. I expect to be at Yarmouth, Thursday or Friday. With best and kindest regards to Mrs. Nelson, and all friends, believe me, ever your affectionate brother,

NELSON AND BRONTE.

Hardy, Parker desire their regards. I have a hundred sharp-shooters on board that fire so well, I am told, they can *for Philip's right eye*—say for Paul's.

TO ADMIRAL THE EARL OF ST. VINCENT, K.B.

[From Clarke and M'Arthur, vol. ii. p. 258. Lord Nelson arrived at Spithead on the 21st of February, and on the 23rd, obtained leave of absence for three days to go to Town. On the 26th, he was directed to embark 600 Troops, under Lieutenant-Colonel the Honourable William Stewart, and he was informed that Sir Hyde Parker having left London for Yarmouth, he was to cause the Ships destined for his Squadron to proceed to that place. On the 2nd of March, Lord Nelson sailed in the St. George from Portsmouth with seven Sail of the Line, Frigates, and small Vessels, for the Downs, and shortly after, arrived at Yarmouth, the rendezvous of Sir Hyde Parker's Squadron.]

1st March, 1801.

The wind was yesterday at S.S.W., which has prevented Warrior, Defence, and Agincourt from sailing. Time,[6] my dear Lord, is our best Ally, and I hope we shall not give her up, as all our Allies have given us up. Our friend here is a little nervous about dark nights and fields of ice, but we must brace up; these are not times for nervous systems. I want Peace, which is only to be had through, I trust, our still

---

[5] Then recently appointed Lord Chancellor.

[6] Like all great men, Nelson was deeply impressed with the value of *time*. In conversation with the late General William Twiss, Colonel Commandant of the Royal Engineers, Lord Nelson observed, "Time, Twiss—time is everything; five minutes makes the difference between a victory and a defeat."—(From the information of W. E. Surtees, Esq.)

invincible Navy.   I have not seen Captain Thesiger[7] here, I
shall receive him with much pleasure; if he is still in Town
pray send word to him to meet me in the Downs or Yarmouth.   I have written to Troubridge relative to Miller's
monument.

March 2nd, getting under sail.   I am always happy when
my conduct meets with your approbation, and whilst I remain
in the service my utmost exertions shall be called forth: for
although, I own, I have met with much more honours and
rewards than ever my most sanguine ideas led me to expect,
yet I am so circumstanced that probably this Expedition will
be the last service ever performed by your obliged and affectionate friend,

NELSON AND BRONTE.[8]

TO LADY HAMILTON.

[From " Lord Nelson's Letters to Lady Hamilton," vol. i. p. 32.]

[March, 1801.]

You say, my dearest Friend, why don't I put my Chief forward?   He has put me in the front of the battle, and Nelson
will be first.   I could say more; but will not make you uneasy, knowing the firm friendship you have for me.   The St.
George will stamp an additional ray of glory to England's
fame, if Nelson survives; and that Almighty Providence, who
has hitherto protected me in all dangers, and covered my
head in the day of battle, will still, if it be his pleasure,

---

[7] Captain Sir Frederick Thesiger, uncle of Sir Frederick Thesiger, Her Majesty's
Attorney-General.   He had served with such distinction, as a Captain in the Rus-
sian Navy, against the Swedes, that he received the Cross of St. George from the
Empress Catherine.   This gallant Officer, who was then only a Commander in our
Navy, accompanied Lord Nelson to Copenhagen, as a Volunteer, and is often honour-
ably mentioned for his gallant conduct.   He was Posted in 1801, and died in
August 1805, being then Agent for Prisoners of War at Portsmouth.

[8] In reply to this letter, Lord St. Vincent wrote to him :—" Be assured, my dear
Lord, that every *public* act of your life has been the subject of my admiration,
which I should have sooner declared, but that I was appalled by the last sentence
of your letter; for God's sake, do not suffer yourself to be carried away by any
sudden impulse.   With many thanks for the spur you have given to the movement
of the Ships at Spithead, believe me to be yours most affectionately, ST. VINCENT."
—*Clarke and M'Arthur,* vol. ii. p. 258.

U 2

support and assist me. Keep me alive, in your and Sir William's remembrance. My last thoughts will be with you both, for you love and esteem me. I judge your hearts by my own. May the Great God of Heaven protect and bless you and him! is the fervent prayer of your and Sir William's unalterable friend, till death,

NELSON AND BRONTE.

TO CAPTAIN SIR EDWARD BERRY.

[Autograph, in the possession of Lady Berry.]

St. George, Yarmouth, March 9th, 1801.

My dear Berry,

Last night I received your letter directed to Lothian's hotel. Why won't you come here for a day, and look at us? As to the plan for pointing a gun truer than we do at present, if the person comes I shall of course look at it, and be happy, if necessary, to use it; but, I hope, we shall be able as usual to get so close to our Enemies that our shot cannot miss their object, and that we shall again give our Northern Enemies that hail-storm of bullets which is so emphatically described in the Naval Chronicle, and which gives our dear Country the Dominion of the Seas. We have it, and all the Devils in Hell cannot take it from us, if our Wooden walls have fair play. With my best respects to Doctor Forster and all my friends at Norwich, believe me ever, my dear Berry, your faithful and affectionate,

NELSON AND BRONTE.

TO — PILLANS, ESQ., GRAND MASTER OF THE ANCIENT ORDER OF GREGORIANS.

[Autograph, in the possession of W. F. Patteson, Esq.]

St. George, Yarmouth, March 11th, 1801.

Sir,

On my arrival in England I received a letter from you acquainting me that the Ancient Order of Gregorians at Norwich had elected me a Member; I have therefore, Sir, to request that you will do me the favour to present to the Society my thanks for the great honour they have been

pleased to confer upon me, and to assure them that my future
exertions shall not be wanting to merit the continuance of
their good opinion.   I have the honour to be, Sir, with great
respect, your most obedient and obliged,

NELSON AND BRONTE.

TO CAPTAIN SAMUEL HOOD, H.M. SHIP VENERABLE.

[Autograph, in the possession of Sir Alexander Hood, Bart.]

St. George, March 13th, 1801.

My dear Hood,
   Many thanks for your kind letter, and believe me there is
not a man breathing that loves you more than myself.   I am
glad you have quitted that d——d Courageux; she would
have drowned you in chase of an Enemy's Squadron.   I have
directed four Crosses[8] to be made, and they are this day sent to
Mr. Davison's, I expect.   I send you an order—*No*, I have
wrote to Davison to deliver it to Troubridge, who will send it
you; it is to be worn round your neck like the Order of St.
Anne.   I send you a piece of Ribbon to suspend it by.   We
sail to-morrow for Yarmouth; I only hope Cornwallis[9] will
meet the French Fleet, and that you will be in company.
Ever, my dear Hood, your obliged and affectionate,

NELSON AND BRONTE.

TO ALEXANDER DAVISON, ESQ.

[From Clarke and M'Arthur, vol. ii. p. 259.   The Squadron sailed from Yar-
mouth on the 12th of March, and consisted of the London, 98, Sir Hyde Parker,
Knt., Admiral of the Blue; First Captain,William Domett; Second Captain, Robert
Waller Otway;—St. George, 98, Lord Nelson, K.B., Vice Admiral of the Blue;
Captain Thomas Masterman Hardy;—Bellona, 74, Captain Sir Thomas Boulden
Thompson; Defence, 74, Captain Lord Henry Paulet; Ganges, 74, Captain
Thomas Francis Fremantle; Monarch, 74, Captain James Robert Mosse; Ramilies,
74, Captain James William Taylor Dixon; Russell, 74, Captain William Cuming;
Saturn, 74, Captain Robert Lambert; Warrior, 74, Captain Charles Tyler; Ardent,
64, Captain Thomas Bertie; Agamemnon, 64, Captain Robert Devereux Fancourt;
Polyphemus, 64, Captain John Lawford; Raisonable, 64, Captain John Dilkes;
Veteran, 64, Captain Archibald Collingwood Dickson; Glatton, 54, Captain William

---

   [8] Of the Order of St. Ferdinand and Merit.
   [9] His old friend Admiral Cornwallis had succeeded the Earl of St. Vincent in the
command of the Channel Fleet.

Bligh; Isis, 50, Captain James Walker. Frigates: Desirée, 40, Captain Henry Inman; Amazon, 38, Captain Edward Riou; Blanche, 36, Captain Graham Eden Hamond; Alcmene, Captain Samuel Sutton; Jamaica, 26, Captain Jonas Rose; Hyæna, 20, Captain William Granger; Arrow, 20, Captain William Bolton; Dart, 30, Captain John Ferris Devonshire; Pylades, 18, Captain James Boorder; Cruiser, Captain James Brisbane; Harpy, 18, Captain William Birchall. Bomb-Vessels: Terror, 8, Captain Samuel Campbell Rowley; Volcano, 8, Captain J. Watson; Explosion, 8, Captain J. H. Martin; Hecla, 8, Captain R. Hatherill; Zebra, 8, Captain Edward Sneyd Clay; Sulphur, 8, Captain Hender Whitter; Discovery, 8, Captain John Conn. Fire-Ships: Otter, Captain George M'Kinley; and Zephyr, Captain C. Upton. Gun-Brigs: Biter, 12, Lieutenant Norman; Hasty, 12, Lieutenant W. Charlton; Blazer, 12, Lieutenant J. Tiller; Bruiser, 12, Lieutenant L. D. Bruce; Tigress, 12,　　　　　　　　; Force, 12, Lieutenant F. Tokely; Pelter, 12, Lieutenant J. Walsh; Teazer, 12, Lieutenant T. L. Robins; and Sparkler, 12, Lieutenant J. Stevens. Cutters: Fox, 12, Lieutenant R. Balfour; Hazard, 6, Thomas Marsh, Master. Schooner: Eling, 14, Lieutenant W. Peake. Luggers: Rover, 14, Lieutenant J. J. Duffy; Lark, 14, Lieutenant J. H. Wilson. The following Ships soon after joined the Fleet: Defiance, 74, Thomas Graves, Esq., Rear Admiral of the White; Captain Richard Retalick; Zealous, 74, Thomas Totty, Esq., Rear-Admiral of the Blue; Captain Samuel Hood Linzee; Edgar, 74, Captain George Murray; Elephant, 74, Captain Thomas Foley; Vengeance, 74, Captain George Duff; Brunswick, 74, Captain G. H. Stephens.

Latitude 57° N., 16th March, 1801.

Our weather is very cold, we have received much snow and sharp frost. I have not yet seen my Commander-in-Chief, and have had no official communication whatever. All I have gathered of our first plans, I disapprove most exceedingly; honour may arise from them, good cannot. I hear we are likely to anchor outside Cronenburg Castle, instead of Copenhagen, which would give weight to our negotiation: a Danish Minister would think twice before he would put his name to war with England, when the next moment he would probably see his Master's Fleet in flames, and his Capital in ruins; but 'out of sight out of mind,' is an old saying. The Dane should see our Flag waving every moment he lifted up his head. I am, &c.,

NELSON AND BRONTE.

TO ADMIRAL SIR HYDE PARKER.

[From Clarke and M'Arthur, vol. ii. p. 259. On the 15th of March, 1801, the Admiralty issued the following "Secret" Orders to Sir Hyde Parker:—

"The Right Honourable Henry Dundas, one of his Majesty's Principal Secretaries of State, having, in his letter of yesterday's date, signified to us his Majesty's pleasure that whether the discussion supposed to be now pending with the Court

of Denmark should be terminated by an amicable arrangement, or by actual hostilities, the Officer commanding the Fleet in the Baltic should, in either case, (as soon
as the Fleet can be withdrawn from before Copenhagen consistently with the attain-
ment of one or the other of the objects for which he is now instructed to take that
station,) proceed to Revel; and if he should find the Division of the Russian Navy
usually stationed at that Port, still there, to make an immediate and vigorous attack
upon it, provided the measure should appear to him practicable, and such as in his
judgment would afford a reasonable prospect of success in destroying the Arsenal,
or in capturing or destroying the Ships, without exposing to too great a risk the
Fleet under his command.

"And Mr. Dundas having further signified to us his Majesty's pleasure that,
consistently with this precaution, the said Officer should be authorized and directed
to proceed successively, and as the season and other operations will permit, against
Cronstadt, and in general by every means in his power to attack and endeavour to
capture or destroy any Ships of War or others belonging to Russia, wherever he
can meet with them, and to annoy that Power as far as his means will admit, in every
manner not incompatible with the fair and acknowledged usages of war; And that
with respect to Sweden, should the Court of Stockholm persist in her hostile engagements with that of Petersburgh against this Country, the same general line of
conduct as hath been stated with respect to the Ships and Ports of the latter,
should govern the said Officer commanding the Fleet, in his proceedings against
those of Sweden; but that, in the contrary supposition (conceived not to be impossible) of this Power relinquishing her present hostile plans against the rights and
interests of this Country, and of her renewing, either singly or in concert with Denmark, her ancient engagements with his Majesty, it will in such case be the duty
of the said Officer to afford to Sweden every protection in his power against the
resentment and attacks of Russia; and Mr. Dundas having also signified that his
Majesty being no less desirous of bringing the existing dispute with Sweden to this
latter issue, than he has shown himself so disposed with respect to Denmark, and
upon the same principles, it will therefore be requisite that the said Officer commanding in the Baltic should make such a disposition of his force, as may appear
best adapted to facilitate and give weight to the arrangement in question, provided
it should be concluded with the Court of Denmark within the forty-eight hours
allowed for this purpose, and the proposal of acceding to it which will be made to
that of Sweden should be entertained by the latter, You are, in pursuance of his
Majesty's pleasure, signified as above mentioned, hereby required and directed to
proceed, without a moment's loss of time, into the Baltic, and to govern yourself
under the different circumstances before stated to the best of your judgment and
discretion, in the manner therein pointed out, transmitting from time to time to our
Secretary, for our information, an account of your proceedings, and such information as you may conceive to be proper for our knowledge. Given under our hands
and seals, the 15th March, 1801. St. Vincent, T. Troubridge, J. Markham."
—Original.]

                                                          24th March, 1801.
     My dear Sir Hyde,
     The conversation we had yesterday has naturally, from its
importance, been the subject of my thoughts; and the more I
have reflected, the more I am confirmed in opinion, that not a
moment should be lost in attacking the Enemy: they will
every day and hour be stronger; we never shall be so good a

match for them as at this moment.   The only consideration in
my mind is, how to get at them with the least risk to our
Ships.   By Mr. Vansittart's[1] account, the Danes have taken
every means in their power to prevent our getting to attack
Copenhagen by the Passage of the Sound.   Cronenburg has
been strengthened, the Crown Islands fortified, on the outermost of which are twenty guns pointing mostly downwards,
and only eight hundred yards from very formidable batteries
placed under the Citadel, supported by five Sail of the Line,
seven Floating batteries of fifty guns each, besides Small-craft,
Gun-boats, &c. &c.; and that the Revel Squadron of twelve
or fourteen Sail of the Line are soon expected, as also five
Sail of Swedes.   It would appear by what you have told me
of your instructions, that Government took for granted you
would find no difficulty in getting off Copenhagen, and in
the event of a failure of negotiation, you might instantly
attack; and that there would be scarcely a doubt but the
Danish Fleet would be destroyed, and the Capital made so
hot that Denmark would listen to reason and its true interest.
By Mr. Vansittart's account, their state of preparation exceeds
what he conceives our Government thought possible, and that
the Danish Government is hostile to us in the greatest possible
degree.   Therefore here you are, with almost the safety,
certainly with the honour of England more intrusted to you,
than ever yet fell to the lot of any British Officer.   On your
decision depends, whether our Country shall be degraded in
the eyes of Europe, or whether she shall rear her head higher
than ever: again do I repeat, never did our Country depend
so much on the success of any Fleet as on this.   How best to
honour our Country and abate the pride of her Enemies, by
defeating their schemes, must be the subject of your deepest
consideration as Commander-in-Chief; and if what I have to
offer can be the least useful in forming your decision, you are
most heartily welcome.

I shall begin with supposing you are determined to enter
by the Passage of the Sound, as there are those who think, if
you leave that Passage open, that the Danish Fleet may sail

---

[1] Mr. Nicholas Vansittart (now Lord Bexley) had shortly before been sent in
the Blanche, to treat with the Danish Court, with the hope of preventing hostilities.

from Copenhagen, and join the Dutch or French. I own I have no fears on that subject; for it is not likely that whilst their Capital is menaced with an attack, 9000 of her best men should be sent out of the Kingdom. I suppose that some damage may arise amongst our masts and yards; yet perhaps there will not be one of them but could be made serviceable again. You are now about Cronenburg: if the wind be fair, and you determine to attack the Ships and Crown Islands, you must expect the natural issue of such a battle—Ships crippled, and perhaps one or two lost; for the wind which carries you in, will most probably not bring out a crippled Ship. This mode I call taking the bull by the horns. It, however, will not prevent the Revel Ships, or Swedes, from joining the Danes; and to prevent this from taking effect, is, in my humble opinion, a measure absolutely necessary—and still to attack Copenhagen. Two modes are in my view; one to pass Cronenburg, taking the risk of damage, and to pass up the deepest and straightest Channel above the Middle Grounds; and coming down the Garbar or King's Channel, to attack their Floating batteries, &c. &c., as we find it convenient. It must have the effect of preventing a junction between the Russians, Swedes, and Danes, and may give us an opportunity of bombarding Copenhagen. I am also pretty certain that a passage could be found to the northward of Southolm for all our Ships; perhaps it might be necessary to warp a short distance in the very narrow part. Should this mode of attack be ineligible, the passage of the Belt, I have no doubt, would be accomplished in four or five days, and then the attack by Draco could be carried into effect, and the junction of the Russians prevented, with every probability of success against the Danish Floating batteries. What effect a bombardment might have, I am not called upon to give an opinion; but think the way would be cleared for the trial. Supposing us through the Belt with the wind first westerly, would it not be possible to either go with the Fleet, or detach ten Ships of three and two decks, with one Bomb and two Fire-ships, to Revel, to destroy the Russian Squadron at that place? I do not see the great risk of such a detachment, and with the remainder to attempt the business at Copenhagen. The measure may be thought bold, but I am of opinion the boldest measures are the safest; and our Country demands a most vigorous exertion of her force, directed with judgment. In supporting you, my dear Sir Hyde, through the arduous and important task you have undertaken, no exertion of head or heart shall be wanting from your most obedient and faithful servant,

NELSON AND BRONTE.

TO CAPTAIN GEORGE MURRAY, H.M. SHIP EDGAR.

[Autograph, in the possession of his Royal Highness Prince Albert.]

[Towards the end of March, 1801.]

My dear Murray,

I was glad to see you placed where you are, for it is a post of great consequence. I take for granted you will follow the last Ship; and I hope the guns of Cronenburg will be lessened, and the *heads* too, by that time. God will prosper us if we conduct ourselves well. Ever yours faithfully,

NELSON AND BRONTE.

TO CAPTAIN THOMAS BERTIE, H.M. SHIP ARDENT.

[From the "Naval Chronicle," vol. xxvi. p. 16.]

28th March, 1801.

My dear Bertie,

I thank you for your truly kind note, and am very sorry that anything should have caused you a moment's uneasiness. Fremantle and Stewart[2] are perfect good friends. I will talk to your Pilot; but I do not much mind what they say. Our Ships will ride anywhere, and the wind which makes a sea will send us to our destination. Last night the Governor of Cronenburg had *no* orders to fire on us; but the Devil trust them—I will not. Wishing you, with myself, every success, in all our undertakings, believe me ever, my dear Bertie, your faithful and affectionate friend,

NELSON AND BRONTE.

[2] Lieutenant-Colonel the Honourable William Stewart, second surviving son of John, 7th Earl of Galloway, K.T., afterwards Lieutenant-General Sir William Stewart, G.C.B. He commanded the Troops employed in this expedition; and distinguished himself in the command of a Division at the Battles of Albuhera, Vittoria, Pyrenees, Nive, and Orthes, and died in January, 1827.

BATTLE OF COPENHAGEN.

The most interesting account of the Expedition to the Baltic, and of the BATTLE OF COPENHAGEN, is that which occurs in Clarke and M'Arthur's " Life of Lord Nelson," who state that it was written " by an Officer who was with Lord Nelson." The extracts in that work commence with the words " Lord Nelson's plan would have been to have proceeded with the utmost despatch," &c., (*vide* p. 300, *post*,) but the Nelson Papers contain the *previous* part of the Narrative, which proves it to have been written for Drs. Clarke and M'Arthur's work, by the Honourable Colonel Stewart, who commanded the Troops embarked. The entire Narrative is now given :

"NARRATIVE OF EVENTS CONNECTED WITH THE CONDUCT OF LORD NELSON IN THE BALTIC, 1801.

" The Writer of this Narrative repaired to Portsmouth, on the 26th of February, 1801, in command of a detachment of Troops, which consisted of the 49th Regiment, about 760 rank and file, commanded by the Lieut.- Colonel Brock, and of a company of a Rifle corps, (now the 95th regiment,) 100 rank and file, commanded by Captain Sidney Beckwith. His instructions were to put himself under the orders of the Admiral commanding a Fleet destined for a special service in the North Sea.

" On the 27th of February, in the forenoon, the troops proceeded to South Sea Common, awaiting orders to embark. Lord Nelson arrived from London about ten, A.M. He sent for me immediately on his arrival, to Major-General Whitelocke's : on first acquaintance with Lord Nelson, I witnessed the activity of his character ; he said that ' not a moment was to be lost in embarking the troops, for he intended to sail next tide.' Orders were sent for all boats, and the whole were on board of the men-of-war, before mid-day. Lord Nelson, in three hours after, left the Sally-port for the St. George ; this Ship was commanded by his old friend Captain Hardy, (now Sir Masterman,) and was under considerable repair at Spithead. No time, however, was to be lost ; the caulkers and painters were detained on board, and we proceeded with them to St. Helen's, Lord Nelson observing that ' if the wind proved fair in the morning, they should be sent up the harbour, but if unfair, no time would have been lost.' The wind became fair in the course of the night, and we got under weigh at daylight on the 28th ; I do not remember by what number of Ships we were accompanied. Nothing particular occurred until our arrival in the Downs : the seine was frequently hauled, by Lord Nelson's directions, and the eagerness and vivacity which he showed upon the occasion, to the great delight of the seamen, early pointed out to me the natural liveliness of his character, even in trivial matters. Another trait may be worthy of remark, as illustrative of much *nâiveté*. His Lordship was rather too apt to interfere in the working of the Ship, and not always with the best success or judgment. The wind, when off Dungeness, was scanty, and the Ship was to be put about ; Lord Nelson would give the orders, and caused her to miss stays. Upon this he said, rather peevishly, to the Master, or Officer of the Watch, (I forget which,) ' Well, now, see what we have done. Well, Sir, what mean you to do now ?' The Officer saying with hesitation, ' I don't exactly know, my Lord ; I fear she won't do,' Lord Nelson turned sharply towards the cabin, and replied, ' Well, I am sure if you do not know what to do with her, no more do I either.' He went in, leaving the Officer to work the Ship as he liked. When in the Downs, the Warrior standing in from the southward, got on the Goodwin Sands, but was not much damaged. Lord Nelson ex-pressed what, for him, was a considerable degree of displeasure at the circumstance :

I always perceived that he felt much more than he gave vent to, when dissatisfied with the conduct of others. He visited, on shore at Deal, his old friend Admiral Lutwidge.

" We sailed on the succeeding morning, and entered Yarmouth Roads on the 6th or 7th of March. The St. George was the first three-decker which had so done. The flag of Sir Hyde Parker, the Commander-in-Chief, was flying on board of one of the Ships of the station, but was removed to the London on her arrival next day. Sir Hyde was on shore, and I remember that Lord Nelson regretted this. He reported his arrival, and his intention of waiting on him the next morning. We breakfasted that morning, as usual, soon after six o'clock, for we were always up before daylight. We went on shore, so as to be at Sir Hyde's door by eight o'clock, Lord Nelson choosing to be amusingly exact to that hour, which he considered as a very late one for business.

" Lord Nelson's plan would have been to have proceeded with the utmost dispatch, and with such Ships as were in readiness, to the mouth of Copenhagen Harbour ; then and there to have insisted on amity or war, and have brought the objects of Messrs. Drummond and Vansittart's negotiation to a speedy decision. He would have left orders for the remainder of the Fleet to have followed in succession, as they were ready, and by the rapidity of his proceedings have anticipated the formidable preparations for defence which the Danes had scarcely thought of at that early season. The delay in Yarmouth Roads did not accord with his views. An order from the Admiralty arrived on the 11th of March, in consequence of which the Fleet put to sea on the succeeding day. The land troops were equally distributed on board of the Line-of-Battle Ships, and I, repairing to the London, had not an opportunity of being with Lord Nelson, until our arrival off the Sound. Our Fleet consisted of about fifty Sail ; of these forty were Pendants, sixteen being of the Line. On the 15th, we encountered a heavy gale of wind, which in some measure scattered the Fleet, and prevented our reaching the Naze until the 18th. On the next day, when off the Scaw, the whole were nearly collected ; a north-west wind blew, and an opportunity appeared to have been lost of proceeding through the Cattegat. Every delay, however trifling, gave cause for regret, and favoured the views of the Northern Coalition. The openness of those seas had rarely been equalled at this season of the year, and in particular called for activity in our movements. The Commander-in-Chief had probably, however, instructions by which he acted ; and if so, this, in addition to numerous instances of a similar nature, proves the propriety of discretionary powers, whenever success is to depend on energy and activity. Lord Nelson was, as I understood, greatly vexed at the delay.

" On the 21st it blew hard : we anchored for twenty-four hours, and did not arrive off the point of Elsineur until the 24th. The Blanche Frigate, with Mr. Vansittart on board, preceded the Fleet from the Scaw, and, landing him at Elsineur on the 20th, he joined Mr. Drummond at Copenhagen. The terms demanded by these gentlemen having been rejected, they returned to our Fleet on the 24th, and left us for England on the succeeding day. The wind was again strong and favourable, and expectation was alive that we should have sailed through the Sound on the 25th : it was, however, generally understood, that the formidable reports which had been made by Mr. Vansittart, and by the Pilots whom we had brought with us, as to the state of the batteries at Elsineur, and of the defensive situation of Copenhagen, induced the Commander-in-Chief to prefer the circuitous passage by the Great Belt. Lord Nelson, who was impatient for action, was not much deterred by these alarming representations ; his object was to go to Copenhagen, and he said,

' Let it be by the Sound, by the Belt, or anyhow, only lose not an hour.' On the 26th the whole Fleet accordingly sailed for the Great Belt; but after proceeding for a few leagues along the Coast of Zealand, the plan was suddenly changed.[1] This arose partly in consequence of some suggestions from Captain George Murray of the Edgar, who was to have led the Fleet through the intricate channels, partly on account of some difficulty appearing in our course, (one or two of the smaller craft being on the rocks,) but chiefly at the instigation of Lord Nelson, who went on board the London, about ten A.M. Be the reasons as they may, the Fleet returned to its former anchorage before sunset. As if a more than sufficient time had not been given for the Danes to prepare their defence, another message was sent, on the 27th of March, to the Governor of Elsineur, Stricker, to discover his intentions relative to opposing our Fleet, if it were to pass the Sound. He replied, ' I have the honour to inform your Excellency, that his Majesty the King of Denmark did not send away the Chargé d'Affaires; but that on his own demand he obtained a passport. As a Soldier, I cannot intermeddle with politics; but I am not at liberty to suffer a Fleet, whose intention is not yet known, to approach the guns of the Castle of Cronenburg, which I have the honour to command. In case your Excellency should think proper to make any proposals to the King of Denmark, I wish to be informed thereof before the Fleet approaches nearer to the Castle.' Sir Hyde Parker replied, ' that finding the intentions of the Court of Denmark to be hostile against his Britannic Majesty, he regarded his Excellency's answer as a declaration of war; and, therefore, agreeably to his instructions, could no longer refrain from hostilities, however reluctant it might be to his feelings. But, at the same time, the Admiral would be ready to attend to any proposals of the Court of Denmark for restoring the former amity and friendship which had for so many years subsisted between the two Courts.'

" On the 26th of March, the Elephant, Captain Foley, and another 74, had joined the Fleet, bringing the melancholy intelligence of the loss of the Invincible, 74 guns, Rear-Admiral Totty, Captain Rennie, one of our Squadron, on the sandbank called Hammond's Knowl. On the 29th, Lord Nelson shifted his Flag from the St. George to the Elephant, commanded by his intimate friend, Captain Foley, in order to carry on operations in a lighter Ship. Both the 28th and 29th of March were unfortunately calm: orders had, however, been given for the Fleet to pass through the Sound as soon as the wind should permit. At day-light, on the morning of the 30th, it blew a topsail breeze from N.W. The signal was made, and the Fleet proceeded in the order of Battle previously arranged; Lord Nelson's division in the Van, the Commander-in-Chief's in the Centre, and Admiral Graves's in the

---

[1] It is stated in the Memoir of Admiral Sir Robert Waller Otway, Bart., G.C.B., in Ralfe's *Naval Biography*, (a copy of which was placed in the Editor's hands by that Officer,) that the alteration made in the approach of the Fleet to Copenhagen was suggested by him. He was then Captain of the London, after the Council of War, at which he was not present, broke up, he succeeded in convincing Sir Hyde Parker, that the Sound was the best route:—" The Fleet was again brought to, and Captain Otway was sent to apprise Lord Nelson of the reasons. On explaining to his Lordship the alteration that had been made in the route, he exclaimed—' I don't care a d—n by which passage we go, so that we fight them!' He determined to return with Captain Otway to the Commander-in-Chief, and in consequence of the wind blowing fresh, was hoisted out in one of the Boats; and on his arrival on board the London, everything was finally arranged agreeably to the plan suggested by Captain Otway."

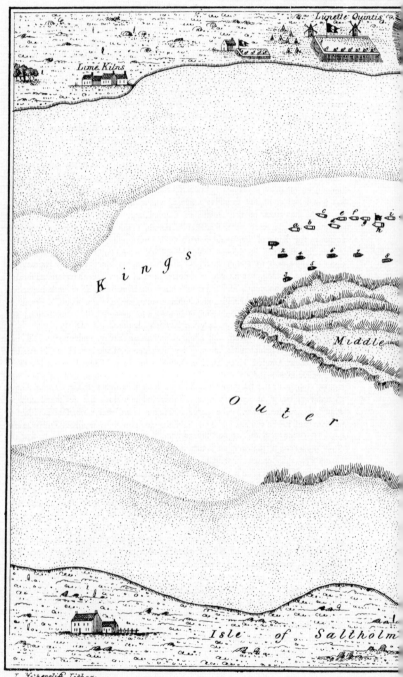

Lunette Quintis

Lime Kilns

Kings

Middle

Outer

Isle of Saltholm

J. Netherclift Lithog:

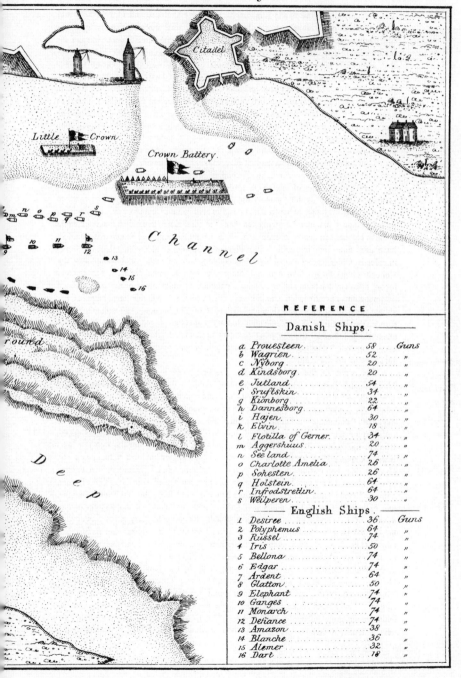

Citadel

Little — Crown

Crown Battery.

m n o p q r s

9 10 11 12 13 14 15 16

C h a n n e l

Ground

D e e p

REFERENCE

——— Danish Ships. ———

			Guns
a	Prouesteen	58	Guns
b	Wagrien	52	„
c	Nyborg	20	„
d	Kindsborg	20	„
e	Jutland	54	„
f	Sruftskin	34	„
g	Kionborg	22	„
h	Dannesborg	64	„
i	Hajen	30	„
k	Elvin	18	„
l	Flotilla of Gerner	34	„
m	Aggershuus	20	„
n	Seeland	74	„
o	Charlotte Amelia	26	„
p	Sohesten	26	„
q	Holstein	64	„
r	Infrodstretlin	64	„
s	Weilperen	30	„

——— English Ships. ———

			Guns
1	Desiree	36	Guns
2	Polyphemus	64	„
3	Russel	74	„
4	Iris	50	„
5	Bellona	74	„
6	Edgar	74	„
7	Ardent	64	„
8	Glatton	50	„
9	Elephant	74	„
10	Ganges	74	„
11	Monarch	74	„
12	Defiance	74	„
13	Amazon	38	„
14	Blanche	36	„
15	Alcmer	32	„
16	Dart	18	„

Rear: Captain Murray in the Edgar, with the Fleet of Bomb and Gun vessels, took their station off Cronenburg Castle on the preceding morning; and, upon the first Danish shot, opened their fire upon the Castle. The semi-circular form of the land off Elsineur, which was thickly lined with batteries, caused our Fleet to pass in a form truly picturesque, and nearly similar. It had been our intention to have kept in mid-channel, the forbearance of the Swedes not having been counted upon, the lighter Vessels were on the larboard side of our Line of Battle, and were to have engaged the Helsinburg shore: not a shot, however, was fired, nor any batteries apparent, and our Fleet inclined accordingly to that side, so as completely to avoid the Danish shot which fell in showers, but at least a cable's length from our Ships. The Danish batteries opened a fire, as we understood, of nearly 100 pieces of cannon and mortars, as soon as our leading Ship, the Monarch, came abreast of them; and they continued in one uninterrupted blaze during the passage of the Fleet, to the no small amusement of our crews; none of whom received injury, except from the bursting of one of our own guns. Some of our leading Ships at first returned a few rounds, but, perceiving the inutility, desisted. The whole came to anchor about mid-day, between the Island of Huen and Copenhagen; the division under Captain Murray following, as soon as the main body had passed: as is usually the case in sea-bombardments, little or no damage was afterwards found to have been done by our shells. Our Fleet was no sooner at anchor, than the Commander-in Chief, accompanied by Lord Nelson, two or three Senior Captains, the Commanding Officer of the Artillery and of the troops, proceeded in a schooner to reconnoitre the harbour and channels. We soon perceived that our delay had been of important advantage to the Enemy, who had lined the northern edge of the shoals near the Crown batteries, and the front of the harbour and arsenal, with a formidable Flotilla. The Trekroner battery appeared, in particular, to have been strengthened, and all the buoys of the Northern and of the King's Channels had been removed. Having examined these points with some attention, the party returned to the London.

"The night of the 30th of March was employed by some of the intelligent Masters and Pilots, under the direction of Captain Brisbane, in ascertaining the Channels round the great shoal called the Middle Ground, and in laying down fresh buoys, the Danes having either removed or misplaced the former ones. On the next day, the Commander-in-Chief and Lord Nelson, attended, as before, with the addition of all the Artillery Officers, proceeded in the Amazon Frigate, Captain Riou, to the examination of the Northern Channel, and of the Flotilla from the eastward. Captain Riou became on this occasion first known to Lord Nelson, who was struck with admiration at the superior discipline and seamanship, that were observable on board the Amazon during the proceedings of this day. The Danish Line of Defence was formed in a direct line eastward from the Trekroner Battery, and extended at least two miles along the Coast of Amak: it was ascertained to consist of the hulls of seven Line-of-Battle Ships with jury masts, two only being fully rigged, ten Pontoons or Floating Batteries, one Bomb-ship rigged, and two or three Smaller craft. On the Trekroner, appeared to be nearly seventy guns; on the smaller battery, in-shore, six or seven guns; and on the Coast of Amak, several batteries which were within a long range of the King's Channel. Off the Harbour's mouth, which was to the westward of the Trekroner, were moored four Line-of-Battle Ships and a Frigate; two of the former and the latter were fully rigged. Their whole Line of Defence, from one extreme point to the other, might embrace an extent of nearly four miles. The Dockyard and Arsenal were in line nearly south, within the Trekroner, about half a mile distant. A few shot were fired at the Amazon whenever we approached the leading Ship of their Line. The Officers of Artillery were desired to ascertain, whether, in the event of the Line of Defence being in part or wholly removed, they could place their Bomb-ships, of which there were seven, so as to play with effect on the Dockyards and Arsenal. After some hours' survey, the Amazon returned to the Fleet, when the opinions of the Artillery Officers were given in the affirmative, if the Flotilla to the eastward of the Crown Batteries were only removed. A Council of War was held in the afternoon, and the mode which might be advisable for the Attack was considered: that from the eastward appeared to be preferred. Lord Nelson offered his services, requiring ten Line-of-Battle Ships, and the whole of the Smaller Craft. The Commander-in-Chief, with sound discretion, and in a handsome manner, not only left everything to Lord Nelson for this detached service, but gave two more Line-of-Battle Ships than he demanded. During this Council of War, the energy of Lord Nelson's character was remarked : certain difficulties had been started by some of the members, relative to each of the three Powers we should either have to engage, in succession or united, in those seas. The number of the Russians was, in particular, represented as formidable. Lord Nelson kept pacing the cabin, mortified at everything which savoured either of alarm or irresolution. When the above remark was applied to the Swedes, he sharply observed, ' The more numerous the better ;' and when to the Russians, he repeatedly said, ' So much the better, I wish they were twice as many, the easier the victory, depend on it.' He alluded, as he afterwards explained in private, to the total want of tactique among the Northern Fleets; and to his intention, whenever he should bring either the Swedes or Russians to Action, of attacking the head of their Line, and confusing their movements as much as possible. He used to say, ' Close with a Frenchman, but out-manœuvre a Russian.' The night of the 31st of March was employed, as the preceding, in ascertaining, even by buoy lights, the course of the upper channel. Captain Brisbane was particularly active on this service, conducted under Lord Nelson's immediate directions.

On the forenoon of the 1st of April, the whole Fleet removed to an anchorage within two leagues of the Town, off the N.W. end of the Middle Ground. It was intended that the Division under Lord Nelson should proceed from this point through the Northern Channel. His Lordship, accompanied by a few chosen friends, made his last observations during that morning on board the Amazon, and about one o'clock returning to the Elephant, he threw out the wished for signal to weigh. The shout with which it was received throughout the Division was heard to a considerable distance; the Ships then weighed, and followed the Amazon in succession through the narrow channel. The wind was light, but favourable, and not one accident occurred. The buoys were accurately laid down, and the Smaller Craft distinctly pointed out the course : the gallant Riou led the way—the scene was perfect. About dark, the whole Fleet was at its anchorage off Draco point; the headmost of the Enemy's line not more than two miles distant. The small extent of the Anchoring-ground, as the Fleet did not consist of less than thirty-three Pendants, caused the Ships to be so much crowded, which the calmness of the evening increased, that had the Enemy but taken due advantage of it by shells from Mortar-boats, or from Amak Island, the greatest mischief might have ensued. They threw two or three about eight P.M., which served to show that we were within range. The Danes were, however, too much occupied during this night in manning their Ships, and strengthening their Line; not from immediate expectation, as we afterwards learned, of our Attack—conceiving the Channel impracticable to so large a Fleet, but as a precaution against our nearer approach. Our Guard-boats were actively employed between us and the Enemy, and Captain Hardy even rowed to their leading Ship; sounding round her, and using a pole when he was apprehensive of being heard. His chief object was to ascertain the bearing of the eastern end of the Middle Ground—the greatest obstacle, as it proved, that we had to contend with.

"On board the Elephant, the night of the 1st of April was an important one. As soon as the Fleet was at anchor, the gallant Nelson sat down to table with a large party of his comrades in arms. He was in the highest spirits, and drank to a leading wind, and to the success of the ensuing day. Captains Foley, Hardy, Fremantle, Riou, Inman, his Lordship's Second in Command, Admiral Graves, and a few others to whom he was particular attached, were of this interesting party; from which every man separated with feelings of admiration for their great leader, and with anxious impatience to follow him to the approaching Battle. The signal to prepare for Action had been made early in the evening. All the Captains retired to their respective Ships, Riou excepted, who with Lord Nelson and Foley arranged the Order of Battle, and those instructions that were to be issued to each Ship on the succeeding day. These three Officers retired between nine and ten to the after-cabin, and drew up those orders that have been generally published, and which ought to be referred to as the best proof of the arduous nature of the enterprise in which the Fleet was about to be engaged. From the previous fatigue of this day, and of the two preceding, Lord Nelson was so much exhausted while dictating his instructions, that it was recommended to him by us all, and, indeed, insisted upon by his old servant, Allen, who assumed much command on these occasions, that he should go to his cot. It was placed on the floor, but from it he still continued to dictate. Captain Hardy returned about eleven, and reported the practicability of the Channel, and the depth of water up to the Ships of the Enemy's line. Had we abided by this report, in lieu of confiding in our Masters and Pilots, we should have acted better. The orders were completed about one o'clock, when half a dozen Clerks in the foremost cabin proceeded to transcribe them. Lord Nelson's impatience again showed itself; for instead of sleeping undisturbedly, as he might have done, he was every half hour calling from his cot to these Clerks to hasten their work, for that the wind was becoming fair: he was constantly receiving a report of this during the night. Their work being finished about six in the morning, his Lordship, who was previously up and dressed, breakfasted, and about seven made the signal for all Captains. The instructions were delivered to each by eight o'clock; and a special command was given to Captain Riou to act as circumstances might require. The Land-forces and a body of 500 seamen were to have been united under the command of Captain Fremantle and the Honourable Colonel Stewart, and as soon as the fire of the Crown Battery should be silenced, they were to storm the work and destroy it. The Division under the Commander in-Chief was to menace the Ships at the entrance of the Harbour, the intricacy of the Channel would, however, have prevented their entering; Captain Murray in the Edgar was to lead :"

ORDERS FOR THE ATTACK.

[From the " Naval Chronicle," vol. v. p. 335.]

As Vice-Admiral Lord Nelson cannot with precision mark the situation of the different descriptions of the Enemy's Floating Batteries and smaller Vessels, lying between their two-decked Ships and Hulks, the Ships which are to be opposed to the Floating Batteries, &c. &c., will find their stations by observing the stations of the Ships to be opposed to the two-decked Ships and Hulks.

LINE OF BATTLE.[3]

These Ships are to fire in passing on to their stations.
{ Edgar
Ardent
Glatton
Isis
Agamemnon* }
Are to lead in succession.

The Edgar to anchor abreast of No. 5, (a sixty-four gun Ship, Hulk). The Ardent to pass the Edgar, and anchor abreast of Nos. 6 and 7. The Glatton to pass the Ardent, and anchor abreast of No. 9, (a sixty-four gun Ship Hulk.) The Isis to anchor abreast of No. 2, (a sixty-four gun Ship, Hulk). The Agamemnon to anchor abreast of No. 1.

Bellona,*
Elephant,
Ganges,
Monarch,
Defiance,
Russell,*
Polyphemus,
} To take their station and anchor, as is prescribed by the following arrangement.

MEMORANDUM.—No. 1 begins with the Enemy's first Ship to the southward.

No.	Rate.	Supposed Number of guns mounted on one side.	Station of the Line as they are to anchor and engage.
1	74	28	Agamemnon.* Desirée is to follow Agamemnon, and rake No. 2.
2	64	26	Isis.
3 4	Low Floating Batteries, Ship-rigged, rather lay within the Line	10 10	It is hoped the Desirée's fire will not only rake No. 1, but also rake these two Floating Batteries. Capt. Rose is to place the six Gun Brigs so as to rake them also.

³ The Ships marked thus (*) were not in Action, being on Shore; though, from their situation, they were exposed to the Enemy's fire.

No.	Rate.	Supposed Number of guns mounted on one side.	Station of the Line, as they are to anchor and engage.
5	64	27	Edgar.
6 }	Pontoon	10 }	Ardent.
7 }	Frigate Hulk	12 }	
8 }	Small—no guns visible,		Glatton.
9 }	64	20 }	
10	Ship Gun-boat of 22 guns	11 }	Bellona,* to give her at-
11 }	Pontoons, or	12 }	tention to support the
12 }	Floating Batteries . .	12 }	Glatton.
13	74	36	Elephant.
14 }	Pontoons, or	12 }	Ganges.
15 }	Floating Batteries . .	12 }	
16	64	30	Monarch.
17	64	30	Defiance.
18	64	30	Russell.*
19	64	30	Polyphemus.
20 {	A small Ship, supposed a Bomb,	11	

The six Gun-boats, Captain Rose is to place with the Jamaica, to make a raking fire upon No. 1. The Gun-boats, it is presumed, may get far enough astern of No. 1, to rake Nos. 3 and 4 ; and Captain Rose is to advance with the Ship and Vessels under his orders, to the Northward, as he may perceive the British fire to cease where he is first stationed.

Nos. 1, 2, 3, and 4, being subdued, which is expected to happen at an early period, the Isis and Agamemnon are to cut their cables, and immediately make sail and take their station ahead of the Polyphemus, in order to support that part of the Line. One Flat Boat manned and armed, is to remain upon the off side of each Line of Battle Ship. The remaining Flat Boats, with the Boats for boarding, which will be sent by Admiral Sir Hyde Parker under the command of the First Lieutenant of the London, are to keep as near to the Elephant as possible, but out of the line of fire, and to be ready to receive the directions of Lord Nelson.

The four Launches with anchors and cables, which will be sent by Admiral Sir Hyde Parker, under the command of a Lieutenant of the London, to be as near to the Elephant as

possible, out of the line of fire, ready to receive orders from
Vice-Admiral Lord Nelson.

The Alcmene, Blanche, Arrow, Dart, Zephyr, and Otter,
Fire-Ships, are to proceed under the orders of Captain Riou,
of the Amazon, to perform such service as he is directed by
Lord Nelson.

" The above were Lord Nelson's judicious dispositions for this memorable day.
With the returning light, the wind had been announced as becoming perfectly fair.
The Pilots, who were, in general, Mates of Trading Vessels from the Ports of Scotland and North of England to the Baltic, and several of the Masters in the Navy,
were ordered on board the Elephant between eight and nine o'clock. A most
unpleasant degree of hesitation prevailed amongst them all, when they came to the
point about the bearing of the east end of the Middle Ground, and about the exact
line of deep water in the King's Channel. Not a moment was to be lost; the wind
was fair, and the signal made for Action. Lord Nelson urged them to be steady, to
be resolute, and to decide. At length Mr. Brierley, the Master of the Bellona,
declared himself prepared to lead the Fleet; his example was quickly followed by
the rest, they repaired on board of their respective Ships, and at half-past nine, the
signal was given to weigh in succession. This was quickly obeyed by the Edgar,
who proceeded in a noble manner for the Channel. The Agamemnon was to follow,
but happened to take a course in a direct line for the end of the shoal.
The Polyphemus' signal, Captain Lawford, was then made, and this change in
the Order of Sailing was most promptly executed. The Edgar was, however,
unsupported for a considerable time; when within range of the Provestein, she
was fired at, but returned not a shot until she was nearly opposite to the number which was destined for her by the instructions—she then poured in her broadsides with great effect. The Polyphemus was followed by the Isis, Bellona, and
Russell; the former, commanded by Captain Walker, took her station most gallantly,
and had the severest berth this day of any Ship, the Monarch perhaps not excepted.
The Bellona and Russell, in going down the Channel, kept too close on the starboard shoal, and ran aground; they were, however, within range of shot, and
continued to fire with much spirit upon such of the Enemy's Ships as they could
reach. An instance of Lord Nelson's presence of mind now occurred, and which,
if I mistake not, was as follows :—In going down the Channel, the water was
supposed to shoal on the larboard shore, each Ship had been ordered to pass her
leader on the starboard side. When it came to the turn of the Elephant, his
Lordship, thinking that the two above-mentioned Ships had kept too far in that
direction, made the signal to close with the Enemy. Perceiving that this was not
done, which their being aground unknown to him was the cause of, he ordered the
Elephant's helm to starboard, quitted the intended Order of Sailing, and went within
those Ships. The same course was consequently followed by the succeeding Ships,
and the major part of our Fleet might thus, in all probability, have been saved from
going on shore. In succession, as each Ship arrived nearly opposite to her number
in the Danish line, she let her anchor go by the stern, the wind nearly aft, and
presented her broadside to the Enemy.

" The Action began at five minutes past ten. In about half an hour afterwards,
the first half of our Fleet was engaged, and before half past eleven, the Battle
became general. The Elephant's station was in the centre, opposite to the Danish
Commodore, who commanded in the Dannebrog, 62, Commodore Fischer, Captain

F. Braun. Our distance was nearly a cable's length, and this was the average distance at which the Action was fought; its being so great, caused the long duration of it. Lord Nelson was most anxious to get nearer; but the same error which had led the two Ships on the shoal, induced our Master and Pilots to dread shoaling their water on the larboard shore: they, therefore, when the lead was a quarter less five, refused to approach nearer, and insisted on the anchor being let go. We afterwards found, that had we but approached the Enemy's line, we should have deepened our water up to their very side, and closed with them: as it was, the Elephant engaged in little more than four fathom. The Glatton had her station immediately astern of us; the Ganges, Monarch, and Defiance a-head; the distance between each not exceeding a half cable. The judgment with which each Ship calculated her station in that intricate Channel, was admirable throughout. The failure of the three Ships that were aground, and whose force was to have been opposed to the Trekroner battery, left this day, as glorious for seamanship as for courage, incomplete. The lead was in many Ships confided to the Master alone; and the contest that arose on board the Elephant, which of the two Officers who attended the heaving of it should stand in the larboard chains, was a noble competition, and greatly pleased the heart of Nelson, as he paced the quarter-deck. The gallant Riou, perceiving the blank in the original plan for the attack of the Crown Battery, proceeded down the Line with his Squadron of Frigates, and attempted, but in vain, to fulfil the duty of the absent Ships of the Line. His force was unequal to it; and the general signal of recall, which was made about mid-action by the Commander-in-Chief, had the good effect of, at least, saving Riou's Squadron from destruction.

"About one P.M., few if any of the Enemy's heavy Ships and Praams had ceased to fire. The Isis had greatly suffered by the superior weight of the Provestein's fire; and if it had not been for the judicious diversion of it by the Desirée, Captain Inman, who raked her, and for other assistance from the Polyphemus, the Isis would have been destroyed. Both the Isis and Bellona had received serious injury by the bursting of some of their guns. The Monarch was also suffering severely under the united fire of the Holstein and Zealand; and only two of our Bomb-vessels could get to their station on the Middle Ground, and open their mortars on the Arsenal, directing their shells over both Fleets. Our Squadron of Gun-brigs, impeded by currents, could not, with the exception of one, although commanded by Captain Rose in the Jamaica, weather the eastern end of the Middle Ground, or come into Action. The Division of the Commander-in-Chief acted according to the preconcerted plan; but could only menace the entrance of the Harbour. The Elephant was warmly engaged by the Dannebrog, and by two heavy Praams on her bow and quarter. Signals of distress were on board the Bellona and Russell, and of inability from the Agamemnon. The contest, in general, although from the relaxed state of the Enemy's fire, it might not have given much room for apprehension as to the result, had certainly, at one P.M., not declared itself in favour of either side. About this juncture, and in this posture of affairs, the signal was thrown out on board the London, for the Action to cease.

"Lord Nelson was at this time, as he had been during the whole Action, walking the starboard side of the quarter-deck; sometimes much animated, and at others heroically fine in his observations. A shot through the mainmast knocked a few splinters about us. He observed to me, with a smile, 'It is warm work, and this day may be the last to any of us at a moment;' and then stopping short at the gangway, he used an expression never to be erased from my memory, and said with emotion, 'but mark you, I would not be elsewhere for thousands.' When the signal, No. 39, was made,[4] the Signal Lieutenant reported it to him. He continued his walk, and did not appear to take notice of it. The Lieutenant meeting his Lordship at the next turn asked, 'whether he should repeat it?' Lord Nelson answered, 'No, acknowledge it.' On the Officer returning to the poop, his Lordship called after him, 'Is No. 16 [5] still hoisted?' the Lieutenant answering in the affirmative, Lord Nelson said, 'Mind you keep it so.' He now walked the deck considerably agitated, which was always known by his moving the stump of his right arm. After a turn or two, he said to me, in a quick manner, 'Do you know what's shown on board of the Commander-in-Chief, No. 39?' On asking him what that meant, he answered, 'Why, to leave off Action.' 'Leave off Action!' he repeated, and then added, with a shrug, 'Now, damn me if I do.' He also observed, I believe, to Captain Foley, 'You know, Foley, I have only one eye—I have a right to be blind sometimes;' and then with an archness peculiar to his character, putting the glass to his blind eye, he exclaimed, 'I really do not see the signal.' This remarkable signal was, therefore, only acknowledged on board the Elephant, not repeated. Admiral Graves did the latter, not being able to distinguish the Elephant's conduct: either by a fortunate accident, or intentionally, No. 16 was not displaced. The Squadron of Frigates obeyed the signal, and hauled off. That brave Officer, Captain Riou, was killed by a raking shot, when the Amazon showed her stern to the Trekroner. He was sitting on a gun, was encouraging his men, and had been wounded in the head by a splinter. He had expressed himself grieved at being thus obliged to retreat, and nobly observed, 'What will Nelson think of us?' His Clerk was killed by his side ; and by another shot, several of the Marines, while hauling on the main-brace, shared the same fate. Riou then exclaimed, ' Come then, my boys, let us die all together!' The words were scarcely uttered, when the fatal shot severed him in two. Thus, and in an instant, was the British service deprived of one of its greatest ornaments, and society of a character of singular worth, resembling the heroes of romance.

" The Action now continued with unabated vigour. About two, P.M. the greater part of the Danish Line had ceased to fire : some of the lighter Ships were adrift, and the carnage on board of the Enemy, who reinforced their crews from the Shore, was dreadful. The taking possession of such Ships as had struck, was, however, attended with difficulty ; partly by reason of the batteries on Amak Island protecting them, and partly because an irregular fire was made on our Boats, as they approached, from the Ships themselves. The Dannebrog acted in this manner, and fired at our boat, although that Ship was not only on fire and had struck, but the Commodore, Fischer, had removed his Pendant, and had deserted her. A renewed attack on her by the Elephant and Glatton, for a quarter of an hour, not only completely silenced and disabled the Dannebrog, but, by the use of grape, nearly killed every man who was in the Praams, ahead and astern of that unfortu

---

[4] " To discontinue the engagement." Southey, " upon the highest and most unquestionable authority," states that Sir Hyde Parker made this signal " under a mistaken judgment, but from a disinterested and generous feeling," fearing that the Squadron would be defeated, the wind and current preventing his bringing his own Division to its assistance. " ' The fire,' he said, ' was too hot for Nelson to oppose ; a retreat, he thought must be made:—he was aware of the consequences to his own personal reputation ; but it would be cowardly in him to leave Nelson to bear the whole shame of the failure, if shame it should be deemed."' Mr. James also takes this view of the circumstance in his " Naval History."

[5] " For close Action," which had been flying from the beginning.

nate Ship. On our smoke clearing away, the Dannebrog was found to be drifting in flames before the wind, spreading terror throughout the Enemy's Line. The usual lamentable scene then ensued; and our Boats rowed in every direction, to save the crew, who were throwing themselves from her at every port-hole; few, however, were left unwounded in her after our last broadsides, or could be saved. She drifted to leeward, and about half-past three blew up. The time of half-past two, brings me to a most important part of Lord Nelson's conduct on this day, and about which so much discussion has arisen: his sending a Flag of Truce on shore. To the best of my recollection, the facts were as follow. After the Dannebrog was adrift, and had ceased to fire, the Action was found to be over, along the whole of the Line astern of us; but not so with the Ships ahead and with the Crown batteries. Whether from ignorance of the custom of war, or from confusion on board the Prizes, our Boats were, as before mentioned, repulsed from the Ships themselves, or fired at from Amak Island. Lord Nelson naturally lost temper at this, and observed, ' That he must either send on shore, and stop this irregular proceeding, or send in our Fire-ships and burn them.' He accordingly retired into the stern gallery, and wrote, with great dispatch, that well-known Letter addressed to the Crown Prince, with the address, ' To the Brothers of Englishmen, the brave Danes, &c.:'[6] and this Letter was conveyed on shore through the contending Fleets

---

[6] " In order to show that no hurry had ensued upon the occasion, he sent for a candle to the cockpit, that he might affix a larger seal than usual. The letter being written and carefully folded, he sent for a stick of sealing wax: the person dispatched for the wax had his head taken off by a cannon-ball; which fact being reported to the Admiral, he merely said, ' Send another messenger for the wax.' It was observed to him, that there were wafers on his table. ' Send for the sealing wax,' he repeated. It was done, and the letter sealed with a large quantity of wax, and a perfect impression. ' May I take the liberty of asking, why, under so hot a fire, and after so lamentable an accident, you have attached so much importance to a circumstance apparently trifling ?' ' Had I made use of a wafer,' he replied, ' the wafer would have been still wet when the letter was presented to the Crown Prince ; he would have inferred that the letter was sent off in a hurry; and that we had some very pressing reasons for being in a hurry. The wax told no tales."—Clarke and M'Arthur. Ed. Fisher, 8vo, vol. ii. p. 405. This anecdote is corroborated by a Letter from the late Mr. Thomas Wallis, who was then Purser of the Elephant, dated Brighton, 11th October 1843, to B. R. Haydon, Esq., the Historical Painter, who, wishing to paint the scene, had applied to Mr. Wallis for information. Mr. Wallis died towards the end of 1843 :—

" I shall be most happy to give you all the information in my power, relative to the Copenhagen affair, especially the circumstances attending that important event, the sending on shore, in the midst of the Action, Lord Nelson's celebrated Note, addressed ' to the Brothers of the Englishmen, the Danes.' Lord Nelson wrote the Note at the casing of the rudder-head, and as he wrote, I took a copy, both of us standing. The original was put into an envelope, and sealed with his Arms; at first I was going to seal it with a wafer, but he would not allow this to be done, observing that it must be sealed, or the Enemy would think it was written and sent in a hurry. The man I sent below for a light, never returned, having been killed in his way. To the best of my recollection, the Admiral wore a plain sort of a blue great coat, epaulettes, or gold lace, but on his breast were his several Orders, and he wore a plain cocked hat. Civilians in those days were not required to wear a uniform ; my dress was a plain blue coat, blue trowsers, with a white kerseymere

by Captain Sir Frederick Thesiger, who acted as his Lordship's Aid-de-camp ; and found the Prince near the Sally-port, animating his people in a spirited manner.

Whether we were actually firing at that time in the Elephant or not, I am unable to recollect; it could only have been partially, at such of the farther Ships as had not struck. The three Ships ahead of us were, however, engaged; and from the superiority of the force opposed to them, it was by no means improbable that Lord Nelson's observing eye pointed out to him the expediency of a prudent conduct. Whether this suggested to him the policy of a Flag of Truce or not, two solid reasons were apparent, and were such as to justify the measure: viz., the necessity of stopping the irregular fire from the Ships which had surrendered— and the singular opportunity that was thus given, of sounding the feelings of an Enemy, who had reluctantly entered into the war, and who must feel the generosity of the first offer of amity coming from a conquering foe. If there were a third reason for the conduct of the noble Admiral, and some of his own Officers assert this, it was unnecessary that it should have been expressed; it was certainly not avowed, and will for ever remain a matter of conjecture.[7] While the Boat was absent, the animated fire of the Ships ahead of us, and the approach of two of the Commander-in-Chief's division, the Ramilies and Defence, caused the remainder of the Enemy's Line to the eastward of the Trekroner to strike : that formidable Work continued its fire, but fortunately at too long a range to do serious damage to any one except the Monarch, whose loss in men, this day, exceeded that of any Line-of-Battle Ship during the war. From the uninjured state of this Outwork, which had been manned at the close of the Action with nearly 1500 men, it was deemed impracticable to carry into execution the projected plan for storming it; the Boats for this service had been on the starboard side of each Ship during the Action. The firing from the Crown Battery and from our leading Ships did not cease until past three o'clock, when the Danish Adjutant-General, Lindholm, returning with a Flag of Truce, directed the fire of the battery to be suspended. The signal for doing the same, on our part, was then made from our Ship to those engaged. The Action closed after five hours' duration, four of which were warmly contested.

" The answer from the Prince Regent was to inquire more minutely into the purport of the message. I should here observe, that previous to the Boat's getting on board, Lord Nelson had taken the opinion of his valuable friends, Fremantle and Foley, the former of whom had been sent for from the Ganges, as to the practicability of advancing with the Ships which were least damaged, upon that part of the Danish Line of Defence yet uninjured. Their opinions were averse from it ; and, on the other hand, decided in favour of removing our Fleet, whilst the wind yet held fair, from their present intricate Channel. Lord Nelson was now prepared how to act when Mr. Lindholm came on board, and the following answer was returned to the Crown Prince by Captain Sir Frederick Thesiger: ' Lord Nelson's object in sending the Flag of Truce was humanity; he therefore consents that hostilities shall cease, and that the wounded Danes may be taken on shore. And Lord Nelson will take his prisoners out of the Vessels, and burn and carry off his prizes as

---

waistcoat. The decks, as you observe, were perfectly clear fore and aft, and the place where the Note was written was at the extreme after-part of the Ship. Captain Foley commanded the Elephant: Captain Thesiger, to the best of my remembrance, held no command, but was merely a volunteer on board Sir Hyde Parker's Flagship, and, in consequence of his knowledge of Copenhagen and the Danish language, he was considered the fittest Officer to be entrusted with the Flag of Truce."

[7] *Vide* Lord Nelson's explanation of his motives, pp. 345, 358, *post.*

he shall think fit. Lord Nelson, with humble duty to his Royal Highness the
Prince of Denmark, will consider this the greatest victory he has ever gained, if it
may be the cause of a happy reconciliation and union between his own most
gracious Sovereign, and his Majesty the King of Denmark.' His Lordship, having
finished this letter, referred the Adjutant-General to the Commander-in-Chief, who
was at anchor at least four miles off, for a conference on the important points which
the latter part of the message had alluded to ; and to this General Lindholm did
not object, but proceeded to the London. Lord Nelson wisely foresaw, that, exclusive of the valuable opportunity that now offered itself for a renewal of Peace,
time would be gained by this long row out to sea, for our leading Ships, which were
much crippled, to clear the shoals, and whose course was under the immediate fire
of the Trekroner. The Adjutant-General was no sooner gone to the London, and
Captain Thesiger despatched on shore than the signal was made for the Glatton,
Elephant, Ganges, Defiance, and Monarch, to weigh in succession. The intricacy
of the Channel now showed the great utility of what had been done ; the Monarch,
as first Ship, immediately hit on a shoal, but was pushed over it by the Ganges
taking her amid-ships. The Glatton went clear, but the Defiance and Elephant ran
aground, leaving the Crown Battery at a mile distance ; and there they remained fixed,
the former until ten o'clock that night, and the latter until eight, notwithstanding
every exertion which their fatigued crews could make to relieve them. Had there
been no cessation of hostilities, their situation would certainly have been perilous ;
but it should be observed, on the other hand, that measures would in that case have
been adopted, and they were within our power, for destroying this formidable Work.

"The Elephant being aground, Lord Nelson followed the Adjutant-General,
about four o'clock, to the London, where that negotiation first began, which ter
minated in an honourable Peace. He was low in spirits at the surrounding scene
of devastation, and particularly felt for the blowing up of the Dannebrog. 'Well !'
he exclaimed, 'I have fought contrary to orders, and I shall perhaps be hanged :
never mind, let them.' Lindholm returned to Copenhagen the same evening, when
it was agreed that all Prizes should be surrendered, and the suspension of hostilities
continue for twenty-four hours ; the whole of the Danish wounded were to be
received on shore. Lord Nelson then repaired on board the St. George, and the
night was actively passed by the Boats of the Division which had not been engaged,
in getting afloat the Ships that were ashore, and in bringing out the Prizes. The
Desirée frigate, towards the close of the Action, going to the aid of the Bellona
became fast on the same shoal; but neither these Ships, nor the Russell, were
in any danger from the Enemy's batteries, as the world has frequently since been
led to suppose."—*Colonel Stewart's Narrative* in *Clarke and M'Arthur*, vol. ii.
pp. 261—274.

"At the Battle of Copenhagen," says Mr. Ferguson, the Surgeon of the Elephant,
"I was amongst the companions of the hero. The attempt was arduous in the extreme, no common mind would have dared to conceive it ; but it was suited to the
exalted enterprise of Lord Nelson. As *his* was the invigorating spirit of the Council
that planned the attack, so in the execution *he* only could have commanded success.
During the interval that preceded the Battle, I could only silently admire when I
saw the first man in all the world spend the hours of the day and night in Boats,
amidst floating ice, and in the severest weather; and wonder when the light showed
me a path marked by buoys, which had been trackless the preceding evening. On
the 1st of April, in the afternoon, we took our departure with twelve Sail of
the Line, and a proportional number of smaller Vessels, from the main body of
the Fleet, then lying about four miles below Copenhagen, and coasted along the

outer edge of the shoal called the Middle Ground, until we doubled its farthest extremity, when the Fleet cast anchor. This shoal, of the same extent as the sea-front of the Town, lies exactly before it, at about three-quarters of a mile in distance; the interval between it and the shore had deep water, and is called the King's Channel: there the Danes had arranged their Line of Defence as near the Town as possible. It consisted of nineteen Ships and Floating Batteries, flanked at the Town's extremity by two artificial Islands at the mouth of the Harbour, called the Crown Batteries, and extended for about a mile along the whole front of the Town, leaving intervals for the batteries on shore to play. As our own anchor dropped at eight in the evening, Nelson emphatically called out, 'I will fight them the moment I have a fair wind.' He spent the whole night in consultation.

"About half-past nine, A.M. of the 2nd of April, the signals of the different Ships having been made, repeated, and answered, we had the mortification to see the Agamemnon get upon the edge of the shoal, on the first attempt to leave her anchorage, where she remained immoveable. A similar misfortune followed in succession to the Russell and Polyphemus; and in addition to all this, the Jamaica frigate, with a convoy of Gun-boats and Small craft, having fallen in with the counter-current, made the signal of inability to proceed. A mind less invincible than Nelson's might have been discouraged: though the Battle had not commenced, yet he had approached the Enemy; and he felt that he could not retreat to wait for reinforcements, without compromising the glory of his Country. The signal to bear down was still kept flying. His agitation during these moments was extreme: I shall never forget the impression it made on me. It was not, however, the agitation of indecision, but of ardent, animated patriotism panting for glory, which had appeared within his reach, and was vanishing from his grasp."—*Clarke and M'Arthur*, vol. ii. pp. 266, 267.

TO VICE-ADMIRAL SIR HYDE PARKER.

[From the Letter-Book, and the "London Gazette" of the 15th of April 1801.]

Elephant, off Copenhagen, 3rd April, 1801.

Sir,

In obedience to your directions to report the proceedings of the Squadron named in the margin,[8] which you did me the honour to place under my command, I beg leave to inform you, that having, by the assistance of that able Officer, Captain Riou, and the unremitting exertions of Captain Brisbane, and the Masters of the Amazon and Cruizer in particular, buoyed the Channel of the Outer Deep, and the position of the Middle Ground, the Squadron passed in safety, and anchored off Draco the evening of the 1st; and that yesterday morning I made the signal for the Squadron to weigh, and to engage the

---

[8] Elephant, Defiance, Monarch, Bellona, Edgar, Russell, Ganges, Glatton, Isis, Agamemnon, Polyphemus, Ardent; [Frigates]—Amazon, Desirée, Blanche, Alcmene; Sloops—Dart, Arrow, Cruizer, and Harpy; Fire-Ships—Zephyr and Otter; Bombs—Discovery, Sulphur, Hecla, Explosion, Zebra, Terror, and Volcano.

Danish Line, consisting of six Sail of the Line, eleven Floating Batteries,[9] mounting from twenty-six twenty-four pounders to eighteen eighteen-pounders, and one Bomb-Ship, besides Schooner Gun-Vessels. These were supported by the Crown Islands, mounting eighty-eight cannon, and four Sail of the Line, moored in the Harbour's Mouth, and some Batteries on the Island of Amak.

The Bomb-Ship and Schooner Gun-Vessels made their escape. The other seventeen Sail are sunk, burnt, or taken, being the whole of the Danish Line to the southward of the Crown Islands, after a battle of four hours.[1]

From the very intricate navigation, the Bellona and Russell unfortunately grounded, but although not in the situation assigned them, yet so placed as to be of great service. The Agamemnon could not weather the shoal of the middle, and was obliged to anchor, but not the smallest blame can be attached to Captain Fancourt: it was an event to which all the Ships were liable. These accidents prevented the extension of our Line by the three Ships before mentioned, who would, I am confident, have silenced the Crown Islands, the two outer Ships in the harbour's mouth, and prevented the heavy loss in the Defiance and Monarch; and which unhappily threw the gallant and good Captain Riou, (to whom I had given the command of the Frigates and Sloops named in the margin,[2] to assist in the attack of the Ships at the harbour's mouth) under a very heavy fire. The consequence has been the death of Captain Riou, and many brave Officers and men in the Frigates and Sloops.

The Bombs were directed and took their stations abreast of the Elephant, and threw some shells into the Arsenal. Captain Rose, who volunteered his services to direct the Gun-brigs, did everything that was possible to get them forward, but the current was too strong for them to be of service during the Action; but not the less merit is due to Captain Rose, and, I believe, all the Officers and crews of the Gun-Brigs, for their exertions.

---

[9] In the copy in the *Letter-Book*, "*Seven* Sail of the Line, and *ten* Floating Batteries."

[1] "*About* four hours."—*Ibid.*

[2] Blanche, Alcmene, Dart, Arrow, Zephyr, and Otter.

The Boats of those Ships of the Fleet who were not ordered on the attack, afforded us every assistance; and the Officers and men who were in them merit my warmest approbation.

The Desirée took her station in raking the southernmost Danish Ship of the Line, and performed the greatest service. The Action began at five minutes past ten—the Van led by Captain George Murray of the Edgar, who set a noble example of intrepidity, which was as well followed up by every Captain, Officer, and Man in the Squadron.

It is my duty to state to you the high and distinguished merit and gallantry of Rear-Admiral Graves. To Captain Foley, who permitted me the honour of hoisting my Flag in the Elephant, I feel under the greatest obligations; his advice was necessary on many and important occasions during the Battle. I beg leave to express how much I feel indebted to every Captain, Officer, and Man, for their zeal and distinguished bravery on this occasion. The Honourable Colonel Stewart did me the favour to be on board the Elephant; and himself, with every Officer and Soldier under his orders, shared with pleasure the toils and dangers of the day.

The loss in such a Battle has naturally been very heavy. Amongst many other brave Officers and men who were killed, I have with sorrow to place the name of Captain Moss, of the Monarch, who has left a wife and six children to lament his loss; and among the wounded, that of Captain Sir Thomas Boulden Thompson, of the Bellona. I have the honour to be, &c.,

NELSON AND BRONTE.

NOTES SENT BY LORD NELSON, WITH A FLAG OF TRUCE, TO COPENHAGEN, DURING THE ACTION OF THE 2ND APRIL, 1801.

[Letter-Book.]

TO THE BROTHERS OF ENGLISHMEN, THE DANES.

Lord Nelson has directions to spare Denmark, when no longer resisting; but if the firing is continued on the part of Denmark, Lord Nelson will be obliged to set on fire all the Floating-batteries he has taken, without having the power of saving the brave Danes who have defended them. Dated on board his Britannic Majesty's Ship Elephant, Copenhagen Roads, April 2nd, 1801.

> NELSON AND BRONTE, Vice-Admiral, under the Command of Admiral Sir Hyde Parker.

TO THE GOVERNMENT OF DENMARK.

[Letter-Book.]

Elephant, 2nd April, 1801.

Lord Nelson's object in sending on shore a Flag of Truce is humanity : he, therefore, consents that hostilities shall cease till Lord Nelson can take his prisoners out of the Prizes, and he consents to land all the wounded Danes, and to burn or remove his Prizes. Lord Nelson, with humble duty to His Royal Highness, begs leave to say, that he will ever esteem it the greatest victory he ever gained, if this Flag of Truce may be the happy forerunner of a lasting and happy union between my most gracious Sovereign and his Majesty the King of Denmark.

> NELSON AND BRONTE.

LIST OF THE KILLED AND WOUNDED IN THE ATTACK ON THE ENEMY'S LINE OF DEFENCE, BATTERIES, ETC. ON THE 2ND OF APRIL.

Edgar.—Twenty-four Seamen, two Marines, three Soldiers of the 49th Regiment, killed ; seventy-nine Seamen, seventeen Marines, eight Soldiers of the 49th Regiment, wounded.—Total 133.

Monarch.—Thirty-five Seamen, twelve Marines, eight Soldiers of the 49th Regiment, killed ; one hundred and one Seamen, thirty-four Marines, twenty Soldiers of the 49th Regiment, wounded.—Total 210.

Bellona.—Nine Seamen, two Marines, killed ; forty-eight Seamen, ten Marines, five Soldiers, wounded.—Total 74.

Defiance.—Seventeen Seamen, three Marines, two Soldiers, killed ; thirty-five Seamen, five Marines, seven Soldiers, wounded.—Total 69.

Isis.—Twenty-two Seamen, four Marines, two Soldiers of the Rifle Corps, killed; sixty-nine Seamen, thirteen Marines, two Soldiers of the Rifle Corps, wounded.— Total 112.

Amazon.—Ten Seamen, one Marine, killed; sixteen Seamen, five Marines, wounded.—Total 32.

Glatton.—Seventeen killed, thirty-four wounded.—Total 51.

Desirée.—Three wounded.

Blanche.—Six Seamen, one Marine, killed; seven Seamen, two Marines, wounded.—Total 16.

Polyphemus.—Four Seamen, one Marine, killed; twenty Seamen, four Marines, wounded.—Total 29.

Elephant.—Four Seamen, three Marines, one Soldier of the Rifle Corps, killed; eight Seamen, one Marine, two Soldiers of the Rifle Corps, wounded.—Total 19.

Alcmene.—Five Seamen killed; twelve Seamen, two Marines, wounded.—Total 19.

Dart.—Two killed; one wounded.—Total 3.

Ganges.—Five killed; one missing.—Total 6.

Russell.—Five Seamen, one Marine, wounded.—Total 6.

Ardent.—Twenty-nine Seamen and Marines killed; sixty-four Seamen and Marines wounded.—Total 93.

OFFICERS KILLED.

Edgar.—Edmund Johnson, First Lieutenant; Lieutenant Benjamin Spencer, Marines.

Defiance.—George Gray, Lieutenant; Matthew Cobb, Pilot.

Elephant.—Captain James Bawden, of the Cornish Miners, Volunteer in the Rifle Corps; Mr. Henry Yaulden, Master's Mate.

Polyphemus.—Mr. James Bell, Midshipman.

Isis.—Mr. Daniel Lamond, Master; Mr. Henry Long, Lieutenant of the Marines; Mr. George M'Kinlay, Mr. Thomas Ram, Midshipmen; Mr. Grant, Lieutenant of the Rifle Corps.

Ganges.—Mr. Robert Stewart, Master.

Dart.—Mr. Edwin Sandys, Lieutenant.

Glatton.—Mr. Alexander Nicholson, Pilot.

Monarch.—Captain Robert Mosse.

Amazon.—Captain Edward Riou; Hon. George Tucket,[1] Midshipman; Mr. Jos. Rose, Captain's Clerk.

Ardent.—Mr. George Hoare, Midshipman.

OFFICERS WOUNDED.

Edgar.—Joshua Johnson, Second Lieutenant; William Goldfinch, Fifth Lieutenant; Mr. Gahagan, Mr. Whimper, Mr. Ridge, Mr. Proctor, Mr. Domett, Midshipmen, slightly.

Defiance.—Mr. Paterson, Boatswain; Mr. Gallaway, Midshipman; Mr. Niblet, Captain's Clerk; Mr. Stephenson, Pilot.

Elephant.—Mr. Robert Gill, Midshipman of the St. George, Mr. Hugh Mitchell, Midshipman.

Alcmene.—Mr. Henry Baker, acting Third Lieutenant; Mr. Charles Meredith, Lieutenant of the Marines; Mr. Charles Church, Boatswain; Mr. G. A. Spearing, Master's Mate; Mr. Pratt, Pilot.

Polyphemus.—Mr. Edward Burr, Boatswain.

Desirée.—Mr. King, Lieutenant, slightly.

Isis.—Mr. Richard Cormack, Lieutenant; Mr. Reuben Pain, Mr. Simon Frazer, Mr. Charles Jones, Midshipmen.

Ganges.—Mr. Isaac Davis, Pilot, badly.

Glatton.—Mr. Tindall, Lieutenant; Mr. Robert Thompson, Master's Mate; Mr. John Williams, Midshipman.

Monarch.—Mr. William Minchin, Lieutenant; Mr. James Marrie, Lieutenant of Marines; Mr. James Dennis, Lieutenant of the 49th Regiment; Mr. Henry Swimmer, Mr. W. J. Bowes, Mr. Thomas Harlowe, Mr. George Morgan, Mr. Philip le Vesconte, Midshipmen; Mr. William Joy, Boatswain.

Bellona.—Sir T. B. Thompson, Bart.,[2] Captain, lost his leg; Mr. Thomas Southey, Lieutenant; Mr. Thomas Wilks, Lieutenant, slightly; Captain Alexander Sharp, of the 49th Regiment, badly; Mr. James Emmerton, Master's Mate; Mr. ——— Anderson, Mr. Edward Daubeny, Mr. William Sitford, Mr. Fig, Midshipmen.

---

[1] *Sic*, but a mistake for the Honourable *John* Tuc*h*et.

[2] *Sic*, but a mistake, as he was not made a *Baronet* until 1806.

Amazon.—Mr. James Harry, Mr. Philip Horn, Master's Mates.

KILLED.—Officers 20
　　　　Seamen, Marines, and Soldiers 234
　　　　　　　　　　　　　　　　　　———　254
WOUNDED.—Officers 48
　　　　Seamen, Marines, and Soldiers 641
　　　　　　　　　　　　　　　　　　———　689

Total Killed and Wounded,　943

Lord Nelson's Dispatch was transmitted to the Admiralty by Sir Hyde Parker, with the following Letter:—

TO EVAN NEPEAN, ESQ., ADMIRALTY.

[From the " London Gazette," of April 15th, 1801.]

" London, Copenhagen Roads, 6th April, 1801.
　" Sir,
　" You will be pleased to acquaint the Lords Commissioners of the Admiralty, that since my letter of the 23rd of March, no opportunity of wind offered for going up the Sound until the 25th, when the wind shifted in a most violent squall from the S.W. to the N.W. and North, and blew with such violence, and with so great a sea, as to render it impossible for any Ship to have weighed her anchor. The wind and sea were even so violent as to oblige many Ships to let go a second anchor, to prevent them from driving, notwithstanding they were riding with two cables on end; and by the morning, the wind veered again to the southward of the west.

　" On the 30th of last month, the wind having come to the northward, we passed into the Sound with the Fleet, but not before I had assured myself of the hostile intentions of the Danes to oppose our passage, as the papers marked Nos. 1, 2, 3, and 4, will prove; after this intercourse there could be no doubt remaining of their determination to resist.

　" After anchoring about five or six miles from the Island of Huen, I reconnoitred with Vice Admiral Lord Nelson, and Rear-Admiral Graves, the formidable Line of Ships, Radeaus, Pontoons, Galleys, Fire Ships, and Gun-Boats, flanked and supported by extensive Batteries on the two Islands called the Crowns, the largest of which was mounted with from fifty to seventy pieces of cannon. These were again commanded by two Ships of seventy guns, and a large Frigate, in the inner Road of Copenhagen, and two sixty-four gun Ships (without masts) were moored on the Flat, on the starboard side of the entrance into the Arsenal. The day after, the wind being southerly, we again examined their position, and came to the resolution of attacking them from the southward.

　" Vice-Admiral Lord Nelson having offered his services for conducting the attack, had, some days before we entered the Sound, shifted his Flag to the Elephant, and after having examined and buoyed the Outer Channel of the Middle Ground, his Lordship proceeded with the twelve Ships of the Line named in the margin,[1] all

---

[1] Elephant, Defiance, Monarch, Bellona, Edgar, Russell, Ganges, Glatton, Isis, Agamemnon, Polyphemus, Ardent.

the Frigates, Bombs, Fire-Ships, and all the small Vessels, and that evening anchored off Draco Point, to make his disposition for the attack, and wait for the wind to the southward. It was agreed between us that the remaining Ships with me, should weigh at the same moment his Lordship did, and menace the Crown Batteries, and the four Ships of the Line that lay at the entrance of the Arsenal, as also to cover our disabled Ships as they came out of Action.

" I have now the honour to enclose a copy of Lord Nelson's report to me of the Action on the 2nd instant. His Lordship has stated so fully the whole of his proceedings on that day, as only to leave me the opportunity to testify my entire acquiescence and testimony of the bravery and intrepidity with which the Action was supported throughout the Line.

" Was it possible for me to add anything to the well-earned renown of Lord Nelson, it would be by asserting, that his exertions, great as they have heretofore been, never were carried to a higher pitch of zeal for his Country's service.

" I have only to lament that the sort of attack, confined within an intricate and narrow passage, excluded the Ships particularly under my command from the opportunity of exhibiting their valour; but I can with great truth assert, that the same spirit and zeal animated the whole of the Fleet; and I trust that the contest in which we are engaged, will on some future day afford them an occasion of showing that the whole were inspired with the same spirit, had the field been sufficiently extensive to have brought it into action.

" It is with the deepest concern I mention the loss of Captains Mosse and Riou, two very brave and gallant Officers, and whose loss, as I am well informed, will be sensibly felt by the families they have left behind them; the former a wife and children, the latter an aged mother. From the known gallantry of Sir Thomas Thompson on former occasions, the Naval service will have to regret the loss of the future exertions of that brave Officer, whose leg was shot off. For all other particulars I beg leave to refer their Lordships to Captain Otway, who was with Lord Nelson in the latter part of the Action, and able to answer any questions that may be thought necessary to put to him. A Return of the Killed and Wounded you will receive herewith. I have the honour to be, &c.

" H. Parker.

" P.S.—The promotions and appointments that have taken place on this occasion will be sent by the next opportunity that offers; but I cannot close this without acquainting their Lordships that Captain Mosse being killed very early in the Action, Lieutenant John Yelland continued it with the greatest spirit and good conduct; I must, therefore, in justice to his merit, beg leave to recommend him to their Lordships' favour."

The following was the Official account of the Battle, transmitted to his Royal Highness the Crown Prince, by the Danish Commander-in Chief, Olfert Fischer, whose mis-statements occasioned the remarkable Correspondence between Lord Nelson and the Danish Adjutant-General Lindholm, which will be found in a subsequent page:—

" On the 1st of April, at half-past three in the afternoon, two Divisions of the English Fleet, under the Command of Vice-Admiral Lord Nelson and a Rear-Admiral, weighed anchor, and stood eastwards and by south of the Middle Passage of the Road, where they anchored. This Force consisted of twelve Ships of the Line, and several large Frigates, Gun-boats, and other smaller Vessels, in all thirty-one Sail.

" On the 2nd of April, at three quarters past nine in the morning, the wind S.E., both the Vessels to the south, and the Vessels to the north of the Middle Road, weighed anchor. The Ships of the Line and heavy Frigates under Lord Nelson steered for the Konigstiefe, to take their Station in order, along the Line of Defence, confided to me. The Gun-boats and smaller Vessels took their Station nearer to the Town; and the Division of Admiral Parker, consisting of eight Ships of the Line and some Small Vessels, steered with a press of sail southwards to the right wing of Defence. At half-past ten, the foremost Ships of Admiral Nelson's Division passed the southern-most Ships of the Line of Defence. I gave those Ships that were within shot the Signal for Battle. The Block Ships Provestein and Vagrien, and immediately after these the Jutland, between which and the Block Ship Dannebrog, the leading English Ship (of 74 guns) fixed her station by throwing out one of her rear anchors, obeyed the Signal by a well-directed and well-supported fire. By degrees the rest of the Ships came up, and as they sailed past on both sides of the Ships already at anchor, they formed a thick Line, which, as it stretched northwards to the Ship of the Line, the Zealand, engaged not more than two-thirds of the Line of Defence committed to me; while the Three Crowns Battery, and the Block Ships Elephant and Mars, with the Frigate Hjelperen, did not come at all into the Action. In half an hour the Battle was general. Ten Ships of the Line, among which was one of eighty guns, the rest chiefly Seventy-fours, and from six to eight Frigates, on the one side. On the other, seven Block Ships, of which only one of seventy-four guns; the rest of sixty-four and under, two Frigates, and six Small Vessels. This was the respective strength of the two parties. The Enemy had on the whole two Ships to one, and the Block Ship Provestein had, besides a Ship of the Line, and the Rear-Admiral, two Frigates against her, by which she was raked the whole time, without being able to return a shot.

"If I only recapitulate historically what your Highness, and along with you a great portion of the Citizens of Denmark and Europe, have seen, I may venture to call that an unequal Combat, which was maintained and supported for four hours and a half with unexampled courage and effect, in which the fire of the superior force was so much weakened for an hour before the end of the Battle, that several English Ships, and particularly Lord Nelson's, were obliged to fire only single shots; that this Hero himself, in the middle and very heat of the battle, sent a Flag of Truce on shore to propose a cessation of hostilities; if I add, that it was announced to me that two English Ships of the Line had struck, but being supported by the assist-ance of fresh Ships, again hoisted their Flags, I may, in such circumstances, be permitted to say, and I believe I may appeal to the Enemy's own confession, that in this Engagement Denmark's ancient Naval reputation blazed forth with such in-credible splendour, that I thank Heaven all Europe are the witnesses of it. Yet the scale, if not equal, did not decline far to the disadvantage of Denmark. The Ships that were first and most obstinately attacked, even surrounded by the Enemy, the incomparable Provestein fought till almost all her guns were dismounted. But these Vessels were obliged to give way to superior Force, and the Danish fire ceased along the whole Line from north to south.

"At half-past eleven, the Dannebrog Ship of the Line, which lay alongside Admiral Nelson, was set on fire. I repaired with my Flag on board the Holstein, of the Line belonging to the North wing. But the Dannebrog long kept her Flag flying in spite of this disaster. At the end of the Battle she had two hundred and seventy men killed and wounded. At half past two, the Holstein was so shattered, and had so many killed and wounded, and so many guns dismounted, that I then caused the Pendant to be hoisted, instead of my Flag, and went on shore to the battery of the Three Crowns, from which I commanded the North wing, which was slightly engaged with the Division of Admiral Parker, till about four o'clock, when I received orders from your Royal Highness to put an end to the Engagement. Thus the quarter of the Line of Defence from the Three Crowns to the Frigate Hjelperen, was in the power of the Enemy; and the Hjelperen thus finding herself alone, slipped her cables and steered to Stirbfen. The Ship Elwin, after she had received many shots in the hull, and had her masts and rigging shot away, and a great number killed and wounded, retreated within the Crowns. The Gun-boats Nyburg and Aggershuus, which last towed the former away, when near sinking, ran ashore; and the Gernershe Floating battery, which had suffered much, together with the Block Ship Dannebrog, shortly after the Battle, blew up. Besides the visible loss the Enemy have suffered, I am convinced their loss in killed and wounded is considerable. The advantage the Enemy have gained by their Victory, too, consists merely in Ships which are not fit for use, in spiked cannon, and gunpowder damaged by sea water. The number of killed and wounded cannot yet be exactly ascertained; but I calculate it from sixteen to eighteen hundred men. Among the former it is with grief that I mention the Captain of the Block Ship Indosforetten, and the Frigate Cronenberg, Captain Thara, and first Lieutenant Hauch, with several other brave Officers. Among the wounded, the Commander of the Dannebrog, who, besides other wounds, has lost his right hand. I want expressions to do justice to the unexampled courage of the Officers and Crews. The Battle itself can only enable you to form an idea of it.

"OLFERT FISCHER."

"A LIST OF THE DANISH NAVAL FORCE CALLED THE LINE OF DEFENSION, OPPOSED TO THE BRITISH FLEET UNDER THE COMMAND OF ADMIRAL LORD NELSON, BEFORE COPENHAGEN, APRIL 2ND 1801; WITH REMARKS" COPIED FROM A PAMPHLET PUBLISHED IN ENGLISH, AT COPENHAGEN.

[From the "Naval Chronicle," vol. vi. p. 120.]

Names.	Description.	Commanders.	No.	Guns.	Men.	Remarks.
Provestein,	Block-ship,	Captain Lassen,	1	56	515	Taken and burnt. Forsaken when the Guns were useless.
Vagrien,	Ditto,	Aid-de-Camp Risbrigh,	2	48	361	Ditto.
Rendsborg,	Pram,	Captain-Lieut. Egede,	3	20	216	Driven on the shoals, and burnt by the enemy.
Nyborg,	Ditto,	Captain-Lieut. Rothe,	4	20	209	Escaped, afterwards sunk.*
Jylland,	Block-ship,	Captain Brandt,	5	48	396	Taken. Since burnt by the enemy.
Suerfisken,	Radeau,	Lieut. Sommerfeldt,	6	20	117	Taken. Ditto.*
Kronborg,	Block-ship,	Lieutenant Hauch,	7	22	196	Taken. Ditto.*
Hagen,	Radeau,	Lieutenant Moller,	8	20	155	Taken. Ditto.*
Dannebrog,	Block-ship,	Captain F. Broun,	9	62	336	Caught fire, and blew up after the action.
Elven,	Small repeat. frig.	Lieutenant Holsteen,	10	6	80	Escaped.
Grenier's redeau,	No. 1,	Lieutenant Willemoes,	11	24	120	Ditto.*
Aggershuus,	Pram,	Lieutenant Fasting,	12	20	213	Ditto. Afterwards sunk.
Syælland,	Ship of the Line,	Captain Harboe,	13	74	529	Driven by the waves under the Trekroner battery, and taken after the armistice. Since burnt.
Charlotte Amalia,	Block-ship,	Captain Kofod,	14	26	225	Taken, and afterwards burnt.
Söhesteen,	Radeau,	Lieutenant Middlebo,	15	18	126	Ditto.*
Holsteen,	Ship of the Line,	Captain Ahrenfeldt,	16	60	400	Taken, and put in sailing condition by the enemy, and carried away as a trophy.
Indfodstratten,	Block-ship,	Captain Thura,	17	64	390	Taken. Afterwards burnt.
Hjelperen,	Frigate,	Capt.-Lt. Lillienshield,	18	20	265	Escaped.

Total 628 guns, 4849 men.

"THE FORCE REMAINING IN THE ROAD TO DEFEND THE HARBOUR, UNDER THE ORDERS OF CHAMBERLAIN STEIN BILLE.

Names.	Description.	Commanders.	No.	Guns.
Elephanten,	Block-ship,	Captain Von Thura,	19	70
Mars,	Ditto,	Captain Gyldenfeldt,	20	64
Dannemark,	Ship of the Line,	Chamberlain Stein Bille	21	74
Trekoner,	Ditto,	Captain Riegelsten,	22	74
Iris,	Frigate,	Captain W. Brown,	23	40
Sarpen and Nidelven.	Brigs.			of 18 guns each.

"Twelve Chebecks, each of two . . 24 pounders.
Two   ditto   ditto   . . 12 ditto.
The Great Trekroner Battery of thirty 24 ditto.
Ditto   thirty-eight 36 ditto.
Ditto   one 96 ditto, carronade,
Provided with three furnaces to heat balls.

"The Ships and Vessels marked thus *, were placed a little behind the others on account of their weakness, but in the evening of the 1st of April, Commodore Fischer seeing the great number of the Enemy, ordered them to come into the line. It can easily be perceived that this Defension was to answer no other end than to keep a wise Enemy at too great a distance to bombard the Town; or to make an audacious Enemy so great a resistance, as would cost them many men, and endanger their Ships in such a degree, as to render their future proceedings of little consequence. The result has answered these expectations. The Enemy taking the advantage of the defension being immoveable, attacked the weakest part thereof, but were so warmly received, and met with such a long and unexpected resistance, that they preferred negotiation to hostility.

"SOUTH WING OF DEFENSION.

"WHAT STATE THE SHIPS WERE IN WHICH COMPOSED THE LINE OF DEFENSION, WITH THE NUMBER OF GUNS, AND WEIGHT OF METAL EACH SHIP CARRIED.

Provestein, { An old Three-decker, cut down to two decks, dismantled and condemned. Twenty-eight guns of thirty-six-pounders, and and twenty-eight of twenty-four-pounders.

Vagrien, { An old Two-decker, quarter-deck cut down. Condemned. All her guns of twenty-four pounders.

Rendsborg, { An old Pram for the transport of cavalry, with masts and sails; her guns of twenty-four pounders.

Nyborg, Ditto, completely rigged. Her guns of twenty-four-pounders.

Jylland, { An old Two-decker condemned, without poop or masts. Twenty-four guns of twenty-four pounders, and twenty-four of twelve-pounders.

Suerfisken, { Square Floating-battery with masts. The guns of eighteen-pounders.

Kronborg, { An old condemned Frigate, cut down and dismantled. The guns of twenty-four-pounders.

Hagen, A Battery, like the Suerfisken. The guns of eighteen-pounders,

Dannebrog, { An old condemned Two-decker, cut down and dismantled. The guns twenty-four of twenty-four-pounders, twenty-four of twenty-two-pounders, and fourteen of eight-pounders.

Elven, { A small Repeating vessel rigged. The guns of twenty four-pounders.

Grenier's float,   Old, and without masts. The guns of twenty-four-pounders.

Aggershuus, { An old cavalry Transport, without masts or sails. Her guns of twenty-four-pounders.

Syælland, { A Two-decker, condemned and unrigged. The guns thirty of twenty four-pounders, thirty of eighteen-pounders, and fourteen of eight-pounders.

Charlotte Amalia, { A condemned Indiaman. Condemned and dismantled. The guns of twenty-four pounders.

Söhesten, { A Battery, like the Suerfisken. The guns of twenty-four-pounders.

Holsteen, { A Two-decker newly repaired, and able to serve for twelve years. The guns twenty-four of twenty-four pounders, twenty-four of twelve pounders, and twelve of eight-pounders.

Indfodstratten, { An old condemned Two-decker, cut down and dismantled. Twenty-six guns of twenty-four-pounders, twenty-six of twelve pounders, and twelve of eight-pounders.

Hjelperen, { A good completely rigged Frigate. The guns of thirty six-pounders.

" NORTH WING OF DEFENSION.

" THE BATTERY OR ISLAND OF TREKRONER.

" Mars of 64 guns. An old Two-decker, condemned and without masts.
Elephanten of 70 guns.   Ditto.

This Wing, which properly defended the entry of the Harbour, was likewise supported by the advanced Battery of the Citadel, and by a moveable Squadron situated behind, which consistsd of the

Dannemark . . . . 74 guns
Trekroner 74
Iris 40
Sarpen and Nidelven, Brigs of 18 guns each,

under the orders of Chamberlain Bille.

" REMARKS.

" The Frigates that raked the Provestein fore and aft, were at anchor opposite the battery on Almak Island, at about 3400 Danish feet distance. The guns of the outermost fortifications at the S. E. of Copenhagen, being 4600 Danish feet distant from the nearest Ships of the Defension, were of no service while the Action lasted: they began to fire when the Enemy took possession of the abandoned Ships, but it was at the same time that the parley appeared. Parker's Division was engaging at a great distance; the Block-ships of the north wing and the Trekroner battery kept him in awe, as well as Nelson's van, so that Parker's motions could have no other tendency than to hinder this part of the Defension from assisting the others, and to keep Stein Bille's Squadron from coming out to take possession of those English Ships which had struck, or to succour the nearest part of the fighting Wing. The Citadel, too far behind to use its guns, threw several shells, but soon left off on account of its great distance. The Foe had not only the advantage of the

wind, which sent the smoke on our Ships, but likewise of the current, which permitted them to stop where they thought proper by means of a stern anchor, and
thereby were enabled judiciously (as Commodore Fischer mentions in his report)
to assist, cover, or draw back their Ships, in order to distribute the damage so
equally on all, that none should be totally lost, but that they might all, at least in
appearance, safely come out of so warm a fight. The Danes had the misfortune,
half an hour after the Action began, to have the Rendsborg Pram's cable shot off,
which caused her to drive on a bank behind the line, with her bows towards the
Enemy, so that she became useless. The second misfortune, which happened almost
immediately, was the Dannebrog's catching fire. The third, that the Syælland's
cables were shot away. The fourth was that the Chief of the Infodstratten was killed
by the same fire from the Enemy. The fight was, nevertheless, continuing, and the
fire of the southerly fortification of the Town became effective, as well as that of
the Block-ships, the Mars and Elephanten, and the Trekroner battery, by the approach of the Enemy, when Lord Nelson sent a parley on shore: he thereby gained
time to succour those of his Ships that had struck, to help others off that were
aground, and to take a quiet possession of those wrecks that were either surrendered
or forsaken."

A very interesting account of the Battle of Copenhagen is given by the celebrated
Historian, Niebuhr, who was then in that City, in a series of letters to Madame
Hensler, written during the Action; a translation of which letters is published in
Tait's Magazine for June last. Niebuhr not only represents Nelson's conduct
as having been absurdly undignified, but he says, that "two English Ships of
the Line struck, but could not be taken;"—that "the Enemy have burnt several
of their own disabled Ships, more are said to have been thus burnt than they
have captured from us!" and that "their loss is reported to amount to 2000 men,
killed and wounded." It is also proper to refer to Monsr. Thiers' recent animated
description of the Battle; and the generous admiration of Nelson, which that
distinguished writer exhibits, is security that he will gladly avail himself of the
authentic information of Nelson's conduct, which this Volume affords, to correct his
mis-statements; for he will here find ample evidence, that Nelson was neither
"almost beaten," nor that, "had the firing continued a few moments longer, Nelson's
Fleet, almost disabled, would have been obliged to retire, half destroyed." Monsr.
Thiers will find, also, that Nelson had no other motive for sending the Flag of Truce,
than humanity to a conquered but brave and noble Foe.

Other accounts of the Battle of Copenhagen will be found in James' *Naval
History*, vol. v. p. 65, *et seq.*; in Southey's *Life of Nelson*: and in a Letter from an
Officer of the Ganges, in the *Naval Chronicle*, vol. v. p. 338.

Colonel Stewart's Narrative contains some farther particulars of much interest:—
"Early in the morning of the 3rd of April, when it was scarcely light, Lord Nelson repaired in his gig, (his usual conveyance,) on board of our Ship, the Elephant,
conceiving that we were still aground. The fatigue and cold of a long row in a
northern sea, and at that early hour, and after the most severe exertions both of
body and mind for several successive days, had no effect in causing this uncommon
man either to indulge in rest, or for an instant to forget those whose fate he valued.
His delight and praises at finding us afloat were unbounded, and recompensed all
our misfortunes. He took a hasty breakfast and then rowed to such of the Prizes,
as were not yet removed from the Danish shore; and here he gave another proof of
the eccentricity, as well as boldness, of his character. Finding that one of the Line-
of-Battle Ships, the Zealand, which had struck the last, and was under the immediate

protection of the Trekroner, had refused to acknowledge herself to be a captured Ship, and made some quibble about the Colours and not the Pendant having been hauled down, his Lordship ordered one of our Brigs to approach her, and proceeded in his gig to one of the Enemy's Ships which were within that battery, in order to communicate with the Commodore, whose flag was flying on board of the Elephanten. When he got alongside, he found it to be his old acquaintance, Müller, whom he had known in the West Indies. He invited himself on board, and acted with so much ability and politeness towards his friend and the Officers assembled, that he not only explained and gained the point in dispute about the Zealand, but left the Ship, as much admired by his Enemies, as he had long been by those who were his intimate friends in his own Fleet. This day was actively employed in refitting the Squadron, securing the Prizes, distributing the prisoners, and in negotiating with the shore. It was resolved that Lord Nelson should wait on the Prince Regent on the ensuing day.

" On the 4th of April, his Lordship left the Ship, accompanied by Captains Hardy and Fremantle, and was received with all possible attention from the Prince. The populace showed a mixture of admiration, curiosity, and displeasure. A strong guard secured his safety, and appeared necessary to keep off the mob, whose rage, although mixed with admiration at his thus trusting himself amongst them, was naturally to be expected. The events of the 2nd had plunged the whole Town into a state of terror, astonishment, and mourning; the oldest inhabitant had never seen a shot fired in anger at his native Country. The Battle of that day, and the subsequent return of the wounded to the care of their friends on the 3rd, were certainly not events that could induce the Danish Nation to receive their conqueror, on this occasion, with much cordiality. It perhaps savoured of rashness in Lord Nelson thus early to risk himself amongst them; but with him, his Country's cause was paramount to all personal consideration.

" The negotiation continued, and the interim between the 4th and 9th of April was employed in destroying the Prizes, refitting the Fleet, and in taking a position with the Bomb-vessels and Gun-brigs, in order to open the bombardment, in the event of hostilities being renewed. On the 9th, Lord Nelson landed again, and was accompanied by the Adjutant-General Lindholm, who came to receive him, and whose attention was marked throughout; and by Lieutenant-Colonel Stewart, Captain Parker, the Rev. Mr. Scot, &c. He was escorted to the Palace, surrounded by an immense crowd, who showed more satisfaction on this occasion than on the preceding one. The Commissioners, who were appointed to adjust the terms of an Armistice, proceeded to business without delay. On the seventh Article of this Treaty much difficulty arose, and the negotiation was likely to have been broken off on the point of duration. The Danish Commissioners candidly avowed their apprehension of the Court of Russia: Lord Nelson assured them, with a degree of candour not quite customary in diplomacy, that his reason for requiring so long a term as sixteen weeks, was that he might have time to act against the Russian Fleet, and then return to them. The point not being acceded to on either side, one of the Danish Commissioners hinted at the renewal of hostilities. Upon which Lord Nelson, who understood French sufficiently to make out what the Commissioner said, turned to one of his friends with warmth, and said, ' Renew hostilities ! Tell him that we are ready at a moment; ready to bombard this very night.' The Commissioner apologized with politeness, and the business went on more amicably. The duration of the Armistice could not, however, be adjusted; and the conference broke up at two o'clock, for reference to the Crown Prince. A Levée was consequently held in one of the state rooms, the whole of which were without furniture, from the apprehension of a bombardment. His Lordship then proceeded to a grand dinner up stairs, the Prince leading the way. Lord Nelson, leaning on the arm of a friend, whispered, ' Though I have only one eye, I see all this will burn very well:' he was even then thinking more about the bombardment than about the dinner. During the entertainment, which was laid for fifty covers, Lord Nelson sat on the Prince's right hand, and much cordiality prevailed. They were afterwards closeted together for some time, and the Prince at length acceded to an Armistice of fourteen weeks' duration; to which Lord Nelson assenting, with the reservation of the approval of the Commander-in-Chief, the party returned on board."—*Clarke and M'Arthur.*

Intelligence of the Battle of Copenhagen reached the Admiralty on the 15th of April, and Lord St. Vincent thus immediately acknowledged Lord Nelson's dispatch:—

"Admiralty, April, 1801.

" My dear Lord,

" It is impossible for me to describe the satisfaction expressed by his Majesty, his confidential Servants, and the whole body of the People, at the conduct of your Lordship, and the Officers, Seamen, Marines, and Soldiers, who served under your auspices on the 2nd Instant ; and all are equally well disposed to give credit to your zeal as a negotiator. You cannot have a stronger proof, than in your appointment to succeed Admiral Sir Hyde Parker in the command of the Baltic Fleet, on the conduct of which, the dearest interests of this Nation depend ; and, although the death of the late Emperor of Russia appears to have made a material change in the politics of the Court of Petersburgh, it is absolutely necessary to be prepared for the sudden changes which too frequently happen in the political hemisphere. I will seize the first opportunity to convey to the King the high estimation in which you hold our friend Colonel Stewart : he is the bearer of this, and will, I am persuaded, be of great use to you, both in negotiating and fighting, if there should be again occasion. That the same Divine influence which has hitherto prospered all your Lordship's exertions in the cause of your Country, may continue to hover over you, is the fervent prayer of your truly affectionate, St. Vincent." *Clarke and M'Arthur.*

On the 16th of April, Lord St. Vincent, First Lord of the Admiralty, " called the attention of the House of Lords to the recent Victory obtained over the Danes. He paid a very handsome compliment to the several persons engaged in the Expedition, whose conduct upon this occasion, in his opinion, far surpassed anything that was to be found in the glorious annals of the British Navy. He then moved the Thanks of the House to Admiral Sir Hyde Parker, for the Victory obtained over the Danish Fleet on the 2nd of Apri last, and also that the Thanks of the House should be given to Vice-Admiral Lord Nelson; to Rear-Admiral Graves; to the Honourable Colonel Stewart, of the 49th Regiment of Foot; together with the Officers, Marines, and Sailors, serving on board the British Fleet.

" Lord Grenville said it would be impossible for him to add anything to the impression which the House must already have felt with regard to the merits of those great and gallant Officers who had so recently obtained so signal and brilliant a Victory. The noble Earl, whose great professional knowledge the Country had already felt the benefit of, and which was fully known to every Noble Lord in that House, had, in his short and emphatic address, just described this Victory in a manner which spoke more forcibly to the feelings and understandings of men, than the most elaborate oratory could do. He had truly described it as a Victory which was not equalled by any that had ever been achieved by the Navy of Great Britain.

It was not, therefore, for the purpose of adding anything to the praise of those gallant Officers that he then addressed their Lordships. He rose merely to say a few words upon the subject in a political point of view. In the first place, he would inform their Lordships, that the Expedition which led to this Victory had been planned by his Majesty's late Ministers; but, at the same time, he must give the present Ministers, and, particularly, that Noble Lord who now presided with such distinguished ability at the Admiralty Board, the credit of having forwarded it with such astonishing dispatch, as to render the object of it completely successful. It was impossible for him to find words to express the sense he entertained of the valour and abilities of the noble Admiral who bore a principal share in the late Victory, which was not equalled by his most splendid victory at Aboukir. But great as was his merit as an Officer and a Conqueror, he should value those two Victories gained by him, more from the importance of their political consequences, than from the valour and talents displayed in achieving them. The Victory at Aboukir was followed by the greatest advantages to this Country; and the late Victory in the Baltic, which terminated the Northern War as soon as it had been begun, would be productive of consequences still more important and beneficial. His Lordship concluded with giving his most hearty concurrence to the motion.

" The EARL OF WESTMORLAND said he could not give a silent vote : he must add the testimony of his approbation and applause to what had been already said of those gallant Officers—whose greatest merit, however, was that of having been praised by the noble Earl at the head of the Admiralty—*laudari a laudato viro.*

" The DUKE OF CLARENCE said, it might appear presumptuous in him to rise and add approbation to what was already mentioned ; yet he would just say, that great praise was owing to the late First Lord of the Admiralty, for the peculiar choice he had made of Commanders for the Expedition, and great praise also to the present Noble Earl who had dispatched it with a celerity and promptitude that led almost to sure and instant success. He complimented Lord Nelson highly on his courage and intrepidity, which Fortune seemed to back in every enterprise in which he was engaged ; and acknowledged his own personal obligation, as a Prince of the Blood, to the gallant Commanders, and to the whole Fleet, for the accomplishment of a Victory, which probably in its effect would restore the possessions on the Continent to his Family, together with the peace and security of the British Empire, and of Europe.

" LORD HOOD could not content himself with giving a silent vote, because he had been personally convinced, while he had the honour of having those two illustrious Officers serving under him, that it was impossible there could be two more courageous and able Commanders, or who were more zealous in their Country's Cause."

The Motions were agreed to; and the Thanks were ordered to be communicated to the respective Commanders.

In the HOUSE OF COMMONS, on the same day,—

" MR. ADDINGTON (Chancellor of the Exchequer, rose to move the Thanks of the House to the Officers and Seamen of the Northern Fleet, for the distinguished zeal and gallantry which they had shown in the Action of the 2nd of April. He must say, that no Action had taken place in the course of the present war, which contributed more to sustain the character and to add to the lustre of the British Arms. For its execution, Sir Hyde Parker, Lord Nelson, and Rear-Admiral Graves, three most distinguished Officers. had been selected ; and, thus prepared, the Armament proceeded to the North. 'To enter into all the particulars of the Service was unnecessary; it was sufficient, therefore, to say, that the Fleet, after passing the Sound, advanced to Copenhagen. Such was the situation of the Enemy's force, that all our Ships could not possibly be engaged. In these circumstances, Sir Hyde Parker had, with a degree of judgment which reflected the highest credit on his choice, appointed Lord Nelson, whose name had already been covered with splendour and renown, to the execution of the important enterprise. Great, however, as was the courage, the skill, and the success which had been formerly displayed by this illustrious Commander at Aboukir, it was not greater than that which had been exhibited in the Attack upon the Fleet moored for the defence of Copenhagen. But this was not all. After the Line of Defence was destroyed, and whilst a tremendous fire was still continued, Lord Nelson retired to his cabin, and addressed a letter to the Prince Royal of Denmark. He then asked that a Flag of Truce might be admitted to land, adding at the same time, that if this was denied, he must be obliged to demolish the Floating Batteries which were in his power; and that in such case he could not answer for the lives of the brave men by whom they had been defended. To the answer, which required to know the motive of such a message, his reply was—that his only motive was humanity; that his wish was to prevent the further effusion of blood; and that no Victory which he could possibly gain would afford him so much pleasure as would result from being the instrument of restoring the amicable intercourse which had so long existed between his Sovereign and the Government of Denmark. Lord Nelson in consequence went on shore, and was received by a brave and generous people—for brave they had shown themselves in their Defence, and generous in the oblivion of their loss—with the loudest and most general acclamations. The Prince Royal of Denmark had also received his Lordship in a manner conformable to his high character. The Negotiation which ensued between them it would be highly improper for him now to state; but this he must observe, that Lord Nelson had shown himself as wise as he was brave, and proved that there may be united in the same person, the talents of the Warrior and the Statesman. The manner in which he spoke of Admiral Graves, Colonel Stewart, and the rest of the Gentlemen who had co-operated with him, showed the kindness of his nature and the gallantry of his spirit. He gave, in fact, due praise for their good conduct to all. Mr. Addington concluded a very complimentary Speech by moving a Vote of Thanks to Sir Hyde Parker 'for the able and judicious disposition which he had made of the Fleet under his Command, when the Line of Defence before Copenhagen was forced, and a signal Victory obtained.'

LORD HAWKESBURY, Secretary of State for Foreign Affairs, said, in seconding the motion of his Right Honourable friend, he should say a very few words, preserving a silence as to the progress of the expedition to ultimate victory, that having been so ably detailed by his Right Honourable friend. It was with sincere satisfaction he contemplated that not a drop of British or Danish blood which had been spilled, could be attributed to this Country, proposals for an amicable arrangement having been made to the last by England. It was the injustice of the Enemy that at length compelled us to draw the sword, in spite of every effort to the contrary, short of the complete abandonment of that very principle, which was the object of the contest. The Victory of the 2nd of April must be considered as more important to the interests of the Country, and as leading to events that must be contemplated with satisfaction and exultation.

MR. PITT said, he did not rise to detain the House one moment, but to declare his sincere concurrence in the motion and the sentiments offered by his Honourable friend.

MR. GREY said, he also rose to express his entire concurrence in the motion, and he trusted there would not be a dissentient voice upon the occasion. He not only wished to thank the Officers and men employed upon the expedition, but to applaud the merit to which Government were entitled for the vigour displayed in its equipment and dispatch. He was happy to hear the sentiments of moderation expressed by the Right Honourable gentleman, and the prospects which might be entertained of a just and equitable peace. An observation had been made by the noble Lord which he thought might have been spared, as leading to an opposition of sentiment, which he deprecated upon the present occasion. He was determined, however, that nothing should prevent him from joining in the expression of that joy and satisfaction which every one most feel. He could not help observing, that what had been assumed by the noble Lord relative to the cause of the war, was assumed without any documents being before the House to support it, no communication upon the subject having been made from the Throne; and this was, perhaps, the only war in which this Country had been engaged, where the first information received of it by the House, was a motion for a Vote of Thanks, in consequence of a brilliant and decisive Victory, without any previous communication whatever upon the subject.

MR. SHERIDAN said, that whatever difference of opinion might exist relative to our dissensions with the Northern Powers, he should have hoped it would not have been brought into discussion; and he applauded the forbearance and moderation of his Honourable friend, in declining to take notice of certain observations from the other side of the House, which might have been as well avoided, with respect to which, he still retained the opinion he formerly had, relative to our contest with the Northern Powers. On the subject more immediately before the House, only one sentiment could be entertained, that of admiration and gratitude, which words were inadequate to express, particularly towards that noble Lord, who could gain the plaudits and acclamations of a vanquished enemy. After the motions of Thanks were disposed of, there remained a more melancholy duty to perform, to pay a tribute of respect and gratitude to the two gallant Officers who had lost their lives on this occasion. He understood one of those Officers had left an aged mother, and the other a widow and orphan family, by no means in affluent circumstances, to whom he trusted the spontaneous benevolence of his Majesty would extend the means of comfort, as a small compensation for the heavy loss they had sustained.

MR. WILBERFORCE said a few words expressive of his approbation of the motion, and congratulating the Country on the moderation displayed by his Majesty's Ministers.

The Vote of Thanks to Sir Hyde Parker was then put, and carried, *nem. con.*

The Thanks of the House were then voted, in like manner, to Lord Nelson, Admiral Graves, and Colonel Stewart, of the 49th Regiment, and the other Officers.

The approval and acknowledgment of the conduct of the Seamen, Soldiers, and Marines, were also passed, *nem. con.*

MR. ADDINGTON then moved an Address to His Majesty, that a Monument might be erected to the memory of Captains Riou and Mosse in the Cathedral of St. Paul. He said, at the same time, that due attention should be paid to their surviving Relatives.—The motion was agreed to."

It was not until a month after the news of the Battle reached London, that the Rewards conferred upon the two Admirals present were officially announced. On the 19th of May, the "London Gazette" stated that, "The King has been pleased to grant the dignity of a Viscount of the United Kingdom of Great Britain and Ireland to the Right Honourable Horatio Baron Nelson, Knight of the Most Honourable Order of the Bath, and Vice-Admiral of the Blue Squadron of his

Majesty's Fleet, and the heirs male of his body lawfully begotten, by the name, style, and title of Viscount Nelson of the Nile, and of Burnham Thorpe, in the county of Norfolk.[1]

"The King has also been pleased to nominate and appoint Thomas Graves, Esquire, Rear-Admiral of the White, to be one of the Knights Companions of the Most Honourable Order of the Bath."

Medals were *not* conferred upon the Captains, nor did the City of London vote its Thanks to Lord Nelson and his Companions—omissions which he deeply felt, and which became the subjects of an extraordinary Correspondence.

It is also remarkable that the Battle should not have been expressly mentioned in the King's Speech on proroguing Parliament, in October following—there being no other allusion to it than that "the distinguished valour and eminent services of my forces by sea and land, which at no period have been surpassed, are entitled to my warmest acknowledgments," in which "acknowledgment" the Militia, Fencibles, Yeomanry, and Volunteers, were included.

TO ADMIRAL SIR HYDE PARKER, BART., COMMANDER-IN-CHIEF.

[Autograph, in the possession of Admiral Sir Robert Waller Otway, Bart., G.C.B., who was then Captain of the London, Sir Hyde Parker's Flag Ship.]

St. George, 3 A.M.
[3rd April, 1801.]

My dear Sir Hyde,

One of the Ships which struck during yesterday's Battle, was by some oversight not taken possession of. I directed Lord Henry Paulet, late last night, to do so. His Boats, I find, were fired at, and not allowed to come alongside, saying they had not surrendered, as their Pendant was still flying. This is a most disgraceful subterfuge, as this Ship had ceased firing, on hauling down her Colours. I think you had better demand her in a peremptory manner; and I recommend your sending Otway[2] for that purpose. In much haste, sincerely yours,

NELSON AND BRONTE.

[1] See a Copy of the PATENT in the APPENDIX.

[2] On the copy of this Note, sent to the Editor, Admiral Sir Robert Otway wrote: "This Note was given to me by Sir Hyde Parker, with his directions to act upon it according to my judgment. I have the satisfaction of adding, that I had the Ship in question (which was a 74) given up to me by the Danish Commodore.—R. W. OTWAY, Admiral of the White." The Ship, the Holstein, was recovered by Captain Otway, by a very extraordinary *ruse*, which is described in the memoir of that gallant Officer, in Ralfe's "Naval Biography."

TO THE RIGHT HONOURABLE HENRY ADDINGTON.

[Autograph, in the Sidmouth Papers.]

St. George, Copenhagen Roads, April 4th, 1801.

My dear Sir,

It was by your own desire that I trouble you with a letter, after having tried the contest afloat with Denmark. I shall not trouble you with a history of battles. Suffice it to say, as far as we could, we have, by the blessing of God been completely victorious. Circumstances threw me in the way of communicating with the Prince Royal of Denmark, and it has led to some messages passing between the shore and Sir Hyde Parker. I own I do not build much hopes on the success of negotiation, as it appears clearly to me that Denmark would at this moment renounce all her alliances to be friends with us, if fear was not the preponderating consideration. Sir Hyde Parker thought that probably some good might arise, if I went on shore to converse with his Royal Highness; I therefore went yesterday noon, dined in the Palace, and, after dinner, had a conversation of two hours alone with the Prince, (that is, no Minister was present,) only his Adjutant-General, Lindholm, was in the room.

His Royal Highness began the conversation by saying how happy he was to see me, and thanked me for my humanity to the wounded Danes. I then said it was to me, and would be the greatest affliction to every man in England, from the King to the lowest person, to think that Denmark had fired on the British Flag, and became leagued with her Enemies. His Royal Highness stopped me by saying, that Admiral Parker had declared war against Denmark. This I denied, and requested his Royal Highness to send for the papers, and he would find the direct contrary, and that it was the furthest from the thoughts of the British Admiral. I then asked if his Royal Highness would permit me to speak my mind freely on the present situation of Denmark, to which he having acquiesced, I stated to him the sensation which was caused in England by such an unnatural alliance with, at the present moment, the furious enemy of England. His answer was, that when he made the alliance, it was for the protection of their trade, and that Denmark would never be the enemy of England, and that the

Emperor of Russia was not the enemy of England when this treaty was formed; that he never would join Russia against England, and his declaration to that effect was the cause of the Emperor (I think he said) sending away his Minister; that Denmark was a trading Nation, and had only to look to the protection of its lawful commerce. His Royal Highness then enlarged on the impossibility of Danish Ships under Convoy, having on board any contraband trade; but to be subjected to be stopped—even a Danish Fleet by a pitiful Privateer, and that she should search all the Ships, and take out of the Fleet any Vessels she might please—was what Denmark would not permit. To this my answer was simply, ' What occasion for Convoy to fair trade ?' To which he answered, ' Did you find anything in the Convoy of the Freya ?'[3] and that no Commander could tell what contraband goods might be in his Convoy, &c. &c.; and as to merchants, they would always sell what was most saleable; that as to swearing to property, I would get anything sworn to which I pleased.' I then said, ' Suppose that England, which she never will, was to consent to this freedom and nonsense of navigation, I will tell your Royal Highness what the result would be—ruination to Denmark; for the present commerce of Denmark with the warring Powers was half the Neutral carrying trade, and any merchant in Copenhagen would tell you the same. If all this freedom was allowed, Denmark would not have more than the sixth part; for the State of Hamburgh was as good as the State of Denmark, in that case; and it would soon be said, we will not be stopped in the Sound—our Flag is our protection; and Denmark would lose a great source of her present revenue, and that the Baltic would soon change its name to the Russian Sea.' He said this was a delicate subject; to which I

---

[3] On the 25th of July 1800, a small Squadron, under Captain Baker of the Nemesis, fell in with the Danish frigate Freya, and her Convoy, off Ostend. The intention to search the Convoy being resisted by the Freya, a spirited Action ensued, and the Dane, after a most gallant resistance against a very superior force, struck his colours, and, with his Convoy, was carried into the Downs. Lord Whitworth was immediately sent to Denmark, with a Fleet under Vice-Admiral Dickson; and on the 28th of August a Convention was signed, by which it was agreed that the Freya and her Convoy should be repaired at the expense of Great Britain, and released, and that the question of the right of this Country to examine Convoys should be afterwards discussed in London.

replied that his Royal Highness had permitted me to speak out. He then said, ' Pray answer me a question ; for what is the British Fleet come into the Baltic ?' My answer—' To crush a most formidable and unprovoked Coalition against Great Britain.' He then went on to say that his Uncle[4] had been deceived ; that it was a misunderstanding, and that nothing should ever make him take a part against Great Britain ; for that it could not be his interest to see us crushed, nor, he trusted, ours to see him : to which I acquiesced. I then said there could not be a doubt of the hostility of Denmark ; for if her Fleet had been joined with Russia and Sweden, they would assuredly have gone into the North Sea, menaced the Coast of England, and probably have joined the French, if they had been able. His Royal Highness said his Ships never should join any Power against England ; but it required not much argument to satisfy him that he could not help it.

In speaking of the pretended union of the Northern Powers, I could not help saying that his Royal Highness must be sensible that it was nonsense to talk of a mutual protection of trade, with a Power who had none, and that he must be sensible that the Emperor of Russia would never have thought of offering to protect the trade of Denmark, if he had not had hostility against Great Britain. He said repeatedly, ' I have offered to-day, and do offer my mediation between Great Britain and Russia.' My answer was, ' A mediator must be at peace with both parties. You must settle your matter with Great Britain. At present you are leagued with our Enemies, and are considered naturally as a part of the effective force to fight us.' Talking much on this subject, his Royal Highness said, ' What must I do to make myself equal ?' Answer— ' Sign an Alliance with Great Britain, and join your Fleet to ours.' His Royal Highness—' Then Russia will go to war with us ; and my desire, as a commercial Nation, is to be at peace with all the world.' I told him he knew the offer of Great Britain, either to join us, or disarm. ' I pray, Lord Nelson, what do you call disarming ?' My answer was, ' That I was not authorized to give an opinion on the subject, but I considered it as not having on foot any force beyond the cus-

tomary establishment.' Question—'Do you consider the
Guard-ships in the Sound as beyond that common establishment?' Answer—'I do not.' Question—'We have always
had five Sail of the Line in the Cattegat and Coast of Norway.'
Answer—'I am not authorized to define what is exactly disarming, but I do not think such a force will be allowed.'
His Royal Highness—'When all Europe is in such a dreadful
state of confusion, it is absolutely necessary that States should
be on their guard.' Answer—'Your Royal Highness knows
the offers of England to keep twenty Sail of the Line in the
Baltic.' He then said, 'I am sure my intentions are very
much misunderstood;' to which I replied, that Sir Hyde
Parker had authorized me to say that, upon certain conditions
his Royal Highness might have an opportunity of explaining
his sentiments at the Court of London—'I am not authorized
to say on what conditions exactly.' Question—'But what do
you think?' Answer—'First, a free entry of the British
Fleet into Copenhagen, and the free use of every thing we may
want from it.' Before I could get on, he replied quick, 'That
you shall have with pleasure.' 'The next is, whilst this
explanation is going on, a total suspension of your treaties
with Russia. These, I believe, are the foundation on which
Sir Hyde Parker only can build other articles for his justification in suspending his orders, which are plain and positive.'
His Royal Highness then desired me to repeat what I had
said, which having done, he thanked me for my open conversation; and I having made an apology if I had said anything
which he might think too strong, his Royal Highness very
handsomely did the same, and we parted; he saying that he
hoped we would cease from hostilities to-morrow, as on such
an important occasion he must call a Council. My reception
was such as I have always found it—far beyond my deserts.

I saw Count Bernstoff[5] for a moment, and could not help
saying he had acted a very wrong part in my opinion, in involving the two Countries in their present melancholy situation, for that our Countries ought never to quarrel. I had not
time to say more, as the Prince sent for me, and Count Bernstoff was called the moment I came out of the room. The

---

[5] Danish Minister for Foreign Affairs.

King's brother and his son desired I might be presented to them, which I was, and then returned on board. Yesterday evening I received from General Adjutant Lindholm, the English papers to March 24th, with a hope that what I had said to the Prince would make peace. I find all the Country hate both the Russians and Swedes. Again begging your pardon for this long letter, I will only add that I am ever your most obliged,

NELSON AND BRONTE.

TO ADMIRAL THE EARL OF ST. VINCENT, K.B.

[From Clarke and M'Arthur, vol. ii. p. 276.]

[Apparently about April 5th, 1801.]

Whether Sir Hyde Parker may mention the subject to you, I know not, for he is rich, and does not want it. Nor is it, you will believe me, from any desire I possess to get a few hundred pounds, that actuates me to address this letter to you; but, my dear Lord, justice to the brave Officers and men who fought on that day. It is true, our opponents were in Hulks and Floats only adapted for the position they were placed in; but that made our battle so much the harder, and victory so much the more difficult to obtain. Believe me, I have weighed all circumstances, and in my conscience I think that the King should send a gracious Message to the House of Commons, for a gift to this Fleet; for what must be the natural feelings of the Officers and men belonging to it, to see their rich Commander-in-Chief burn all the fruits of their victory, which, if fitted up and sent to England, as many of them might have been by dismantling part of our Fleet, would have sold for a good round sum? Having mentioned the subject, I shall leave it to the better judgment of your lordship and Mr. Addington. I am, &c.,

NELSON AND BRONTE.

TO LIEUTENANT . . . ., WARRIOR.

[Letter-Book.]

St. George, Copenhagen Roads, 8th April, 1801.

Sir,

Most assuredly you did perfectly right in reporting to me
(if your assistance was of no use) the Bellona and Russell
being aground, in order that I might direct the necessary
measures for getting them afloat. But as the transaction had
slipped my memory until reminded of it by you, I must now
say, that I think, at such a moment, the delivery of anything
like a desponding opinion, unasked, was highly reprehensible,
and deserved much more censure than Captain Foley (I suppose was the person you allude to) gave you. As far as my
opinion goes, I repeat, that, although you were right in acquainting me with the situation of the Bellona and Russell,
if you were not wanted there, yet I think you wrong in
giving a desponding opinion unasked, but which I should
not have recollected, if your letter had not brought it fresh to
my mind. I had so much pleasure in seeing every Officer
and man do his duty on the 2nd, that I should not have recollected an unintentional error, much less a slip of the tongue.
I am, &c.,

NELSON AND BRONTE.

TO THE RIGHT HONOURABLE HENRY ADDINGTON.

[Autograph, in the Sidmouth Papers. On the 9th of April an Armistice was
agreed upon, and Sir Hyde Parker sent a copy of it to the Admiralty by Colonel
the Honourable William Stewart, which was published in the " London Gazette,"
of the 21st of April, 1801.

ARMISTICE.

The Danish Government on the one hand, and Admiral Sir Hyde Parker, Knight,
Commander-in-Chief of His Britannic Majesty's Naval Forces in the Road of
Copenhagen on the other, being from motives of humanity, equally anxious to put
a stop to the further effusion of blood, and to save the City of Copenhagen from the
disastrous consequences which may attend a further prosecution of hostilities
against that City, have mutually agreed upon a Military Armistice, or Suspension of
Arms.

His Danish Majesty having for that purpose appointed Major-General Ernest
Frederick Waltersdorff, Chamberlain to His Danish Majesty, and Colonel of a
Regiment, and Adjutant-General Hans Lindholm, Captain in His Danish Majesty's
Navy, his Commissioners for agreeing about the Terms of the said Armistice ; and

Admiral Sir Hyde Parker, Knight, having with the same view duly authorized the Right Honourable Horatio Lord Nelson of the Nile, Knight of the Most Honourable Order of the Bath, Duke of Bronté in Sicily, Knight of the Grand Cross of the Order of St. Ferdinand and of Merit, and of the Imperial Order of the Crescent, Vice-Admiral in the Fleet of His Britannic Majesty's Service, and the Honourable William Stewart, Lieutenant-Colonel in his Britannic Majesty's Service, and Member of Parliament, and Commanding a Detachment of His Britannic Majesty's Forces embarked, these said Commissioners have met this day, and having exchanged their respective powers, have agreed upon the following terms :—

" Article I.—From the moment of the signature of this Armistice, all hostilities shall immediately cease between the Fleet under the command of Admiral Sir Hyde Parker and the City of Copenhagen, and all the armed Ships and Vessels of His Danish Majesty in the Road or Harbour of that City, as likewise between the different Islands and Provinces of Denmark, Jutland included.

" Article II.—The armed Ships and Vessels belonging to His Danish Majesty, shall remain in their present actual situation as to armament, equipment, and hostile position ; and the Treaty commonly understood as the Treaty of Armed Neutrality shall, as far as relates to the co-operation of Denmark, be suspended, while the Armistice remains in force.

" On the other side, the armed Ships and Vessels under the command of Admiral Sir Hyde Parker, shall in no manner whatsoever molest the City of Copenhagen or His Danish Majesty's armed Ships and Vessels, and the Coasts of the different Islands and Provinces of Denmark, Jutland included ; and in order to avoid every thing which might otherwise create uneasiness or jealousy, Sir Hyde Parker shall not suffer any of the Ships or Vessels under his command to approach within gunshot of the armed Ships or Fort of His Danish Majesty in the Road of Copenhagen : this restriction shall not however extend to Vessels necessarily passing or repassing through the Gaspar, or King's Channel.

" Article III.—This Armistice is to protect the City of Copenhagen, as also the Coasts of Denmark, of Jutland, and the Islands included, against the attack of any other Naval Force which His Britannic Majesty may now or hereafter, during its remaining in force, have in these seas.

" Article IV.—The Fleet of Admiral Sir Hyde Parker shall be permitted to provide itself at Copenhagen, and along the Coasts of the different Islands and Provinces of Denmark and Jutland included, with everything which it may require for the health and comfort of the Crews.

" Article V.—Admiral Sir Hyde Parker shall send on shore all such subjects of His Danish Majesty as are now on board the British Fleet under his command, the Danish Government engaging to give an acknowledgment for them, as also for all such wounded as were permitted to be landed after the Action of the 2nd instant, in order that they may be accounted for in favour of Great Britain, in the unfortunate event of the renewal of hostilities.

" Article VI.—The Coasting trade carried on by Denmark, along all such parts of her Coast as are included in the operation of this Armistice, shall be unmolested by any British Ships or Vessels whatever, and instructions given accordingly by Admiral Sir Hyde Parker.

" Article VII.—This Armistice is to continue uninterrupted by the contracting Parties for the space of fourteen weeks from the signature hereof ; at the expiration of which time, it shall be in the power of either of the said Parties to declare a cessation of the same, and to recommence hostilities, upon giving fourteen days' previous notice.

"The conditions of this Armistice are upon all occasions to be explained in the most liberal and loyal manner, so as to remove all ground for farther disputes, and to facilitate the means of bringing about the restoration of harmony and good understanding between the two Kingdoms.

"In faith whereof, we the undersigned Commissioners, in virtue of our full powers, have signed the present Armistice, and have affixed to it the Seal of our Arms.

"Done on board His Britannic Majesty's Ship the London, in Copenhagen Roads, April 9th, 1801.

(*L.S.*)   "NELSON AND BRONTE.

(*L.S.*)   "WILLIAM STEWART.

(*L.S.*)   "ERNEST FREDERICK WALTERSDORFF.

(*L.S.*)   "HANS LINDHOLM.

"In pursuance of my above-mentioned authority, I ratify this document with my hand.

(*L.S.*)   "FREDERICK.

"Ratified by me,

(*L.S.*)   "HYDE PARKER, Admiral and Commander-in-Chief of His Britannic Majesty's Fleet.]

St. George, April 9th, 1801.

My dear Sir,

A negotiator is certainly out of my line, but being thrown into it, I have endeavoured to acquit myself as well as I was able, and in such a manner as I hope will not entirely merit your disapprobation. If it unfortunately does, I have only to request that I may now be permitted to retire, which my state of health, and inconvenience from the loss of my limb has long rendered necessary. I trust you will take into consideration all the circumstances which have presented themselves to my view. 1st. We had beat the Danes. 2nd. We wish to make them feel that we are their real friends, therefore have spared their Town, which we can always set on fire; and I do not think, if we burnt Copenhagen it would have the effect of attaching them to us; on the contrary, they would hate us. 3rd. They understand perfectly that we are at war with them for their treaty of Armed Neutrality made last year. 4th. We have made them suspend the operations of that treaty. 5th. It has given our Fleet free scope to act against Russia and Sweden; 6th, which we never should have done, although Copenhagen would have been burnt, for Sir Hyde Parker was determined not to have Denmark hostile in his rear. Our passage over the Grounds might have been very seriously interrupted by the batteries near Draco. 7th. Every reinforcement, even a Cutter, can join us without molestation, and also provisions,

stores, &c.   8th. Great Britain is left with the stake of all the
Danish property in her hands, her Colonies, &c., if she refuses
peace.   9th. The hands of Denmark are tied up; ours are
free to act against her confederate Allies. 10th. Although
we might have burnt the City, I have my doubts whether we
could their Ships.   They lay in this way :

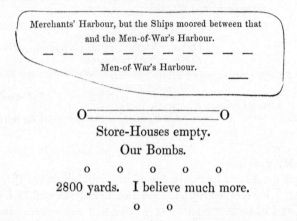

Men-of War's Harbour.

O⸻O

Store-Houses empty.

Our Bombs.

o   o   o   o   o

2800 yards.   I believe much more.

o   o

Therefore our shells have only the width of a Line of Battle
Ship, and every Ship must be separately burnt, for they have
plenty of room to haul any Ship on fire clear of the others.
All these considerations weighed deeply in my mind; added
to which, having shown them that it was not because we feared
fighting them that we negotiated, but for the cause of humanity
towards Denmark, and the wish to conciliate their affections;
all these matters have affected my mind, nor shall I have a
moment's rest, till I know, at least, that I am not thought to
have done mischief.   After we had forced the expression ot
the suspension of the treaty of Armed Neutrality, a point very
difficult for fear of Russia, I said to the Prince, ' Now, Sir,
this is settled, suppose we write Peace instead of Armistice ?'
to which he replied, that he should be happy to have a peace,
but he must bring it about slowly, so as not to make new
wars.   We talked whether some method could not be thought
of, to prevent the mortifications to which Ships of War with
Convoys were liable, by being stopped; to which I answered,
I thought there might very easily.   I did not enter further

on the subject with him, although I did to his Adjutant-General of the Fleet, Lindholm, who seems much in his confidence. My idea is, that no Convoys shall be granted to any Vessels bound to Ports at war with us; and that if any such Convoy is granted, that it shall be considered as an act of hostility; and that if any Vessel under Convoy proceeds to an Enemy of England's Port, that the owner shall lose the value of his Ship and cargo, and the Master be severely punished. On those foundations I would build a prevention against future disputes; but all these matters I leave to wiser heads, and shall only assure you that I am truly, with the greatest respect, your most faithful and obedient servant,

NELSON AND BRONTE.

I have the pleasure to tell you that Count Bernstoff was too ill to make me a visit yesterday. I had sent him a message to leave off his Ministerial duplicity, and to recollect he had now British Admirals to deal with, who came with their hearts in their hands. I hate the fellow.

Colonel Stewart, a very fine gallant man, will give you every information.

TO ADMIRAL THE EARL OF ST. VINCENT, K.B.

[From Clarke and M'Arthur, vol. ii. p. 276.]

St. George, 9th April, 1801.

Just returned from getting the Armistice ratified. I am tired to death. No man but those who are on the spot can tell what I have gone through, and do suffer. I make no scruple in saying, that I would have been at Revel fourteen days ago; that without this Armistice the Fleet would never have gone but by order from the Admiralty; and with it, I dare say, we shall not go this week. I wanted Sir Hyde to let me at least go and cruise off Carlscrona, to prevent the Revel Ships from getting in. I said, I would not go to Revel to take any of those laurels which I was sure he would reap there. Think for me, my dear Lord, and if I have deserved well, let me retire; if ill, for heaven's sake supersede me, for I cannot exist in this state. I am, &c.,

NELSON AND BRONTE.

TO THE RIGHT HONOURABLE LORD MINTO.

[Autograph, in the Minto Papers.]

Copenhagen Roads, April 9th, 1801.

My dear Lord,

I cannot let an Officer go to Berlin, without sending a line to be forwarded to Vienna, to say I am still alive, although not well; and also to say that George[4] is alive, well, and a very good young man. You ought to get him made a Captain. God knows it is of no use being with me for promotion, for not one out of the St. George is promoted by Sir Hyde Parker. You will see, probably, that my Flag flew in the Elephant, the 2nd, as the St. George drew too much water. It was hard fought, but God blessed my endeavours with success. Before you condemn the Armistice, hear all the reasons: they are weighty, and most important. Without it we should have gone no further this year, and with it not half so far as I wish. Pray present my humble duty to the Queen of Naples. I have this night a letter from the King of Naples, but I have not time to finish my numerous letters of business. To Lady Minto and your family, everything which is kind. George is fitting out a Danish seventy-four, therefore does not know of this opportunity. Ever yours affectionately,

NELSON AND BRONTE.

TO SIR BROOKE BOOTHBY, BART.

[From a Copy in the Nelson Papers.]

St. George, Copenhagen Roads, April 9th, 1801.

My dear Sir Brooke,

I am well; the Battle was, I must allow, hard fought, but our success was complete. Of the eighteen Vessels of all descriptions, seventeen are sunk, burnt, and taken. I ought to be ashamed, after such a neglect of your kind letter, of writing so short a one, but time is not mine: therefore, forgive me! I but wish to finish Paul, and then retire for ever. Believe me, your most obliged,

NELSON AND BRONTE.

---

[4] Now Rear-Admiral the Honourable George Elliott, C.B.

TO ADMIRAL THE EARL OF ST. VINCENT, K.B.

[From Clarke and M'Arthur, vol. ii. p. 278.]

14th April, 1801.

Captain Bligh[5] has desired my testimony to his good conduct, which, although, perfectly unnecessary, I cannot refuse :
his behaviour on this occasion can reap no additional credit
from my testimony. He was my second, and the moment
the Action ceased, I sent for him, on board the Elephant, to
thank him for his support. I am sure of your goodness to
Thompson.[6] I am, &c.,

NELSON AND BRONTE.

TO ADMIRAL THE EARL OF ST. VINCENT, K.B.

[From Clarke and M'Arthur, vol. ii. p. 278, who state, that after mentioning the
names of Lieutenants Bolton, Pearce, and others, whom he considered as his
children, and who had not been promoted, he generously added :—]

[About 14th April, 1801.]

I can only say, that the first I must name, can be no other
than the First Lieutenant of the Elephant—no acquaintance,
and one intended to be advanced by Sir Hyde Parker. Captain Devonshire, after Brisbane, highly deserved to be made
Post. I am, &c.

NELSON AND BRONTE.

TO GENERAL-ADJUTANT LINDHOLM.

[Letter-Book, and Copy in the Nelson Papers. Between the 2nd and 9th
of April, during the negotiation for the Armistice, Lord Nelson was employed
in getting out and destroying his Prizes, except the Holstein, which was sent
to England. On the 12th, Sir Hyde Parker sailed from Copenhagen Road with
the Fleet, except the St. George, and one or two Frigates ; and to the astonish··
ment of the Northern world, entered the Baltic, along the Grounds, between
the Islands of Amak and Saltholm, intending to attack the Russian Squadron in
Revel. Hearing, however, that the Swedish Squadron was at sea, Sir Hyde proceeded
to the northern extremity of the Island of Bornholm; but the Swedes had taken refuge
in Carlscrona. Lord Nelson hastened to join the Commander-in-Chief; and the

---

[5] Captain William Bligh, of the Glatton, who had commanded the Director at
Camperdown, and received the Medal: he died a Vice Admiral in December, 1817.

[6] Captain Sir Thomas Boulden Thompson, who had lost his leg in command of
the Bellona: he has been often before mentioned. Vide vol. iii. p. 90.

extraordinary efforts which he made for that purpose are thus described in a letter from Mr. Brierly, Master of the Bellona, dated on the 19th of April:—

" This day the St. George got her guns on board the American Ship, for the purpose of going over the Grounds, to the southward of Copenhagen, where Sir Hyde Parker, with the Fleet, had sailed two days before ; but the wind being foul, prevented us moving. At six, P.M., Lord Nelson received advice, per letter, from Sir Hyde Parker, of a Swedish Squadron being seen by one of our look-out Frigates. The moment he received the account, he ordered a Boat to be manned, and without even waiting for a boat cloak (though you must suppose the weather pretty sharp here at this season of the year), and having to row about twenty-four miles with the wind and current against him, jumped into her, and ordered me to go with him, I having been on board that Ship to remain till she had got over the Grounds. All I had ever seen or heard of him, could not half so clearly prove to me the singular and unbounded zeal of this truly great man. His anxiety in the Boat for nearly six hours (lest the Fleet should have sailed before he got on board one of them, and lest we should not catch the Swedish Squadron) is beyond all conception. I will quote some expressions in his own words. It was extremely cold, and I wished him to put on a great coat of mine which was in the boat : ' No, I am not cold ; my anxiety for my Country, will keep me warm. Do you not think the Fleet has sailed ?' —' I should suppose not, my Lord.'—' If they are, we shall follow them to Carlscrona in the Boat, by God !'—I merely state this to show how his thoughts must have been employed. The idea of going in a small Boat, rowing six oars, without a single morsel of anything to eat or drink, the distance of about fifty leagues, must convince the world, that every other earthly consideration than that of serving his Country, was totally banished from his thoughts. We reached our Fleet by midnight, and went on board the Elephant, Captain Foley, where I left his Lordship in the morning, and returned to my Ship. In our late Action, nothing but his superior abilities, as well as bravery, could have given us so decided a victory, when four of our Ships ran a-ground, and in the heat of battle."—*Naval Chronicle*, vol. v. p. 452.]

St. George, at Sea, 22nd April, 1801.

My dear Sir,

Commodore Fischer having, in a Public letter,[7] given an account to the world of the Battle of the 2nd, and called upon his Royal Highness as a witness to the truth of it, I therefore think it right to address myself to you, for the information of his Royal Highness, as, I assure you, had this Officer confined himself to his own veracity, I should have treated his Official letter with the contempt it deserved, and allowed the world to appreciate the merits of the two contending Officers. I shall make a few, and very few, observations on his letter. He asserts the superiority of numbers on the part of the British ; it will turn out, if that is of any consequence, that the Danish Line of Defence, to the southward of the Crown Islands, was much stronger, and more numerous, than the British. We had only five Sail of Seventy-fours, two Sixty-fours, two Fifties, and one Frigate engaged; a Bomb-vessel towards the latter end threw

[7] Vide p. 320, ante.

some shells into the Arsenal. Two Seventy-fours, and one Sixty-four, by an accident grounded on the Crown Islands, and the Elephant and Mars would have had full employment, and, by the assistance of the Frigates, who went to try alone what I had directed the three Sail of the Line that grounded to assist them in, I have reason to hope they would have been equally successful, as that part of the British Line engaged.

I am ready to admit that many of the Danish Officers and men behaved as well as men could do, and deserved not to be abandoned by their Commander. I am justified in saying this, from Commodore Fischer's own declaration. In his letter he states that, after he quitted the Dannebrog, she long contested the battle. If so, more shame for him to quit so many brave fellows. *Here* was no manœuvring : *it was* downright fighting, and it was his duty to have shown an example of firmness becoming the high trust reposed in him. He went in such a hurry, if he went before she struck, which but for his own declaration I can hardly believe, that he forgot to take his Broad Pendant with him ; for both Pendant and Ensign were struck together, and it is from this circumstance that I claimed the Commodore as a prisoner of war. He then went, as he said, on board the Holstein, the brave Captain of which did not want him, where he did not hoist his Pendant. From this Ship he went on shore, either before or after she struck, or he would have been again a prisoner. As to his nonsense about Victory, his Royal Highness will not much credit him. I sunk, burnt, captured, or drove into the harbour the whole Line of Defence to the southward of the Crown Islands.

He says he is told that two British Ships struck. Why did he not take possession of them ? I took possession of his, as fast as they struck. The reason is clear—that he did not believe it. He must have known the falsity of the report, and that no fresh British Ships did come near the Ships engaged. He states, that the Ship in which I had the honour to hoist my Flag fired latterly only single guns. It is true ; for steady and cool were my brave fellows, and did not wish to throw away a single shot. He seems to exult that I sent on shore a Flag of Truce. Men of his description, if they ever are victorious, know not the feeling of humanity. You know, and his Royal Highness knows, that the guns fired from the shore could only fire through the Danish Ships, which had surrendered, and that if I fired at the shore it could only be in the same manner. God forbid I should destroy a non-resisting Dane! When they became my prisoners, I became their protector. Humanity alone could have been my object, but Mr. Fischer's carcase was safe, and he regarded not the sacred call of humanity. His Royal Highness thought as I did. It has brought about an Armistice, which I pray the Almighty may bring about a happy reconciliation between the two Kingdoms. As I have not the names of all the Ships correct, only of the thirteen, including the seven Sail of the Line which struck, remained at anchor, and fell into my possession after the battle, I shall therefore be very much obliged to you for a correct list of their names, and the number of men, if possible, to be obtained, on board each, and the numbers sent from the shore during the Action; my earnest wish is to be correct; and believe me, dear Sir, with great esteem, your most obedient Servant,

NELSON AND BRONTE.[8]

[8] To the above Letter, Adjutant-General Lindholm wrote the following gentlemanly reply:—

" Copenhagen, May 2nd, 1801.

" My Lord,

" Your Lordship has imposed upon me a very painful task, by desiring me to communicate to his Royal Highness the Crown Prince the contents of that letter with which your Lordship has favoured me, the 22nd April, and in which you have treated Commodore Fischer with a severity, which, as a Brother-officer, I cannot but think too great indeed. I conceive that your Lordship has felt a certain degree of displeasure at that incorrectness which you have thought to find in Commodore Fischer's official Report, but your Lordship did not fully consider, at that moment, that he himself might have received [an] incorrect Report, a fatality to which every Commander-in-Chief is exposed. I flatter myself, from your Lordship's well-known candour and indulgence, that you will not think it presuming in me, or contrary to the respect I feel for your Lordship, if I take the liberty of offering you some few observations, in vindication of the conduct of Commodore Fischer. But, first, let me have the honour to assure your Lordship, that I have not communicated to that Officer your letter of the 22nd of April, and that what I take the liberty of offering your Lordship is absolutely my private and individual opinion.

" Your Lordship thinks that Commodore Fischer has over-rated the forces by which he was attacked, and under-rated his own; or that he wrongly asserts the superiority of numbers on the part of the British. I must confess that I am now, as I have always been, of opinion, that the Squadron with which your Lordship attacked our southern Line of Defence, say all those Ships and Vessels lying to the southward of the Crown Battery, was stronger than that Line. I will say nothing about our not having had time sufficient to man our Ships in the manner it was intended, they being badly manned, both as to number, and as to quality of their crews, the greatest part of which were landsmen, people that had been pressed, and who never before had been on board a Ship, or used to the exercise of guns. I will not mention our Ships being old and rotten, and not having one-third of their usual com-

MEMORANDA RESPECTING THE BATTLE OF COPENHAGEN.

[Autograph, in the Nelson Papers.]

Lindholm ought to have omitted the guns of the Russell, Bellona, Agamemnon, Amazon, Alcmene, Blanche, Dart, and

plement of Officers. I will confine myself to the number of guns, and from the Ships named in your Lordship's official Report, and there I find that your Squadron carried 1058 guns, of much greater calibre than ours, exclusive of carronades (which did our Ships so much injury,) also exclusive of your Gun-brigs and Bomb-vessels.

" Now, I can assure your Lordship, upon my honour, that to my certain knowledge the number of guns on board of those eighteen Ships and Vessels of ours which were engaged (including the small Ship, the Elbe, which came into the harbour towards the end of the Action,) amount to 634. I have not included our eleven Gun-boats, carrying each two guns, as a couple of them had only an opportunity of firing a few shot. Nor need I to mention the Crown Battery, on which sixty-six guns were mounted, as that Battery did not fairly get into Action, and only fired a few random shot. When Commodore Fischer left the Dannebroge, that Ship was on fire, had many killed, several of its Officers wounded, and others suffered much. It was, I conceive, the duty of the Commander to remove his Broad Pendant to another Ship, and he went on board the Holstein, from whence he commanded the Line of Defence, and where he remained two hours, his Broad Pendant flying on board the said Ship. When this Ship was mostly disabled, the Commodore went to the Crown Battery, who also was under his command. He would, in my humble opinion, have been justified, from the wound he received on his head, to quit the command altogether, when he left the Dannebroge, and no blame could ever have attached for it to his character as a soldier. I have given myself every possible pain to be informed whether Commodore Fischer's Pendant had been removed before or after the Ship struck, and the Officers all agree in declaring, that the Broad Pendant, had been replaced by a Captain's Pendant, both on board the Dannebroge and the Holstein, previous to those Ships hauling down their Ensign. It is even remarkable that on board the Dannebroge, the man who had taken down the Broad Pendant, and hoisted the Captain's Pendant, was killed when coming down the shrouds, and fell upon deck with the Commodore's Pendant in his hand.

" I do not conceive that Commodore Fischer had the least idea of claiming as a victory, what, to every intent and purpose, was a defeat. He has only thought that this defeat was not an inglorious one, and that our Officers and men displayed much bravery and firmness, against force so superior in every respect. Your Lordship's Report, and your letter to me, prove it. I confess that your Lordship took all the Vessels opposed to you, except five, carrying together eighty-six guns. I am of opinion, with your Lordship, that three Ships of seventy-four guns each, would have been a hard match for the Three Crown Battery, but they certainly would have been forced to go away. As to your Lordship's motives for sending a Flag of Truce to our Government, it can never be misconstrued, and your subsequent conduct has sufficiently shown that humanity is always the companion of true valour. You have done more : you have shown yourself a friend of the re-establishment of peace and good harmony between this Country and Great Britain. It is therefore with the sincerest esteem I shall always feel myself attached to your Lordship, and it is with the greatest respect I have the honour to subscribe myself, my Lord, your Lordship's most obedient and most humble servant,—H. LINDHOLM."—*Autograph*, in the Nelson Papers.

Arrow, as the two first were aground, and although within
random shot, yet were unable to do that service expected
from Seventy-four-gun Ships. The Agamemnon was not
within three miles; the others, Frigates and Sloops, were
exposed to a part of the Crown battery and the Ships in the
other Channel, but not fired upon by the eighteen Sail drawn
up to the southward of the Crown Islands; therefore, 366
guns are to be taken from the British and 166 guns added to
the Danes—viz., 66 Crown batteries (I think there were 88)
and 100 for the Batteries on a mark, besides random shot
from the Ships in the other Channel, [total, &c.] therefore,
the account ought to stand thus:—

Guns by Lindholm's account 1058
Deduct as by other side 366
British force in Action 692

Danish force by Lindholm's account . . 634
To which add—I say, at least 166

Danish force 800
British force 692

Superiority of the Danes 108

TO HERCULES ROSS, ESQ., ROSSIE CASTLE, N. B.

[Autograph, in the possession of Horatio Ross, Esq.]

St. George, Baltic, April 23rd, 1801.

My dear Friend,

Your letter respecting your nephew[9] I received at Yarmouth,
at the time Mr. Davison was with me, and I put the case into
his hands, who seemed to admit the justness of it, and did not
know so much of the matter of fact before, and I hope all is
amicably settled with your nephew long before this time. You
must forgive my not answering your letter, as I have truly had
my head full of things of some importance to our Country.
Affairs now bear an aspect of reconciliation with the North,

[9] Mr. Ross's nephew, Mr. Hercules Ross, claimed the right of being Co-agent
with Mr. Davison to the Captors of the Cape of Good Hope.

for we are now returning to an anchorage near Copenhagen, having looked at the Swedes in Carlscrona, for Sir Hyde Parker has received a notification from the Russian Minister at Copenhagen, that his Master will not go to war with us. I trust all these events will bring about an honourable Peace, and allow me to get a little of that repose which my shattered carcase so much wants. In every situation, believe me I feel myself, as ever, your truly obliged friend,

NELSON AND BRONTE.

I beg, although unknown, that you will present my respects to Mrs. Ross, and also to Mrs. Parish and her family, when you write to Hamburgh.

TO HIS ROYAL HIGHNESS THE DUKE OF CLARENCE.

[From Clarke and M'Arthur, vol. ii. p. 284. Intelligence of the death of the Emperor Paul having reached this Country, the Admiralty issued orders to Sir Hyde Parker, dated on the 17th of April, 1801, stating "that a communication having been received from the Court of Petersburgh, in consequence of that event, affording some reason to hope that his successor, the present Emperor, will not persevere in those measures of violence and unprovoked aggression towards his Majesty, which were on the point of involving the two Countries in actual hostilities, and that his Majesty, uniformly actuated by the wish he has already so frequently manifested of averting this calamity, and re-establishing the ancient relations of peace and amity with Russia, has signified his commands that such measures should immediately be adopted as may appear most conducive to this desirable object, and to prevent, as far as lies in his Majesty's power, any fresh obstacles being thrown in the way of accommodation,"—his Majesty had therefore signified his pleasure that the directions contained in the order to Sir Hyde Parker of the 15th of March, [vide p. 295, ante,] "for an attack on the Russian Fleets at Revel and Cronstadt should for the present be suspended;" Sir Hyde Parker was desired "to use his best endeavours to ascertain as soon as possible (by sending a Flag of Truce, if necessary, to Revel, or some other Port of Russia, for this purpose) whether the embargo laid on British Ships by the late Emperor had been taken off, and their crews released." If the answer was in the affirmative, he was "to suspend, without limitation of time, or other condition, all hostile proceedings against the Ships or Ports of Russia; but if, (contrary to his Majesty's expectation,) no order to the above effect shall have been given by the present Emperor, and even in case no positive assurance should be obtained of such being his intention," Sir Hyde Parker was, in such case, "authorized and directed to offer a suspension of hostilities, provided you shall be given to understand that the Court of St. Petersburgh is disposed to enter into, or is actually engaged in, an amicable discussion with his Majesty, with a view to the satisfactory adjustment of any existing differences, and on condition also that during such suspension of hostilities, and until it shall be accompanied by the removal of the embargo, and the liberation of the British Ships, the Division of the Russian Fleet now at Revel shall not take advantage of it to join the Division at Cronstadt, or *vice versâ*, that it shall be further understood, that hostilities may be commenced by either party at the expiration of twelve hours after they shall have given a notice in writing to that effect." The order then proceeded in these words :—

"As this event can only happen in the very improbable case of the present Emperor rejecting his Majesty's offers of conciliation and friendship, and of his refusing to acquiesce in his Majesty's just expectations respecting the removal of the embargo, and the liberation of the British seamen now detained in Russia, in which case his Majesty would be under the necessity of recurring to those measures which the conduct of the late Emperor had reluctantly compelled him to adopt; it is only in the supposition of your receiving the most unequivocal proofs that the Court of Petersburgh, under the present change, persists in a system of determined hostility to this Country, and of the proposals you are hereby authorized to make, founded on a contrary supposition, being totally rejected, and in such a manner as leaves no doubt on this point, that you are to consider yourself at liberty to follow the directions contained in our order to you of the 15th ultimo, without waiting for further instructions from this Country.

"And whereas Lord Hobart has also acquainted us, that in case the Court of Stockholm should manifest a friendly disposition, and should make any proposal to you for a suspension of hostilities, his Majesty is pleased to consent that you should comply with that proposal, provided it be accompanied with a specific assurance in writing from the proper authorities at that Court, that the King of Sweden relinquishes all hostile engagements against this Country, and, particularly, those contained in the Treaty signed at Petersburgh on the 16th of December last, and that he will forthwith disarm, and re-establish the ancient relations of peace and amity between the two Countries, in conformity to the Treaties, on the strict and respective observance of which, the continuance of those advantages must depend;" and Sir Hyde Parker was directed to govern himself accordingly.—*Original.*]

Kioge Bay, 27th April, 1801.

Sir,

I feel infinitely your Royal Highness's kindness by your expressions of attachment to me in the House of Peers,[1] which I am sure your Royal Highness will believe that no conduct of mine shall ever be likely to diminish. As I think that all our fighting is over in the North, I am going to England : my health and circumstances absolutely require it. Admiral Graves desires me to present his dutiful thanks to your Royal Highness, for the very handsome manner you spoke of him. We are now, I believe, waiting for orders from home what is next to become of us. I would strongly recommend keeping our seamen actively employed ; for there has been, I suspect, something very wrong going on in many of our Ships, instigated in England. Believe me, for ever, your Royal Highness's faithful servant,

NELSON AND BRONTE.

[1] Vide p. 328, ante.

TO SAMUEL BARKER, ESQ., YARMOUTH.

[From a Fac-simile, in the possession of J. Baas, Esq.]

St. George, Kioge Bay, April 27th, 1801.

My dear Sir,

I feel truly sensible of your kind congratulations on the success of His Majesty's Arms; the spirit and zeal of the Navy I never saw higher than in this Fleet, and if England is true to herself, she may bid defiance to Europe. The French have always, in ridicule, called us a Nation of shop-keepers—*so*, I hope, we shall always remain, and, like other shopkeepers, if our goods are better than those of any other Country, and we can afford to sell them cheaper, we must depend on our shop being well resorted to. If I land at Yarmouth, I shall most assuredly pay my personal respects to you, not only as a gentleman who has shown [me] great civilities, but also as the Chief magistrate of a Borough of which I have the honour to be a Freeman. I beg you will have the goodness to present my best respects and good wishes to every individual of the Corporate body, and believe me, my dear Sir, your truly obliged,

NELSON AND BRONTE.

___

TO ADJUTANT-GENERAL LINDHOLM.

[From a Copy in the Nelson Papers.]

St. George, May 3rd, 1801.

My dear Sir,

I was yesterday evening favoured with your reply to my letter of the 22nd of April, and I have no scruple in assuring you, that if Commodore Fischer's letter had been couched in the same manly and honourable manner, that I should have been the last man to have noticed any little inaccuracies which might get into a Commander-in-Chief's public letter; and if the Commodore had not called upon his Royal Highness for the truth of his assertions, I never should have noticed his letter. You have stated truly the force which would have been brought into Action, but for the accidents of their getting aground, and, except the Desirée Frigate, no other Frigate or Sloop fired a gun to the southward of the Crown Islands.

I have done ample justice to the bravery of nearly all your
Officers and men; and as it is not my intention to hurt your
feelings or those of his Royal Highness, but on the contrary,
to try and merit your esteem, I will only say, that I am confident you would not have wrote such a letter. Nothing, I
flatter myself, in my conduct ought to have drawn ridicule on
my character, from the Commodore's pen; and you have
borne the handsomest testimony of it, in contradiction to his.
I thought then, as I did before the Action and do now, that it
is not the interest of our Countries to injure each other. I am
sorry that I was forced to write you so unpleasant a letter;
but for the future I trust that none but pleasant ones will pass
between us, for I assure you that I hope to merit the con-
tinuation of your esteem, and of having frequent opportunities
of assuring you how I feel interested in being your sincere and
faithful friend,

NELSON AND BRONTE.

TO EVAN NEPEAN, ESQ., ADMIRALTY.

[Letter-Book. On the 5th of May, dispatches arrived, dated on the 21st of April,
appointing Lord Nelson successor to Sir Hyde Parker, as Commander-in-Chief.
" The first signal which Lord Nelson made, as Commander-in-Chief, was to
hoist in all launches, and prepare to weigh. This at once showed how different a
system was about to be pursued; it having been intended that the Fleet should
await at anchor fresh instructions from England relative to the state of the Northern
affairs, an account of which had but lately been dispatched. Lord Nelson, who foresaw every bad consequence from this inactive mode of proceeding, owed his bad
health more to chagrin than to any other cause. The joy with which the signal was
received not only manifested what are the customary feelings on those occasions,
but was intended as peculiarly complimentary to the Admiral. On the 7th of May
1801, the Fleet left Kioge Bay, and, proceeding towards Bornholm, anchored, in
blowing weather, off that Island. The greater part was here left to watch the
motions of the Swedes; and with a chosen Squadron, consisting of his ten best
sailing Seventy-fours, two Frigates, a Brig, and a Schooner, Lord Nelson sailed for
the Port of Revel. He wished for further satisfaction respecting the friendly disposition of the Russians, and thought that the best method of putting this to the proof,
would be to try how he should be received in one of their Ports. He sincerely
desired peace, but had no apprehension of hostilities. Exclusive of a wish to show
the activity of his Fleet, he had two other objects in view, personally to wait on the
Emperor, and congratulate him on his accession to the Throne, and also to promote the release of the British Merchant Ships and seamen, who had been detained
by the Emperor Paul."—*Colonel Stewart's Narrative.*]

Sir,   George, Kioge Bay, 5th May, 1801.

I beg leave to acknowledge the receipt of their Lordships'
Commission, appointing me Commander-in-Chief; and I

request you will assure their Lordships, that I will endeavour
to execute the high trust reposed in me, as well as my abilities,
and a most wretched state of health, will allow. I am, &c.,

NELSON AND BRONTE.

TO EVAN NEPEAN, ESQ., ADMIRALTY.

[Letter Book.]

St. George, Kioge Bay, 5th May, 1801.

Sir,

Captain Domett[1] having consented to serve as my First
Captain, I have to acquaint you that, agreeable to their Lord-
ships' direction, I have given him a Commission accordingly.
I am, &c.   NELSON AND BRONTE.

TO EVAN NEPEAN, ESQ., ADMIRALTY.

[Letter-Book.]

St. George, Kioge Bay, 5th May, 1801.

Sir,

I have to acknowledge the receipt of your letter of the
22nd ultimo, enclosing a copy of a letter from Lord Hobart
to their Lordships, acquainting them that the King has thought
fit to approve of the Convention entered into with the Court
of Denmark for a suspension of hostilities,[2] and their Lordships'
directions to me to cause the several stipulations therein
contained to be punctually observed, to all which due obedience shall be paid. I am, &c.

NELSON AND BRONTE.

TO ALEXANDER DAVISON, ESQ., ST. JAMES'S SQUARE.

[Autograph, in the possession of Colonel Davison.]

My dear Davison,   May 5th, 1801.

A Command never was, I believe, more unwelcomely received by any person than by myself. It may be at the expense

---

[1] Afterwards Admiral Sir William Domett, G.C.B., who commanded the Royal
George in the Battle of the 1st of June 1794, and had been Captain of the Fleet to
Sir Hyde Parker. He died in May 1828.

[2] Vide the next page.

of my life; and therefore, for God's sake, at least, for mine, try if I cannot be relieved. The time was, a few months ago, that I should have felt the honour, and I really believe that I should have seen more of the Baltic, the consequence of which I can guess. But nothing, I believe, but change of climate can cure me, and having my mind tranquil. I grieve for Maurice,[3] but I hope he will recover and do well. I hope yet within a month to be in England. With my thankful respects to Mrs. Davison and your family, believe me ever, my dear Davison, your truly obliged friend,

NELSON AND BRONTE.

I will endeavour to collect my ideas on the subject of money matters; but, as you observe, every one pulls at me. The Subscription Book of the Fleet to be delivered to the Committee at Lloyd's, and a Clerk, I suppose, will be sent to the different persons for the subscription. I dare say you have paid mine. Sir Hyde is just gone; he is very low.

TO ADMIRAL THE EARL OF ST. VINCENT, K.B.

[From Clarke and M'Arthur, vol. ii. p. 285.]

[5th May, 1801.]

I am, in truth, unable to hold the very honourable station you have conferred upon me : Admiral Graves also is so ill, as to keep his bed. I know not exactly the purport of Fremantle's mission.[2] If Sir Hyde were gone, I would now be under Sail, leave six Sail of the Line off Bornholm to watch the Swedes and to cover our communication, and go to Revel, where I should at least, if not too late, prevent the junction of the two Squadrons : that I shall never suffer. I will have all the English Shipping and property restored; but I will do nothing violently; neither commit my Country, nor suffer Russia to mix the affairs of Denmark or Sweden with the detention of our Ships. Should I meet the Revel Squadron, I shall make them stay with me until all our English Ships

---

[3] His eldest brother, Mr. Maurice Nelson, who died of a brain fever, after a few days' illness, on the 24th of April.

[2] Captain Fremantle of the Ganges was sent to St. Petersburgh with a communication to the Russian Government.

join; for we must not joke. As the business will be settled in a fortnight, I must entreat that some person may come out to take this command.

NELSON AND BRONTE.

TO THE RIGHT HONOURABLE HENRY ADDINGTON.

[Autograph, in the Sidmouth Papers.]

St. George, May 5th, 1801.

My dear Sir,

I feel very much flattered by your truly kind letter, and also for the kind expressions you were so good as to send me by Colonel Stewart. I am sorry that the Armistice is only approved under *all* considerations.[3] Now I own myself of opinion that every part of the *all* was to the advantage of our King and Country. I stated many of my reasons for thinking it advantageous. We knew not of the death of Paul,[4] or a change of sentiments in the Court of Prussia, if her sentiments are changed. My object was to get at Revel before the frost broke up at Cronstadt, that the twelve Sail of the Line might be destroyed. I shall now go there as a friend, but the two Fleets shall not form a junction, if not already accomplished, unless my orders permit it. My health is gone, and although I should be happy to try and hold out a month or six weeks longer, yet death is no respecter of persons. I own, at present, I should not wish to die a natural death—but to the last, believe me, dear Sir, your most obliged,

NELSON AND BRONTE.

---

[3] On the 22nd of April, the Lords of the Admiralty transmitted to Lord Nelson a copy of the following Letter to them from Lord Hobart, Secretary of State for Foreign Affairs :—

"Downing street, 20th April 1801.

"Having laid before the King your Lordships' letter of this date, I have received his Majesty's commands to acquaint your Lordships, that, upon a consideration of all the circumstances, his Majesty has thought fit to approve of it, and has, in consequence, been graciously pleased to direct that the several stipulations therein contained should punctually be observed, and that your Lordships should give such orders as may be necessary for carrying them into execution. I am, &c., HOBART." —*Copy*, in the possession of the Right Hon. John Wilson Croker.

[4] The Emperor Paul died on the 24th of March 1801.

A A 2

TO SIR ANDREW SNAPE HAMOND, BART., COMPTROLLER OF THE NAVY.

[Autograph, in the possession of Vice-Admiral Sir Graham Eden Hamond, Bart., K.C.B.]

[No date.]

My dear Sir Andrew,

I feel very much obliged by your kindness to my brother,[2] and I trust he will get one rise more in the Navy Office—I mean a Seat at the Board. All must acknowledge he is fit for it, and I am sure he would do his utmost to support and assist you. I desired Davison to say, your son[3] was well. He is gone to look into Carlscrona; I can assure you that a better, or more diligent Officer is nowhere to be found. I hope very soon to see you in England, for my health will not permit my remaining here, and I think we shall have no more fighting. I beg my compliments to Lady Hamond, and that you will believe me, as ever, your most obliged and affectionate,

NELSON AND BRONTE.

TO HIS EXCELLENCY COUNT BERNSTORFF, DANISH MINISTER.

[Letter-Book.]

St. George, Kioge Bay, May 6th, 1801.

Sir,

I have the honour to acquaint your Excellency that the King, my Master, having approved of the Armistice concluded between Denmark, its Provinces, Jutland, and the Islands, and the Lords of the Admiralty having, in consequence, directed me to strictly adhere to the terms, I have to assure you that the strictest orders are given by Sir Hyde Parker for that purpose; and I hope that your Excellency will take care that orders are given to the same purpose from the Government of Denmark, particularly in Holstein, as I have heard

---

[2] His eldest brother, Maurice Nelson.

[3] The present Vice Admiral Sir Graham Eden Hamond, Bart., K.C.B., who was then Captain of the Blanche, of 36 guns. In a letter to Mr. Davison, dated on the 13th of April, Lord Nelson said, " I am glad Maurice has got Hartwell's place. I shall write Sir Andrew by the Brig, and say, which is true, that no Ship in the world can be better conducted, in every respect, than Captain Hamond's: he is gone off Carlscrona."

that in some parts of Holstein it was thought the Armistice did not extend to that Province. With every sentiment of respect, and a most cordial wish for a return of that ancient amity between our two gracious Sovereigns, so conducive to the true happiness and prosperity of both Countries, I have the honour to be, &c.,

NELSON AND BRONTE.

TO HIS EXCELLENCY COUNT BERNSTORFF.

[Letter-Book.]

St. George, Kioge Bay, May 6th, 1801.

Sir,

Admiral Sir Hyde Parker having received a number of letters, informing him that many Vessels with corn from the Baltic, bound for England, have been arrested in the Ports of Norway, and as both Sir Hyde Parker and myself flatter ourselves that there must be some mistake in these detentions, (although the Officers in Norway have said it was by order of Government,) which will, on the receipt of this letter, be immediately rectified by your Excellency; for, as Sir Hyde Parker has done everything his Royal Highness wishes, to give facility to the getting provisions to the poor people of Norway, I will not suffer myself to think that it could be the intention of the Danish Government to receive provisions by permission of the British Admiral, and to send orders for the seizure of corn bound to England.

I therefore hope and believe that the Government of Denmark will give instant orders that all the corn stopped in Norway, bound for England, shall be given up, and directions given that no detention shall be made in future; for your Excellency may be assured, it would be very unpleasant to me to be obliged to take any measures in this (I hope) returning amity between the two Countries, which would be unpleasant. I have the honour to be, &c.,

NELSON AND BRONTE.

TO EVAN NEPEAN, ESQ., ADMIRALTY.

[Letter-Book.]

St. George, at Anchor, off Falsterholm, May 7th, 1801.

Sir,

I beg leave to inform you, that I directed the Fleet to be got under sail yesterday morning; but the wind coming strong to the eastward, I was obliged to anchor here. It is my intention to leave Captain Murray,[5] till relieved by Rear-Admiral Totty,[6] off Bornholm, with seven Sail of the Line and a proper number of attendant Frigates and Small craft. Under the present circumstances, I have thought it right to address a letter to the Swedish Admiral in respectful terms, signifying my wish, that the Swedish Fleet would not come to sea, as I should be sorry, out of respect to the Emperor of Russia, to see hostilities committed, which must be the case, if they put to sea.

I have directed all the Bombs, Fire-ships, and Gun-brigs, to be placed under the directions of Captain Inman,[7] of the Desirée, and to keep them as much as possible at anchor under Bornholm; for in bad weather they are bad cruizers. With eleven Sail of the Line, a Frigate, and two Sloops, it is my intention to show myself in the Gulf of Finland; but in such a manner, as I trust will be taken as a compliment by the Emperor of Russia, and at the same time, with the precaution, that if the whole Empire of Russia was hostile to us, their Lordships may be perfectly at ease for the safety of the Squadron, in spite of all the power of Russia.

I cannot omit this opportunity of testifying, that I never saw more zeal or a desire to distinguish themselves, than in this Fleet; and it must be with real sorrow, when I am forced to state that the probability is, that very soon I must be separated

---

[5] Captain George Murray. This gallant Officer, who wore a Medal for the Battle of St. Vincent, in which he commanded the Colossus, died a Vice-Admiral, and a Knight Commander of the Bath, in February 1819.

[6] Rear Admiral Thomas Totty died of the yellow fever in the West Indies, in June 1802.

[7] Captain Henry Inman: he commanded the Triumph in Sir Robert Calder's Action of the 22nd July 1805, and died Naval Commissioner at Madras on the 15th of July 1809, ten days after his arrival.

from them; either my decline must finish my earthly career, or a change of climate is the only prospect of the restoration of my health.　I send this by way of Hamburgh, through Sir James Crauford.[8]　I am, &c.,

NELSON AND BRONTE.

TO ADMIRAL THE EARL OF ST. VINCENT, K.B.

[From Clarke and M'Arthur, vol. ii. p. 285.]

May 7th, 1801.

It is no compliment, for it is true, that except those who have served in your school, I find such a deficiency of resource, that even I, who never had any compared with twenty who served in the Mediterranean, am astonished: but by seeing others get on with the Service, it is surprising what example effects.　I shall endeavour to do my best whilst I remain; but, my dear Lord, I shall either soon go to Heaven, I hope, or must rest quiet for a time.　My little trip into the Gulf of Finland will be, I trust, of National benefit, and I shall be kind or otherwise, as I find the folks.　I am, &c.,

NELSON AND BRONTE.

TO THE RIGHT HONOURABLE HENRY ADDINGTON.

[Autograph, in the Sidmouth Papers.]

May 8th, 1801.　Foul wind, blows fresh.

My dear Sir,

　　Forgive me for one moment, but so much having been said, both by friends and enemies, why I sent on shore a Flag of Truce on the 2nd of April, and but few seemed pleased with the Armistice, I take the liberty of sending the reasons why I sent the Flag of Truce, and also my reasons why I think the Armistice was a proper measure.　If you and some other friends approve, I care not.　I have dispersed the reasons to several hands, for I feel hurt.　Trusting that God Almighty will allow me to present myself at your door, believe me, for ever, yours, most obliged,

NELSON AND BRONTE.

---

[8] Envoy to Lower Saxony, and Resident with the Hans Towns.

TO THE RIGHT HONOURABLE HENRY ADDINGTON.

[From a Copy, in the Sidmouth Papers.]

[May 8th, 1801.]

My dearest Friend,

As both my friends and enemies seem not to know why I sent on shore a Flag of Truce—the former, many of them, thought it was a *ruse de guerre*, and not quite justifiable; the latter, I believe, attributed it to a desire to have no more fighting, and few, very few, to the cause that I felt, and which I trust in God I shall retain to the last moment, *humanity.* I know it must to the world be proved, and therefore I will suppose you all the world to me. First, no Ship was on shore near the Crown batteries, or anywhere else, within reach of any shore, when my Flag of Truce went on shore. The Crown batteries, and the batteries on Armak and in the Dockyard, were firing at us, one half their shot necessarily striking the Ships who had surrendered, and our fire did the same, and worse, for the surrendered Ships had four of them got close together, and it was a massacre. This caused my Note. It was a sight which no real man could have enjoyed. I felt when the Danes became my prisoners, I became their protector; and if that had not been a sufficient reason, the moment of a complete victory was surely the proper time to make an opening with the Nation we had been fighting with.

When the Truce was settled, and full possession taken of our Prizes, the Ships were ordered, except two, to proceed and join Sir Hyde Parker, and in performing this service, the Elephant and Defiance grounded on the Middle Ground. I give you, verbatim, an answer to a part of a letter from a person high in rank[9] about the Prince Royal, which will bear testimony to the truth of my assertions :—'As to your Lordship's motives for sending a Flag of Truce to our Government, it never can be misconstrued; and your subsequent conduct has sufficiently shown that humanity is always the companion of true valour. You have done more. You have shewn yourself a friend of the re-establishment of peace and good harmony between this Country and Great Britain.'

---

[9] Adjutant-General Lindholm. Vide p. 347, ante.

ON THE ARMISTICE.

Much having been said relative to the bad terms of the Armistice made with Denmark, I wish to observe, first, that the Armistice was only intended [to be] a Military one, and that all Political subjects were left for the discussion of the Ministers of the two Powers. Peace, Denmark could not in the moment make with you, as the moment she made it with you, she would lose all her Possessions except the Island of Zealand, and that also, the moment the frost set in; therefore, there was no damage we could do her equal to the loss of everything. Our destruction would have been Copenhagen and her Fleet; then we had done our worst, and not much nearer being friends. By the Armistice we tied the arms of Denmark for four months from assisting our Enemies and her Allies, whilst we had every part of Denmark and its Provinces open to give us everything we wanted. Great Britain was left the power of taking Danish Possessions and Ships in all parts of the world, whilst we had locked up the Danish Navy, and put the key in our pocket; time was afforded the two Countries to arrange matters on an amicable footing; besides, to say the truth, I look upon the Northern League to be like a tree, of which Paul was the trunk, and Sweden and Denmark the branches. If I can get at the trunk, and hew it down, the branches fall of course; but I may lop the branches, and yet not be able to fell the tree, and my power must be weaker when its greatest strength is required. If we could have cut up the Russian Fleet, that was my object. Denmark and Sweden deserved whipping, but Paul deserved punishment. I own I consider it as a wise measure, and I wish my reputation to stand upon its merits.

TO SIR JAMES CRAUFORD, ENVOY EXTRAORDINARY TO THE CIRCLE OF LOWER SAXONY.

[Letter-Book.]

St. George, Baltic, May 8th, 1801.

Sir,

I have to request that you will have the goodness to forward my dispatch to Mr. Nepean, when the Packet sails for

England. It is not of that importance which requires a Packet to be sent on purpose. Sir Hyde Parker having left the Fleet for England, this command, for the moment, is conferred upon me. We can have nothing new here, and under present circumstances, I hope the Swedish Fleet will not put to sea; for if they do, I must try and take them. But to prevent anything happening, I shall give this notice to the Swedish Admiral. With every respect, believe me, &c.,

NELSON AND BRONTE.

TO THE EARL OF CARYSFORT, K.B., ENVOY EXTRAORDINARY
TO THE KING OF PRUSSIA.

[Letter-Book.]

St. George, Baltic, May 8th, 1801.

My dear Lord,

Sir Hyde Parker being ordered to England, the command of the Fleet has been, for the moment, given to me, the duties of which I shall endeavour to execute, as well as my abilities and bad health will allow me. It is my intention to send into Carlscrona a letter to the Swedish Admiral; for, under present circumstances, it would be unpleasant to have a battle with the Swedes: therefore, if anything happens after the receipt of my letter, the blame will rest with them.

I hope Lord St. Helens will be at Berlin, on his way to Russia; and it is my intention to proceed with a part of the Fleet into the Gulf of Finland; but in such a moment, and with such notice, that I wish the new Emperor to see its coming to Revel as a great compliment, as I shall carry neither Bomb-ship, Fire-Ship, nor any of the Flotilla—only twelve Sail of the Line, with some Frigates, Sloops, &c.,—as fine Ships, and in as good order, as any in Europe. Although this is my present plan, yet much must depend on the reception which Sir Hyde Parker's letter and messenger have met with at Petersburgh. Let matters turn out as they may, we have force enough to bid defiance to the whole Baltic Fleet; but I hope that all will end amicably. I beg your Lordship to believe me, &c.

NELSON AND BRONTE.

TO HIS EXCELLENCY THE SWEDISH ADMIRAL.

[Letter-Book.]

St. George, Baltic, May 8th, 1801.

Sir,

The late Commander-in-Chief of the British Fleet in the Baltic having, by request of the Emperor of Russia, allowed the Swedish trade in the Baltic to pass unmolested, I should be sorry that any event could happen which might disturb for a moment the returning amity (I hope) between Sweden and Great Britain. I beg leave, therefore, to apprise your Excellency, that I have no orders to abstain from hostilities, should I meet the Swedish Fleet at sea, which, as it lies in your power to prevent, I am sure you must take this communication as the most friendly proceeding on my part, and communicate it to your august Sovereign, begging your Excellency to believe me, with every sentiment of respect, &c.

NELSON AND BRONTE.

TO ALEXANDER COCKBURN, ESQ., CONSUL-GENERAL IN LOWER SAXONY, AND WITH THE HANS TOWNS.

Baltic, May 8th, 1801.

Dear Sir,

It is so very uncertain how long a stay our Fleet may make in the Baltic, that we can only be supplied for our daily consumption, nor look forward beyond a week, therefore I send you a paper, that Mr. Adey, or any other merchant, may give me their proposals upon it; and it must be noticed, that the lowest price and the best provisions must both combine. Dantzic, while our Squadron is off Bornholm, is as convenient, with certain winds, as Rostock.

Sir Hyde Parker left the Fleet the same day that you did; and I had thought that you had intended staying the result of a messenger, who arrived the same night I had the pleasure of seeing you. I am, dear Sir, &c.

NELSON AND BRONTE.

TO ADMIRAL THE EARL OF ST. VINCENT, K.B.

[From Clarke and M'Arthur, vol. ii. p. 278.]

8th May, 1801.

I dare say Sir Hyde Parker has recommended to your notice Lieutenant Joshua Johnson, of the Edgar. At the commencement of the Action he was Second Lieutenant; but the First being very soon killed, he acted as such until his left arm was shot off. He refused the idea of being sent to England, and hoped that Captain Murray would be content by the First Lieutenant's duty being done by a one-armed Officer. He is now perfectly recovered, and doing his duty as First Lieutenant. All his conduct has been so highly creditable, that I should be unjust not to recommend him to your Lordship's protection.[1]   I am, &c.,

NELSON AND BRONTE.

TO HIS EXCELLENCY THE COUNT PAHLEN, RUSSIAN MINISTER FOR FOREIGN AFFAIRS.

[Letter-Book.]

St. George, May 9th, 1801.

Sir,

I am this moment honoured with your Excellency's letter of April 22nd, O.S., covering two letters from Lord Carysfort. I am happy in this opportunity of assuring your Excellency, that my orders towards Russia from England are of the most pacific and friendly nature; and I have to request, that you will assure his Imperial Majesty, that my inclination so perfectly accords with my orders, that I had determined to show myself with a Squadron in the Bay of Revel, (or at Cronstadt, if the Emperor would rather wish me to go there,) to mark the friendship which, I trust in God, will ever subsist between our two gracious Sovereigns; and it will likewise be of great service, in assisting to navigate to England many of the English Merchant-vessels, who have remained all the winter in Russia.

I have taken care in the Squadron which I bring up

---

[1] He was immediately promoted, and died a Commander, about 1831.

with me, that there shall be neither Bomb-Ship, Fire-Ship,
nor any of the Flotilla, in order to mark the more strongly,
that I wish it to be considered as a mark of the greatest
personal respect to his Imperial Majesty. I beg leave to assure
your Excellency that I shall feel truly happy in the opportunity of assuring you personally how much I feel your Excellency's obliged and obedient humble Servant,

NELSON AND BRONTE.

P.S.—The command of the British Fleet has been conferred upon me ; and Sir Hyde Parker has returned to
England.

TO REAR-ADMIRAL TOTTY.

[Letter-Book.   This Letter was left with Captain Murray, on the 9th of May, to
be delivered to Rear-Admiral Totty on his arrival from England.]

Dear Sir,   [About May 9th, 1801.]
I leave the Saturn, in order that you may take a convenient
time for removing your Flag, &c. to her, as Sir Hyde Parker
says, she is the Ship which he understands is destined for
you, and that Captain Brisbane[2] is to be your Captain. He is
at this moment acting in the Ganges; but the moment Captain Fremantle[3] joins from Petersburgh, I shall send him down
in the Dart, when Captain Lambert[4] will join Alcmene, and
Captain Devonshire,[5] the Dart.

You will see, that I wish to keep your Squadron strong
enough to master the Swedes, if they have the impertinence
to come to sea. Therefore you will keep, with the Ships
which arrive from England, with you, seven Sail of the Line ;
sending the Edgar, (and Ruby, if Sir Edward Berry is in

---

[2] Captain James Brisbane. He was nominated a Companion of the Bath in 1815,
and commanded Lord Exmouth's Flag-ship, the Queen Charlotte, at Algiers, in
1816, for his services on which occasion he was Knighted : he died a Post Captain
in 1827.

[3] Captain Thomas Francis Fremantle, so often mentioned.

[4] Captain Robert Lambert : he died a Vice-Admiral of the Blue in September
1836.

[5] Captain John Ferris Devonshire. This zealous Officer, who is mentioned in the
Preface to the First Volume, became a Retired Rear-Admiral, was made a Com-
mander of the Order of the Guelphs, and Knighted by Patent in 1834, and died in
February 1839.

her,) and any other Ships you please, except the Ardent and
Glatton, to join me in the Gulf of Finland,—most probably
at Revel. All your bad-sailing Small craft you had better put
under the directions of Captain Inman. You will not, I am
sure, fail to let me know, if any extraordinary occurrence
should take place. My absence probably will not exceed
fourteen days; but you may rely on your being timely
acquainted with all my movements; and I beg you will
believe me, dear Sir, your very obedient Servant,

NELSON AND BRONTE.

TO HIS EXCELLENCY THE COMMANDER-IN-CHIEF OF HIS
IMPERIAL MAJESTY'S SHIPS AT REVEL.

[Letter-Book.]

St. George, May 11th, 1801.

Sir,

I beg leave to inform you of my intention to anchor a
Squadron of His Britannic Majesty's Ships in the Bay of
Revel, of which intention I have informed Count Pahlen,
and his Excellency the Governor of Revel. I have therefore
to request, that you will have the goodness to allow some of
your Officers and Pilots to come on board me, in order that the
Squadron may be anchored in a good berth. I have the
honour to be, &c.,

NELSON AND BRONTE.

TO BENJAMIN GARLIKE, ESQ., SECRETARY OF EMBASSY AT ST.
PETERSBURGH.

[Letter-Book.]

St. George, entrance of the Gulf of Finland, May 11th, 1801.

Sir,

I send you copies of my letters to His Excellency Count
Pahlen, and to the Swedish Admiral, which will put you in
full possession of my situation and intentions; and, as Sir
Hyde Parker, the late Commander-in-Chief has shown the
greatest attention in abstaining from all hostilities in the
Baltic, conformably to the wishes expressed by the Emperor

of Russia, and my orders from England being of the most pacific and friendly tenour, I have thought it the very highest compliment I could pay His Imperial Majesty to come into the Gulf of Finland, with a small Squadron of His Majesty's Ships. The body of the Fleet I have left in the Baltic, and to avoid anything which could give an appearance of warlike movements, neither Bomb-Ship, Fire-Ship, nor one of the Flotilla has attended me ; and I trust that the Court of Russia will see my conduct in its proper point of view.

I am also particularly anxious, respecting the situation of our seamen and Merchants-ships detained last Autumn in the Russian Ports; and as I hope they are entirely liberated, I wish you to call a meeting of the Merchants, that I may know how I can best assist them in getting their Ships to England, or in any way be useful to them. I shall very anxiously wait, I hope in Revel, the return of the messenger, who carries this letter, and I beg you to believe me, Sir, with great respect, your most obedient Servant,

NELSON AND BRONTE.

TO NICHOLAS VANSITTART, ESQ.[a]

[Autograph, in the possession of Lord Bexley. " A favourable wind brought us, on the 12th of May, into Revel Roads, where Lord Nelson was rather disappointed at not finding the Russian Fleet; the early breaking up of the ice had enabled it to proceed to Cronstadt, three days before our arrival. We came to anchor in the outer bay, and a friendly message was sent on shore to the Governor, General Sacken, inquiring whether a salute was intended to be fired? Lord Nelson stated his being ready to return the same, and assured him of the above-mentioned friendly objects which he had in view in entering a Russian Port. Cordial declarations of amity were returned, and a salute promised; this, however, being neglected, the Admiral again sent on shore, and was informed that the delay had arisen from the misconduct of the Officer commanding the Artillery, who had been put under arrest in consequence, and that the salute should be given. This was accordingly done, but at so late an hour that our salute was not returned until the next morning. Lord Nelson having been invited by the Governor, went on shore about noon on the 13th of May, and was received with all military honours. His letter having been forwarded to the Emperor, great activity was exerted in providing the Fleet with fresh meat and vegetables. The joy which pervaded the whole Empire on the death of Paul was manifest at Revel ; nor were the disgraceful circumstances that attended his death by any means concealed : the re-establishing a good understanding with England appeared, on the other hand, to give general satisfaction, and we were cordially received by the

------

a. Now Lord Bexley.   Vide p. 296, ante.

inhabitants, as well as the military. On the 14th of May the Governor returned Lord Nelson's visit, on board the St. George; he was accompanied by young Pahlen, the Minister's son, who commanded a regiment of hussars in garrison there, and by other military commanders. They were shown over every part of the Ship by Lord Nelson, and it was observable that the Cossack officers gave infinitely more attention to what they saw, than did any of the Russians. The interval between this and the 16th of May was employed by his Lordship in observation, and in acquiring information of the Harbour, Mole, and Anchorage. It was decidedly his opinion, that had the Russian Fleet been hostile, it might have been attacked with success by firing the wooden Mole, behind which it is always moored during the winter months; a position seemed also to present itself for a three-decker across the mouth of the harbour, by which Ship the whole dock might have been raked from end to end."—*Colonel Stewart's Narrative.*]

St. George, Gulf of Finland, May 12th, 1801.

My dear Sir,

I feel, I assure you, most infinitely obliged by your truly kind and satisfactory letter of April 8th, for I know from experience how difficult it is for an Officer to have his feelings properly represented at home. You did me full justice that I wanted to get at an Enemy as soon as possible to strike a *home* stroke, and that Paul was the Enemy most vulnerable, and of the greatest consequence for us to humble. On the 2nd of April, we could have been at Revel, and I know nothing at present which could have prevented our destroying the whole Russian force at that Port. It would have brought, if not Paul to his senses, yet most probably both Sweden and Denmark; but mankind form opinions on what has happened, and seldom do that justice which both you and Mr. Addington did to my opinion, formed on the information and circumstances before me. The difficulty was to get our Commander-in-Chief to either go past Cronenburg or through the Belt, because, what Sir Hyde thought best, and what I believe was settled before I came on board the London, was to stay in the Cattegat, and there wait the time when the whole Naval force of the Baltic might choose to come out and fight—a measure, in my opinion, disgraceful to our Country. I can only again repeat how much I feel your goodness in explaining the motives which actuated my conduct; and I beg you to believe me, dear Sir, your truly obliged,

NELSON AND BRONTE.

His Majesty's Ministers will be able to form a decisive opinion on the future plans of the Emperor Alexander from his conduct at this moment. You will see, of course, all the papers which I send to the Admiralty.

May 17th.—I hope you will read Count Pahlen's last letter : it is a very curious one. *The Revel Fleet* he considers as safe. I left Revel this morning where everybody has been kind to us.

TO ALEXANDER DAVISON, ESQ., ST. JAMES'S SQUARE.

[Autograph, in the possession of Colonel Davison.]

St. George, off Otkensholm Light-house, Gulf of Finland,
May 12th, 1801.

My dear Davison,

As it is in vain for me to urge the justness of my cause.[3] If justice is fled from our Island, it is useless to torment either myself or you on a business which must long ago be decided, (I mean before you read this letter.) If it is given against me, I have only to lament that the hand of power has robbed me ; for I cannot doubt but if I could have appeared before a Jury, and told truth, that the Earl's cause would not have held water. But never mind, I hope another Admiral is on his way to supersede me ; for why am I to be kept here to die a natural death? I did not bargain for that when I came to the Baltic. It is now sixteen days that I have not been able to get out of my cabin ; and Admiral Graves has been as many in bed. The Country may do very well to fight a battle, but no man of common sense would remain ; but, fight or not fight, as they please, I stay no longer than I get down, which I hope will be by June 1st,.if I live so long. In forty-eight hours I shall have formed my opinion of the future plans of Alexander towards us ; and I hope our Ministry, from the papers I shall send them of my reception and treatment, will be fully equal to decide every [thing] which the Russian Ministry intend doing in the present state of affairs. I have not forgot the cause of our Merchants, and I have wrote strongly, although I trust friendly, to Count Pahlen on the subject, and I have desired our Chargé d'Affaires at Peters-

---

[3] His Law-suit with the Earl of St. Vincent, respecting Prize-money, before mentioned, which was eventually decided in Lord Nelson's favour.

burgh, to call a meeting of the British Merchants, in order that I may know how best to be useful to them ; for whilst I do stay in the Baltic, mine shall be a life of activity, and as far as my abilities enable me, useful to my Country. By the 12th of June, I shall assuredly take you by the hand, and hope you have entirely got rid of the gout. May God bless you, my dear Davison, and believe me ever your obliged and affectionate friend,

NELSON AND BRONTE.

TO EVAN NEPEAN, ESQ., ADMIRALTY.

[Letter-Book.]

St. George, Revel Bay, May 15th, 1801.

Sir,

Under the Armistice with Denmark, I should wish very much to have their Lordships' directions whether our Merchant-ships ought to pay the Sound dues? I own myself of opinion that, considering Denmark as an Enemy, she has no right to expect that we are to pay her any money, and that our Merchant-ships may pass the Belt, if they choose. But situated as the North of Europe is at this moment, the Admiral who will command here, must be very anxious to receive their Lordships' directions as soon as possible on this subject. I am, &c.,

NELSON AND BRONTE.

TO ADMIRAL THE EARL OF ST. VINCENT, K.B.

[From Clarke and M'Arthur, vol. ii. p. 285.]

Revel Bay, 16th May, 1801.

To your Lordship, I shall confine myself to what we clearly could have done with our Baltic Fleet, such as it was after the conclusion of the Armistice with Denmark. I shall not say more of the Swedes, than as we saw their force at Carlscrona, where they had wisely retired when they *saw our Frigates* in the Baltic. On the 19th of April, we had eighteen Sail of the Line and a fair wind. Count Pahlen came and resided at this place, evidently to endeavour to prevent any hostilities against the Russian Fleet here, which was, I decidedly say, at our mercy. Nothing, if it had been right to make the attack, could have saved one Ship of them in two hours after our entering the Bay; and to prevent their destruction, Sir Hyde Parker had a great latitude for asking for various things for the suspension of his orders; but I hope all is for the best, and that the Emperor has not deceived us. On Wednesday, the 29th of April, the Bay of Revel was clear of firm ice; and, on that day, the ice in the Mole, about six feet thick, was cut, and three Sail of the Line got out, and moored on the eastern side of the Bay, absolutely unprotected except by a battery of six guns. By the Sunday, they were all out, fourteen Sail of Ships; but I am not certain yet, whether the Fleet was ten, eleven, or twelve Ships of the Line—two were three-decked Ships : they sailed for Cronstadt the same day. I hope you will approve of our coming here; we now know the navigation, should circumstances call us here again. All the folks are thieves, and think us fair game. Hardy and myself have managed the whole business here. I am, &c.,

NELSON AND BRONTE.

TO HIS EXCELLENCY COUNT PAHLEN.

[Letter-Book.]

St. George, Revel Bay, May 16th, 1801.

Sir,

I am this moment honoured with your Excellency's letter ;[6] and I only beg leave to refer you again to my letter of the 9th of May. You will there see, that not one-seventh part of

---

[6] "S. E. MYLORD NELSON.

"St. Petersbourg, ce 2 Mai, [i. e. 13th May, N.S.] 1801.

"Mylord,

"La lettre que votre Excellence m'a fait l'honneur de m'écrire en date du 9 Mai, a été pour moi l'objet de la plus grande surprise. Elle me confirme l'assurance des dispositions pacifiques de la Grande Bretagne, et en même tems elle m'annonce votre intention, Mylord, de venir avec toute la flotte sous vos ordres à la rade de Revel, ou à celle de Cronstadt. L'Empéreur, mon Maître, ne juge point une semblable démarche compatible avec le vif désir manifesté par Sa Majesté Britannique, de rétablir la bonne intelligence, qui a regné si longtems entre les deux Monarchies. Sa Majesté Impériale la trouve au contraire entièrement opposée à l'esprit des instructions de la Cour de Londres, telles qu'elles lui sont annoncées par le Lord Hawkesbury. En conséquence, Sa Majesté m'ordonne de vous déclarer, Mylord,

B B 2

the Fleet in point of numbers were coming into the Gulf
of Finland ; and that, as my intention was to pay a very particular respect to His Imperial Majesty, I submitted it to His
pleasure, which Port he would wish me to come to, Revel or
Cronstadt.

que le seul garant qu'Elle accepte de la loyauté de vos intentions, est le prompt
éloignement de la flotte que vous commandez, et qu'aucune négociation avec votre
Cour ne pourra avoir lieu, tant qu'une force navale sera à la vue de ses ports.

" L'Empéreur persiste toujours dans ses dispositions de terminer à l'aimable les
differends survenus entre les deux Cours. Sa Majesté déferera avec plaisir aux
demandes que le Roi votre Maitre lui adressera par la voie d'une négociation
amicale et qui seront fondées sur la justice ; mais toute démonstration qui donnerait
à ces demandes l'air de conditions, ne peut que faire manquer l'effèt qu'on s'en
propose.

" Sa Majesté attend de vôtre prudence, Mylord, qu'en donnant à cette déclaration
toute l'attention qu'elle mérite, vous aurez soin de prevenir tout ce qui s'opposerait
aux vœux mutuels de nos Souverains pour la conservation de la paix, et rien n'y
serait plus contraire, que la prolongation du séjour de la flotte Anglaise dans nos
parages.

"Les lumières de votre Excellence ne me permettent pas d'ailleurs de douter,
qu'elle sentira combien sa réponse peut être décisive pour déterminer la conduite
future de la Cour de Russie, et qu'elle ne voudra point se rendre personnellement
responsable des suites qu'entrainerait sa resistance aux justes représentations con-
tenues dans la présente. Il serait très pénible à mon auguste Maître de renoncer
aux voies de conciliation, mais il ne differera pas un instant de déployer les forces que
la Providence a mises entre ses mains si la moindre atteinte à la dignité de sa
Couronne lui en impose malheureusement l'obligation toujours sacrée pour lui.

" J'ai l'honneur d'être, avec une considération très distinguée, Mylord, de vôtre
Excellence, le très humble et très obéissant serviteur, LE COMTE DE PAHLEN."—
Original, in the possession of the Right Hon. John Wilson Croker.

" This Letter," says Colonel Stewart, " reached Lord Nelson about three P.M.
on the 16th of May, and was accompanied by a letter from Governor Sacken, expressing a wish that the British Fleet should retire from the anchorage of Revel.
Lord Nelson received it a few minutes before dinner-time ; he appeared to be a good
deal agitated by it, but said little, and did not return an immediate reply. During
dinner, however, he left the table, and in less than a quarter of an hour sent for
his Secretary to peruse a letter which, in that short absence, he had composed.
The signal for preparing to weigh was immediately made ; the answer above mentioned was sent on shore ; and although contracts had been entered into for fresh
provisions, &c. for the Fleet, his Lordship would not admit of the least delay, but
caused it to weigh, and to stand as far to sea as was safe for that evening. It was
only dark for an hour or two, during which time we lay to, and at dawn of day proceeded down the Baltic ; a Brig was left to bring off the provisions, and settle the
contracts. When off Bornholm, we were joined by the Squadron under Captain
Murray. A detachment from the Fleet was then sent off to Kioge Bay, where a
British merchant established in Denmark, Mr. Balfour, had contracted for the
supply of fresh provisions, under the sanction of the Danish government. Another
detachment was sent on the same errand to Dantzic, and Lord Nelson himself
proceeded with a few Ships to Rostock Bay."—*Narrative* in *Clarke and M‘Arthur*.

Your Excellency will have the goodness to observe to the Emperor, that I did not even enter into the outer Bay of Revel, without the consent of their Excellencies the Governor and Admiral. My conduct, I feel, is so entirely different to what your Excellency has expressed in your letter, that I have only to regret, that my desire to pay a marked attention to His Imperial Majesty has been so entirely misunderstood. That being the case, I shall sail immediately into the Baltic.

Requesting again, that your Excellency will express to His Imperial Majesty my ardent desire to have shown him all the respect in the power of your Excellency's most obedient, &c.,

NELSON AND BRONTE.

TO ADMIRAL THE EARL OF ST. VINCENT, K.B.

[From Clarke and M'Arthur, vol. ii. p. 286.]

May 17th, 1801.

The answer from Count Pahlen, with all my correspondence is under cover to Mr. Nepean ; after such an answer, I had no further business here. Has the Count any meaning in his gross falsehoods, or has it been an entire misunderstanding of my letter ? Time will show ; but I do not believe he would have written such a letter, if the Russian Fleet had been in Revel. A word for myself : since the 27th of April, I have not been out of my cabin, except in being obliged to do the civil thing at Revel ; nor do I expect to go out, until I land in England, or am carried out of the Ship. I therefore most earnestly hope that some worthy Admiral will be arrived to command this Fleet, which I can truly say is deserving of any Officer ; for more zeal and desire to distinguish themselves I never saw. In four days I hope to join Admiral Totty, off Bornholm. I am, &c.,

NELSON AND BRONTE.[7]

---

[7] Lord St. Vincent wrote to Lord Nelson on the 31st of May,—" I have the deepest concern at learning from Lieutenant Colonel Hutchinson, that your health has suffered in so material a degree. To find a proper successor, your Lordship well knows, is no easy task ; for I never saw the man in our Profession, excepting yourself and Troubridge, who possessed the magic art of infusing the same spirit into others,

TO REAR-ADMIRAL THOMAS TOTTY.

[Letter-Book.]

St. George, Gulf of Finland, 17th May, 1801.

Sir,

As I am proceeding to join you with all expedition, it is my desire that you do not allow any of His Majesty's Ships or Vessels to go up the Gulf of Finland, and that you will endeavour to keep the Squadron with you as much together as possible. I request a Vessel may cruize to the N.E. of Bornholm, to point out to me your situation.

I have directed Captain Boys[8] to wait four hours for letters to take to England; but beg he may not be detained a moment longer. I am, Sir, &c.,

NELSON AND BRONTE.

TO EVAN NEPEAN, ESQ., ADMIRALTY.

[Letter-Book.]

St. George, Gulf of Finland, May 17th, 1801.

Sir,

I beg you will inform their Lordships, that my state of health is such, that I feel at present unable to execute the high trust reposed in me, with either comfort to myself, or benefit to the State. I have, therefore, earnestly to request their Lordships' permission to return to England, in order to try and re-establish my health. I am, &c.

NELSON AND BRONTE.

which inspired their own actions, exclusive of other talents and habits of business, not common to Naval characters. But your complaint demands prompt decision : we have, therefore, fixed on Admiral Pole. Your Lordship's whole conduct, from your first appointment to this hour, is the subject of our constant admiration. It does not become me to make comparisons : all agree there is but one Nelson. That he may long continue the pride of his Country, is the fervent wish of your Lordship's truly affectionate, ST. VINCENT."—*Clarke and M'Arthur*, vol. ii. p. 236.

[8] Captain Charles Worsley Boys, of the Harpy : he lost a leg while a Midshipman, in Lord Howe's Action, in June 1794; was made a Post Captain in the general promotion of April 1802, and died in command of the Statira, on the 17th of November 1809.

TO EVAN NEPEAN, ESQ., ADMIRALTY.

[Letter-Book.]

Sir,　　　　　St. George, Gulf of Finland, May 17th, 1801.

You will know by my letter of the 7th, of my intentions to proceed with a Squadron into the Gulf of Finland. I now have to acquaint you, that having left Captain Murray with seven Sail of the Line and all the Small craft, off Bornholm, I arrived, and anchored with the consent of the Governor and Russian Admiral, in the outer part of the Bay of Revel on the 13th, where the greatest civilities were shown the Squadron; but as I found that none of our Merchant-ships were actually at liberty to sail, I left Revel this morning, and am proceeding to join the Squadron left off Bornholm. I have the honour to be, &c.,

NELSON AND BRONTE.

TO HIS EXCELLENCY THE EARL OF CARYSFORT, K.P.

[Letter-Book.]

St. George, off Gothland, May 19th, 1801.

My dear Lord,

As it may be pleasant for you and particularly for Lord St. Helens, if he passes by Berlin, to know everything which relates to the Court of Russia, I send your Lordship copies of some letters which have passed between Count Pahlen and myself. You will have your opinion, as I have mine, that he never would have wrote such a letter, if the Fleet had been at Revel in April. Mine was a desire to mark a particular civility which, as it was not treated in the way I think handsome, I left Revel on Sunday the 17th, and here I am. From all the Russian Officers at Revel, I received the most attentive behaviour, and I believe they are as much surprised at the answer as I was.

Sir Hyde Parker's letter on the subject of the release of the British Merchant-ships has not been answered. I hope all is right; but as seamen are but bad negotiators—for we put the matter to issue in five minutes what Diplomatic forms would be five months doing—I shall have a frequent communication with Rostock, if our stay in the Baltic is prolonged.

The Swedish Admiral has sent my letter to his King. I have just received a letter from Count Bernstorff; and under our present circumstances I have only to say, that a good understanding is kept alive between us and Denmark. Although I am sensible that all which I send you is of no consequence, still I know from experience that to know there is nothing very particular passing, is comfortable. Our Fleet is twenty-two Sail of the Line, and forty-six Frigates, Bombs, Fire-ships, and Gun-Vessels, and in the Fleet not one man in the Hospital ship—a finer Fleet never graced the Ocean. Ever, my dear Lord, your most obliged and obedient Servant,

NELSON AND BRONTE. .

TO HIS EXCELLENCY COUNT PANIN.

[Letter-Book.]

St. George, May 20th, 1801.

Sir,

I have received the honour of your Excellency's letter by Admiral Tchitchagoff,[9] and have conversed freely with the Admiral on the several points to which your Excellency referred Sir Hyde Parker, the late Commander-in-Chief; and I trust that my full and explicit Declaration will remove

---

[9] "A S. E. MILORD NELSON-BRONTE.

"St. Petersbourg, ce 29 Avril, V. S., 1801.
"Milord,

"Celui que a su mériter le titre honorable de votre ami est sûr de trouver partout l'accueil le plus distingué. Mr. le Capitaine Fremantle ne pouvoit pas sans doute nous apporter une meilleure recommandation, et je me flatte que le rapport qu'il fera à votre Excellence de son séjour dans cette Capitale la convaincra de l'empressement que j'ai eu à remplir vos intentions; il me laisse cependant le regret de n'avoir pas eu le tems de lui prouver combien je suis jaloux de toutes les occasions de mettre au jour les sentimens que j'ai voués au héros du Nil. Mr. Fremantle m'ayant dit que votre Excellence n'avoit encore aucune nouvelle d'Egypte depuis le débarquement des troupes Angloises, j'éprouve une satisfaction particulière d'être le premier à vous transmettre, Milord, la nouvelle des succès de l'Armée Britannique, dans ce pays témoin de votre gloire. Agréez en mes sincéres felicitations. Je ne saurois terminer ces lignes sans recommander aux bontés de votre Excellence Mr. le Contre-Amiral Tchitchagoff, porteur de la présente, chargé d'une commission particulière pour Mr. l'Amiral Parker. C'est un des Officiers les plus distingués de la Marine Impériale. J'ai l'honneur d'être, avec une haute considération, Milord, de votre Excellence le très humble et très obéissant serviteur, PANIN."—*Autograph*, in the possession of the Right Honourable John Wilson Croker.

every impression, which would militate for a moment against the returning peace and harmony between our august Masters, and which, from the bottom of my heart I hope, never again to see interrupted. With every sentiment of respect, believe me, your Excellency's most obedient Servant,

NELSON AND BRONTE.

MANIFESTO.

[Letter-Book.]

Admiral Tchitchagoff having declared to me this day, that His Imperial Majesty the Emperor of all the Russias, has the greatest desire to return to his amicable Alliance with the King of the United Kingdom of Great Britain and Ireland, my most gracious Sovereign, I have, therefore, the pleasure to say, that I can declare the wishes of my Sovereign to return to His ancient friendly Alliance with the Court of Russia, and that my orders,[1] on such a Declaration being given on the part of His Imperial Majesty, are clear and decisive to commit no act of hostility against anything appertaining to the Emperor of Russia. And I likewise declare, that the wishes of His Imperial Majesty respecting the freedom of the trade, both of Denmark and Sweden, in the Baltic, have been fully complied with.

Given on board His Britannic Majesty's Ship, St. George, in the Baltic, May 20th, 1801.

NELSON AND BRONTE.

TO LADY PARKER.

[Autograph, in the possession of Mrs. Ellis.]

St. George, Baltic, May 21st, 1801.

My dear Lady,

It was only when Admiral Totty joined me that I received your most truly kind and affectionate letter of April ———. Believe me, when I say that I am as sensible as ever that I owe my present situation in life to your and good Sir Peter's partiality for me, and friendly remembrance of Maurice Suck-

[1] Vide p. 349, ante.

ling. I am sorry to hear you so complaining, but I trust the summer will completely repair your health. The air of the Baltic has completely done me up, and I have my serious doubts, if Lord St. Vincent do not very soon send out an Admiral to supersede me, that I never shall leave this Country. Pray remember [me] most gratefully to dear Sir Peter, affectionately to Admiral Parker and all your family; and believe me, as ever, your obliged and grateful,

NELSON AND BRONTE.

Murray, Foley, and Fremantle, are now on board: they desire their kind thanks and best regards.

TO ALEXANDER DAVISON, ESQ.

[Autograph, in the possession of Colonel Davison.]

St. George, May 22nd, 1801.

My dear Davison,

By a letter from Sir Andrew Hamond, given to Lord St. Helens, I first heard of the death of my dear brother Maurice. As the dead cannot be called back, it is of no use dwelling on those who are gone. I am sure you will do everything which is right for his poor blind wife. I hope he has left her well provided for; if not, I beg you will take the trouble to arrange a proper and ample subsistence, and I will make it up.[1] It is the only true regard I can pay to his memory. He was always good and kind to me; but enough on this subject: I know your sincere friendship for him. Your letters are on board Admiral Totty, with Parker,[6] and I have not yet joined him. I shall see you in a very few days; till then I shall only say God bless you. I am very unwell. Since April 27th, I have only been once out of my cabin. Ever yours affectionately,

NELSON AND BRONTE.

Pray send the enclosed.

---

[1] Mr. Maurice Nelson lived many years with a Miss Sarah Ford, who accidentally lost her sight, and became a cripple. Mr. Nelson was supposed to have married her from compassion for her helpless condition, and she bore his name. Lord Nelson, who always treated her as his brother's widow, allowed her an annuity; and after his death, she received assistance from Lady Hamilton. She died in 1810 or 1811.

[6] Captain Edward Thornborough Parker, who is frequently mentioned in subsequent Letters.

TO ADMIRAL THE EARL OF ST. VINCENT, K.B.

[From Clarke and M'Arthur, vol. ii. p. 286. About this time Lord Nelson received Secret Orders, addressed on the 6th of May to Sir Hyde Parker (though he had been superseded by Lord Nelson,) conveying the King's pleasure, that, as it appears possible the Swedish Squadron, taking advantage of the return of the Fleet under your command to Kioge Bay, may entertain an intention of forming a junction with the Russians, either at Revel or Cronstadt, or with the Danish Fleet at Copenhagen, you should be directed, either with the whole, or with such part of the Fleet as may be adequate to the purpose, to take such a position as you may conceive best calculated to prevent such a movement on the part of the Swedish Squadron. You are, in pursuance of his Majesty's command signified to us, hereby required and directed to place yourself in such a position, either with the whole or a part of your Fleet, as you may judge best adapted to that purpose accordingly, subject, however, to the restriction of your not going to the northward of Carlscrona, so long as the Swedish Fleet shall not proceed up the Baltic; and, with a view to remove any anxiety that may be felt by the Swedish Court with respect to your intentions, you are to take the earliest opportunity of communicating to that Court, that you are expressly instructed to commit no act of hostility whatsoever against the Ships of his Swedish Majesty, provided that he shall direct his Fleet to remain in the Port of Carlscrona; but that, in the event of its leaving that Port, you have received orders to use every means in your power to prevent its junction with the Naval forces either of Russia or Denmark.

"In the event of the Swedish Fleet having already sailed to Revel or Cronstadt before you shall receive these orders, you are, in such case, to take such a position off Revel as may be best adapted for preventing any further junction being effected by the Ships there with the force at Cronstadt, or vice versâ; and if, after the arrival of the Swedish Fleet at either of the places above-mentioned, the Officer commanding it should be desirous of returning to Carlscrona, you are, in that case, upon a proper intimation being made to you, to allow this movement to be made without any opposition; and as soon as it shall have taken place, return to the position you are directed to take in the more probable case of the Swedish Fleet having remained at Carlscrona, instead of proceeding up the Baltic, unless in consequence of any communication from his Majesty's Ambassador to the Court of Russia, you should judge it more advisable to remain in the Gulf of Finland."

Sir Hyde Parker was then directed to regulate his conduct according to the information he might receive from Lord St. Helens, Ambassador to the Court of Petersburgh, " and to proceed in conformity with your former instructions, and particularly to those contained in our order to you of the 15th of March last, against the Ports, Arsenals, and Shipping of Russia and Sweden, if, contrary to every expectation, you should receive information from Lord St. Helens that every hope of amicable adjustment is at an end."

" With respect to Denmark, no step can be taken against her within the limits of the Armistice, but at the expiration thereof, you are hereby authorized and directed to renew hostilities against that Power, unless the grounds of difference between the two Countries shall in the meantime be removed, either by direct negotiation, or through the intervention of the Court of Petersburgh, of which information will be conveyed to you by his Majesty's Ambassador at that Court."—*Original.*]

May 22nd, 1801.

I send you a plan of the Bay of Revel, drawn by our friend Colonel Stewart, who is an excellent and indefatigable young man, and, depend upon it, the rising hope of our Army. As there is no other plan in existence, perhaps you will direct a copy to be lodged in the Hydrographer's Office. The Fleet when out of the Mole, always moor on the east side of the Bay, the outer Ship is supposed to be protected by the Fort, which is marked; there are, it is true, a number of guns, but as the Officer who goes there is not to be supposed to mind guns, if he can get in and out again, in my opinion the Revel Fleet, whether in or out of the Mole, would be destroyed by a vigorous attack; and that it may, if the Russians again give us offence, is the sincere wish of your affectionate sick friend,

NELSON AND BRONTE.

P.S.—You have often spoke of that worthy officer Admiral George Montagu:[4] I own, I long from his character to give up this Fleet to him, or some other good man. May 24th.— The death of my dear brother, which I received only yesterday, has naturally affected me a good deal; and if I do not get some repose very soon, another will go. Six sons are gone, out of eight; but I hope yet to see you, and to cheer up once more.

TO HIS EXCELLENCY LORD ST. HELENS, AMBASSADOR AT THE COURT OF ST. PETERSBURGH.

[Letter-Book.]

St. George, off Bornholm, May 22nd, 1801.

My Lord,

I never before regretted having a fair wind; but your quick voyage is of so much more importance than mine, that I sincerely regret your not having a fair wind. I send your Excellency copies of some letters of mine, which in conversation you may have occasion to refer to. Captain Thesiger, who will have the honour of delivering this letter, has been for many years a Captain in the Russian Navy; but left it two years ago, from the extraordinary conduct of the late Emperor. I have sent a fast sailing Lugger to attend on your Mission,

---

[4] Admiral George Montagu: he was appointed a Knight Grand Cross of the Bath, on the extension of the Order in January 1815, and died in December 1829.

the progress and result of which, as far as may be proper for me
to be made acquainted with, I must be in a state of constant
anxiety to know, that the Fleet may be collected ready for a
push, should the Russian Fleet make any movements indicating an intention of going to sea. I trust to your Excellency
allowing Captain Sotheron[5] to give me notice of it, by one
of the small Vessels. I have not a word of news.

Wishing your Excellency every success, I have the honour
to be, &c.,

NELSON AND BRONTE.

TO CAPTAIN SOTHERON, H.M. SHIP LATONA.

[Letter-Book.]

St. George, off Bornholm, 22nd May, 1801.

Sir,

I send the Lark lugger with dispatches for Lord St. Helens.
The Lieutenant of her has my orders to put himself under
your directions, for the purpose of waiting on the Mission.
Should the Russian Fleet make any movements indicating an
intention of putting to sea, you are immediately to make it
known to Lord St. Helens, in order that I may be apprised of
their so doing. I am, &c.,

NELSON AND BRONTE.

TO A. H. STEWARD, ESQ., YARMOUTH.

[Autograph, in the possession of the Rev. A. H. Steward, of Whitton, near Ipswich.]

St. George, May 23rd, 1801.

My dear Sir,

I have thousands of thanks to give you for the great trouble
you have had in receiving my letters and packages, and for
many things which you have had the goodness to send me;
and if it pleases God, I hope to return you my sincere thanks
and to repay you the money you must have laid out for, dear
Sir, yours truly obliged,

NELSON AND BRONTE.

---

[5] Captain Frank Sotheron, of the Latona: he died an Admiral of the White, in
February 1839.

TO ALEXANDER DAVISON, ESQ.

[Autograph, in the possession of Colonel Davison.]

St. George, May 23rd, 1801.

My dear Friend,

I shall not repeat my feelings for the death of poor Maurice. You have ever done everything which was kind towards him. Your sentiments about poor Mrs. Nelson (for such I shall always call her) agree so perfectly with my own, that it is unnecessary to say anything farther. You are overwhelming me with favours, but my heart is grateful. I have only time to say, that if I do not see you in fourteen days, probably I never may. Be that as it may, I shall always be, till death, your most obliged and affectionate friend,

NELSON AND BRONTE.

TO CAPTAIN DEVONSHIRE, COPENHAGEN ROAD.

[Autograph, in the possession of Lady Devonshire.]

St. George, May 23rd, 1801.

Dear Sir,

I am sorry that it is necessary to send any Captain to the Alcmene, which will render it necessary for you to return to the Dart; but if you will take my advice, make the best of the case, for as it must be, it is of no use going against the arrangement of the First Lord of the Admiralty; but reports say, that Captain M'Kinley[6] is not confirmed Post, as the Admiralty consider it as their vacancy, and I think it very possible you may be intended for that vacancy; and that it may prove so, is the sincere wish of your most faithful Servant,

NELSON AND BRONTE.

Join me off Rostock.

---

[6] Captain George M'Kinley, of the Otter: now a Vice-Admiral of the Blue.

TO REAR-ADMIRAL HOLLOWAY.

[Autograph, in the possession of Admiral Sir Robert Otway, Bart., G.C.B.]

St. George, May 23rd, 1801.

My dear Holloway,

Only this morning I received your truly kind letter of congratulation of April 18th: from my heart I wish you had been here, and if this Northern business is not settled, they must send more Admirals. I am going home immediately or I shall be dead with a consumption, the keen air of the North has cut me to the heart. Graves has kept his bed for a month, but I suspect with a different complaint to mine. I beg you will present my best respects to Mrs. Holloway, and say, her relation, Lyons, is in great truth a very fine lad, and is continued rated, which is a proof of it. With best regards to all, at Portsmouth, of our friends, believe me, dear Holloway, your faithful and obliged,

NELSON AND BRONTE.

TO EVAN NEPEAN, ESQ., ADMIRALTY.

[Letter-Book.]

St. George, at Sea, 23rd May, 1801.

Sir,

On the 17th, having dispatched the Harpy with information of my proceedings to that date, I have now further to request that you will acquaint their Lordships, that Captain Murray, with four Sail of the Line, joined me off the North end of Gothland, having been relieved on his station off Bornholm by Rear-Admiral Totty.

From the returns of bread, I judged it proper to put the Ships' companies to two-thirds allowance of that species of provisions; but, from the report I have received from Dantzic, and a similar one I expect from Rostock, I hope that the Fleet will get an ample supply of bread and flour, and at a cheaper rate than it can be purchased in England; and supplies of fresh beef will be as much as we wish, and, I hope, not exceeding fourpence or fourpence half-penny per pound. I believe it will not cost Government anything more for water;

and I beg you will assure their Lordships, that my utmost endeavours shall be used to keep this Fleet in a perfect state for any service, at the smallest possible expense; for I am fully aware of the necessity of economy in every Department of the State, and what abuses have crept in from the want of due attention.

I have sent Captains Murray, Foley, and Tyler,[8] in their respective Ships, to Dantzic to get supplies, and to endeavour to fix everything at the lowest possible price; but in this Country the price of provisions rises and falls as the London market demands. As soon as I am complete master of this subject, their Lordships shall know the particulars. Whether wine can be got reasonably in this Country, I have my doubts. Sir Hyde Parker bought some in Denmark; but I am not acquainted with the price. But I own myself a strong advocate for serving wine to the Ships' companies instead of spirits. Respecting stores for the Fleet, I have directed an account to be made out of the spars expended in consequence of the Action of April 2nd: as to rope, those who have been industrious have more rope than when the Fleet sailed from England; for the greatest quantity of rope has been made from the wounded cables of the prizes, which were all new. And I give their Lordships as my opinion, that not a rope-yarn can be carried away or expended, (except by Battle,) between this period and September 1st, and I may, with truth, congratulate their Lordships on there being, at this moment, twenty Sail of the Line in the Baltic, as efficient Ships as any in Europe. I do not reckon on the Ardent and Glatton; for they sail so very heavy, that no rapid movement could be made with them in the Line or Order of Sailing.

On the whole, I may take upon me to say that, although we may have imaginary wants, yet, thank God! we have no real ones, from one end of the Fleet to the other. I shall anchor with some of the Ships off Rostock, to get bread and beef. Some will be watering in Kioge Bay; eight Sail of the Line will always be off Bornholm to watch the Swedes. In short, the Fleet shall always be in motion; and, as far as

---

[8] Captain, afterwards Admiral Sir Charles Tyler, G.C.B., who was severely wounded in command of the Tonnant at Trafalgar; and died in September 1835.

lies in my power, complete in every respect for real service. On the 20th, at night, I fell in with the Latona, having on board his Excellency Lord St. Helens, with whom I had three hours' conversation; and their Lordships may rely that everything shall be done on my part to promote the happy termination of his Lordship's mission.   I have the honour, &c.

NELSON AND BRONTE.

The Shannon reported the Swedish Fleet, top-gallant masts struck generally, but got up on particular days, seven Sail of the Line, and three Frigates.   I have a report from Vessels spoke, that the Swedish Flotilla is returned to Stockholm.

TO EVAN NEPEAN, ESQ., ADMIRALTY.

[Letter-Book.]

St. George, 23rd May, 1801.

Sir,

On the 20th, a Russian Frigate, having on board Rear-Admiral Tchitchagoff, delivered me copies of answers to Sir Hyde Parker's letter of April 26th; and having had a good deal of conversation with the Rear-Admiral, we exchanged the Declarations sent herewith, which, I feel, is in strict compliance with the spirit of part of their Lordships' orders of April 17th.

I also send copies of letters, which I have judged it proper to write to the Swedish Admiral. The Russian Frigate sailed at eight o'clock in the morning for Petersburgh, and the Latona parted company at twelve at night. I have sent two Small craft with the Latona, in order to keep up a constant communication.   I have the honour, &c.

NELSON AND BRONTE.

TO HIS EXCELLENCY ADMIRAL CRONSTEDT, CARLSCRONA.

[Letter-Book.]

St. George, at Sea, 23rd May, 1801.

Sir,

In the correspondence which your Excellency has held with the late Commander-in-Chief of the British Fleet in the

Baltic, I do not see, in return to his Declaration that the trade
of Sweden in the Cattegat and Baltic would be allowed to
pass unmolested by the British Cruizers, any return of Declarations on the part of Sweden, I have therefore to request, that
your Excellency will return an explicit Declaration, that
the trade of Great Britain shall not be molested, in any
manner, in the Cattegat and Baltic by the Swedes.

Your Excellency's judgment will show the necessity of this
mutual Declaration. I have the honour, &c.

                                        NELSON AND BRONTE.

                ――――――――――

                TO EVAN NEPEAN, ESQ., ADMIRALTY.

[Letter-Book. " The keeping his Fleet continually on the alert, and thus amply
furnishing it with fresh water and provisions, were the objects of his Lordship's un-
remitted care; and to this may in a great measure be ascribed the uniform good health
and discipline which prevailed. Another point to which he gave nearly equal attention, was his economy of the resources of his Fleet in regard to stores; their consumption was as remarkable for its smallness in the Baltic, as it was in the Fleet
that was afterwards under his command in the Mediterranean. His hour of rising
was four or five o'clock, and of going to rest about ten; breakfast was never later
than six, and generally nearer to five o'clock. A midshipman or two were always of
the party; and I have known him send during the middle watch to invite the little
fellows to breakfast with him, when relieved. At table with them, he would enter
into their boyish jokes, and be the most youthful of the party. At dinner he invariably had every Officer of his Ship in their turn, and was both a polite and hospitable host. The whole ordinary business of the Fleet was invariably dispatched,
as it had been by Earl St. Vincent, before eight o'clock. The great command of
time which Lord Nelson thus gave himself, and the alertness which this example
imparted throughout the Fleet, can only be understood by those who witnessed it,
or who know the value of early hours. The Russian Frigate Venus, with Admiral
Tchitchagoff on board, met us on our return to Bornholm; she had been in
search of us, with the answer to some pacific overtures that had passed between Sir
Hyde Parker and the Russian Government, and which was of the most friendly
description. Lord St. Helens also met us in the Latona, on his way to Petersburgh on a special mission. At Rostock not an hour was lost in procuring fresh
provisions for the Fleet. The greatest veneration was here shown to the name of
Nelson; and some distant inland Towns of Mecklenburg sent even Deputations,
with their public books of record, to have his name written in them by himself.
Boats were constantly rowing round his Flag-ship, the St. George, with persons of
respectability in them, anxious to catch a sight of this illustrious man. He did not
again land whilst in the Baltic; his health was not good, and his mind was not at
ease: with him, mind and health invariably sympathized."—*Colonel Stewart's Narrative.*]

                        St. George, off Rostock, 24th May, 1801.
    Sir,
    Having joined Rear-Admiral Totty off Bornholm yester-
day morning at three o'clock, and in the course of the day

having arranged the business of the Squadron, and placed under his command the Ships named in the margin,[1] exclusive of the Small craft, which are kept generally at anchor under Bornholm, under the direction of Captain Inman, who has had great merit in keeping them in proper discipline, and as no person at Bornholm could give them money for their bills, or, indeed, take them, I have directed Captain Inman to bring some of them to Rostock; and I must draw for money and supply them. As this proceeding may not be strictly regular, yet as all difficulties give way with me to the benefit of the King's service, I trust their Lordships will take care that I may not be censured for irregularity by the different Boards, if what I do is really for the good of the service.

Having sent the Ganges, Defence, and Veteran to water in Kioge Bay, I left Rear-Admiral Totty in the evening, and anchored here this afternoon with eight sail of the Line, a Frigate, &c. I am so anxious to acquaint their Lordships with the apparent favourable change in the language of the Court of Russia, and of the observations made by Captain Fremantle on the state of the Russian Fleet, that I send the Speedwell; as I am of opinion their Lordships cannot be too minutely acquainted with every circumstance that passes in these critical times. I have the honour to be, &c.

NELSON AND BRONTE.

TO EVAN NEPEAN, ESQ., ADMIRALTY.

[Letter Book.]

St. George, May 24th, 1801.

Sir,

Not wishing to detain Lord St. Helens one moment, I gave to his Lordship all the papers I had received from Rear-Admiral Tchitchagoff and from Captain Fremantle, and directed the Lynx to bring them to me the next day, when Lord St. Helens would have had time to copy them, and to write his letter for England. But, as the Lynx is not arrived, and the

---

[1] Saturn, Zealous, Powerful, Vengeance, Ramilies, Bellona, Ruby, Raisonnable, Shannon, Jamaica, Cruizer, and Lynx.

wind perfectly fair for passing the Belt, I have determined to
send off the Speedwell, and to recite, as well as my memory
will allow, the tenour of the papers sent me, and the conversation which passed with the Russian Admiral.

No. 1, was a very civil letter from Count Pahlen, saying
that he was directed by the Emperor to send Admiral
Tchitchagoff to hold a confidential communication with the
Commander-in-Chief of the British Fleet, supposed to be (of
course) Sir Hyde Parker, and that I might give full credit to
all he said on this occasion. He began by stating the ardent
desire the Emperor had shown from the moment he had
commenced his reign, to return to his ancient amity between
Russia and Great Britain, and that he fully expected a similar
desire on the part of Great Britain ; that Lord Hawkesbury's
letter was announcing that hostilities would not be carried on
in the Baltic, and that such orders had been sent to Sir Hyde
Parker ; that Sir Hyde Parker's letter was amicable, but held
forth a threat, that it could only remain so, in case the British
Shipping were immediately given up ; and that this threat
was in opposition to Lord St. Helens' letter. To which I
replied, that Sir Hyde Parker's instructions were drawn up in
forty-eight hours after it was known the death of the Emperor
Paul ; and that, certainly, he was instructed to send to
Petersburg, to learn the disposition of the Court of Petersburg, and whether our Ships had been restored, in order
that he might regulate his conduct by that of Russia ; but
that Sir Hyde Parker had shown the utmost complaisance to
the wishes of the Emperor of Russia, by abstaining from all
hostility against the trade of the Powers in the Baltic ; and
that the spirit of the instructions were—' if the Emperor wishes
to be sincere friends with us, that then we wished to be
sincere friends with him ; which Admiral Tchitchagoff having
asserted in the name of the Emperor, I said—if that is the
case, and you will declare it in writing, I will make your Court
perfectly at ease about the disposition of my most gracious
Sovereign.' And the Admiral having made the strongest
declaration of the desire, on the part of the Emperor, to
return to his ancient amity with Great Britain, and to see
the peace of the North re-established, I then gave him the
paper transmitted herewith ; on receiving which, he said he

could almost assure me that his Emperor would order the immediate restitution of the British shipping. As I knew Lord St. Helens was on the point of arriving, I did not choose to enter into the subjects of Danish and Swedish [Ships] detained, which he wished to have had my opinion upon: I only generally said, that the Treaty of December last was looked upon, in England, by all ranks, as a most scandalous attempt to injure Great Britain. We parted the best possible friends. I have the honour to be, &c.

NELSON AND BRONTE.

TO WILLIAM BECKFORD, ESQ.

[Autograph, in the possession of the Duchess of Hamilton and Brandon.]

St. George, Bay of Rostock, May 24th, 1801.
This day week was at Revel, in the Gulf of Finland.

My dear Sir,

I have to give you many thanks for your truly kind and friendly letter of April 29th. It is not tiresome being congratulated on good fortune from those you believe sincere, but it is far different if you know the writers hate you, and wish you had miscarried; and, as I have had so many proofs of your real kindness for me I feel truly gratified by your remembrance. I hope Lord St Helens will arrange amicably our affairs with the Northern Powers; and as to France, if she dares to stir off her shores, I only wish our seamen to meet them half seas over. As to myself, I am knocked up, and only want to enjoy, during this negotiation, a little repose, to enable me, if better men will not come forth, to meet these Northern blades. They do not want for courage, that is certain; but in the management of their Fleet, they would, I am [sure,] miserably fail; and two-thirds of their numbers must beat them, if we make use of the skill God Almighty has blessed us with. I trust I shall be, in eight or ten days, in London, and shall have the greatest pleasure in apprising you personally with what esteem and real regard I feel myself your truly obliged,

NELSON AND BRONTE.

My patronage to Mr. Tomkins is not worth a farthing;

and I hear that a print is coming out, done by Captain
        , dedicated to me: if, under these circumstances,
my [name] can be of any use to Mr. T. he is heartily welcome
to it.

TO MESSRS. THOMSON AND POWER.

[Letter-Book.]

St. George, Rostock, May 25th, 1801.

Gentlemen,

I am favoured with your polite letter of May   , and I
have to thank you for your expression of regard and esteem,
and I assure you that I never shall forget the kindness I
experienced in Hamburgh. I truly felt for the situation which
that City was lately placed in; and if at any time it should be
in my power to assist in maintaining the freedom of that
ancient and respectable City, (so useful to Europe in general,)
it would afford me infinite satisfaction.

Respecting provisions for the Fleet, my duty points out that
I am to obtain them at the lowest prices, and of the best
qualities: whoever is willing to make proposals, the road is
open; and the person who will serve Government on the best
terms is the person whom I must employ, without partiality,
favour, or affection. I am, &c.

NELSON AND BRONTE.

TO EVAN NEPEAN, ESQ., ADMIRALTY.

[Letter-Book.]

St. George, off Rostock, May 25th, 1801.

Sir,

I dispatched the Speedwell early this morning, with an
account of my proceedings up to last night; and in the
course of to-day the Lynx returned with Count Pahlen's
letters from Lord St. Helens, copies of which I now send you.
When his Lordship joined the Squadron, I gave him the
original Declaration made by the Russian Admiral Tchitchagoff, as it was my wish not to detain him for a moment. It
is with real concern I find he has not returned either that, or
a copy.

His Lordship has sent letters for Lord Hawkesbury; probably it may be enclosed in them; but the purport of the
Declaration is, what I stated in a letter to you, forwarded
in the Speedwell. I enclose for their Lordships' perusal a
few words that the Emperor of Russia said to Captain Skene,[9]
after stopping the carriage he was riding in at Petersburgh. I
am, &c.

NELSON AND BRONTE.

TO ALEXANDER DAVISON, ESQ., ST. JAMES'S SQUARE.

[Autograph, in the possession of Colonel Davison.]

Bay of Rostock, May 25th, 1801.

My dear Davison,
　　The morning I sailed from Yarmouth, I wrote you a letter,
and several others, which were put on board a Ship left
behind, in which I requested you to give Mrs. William Nelson[1]
£100 for me, and I do not hear, either from you or any person,
that the letter got safe to you. Respecting poor Maurice's
wife, if her necessities require it, every farthing which his
kindness gave me shall be used, if she wants it; therefore, I
beg you will be everything generous towards her, for she
shall ever be by me considered as his honoured wife. Every
moment I am looking out for a new Admiral. May God
bless you, and believe me ever your affectionate friend,

NELSON AND BRONTE.

This day comes on my trial with the great Earl. May the
just gain it. Pray send the inclosed. Harpy and Speedwell
must have arrived.

TO REAR-ADMIRAL TOTTY.

[Letter-Book.]

St. George, Rostock Bay, 26th May, 1801.

My dear Sir,
　　I am favoured with your letter of yesterday; and the
Swedish Cutter brought almost a duplicate of the Admiral's

---

[9] Captain Alexander Skene: he was posted in April 1802, and died about 1824.
[1] Wife of his brother, the Reverend William, afterwards Earl Nelson.

letter, and a Declaration from the King of Sweden, that all British Merchant-ships were to pass unmolested.

Mr. Cockburn, the Consul for Lower Saxony, is gone, I fancy, off Bornholm in search of me; but an express was sent after him, and it was hoped to arrive time enough at Stralsund to prevent his embarkation. I hope the Russian Brig's going to England, is a good omen for a peace; indeed, my opinion is, that we shall have it in the North.

I have reason to believe, that a combination has been entered into against us, to make us pay nearly double the market-price for both beef and bread; but offers are to come off this morning, and I am fixed not to give more than five pence a pound for beef, and thirty shillings a hundred weight for bread, unless by order from the Admiralty. I suspect the combination has reached Dantzic. What a set of villains, if it is so! I shall send off the Lynx the moment I can settle anything about supplies; and if the Alkmaar brings you good accounts, I shall continue sending two Ships of the Line, with some Small craft, to that place.

I approve very much of your completing the Ships with water. The Foreign flags had better be distributed, particularly to the Frigates and large Brigs. Reports are from the Ships arrived from Kioge Bay, that two Ships of the Line, English, are in Copenhagen Roads: nothing new from England or the Continent. The Lynx shall sail to-morrow. Believe me, dear Sir, your most obliged servant,

NELSON AND BRONTE.

Admiral Graves thinks he is better; but others think the contrary.

TO THE SWEDISH ADMIRAL, AT CARLSCRONA.

[Letter-Book.]

St. George, Bay of Rostock, May 26th, 1801.

Sir,

I am this moment honoured with your Excellency's letter of May 24th, enclosing a copy of his Swedish Majesty's Proclamation respecting the British Merchant-ships; for which I feel much obliged.

As his Excellency Lord St. Helens is arrived about this

time at St. Petersburgh, as Ambassador from my most gracious
Sovereign to his Imperial Majesty, I hope that a very few
days will restore the ancient amity between our Countries, so
conducive to the true interest of both; and that I shall have an
opportunity, in person, of assuring your Excellency with what
respect, I am your most obedient servant,

NELSON AND BRONTE.

TO HIS EXCELLENCY COUNT PAHLEN.

[Letter-Book. " The day after Lord Nelson's arrival off Rostock, on the 26th of
May, 1801, a Russian Lugger brought the reply from Count Pahlen, to his letter
written on leaving Revel. The effect intended by that letter had been fully felt at
Petersburgh: a more flattering communication was, perhaps, never made from a
Sovereign to the subject of another Power, than was conveyed in the Minister's reply.
It apologized for any misconception of his Lordship's views in having entered Revel
Roads, it expressed an anxious wish that Peace should be restored on the most
solid basis; and in a particular manner invited Lord Nelson to Petersburgh, in
whatever mode might be most agreeable to himself. The Lugger, on leaving our
Fleet with Lord Nelson's answer to this gracious letter, fired a salute, an act
which implies much more in the Russian service than in many others. Lord Nelson
observed to his Secretary, on his return from the shore, ' Did you hear that little
fellow salute? Well, now, there is peace with Russia, depend on it: our jaunt to
Revel was not so bad, after all."—*Colonel Stewart's Narrative.*]

St. George, Rostock Bay, 10 o'clock at Night, 26th May, 1801.

Sir,

I am this moment honoured with your Excellency's flattering letter of May 6th, O. S.,[2] and I assure you that his
Imperial Majesty's justice has filled the idea I had formed of

---

[2] " A S. E. MYLORD NELSON BRONTE.

" St. Petersbourg, le 6 Mai, 1801.

" Mylord,

" Je ne saurais donner à vôtre Excellence un témoignage plus éclatant de la
confiance que l'Empéreur mon Maître lui accorde qu'en lui annonçant l'effet qu'a
produit sa lettre du 16 de ce mois. Sa Majesté Impériale a ordonné sur le
champ la levée de l'Embargo mis sur les Navires Anglais. Cette mesure aurait été
remplie depuis longtems si des circonstances antérieures à Son règne n'eussent pas
donné lieu à une démonstration hostile de vôtre Gouvernement, dans le Nord, et
mon auguste Maître se livre avec plaisir à l'impulsion de son amour pour la justice dès
l'instant où l'Europe ne peut plus être abusée par les apparences sur les motifs qui
le font agir.

" Je regrette vivement, Mylord, que vôtre lettre précédente ait produit un
mésentendu, mais celui qui connait comme vous les loix de l'honneur et de la
vraie dignité ne peut en être surpris. Sa Majesté Impériale me charge de mander à
vôtre Excellence, qu'elle sera charmée de faire la connaissance personnelle du

his excellent heart and head; and I am sure the handsome
manner in which the embargo has been taken off the British
Shipping, will give the greatest pleasure to my good and
gracious Sovereign.

I am truly sensible of the great honour done me by the
invitation of his Imperial Majesty, and at a future time I hope
to have the pleasure of presenting my humble duty. I have
now only to pray, that a permanent (which must be honourable) Peace may be established between our gracious Sovereigns, and that our august Masters' reigns may be blessed
with every happiness which this world can afford; and I beg
that your Excellency will believe that I am, with the greatest
respect, your most obedient and very humble servant,

NELSON AND BRONTE.

MEMORANDUM.

[From "The Athenæum."]

[May, 1801.]

Mem.—I wish the Harpy to be sent to me with any
dispatches, as I intend to send her to England, the first Vessel.
I recommend sending the Dart, and a good, clever Purser, to
Dantzic, to purchase bullocks and biscuits, if to be had reasonable and good, as our Ships are getting short of that article.
The Dart can bring, at this season, twenty head of cattle;
the hay for their use must be calculated separately, and the
meat, delivered on board the Fleet off Bornholm, ought not
to exceed fourpence or fivepence. The Alkmaar will be a
good Ship to send for bullocks. The Purser must send for
greens, or they must be purchased and charged against them.
The following rates have been thought very reasonable for
the Pursers:—7s. 6d. for Three deckers, 5s. for Two deckers,
and 2s. 6d. for Frigates.

héros du Nil, et de vous voir à sa Cour, si vos instructions vous permettent de
quitter la Flotte et d'aborder avec un seul Vaisseau dans un de nos Ports. J'ai
l'honneur d'être, avec la plus haute considération, Mylord, de vôtre Excellence, le
très humble et très obéissant serviteur, LE COMTE DE PAHLEN."—*Original*, in
the possession of the Right Hon. John Wilson Croker.

TO THE RIGHT HONOURABLE HENRY ADDINGTON.

[Autograph, in the Sidmouth Papers.]

St. George, Rostock, May 27th, 1801.

My dear Sir,

I do not trouble you often with letters, as your time must be much more essentially employed than in reading any opinions of mine. As I send the facts themselves to the Admiralty, Ministers can draw much better conclusions from them than a mere Sea-officer; but as it was the wish of Lord St. Helens for me to give my opinion, from what I had seen in Russia, and my communication with them, I readily gave it—viz., The Emperor of Russia and his Ministers wish for peace with us, but at the same time it is wished to hold up his character, therefore it is wished that he should have the appearance of arranging the peace of the North, and I am confident more would be given up by paying the Emperor that compliment than if we attempted to lay down the law; and his Lordship was pleased to say that he should let the negotiation take that turn. Respecting Privateers, I own I am decidedly of opinion that with very few exceptions they are a disgrace to our Country; and it would be truly honourable never to permit one after this war. Such horrid robberies have been committed by them in all parts of the world, that it is really a disgrace to the Country which tolerates them; and the conduct of too many of our Vice-Admiralty Courts has no wonder made neutral Nations think of preventing such iniquitous proceedings; but as I shall, if alive, have the honour of seeing you in a very few days, I will only say that, I am, with the greatest respect, your most faithful and obliged,

NELSON AND BRONTE.

Lord St. Helens would be at Petersburgh about yesterday. My complaint, I flatter myself, is better within these last two days; but we have lost so many of our finest young men by the disorder, and I know it is so deceitful, and no one will tell me anything of my disorder, that I only rely on Providence; I own I have no inclination to die a natural death at present; I ought to have returned with my good and excellent friend Colonel Stewart.

TO MR. RICHARD BOOTH, PURSER OF THE LONDON.

[Letter-Book.]

St. George, Rostock Bay, 28th May, 1801.

Sir,

I have received a letter from Captain Murray, enclosing a statement of the prices of the different articles that can be procured at Dantzic, for the use of the Fleet. With respect to the beef supplied in the Bay, and which may be sent to the Fleet alive, and the bread—provided the Captains think it good in quality—I approve of the prices, and authorize you to furnish what may be required by the Ships that may arrive in the Bay, and also to send to the Squadron off Bornholm such bread and live cattle, which the Ships, as they are ordered away, can conveniently carry ; and I shall give directions for the hides and tallow to be taken care of, and returned, as you recommend. I also desire you will purchase 4000 pounds of cheese, at the price you mention, taking care that it answers to the sample you have sent.

As to the wine and spirits, I disapprove of the price altogether ; the flour I think not good in quality, and desire none may be bought, unless better can be got by adding a trifle to the price. In that case, I wish about 4000 lbs to be put on board each 74 Gun-ship, and smaller Vessels in proportion, for the purpose of being served in lieu of part of the allowance of bread : but no pease are wanted. The continuance of the Fleet in the Baltic being very uncertain, you must regulate your engagements accordingly, and not purchase more at a time than can be brought away in the Squadron of three or four Sail of the Line, and a few Small-craft, which it is my intention to keep in the Bay of Dantzic.

In order to recompense you for the trouble you may have on this occasion, I shall recommend to the Admiralty to direct, that you be allowed two and a half per cent. on the money laid out, and your expenses paid for living on shore, trusting that you will use your best endeavours to procure everything you are authorized to buy, at the cheapest rate, and of the best quality. You are hereby authorized to draw bills on the Commissioners of the Victualling [Board] for the amount of what you purchase, taking care to get receipts from the different Pursers for what you may supply, and vouchers from the proper Officers, that it was good in the kind, as well as a certificate from some of the most respectable merchants, that all your purchases were made at the cheapest rate, and bills drawn at the proper Exchange.　I am, &c.,

NELSON AND BRONTE.

TO REAR-ADMIRAL TOTTY.

[Letter-Book.]

St. George, Bay of Rostock, May 29th, 1801.

My dear Sir,

This morning, the Ganges, London, and Hyæna, sail for Dantzic; for I find that supplies of bread, flour, cheese, and beef, can be procured for very near half the price which they can be purchased for at Rostock, for a most wicked combination is entered into against us; but I shall match them by buying scarcely anything.

The Ships, Russell and Veteran, will join you in four or five days, and then I would have you send to Dantzic two other Ships, to receive provisions from Mr. Booth, who, if he will accept it, I have appointed to purchase the articles before mentioned; and I desire you will direct any Ships you send, for the Surgeons and Pursers to complete their necessaries. Mr. Booth is very pressing for the hides and tallow to be returned as expeditiously as possible, as the loss on these articles will fall upon Government. The Gun-brigs have nothing else to do, and the best sailers of them must be employed on this service.

When Captain Murray joins, if you are disposed to go to Dantzic yourself, leave the Squadron to his charge with a copy of your orders; for Rear-Admiral Graves is not in a condition to undertake business. Captain Inman, with part of his Squadron, will go from here in about three days, as complete for six weeks as I can make them; therefore, some of the other Bombs and Small-craft may go to Dantzic directly, and get supplies. I wrote to Mr. Booth yesterday by the Fox Cutter; therefore, (although I hope he has not,) if he *has* joined you, I wish him to return to

Dantzic, and fulfil my instructions to him. The Ramilies
having been represented to me as having the appearance of
scurvy on board her, I desire she may be sent to join Captain
Fremantle at Dantzic Bay. Whenever the Squadron with
you can average six weeks bread with flour at whole allowance, then I wish the Ships to be put at full allowance, serving
half a pound of flour. I send you a copy of my letter to Mr.
Booth. I am, &c.,

NELSON AND BRONTE.

MEMORANDA.

[Letter-Book. No date is given to these Memoranda, which are inserted as they
occur in the Letter-Book ; but they would seem to have been written before the end
of May 1801.]

That in all places of the King of Denmark's Dominions,
they should perfectly understand our right to have the free
use of the markets, and the liberty to obtain whatever refresh-
ments are wanted for the health of the crews.

That Vessels will be sent to Moen Island, Holstein, Jutland, &c., in order to purchase supplies, as we have a right to
do by the fourth article of the Treaty.

To obtain a general order to the Governor and Head Officers of the Government in each place, to conform to the
article, and not to throw obstructions in the way of *our* free
communication with every part of the shore.

I am answerable that no breach of the Treaty shall take
place, in the first instance, from me ; and it is my duty to
take care that it is fully complied with, on the part of Denmark. The Officers will, in future, be permitted to go on
shore, to walk, and take other recreations necessary for their
health, and as Lord Nelson holds himself responsible for their
good conduct, he expects that they are not to be annoyed by
guards, which Lord Nelson is sorry to observe has been the
case at Kioge. As Lord Nelson hopes that the ancient amity
between the two Countries is on the point of being restored,
Lord Nelson expects that the most generous conduct will be
pursued on the part of Denmark towards all the Officers and
men of the British Fleet.

TO CAPTAIN GEORGE MURRAY.

[Autograph, in the possession of George Murray, Esq.]

June 1st, 1801.

My dear Murray,

Although you like to be a Commodore, I find you have no inclination to be a *Contractor*. Now as I find no honest men but Commodores, you must necessarily, if you will be a Commodore, become a Contractor. Myself and Hardy are Contractors; Lord Henry[5] is just established a Commodore and a Contractor; only I charge you, being a brother Contractor, not to let the world know how much you make by it! Be that as it may, ever believe me, my dear Murray, your obliged and faithful friend,

NELSON AND BRONTE.

Pylades goes for England the moment any news comes from Lord St. Helens.

Graves has the Red Ribbon, I a Viscount.

TO EVAN NEPEAN, ESQ., ADMIRALTY.

[Letter-Book.]

St. George, Rostock Bay, 1st June, 1801.

Sir,

I herewith enclose a translation of two letters, and a Declaration received from the Swedish Admiral. I beg you will assure their Lordships that I should have forwarded them sooner, but could not get them translated before yesterday. Their Lordships must not be surprised at seeing my letter to the Swedish Admiral, of the 8th ultimo, and his answer thereto, inserted in the papers, as they were in the ' Hamburgh Gazette,' a few days after my receiving the answer. I am, &c.

NELSON AND BRONTE.

[5] Lord Henry Paulet, Captain of the Defence: he was second son of George, 12th Marquis of Winchester, and died a Vice-Admiral and a Knight Commander of the Bath, in January 1832.

TO REAR-ADMIRAL TOTTY.

[Letter-Book.]

Sir,   St. George, June 2nd, 1801.

I have just heard that the Governor of the Island of Bornholm has prevented vegetables and other articles from being
sold to the crews of his Majesty's Ships, in direct defiance of
the Armistice between the Commander-in-Chief of the British
Fleet and the Court of Denmark. I therefore send you an
authenticated copy of the fourth Article of the Treaty,[6] which,
if the report is true, I desire that you will send on shore to
the Governor, and demand his compliance therewith. If he
refuses, you are to consider it as a breach of the Treaty on his
part, for which he must be answerable to his Government.
And you will prevent, until he complies with the Treaty, all
Vessels from leaving the Island; for his conduct cannot be
justified by his Court, unless it means to break the Treaty.
I am, &c.,

NELSON AND BRONTE.

TO ALEXANDER JOHN BALL, ESQ., COMMISSIONER OF HIS MAJESTY'S NAVY, GIBRALTAR.

[Autograph, in the possession of Sir William Keith Ball, Bart.]

St. George, Kioge Bay, June 4th, 1801.

My dear invaluable Friend,

Although I may not answer letters regularly, or perform
many other little acts which the world deem as of the very
utmost importance, and for the omission of which, it is necessary to cut each other's throats, although I own I fail most
miserably (towards my real friends in particular) in those
things, yet believe me, Ball, my heart entertains the very
warmest affection for you, and it has been no fault of mine,
and not a little mortification, that you have not the Red ribbon
and other rewards that would have kept you afloat, and not to
have made you a Commissioner; but as, I trust, the war is at a
close, you must, like Lord Hood,[7] take your Flag when it comes

---

[6] *Armistice.* Vide p. 338, ante.

[7] Admiral Viscount Hood was Commissioner of the Navy at Portsmouth in September 1780, when promoted to be a Rear-Admiral of the Blue.

to you, for who is to command our Fleets in a future war? for whatever peace we may make under the present government of France cannot be lasting. I pity the poor Maltese; they have sustained an irreparable loss in your friendly counsel and an able director in their public concerns: you was truly their father, and, I agree with you, they may not like step-fathers; however, I hope that you will find as much pleasure in your new office as it is possible for it to afford, although I am sure it will not be equal to your merit.

As I know you have always been kind to me, I know you will be sorry to hear that I have been even at *Death's* door, apparently in a consumption. I am now rallied a little, but the disorder is in itself so flattering that I know not whether I am really better, and no one will tell me, but all in the Fleet are so truly kind to me, that I should be a wretch not to *cheer up.* Foley has put me under a regimen of milk, at four in the morning; Murray has given me lozenges, and all have proved their desire to keep my mind easy, for I hear of no complaints, or other wishes than to have me with them. Hardy is as good as ever, and with Domett, join their kindest regards. I have also on board Colonel Stewart, who commands our *little* Army; he remembers you at St. Domingo. I am just returned from the Gulf of Finland, Revel; and met Lord St. Helens at the entrance; by this, I am sure Peace must be signed with Russia, and Denmark and Sweden have so completely lost their consequence by joining against us, that they must submit to what we settle with Russia. The Northern Fleets are only formidable in point of numbers; in every other respect they are insignificant; and, if our Fleet is active, in the spring of the year, may be got at separately; late in the summer they have their numerous Flotilla, who can join in spite of all our efforts to prevent them, for there is a complete navigation inside, and amongst 10,000 Islands. I hope this will find you in England, as I know your American affairs claim your attention; it is, I trust, [needless] my dear Ball, to assure you, that if it ever should be in my power in any way to be useful, that nothing could give me greater happiness; for believe me at all times, and places, for ever your sincere, affectionate, and faithful friend,

NELSON AND BRONTE.

TO REAR-ADMIRAL TOTTY.

[Letter-Book. " After being at anchor some days off Rostock, the Fleet was getting under weigh for Kioge Bay, when the Duke of Mecklenburg Strelitz, brother of Queen Charlotte, the Consort of George III., was announced to be coming from Butzow, to wait on Lord Nelson. His Royal Highness was received with all the attention which the sudden visit could give time for, and was shown by Lord Nelson through every part of the Ship. The Fleet returned to Kioge Bay on the 5th or 6th of June, but remained there only a few days to complete their water, which could not be done at Rostock, and to arrange the stations of the various squadrons that were constantly kept on the move. Lord Nelson's principle was to keep all hands employed; and he used to say, 'No matter how, and no matter where.' In the meantime, communications of the most pacific nature were passing between us and the Courts of the Northern Confederacy. Denmark and Sweden only waited for the decision of Russia, to accede to a general Peace; and Prussia had not declared herself decidedly hostile during any part of the campaign. The Enemy's Fleets, with the exception of a single Ship for the instruction of the Danish Naval Academy, were confined to their Ports, and the intercourse of commerce, excepting coastways, was temporarily suspended: by the good arrangements, however, of Lord Nelson, nothing occurred on the face of these Northern seas, which could in the smallest degree tend to interrupt negotiation, or the returning good understanding between the Confederates and Great Britain."—*Colonel Stewart's Narrative.*]

St. George, Kioge Bay, June 5th, 1801.

My dear Sir,

Nothing from England! which to me is very astonishing. I send you the Vanguard and Asia; therefore you can either send one or two Ships to Dantzic, merely to receive forty or fifty bullocks each, for the use of the Fleet; for at this place we can get none, but at such a price as I cannot feel justifiable at suffering. As bread and flour can only be procured in small quantities, it is better not to keep many Ships in Dantzic Bay; for I expect an order, the moment the Peace is signed with Russia, to withdraw all our Ships from the Baltic. I would, therefore, have you open any letters which may come for me from Lord St. Helens; and if you find that either the peace is actually signed, or that there is a fair prospect that it will soon be signed, in either of these cases I desire that you will send to Dantzic directions for Mr. Booth to close his accounts as expeditiously as possible, and for the Ships to join you off Bornholm. If one is necessary to remain to bring off any bread or flour ordered by Mr. Booth, you will direct a Sixty-four to remain.

You will see the propriety of keeping the contents of Lord

St. Helens' letters a profound secret, be they peace or war; for the curiosity of every one to hear news, and to write it to England, is so great, that much harm arises from it. Our Dantzic supplies of bread will help us a little, but surely the Admiralty will either send us provisions, or direct some contracts to be made in this Country; for I can never believe that the present Board of Admiralty do not think of our wants; and if I was to make any great purchases, they might be displeased at my supposing that they had not provided for the wants of a Fleet under their nose. If I were in the Mediterranean, circumstanced us we are, I should, of course, act very differently. As we can get no fresh beef here, I wish you would send down the Ships which have last come from Dantzic, and let them bring us a few bullocks. The moment the wind comes westerly, something must arrive; it is, this day, thirty days without the scratch of a pen. You shall have your letters and the news, in half an hour afterwards.

Sir Thomas Graves is still very ill; so much so, that he begged I *would not* go and see him, as the pleasure he had in seeing me did him harm, when he was left. I fear he is in a bad way. In the St. George we have got the influenza. Whenever the London joins you, send her to me. Ever, my dear Sir, your obedient servant,

NELSON AND BRONTE.

TO HIS EXCELLENCY CHEVALIER DE LIZAKOWITZ, ENVOY FROM RUSSIA TO COPENHAGEN.

[Letter-Book.]

St. George, Kioge Bay, June 7th, 1801.

Sir,

From the very flattering manner in which I was received by Admiral Spendow, General Sacken, the Governors, Civil and Military, at Revel, and from the very handsome letter of Count Pahlen of May 6th, (O.S.,) conveying the Emperor's orders for liberating all the English Ships in his Ports, I look forward, as to a certainty, of the ancient amity between our two Sovereigns being renewed and cemented, I trust stronger than ever. I therefore beg leave not only to introduce myself to your Excellency, but also to present my friend, the Honourable Colonel Stewart, who will do me the favour of delivering this letter. In a very few days I expect letters from Lord St. Helens; whenever they arrive, I shall be happy in communicating their contents to you, and at all times it will be a pleasure to assure your Excellency with what respect I am, your most obedient servant,

NELSON AND BRONTE.

TO HERCULES ROSS, ESQ., ROSSIE CASTLE, N. B.

[Autograph, in the possession of Horatio Ross, Esq., Lord Nelson's godson, alluded to in this letter.]

St. George, Kioge Bay, June 9th, 1801.

My dear Friend,

Your kind letter of May 22nd, I received last night, and I sincerely hope that your nephew's affairs with my valuable friend Davison, will end in an amicable manner. I can assure you that Davison is a man of as strict honour as any in Europe.

You do me a great deal of honour in wishing me to stand godfather for your next child; I accept the duty with much pleasure, and hope that the future Horatio, or a, will be an addition of happiness to you and Mrs. Ross; and if ever I travel into Scotland, I pledge myself not to pass Rossie Castle; but Peace—the blessings of Peace, must first shed its benign rays over us, and under the present Ruler of France I see but little prospect of that happy event. Buonaparte's power exists by war, and as France must in time be tired of it, I think his life will be cut short. I hope that we are on the eve of peace with Russia, and both Sweden and Denmark have so given up their independence to her, that if Russia makes peace, the others must. I hope very soon to be in England, for the keen air of the North has not agreed with a constitution so long used to Southern climates. I beg you will present my best compliments to Mrs. Ross; I shall never forget the open heart of her good mother; and do you believe me, ever your most faithful and affectionate friend,

NELSON AND BRONTE.

TO ADJUTANT-GENERAL LINDHOLM.

[Letter-Book.]

St. George, Kioge Bay, 11th June, 1801.

My dear Sir,

As you say that you intend me the favour of coming on board the St. George, I will not put my feelings on paper on the subject of your letter. I trust that, if any serious insult has been offered ·by any persons to British Officers, they will be brought to punishment. I expect the Eling Schooner here this day. I shall always feel pleasure in complying with the wishes of His Royal Highness, as far as is consistent with my duty as a 'British Admiral, who is bound to suffer no insult to be offered to the Flag of his Royal Master, or one of his Subjects to be ill-treated with impunity.

With every sentiment of respect and esteem, believe me, dear Sir, your obedient Servant,

NELSON AND BRONTE.

TO REAR-ADMIRAL TOTTY.

[Letter-Book.]

St. George, in Kioge Bay, June 11th, 1801.

My dear Sir,

As I think that we must all be on the move homewards, I desire that you will direct all the Bombs, and such of the Gun-brigs as you do not want to carry the hides and tallow, to Dantzic, to proceed and join me in this Bay; and I wish you to write, by the first Vessel that goes to Dantzic, to Mr. Booth, and say that he must attend to my instructions to him, sent by the Fox Cutter in May from Rostock; and that, so far from laying in a large stock of bullocks, that I desire he will only keep just enough to supply our Ships for a very few days, and be prepared to settle his accounts, and come from Dantzic at a very short notice. A week from this date, all must be settled one way or the other.

Reports say that Victuallers are lying at Yarmouth, ready to sail; probably they are waiting the issue of Lord St. Helens' negotiation. In Denmark, we shall no longer find

an Enemy; they have too much to lose by the renewal of
hostilities. At this moment, generally speaking, they hate
us; but they are determined not to give up their Colonies,
Ships, &c. In the Nation we shall not be forgiven our having
the upper hand of them: I only thank God we have, or they
would try and humble us to the dust. The Edgar, Elephant,
&c. you will send here; then Murray shall be put in order.
I hope none of your Ships have suffered in the late gale of
wind. As you will not, I believe, want the Dart, return her
to me as soon as possible. The moment any Vessel comes
from England, your letters, &c. shall be sent off. I feel
much flattered at your kind wishes for my remaining with
the Fleet; but, although my health is perfectly re-established,
yet, as the Admiralty cannot know it, I trust they have had
consideration to my situation, and directed another Admiral
to supersede me. Sir Thomas Graves is represented to be
getting better; but, as yet, is unable to get out of his cabin.

I have two Lieutenants of Gun-brigs in confinement for
trial; and if you have any that behave ill, I will bring them
to an account for their conduct, before a Court-martial. I
send you the two last newspapers; and am, with every sentiment of esteem, dear Sir, your most obliged and obedient
servant,   NELSON AND BRONTE.

TO CAPTAIN SIR EDWARD BERRY, H. M. S. RUBY, OFF BORNEO.

[From a Copy in the Nelson Papers.]

St. George, Kioge Bay, June 11th, 1801.

My dear Sir Edward,

I would not go to St. Petersburgh[8] if they would hire me. I
have not been out of the Ship, nor do I intend it, till I happily
arrive in England. They hate us in Denmark for, as they
say, our hard terms which Duckworth and General Trigge[9]
have imposed on their Islands. Your ever affectionate,

NELSON AND BRONTE.

[8] Sir Edward Berry wrote on this Letter:—" I suggested the idea of the appearance of some of our Ships at St. Petersburgh, as well as the presence of his Lordship, from an idea that it would have great weight in that Cabinet at this crisis.—
E. B."

[9] In March 1801, an Expedition under Rear-Admiral Duckworth and Lieutenant
General Trigge, captured St. Thomas and other Danish Islands in the West
Indies.

TO ALEXANDER DAVISON, ESQ.

[Autograph, in the possession of Colonel Davison.]

St. George, Kioge Bay, June 11th, 1801.

My dear Davison,

Why have I been kept here, when, for anything which could be known, I ought long since to have been dead? unless, indeed, the Admiralty thought I had as many lives as a cat; or was it a matter of indifference to them whether I lived or died? But that great and good Being, who has so often taken care of me, has still protected me, and I am recovered, contrary, I am sure, to the expectation of myself, and every one in this Fleet : and, within these last four days, am got stronger and better than I almost ever felt myself—no thanks to one of them. All my friends in the Fleet have been more than kind to me. If I had not been so ill, I should, perhaps, not have believed how much I [am] respected, I may almost say beloved, in the Fleet. Even Admiral Totty, an entire stranger to me, writes me—'Your Lordship talks of going to England. I hope in God you will not stir from the Baltic until everything is settled, and you take us all with you.' I know, my dear Friend, that it will give you pleasure that I can do my duty as well as any of the very strict gentlemen, and still have the affection of the whole body. But enough of myself.

I am sure you have done everything which is proper and kind for poor Mrs. Nelson: be liberal, and let her want for no comfort. I never wanted to make money of any one. The dead cannot do any more kindness than to repose a confidence in the living. Never shall poor Maurice, can he know what is going on, be sorry for his goodness to me. It is now thirty-seven days since I have had a scrap of a pen from England, and all our eyes are strained, looking anxiously for some Vessel with orders, in the event of either a renewal of War, or a Peace. The moment the wind comes from the eastward, I shall hear from Petersburgh, and I cannot doubt but that the Peace will be signed; and if not, the Russian Fleet will not come into the Baltic this year. The Danes are very much irritated at the hard terms imposed upon their West India Islands, and so every one

must think them. When we look at the terms granted by
the French to our Islands last War, we ought to blush. I
trust Government will not allow such an example against us,
some day, and that the income of all Military absentees
should be confiscated if they serve their King! Oh, God, I
blush. But I shall leave this to Mr. Addington's good heart.
I have had a letter from Mr. Ross, respecting the case of his
nephew. You will recollect I put his case into your hands at
Yarmouth. I have wrote him, that he would find you, *such
as you are,* in truth, almost without an equal, and that I was
sure you would do whatever was honourable and right.
Colonel Stewart has been very unwell: the keen cold cuts us
to pieces. I have never been on shore, except on the business
of the Armistice at Copenhagen, and to return the visit of the
Admiral and Governor at Revel. The Queen's Brother[7]
accepted of my apology. I presented him with one of your
last Medals, which are beautiful, and the University of Rostock with another. He sent off a petition that I would write
my name, and I sent him your Medal, which produced the
flattering letter I send herewith.[9] What obligations I am
under to you! but ever believe me your grateful friend,

NELSON AND BRONTE.

Pray send the enclosed. Captain Parker desires his
respects.

TO CAPTAIN SAMUEL SUTTON,[1] H. M. SHIP AMAZON.

[Letter-Book.]

St. George, Kioge Bay, June 11th, 1801.

Sir,

Having received information that a Ship is bound from
Copenhagen to Norway, loaded with cannon, and also that

---

[7] The Duke of Mecklenburg Strelitz, who came on board the St. George, at
Rostock. *Vide* p. 402, *ante.*

[9] A Letter, now in the possession of Colonel Davison, from "Oloff Gerhard
Tyckson, Senior and Professor of Oriental of the University, Counsellor of the
Court," dated Rostock, 5th June, 1801, written in a strain of hyperbolical compli-
ment.

[1] This gallant Officer, who, as will appear from Lord Nelson's letters, became
his intimate friend, was present as a Midshipman in five general Actions; was a
Lieutenant of the Culloden in Lord Howe's Action in 1794; commanded the Alcmene

some other Vessels are about sailing from Copenhagen, loaded
with Naval stores, contrary to the terms and spirit of not only
the Armistice, but also to the kindness of Sir Hyde Parker
and the British Government, who allowed provisions to pass
from Denmark into Norway, I therefore desire that you will
proceed through the Belt, and cruize between the Koll and
the Island of Zealand, and endeavour to intercept the Ships
and Vessels above described, as also all other Vessels which
may be bound from Copenhagen, or other parts of the Danish
Dominions, to Norway, Iceland, Ferro, or Greenland, loaded
with warlike stores, or Naval stores; and you will send such
Ships as you may seize of the above description to England.
And, as there is a Squadron of Danish Ships of War in
Norway, who may wish to get to Copenhagen, it is my
directions that you do your utmost in endeavouring to prevent
their coming to Copenhagen: but you are to acquaint the
Commander of your orders; and if he consents to remain
with you till you receive directions from me, or any other
your superior Officer, for your conduct, in that case you are
to allow him or them to keep their Colours flying. But, if
they refuse your reasonable request, it is my directions that
you use your utmost endeavours to take possession of him or
them, and acquaint me, or the Secretary of the Admiralty, as
the case may require, of your proceedings. I am, Sir, &c.

NELSON AND BRONTE.

TO ADJUTANT-GENERAL LINDHOLM.

[Letter-Book.]

St. George, June 12th, 1801.

My dear Sir,

I am very sorry to hear you complain of indisposition, but
I sincerely hope that a day's rest will perfectly recover you.
As you promise me the favour of coming on board the St.
George very soon, I will not enter into the subject of what

---

at Copenhagen, and, after the Battle, succeeded Captain Riou in the Amazon. In
1803, he was for a short time Flag-Captain to Lord Nelson in the Victory: in
1805 he commanded the Amphion, in an Action with four Spanish Frigates: he
was promoted to the rank of Rear-Admiral of the Blue in July 1821; and died a
Rear-Admiral of the Red, in June 1832.

has happened at Copenhagen till that time; I have very much to say on many things which are passing in that City.

Respecting my permitting a Danish Frigate to pass from Norway to Copenhagen, I beg leave to inform his Royal Highness, that I have no power whatever to grant such permission. On the contrary, the Government of Denmark having refused to allow of Norway being included in the Armistice, I believe that there would be no impropriety in any English Man-of-War attacking them in the Ports of Norway, much less, if they put to sea, as Denmark has refused the temporary neutrality for that Kingdom; but I have no doubt the British Government will do everything of that nature, which his Royal Highness may think proper to *ask*.

Being on the subject of Norway, I think it my duty to ask that it may be given in the name, and by the authority, of the Prince, an assurance that during the time which Sir Hyde Parker, and since the British Government, have given permission for provisions to be sent to Norway, that no warlike stores have been, or will be, sent into Norway, and that no Gun-Vessels have, or will be, sent from Norway to Copenhagen, during the time the kindness of the British Government is continued to be received by the Danish Government.

Sincerely hoping that each Country may see its true interests in uniting closer than ever together, I have the pleasure to subscribe myself, your most obliged and faithful servant,

NELSON AND BRONTE.

Should his Royal Highness wish to send a Brig of War to England with dispatches, the Commander had better receive a letter from me, in order to prevent the possibility of any misunderstanding with the British Cruizers in the North Sea.

TO ADJUTANT-GENERAL LINDHOLM.

[Letter-Book.]

St. George, Kioge Bay, 12th June, 1801.

My dear Sir,
I cannot sufficiently thank you for your kind remembrances of me, by Colonel Stewart, and I sincerely hope that some

day very near, we shall meet in real Peace, for at present all does not seem cordial as it ought; and yet I should have thought that the unprecedented kindness of our Minister would have made the whole Nation grateful. It never happened in the annals of the world, that, after shot had been fired, the property seized had not been immediately confiscated; but the King has shown a magnanimity and kindness towards Danish subjects, which cannot fail to make a sensible impression on the mind of his illustrious Nephew; and I trust in God, that the return of affection from his Royal Highness will, with the blessing of God, be the means of restoring and cementing closer the bonds of union between our two dear Countries. I beg you will believe me, my dear General, your obliged and affectionate servant,

NELSON AND BRONTE.

I beg to be remembered to your Son.

TO EVAN NEPEAN, ESQ., ADMIRALTY.

[Letter-Book.]

St. George, Kioge Bay, 12th June, 1801.

Sir,

Herewith, I enclose you remarks made on the passage of the Belt, also drawings of the same, which I beg you will be pleased to lodge in the records of the Admiralty, that they may be referred to, in case they are wanted. I am, &c.,

NELSON AND BRONTE.

TO EVAN NEPEAN, ESQ., ADMIRALTY.

[Letter-Book.]

St. George, Kioge Bay, 12th June, 1801.

Sir,

I am to acquaint you, for the information of the Lords Commissioners of the Admiralty, that the general conduct of Denmark has been so entirely different from what the Armistice points out, that I do not think myself at liberty to proceed as I should think right, until I get their Lordships' instructions, which I trust will be soon. The Armistice, except their Ships being absolutely hauled out, has been totally disregarded. Ships have been masted, guns taken on board, Floating batteries prepared; in short, everything is doing, as my reporters say, in defiance of the Treaty, except hauling out, and completing their rigging.

The moment I receive information, that peace is made with Russia, I shall go over the Grounds, and anchor in Copenhagen Roads, ready to act as circumstances may require, and their Lordships may direct, leaving eight Sail of the Line to watch the Swedes. I think it proper to send the Pylades immediately on receiving the above intelligence; otherwise I should not have sent her until a Vessel had arrived from Petersburgh, which I have now reason to expect every day, as Lord St. Helens has three small Vessels with him, besides the Latona. I am, &c.,

Nelson and Bronte.

TO ADMIRAL THE EARL OF ST. VINCENT, K.B.

[From Clarke and M'Arthur, vol. ii. p. 287.]

12th June, 1801.

I feel truly thankful, my dear Lord, for your complying with my request; and your very kind way of relieving me, and seeing the Fleet resigned into such good hands, really has set me up. I shall give my friend Charles Pole[2] every information in my power.

June 14th. Kioge Bay. I hope the reply of the Admiralty to my letter of this day, will be clear and explicit, whether the Commander-in-Chief is at liberty to hold the language becoming a British Admiral? which very probably, if I am here, will break the Armistice, and set Copenhagen in a blaze. I see everything which is dirty and mean going on, and the Prince Royal at the head of it; but your astonishment will cease, when I assure [you] that a French Republican Officer, in his uniform, feathers, &c., is always

----

[3] Afterwards Admiral Sir Charles Morice Pole, Bart. and G.C.B.; he was one of Nelson's early friends, (*vide* vol. i. pp. 37, 38, *et passim*,) and died, Admiral of the Fleet, in September 1830.

with his Royal Highness. The measure is so indelicate towards England, that you will not be surprised, if everything which is sacred amongst Nations of Honour should be broken. The Armistice, except their Ships being absolutely hauled out, has been totally disregarded. Ships have been masted, guns taken on board, Floating batteries prepared ; and except hauling out and completing their rigging, everything has been done in defiance of the Treaty. I do not, under our present circumstances, feel myself at liberty to pass over the Grounds with a part of the Fleet; but the moment I receive an assurance that the business of Russia is settled, I shall pass into Copenhagen Roads with all the Fleet, except eight Sail of the Line to watch the Swedes until they are settled. My heart burns, my dear Lord, at seeing the word of a Prince, nearly allied to our good King, so falsified ; but his conduct is such, that he will lose his Kingdom if he goes on, for Jacobins rule in Denmark. I have made no representations yet, as it would be useless to do so until I have the power of correction. All I beg in the name of the future Commander-in-Chief is, that the orders may be clear; for enough is done to break twenty Treaties, if it should be wished, or to make the Prince Royal, and his Republican companion, humble themselves before British generosity. I am, &c.,

NELSON AND BRONTE.

TO EVAN NEPEAN, ESQ., ADMIRALTY.

[Letter-Book. " The St. George made her last cruise, with Lord Nelson's Flag on board, off Bornholm, between the 9th and 13th of June, on which latter day he received the sanction of the Admiralty for his return to England, and the instructions of his Majesty George III. to invest Rear-Admiral Graves with the Order of the Bath. This ceremony was performed, with all the possible dignity, on the 14th of June, on the quarter-deck of the St. George, Lord Nelson laying the sword on the Rear-Admiral's shoulder in the name of the King; he accompanied this by a very dignified and animated speech : never was Knight more honourably invested. Sir Charles Morice Pole arrived a few days afterwards in the Æolus frigate, and received the chief command. Lord Nelson's resignation was attended with infinite regret to the whole Fleet, and there was a complete depression of spirits upon the occasion."—*Colonel Stewart's Narrative.*]

Sir,   St. George, Kioge Bay, 13th June, 1801.

I am to acknowledge the receipt of your letter of the 31st May, signifying to me their Lordships' permission for my return to England, for the re-establishment of my health, agreeably to my request, the 17th of last month. I beg you will assure their Lordships, that I feel much flattered by the very handsome manner, in which they have expressed their acquiescence.[3] I have the honour to be, &c.,

NELSON AND BRONTE.

TO CAPTAIN SIR EDWARD BERRY, H. M. SHIP RUBY.

[Autograph, in the possession of Lady Berry.]

St. George, Kioge Bay, June 15th, 1801.

My dear Sir Edward,

There is a report, and very generally believed, that the embargo on Russian and Danish Ships is taken off: if so, our Ministry must be convinced that all is peace in the North. I have desired twenty Marines to be sent to you, as you are short of complement, and whatever I can do to make your Ruby comfortable, you are sure I shall be happy in doing, for believe me ever, my dear Sir Edward, your obliged and affectionate friend,

NELSON AND BRONTE.

Yesterday I Knighted Sir Thomas Graves, and Invested him with the Ensigns of the Order of the Bath, in the most public and best manner our circumstances would admit of.[4]

---

[3] " TO VICE-ADMIRAL LORD NELSON, K.B.

" My Lord, " Admiralty Office, 31st May, 1801.

" I have received and communicated to my Lords Commissioners of the Admiralty your Lordship's letter of the 17th instant . . . . and I have it in command from their Lordships to acquaint you, in answer thereto, that an arrangement will be made, with as little delay as possible, for relieving your Lordship in your command.

" I have their Lordships' further commands to acquaint your Lordship, that your services in the Baltic have met their entire approbation, and to assure you that they feel the greatest concern that the state of your health should render it necessary you should quit the command, by which your Country must be deprived (though it is hoped only for a short time) of the advantage of your Lordship's talents and experience, which have been so conspicuous on all occasions. I have the honour to be, &c.—EVAN NEPEAN."—Original.

[4] The following description of the Investiture of Rear-Admiral Sir Thomas Graves is taken from the Naval Chronicle, vol. v. p. 532:

" His Majesty's Ship St. George, Kioge Bay, June 14th.

" A Chair was placed on the gratings of the sky-light, on the quarter-deck, with

TO JOHN JULIUS ANGERSTEIN, ESQ., LLOYD'S COFFEE-HOUSE.

[Letter-Book.]

St. George, Kioge Bay, 15th June, 1801.

Sir,

I am honoured with the receipt of your letter, and I beg to assure you that your desire shall be strictly complied with. Di-

the Royal Standard suspended over it, showing the King's Arms; the Chair was covered with the Union Flag; a Guard was ranged on each side the quarter-deck, consisting of the Marines, and a detachment of the Rifle Corps; and the Captains of the Fleet attended in their full-dress uniforms.

" The Royal Standard was hoisted the moment of the Procession beginning, which took place in the following order:—

" Lord Nelson came up the ladder in the fore part of the quarter deck, and made three reverences to the Throne. He then placed himself on the right hand side of it. Captain Parker, bearing the Sword of State (being that which was presented to Lord Nelson by the Captains of His Majesty's Fleet, who fought under his Command at the Battle of the Nile), followed Lord Nelson and placed himself on his right side, a little in advance, making three reverences to the Throne, and one to Lord Nelson. His Lordship's Secretary, Mr. Wallis, then followed, bearing in his hand, on a satin cushion, the Ensigns of the Order, making similar reverences to the Throne, and to Lord Nelson. Captain Parker then read the Duke of Portland's order to Lord Nelson; which ended, Rear-Admiral Graves was introduced between Captains Hardy and Retalick, making three reverences to the Throne and one to Lord Nelson. The Rear-Admiral then kneeled down, and Lord Nelson, in the name of His Majesty, laid the Sword on the shoulders of the Rear-Admiral; the Knight Elect then rose, and, bending his body a little forward, Lord Nelson, with the assistance of Captains Hardy and Retalick, put the Riband over the new Knight's right shoulder, and placed the Star on his left breast. Lord Nelson then said:

" Sir Thomas Graves, having fulfilled the commands of His Majesty, in Investing you with the Ensigns of the Most Honourable and Military Order of the Bath, I cannot but express how much I feel gratified that it should have fallen to my lot to be directed to confer this justly merited honour, and special mark of Royal favour upon you; for I cannot but reflect, that I was an eye witness of your high merit and distinguished gallantry on the memorable 2nd of April, and for which you are now so honourably rewarded. I hope that these Honours conferred upon you will prove to the Officers in the Service, that a strict perseverance in the pursuit of glorious Actions, and the imitation of your brave and laudable conduct, will ever ensure them the favours and reward of our most gracious Sovereign, and the thanks and gratitude of our Country."

" The Procession then retired in the same manner it came, except the new Knight, who went first, making one reverence to Lord Nelson, and three to the Throne. The moment the Riband was put over Sir Thomas Graves' shoulder, the signal being made preparative, the whole Fleet fired a Salute of twenty-one guns. When the ceremony was finished, the Standard was hauled down. The Troops and Marines, on hoisting the Standard, presented their arms, and the drums beat a march; the Troops kept their arms presented during the Ceremony, and on the Standard being hauled down, a march was likewise beat."

rections have been given to the different Captains under my command to make a true report of the names of every person killed and wounded (with remarks on their wounds) on board their respective Ships in action, off Copenhagen. I feel— and I am certain every Officer and man in the Fleet does the same—much indebted to the Gentlemen of the Committee for the attention they pay, and trouble they experience, on this occasion. I hope in a few days to have it in my power to pay my respects personally to them. Believe me, &c.,

NELSON AND BRONTE.

TO ALEXANDER DAVISON, ESQ., ST. JAMES'S SQUARE.

[Autograph, in the possession of Colonel Davison.]

St. George, June 15th, 1801.

My dear Davison,

Captain Middleton of the Flora Frigate brought home a small box for me from Mr. Tyson. Pray get it, and keep it till my arrival, which, I trust, will be as soon as this letter. The Subscription Book has been sent, and I hope is arrived before this time. Ever yours faithfully,

NELSON AND BRONTE.

The wind is fair for Admiral Pole: he must be here to-day.

Secret.—They are not Sir Hyde Parker's real friends who wish for an inquiry. His friends in the Fleet wish everything of this Fleet to be forgot, for we all respect and love Sir Hyde; but the dearer his friends, the more uneasy they have been at his *idleness*, for that is the truth—no criminality. I believe Sir H. P. to be as good a subject as his Majesty has.

TO ADJUTANT-GENERAL LINDHOLM.

[Letter-Book.]

St. George, in Kioge Bay, June 16th, 1801.

My dear Sir,

I have been favoured with your letter, and shall always feel the most perfect esteem for you, as I am sure you must be the friend of the two Countries—England and Denmark—

formed to love and to assist each other. The best friends may quarrel; but I trust we never can be real enemies. You forgot to answer my serious question about Norway; for I trust both our Nations have been upon honour, respecting the Armistice; and reports so injurious to Denmark have been brought me—but which I never could give credit to, or I should, of course, have asked some questions—such as, that instead of your Fleet remaining precisely in the same state they were at the signing of the Armistice, they have been caulked and fitted for service; that even Ships have been preparing as Floating-batteries; that masts have been put in some of your Ships, and many such stories,—not one of which I believe, for his Royal Highness has too just a sense of honour to break his word, and a sacred Armistice, and I am sure neither yourself or General Waltersdorff[5] would have suffered it. The report arose from some Republican rascal, I am sure, that wished to see all Monarchies overturned. May our Monarchs send all Republicans to the Devil, is my sincere prayer. I beg, with all humility, my humble duty to his

[5] It appears, from the following letter from Count Waltersdorff, that Lord Nelson had written to him on the 12th of June:—

"My Lord,　　　　　　　　　　"Copenhagen, June 15th, 1801.

"I received yesterday, in the country, your Lordship's favour of the 12th instant, and I cannot sufficiently express how much I am sensible of the honour your Lordship has done me. It will give me the most heartfelt pleasure to see your Lordship soon again in perfect peace, and I hope that moment cannot be far distant, as we have now received the agreeable intelligence of his Britannic Majesty having, on the 4th instant, ordered the embargo on all Russian and Danish Ships to be taken off. This step must, of course, be considered as the forerunner of peace, It creates here the most agreeable sensation, and will soon re-establish a perfect cordiality between our two Nations and Governments. Whoever may be the respective Ministers who shall sign the Peace, I shall always consider your Lordship as the Pacificator of the North, and I am sure that your heart will be as much flattered by that title, as by any other which your grateful Country has bestowed on you. I shall esteem myself extremely happy, if aught in my conduct, during the conferences which I had the honour of having with your Lordship on board the London, can entitle me to a place in your Lordship's esteem and remembrance. My son, who is highly flattered by the honour of being remembered by your Lordship, begs you to accept the assurance of his respectful attachment. If your Lordship will favour me with a copy of the history of your life, I will put it immediately into his hands, and I am sure it will leave many useful and lasting lessons in his memory and his heart. Permit me, my Lord, to assure you of the high regard and sincere respect with which I have the honour to be, my Lord, your Lordship's most obedient and most humble servant,—ERNEST FREDERICK WALTERSDORFF."—*Autograph*, in the possession of the Right Hon. John Wilson Croker.

Royal Highness; assure him how strongly I have ever ex-pressed myself of his attachment to England, and of his declaration, 'that no power on earth should ever make him the enemy of England.' I rejoice with you on the near approach of peace between our Countries; and it must be all our duties to turn all French Republicans out of our Monarchical Go-vernments. Ever, my dear Sir, your most obliged,

NELSON AND BRONTE.

I hope yet to see you, according to your kind promise, as my successor is not arrived.

TO REAR-ADMIRAL TOTTY.

[Letter-Book.]

St. George, Kioge Bay, 15th [query 18th] June, 1801.

My dear Admiral,

I requested Captain Domett to write you a few lines on the arrival of the Phœnix Cutter, directing what occurred to me as proper to be done at the moment, which was briefly to have the Fleet as much collected, as the nature of the service would admit, for the disposal of Admiral Pole; and that, as a Fleet of Victuallers are on the point of arriving, all sup-plies of provisions, except bullocks, which were to go on as before; but that it was not necessary to leave a supply of 1000 head of cattle, as supposed by Mr. Booth. From this moment it would not be necessary to have any bought up from Government-account, as the expense of keeping them, and occasional accidents, would very soon make the beef *very* dear, instead of very cheap. We have got our meat here at seven-pence a *lb.*, at no risk, and brought alongside. Therefore, I beg you will give Mr. Booth directions to close all his ac-counts; and, Mr. Foley and Gibson—I believe are their names—will supply us cheerfully at the market prices, with all we want, from Dantzic. I had wrote to Murray by the Fox, to purchase ten spars fit for topmasts, which I hope has been done by the senior Captain who next went there, and if any spars for topsail-yards are wanted, they may also be pur-chased, with a little oak-plank; but no expense is to be incurred

in making topmasts, &c., ashore. Each Ship is to make her
own; and I strongly recommend Lord St. Vincent's plan of
having them not tapered away towards the hounds. Eight
or nine Sail of the Line you are to keep with you, which will
afford one or two always going to Dantzic to refresh, and to
bring bullocks for the Ships off Bornholm. The Shannon
can go to Dantzic, and Captain Pater[1] can, if he pleases, get
everything he wants. The Fleet to be put to whole allowance of bread species—that is, half a pound of bread, half a
pound of flour—this mode to continue till all the flour purchased in the Baltic, has been expended.

Respecting Bornholm, it appears like the conduct of all
the rest of Denmark,—a conduct of enmity towards us; which,
if *real*, is extraordinary. But we shall very soon bring them to
their senses, if we are forced to begin again. I hope the news
from Russia is with you, and that it will tell you all is
peace. In that case, great part of the Fleet will go over
the Grounds, and be preparing for the Danes, if they are
saucy; or be ready to proceed for England; which, I think,
most probable.

Allow me now, my dear Sir, both as a public and a private
man, to express to you how much I feel indebted to you as
an Admiral, for your truly Officer-like manner of conducting
the King's service, and also, for the truly kind and handsome
manner you have ever expressed yourself towards myself. I
regret that circumstances have so turned out (from Sir Thomas
Graves' ill-health, and my own miserable constitution) that I
have not had more of the pleasure of your company, and opportunities of cultivating your more intimate acquaintance;
for believe, my dear Sir, that with the very highest respect
for your character, I feel myself your most obliged and affectionate servant,   NELSON AND BRONTE.

I send a Memorandum, which I request you will have the
goodness to issue in General Orders.

---

[1] Captain Charles Dudley Pater, of the Shannon: he died a Rear-Admiral of the
White, in February 1818.

MEMORANDUM.

[Letter-Book. Lord Nelson quitted the command in the Baltic on the 19th of June, and sailed in the Kite Brig, commanded by Captain Digby, for England, being unwilling to take a larger Vessel from the Fleet.]

St. George, Kioge Bay, 18th June, 1801.

Lord Nelson has been obliged, from the late very bad state of his health, to apply to the Lords Commissioners of the Admiralty for leave to return to England, which their Lordships have been pleased to comply with. But Lord Nelson cannot allow himself to leave the Fleet, without expressing to the Admirals, Captains, Officers, and Men, how sensibly he has felt, and does feel, all their kindness to him, and also how nobly and honourably they have supported him in the hour of Battle, and the readiness which they have shown to maintain the honour of their King and Country on many occasions which have offered; and had more opportunities presented themselves, Lord Nelson is firmly persuaded, they would have added more glory to their Country.

Lord Nelson cannot but observe, with the highest satisfaction which can fill the breast of a British Admiral, that (with the exception of the glaring misconduct of the Officers of the Tigress and the Cracker Gun-brigs, and the charges alleged against the Lieutenant of the Terror Bomb,) out of 18,000, of which the Fleet is composed, not a complaint has been made of any Officer or Man in it; and he cannot but remark, that the extraordinary health of this Fleet, under the blessing of Almighty God, is to be attributed to the great regularity, exact discipline, and cheerful obedience of every individual in the Fleet.

The Vice-Admiral assures them, that he will not fail to represent to the Lords Commissioners of the Admiralty their highly praiseworthy conduct; and if it pleases God that the Vice-Admiral recover his health, he will feel proud, on some future day, to go with them in pursuit of further glory, and to assist in making the name of our King and Country beloved and respected by all the world.

TO ADMIRAL THE EARL OF ST. VINCENT, K.B.

[Autograph, in the possession of Vice-Admiral Sir William Parker, Bart., G.C.B.
Lord Nelson arrived at Yarmouth on the 1st of July, immediately visited the
Hospitals to which the wounded at Copenhagen had been conveyed, and then pro-
ceeded to London.]

July 1st, 1801.

My dear Lord,

Although most probably you have many letters from Lord
St. Helens, later than mine, yet I send Parker with mine of
the 5th June ; and also with some others, which, although
most flattering to my vanity, will not, I trust, be unacceptable
to your Lordship. In the course of the morning I shall do
myself the pleasure of being at the Admiralty, and of
assuring you in person how much I am your affectionate,

NELSON AND BRONTE.

TO R. NELSON, ESQ., PLYMOUTH DOCK, DEVON.

[Autograph, in the possession of Mrs. Taylor, of Albemarle Street.]

London, July 7th, 1801.

Dear Sir,

I received your kind letter from Plymouth, and congratulate
you on the birth of a grandson, who I am much flattered with
your intention to call after me. I trust that the name of
NELSON will remain with credit to our Country for many ages,
and although I do not yet despair but that I may have fruit
from *my* own loins, yet the honour of the Nelson family will
not, I am confident, be lost by yours. I beg my compliments
to Colonel Nelson, and that you will believe me, your most
obliged servant,　　　　　　NELSON AND BRONTE.

I beg my compliments to Mr. Marshall.

TO THE RIGHT HONOURABLE HENRY ADDINGTON.

[Autograph, in the Sidmouth Papers.]

July 8th, 1801.

My dear Sir,

Prince Castelcicala[6] has been so pressing that I should bear
my testimony to you of the fidelity of the King of the Two

---

[6] Envoy from the King of Naples.

Sicilies, and his fear that the loss of the Island of Sicily may be the consequence of the want of assistance from this Country, that it has struck me forcibly that the former plan of the French is still likely to be carried into effect, either by treaty or by force. I dare say that plan is much better known to you than to me, although having for a length of time seen the correspondence both public and private, from all the Neapolitan Ministers to their Government and to the Queen of Naples, I am perfectly acquainted with the views of the several Powers. The plan of the French Directory was, not to have an Army of French in Italy on a peace, but to make all the Powers of Italy dependent upon them; in order to do this, Corsica was to be taken from *us*, Elba, Sardinia, Sicily, if possible, Malta, Corfu, and these could be easily kept, and would awe their enemies in Italy (if any turned against them), and support their friends, and cut our trade both with Italy and Turkey to pieces; indeed, we could have none. From Castelcicala's conversation, I think, that either by a forced treaty with the King of Naples, or by force of arms, these people will attempt, and even are attempting, the getting Sicily, which will be a very severe stroke upon us. Forgive me, being thus impertinent, but I could not have an opportunity of conversing with you, which I wished, on various subjects. I send a letter from Sir John Acton to Sir William Hamilton. Ever, my dear Sir, your obliged,

NELSON AND BRONTE.

TO REAR-ADMIRAL HOLLOWAY.

[Autograph, in the possession of Admiral Sir Robert Otway, Bart., G.C.B.]

My dear Holloway,[7]   July 8th, 1801.

Otway is as good as an angel. London will not come home, I suppose, till the rest of the Baltic Fleet—unless a part of them are ordered home. She will, most probably, be docked. Lyons is on board the St. George; a very good young man.

---

[7] This letter was written in reply to one from Admiral Holloway, asking Lord Nelson his opinion of Captain Otway, of the London, who had then proposed for the hand of Miss Holloway, now Lady Otway, the Admiral's daughter, whom he married on the 15th of the following month.

He will, of course, remain there till you otherwise dispose of
him. Many thanks for all your kind congratulations. Ever
yours faithfully,

NELSON AND BRONTE.

TO ADMIRAL THE EARL OF ST. VINCENT, K.B.

[Autograph, in the possession of Vice-Admiral Sir William Parker, Bart., G.C.B.]

Staines, July 12th, 1801.

My dear Lord,

Before I saw you yesterday, and afterwards, I was so unwell
with the pain in my stomach, that I have been forced to get
again into the Country; and therefore have been obliged to
make my apologies to Lord Hobart [8] for not dining with him
on Tuesday, and I hope his Lordship will forgive me. Large
dinners truly alarm me.

I have to send you a letter from Lieutenant Walpole.[9]
I have no right to ask you to do anything: probably he would
have been made, if he had not come home with Sir Hyde.
Most sincerely do I congratulate you on the good news from
the Baltic; and believe me ever yours faithfully,

NELSON AND BRONTE.

TO THE RIGHT HONOURABLE HENRY ADDINGTON.

[Autograph, in the Sidmouth Papers.]

July 18th, 1801.

My dear Sir,

I take the liberty of sending you the manner it is my wish
to have the Barony of Nelson extended,[1] which I trust will

---

[8] Secretary of State for Foreign Affairs.

[9] Apparently the Honourable William Walpole, son of Horatio, 2nd Earl of Orford, who was made a Commander in 1806, Posted in November 1809, and died in
June 1814.

[1] To prevent the extinction of his Peerages, from failure of heirs male of his own
body, Lord Nelson, obtained, on the 18th of August, 1801, a *new* Barony of Nelson,
entitled the "BARONY OF NELSON OF THE NILE AND OF HILBOROUGH, IN THE
COUNTY OF NORFOLK," which was limited, in default of his issue male, to his Father
and the heirs male of his body, failing which, to the heirs male of the bodies of
his Sisters, Mrs. Bolton and Mrs. Matcham respectively. His Foreign Orders were,
as he requested, fully described in the Patent, which declares the Royal pleasure
that every person who may succeed to the Barony thereby created, shall use the
surname of NELSON only. (*Vide* APPENDIX, No. II.) In reply to Mr. Addington's

have your approbation; and it is also my earnest wish, that my Foreign honours may be stated fully in the Patent and Gazette, for feeling as I do that they were honourably obtained, and that the title of Duke of Bronté and the Order of St. Ferdinand and of Merit, having been approved under the King's Sign Manual, and that the Turkish Order having met, through Lord Spencer, the approbation of the King, I am anxious to have them told to the world, but the fact [is] I have not thought it right to pay for any *Honours* obtained for military service to the Herald's Office.[2] I have seen Lord St. Vincent and submit to your and his partiality. Whilst my health will allow, I can only say, that every exertion of mine shall be used to merit the continuance of your esteem ; and believe me, my dear Sir, your obedient and faithful,

NELSON AND BRONTE.

I hope the news of the surrender of Alexandria is true, but I suspect the channel, for *viâ* Constantinople, you would have had it much sooner, unless by very favourable winds.

TO THE HONOURABLE MR. YORKE.[3]

[Autograph.]

My dear Sir,   Lotmar's H otel, July 20th, 1801.

I beg leave to introduce to you my relation, Lieut.-Colonel Suckling, late of the 3rd Dragoon Guards, and at the same time to express, that I am very anxious for his appointment to the situation of Barrack-master.[4] Whenever you can comply with his request, it will be a great obligation conferred upon, dear Sir, your most obedient servant,

NELSON AND BRONTE.

letter, asking the King's approbation of the new creation, his Majesty thus graciously signified his consent:—

"Weymouth, July 28th, 1801.

" The King is so thoroughly satisfied with the services and ardour of Viscount Nelson, that he cannot make the smallest objection to the preservation of the Barony in his Father's family, agreeable to the paper Mr. Addington has transmitted, and which is now returned."—*Autograph*, in the possession of the Hon. Miss Addington.

² Vide vol. ii. p. 401.

³ The Right Honourable Charles Philip Yorke, half-brother of Philip, 3rd Earl of Hardwicke, K.G., afterwards First Lord of the Admiralty: he died in March 1834.

⁴ Colonel Suckling wrote on the back of this letter, " The appointment was granted before there was an opportunity of delivering this letter."

MEMORANDA BY LORD NELSON, ON THE DEFENCE OF THE THAMES, ETC.

[Autograph in the Admiralty. In the summer of 1801, Buonaparte collected a Flotilla and large Army at Boulogne, with the avowed design of invading England. Vigorous measures were accordingly taken to resist the attempt, and it was determined to place a large force consisting of Frigates, Brigs, and smaller Vessels, under the command of Lord Nelson, between Orfordness and Beachy Head. Lord St. Vincent's (the First Lord of the Admiralty) views on the subject were thus described in a letter to Admiral Lutwidge, the Commander-in-Chief in the Downs, dated Admiralty, 24th of July, 1801. " The state of the Enemy's preparations on different parts of the Coast in the Channel, particularly opposite to you, beginning to wear a very serious appearance, and all our intelligence agreeing that a descent on some part of the Coast is actually intended, it has naturally been matter of consideration, what measures would be most advisable to be taken for our defence ; and after viewing the subject in every shape in which it could present itself, no plan appears to me to be so effectual for frustrating the Enemy's designs, as that of placing the whole of the Force applicable to that particular service, under the command of a Flag-Officer who will have no other duty to perform, than that of attending to this important object. I am aware that the measure I have mentioned will materially interfere with your command in the Downs ; and I can assure you, with great truth, that I have so much respect both for your public and private character, that I should not have taken this, or any other measure that might be in any respect unpleasant to you, if I had thought it could have been avoided without detriment to the Public service. The Officer I have fixed upon is Viscount Nelson, who will, I think, hoist his Flag in one of the Frigates, and proceed immediately to the coast of France, to settle the necessary arrangements with the Officers, now employed there. The command in the Downs will of course be left in your hands, with the superintendence of what is generally understood to be the port-duty, while it may be requisite to continue Lord Nelson in this situation."—*Clarke and M'Arthur.*

Lord Nelson assumed his command by hoisting his Flag in L'Unité Frigate, at Sheerness, on the 27th of July, and, two days before, submitted to the Admiralty the following OBSERVATIONS ON THE DEFENCE OF THE THAMES.]

25th July, 1801.

Besides the stationed Ships at the different posts between the North Foreland and Orfordness, as many Gun-vessels as can be spared from the very necessary protection of the Coast of Sussex and of Kent to the westward of Dover, should be collected, for this part of the Coast must be seriously attended to ; for supposing London the object of surprise, I am of opinion that the Enemy's object *ought* to be the getting on shore as speedily as possible, for the dangers of a navigation of forty-eight hours, appear to me to be an insurmountable objection to the rowing from Boulogne to the Coast of Essex. It is therefore most probable (for it is certainly proper to believe the French are coming to attack London, and there-

fore to be prepared) that from Boulogne, Calais, and even
Havre, that the Enemy will try and land in Sussex, or the
lower part of Kent, and from Dunkirk, Ostend, and the other
Ports of Flanders, to land on the Coast of Essex or Suffolk ;
for I own myself of opinion that, the object being to get on
shore somewhere within 100 miles of London, as speedily as
possible, that the Flats in the mouth of the Thames will not be
the only place necessary to attend to; added to this, the
Enemy will create a powerful diversion by the sailing of the
Combined Fleet, and the either sailing, or creating such an
appearance of sailing, of the Dutch Fleet, as will prevent
Admiral Dickson[5] from sending anything from off the great
Dutch Ports, whilst the smaller Ports will spew forth its Flotilla,
—viz., Flushing, &c. &c. It must be pretty well ascertained
what number of small Vessels are in each Port.

I will suppose that 40,000 men are destined for this attack, or
rather surprise, of London; 20,000 will land on the west side of
Dover, sixty or seventy miles from London, and the same
number on the east side : they are too knowing to let us have
but one point of alarm for London.   Supposing 200 Craft, or
250, collected at Boulogne, &c., they are supposed equal to
carry 20,000 men.   In very calm weather, they might row
over, supposing no impediment, in twelve hours; at the same
instant, by telegraph, the same number of troops would be
rowed out of Dunkirk, Ostend, &c. &c.   These are the two
great objects to attend to from Dover and the Downs, and
perhaps one of the small Ports to the westward.   Boulogne
(which I call the central point of the Western attack) must be
attended to.   If it is calm when the Enemy row out, all our
Vessels and Boats appointed to watch them, must get into the
Channel, and meet them as soon as possible : if not strong
enough for the attack, they must watch, and keep them company till a favourable opportunity offers.   If a breeze springs
up, our Ships are to deal *destruction;* no delicacy can be
observed on this great occasion.   But should it remain calm,
and our Flotilla not fancy itself strong enough to attack the
Enemy on their passage, the moment that they begin to touch
our shore, strong or weak, our Flotilla of Boats must attack as

---

[5] Admiral Archibald Dickson, Commander-in-Chief in the North Sea.

much of the Enemy's Flotilla as they are able—say only one half
or two-thirds ; it will create a most powerful diversion, for the
bows of our Flotilla will be opposed to their unarmed sterns, and
the courage of Britons will never, I believe, allow one Frenchman to leave the beach.　A great number of Deal and Dover
Boats to be on board our Vessels off the Port of Boulogne, to
give notice of the direction taken by the Enemy.　If it is
calm, Vessels in the Channel can make signals of intelligence
to our shores, from the North Foreland to Orfordness, and
even as far as Solebay, not an improbable place, about seventy
or eighty miles from London.

　A Flotilla to be kept near Margate and Ramsgate, to consist
of Gun-boats and Flat-boats; another Squadron to be stationed
near the centre, between Orfordness and North Foreland, and
the third in Hosely[1] Bay.　The Floating Batteries are stationed
in all proper positions for defending the different Channels,
and the smaller Vessels will always have a resort in the support
of the stationed Ships.　The moment of the Enemy's movement
from Boulogne, is to be considered as the movement of the
Enemy from Dunkirk.　Supposing it calm, the Flotillas are
to be rowed, and the heavy ones towed, (except the stationed
Ships,) those near Margate, three or four leagues to the north
of the North Foreland ; those from Hosely Bay, a little
approaching the Centre Division, but always keeping an eye
towards Solebay ; the Centre Division to advance half-way
between the two.　The more fast Rowing boats, called Thames
Galleys, which can be procured the better, to carry orders, information, &c. &c.

　Whenever the Enemy's Flotilla can be seen, our Divisions
are to unite, but not intermix, and to be ready to execute
such orders as may be deemed necessary, or as the indispensable circumstances may require.　For this purpose, men
of such confidence in each other should be looked for, that (as
far as human foresight can go,) no little jealousy may creep
into any man's mind, but to be all animated with the same
desire of preventing the descent of the Enemy on our Coasts.
Stationary Floating Batteries are not, from any apparent
advantage, to be moved, for the tide may prevent their re-

---

[1] Lord Nelson always wrote " Hollesley " *Hosely* Bay.

suming the very important stations assigned them : they are
on no account to be supposed neglected, even should the
Enemy surround them, for they may rely on support, and
reflect that perhaps their gallant conduct may prevent the
mischievous designs of the Enemy. Whatever plans may be
adopted, the moment the Enemy touch our Coast, be it where
it may, they are to be attacked by every man afloat and on
shore : this must be perfectly understood. *Never fear the event.*
The Flat Boats can probably be manned (partly, at least,) with
the Sea Fencibles, (the numbers or fixed places of whom I am
entirely ignorant of,) but the Flat Boats they may man to be
in grand and sub-divisions, commanded by their own Captains
and Lieutenants, as far as is possible. The number of Flat
Boats is unknown to me, as also the other means of defence
in Small Craft; but I am clearly of opinion that a proportion
of the small force should be kept to watch the Flat-boats from
Boulogne, and the others in the way I have presumed to
suggest. These are offered as merely the rude ideas of the
moment, and are only meant as a Sea plan of defence for the
City of London; but I believe other parts may likewise be
menaced, if the Brest fleet, and those from Rochfort and
Holland put to sea ; although I feel confident that the Fleets
of the Enemy will meet the same fate which has always
attended them, yet their sailing will facilitate the coming over
of their Flotilla, as they will naturally suppose our attention
will be called only to the Fleets.

TO HIS ROYAL HIGHNESS THE DUKE OF CLARENCE.

[From Clarke and M'Arthur, vol. ii. p. 293.]

[About 25th July, 1801.]

Sir,

I have this morning received my commission as Commander-in-Chief of a Squadron of Ships and Vessels employed on a particular service. My command is to extend
from Orfordness to Beachy Head, on both Shores ; but
without interfering with either the Nore or Downs command.
I assure your Royal Highness that I feel my ability to render

service, in this new sort of command, only in my zeal; in many other respects I am sensible of much deficiency, and require that great allowance should be made for me.   I am, &c.,

NELSON AND BRONTE.

TO EVAN NEPEAN, ESQ., ADMIRALTY.

[Original, in the Admiralty.]

Sir,   London, July 26th, 1801.
Captain Parker⁵ of H. M. Ship Sloop Amaranthe, under my command, having represented to me that his Sloop is not ready for sea, and as the services of Captain Parker will be very useful to me in my situation, I have to beg you will request their Lordships to grant him leave to be with me on the service I am employed on.   I am, &c.

NELSON AND BRONTE.

TO EVAN NEPEAN, ESQ., ADMIRALTY.

[Original, in the Admiralty.]

Sir,   Sheerness, July 27th, 1801.
I have to request you will be pleased to inform the Lords Commissioners of the Admiralty with my arrival at this place, and that I have hoisted my Flag on board H. M. Ship Unité, in Sheerness Harbour.   I am, &c.

NELSON AND BRONTE.

TO EVAN NEPEAN, ESQ., ADMIRALTY.

[Letter-Book.]

Sir,   Unité, Sheerness, 28th July, 1801.
I beg leave to send you, for the information of their Lordships, a statement of the Stations the Ships that are here

---

⁵ Captain Edward Thornborough Parker, to whom Lord Nelson became so much attached as to call him "his son." Few events in Nelson's life occasioned him such grief as the death of Captain Parker, from a wound, in September following.

under my command have already taken and are to take. I
am, &c.   NELSON AND BRONTE.

The Redoubt, ⎫
Firm,   ⎪   In the East Swale, under the com-
Haughty,   ⎬ mand of Captain John [James] Shepard[6]
Gallant,   ⎭ of the Redoubt.

Glatton,   ⎫
Vlieter,   ⎬   At the Wallett, Glatton to go.

Batavier,   Pan Sand.

Ardent,   ⎫   In the entrance of Margate Roads, the
Daphne,   ⎬ North Foreland Light about S.W., and the
Serapis,   ⎭ buoy of the Sand N. B. E., at the distance
of a mile and a half, for the purpose of preventing the Enemy
from coming inside Margate Sand, and to be ready to go
round the head of the Sand, in case the Enemy should go up
the Queen's Channel.

Ruby, in Hosely Bay.

Conflict,   ⎫
Monkey,   ⎬   Going to Hosely Bay.

Attack,   ⎧ Thames Stream.   ⎧ Employed by Admiral
Defender,   ⎩ Spill Buoy.   ⎨ Græme[7] to get manned,
                                  ⎩ themselves not manned.

TO ADMIRAL THE EARL OF ST. VINCENT, K.B.

[From Clarke and M'Arthur, vol. ii. p. 294.]

Sheerness, 28th July, 1801.

Everything, my dear Lord, must have a beginning, and we
are literally at the foundation of our fabric of defence. I
agree perfectly with you, that we must keep the Enemy as
far from our own Coasts as possible, and be able to attack
them the moment they come out of their Ports. . . . As soon
as all the orders are given, it is my intention to go to Deal,
and to consult with Admiral Lutwidge. Should the Enemy

---

[6] Captain James Keith Shepard, who died a Vice-Admiral of the Red, in 1843.
Vide vol. i. p. 85.

[7] Vice-Admiral of the White, Alexander Græme, Commander-in-Chief at the
Nore. He died an Admiral of the Red in 1818.

approach our Coasts near the Thames, our Dock-yards can man Flat-boats if they are kept in readiness; and this Yard has 100 men, who can man two Flats which are ordered to be fitted out. If the Unité arrives at the Nore this day, I shall go on board her, in order to show that we must all get to our posts as speedily as possible. I am, &c.

NELSON AND BRONTE.

TO CAPTAIN SIR EDWARD BERRY, H.M.S. RUBY.

[Autograph, in the possession of Lady Berry.]

July 28th, 1801.

My dear Sir Edward,

Although by the Admiralty orders I am not absolutely to take you under my command, yet I am authorized to give you any directions which I may judge proper; therefore I send you two Gun-brigs to be under your command, and I wish them to be exercised, in order to make them fit for any real service. I am only beginning the Defence, and a beginning there must be of all things. I shall send you some Revenue Cutters, who must always be kept on the look-out, so that you may not be surprised in the night by an Enemy close to you. Ever yours faithfully,

NELSON AND BRONTE.

TO VICE-ADMIRAL GRÆME, COMMANDER-IN-CHIEF, AT THE NORE.

[Letter-Book.]

Sir,   Unité, Sheerness, July 29th, 1801.

I have to request that you will direct such Ships, Vessels, and Revenue Cutters, as are or may be placed under my command, (who have not received particular orders from me,) to proceed and put themselves under the command of the Senior Captains, either at the Squadron stationed off Hosely Bay, or the Squadron stationed to the southward of Margate Sand. The Attack and Defender, I have directed, so soon as they are manned, to join the Squadron off Margate Sand. I have the honour to be, &c.

NELSON AND BRONTE.

TO EVAN NEPEAN, ESQ., ADMIRALTY.

[Original, in the Admiralty.]

Leyden, Downs, 30th July, 1801.

Sir,

I beg you will be pleased to acquaint their Lordships that having arranged everything at Sheerness, I thought it right to come here, where I arrived last night, and hoisted my Flag for the present on board the Leyden; I am now employed issuing the necessary directions to the several Ships under my command at this anchorage. I have sent for the Medusa, in which ship I mean to go over to the Coast of France. I am, Sir, &c.,

NELSON AND BRONTE.

TO ADMIRAL THE EARL OF ST. VINCENT, K.B.

[From Clarke and M'Arthur, vol. ii. p. 294.]

Deal, July 30th, 1801.

As I had arranged everything possible for me to do at Sheerness, I thought it best to set off for the Downs by the way of Feversham, as I wished to see Captain Becher[8] on the subject of the Sea-Fencibles. I had previously sent Captain Shepard to desire that a Mr. Salisbury would meet me; as he was a person of respectability, rich, (got it by the fair trade,) and of great influence amongst the Seafaring men on that part of the Coast, particularly about Whitstable. I made him sensible of the necessity of our Ships, which were to be stationed off the Sand-heads, being manned. He thought if the Admiralty, through me, gave the men assurances that they should be returned to their homes, when the danger of the Invasion was passed, that the Sea-folk would go; but that they were always afraid of some trick: this service, my dear Lord, above all others, would be terrible for me : to get up and harangue like a Recruiting Serjeant! I do not think I could get through it; but as I am come forth, I feel that I

---

[8] Captain Alexander Becher: he commanded the Sea Fencibles at Feversham; was Posted in April 1802, and died about 1826.

ought to do this disagreeable service as well as any other, if judged necessary. I hoisted my Flag here this morning. The Medusa is sent for, and I propose going over to the Coast of Boulogne, if possible, to-morrow or next day morning, and to take Captain Fyers[9] of the Artillery with me; to return here, and then to go off Flushing with a Captain Owen[1] of the Nemesis: I have thoughts of fixing a Squadron of Small Vessels under him, if I find him equal to my expectation from his writing, and of stationing Captain Bedford[2] of the Leyden, whose good sense and Officer-like conduct I have heard much commended, to support him off Flushing; and also for Captain Owen to have the chief command of the Ships and Vessels anchored off Margate Sand. I am, &c.

NELSON AND BRONTE.

TO ADMIRAL THE EARL OF ST. VINCENT, K.B.

[From Clarke and M'Arthur, vol. ii. p. 294.]

Deal, July 31st, 1801.

Our force will, by your great exertions, soon get so formidable, that the Enemy will hardly venture out. I shall endeavour in the morning to ascertain the possibility of destroying their Vessels in the Harbour of Boulogne. I send you the Return of men in the Master-Attendant's department in Sheerness yard, (247,) who could man on an emergency the six upper Vessels: for the time must come, if the Enemy approaches, that all work, except fighting, would stand still; therefore I propose, if we have not men to man them at present, that at least the Vessels should be prepared and ready for the Dock-yard men to be put on board, commanded by their own Officers; which could be of the greatest consequence, and they could always get either to the Essex Coast, or towards Margate, in any weather the Enemy would attempt coming over. Other Yards may be also able to do much. I am, &c.   NELSON AND BRONTE.

----

[9] Captain Peter Fyers, of the Artillery; now a Major-General, and a Companion of the Bath.

[1] Now Vice-Admiral Sir Edward William Campbell Rich Owen, G.C.B., G.C.H.

[2] Captain William Bedford: he died a Vice-Admiral of the White, in 1827 or 1828.

TO THE RIGHT HONOURABLE HENRY ADDINGTON.

[Autograph, in the Sidmouth Papers.]

Deal, July 31st, 1801.

My dear Sir,

I beg to thank you for your kind communication of His Majesty's goodness, in granting the extension of the Barony to my Father's family. To-morrow, I am going to the Coast of France, and shall take an Artillery-Officer with me, who will be able to form a judgment as to the possibility of the effect of shells on the Enemy's Vessels at Boulogne. Our means of defence so rapidly increase, that it will soon be almost improbable that the Enemy should attempt to come out of their Ports, on the Coasts near us. You may rely on my zeal (which is all I pretend to) to endeavour to merit the good opinion you are pleased to entertain of me; and ever consider me, your most obliged and obedient servant,

NELSON AND BRONTE.

TO THE EARL OF ST. VINCENT, K.B.

[From Clarke and M'Arthur, vol. ii. p. 295.]

Off Boulogne, 2nd August, 1801.

I have been looking at Boulogne this morning, and see their Line of Vessels, all armed, which lie outside the Port. Captain Fyers, of the Artillery, thinks that they are stationed to add strength to the place. The French are erecting Batteries both for guns and mortars on each side of the Town, as if fearful of an attack. All accounts agree, that fifty or sixty is the full number of Boats, large and small, at Boulogne, and that these can be moved out of the reach of shells; however, I have sent for the Bombs, and will try what can be done. I am, &c.,

NELSON AND BRONTE.

TO CAPTAIN JOHN RUSSEL,[3] H.M. SLOOP GIER, OFF GRAVELINES.

[Autograph, in the possession of his Son, Thomas Russel, Esq., Assistant-Surgeon in the Service of the East India Company.]

Secret.   August 2nd, 1801, 9 p.m.

Dear Sir,

I approve very much of your movement towards Gravelines, and I wish you, when you can ascertain what is the Enemy's force in Dunkirk Roads, to let me know, and whether they are not to be attacked in the night of to-morrow, and what force you would wish to have for that service. I can send you some of the Sloops with Gover's guns, and some Revenue Cutters, and more Gun-brigs. But let me know your opinion, if possible, by to-morrow forenoon's tide. Except to the Captains, (and Pilots, such as are necessary to be consulted) and to whom, enjoin secrecy, do not say a word. I am, dear Sir, your most obedient Servant,

NELSON AND BRONTE.

TO ADMIRAL THE EARL OF ST. VINCENT, K.B.

[From Clarke and M'Arthur, vol. ii. p. 295.]

Medusa, off Boulogne, August 3rd, 1801.

The wind falling nearly to a calm, and, what was worse, coming to the northward, I called the Bombs off after they had fired ten or twelve shells, some of which went as far as the Town, but without any effect that we could see. We have, however, ascertained that we can bombard the Vessels at proper times of tide, and, with the wind to the southward of the west, with great facility. I hope the wind will come westerly, when we can fully try the effect of shells. I am, &c.

NELSON AND BRONTE.

[3] Captain John Russel, of the Gier: he was Posted in 1802; afterwards commanded the Sea Fencibles in Argyleshire, and died between 1809 and 1814.

F F 2

TO ADMIRAL SKEFFINGTON LUTWIDGE, DOWNS.

[Autograph, in the possession of Major Lutwidge.]

August 3rd, 1801, 8 A.M.

My dear Admiral,

Many thanks for your letters and for the accounts from
Captain Richardson[4] and Lieutenant Baker;[5] the Armed Vessels outside of Boulogne are twenty-four, probably intended to
cover the entrance of the Vessels from the westward; but of
the Craft which I have seen, I do not think it possible to *row*
them to England ; and sail they cannot. Yesterday, I ordered
Jamaica and six other Vessels to take their station between
Porté Point and Etaples ; a number of Vessels came yesterday
morning into the Road of Dunkirk ; Captain Russel has his
eye upon them. No fishing-boats have been out yesterday or
this morning ; the wind is so far to the northward, that I doubt
if the Bombs can be sent in this morning to try a few shells.
Ever your obliged,

NELSON AND BRONTE.

If you keep the King George, then the Cygnet will run to
and fro.

TO THE SENIOR CAPTAINS, OFF DIEPPE.

[Letter-Book.]

Sir,   Medusa, August 3rd, 1801.

I returned your old Cruizer, the Stag, and also, the Stag
Revenue Cutter. I have also stationed the Jamaica, Captain
Rose,[6] and six other Vessels, between Etaples and Point Portel ;
therefore, they will be [able] to keep a good look-out further
westward. It is of great consequence, the destruction of the
Enemy's Flat boats ; and I wish you to let me know, if any of

---

[4] Apparently Captain William Richardson, of the Autumn: he was Posted in
1804, and died in August 1818.

[5] Apparently Lieutenant John Baker, elder brother of the late Vice-Admiral Sir
Thomas Baker, K.C.B.: he then commanded the Vixen Gun brig; was made a
Commander in April 1802, was Posted in October 1810; and died in 1838.

[6] Captain Jonas Rose, of the Jamaica, which Ship he commanded at Copenhagen,
(vide p. 314, ante:) he was Posted on the 1st of January, 1801, and died between
1816 and 1820.

the Flat boats, &c., can be bombarded with advantage, either at St. Vallery, Dieppe, or other places along the Coast. I have received Captain Richardson's and Lieutenant Baker's letters. I am, &c.,

　　　　　　　　　　　　　NELSON AND BRONTE.

TO EVAN NEPEAN, ESQ., ADMIRALTY.

[Original, in the Admiralty.]

　　　　　　　　　　Medusa, off Boulogne, August 3rd, 1801.
Sir,

As I understood from Mr. Lawrence, the Naval Storekeeper at Deal, that twelve or fourteen Flat-bottomed Boats would be ready to put in the water the latter end of this week, I wish very much that directions may be given to fit eight of them with brass, eight-inch howitzers, and the remainder with twenty-four-pounder carronades, as I am of opinion that the Enemy may be more annoyed by firing into their small Harbours and little Ports in the night than by greater and larger attacks.

The stores, ammunition, &c., I should think, might be immediately sent from Dover to the Downs, by which means no time would be lost in equipping them for the service intended. They can be stowed on board the larger Ships on this Coast, who will have the best means of furnishing them, manning, &c. I am, &c,

　　　　　　　　　　　　　NELSON AND BRONTE.

TO EVAN NEPEAN, ESQ., ADMIRALTY.

[Autograph, in the Admiralty.]

　　　　　　　　　　Medusa, off Boulogne, August 3rd, 1801.
Sir,

The Enemy have twenty-four armed Vessels anchored outside the Port of Boulogne, for what purpose is difficult to guess, it may be to afford protection to the Vessels chased on the 1st into St. Vallery. The wind is too far to the northward at present for our Bombs to go on the sea-shore. These Vessels anchored before this Port appear to me incapable in the smoothest water of being rowed more than one and a half per hour. No Fishing boats have been out since the 1st. The Enemy are working hard at new batteries. Captain Russel, who is stationed off Calais, received yesterday information that some Vessels had come out of the Harbour of Dunkirk into the Roads; he is, therefore, (there being only one Brig in Calais,) gone to Gravelines, in order to watch them. With our present force from Dieppe to Dunkirk, certainly nothing can with impunity leave the Coast of France one mile. I am, Sir, &c.,   NELSON AND BRONTE.

TO ADMIRAL THE EARL OF ST. VINCENT, K.B.

[From Clarke and M'Arthur, vol. ii. p. 295.]

August 4th.

The wind being at N.E., the Bombs anchored at half-past five, abreast of the Town. What damage has been done cannot be ascertained inside the Pier; on the outside, two large Floating batteries are sunk, and one large Gun-brig cut her cables and ran on shore, where she lies abandoned. The Bombs are very well placed by their Captains, and the Artillery Officers and men have the greatest desire to do their duty. Boulogne is certainly not a very pleasant place this morning: but it is not my wish to injure the poor inhabitants, and the Town is spared as much as the nature of the service will admit. Very little damage has been done to our Bombs. Captain Fyers is slightly wounded in the thigh, but remains at his post. I have paid them all a visit, and the Medusa is at anchor one cable's length from them. I am, &c.,

NELSON AND BRONTE.

P.S.—Since I finished my letter, one or two more Gun-vessels are destroyed.

TO THE RIGHT HONOURABLE HENRY ADDINGTON.

[Autograph, in the Sidmouth Papers.]

Medusa, off Boulogne, August 4th, 1801.

My dear Sir,
    I think I may venture to assure you that the French Army will not embark at Boulogne for the invasion of England;

they are suffering this morning from allowing a collection of
Craft to be assembled in their Port. Five Vessels of different
descriptions are sunk on the outside the Pier by our shells;
they were all fitted with heavy guns, and full of men. What
damage has taken place inside the Pier, cannot be ascertained,
but, judging from the outside, we may suppose it considerable.
Ever, my dear Sir, your most obliged,

NELSON AND BRONTE.

TO ADMIRAL LUTWIDGE.

[Autograph, in the possession of Major Lutwidge.]

Medusa, August 4th, 1801.

My dear Admiral,

The arrangement about the correspondence shall be duly
attended to, but no Fishing-boats are come out since my
appearance. I have given Captain Rose the signals to the
westward, where he is stationed, and Captain Somerville[7] has
also a copy. Captain Owen seems an intelligent Officer.
Our Bombs are at work. Captain Owen can tell you what
we see—two Flats sunk, and one Brig run on shore, evidently
struck by a shell. At Boulogne it is certainly not a pleasant
morning. Captain Fyers is slightly wounded. Ever, my
dear Admiral, your obliged and affectionate,

NELSON AND BRONTE.

TO CAPTAIN SIR EDWARD BERRY, H.M. SHIP RUBY, HOSELY BAY.

[Autograph, in the possession of Lady Berry.]

Medusa, off Boulogne, August 4th, 1801.

My dear Sir Edward,

Pray direct immediately the Monkey and Conflict Gun-
brigs to obey my order sent by this occasion; Captain Owen
thinks they may be very useful. I hope your Ruby is getting
about again; she is a fine Ship, and you will soon be very comfortable in her. We are tormenting the vagabonds here; this

---

[7] Captain Philip Somerville was Posted on the 29th of April, 1802, and died between 1816 and 1820.

morning, five of their armed Flats and a Brig are sunk, and lying on their beam-ends. I do not believe that the French Army will embark from Boulogne. Ever yours faithfully,

NELSON AND BRONTE.

If the Monkey is not complete, or nearly so, with her complement, she may remain till she is.

TO CAPTAIN BEDFORD, H.M. SHIP LEYDEN.

[Letter-Book.]

Medusa, off Boulogne, 4th August, 1801.

Dear Sir,

Lieutenant Fabian,[8] delivered me your letter of yesterday, this morning. I approve of your anchorage of the Gun-brigs. The other Vessels of force will, I suppose, soon be with you, when you will leave the order for the Senior Officer at the Sand-heads, with whoever may be there, in case you are on the other side of the water. The Margate and Harwich Revenue Cutters are directed by me, by way of Sheerness, to attend on the Elder Brethren of the Trinity House, who are in their Yacht, in Margate Roads. I shall be with you in two days. Pray send one of the Smacks to Hosely Bay, with my letter to Sir Edward Berry, or the Commanding Officer.

Our Bombs are at work, and five of the Enemy's Gunvessels are sunk; and upon the whole they have not had a very pleasant morning. I am, dear Sir, &c.

NELSON AND BRONTE.

TO EVAN NEPEAN, ESQ., ADMIRALTY.

[Letter-Book and "London Gazette" of 8th August, 1801.]

Medusa, August 4th, 1801.

Sir,

The Enemy's Vessels, Brigs, and Flats, (Lugger-rigged,) and a Schooner, twenty-four in number, were this morning, at daylight, anchored in a line, in front of the Town of

---

[8] Lieutenant Charles Montagu Fabian: he was made a Commander in 1802; Posted in October 1810; and died between 1816 and 1820.

Boulogne. The wind being favourable for the Bombs to act,
I made the signal for them to weigh, and to throw shells at
the Vessels; but as little as possible to annoy the Town. The
Captains placed their Ships in the best possible position, and
in a few hours three of the Flats and a Brig were sunk; and
in the course of the morning, six were on shore, evidently
much damaged. At six this evening, being high water, five
of the Vessels, which had been aground, hauled with difficulty
into the Mole; the others remained under water. I believe
the whole of the Vessels would have gone inside the Pier, but
for want of water. What damage the Enemy may have sustained beyond what we see, is impossible to tell. The whole
of this affair is of no further consequence, than to show the
Enemy that they cannot with impunity come outside their
Ports. The Officers of the Artillery threw the shells with
great skill; and I am sorry to say that Captain Fyers, of the
Royal Artillery, is slightly wounded in the thigh, by the
bursting of an Enemy's shell, and three seamen are also
wounded. I am, &c.

                                        NELSON AND BRONTE.
One more of the Enemy's Flats is this moment sunk.

TO HIS ROYAL HIGHNESS THE DUKE OF CLARENCE.

[From Clarke and M'Arthur, vol. ii. p. 295.]

                                        August 5th, 1801.

The whole of this business is of no further moment than to
show the Enemy, that, with impunity, they cannot come outside their Ports. I see nothing but a desire on the part of
our Officers and men to get at them. I am now on my way
off Ostend and Flushing, whence I shall cross to either Margate or Hosely Bay. Most cordially do I congratulate your
Royal Highness on the distinguished merits of Captain Keats,[9]
your opinion of him was truly formed. Again let me assure
you how sensibly I feel all your partiality for me, and that I
will ever continue to deserve it. I am, &c.

                                        NELSON AND BRONTE.

[9] Afterwards Admiral Sir Richard Goodwin Keats, G.C.B., who had then recently
distinguished himself in command of the Superb, at the battle of Algesiras.

TO THE SQUADRON.

[From the " Naval Chronicle," vol. vi. p. 160.]

5th August, 1801.

Lord Nelson has reason to be very much satisfied with the Captains of the Bombs, for their placing of the Vessels yesterday. It was impossible that they could have been better situated; and the Artillery Officers have shown great skill in entirely disabling ten of the Armed Vessels out of twenty-four opposed to them, and many others, Lord Nelson believes are much damaged. The Commander-in-Chief cannot avoid noting the great zeal and desire to attack the Enemy in a closer and different combat, which manifested itself in all ranks of persons, and which Lord Nelson would gladly have given full scope to, had the attempt at this moment been proper; but the Officers and others may rely, that an early opportunity shall be given them for showing their judgment, zeal, and bravery. The Hired and Revenue Cutters kept under sail, and performed the duty entrusted to them with a great deal of skill.

NELSON AND BRONTE.

TO ADMIRAL LUTWIDGE.

[Autograph, in the possession of Major Lutwidge.]

Medusa, off Calais, August 6th, 1801.

My dear Admiral,

I know nothing of the De Ruyter and Hind being under my command; if they are, they had better join me off the end of Margate Sand, with the Icarus. I am on my way with the Brilliant and some Cutters, going to Flushing. Our force to the westward is abundant for our part of the Coast. The York and Isis will support all our Small craft. One more Flat sunk in the evening. The wind coming at eight o'clock to the N.W., I ordered the Bombs out of the Road. I believe they must be sick of their stations. Four Vessels are just above water at low water; six were at high water got into the Mole, evidently much damaged. The Commodore is the English Gun-brig taken off Dungeness; she hauled on shore, and is also damaged. I should suppose that they must have lost many men, as at half-past nine till dark, not more than two or three men were aboard each of them. I have sent to the Admiralty to have some Flat boats fitted with brass howitzers, and twenty-four pounder carronades, to fire 57-inch shells. I shall come from Flushing to Margate, and probably pay my respects to you in the Downs. I beg my best respects to Mrs. Lutwidge, and with many thanks for all your goodness to me, believe me ever your obliged and faithful

NELSON AND BRONTE.

TO EVAN NEPEAN, ESQ., ADMIRALTY.

[Original, in the Admiralty.]

Medusa, 6th August, 1801.

Sir

I beg leave to inform you, for the information of my Lords Commissioners of the Admiralty, that in consequence of their dispatches I received last night, relative to the Sea-Fencibles, added to the wind being at present easterly, which will occasion a great delay in my intention of proceeding off Flushing, I have determined to go to Margate Roads, for the purpose of carrying into execution, to the utmost of my power, their Lordships' orders relative to the regulation and distribution of the Sea-Fencibles in that quarter, which I hope will meet their Lordships' approbation. I also beg leave to enclose herewith a copy of a circular letter, which I have sent to the Captains commanding the different districts of the Sea-Fencible corps. I remain, &c.

NELSON AND BRONTE.

P.S.—I have added the Brilliant Frigate, and Monkey and Conflict Gun-brigs, to the Squadron off Flushing.

N. & B.

TO CAPTAINS SHIELD, HAMILTON, SCHOMBERGH, AND EDGE.

[Original, in the Admiralty.]

Medusa, 6th August, 1801.

Sir,

As there can be no doubt of the intention of the French to attempt the Invasion of our Country, and as I trust, and am confident, that if our Seafaring men do their duty, that either the Enemy will give over the folly of the measure, or, if they persist in it, that not one Frenchman will be allowed to set his foot on British soil; it is, therefore, necessary that all good men should come forward on this momentous occasion to oppose the Enemy, and, more particularly, the Sea-Fencibles, who have voluntarily enrolled themselves to defend their Country afloat, which is the true place where Britain ought to be defended, that the horrors of war may not reach the peaceful abodes of our families. And as the Lords Commissioners of the Admiralty have been pleased to appoint me to command the Sea defence of Great Britain, within the limits of your district, it is my duty to request that you will have the goodness to acquaint all the Sea-Fencibles under your command, and all other Sea-faring men and fishermen, that their services are absolutely required at this moment on board the Ships and Vessels particularly appointed to defend that part of the Coast where the Enemy mean to attempt a landing, if unopposed.

I am authorized to assure the Fencibles, and other Sea-faring men who may come forward on this occasion, that they shall not be sent off the Coast of the Kingdom, shall be kept as near their own homes as the nature of the service will admit, and that the moment the alarm of the threatened Invasion is over, that every man shall be returned to their own homes; and also, that during their continuance on board Ship, that as much attention as is possible shall be paid to their reasonable wants. And I flatter myself, that at a moment when all the Volunteer corps in the Kingdom are come forward to defend our land, that the Seamen of Great Britain will not be slow to defend our own proper element, and maintain as pure as our glorious ancestors have transmitted it to us, our undoubted right to the Sovereignty of the Narrow Seas, on which no Frenchman has yet *dared* to sail with impunity. Our Country looks to its Sea defence, and let it not be disappointed.

I shall send Cutters to bring the Sea-Fencibles, and other Sea-faring men to me, in order that I may dispose of them in the way most proper for the defence of our King and Country, and, at the same time, in the most commodious way to the men themselves. I beg your answer as expeditiously as possible, and am, Sir, &c.

NELSON AND BRONTE.

Let me know, as near as possible, the exact numbers; and when they embark correct lists must be sent with them.

TO ADMIRAL THE EARL OF ST. VINCENT, K.B.

[From Clarke and M'Arthur, vol. ii. p. 295.]

6th August, 1801.

My Lord,

The wind being easterly, I have determined to give up for a few days my visit to Flushing, and to do my utmost to get the Fencibles afloat. The information respecting the number of troops assembled at Boulogne cannot be true; it is evidently a lie, most likely fabricated by some scoundrel emigrant in London. I have now more than ever reason to believe, that the Ports of Flushing and Flanders are much more likely places to embark men from, than Calais, Boulogne, or Dieppe; for in Flanders we cannot tell by our eyes what means they have collected for carrying an Army. Captain Fyers' wound is so very painful, that I am sending him to Deal; I am sorry, at this moment, to lose the services of so useful and zealous an Officer. Again and again, I congratulate and rejoice with you on Sir James Saumarez's success: no small degree of merit must attach itself to your Lordship, for nicking the time of sending out that Squadron. I am, &c.,

NELSON AND BRONTE.

TO ALEXANDER DAVISON, ESQ., SWANLAND HOUSE, MORPETH.

[Autograph, in the possession of Colonel Davison.]

Medusa, Margate, 6th August, 1801.

My dear Davison,

Will you forgive my writing to you at this moment, for as you will believe I have more of it than I can lay my hand to. I can venture to assure you that no embarkation of troops can take place at Boulogne. If they

come forth, it must be from Flushing and other Ports in
Flanders. With my best respects to Mrs. Davison and your
family, believe me ever, your obliged and faithful friend,

NELSON AND BRONTE.[1]

TO ADMIRAL THE EARL OF ST. VINCENT, K.B.

[From Clarke and M'Arthur, vol. ii. p. 295.]

Margate Roads, 7th August, 1801.

You have seen a copy of my letter to the Captain of the
Fencibles. As Margate will probably serve as a model for
the situation of all the Sea-Fencibles, I shall confine myself to it; and submit with deference, what in my humble
opinion is best to be done. But as they are only the
thoughts of the moment, you must make due allowances,
and much must require arranging. Of the 2600 Sea-Fencibles
enrolled between Orfordness and Beachy Head, only 385 have
offered themselves to go on board a Ship, and serve at the
Sand-heads, &c.; the Sea-Fencibles of Margate, for instance
consist of 118 men, their occupation is pier-men belonging to
the Margate hoys, and some few who assist Ships up and down
the River. These men say, ' our employment will not allow us
to go from our homes beyond a day or two, and for actual
service:' but they profess their readiness to fly on board, or
on any other duty ordered, when the Enemy are announced
as actually coming on the sea. This, my dear Lord, we must
take for granted is the situation of all other Sea-Fencibles:
when we cannot do all we wish, we must do as well as we can.

----

[1] The above was written on the back of the following Letter from Captain Parker.
The words in Italics were added by Lord Nelson:—

" Medusa, Margate, August 6th, 1801.

" My dear Sir,

" Lord Nelson having received a letter from Lloyd's, acquainting him they have
voted £500 *for the Copenhagen business*, to be laid out in plate for him, desires
me, as he has not time to write himself, to beg you will write to Rundell and
Bridge, and order them to make what you think necessary to add to the rest, to
make a complete set, such as plates, or whatever you may think right. We
left Boulogne yesterday morning, after having annoyed them and their Flotilla considerably. We are now at Margate, and I believe for the purpose of regulating
the gentlemen there, and putting the Sea-Fencibles in order. Lord Nelson says he
shall add a Postscript. I remain your ever obliged, grateful servant,

Turn over.   " E. T. PARKER."

Our Ships fitted for the service, on both shores, between
Orfordness and the North Foreland, want 1900 men, the
River-barges two or three hundred.　Shall I try and arrange,
that when the Invasion is coming, these Ships shall be manned
from particular places?　In that case, we must get as many
volunteers as we can at present to take care of our Ships, and
trust to their being manned at the last moment by the (almost)
scrambling manner I have pointed out; in which case the
unmanned Ships must be brought from the end of Margate
Sand into the Roads, and kept as safe as possible with a few
men.　Respecting the River-barges, out of the twelve ordered
to the Nore, I propose placing four on Whitstable Flat, and
the other on the Essex-side, about Mercey Island: these must
be considered as belonging to the Sea-Fencibles, and in a
certain degree under the orders of those Captains, and the
men exercised on board them.　It is my intention to get over,
if possible, to-morrow to Hosely Bay or Harwich, and to have
a meeting with Captains Schomberg and Edge.　My Flotilla,
I hope, will be finished by Wednesday, and I am vain enough
to expect a great deal of mischief to the Enemy from it.　I
am sure that the French are trying to get from Boulogne;
yet the least wind at W.N.W. and they are lost.　I pronounce
that no embarkation can take place at Boulogne; whenever
it comes forth, it will be from Flanders, and what a forlorn
undertaking! consider cross tides, &c. &c.　As for rowing, that
is impossible. It is perfectly right to be prepared against a mad
Government; but with the active force your Lordship has
given me, I may pronounce it almost impracticable.　I am, &c.

　　　　　　　　　　　　　　NELSON AND BRONTE.

TO THE REVEREND HENRY CROWE, BURNHAM, NORFOLK.

[Autograph, in the possession of John Burnet, Esq., Chelsea.]

　　　　　　　　　　　　Medusa, at Sea, August 8th, 1801.
My dear Sir,

　I felt such pleasure in being remembered by an old Burnham friend, that it is impossible to describe what thoughts
rushed into my mind.　The remembrance of you from my very
childhood, of your many acts of civilities and kindnesses to
me and to my dear father, will always make it pleasant to me

to attend to any recommendation of yours. The Riches I must remember if I recollect myself, and shall be very glad to be useful to the Lieutenant; this is the first moment I heard of his being in our service. Raven and Howard both behave exceedingly well; I have directed their removal to the San Josef, where my Flag will soon fly; Raven is literally as we say, his father's own son; such a likeness in person and manner—*pen in the ear*—I never saw. I beg, my dear Sir, that you will present my very kindest respects to good Sir Mordaunt,[1] and to all your and his family, and beg you to believe me ever your obliged Servant,

NELSON AND BRONTE.

TO EVAN NEPEAN, ESQ., ADMIRALTY.

[Original, in the Admiralty.]

Medusa, off Harwich, 9th August, 1801.

Sir,

I beg leave to assure their Lordships that particular attention shall be paid to what you communicated to me by letter of the 7th instant, respecting the limits of Admiral Dickson's Command. Vessels have been ordered by me to cruise as far as the West Capel, which by the charts take in Flushing, and to that point Admiral Lutwidge's cruizers have always been ordered. I am, Sir,

NELSON AND BRONTE.

TO ADMIRAL THE EARL OF ST. VINCENT, K.B.

[From Clarke and M'Arthur, vol. ii. p. 297.]

King George Cutter, off Harwich, 9th August, 1801.

My dear Lord,

We anchored with the Medusa yesterday under Bawdsey Sand, and our Downs pilots are so ignorant that they would neither carry us into Hosely Bay nor Harwich. I sent off express for Captain Schomberg and Edge, and am now here, half sea-sick, waiting their arrival. The men, I believe, will come forth, when the whole Country prepares for fighting;

---

[1] Sir Mordaunt Martin, Bart.

and all other business stands still; but they are no more
willing to give up their occupations than their superiors . . . .
We are so prepared at this moment, on the Enemy's Coasts,
that I do not believe they could get three miles from their own
shore. Many thanks for your giving my friend Bromwich[2]
the Warden's place at Portsmouth: I will answer for him. I
am, &c.,

NELSON AND BRONTE.

TO CAPTAIN OWEN, H.M. SHIP NEMESIS, BETWEEN GRAVELINES
AND WEST CAPEL.

[Letter-Book.]

Sir,   Medusa, Harwich, 10th August, 1801.

Having received the directions of the Lords Commissioners
of the Admiralty, not to interfere with Admiral Dickson's
Cruizers, stationed off Flushing, you are therefore to issue to
the Vessels, cruizing with you, directions to be very particular
in obeying their Lordships' commands, and you will not go
beyond the limits of your station, nor interfere with those
Cruizers, unless absolutely necessary for the good of His
Majesty's service, in case the Enemy put to sea. I am, &c.,

NELSON AND BRONTE.

Enclosed, to Captain Owen, orders for Ships with him, to
put themselves under my command, and directed Captain
Owen to distribute them, as addressed.

TO ADMIRAL THE EARL OF ST. VINCENT, K.B.

[From Clarke and M'Arthur, vol. ii. p. 297.]

Medusa, Harwich, 10th August, 1801.
My dear Lord,

In truth, I have no desire for anything else, than to get
at a proper time clear of my present command, in which I
am sure of diminishing my little fortune, which at this moment
does not reach 10,000*l.* ; and never had I an idea of gaining
money by accepting it. I wrote to Hardy, to prepare to go

---

² Lieutenant Joseph Bromwich. Vide vol. i. p. 52.

into the San Josef. Do you still think of sending me to the Mediterranean? If not, I am ready to go, for the spur of the occasion, on the Expedition which is in embryo, but to return the moment it is over, for I am afraid of my strength. I am always ready, as far as I am able. I shall be at the Nore by sunset. Mr. Spence, the Maritime surveyor of this Coast, is going to carry the Medusa out by a new Channel. It is necessary I should know all that is to be known of the navigation; and I have been a tolerable Pilot for the mouth of the Thames in my younger days.[3]   I am, &c.,

NELSON AND BRONTE.

TO CAPTAIN SIR EDWARD BERRY, H.M. SHIP RUBY.

[From a Copy in the Nelson Papers.]

Medusa, 10th August, 1801.

My dear Sir Edward,

I am just going to the Nore. You will send your boat to Orford for the Fencibles, and be correct as to the time of the Boats being there or the men may alter their minds, as is possible. You forgot to send the Sick-Ticket, but I send an order for your Lieutenant being received. You will get men: great preparations at Ostend: Augereau commands that part of the Army. I hope to let him feel the bottom of the Goodwin Sand. Ever yours faithfully,

NELSON AND BRONTE.

TO EVAN NEPEAN, ESQ., ADMIRALTY.

[Original, in the Admiralty.]

Medusa, Buoy of the Gun-Fleet, August 10th, 1801.

Sir,

I have reason to be very much pleased with the services of Mr. Græme Spence, who, finding my anxiety to get from Harwich, and the Pilots refusing to take charge of the Ship through the common channel for Ships of War, took charge of the Medusa at high water and brought her over the Naze Flat,

---

[3] Vide vol. i. p. 2.

which was never yet navigated by a Ship of War of this size, and Mr. Spence has given me some better ideas for placing Vlieter and Beschamer, which I have directed their Captains to put in execution. I am, Sir, &c.,

NELSON AND BRONTE.

TO EVAN NEPEAN, ESQ., ADMIRALTY.

[Original, in the Admiralty.]

Medusa, Harwich, 10th August, 1801.

Sir,

Herewith I send you copies of my letters from the Captains Hamilton and Sheilds, and I have also seen and conversed with Captains Schomberg, Edge, Becher, and Rudsdell, on the subject of the embarkation of the Sea-Fencibles. They unanimously agree in one thing, of the loyalty of the men and of their readiness to fight in defence of their King and Country; but as they represent that the Sea-Fencibles are composed of a description of men not generally liable to be impressed, and that they have all an occupation in the several places where they are enrolled : that to the majority of them it would be little short of ruin were they to give up their business, many of the Fencibles are Merchants and Masters of Ships, who have come forward very handsomely, in order to encourage their men; therefore, with deference to their Lordships' better judgment, I beg leave to state that I have directed Cutters to go to such places and receive such volunteers as are to be got, and to remove our Ships now at the Nore into the Bay of Hosely, Wallet, and Margate Roads, that they may be ready to receive the Sea-Fencibles whenever the time arrives that every man must come forth, as when it comes to that point the business cannot last three days. I am led to believe that all our Sea-faring men would come forward with the greatest cheerfulness.

With respect to the River-Barges, it seems by all the Captains' account to be a species of defence which the Sea-Fencibles will attend to with pleasure ; therefore supposing that there are only twelve of these Vessels now at the Nore, I propose that four should be stationed on Whitstable Flats, under the direction (as to the manning and exercising them) of Captain Hamilton and the Captains under his directions; that six should instantly be sent to the mouth of Colchester and Malden river, under the direction of Captain Schomberg, and one in Woodbridge, and one in Orford river, under Captain Edge. Except from the necessity of placing large Ships in the Channels, the defence of our numerous landing-places is better adapted to our River-Barges, than any other which we could adopt, for they require few men to take care of them, and would always be manned in a few minutes from the Fencible Corps. I am led to hope that three hundred volunteers may be obtained from Essex and Suffolk; from Sussex and Kent, not a man has offered. The Fencibles of Ramsgate said to Captain Rudsdell, 'if two Gun-Brigs are assigned to us, we will man them on the spur of the moment;' but our first defence is close to the Enemy's Ports, and when that is broke, others will come forth on our own Coasts; but the Board have taken such precautions by having assigned such a respectable force under my orders, that I venture to express a well-grounded hope, that the Enemy would be annihilated before they get ten miles from their own shores; to accomplish which, nothing shall be wanting in the abilities of, Sir, your most obedient servant,

NELSON AND BRONTE.

TO CAPTAIN BEDFORD, H.M. SHIP LEYDEN.

[Letter-Book.]

[Medusa, at the Nore, August 10th, 1801.

Dear Sir,

I have just received your letter, and return you many thanks for your information respecting Flushing; but I must request you will keep everything as secret as possible, relative to my intentions, and take good care of your new Pilot, until I see you, which I hope will be in twenty-four hours. I shall be glad to have some conversation with him, as from your account, I am in hopes he may be of infinite use.

I have received directions from the Admiralty not to interfere with the Ships under Admiral Dickson's orders, and must therefore request you, when on the Coast of Flushing, to

be particularly guarded on that point, and, as far as the service will admit, never to go beyond the limits; but I think,
upon the whole, you had better remain in your present station until I see you, and keep the Brilliant with you, either
under sail, or as you like; but, above all, be particularly careful
not to let a word drop of what is now passing. I am, &c.

NELSON AND BRONTE.

TO CAPTAIN HAMILTON, MARGATE.

[Letter-Book.]

Medusa, Nore, August 11th, 1801.

Dear Sir,

Four River-Barges I have directed to be sent to Whitstable
Flats, and as they will only have the Master and two men, I
fancy, on board them, it is necessary that they should be laid
in a place of safety, in case of bad weather; and as they are intended to be under the direction of yourself and other Captains
of the Sea-Fencibles under your command, it is to be expected
that the Fencibles of Whitstable will frequently go on board,
and exercise not only the cannon, but get the Barges under
sail, and perform such exercises as may, in your judgment, be
best suited for the defence of that part of the Coast.

The Ardent and Serapis are to come into Margate Roads,
when Fencibles from your part of the Coast come forward and carry them down, and to take care of them when
anchored. Essex and Suffolk volunteer very near 500, who
are going on board the Ships stationed on the Coast of Essex
and Suffolk. Can no inducement get a few volunteers from
all the Craft which have so long been protected? State this
case, and say that if forty or fifty men can be placed in each
of the three Ships stationed at Margate, they can be relieved
by   on the other side. Every Fishing Smack and
Coaster gives one man. I shall sail for the Downs this day.
I hope to hear from you. I am, dear Sir, &c.

NELSON AND BRONTE.

TO EVAN NEPEAN, ESQ., ADMIRALTY.

[Original, in the Admiralty.]

Medusa, Nore, August 11th, 1801.

Sir,

The Medusa came to the Nore last night, in order that I might expedite the business going on here, and will sail for the Downs at two o'clock this afternoon. I have left a letter with Admiral Græme, requesting him to forward the River Barges to the several stations assigned them, and also the other Ships, when Sea-Fencibles can be got in sufficient numbers to navigate them to their several destinations. I have the honour to be, &c.

NELSON AND BRONTE.

TO LADY HAMILTON.

[Extract from " Lord Nelson's Letters to Lady Hamilton," &c., vol. i. p. 44.]

Sheerness, August 11th, 1801.

I came from Harwich yesterday noon; not having set my foot on shore, although the Volunteers, &c. were drawn up to receive me, and the people ready to draw the carriage. Parker had very near got all the honours...... I came on shore; for my business lays with the Admiral, who lives in a Ship hauled on shore, and the Commissioner. Slept at Coffin's; and, having done all that I can, am off for the Downs—to-day, if possible. As far as September 14th, I am at the Admiralty's disposal; but, if Mr. Buonaparte does not choose to send his miscreants before that time, my health will not bear me through equinoctial gales. I wish that Sir William was returned; I would try and persuade him to come to either Deal, Dover, or Margate; for, thus cut off from the society of my dearest friends, 'tis but a life of sorrow and sadness. But *patienza per forza!* The Mayor and Corporation of Sandwich, when they came on board to present me the Freedom of that ancient Town, requested me [to] dine with them. I put them off for the moment, but they would not be let off. Therefore, this business, *dreadful* to me, stands over, and I shall be attacked again when I get to the Downs.　But I will not dine there, without you say, approve; nor, perhaps, then, if I can get off.　Oh! how I hate to be stared at!　I am, &c.,

NELSON AND BRONTE.

TO ADMIRAL THE EARL OF ST. VINCENT, K.B.

[From Clarke and M'Arthur, vol. ii. p. 298.]

Sheerness, 11th August, 1801.

My dear Lord,

I came here last night, and found not one of the River Barges... Our active force is perfect, and possesses so much zeal, that I only wish to catch that Buonaparte on the water, either with the Amazon or Medusa; but himself he will never trust.　He would say, *Allez vous en,* and not *Allons, mes amis!*　I hope these French, if they come this year, mean to do it before the 14th of September, beyond which I fear the season will be too much for me.　I know not, my Lord, at this moment where I had best strike a blow, which I wish to be a very hard one: you have well guessed the place, Flushing, but I must be careful, and not cripple our Gun-Brigs.　At Ostend we cannot get at them, therefore I am anxious for our Howitzer Boats; but they will not keep pace with my wishes.　No person knows of my ideas except Captain Owen, who has been long stationed there under Admiral Lutwidge, and Captains Bedford and Parker.　I am, &c.,

NELSON AND BRONTE.

TO EVAN NEPEAN, ESQ., ADMIRALTY.

[Original, in the Admiralty.]

Medusa, Queen's Channel, August 12th, 1801.

Sir,

Having left all the necessary directions for the River-Barges, and also the alterations in the stations of the Glatton, Alceste, and Alliance, I left the Nore, and am proceeding to the Downs to be ready to perform such service as the times may require.　I am Sir, &c.

NELSON AND BRONTE.

TO THE RIGHT HONOURABLE HENRY ADDINGTON.

[Autograph, in the Sidmouth Papers.]

Medusa, off Margate, August 12th, 1801.

My dear Sir,

Sir Thomas Troubridge has given me permission, in confidence, to send for your perusal the enclosed letter from Sir Alexander Ball: the contents are of sufficient importance to merit your attention, and will, therefore, plead my apology for troubling you with it. When read, please to return it to Sir Thomas.

In my command I can tell you with truth, that I find much zeal and good humour; and should Mr. Buonaparte put himself in our way, I believe he will wish himself *even in Corsica.* I only hope, if he means to come, that it will be before the 14th of September, for my stamina is but ill-suited for equinoctial gales and cold weather. I feel much obliged by your kindness about the extension of my Title, and rely on your good intention for my brother. I hope you will hear of me soon. With every sentiment of respect, believe me, dear Sir, your most obliged,   NELSON AND BRONTE.

TO ADMIRAL THE EARL OF ST. VINCENT, K.B.

[From Clarke and M'Arthur, vol. ii. p. 298.]

Downs, August 13th, 1801.

My dear Lord,

I send you the reports of the Sea-Fencible Captains in Sussex and lower Kent, that you may give them, if you please, to Nepean, but I thought it as well not to lay them before the Board; for the Clerks in all the Public Office chatter so much, that nothing is a secret. I have reports from our Ships off Boulogne by a Neutral just arrived: the account of troops given by the French scoundrels in our pay, is as false as they are. I am certain that in the Towns of Boulogne and the surrounding hills, the total number could not exceed 2000 men. The Galgo arrived in the night from off Ostend; Captain Hawkins[5] assures me, that the Boats col-

-----

[5] Captain Richard Hawkins, of the Galgo: he was Posted in April 1802, and died about 1826.

lected at Ostend and Blakenberg, may amount to sixty or seventy, that he is sure they could not carry more than fifty or sixty men each; he understood that the poor devils of fishermen are sent off for Brest. Where, my dear Lord, is our Invasion to come from? The *time* is gone; owing to the precautions of Government, it cannot happen at this moment, and I hope that we shall always be as much on the alert as our Enemies. We must constantly guard our Coasts and the Flats; for Malden River and the Flats of Whitstable should always be ready for service.

I now come, my Lord, to consider of an attack—Flushing is my grand object; but so many obstacles are in the way, and the risk is so great of the loss of some Vessels, that, under all circumstances, I could hardly venture without a consultation with you, and an arranged plan, with the Board's orders. Might not a grand consultation be held for getting at the Dutch Ships at Helvoet, or to take possession of Flushing? But this must be a week's Expedition for 4000 or 5000 troops. To crush the Enemy at home was the favourite plan of Lord Chatham, and I am sure you think it the wisest measure to carry the war from our own doors. I purpose, if to be done, to take all the Gun-vessels outside the Pier of Boulogne—I should like your approbation. I own, my dear Lord, that this Boat warfare is not exactly congenial to my feelings, and I find I get laughed at for my puny mode of attack. I shall be happy to lead the way into Helvoet or Flushing, if Government will turn their thoughts to it: whilst I serve, I will do it actively, and to the very best of my abilities. I have all night had a fever, which is very little abated this morning; my mind carries me beyond my strength, and will do me up; but such is my nature. I have serious doubts whether I shall be able, from my present feelings, to go to the Mediterranean; but I will do what I can—I require nursing like a child. Pray God we may have peace, and with honour, and then let us start fair with the rest of Europe.

Thanks, joy, and congratulation on our success in Egypt; it makes me better, but I am very sick. Your letter of yesterday is just read. I shall be gone, God willing, to-morrow; but no attack for probably two nights, to throw them off their guard. I am, &c.

NELSON AND BRONTE.

TO EVAN NEPEAN, ESQ., ADMIRALTY.

[Original, in the Admiralty.]

Sir,   Medusa, Downs, August 13th, 1801.

As Captain Thesiger is arrived in England, I beg leave to state to you, for the information of their Lordships, the services of Captain Thesiger, also of the Desirée, and of Lieutenant Charlton of the Hasty Gun-brig, on the 2nd of April last. Captain Thesiger came on board the Elephant, and assisted me during the Action. When the Danish force was nearly subdued, under a very heavy fire from all the batteries, he carried on shore my first letter, and brought off the Adjutant-General, Lindholm, to me. Captain Thesiger was also ever forward to render me, and the Public service, all the assistance in his power, and on every occasion conducted himself to my entire satisfaction. It is my duty also, to state the peculiar merits of the Desirée beyond all other Frigates. She was fixed to a station of the greatest importance, and with such judgment by Captain Inman, that he lost not a man, but cut the Provestein, a Ship carrying 36 and 24-pounders, to pieces. The Desirée grounded, exposed to a battery of three or five guns, which would have tore her to pieces but for the gallantry and skill of Lieutenant Charlton[6] of the Hasty Gun-brig, who dismounted the guns in the battery. The Desirée was also got afloat, contrary to the opinion of many Officers, certainly by the meritorious exertions of the Officers and Men, who did not go to bed for two days and nights. I have thought it my duty to state these highly praiseworthy services, as deserving their Lordships' protection. I have the honour to be, &c.   NELSON AND BRONTE.

TO ALEXANDER DAVISON, ESQ.

[Autograph, in the possession of Colonel Davison.]

Medusa, Downs, August 13th, 1801.

My dear Friend,

I send you a letter from the Treasury. When you touch this money you can make a first payment. *Before* Mr. Buona-

---

[6] Lieutenant William Charlton had then been a Lieutenant nineteen years; and, notwithstanding this high encomium, he was not promoted until 1806: in 1808 he was appointed to the Sappho, and died before 1814.

parte arrives, I cannot, with our preparations, careless as the French Government is of its soldiers, believe them capable of ordering, or the soldiers passive enough to obey such a mad order, as to put to sea. I am very much fagged, and from my soul wish it was all over, and I quiet in my nest again. Have you sent to Rundell and Bridge about the last batch of plate—I mean the Danish batch? How are you? Let us hear of you. I am going to-morrow to the French Coast; but there is nothing to be done on the great Scale. I beg my compliments to Mrs. Davison, and to your children; and believe me ever, my dear Davison, your truly obliged friend,

NELSON AND BRONTE.

TO EVAN NEPEAN, ESQ., ADMIRALTY.

[Autograph, in the Admiralty.]

Medusa, Sea, August 14th, 1801.

Sir,

Your letter to me at Sheerness came to me this morning after my leaving the Downs, and I shall pay due attention to the information of Cherbourg and of Flushing. Would their Lordships wish me to look at Cherbourg? but I suppose it is guarded by the Ships off Havre. I am, Sir, &c.

NELSON AND BRONTE.

TO ADMIRAL LUTWIDGE.

[Autograph, in the possession of Major Lutwidge.]

Medusa, August 14th, 1801.

My dear Admiral,

I am still very unwell, and my head is swelled. I hope you will forgive my not waiting upon you yesterday, but my head was split with pain. If you do not particularly want the King George to-morrow, will you allow her to bring out letters, and also, if the weather is moderate, to tow over two Flat-boats, which I could not bring over? They are on board Captain Martin of the Experience—at least, he has the management of them. In doing this, you will truly oblige your most affectionate,

NELSON AND BRONTE.

TO CAPTAIN RUSSEL, H. M. SLOOP GIER.

[Autograph, in the possession of Thomas Russel, Esq.]

Sir,   Medusa, August 15th, 1801.

I send you dispatches for Renard. I believe you have got the signals of sails necessary to point out the Vessel having dispatches to send, or appointed to receive. You will get the dispatches sent herewith on shore as soon as possible. I am, Sir, &c.   NELSON AND BRONTE.

Return the Fox directly, and I wish you could ascertain whether the French Vessels remain in Dunkirk Roads all night, as I could send my Flotilla to attack them.

Signals I believe are—Ship, Mizen-topsail furled; Brig, Fore-topsail furled; Lugger, Mizen furled; Cutter, Foresail down.

PLAN OF ATTACK ON THE ENEMY'S FLOTILLA AT BOULOGNE.

[From a Copy in the possession of the Right Hon. John Wilson Croker.]

On board the Medusa, off Boulogne, 15th August, 1801.

Eight Flat Boats, with 8-inch howitzers, with a Lieutenant in each, and fourteen men, to be under the direction of Captain Conn.[8] Artillerymen to be in them, as arranged by Captain Brome.

Six flat Boats, with 24-pounder carronades, with a Lieutenant in each, besides Seamen, and eight Marines, with the number of Boats hereafter specified, to be under the command of Captains Somerville, Cotgrave,[9] Jones,[1] and Parker.

This force, under the direction of the four Captains beforementioned, is to be divided into four Squadrons, consisting of   Boats each; and two Boats of each of those Divisions to be particularly allotted and prepared for the purpose of cutting the Enemy's cable and sternfast, and to be furnished with stout hook-ropes, to be the more ready to take them in tow. The others are to attract the opponent Divisions, which is to be done at last quarter-flood, at the Pier-head. When any

---

[8] Captain John Conn: he was Posted in 1802, commanded the Dreadnought at Trafalgar, and was drowned by falling overboard, while Captain of the Swiftsure, in May 1810.

[9] Captain Isaac Cotgrave was Posted in April 1802, and was for many years Agent for French Prisoners at Plymouth. He died in 1814.

[1] Captain Richard Jones, of the Diligence: he was a Lieutenant of the Defence at the Nile, and was then made a Commander. Captain Jones was Posted in April 1802, and died about 1829.

Boats have taken one Vessel, the business is not to be considered as finished; but a sufficient number being left to guard the Prize, the others are immediately to pursue the object, by proceeding on to the next, and so on, until the whole of the Flotilla be either taken, or totally annihilated; for there must not be the smallest cessation until their destruction is completely finished.

The Boats from the Ships are to be armed with pikes, cutlasses, and tomahawks, except the Marines, who, as usual, are to have their muskets, bayonets, and cartouch-boxes filled with ammunition. Every Boat is to have a broad-axe well sharpened, and likewise a carcase, or other combustible, with a match, ready to set the Enemy's Vessels on fire, should it be found impracticable to bring them off; but if it is possible they are to be brought off.

The First Division is to be under the direction of Captain Somerville, who is to attack the Enemy's Vessels at the Eastern end, and to consist of the following Boats:—

Flat Boats	2	
Leyden	4 Boats	
Eugenia	1	
Jamaica	2	
Nile	1	To assemble on board the Leyden.
Argus	1	
Queen	1	
Antelope	1	
	13	Total, 13.

Second Division, to be under Captain Parker, and to attack next to Captain Somerville:—

Flat Boats	2	
Medusa	4	
Snipe	1	
Eclipse	1	
Venus (1)	1	
Queenborough	1	
Hecla	1	To assemble on board the Medusa.
Hunter	1	
Hind	1	
Greyhound	1	
Minx	1	
	15	Total, 15.

Third Division, under Captain Cotgrave, to attack the Enemy with the following Boats, next to Captain Parker :—

Flat Boats	. .	2
York	. . . .	4
Gannet	. . .	1
Explosion	. . .	1
Ferret	. . . .	1
Lively	. . . .	1
Bruiser	. . .	1	To assemble on board the York.
Providence	. .	1
Express	. . .	1
Ranger	. . .	1
Lively	. . . .	1
		—
		15	Total, 15.

Fourth Division, under Captain Jones, to attack the Enemy with the following Boats, at their Westernmost part :—

Flat Boat	. . .	1
Isis	. . . .	4
Diligence	. . .	1
Plumper	. . .	1
Cygnet	. . .	1
Dolphin	. . .	1
Sulphur	. . .	1	To assemble on board the Isis.
Renown	. . .	1
King George	.	1
Active	. . . .	1
Stag	. . . .	1
		—
		14	Total, 14.

All the Boats remaining are to be in readiness, manned and armed, on board the different Ships and Vessels, to put off the moment the firing begins, that they may afford all the assistance in their power.

The Revenue, Hired, and other fast-sailing Cutters, after the firing has commenced, are to keep close in shore, to be ready to tow the Enemy's Vessels out, as they are captured.

Captain Conn, who commands the Division of Howitzer-Boats, which are to assemble on board the Discovery as soon

after sunset as possible, is directed to put off the same time
the signal is given for other Boats, and to row as near as possible to the centre of the Pier-head, and when the attack is
begun by us, or by the Enemy, he is to open his fire from the
howitzers upon the batteries and camp.

It is directed that each Division of Boats be formed into two
Sub-divisions, and to be made fast to one another as close as
possible. The Captain commanding the Division is to lead
one, and any Lieutenant he pleases to appoint, the other.

The Boats are on no account to cut, or separate from one
another, until they are close on board the Enemy.

The Captains commanding the Divisions have permission to
make any additional arrangements in the mode of attack they
may think will more easily facilitate it, and the subordinate
Officers are strictly directed to carry into execution, with the
utmost alacrity and attention, all such orders as they may
receive. The greatest silence is to be observed by all the
people in the Boats, and the oars to be muffled.

The Commander-in-Chief relies with the most perfect confidence on the unanimous exertions of the Officers and Men
under his command, for the complete success of the enterprise.

It is recommended that, at half-past ten, the Boats shall be
manned, and at eleven o'clock by the watch, that the Divisions
of Boats shall, by the signal of six lanterns, hung over the
guns of the Medusa, put off, and row in the order prescribed
under the Medusa's stern, from whence they will start as soon
as all are arrived.

Watchword. . . . . . Nelson.
The Answer . . . . . Bronte.
NELSON AND BRONTE.

MEMORANDA FOR SHIPS.

[Autograph draught, in the possession of the Right Hon. John Wilson Croker.]

15th August, 1801.

Jamaica's Boats to go to the Leyden at Noon, and then the
Jamaica, Gannet, and the three Gun Brigs, with Captain
Rose, to resume their stations.

Ten Revenue Cutters to be sent off at Noon to the eastward, and not to approach the Road till after dark, or the

firing begins; but they are to send their Boat, manned and armed, to the Ship directed.

Captain Somerville to go to the Leyden, and arrange his Division; Captain Cotgrave to the York, and Captain Jones to the Isis.

Captain Bedford to send two of the Howitzer-Boats to the Discovery, calling alongside the Medusa for the two Boats' crews.

Captain Bedford to deliver three Howitzer-boats to the Isis.

NELSON AND BRONTE.

MEMORANDUM RESPECTING MEN IN THE DOCK-YARDS.

[Autograph draught, in the possession of the Right Hon. John Wilson Croker.]

As men are wanted when the Enemy may actually approach our Coast, 100 men under the Master Attendants, could be fixed to man No. and 2; and 30, at least, good men, and very seldom in quarantine, can be had from the Lazarettos in Stangate Creek; therefore Flat boats [*unfinished.*]

Ardent—To go off Margate Sand, as stated in the Mem.
Unité.
Daphne.
Serapis.
Alliance.—Swab Way.
  Ruby, 64.
  Conflict.
  Monkey.

TO ADMIRAL THE EARL OF ST. VINCENT, K.B.

[Original, in the Admiralty.]

Medusa, off Boulogne, August 16th, 1801.

My dear Lord,

I am sorry to tell you that I have not succeeded in bringing out or destroying the Enemy's Flotilla moored in the mouth of the harbour of Boulogne. The most astonishing bravery was evinced by many of our Officers and men, and Captains Somerville, Cotgrave, and Parker, exerted themselves to the utmost. We have lost many brave Officers and men: upwards of 100 killed and wounded. Dear little

Parker, his thigh very much shattered; I have fears for his life. Langford shot through the leg. The loss has been heavy, and the object was great. The Flotilla, Brigs, and Flats, were moored by the bottom to the shore, and to each other with chains; therefore, although several of them were carried, yet the heavy fire of musketry from the shore which overlooked them, forced our people to leave them, without being able, as I am told, to set them on fire. No person can be blamed for sending them to the attack but myself; I knew the difficulty of the undertaking, therefore I ventured to ask your opinion. Your kind letter I received half an hour before the attack; but, my dear Lord, although I disapprove of unnecessary consultations as much as any man, yet [being] close to the Admiralty, I should not feel myself justified in risking our Ships through the Channels of Flushing without buoys and pilots, without a consultation of such men as your Lordship, and also I believe you would think an order absolutely necessary; but that must stand fast, for both Leyden and Medusa have lost all their best men—none else, of course, being sent.

Captain Somerville, who I never saw till a few days ago, showed all the courage and good conduct which was possible, and succeeded completely in the fighting part of the business. Conn, in the command of the Howitzer-Boats, did everything which was possible; indeed all behaved well, and it was their misfortune to be sent on a service which the precautions of the Enemy rendered impossible to succeed in. After all this sorrow for me, my health is not improved; my fever is very severe this morning, but believe me ever, my dear Lord, your obliged and affectionate,

NELSON AND BRONTE.

The Medusa cannot move till she gets some good men, nor, I believe, the Leyden. The Unité would complete both these Ships, taking some Marines. This Ship has lost seventeen killed, and thirty wounded, with two Lieutenants, Master, Mids, &c. Young Cathcart[1] behaved most exceedingly well;

---

[1] The Honourable William Cathcart, eldest son of William Schaw, tenth Lord Cathcart, afterwards General Earl Cathcart, K.T. He was then an Acting Lieutenant; and Captain Parker, in his Official Letter to Lord Nelson, said—" I feel myself at a loss for words to do justice to the Officers and men of the Medusa who were in the Boat with me, and to Lieutenant Langford, the Officers and crew of the same Ship,

he saved Parker from either being killed or a prisoner, for every man in Parker's Flat-boat being killed or wounded, and his Boat drifted from the Brig, alongside a Flat full of men. I shall write to the Admiralty, so soon as I get the reports.

TO EVAN NEPEAN, ESQ., ADMIRALTY.

[Autograph, in the Admiralty. Printed in the "London Gazette" of the 18th August, 1801.]

Medusa, off Boulogne, August 16th, 1801.

Sir,

Having judged it proper to attempt bringing off the Enemy's Flotilla moored in the front of Boulogne, I directed the attack to be made by four Divisions of Boats for boarders, under the command of Captain Somerville, Cotgrave, Jones, and Parker, and a division of Howitzer Boats under Captain Conn. The Boats put off from the Medusa at half-past eleven o'clock last night, in the best possible order, and before one o'clock this morning, the firing began, and I had, from the judgment of the Officers and the zeal and gallantry of every man, the most perfect confidence of complete success; but the darkness of the night, with the tide and half-tide, separated the Divisions; and from all not arriving at the same happy moment with Captain Parker, is to be attributed the failure of success. But I beg to be perfectly understood that not the smallest blame attaches itself to any person; for although the Divisions did not arrive together, yet each (except the fourth Division, which could not be got up before day,) made a successful attack on that part of the Enemy they fell in with, and actually took possession of many Brigs and Flats, and cut their cables; but many of them being aground, and the moment of the Battle's ceasing on board them, the Vessels were filled with volleys upon volleys of musketry, the Enemy

who nobly seconded us in the Barge, until all her crew were killed or wounded; and to the Honourable Mr. Cathcart, who commanded the Medusa's Cutter, and sustained the attack with the greatest intrepidity, until the desperate situation I was left in obliged me to call him to the assistance of the sufferers in my Boat." . . . . . . " The Flat Boat in which I was, being alongside, and as there was not an Officer or man left to govern her, must have fallen into the hands of the Enemy, had not Mr. Cathcart taken her in tow and carried her off." (London Gazette, 18th August, 1802.) This gallant young Officer died, Captain of the Clorinde, at Jamaica, on the 5th of June, 1804, aged twenty-two.

being perfectly regardless of their own men, who must have suffered equally with us. It was therefore impossible to remain on board, even to burn them; but allow me to say, who have seen much service this war, that more determined, persevering courage, I never witnessed, and that nothing but the impossibility of being successful, from the causes I have mentioned, could have prevented me from having to congratulate their Lordships. But although, in value, the loss of such gallant and good men is incalculable, yet in point of numbers it has fallen short of my expectations. I must also beg leave to state that greater zeal and ardent desire to distinguish themselves by an attack on the Enemy, was never shown than by all the Captains, Officers, and Crews of all the different descriptions of Vessels under my command. The Commanders of the Hunter and Greyhound, Revenue-Cutters, went in their Boats, in the most handsome and gallant manner, to the attack. Amongst the many gallant men wounded, I have, with the deepest regret, to place the name of my gallant, good friend and able assistant, Captain Edward T. Parker, also my Flag Lieutenant, Frederick Langford,[2] who has served with me many years; they were wounded in attempting to board the French Commodore.

To Captain Gore,[3] of the Medusa, I feel the highest obligations; and when their Lordships look at the loss of the Medusa on this occasion, they will agree with me, that the honour of my Flag, and the cause of their King and Country, could never have been placed in more gallant hands. Captain Bedford, of the Leyden, with Captain Gore, very handsomely volunteered their services to serve under a Master and Commander; but I did not think it fair to the latter, and I only mention it to mark the zeal of those officers. From the nature of the attack, only a few prisoners were made; a Lieutenant, eight seamen, and eight soldiers, are all they brought off. Herewith I send the report of the several Commanders of Divisions, and a return of killed and wounded. I have the honour to be, &c.　　　NELSON AND BRONTE.

Captain Somerville was the Senior Master and Commander employed.

---

[2] Captain Frederick Langford: he was made a Commander in 1801, Posted in November 1806, and died about 1814.

[3] Captain Gore, afterwards Vice-Admiral Sir John Gore, K.C.B., G.C.H.

AN ACCOUNT OF OFFICERS, SEAMEN, AND MARINES, KILLED
AND WOUNDED, IN THE BOATS OF HIS MAJESTY'S SHIPS AND
VESSELS IN THE ATTACK OF THE FRENCH FLOTILLA MOORED
BEFORE BOULOGNE, ON THE NIGHT OF THE 15TH AUGUST,
1801.

SHIPS.	KILLED.				WOUNDED.			
	Officers.	Seamen.	Marines.	Total Killed.	Officers.	Seamen.	Marines.	Total Wounded.
1st Division.								
Leyden	..	8	3	11	5	20	15	40
Eugenie	..	3	..	3	1	5	..	6
Jamaica	1	3	..	4	1	4	4	9
2nd Division.								
Medusa	2	14	4	20	5	24	6	35
Queenborough (Cutter)	..	1	..	1	..	6	..	6
Minx	..	..	..	..	1	..	..	1
3rd Division.								
York	1 Mid.	2	..	3	1	10	5	16
Gannet	..	1	..	1	..	2	..	2
Ferreter	..	..	..	..	..	3	..	3
Providence	..	..	..	..	..	3	..	3
Express	..	..	..	..	..	4	..	4
Explosion	..	1	..	1	..	2	..	2
Discovery	..	..	..	..	..	1	..	1
4th Division.	4	33	7	44	14	84	30	128
None Killed or Wounded.								

NAMES OF OFFICERS KILLED AND WOUNDED.

Belonging to the Leyden.
{ Lieutenant Thomas Oliver
Lieutenant Francis Dickenson } badly
Captain Young, of the Marines }
Mr. Francis Burney, Master's Mate
Mr. Samuel Spratley, Midshipman } Wounded.

Eugenie.   Mr. William Bussel, Acting Lieut.   Wounded.

Jamaica.
{ Mr. Alexander Rutherford, Master's
Mate . . . .   Killed.
Lieutenant Jeremiah Skelton . .   Wounded.

	Mr. William Gore, Midshipman	Killed.
	Mr. William Bristow, Midshipman	
	Captain Edward Thornbrough Parker,	
	Lord Nelson's Aid-de-Camp	
Medusa.	Lieutenants Charles Pelley, and Frederick Langford	Wounded.
	Mr. William Kirby, Master	
	The Honourable Anthony Maitland,[4] Midshipman	
York.	Mr. Berry, Midshipman . . . . Killed.	
	Mr. Brown, Gunner . . . . . Wounded.	

NELSON AND BRONTE.

Medusa, August 16th, 1801.

Mr. Richard Wilkinson, Commander of the Greyhound Revenue Cutter, wounded; and one Seaman, belonging to the Greyhound, likewise wounded.

TO EVAN NEPEAN, ESQ., ADMIRALTY.

[Original, in the Admiralty.]

Medusa, Downs, 17th August, 1801.

Sir,

I beg you will be pleased to acquaint their Lordships that I arrived at this anchorage last night, and that his Majesty's Ship Leyden arrived this morning. The Dart, Otter, and Savage joined me here. I enclose you the defects of the Savage; and, with their Lordships' approbation, I will order her to Sheerness to be repaired, if it is possible to be done. I am, &c.

NELSON AND BRONTE.

[4] Now Rear-Admiral the Honourable Sir Anthony Maitland, K.C.M.G. and C.B., who commanded the Glasgow at Algiers, in 1816.

TO ADMIRAL THE EARL OF ST. VINCENT, K.B.

[Autograph in the possession of Vice-Admiral Sir William Parker, Bart., G.C.B.]

Medusa, Downs, August 17th, 1801.

My dear Lord,

I send you Captain Somerville's account of a young man,[5] who is wounded, acting in a real vacancy on board the Eugenie (a miserable tool), who behaves exceedingly well, and has passed his examination. He is deserving of a Commission. Also, I send a memorandum of Captain Bedford's for a young man[6] of his. He is willing to take him in the Leyden. Ever yours faithfully,

NELSON AND BRONTE.

TO ADMIRAL THE EARL OF ST. VINCENT, K.B.

[From Clarke and M'Arthur, vol. ii. p. 301.]

17th to 19th August, 1801.

Most Secret.

My dear Lord,

I have real thoughts of attacking the Enemy at Flushing, if it be possible to be done, the moment Leyden and Medusa are manned. In that event I must run great risk, and only beg to be supported in case of failure. P.M. I find by Captain Owen's letters off Flushing, three days ago, that all the Dutch Vessels have moved lower down the Doerlog Channel, evidently to defend it : I will go and look at them ; but attack I cannot, without Pilots, nor without sanction. I own I shall never bring myself again to allow any attack to go forward, where I am not personally concerned ; my mind suffers much more than if I had a leg shot off in this late business. I am writing between poor Parker and Langford ; therefore I must beg great indulgences, only believe that I will do my utmost : I am ready to assist the good Cause, and have no other view in my mind. Had our force arrived, as I intended, 'twas not

---

[5] Mr. William Bussel, Acting Lieutenant of the Eugenie : he was promoted on the following day.

[6] John Little : he was also promoted on the 18th August. Both these Officers were still Lieutenants in 1814.

all the chains in France that could have prevented our folks
from bringing off the whole of the Vessels.

August 18th.—To-night seven Howitzer-Boats will be at
work on them, and if we can get the Commodore's Brig at the
Harbour's mouth on fire, many of them will be burnt. Captain
Conn, whom you got promoted, has, under Captain Ferrier,[7]
the entire direction of this business; and a more zealous, deserving Officer never was brought forward. Captain Ferrier
you do not know; therefore it becomes me to tell you, that
his Ship is in the very first order, and that he is a man of
sense, and as steady as old Time himself: I am much pleased
with his regularity and punctuality. Every one speaks of
Captain Somerville's coolness and gallant conduct. I would
not, for the world, have even my dear Parker promoted at the
expense of Captain Somerville, who was an entire stranger to
me. Believe me, my dear Lord, I have no interest but for
the Public service. I am fixed to look at Flushing, and prepared to attack it, if the Pilots can be persuaded to take
Leyden up; if it be within the pale of possibility, it shall be
attempted. My dear Parker is, I fear, in a very bad way.

August 19th.—I believe Calais could be bombarded, but do
you think it is an object? I should not like the Bombs to go
without me. Heavy sea, sick to death—this sea-sickness I
shall never get over. I am, &c.

NELSON AND BRONTE.

TO THE SQUADRON.

[From the "Naval Chronicle," vol. vi. p. 160.]

Medusa, Downs, August 18th, [1801.]

Vice-Admiral Lord Nelson has the greatest satisfaction in
sending to the Captains, Officers, and men under his command, that were employed in the late attempt on the Enemy's
Flotilla off Boulogne, an Extract[8] of a Letter which he has

---

[7] Captain John Ferrier: he became a Rear Admiral in 1810, and died an Admiral
of the Blue between 1834 and 1836.

[8] " It is not given to us to command success. Your Lordship, and the gallant
Officers and men under your orders, most certainly deserve it; and I cannot sufficiently express my admiration of the zeal and persevering courage with which this

received from the First Lord of the Admiralty, not only approving of their zeal and persevering courage, but bestowing the highest praise on them.

The Vice-Admiral begs to assure them that the Enemy will not have long reason to boast of their security; for he trusts ere long to assist them in person in a way which will completely annihilate the whole of them. Lord Nelson is convinced, that if it had been possible for man to have brought the Enemy's Flotilla out, the men that were employed to do so would have accomplished it. The moment the Enemy have the audacity to cast off the chains which fix their Vessels to the ground, that moment Lord Nelson is well persuaded they will be conducted by his brave followers to a British Port, or sent to the bottom.

NELSON AND BRONTE.

TO CAPTAIN RUSSEL, H.M. SLOOP GIER.

[Autograph, in the possession of Thomas Russel, Esq.]

Medusa, Downs, August 18th, 1801.

Sir,

I am very sorry to hear of the escape of the Enemy from Dunkirk into Calais. I believe yourself, and every Officer under you, kept as good a look-out as was possible; but you may be sure they passed inside of you. Can Calais Mole be bombarded with the chance of destroying these Vessels? Let me know your opinion, and you must now look out that they do not escape from Calais. Has not the Repulse Revenue Cutter joined you? I sent her two days ago. I am Sir, &c.

NELSON AND BRONTE.

---

gallant enterprise was followed up, lamenting most sincerely the loss sustained in it. The manner in which the Enemy's Flotilla was made fast to the ground, and to each other, could not have been foreseen. The highest praise is due to your Lordship, and all under your command who were actors in this gallant attempt. I am, &c., ST. VINCENT."

TO LADY HAMILTON.

[Extracts from " Lord Nelson's Letters to Lady Hamilton," vol. i. p. 48.]

Deal, August 18th, 1801.

I have this morning been attending the Funeral of two young Mids: a Mr. Gore, cousin of Captain Gore, and a Mr. Bristow.[9] One nineteen, the other seventeen years of age. Last night, I was all the evening in the Hospital, seeing that all was done for the comfort of the poor fellows. I am going on board. . . . . I shall come in the morning, to see Parker, and go on board again directly. . . . . You ask me what Troubridge wrote me? There was not a syllable about you in it. It was about my not coming to London; at the importance of which, I laughed; and then he said, he should never venture another opinion. On which, I said—'Then I shall never give you one.' This day, he has wrote a kind letter, and all is over. I have, however, wrote him, in my letter of this day as follows—viz. ' And I am, this moment, as firmly of opinion as ever, that Lord St. Vincent and yourself should have allowed of my coming to Town for my own affairs; for, every one knows, I left it without a thought of myself.' . . . . But this business cannot last long, and I hope we shall have Peace; and I rather incline to that opinion. . . . . I have wrote a line to Troubridge about Darby. Parker will write you a line of thanks, if he is able. I trust in God, he will yet do well! You ask me, my dear Friend, if I am going on more Expeditions? And, even if I was to forfeit your friendship, which is dearer to me than all the world, I can tell you nothing. For, I go out; [if] I see the Enemy, and can get at them, it is my duty: and you would naturally hate me, if I kept back one moment. I long to pay them, for their tricks t'other day, the debt of a drubbing, which, surely, I'll pay: but *when, where, or how,* it is impos-

---

[9] " Lord Nelson followed their bodies to the ground with eight Captains of the Navy, preceded by a file of Marines, who fired three vollies over the place of their interment ; an immense crowd of spectators were present to witness this last tribute of respect to the memory of two gallant young Officers, who were an ornament to that Profession in which they so nobly fell. His Lordship was sensibly affected during the funeral, and was seen to shed tears."—*Naval Chronicle,* vol. vi. 172.

sible, your own good sense must tell you, for me or mortal man to say. I shall act not in a rash or hasty manner, that you may rely, and on which I give you my word of honour.

NELSON AND BRONTE.

TO THE RIGHT HONOURABLE HENRY ADDINGTON.

[Autograph, in the Sidmouth Papers.]

Medusa, Downs, August 21st, 1801.

My dear Sir,

I send you two letters and a Note from General Dumourier.[1] What weight to put upon them you know best. Had our Boats, in my late attempt, arrived at the same moment, the

---

[1] The two Letters alluded to are in the Nelson Papers. The Note alluded to in the first of these Letters has not been found:

"Ottensen par Altona le 6 Aoust, 1801.

"Mon cher Nelson, mon héroïque ami, vous devez avoir trouvé deux ou trois de mes lettres à votre arrivée à Londres. Je désire avoir promptement des nouvelles de votre prétieuse santé; vous êtes encore nécessaire à votre Patrie, et il serait très heureux qu'elle pût vous multiplier, mais vos copies ne sont pas aussi heureuses que l'original. Je ne suis pas assez fort dans votre langue pour vous épargner aujourd'hui la peine de me lire en Francais. Ils s'agit de matières très sérieuses du salut de votre Patrie et de l'Europe; je consigne dans la note ci jointe mes inquiétudes, et c'est à vous que je l'adresse; faites en l'usage que vous croîrez utile; et ajoutez un peu de confiance à mon expérience et à mes méditations. Faites mes tendres compliments à Lord Witworth; je suis pénétré pour lui d'amitié et de reconnaissance, quoiqu'il m'ait oublié.

"J'ai beaucoup étudié pendant 20 ans la matière de cette note; alors c'était comme militaire Français que j'étudiais les moyens de descendre sur vos côtes, à present un intérêt plus noble nous unit à la même cause, celle des Rois, de la Réligion, des Mœurs et des Loix. Leur sort, celui de l'Europe entière, est attaché au salut de votre Patrie, soyez la caution du désir que j'ai d'y contribuer. A cet intérêt général se joint celui de la tendre amitié qui m'unit à vous pour la vie.

"DU MOURIEZ.

"P.S.—Qu'on ne prenne pas l'échange sur les points d'attaque; l'espèce d'embarcations qui composent la flotille n'est propre qu'à traverser la Manche, et ne peut servir ni pour l'Ecosse ni pour l'Irlande."

"Ottensen par Altona, No. 43, le 11 Aoust, 1801.

"Mon héroïque ami, lorsque je vous ai écrit ma lettre du [6me], j'ignorais que vous fussiez chargé de la défense navale de votre Patrie; j'en fais mon compliment autant à votre Nation qu'à vous même. Souvenez vous du désir que vous m'avez témoigné de m'avoir pour votre frère d'armes. Ce n'est pas contre ma patrie que je desire de les porter, mais contre ses usurpateurs et ses tyrans. Vous aurez trouvé ma note importante, et vous l'aurez certainement communiquée à votre ministère. Elle demanderait des détails que je ne pourrais donner que de bouche, sur la carte, et encore mieux sur le terrain. Si on le jugeait utile, vous pourriez m'envoyer chercher par une frégate; je partirais incognito, j'arriverais de même; on pourrait m'ar-

whole would have come over to our shores. Our loss is trifling, all circumstances considered. I purpose looking at Flushing, and if it is possible, I will go up and attack the Ships in that Road; but I fear no Pilots will take charge of our Ships, and it is a melancholy thing when the honour of our Country is obliged to be submitted to a man of that class. Lord St. Vincent tells me he hates Councils, so do I between Military men; for if a man consults whether he is to fight, when he has the power in his own hands, *it is certain that his opinion is against fighting*; but that is not the case at present, and I own I do want good council. Lord St. Vincent is for keeping the Enemy closely blockaded; but I see that they get along shore inside their Sandbanks, and under their guns, which line the Coast of France. Lord Hood is for keeping our Squadrons of Defence stationary on our own shore, (except light Cutters, to give information of every movement of the Enemy;) for the time is approaching when a gale of westerly wind will disperse our light Squadrons. Under Dungeness, Downs, Margate Roads and Hosely Bay are good stations. When men of such good sense, such great Sea Officers, differ so widely, is it not natural that I should wish the mode of defence to be well arranged by the mature consideration of men of judgment? I mean not to detract from my judgment; even as it is, it is well known : but I boast of nothing but my zeal; in that I will give way to no man upon earth. With every sentiment of respect, regard, and esteem, believe me, my dear Sir, your most obliged and obedient servant,

NELSON AND BRONTE.

ranger un logement hors de Londrès, ou bien je me tiendrais auprès de vous pour vous seconder, et en rendant service à votre Patrie et à mon ami Nelson, je pourrais hâter le moment de renverser un gouvernement qui renversera tous les autres s'il dure.

"On vient de me communiquer une lettre d'un capitaine d'une des frégates de la flotte de Brest. Il dit que toute la flotte se pourvoit de vivres pour six à sept mois ce qui supposerait un voyage de long cours. Peut-être est elle destinée, en tout ou en partie, à l'expédition de l'Inde, qui avait été arrangée il y a deux ans pour l'Amiral Villaret. Si cette flotte, ou une de ses divisions, va dans l'Inde, c'est pour prendre possession de Goa, et vous enlever ou le Cap, ou Ceilan ; ce peut-être réellement une destination secondaire, en cas que Bonaparte perde l'espoir de la descente en Angleterre. Il faut pourvoir à tout, sans faux calcul.

"J'attends incessamment de vos nouvelles, et je compte sur votre amitié comme vous pouvez comptez sur la mienne. Farewell, and be happy.

"D."

Last night, at seven o'clock, there was fired from Dunkirk
and Boulogne a *feu de joie.*

Your kind letter of the 19th, I have just received. Captain
Parker, I have great hopes, will in time do well. His thigh
is broken in two places, and so high up, that if it does not
unite, it cannot be amputated. All the rest of the wounded
are doing full as well as could be expected. I beg you will
accept my warmest thanks for your letter. Your kind approbation of my endeavours must be very pleasing to me.

TO CAPTAIN OWEN.

[Letter-Book.]

Medusa, Downs, August 23rd, 1801.

Sir,

The moment the men arrive from   for the Leyden
and Medusa, which I hope will be this day, I shall come immediately off Flushing; and, from your account that I can
get at the Enemy, it is my intention to proceed, with all the
force with me, up either the Welling Channel or the Denloo,
as you shall point out, from your knowledge, as the most
proper. On this side I can get no Pilots, who will take
charge without the buoys being placed; but I rejoice that you
have got some who can lead us the right Channel. You will
keep all your Vessels ready for action, and join me yourself
the moment I get sight of you, that not a moment may be lost
after my arrival. Perhaps you have people with you who can
place Vessels where the buoys used to be lying; if so, we can
hoist single and double flags to mark the Channel. I am,
Sir, &c.,

NELSON AND BRONTE.

TO EVAN NEPEAN, ESQ., ADMIRALTY.

[Original, in the Admiralty, and "London Gazette" of 25th August, 1801.]

Medusa, Downs, August 23rd, 1801.

Sir,

Herewith I transmit you two letters, which I have received
from Captains Rose and Sarradine,[2] giving me an account of

---

[2] Captain George Sarradine: he died a Commander in 1805.

the Boats of the several Vessels under their orders having burnt a quantity of pitch, tar, and turpentine, destroyed three Gun-boats, took two Launches, and a Flat-boat about forty-five feet long, and eighteen or twenty wide, mounted with one brass 8-inch howitzer : this Boat sunk astern of the Hound. The business on the part of our Boats was conducted with much spirit ; and much praise is due to Lieutenant Agassiz [3] of the Hound, and Lieutenant le Viscont [4] of the Jamaica, for their brave example on this occasion. I have the honour to be, &c.

NELSON AND BRONTE.

MEMORANDUM.

[Letter-Book.]

Medusa, Downs, 23rd August, 1801.

Enclosed to the Commissioners of the Customs two letters which I had received from Lieutenant Sayers, commanding the Express, respecting spirits which he had seized on board the Brig Williams, belonging to   , in Cornwall, and stated the conduct of the Tide Surveyor at Deal as highly reprehensible (in my opinion) for not acquainting Lieutenant Sayers when he took the spirits out of the Brig, and for saying that the Vessel could be done nothing to, in consequence of her having a regular clearance from the Port where she took in her cargo of iron. In my opinion she ought to have been detained, to answer for having the spirits on board her.

TO ADMIRAL LUTWIDGE.

[Autograph, in the possession of Major Lutwidge.]

Medusa, West Capel, August 24th, 1801.

My dear Admiral,

Six Pilots say that it is impossible, without buoys or beacons, for our Ships to go to Flushing ; and that if all the

---

[3] Lieutenant James John Charles Agassiz : he was made a Commander in April 1802, and retired as a Post-Captain in September 1840.

[4] Lieutenant Philip le Viscont : he was wounded, while a Midshipman of the Monarch, at Copenhagen, and was made a Lieutenant in the following month. In 1816, he was promoted to the rank of Commander.

buoys and beacons were as usual, that we could not return
without a fair wind and flowing water. Had I known as
much before I sailed from the Downs, I would not have come
such a wild-goose chase; but Captain Owen is close to us,
and I shall know all Captain Owen's ideas. His zeal, I am
afraid, has made him overleap sandbanks and tides, and laid
him aboard the Enemy; but I must clear away these little
obstacles before I can give him scope for intentions. I admire
his desire, and could join most heartily in it; but we cannot do impossibilities, and I am as little used to find out the
impossibles as most folks; and I think I can discriminate
between the impracticable and the fair prospect of success.
I have seen Captain Owen, and find it as I suppose. Ever
yours faithfully,

NELSON AND BRONTE.

TO ADMIRAL THE EARL OF ST. VINCENT, K.B.

[From Clarke and M'Arthur, vol. ii. p. 302.]

My dear Lord,　　　　　　　　At Sea, 24th August, 1801.

I weighed from the Downs: sending, after we were under
sail, for old Yawkins,[5] a knowing one. I examined him and some
others, separately, respecting Flushing; and I find that it is
a very difficult thing to take any Ship of sixteen feet draught
of water up there, and without the marks, almost impossible...
The French have expected me at Flushing every day; therefore I look upon the attempt to be out of the question. I
shall have a stout Squadron under Dungeness, which is a
station far preferable to the Downs, both for watching the
Enemy and as a safe anchorage, and perfectly sure of getting
at them, if they approach that part of the Kingdom. It appears that the Enemy, whether they lie below Flushing or
abreast of it, can quit their anchorage any moment, and go
up inside the Dog Sand, where we cannot follow them. I am
convinced, from what I hear, that the thing is not to be done;
but if the weather be favourable to-morrow, I will look at
them in a Cutter. Captain Owen is an Officer of great zeal,
and wished to have removed all obstacles to get at the Enemy.

------

[5] Master of the King George Hired Cutter.

I never heard of more firmness than was shown by the good and gallant Captain Somerville. I felt much in sending an Officer who has a wife and eight children, all dependent on his life. Although he has not reported himself injured, yet I fear he has suffered in his head, by the bow-gun of a Brig that was fired over him. Your handsome letter will confirm, to the Officers and the men, when sent on necessary yet dangerous duty, that at least the First Lord of the Admiralty values their exertions, although success may not crown their endeavours. I am, &c.,

NELSON AND BRONTE.

TO EVAN NEPEAN, ESQ., ADMIRALTY.

[Autograph, in the Admiralty.]

Medusa, off West Capel, August 25th, 1801.

Sir,

I sailed from the Downs on Sunday, and off the North Foreland was joined by the Squadron from Margate, making in the whole, when united off West Capel, thirty Sail, from sixty-four guns to fourteen, including three Bombs and three Fire-vessels. From my consultation with the Pilots on Sunday afternoon, I had not much hopes of being able to get at the Enemy, supposing they lay even below Flushing; and yesterday afternoon, upon a further consultation with the Pilots, I found that the attempt would be improper, for there were so many *ifs* necessary to bring us out again, that I gave the matter up. But further, to satisfy my own mind, I this morning went on board the King George Hired Cutter, Mr. Yawkins, Master, who carried me up the Welling Channel, four or five leagues from our Ships, and near three from the Enemy; the tide running strong up, and the wind falling, it was necessary to get out again. From this distant observation of Captain Gore and myself, with the local knowledge of Mr. Yawkins, I believe that the Enemy's whole force consisted of a Ship of the Line, Dutch, French Frigate, another small Ship, and two or three Brigs laying close to the Town of Flushing, and abreast of it; which position being likewise abreast of the Dog Sand, would render a successful attack almost impossible, for even supposing ourselves able to get alongside the Enemy, they could whenever they pleased, with the flood tide, cut their cables and retreat towards the Ramakins, and leave us with the impossibility of anything else than silencing the fire from Flushing. Under these circumstances, I hesitated not one moment to direct the Ships and Vessels with me to proceed to the several stations assigned them, which I [cannot] have the honour to transmit, without acquainting their Lordships that I cannot but admire Captain Owen's zeal in his anxious desire to get at the Enemy, but under all the circumstances which I have stated, I could not think myself justifiable in acting against my own judgment. I have the honour to be, &c.,

NELSON AND BRONTE.

TO EVAN NEPEAN, ESQ., ADMIRALTY.

[Original, in the Admiralty.]

Amazon, Downs, 28th August, 1801.

Sir,

I am to request that you will be pleased to lay before the Lords Commissioners of the Admiralty, the enclosed letter which I received from Lieutenant Sayes, Commanding His Majesty's Advice-boat Express; and at the same time move their Lordships to grant an additional number of men to the said Vessel; for, her yards being so square and her breadth great, that I perfectly agree with the Lieutenant that thirty men are not sufficient to manage her; she ought, at least, to have a Cutter's complement. I am, Sir, &c.,

NELSON AND BRONTE.

TO GEORGE SMITH, ESQ., CAMER, KENT.

[Autograph, in the possession of his Son, William Masters Smith, of Camer, Esq.]

Deal, August 31st, 1801.

My dear Sir,

I shall always be happy when it is in my power to do anything you wish me, when I recollect that we are twenty-five years' acquaintance,[5] and that although we have scarcely ever met, yet through the medium of our joint and excellent

[5] Vide vol. i. p. 36.

friend Locker, whose memory I shall revere to the last moment
of my life—we have never lost sight of each other in life.
I have inquired how the farm goes on, I know you have heard
how my carcase has fared.

You know enough of the Sea service to be sensible that
some expenses must attend Mr. Feilding's son[7], and at (I hope)
the close of a war it should be considered well the putting a
lad to sea; however, if the lad comes, you may rely that I shall
have great pleasure in doing every kind thing for him. I shall
never forget our visit to Mr. Feilding, and I beg, my dear
Sir, that you will ever believe me, your most obliged and
obedient,　　　　　　　　　　　　　NELSON AND BRONTE.

TO ALEXANDER DAVISON, ESQ., SWANLAND HOUSE, MORPETH.

[Autograph, in the possession of Colonel Davison.]

August 31st, 1801.

My dear Davison,

Many thanks for your truly kind letter of 22nd. Dear
Parker is as well as can be expected; but whether he is to
live or die, or whether he ever will be able to walk again, even
the Surgeons cannot tell. He has youth on his side, and
that is all that can be said for him. Your conduct respecting
the Head-money is like yourself, and therefore unlike any
other *Agent for Prizes*. I am sure the Captors[8] are obliged to
you for getting so much Head money, for them; and I suppose
the value of the Ship and stores, and brass cannon will be
paid for. On the subject of brass guns, I suppose near thirty
have been saved; and as they are worth £400 or £500 a piece,
they must be looked after. In every Ship I hear they have
brass guns: it will come to be plunder, if not looked after.
Captain Hancock, of the Cruizer Sloop, landed two at Yarmouth, and perhaps has others on board. The Arrow, Captain Brodie, has, I am told, five on board; Captain Dixon,
of the Ramilies, had eighteen on board; and other Ships
had guns. *We ought* to have saved £70,000 worth of brass,

---

[7] Mr. Henry Feilding, the son of the Reverend Allen Feilding, son of the
author of "Tom Jones." Mr. Henry Feilding did not enter the Navy; and he is
now Rector of Blean, near Canterbury.

[8] At Copenhagen.

and at least two Sail of the Line, more than we did: but that is past.

I agree with you, and all my friends, that this is not a service for me, beyond the moment of alarm; but I am *used* and *abused*; and so far from making money, I am spending the little I have. I am after buying a little Farm at Merton—the price £9000; I hope to be able to get through it. If I cannot, after all my labour for the Country, get such a place as this, I am resolved to give it all up, and retire for life. I am aware *none* of the *Ministry* care for me, beyond what suits *themselves;* but my belief is that we shall have Peace. Sir William and Lady Hamilton are with me, and Mrs. Nelson. They join with me in kindest respects to you and Mrs. Davison, and to the children, and ever believe me, my dear Davison, your most obliged and affectionate friend,

NELSON AND BRONTE.

TO CAPTAIN SIR EDWARD BERRY, H.M. SHIP RUBY, HOSELY BAY, SUFFOLK.

[Autograph, in the possession of Lady Berry.]

Amazon, Downs, September 2nd, 1801.

My dear Sir Edward,

Many thanks for your letter, and I am glad that Hosely Bay has been so pleasant to you; but as you are not under my command, I cannot insure your remaining there. You have done well to keep my scolding letter from the Commander of the Eagle, Revenue Cutter. Not one Sea-Fencible has come forth from either Kent or Sussex. The establishment of them was originally bad; for no man liable to be impressed should have been enrolled, unless they had large families. The threat of Invasion is still kept up, and the French are trying to make their grand collection of Boats at Boulogne; but I find it difficult to believe that they can ever get half-way over. Many thanks for your kind inquiries about Parker. He is easy, comfortable, and cheerful; but I shall never believe he will get well till I see him walking. Langford has some pieces of bone coming from his leg, but it is in a fair way.

The Dart is off Dieppe. Sir William, Lady Hamilton, and
Mr. Nelson, are staying a few days with me, which enlivens
Deal. I trust we are on the eve of Peace. Ever believe
me, my dear Sir Edward, your most affectionate,

NELSON AND BRONTE.

TO EVAN NEPEAN, ESQ., ADMIRALTY.

[Original, in the Admiralty.]

Amazon, Downs, 2nd September, 1801.

Sir,
I beg you will be pleased to acquaint the Lords Commissioners of the Admiralty, that the Diligence, and the other
Vessels stationed off Cape Grisnez, were obliged to put into
the Downs this morning in consequence of the strong west
wind ; and, from Captain Jones's account I am apprehensive
that every Ship and Vessel stationed to the westward, on the
opposite Coast, will also be under the necessity of doing the
same. I am, Sir, &c.

NELSON AND BRONTE.

TO EVAN NEPEAN, ESQ., ADMIRALTY.

[Autograph, in the Admiralty.]

Amazon, Downs, 4th September, 1801.

Sir,
I enclose herewith two letters from the the Pilots of the
Galgo and Gier Sloops, and one from Captain Russel, and I
have made it my business to get information to form my
opinion, and it is—the Ships cruizing between West Capel
and Dunkirk, if the wind sets in at N.W., the tides, both
flood and ebb, for half the tides set on the shore—therefore,
if it comes to blow to close reefed topsails, none of our Square-
rigged Vessels can beat off the shore, and have only to trust
to their anchors and cables, and I much fear we should lose
our Gun-brigs and the Sloops of War made from the Whitby
Ships : therefore, I submit to their Lordships whether [as to]
the Squadron under Captain Owen, [he] should not have
latitude to bring his Squadron collectively into Margate Roads
on the appearance of blowing weather, leaving a Cutter or two

I I 2

to look out to give him information. The watching of Calais effectually, is worse in the winter months than off Flushing; for I am told, with the wind at N. W. blowing, that hardly any Ship can beat out of the Bay. Boulogne and Dieppe likewise lay in bights; and if they are closely watched to prevent the passage alongshore, and are liable to the same objection, therefore I am of opinion, and submit to their Lordships' better judgment, that care should be taken to keep our Squadrons compact and in good order, under the same Commanders as at present, or changed as circumstances may require; under Dungeness to be the principal Station. Walmer Roads and Margate Roads, to keep Cutters on the look out off the stations on the French Coast. In fine weather our Squadrons to go out and show themselves, but never to risk either being crippled or drove into the North Seas: thus we shall always be sure of an effective force, ready to act whenever the occasion calls for it; and with the large force their Lordships have appointed for the protection of our Coast, if it is kept in order, I do not see how the Enemy can with impunity put into the Channel. But I submit my opinion with deference, never having been used to the service of the North Seas, and this part of our Channels. I have the honour to be, &c.

NELSON AND BRONTE.

With this last little breeze all our Vessels are full of wants, and the old Gun-brigs, in bad weather, seriously feel their heavy guns.

TO ADMIRAL THE EARL OF ST. VINCENT, K.B.

[From Clarke and M'Arthur, vol. ii. p. 302.]

6th September, 1801.

My dear Lord,

Many thanks for your high opinion of me, expressed in your letter of this day. Worn out I shall soon be; and, if here, why, then I shall be totally unfit for the Mediterranean command. Parker suffers very much to-day, and I am very low. I am, &c.,

NELSON AND BRONTE.

TO EVAN NEPEAN, ESQ., ADMIRALTY.

[Autograph, in the possession of the Right Hon. John Wilson Croker.]

Amazon, Downs, September 6th, 1801.

Sir,

I send you a paper, and a note at the bottom. I have answered Mr. Hill's note,[7] and it will be in London on Tuesday morning. If their Lordships think it proper to save me from such letters, they will be pleased to send proper people to take up whoever comes for Mr. Hill's letter. I have franked it with the following direction:—

"Mr. Hill,
"To be left at the Post-Office till called for."

I am, Sir, your most obedient servant,

NELSON AND BRONTE.

TO MR. HILL.

[Letter Book.]

Amazon, Downs, 6th September, 1801.

Mr. Hill,

Very likely I am unfit for my present command, and whenever Government change me, I hope they will find no difficulty in selecting an Officer of greater abilities; but you will, I trust, be punished for threatening my character. But I have not been brought up in the school of fear, and, therefore, care not what you do. I defy you and your malice.

NELSON AND BRONTE.

TO EVAN NEPEAN, ESQ., ADMIRALTY.

[Original, in the Admiralty.]

Amazon, Downs, 7th September, 1801.

Sir,

I have the honour to transmit you herewith, a letter which I have received from Captain Owen, of the Nemesis,

---

[7] Lord Nelson had received a paper entitled, "Remarks by a Seaman on the Attack at Boulogne," containing severe strictures on Lord Nelson's Official Dispatch; to which was added, "Should Lord Nelson wish the enclosed not to be inserted in the Newspapers, he will please to *enclose by return of Post a bank note of* £100, to Mr. Hill, to be left at the Post Office till called for, London."

giving an account of the sailing of a Dutch sixty-four from Flushing, and of her arrival at Goeree. I am well convinced that Captain Owen has done everything in his power to prevent the Enemy from putting to sea; but from the late bad weather, he was not able to keep his station off West Capel. I am, Sir, &c.

NELSON AND BRONTE.

TO ADMIRAL THE EARL OF ST. VINCENT, K.B.

[Autograph, in the possession of Vice-Admiral Sir William Parker, Bart., G.C.B.]

September 7th, 1801.

My dear Lord,

The Dutch sixty-four is got from Flushing to Goeree, but no blame attaches itself to Captain Owen ; I suppose both Agamemnon and Asia were also blown off their stations. The wind now blows very hard at N.E. Dear Parker is very low to-day, but nothing will surprise me : I never had much hopes. Langford is suffering much pain. Ever, my dear Lord, your affectionate,

NELSON AND BRONTE.

I hope, for the sake of the world, that *Mr. Hill* will be caught. For myself I defy him, and all the rest of the envious crew.

TO ADMIRAL THE EARL OF ST. VINCENT, K.B.

[Autograph, in the possession of Vice-Admiral Sir William Parker, Bart., G.C.B.]

September 8th, 1801.

My dear Lord,

You know Captain Conn's worth : therefore, I will only say, that if he cannot get promotion by being made Sir Thomas Graves' Captain, which Graves would be very glad of, then that he may have either the Swallow, Scout, or Utile, which will be commissioned in a few days. Of course, he is desirous of getting a good Ship, and really he deserves whatever can be done for a very able Officer. I am ever, my dear Lord, your most affectionate,

NELSON AND BRONTE.

I have this moment received your letter about Captain
Foley of the Marines; you are right to take care of your own
first. He is a very good man, or I would not have mentioned
his name. You will wish me at the Devil: Mr. Collet was
Gunner of the Captain on the 14th February, and is so now.
Your Lordship gave him the Prince George. By Sir Charles
Thompson's desire he was removed back to the Captain,
to please a friend of Thompson's. The Admiralty, by letter
from Mr. Nepean, promised me a Second-Rate for him.
His son has served all the War in the Agamemnon and
Captain—has passed, as by enclosed letter. The father is an
excellent Officer; the son a good young man: [9] I presume
not, my dear Lord, to say more. Troubridge tells me, he
fears you were not well yesterday, which makes me sorry.
Cheer up, and be well.

TO ADMIRAL THE EARL OF ST. VINCENT, K.B.

[Autograph, in the possession of Vice-Admiral Sir William Parker, Bart., G.C.B.]

September 9th, 1801.

My dear Lord,

Young Walpole, who was placed by Admiral Pole, third
Lieutenant of the Amazon, has not yet received his confirmed
Commission, which makes him a little uneasy. I shall be
obliged to your Lordship to direct its being sent down to
Deal, which will much oblige your affectionate,

NELSON AND BRONTE.

I hope you are better.

TO HERCULES ROSS, ESQ., ROSSIE CASTLE.

[Autograph, in the possession of Horatio Ross, Esq., the son and heir alluded to
in this Letter.]

Amazon, Downs, September 12th, 1801.

My dear Friend,

I congratulate you most sincerely on the birth of a son and
heir, and from my heart I wish all the wealth and happiness
you possess, and all the honours which have fallen to my lot,

---

[9] A Mr. Isaac Charles Smith Collett, probably the Midshipman alluded to, was
made a Lieutenant on the 9th of September 1801.

may be the young Horatio's. Sir William and Lady Hamilton are with me, and as they have been partakers with me of the hospitality of Mrs. Parish, when at Hamburgh, they desire to join me in good wishes for Mrs. Ross's speedy recovery. Whatever call the Public duty has to my services, yet I must not altogether forget the duty of private friendship. You do not think me capable of forgetting when your house, carriages, and purse were open to me ;[1] and to your kindness probably I owe my life, for Green Bay had very often its jaws open to receive me. But as money never was my object, so I am not much richer than when you knew me, except by my pension. No ; the *two* Parkers[2] have had the sweets of Jamaica, but I would not change with them. I pray God we may have Peace, when it can be had with honour; but I fear that the scoundrel Buonaparte wants to humble us, as he has done the rest of Europe—to degrade us in our own eyes, by making us give up all our conquests, as proof of our sincerity for making a Peace, and then he will condescend to treat with us. He be d——d, and there I leave him; and do you believe me ever, my dear Ross, your old and affectionate friend,

NELSON AND BRONTE.

P.S.—I must beg the favour of you to give the enclosed to the Nurse.

TO EVAN NEPEAN, ESQ., ADMIRALTY.

[Autograph, in the possession of the Right Hon. John Wilson Croker.]

My dear Sir,   Amazon, Downs, September 14th, 1801.

Will you have the goodness to forward the letters sent herewith to the Mediterranean? I wish the wretch[3] had been caught as an example—not but that I am indifferent to all they can say against me, because I know I have always done my duty to the best of my abilities.

The Goeree expedition has a great probability of success, if the secret is well kept, and the weather favours us. Nothing shall be wanting on my part; for six Sail of the Line makes my mouth water. Ever your obliged,

NELSON AND BRONTE.

------

[1] At Jamaica in 1779 and 1780. Vide vol. i. p. 34*.
[2] Admiral Sir Peter Parker, and his son, Vice-Admiral Christopher Parker.
[3] " Mr. Hill."

TO ALEXANDER DAVISON, ESQ.

[Autograph, in the possession of Colonel Davison.]

Amazon, Downs, September 14th, 1801.

My dear Davison,

I have to give you ten thousand thanks for your very friendly offer of assisting me in purchasing the Farm. It is true, it will take every farthing I have in the world, and leave me in your debt, and also in Tyson's;[5] but I hope in a little time to be able at least to pay my debts. Should I really want your help, and know that I have enough in the world to pay you, I shall ask no one else. The Baltic expedition cost me full £2000. Since I left London it has cost me, for Nelson cannot be like others, near £1000 in six weeks. If I am continued here, ruin to my finances must be the consequence, for everybody knows that Lord Nelson *is amazingly rich!* Sir William and Lady Hamilton leave me on the 16th. You will easily guess my feelings at their going. Parker is easy, comfortable and cheerful, whether the thigh will ever unite none can say. Langford is suffering much pain, several pieces of bone of his leg are come away, but they both have youth on their side. I look forward with hope but will not be too sanguine. I yet hope the negotiation is not broken entirely off, for we can never alter the situation of France or the Continent, and ours will become a War of defence; but I hope they will do for the best. A man, a few days ago, sent me a letter demanding a bank note of £100, or he would abuse me in the Papers: I sent it of course to Nepean; the Porter who went to the Post-office for my answer, has been taken up, but he knew not his employer and probably never will be caught. Ever, my dear Davison, believe me, your most obliged friend,

NELSON AND BRONTE.

Sir William, Lady Hamilton, and Mrs. Nelson, desire to join me in best compliments to yourself and Mrs. Davison.

---

[5] His late Secretary.

TO ADMIRAL THE EARL OF ST. VINCENT, K.B.

[From Clarke and M'Arthur, vol. ii. p. 302.]

15th September, 1801.

My dear Lord,

Captain Campbell's[4] spirit we are all acquainted with: the plan[5] is fixed in my mind: and at least the attempt is worthy of an English Admiral. It is one of those judicious enterprises, in which we hazard only a few Boats, and may destroy an Enemy's Squadron. I am, &c.,

NELSON AND BRONTE.

TO EVAN NEPEAN, ESQ., ADMIRALTY.

[Original, in the Admiralty.]

Amazon, Downs, September 17th, 1801.

Sir,

I have communicated your letter to Captain Sarradine, and allow me to say, that although the Hound has certainly lost many men, yet that the Captain has taken all the precautions in his power against the loss of men, and I believe that he has sent many more than four descriptions of the men to the different rendezvous. Captain Sarradine is, I can assure their Lordships, a very zealous and good officer. I am, Sir, &c.

NELSON AND BRONTE.

TO LORD ELDON, LORD HIGH CHANCELLOR.

[From "The Life of the Earl of Eldon," by Horace Twiss, Esq., vol. i. p. 390.]

Amazon, September 17th, 1801.

My Lord,

I feel very much obliged by your open and very handsome answer to my request, which so exactly accords with what my friend Davison told me of your Lordship's character; and allow me to consider myself, in every respect, your most obliged

NELSON AND BRONTE.

---

[4] Captain Patrick Campbell, of the Ariadne, who had distinguished himself in command of the Dart in the preceding year. He died a Vice-Admiral, and a Knight Commander of the Bath, in August 1841.

[5] To attack Goeree.

TO ADMIRAL THE EARL OF ST. VINCENT, K.B.

[From Clarke and M'Arthur, vol. ii. p. 302.]

My dear Lord,　　　　　　　　　　19th September, 1801.

I have given out this day the strictest orders relative to the discipline of the Ships (in particular meant for the Gun-brigs), and to have them always ready for service. The new Gun-brigs are certainly very fine Vessels ; and, if the Commanders of them will keep the sea, I should think they might prevent much smuggling ; but many of them will require changing ; and a proper Boat must be given to each for that service. In short, Officers must be found fit for the command ; and the command not be, merely as a sinecure, fit for them. Much reformation has been adopted ; and, my dear Lord, much, very much, is necessary. The history of the Bomb-tenders will make you stare ; but you know it all.

20th of September.—I am full of grief for the fate of poor Parker ; our only consolation is, that everything has been done which was possible : the breath is not yet gone ; but, I dare say, he cannot last until night. Dr. Baird's kindness and ability will make a lasting impression on me. I am, &c.,

NELSON AND BRONTE.

TO DR. BAIRD.

[From "The Athenæum."]

Amazon, September 20th, 1801.

My dear Doctor,

Your kind letter has given me hopes of my dear Parker ; he is my child, for I found him in distress. I am prepared for the worst, although I still hope. Pray tell me as often as you can. Would I could be useful, I would come on shore and nurse him ; I rely on your abilities, and if his life is to be spared, that you, under the blessing of God, are fully equal to be the instrument. Say everything which is kind for me to Mrs. Parker, and if my Parker remembers me, say, ' God bless him ;' and do you believe me, your most obliged and thankful friend,　　　　　　　　NELSON AND BRONTE.

I have been in real misery. Hawkins will come off, night or day.

TO ALEXANDER DAVISON, ESQ.

[Autograph, in the possession of Colonel Davison.]

Amazon, September 20th, 1801.

My dear Davison,

You will join with me in affliction for the fate of dear good little Parker. Yesterday, at two in the afternoon, I was with him, so was Lady Hamilton, Sir William, and Mrs. Nelson;[1] he was so well that I was for the first moment sanguine in my hopes of his recovery; at 10 o'clock the great artery burst, and he is now at death's door, if not departed this life. You will judge our feelings; and, to mend all, Lady Hamilton with her party went to London this morning. I am pressing for my removal, and I hope to accomplish it. With my best respects to all in your house, believe me, dear Davison, your affectionate and obliged,

NELSON AND BRONTE.

TO DR. BAIRD.

[From " The Athenæum."]

Amazon, September 21st, 1801.

My dear Doctor,

Many thanks for your truly comfortable letter, and I trust that nature, watched and encouraged by your abilities, will yet get him up again. I will send some Madeira in the course of the day; my Steward is on shore at this moment with the key of the store room. Make my best respects to Mr. Parker, and to our dear Parker, say everything which is kind (at proper times). You cannot, be assured, say too much of what my feelings are towards him, and also to Langford, and do you believe me your truly obliged,

NELSON AND BRONTE.

[1] Wife of his brother, the Reverend Dr. Nelson, afterwards Countess Nelson.

TO EVAN NEPEAN, ESQ., ADMIRALTY.

[Original, in the Admiralty.]

Sir,   Amazon, Downs, 21st September, 1801.

The 12th instant I acquainted you that the Merchant-brig Unity, belonging to Bideford, had ran on shore on the Coast of France, and was destroyed by the Enemy; and that I had sent for the Master and Crew to account for so extraordinary a circumstance. The Master landed at Dover, prior to the Cutter's arrival for him; but the Mate and Crew are now on board the Amazon, from whose examination there does not remain scarcely a doubt but that the Brig was run on shore intentionally, or by gross inattention. I therefore suggest to their Lordships whether the circumstance should not be made known to Lloyd's Coffee House. I am, Sir, &c.

NELSON AND BRONTE.

TO LADY HAMILTON.

[Extract from "Lord Nelson's Letters to Lady Hamilton," vol. i. p. 58.]

September 21st, [1801.]   Quarter past Ten o'Clock.

I send you Dr. Baird's comfortable note, this moment received. You will [see] Parker is treated like an infant. Poor fellow! I trust he will get well, and take possession of his room at the Farm.

NELSON AND BRONTE.

TO ALEXANDER DAVISON, ESQ.

[Autograph, in the possession of Colonel Davison.]

Amazon, September 21st, 1801.

My dear Davison,

Dear Parker has rallied again : he has taken new milk and jellies: there is a gleam of hope, and I own I embrace it with avidity. I know you take an interest in his fate, therefore I send you this happy news; and ever believe me, your obliged and affectionate,

NELSON AND BRONTE.

TO DR. BAIRD.

[From " The Athenæum."]

½ past 11, September 22nd, 1801.

My dear Sir,

Although dear Parker has had but a bad night, yet with your nursing I have great hopes ; and, let what will happen, great consolation from your abilities and affectionate disposition ; and believe me ever your obliged,

NELSON AND BRONTE.

Make my respects to Mr. Parker ; and to our Parker say everything which is kind from me when it is proper. I am miserably sea-sick.

TO DR. BAIRD.

[From " The Athenæum."]

September 23rd, 1801.

My dear Sir,

I will not quite despair, but must not be too sanguine in my hopes. Your kindness is everything. I send a line from Lady Hamilton—best respects to Mr. Parker, and believe me your truly obliged,

NELSON AND BRONTE.

TO MISS PARKER, WESTGATE, GLOUCESTER.

[Autograph, in the possession of William Henry Ince, Esq.]

Amazon, September 24th, 1801.

Lord Nelson from his heart congratulates Miss Parker on the happy prospect of her dear brother's recovery. Captain Parker, will be, he hopes, for life, the dear son and friend of

NELSON AND BRONTE.[3]

---

[3] To the above Note, the following addition was made by some friend :—" The above was a flattering account given to Lord Nelson, yesterday, by Captain Bedford, who took it from hearsay, from your brother's asking if the Amazon was sailed. His Lordship sailed this morning at six o'clock, I find, (after staying in port to the last minute,) with his heart full of grief. The Doctor wrote to him, at five o'clock this morning. One o'clock. I have just seen him, and think him worse, and incoherent in his speech."

TO DR. BAIRD.

[From " The Athenæum."]

Amazon, September 24th, 1801.

My dear Sir,

I am truly sorry to hear that you have been so unwell ;
but, indeed, I am not surprised at it, for your kind fatigue for
others has drawn health from you to them. I shall probably
be here by Sunday, and then I hope you will allow me to see
my son, dear Parker; to you I shall always think I owe his
life, and I beg that you will ever consider me as your most
obliged,

NELSON AND BRONTE.

Remember me most kindly to Langford, and give my good
wishes to Mr. Skelton,[4] and all the wounded at the Hospital.

TO ADMIRAL LUTWIDGE.

[Autograph, in the possession of Major Lutwidge.]

Amazon, September 26th, 1801.

My dear Admiral,

I had intended coming on shore this morning to pay my
respects to you and Mrs. Lutwidge, but the weather has put
on such an unfavourable appearance that I must request your
forgiveness of my coming out of the Ship to-day.

Your Secretary was so good as to send me off Mr. Tod-
man's letter. Really some steps must be taken to prevent
the Signal 50 being made every time a Vessel is hauling out
of Boulogne Mole. We shall not believe when the *Wolf* is
coming with not less than twenty Sail of Ships of War, although
he does not appear to see them, and, what he does, not cor-
rectly ; for at 11 A.M. the Isis and York, with the Boulogne
Squadron, was standing over towards Boulogne. The
Anacreon Brig and Cygnet Cutter were three leagues off
Dungeness; the whole of Captain Russel's Squadron were at
anchor in Dover Roads; the Greyhound was half-way over ;
he is correct about the Cape Grisnez Squadron ; I think as

---

[4] Lieutenant Jeremiah Skelton, of the Jamaica. Vide p. 468, ante.

this signal will now create no alarm, that the signal 51 might be made to say, that the Enemy are (with numerary signal) standing from the French Coast towards England: in short some other signals must be adopted, or No. 50 left off, unless it is understood that the signal implies that the Enemy have actually sailed from Boulogne Roads, and are crossing the Channel, or steering as by compass signal shown at the Port. I wish you would mention it at the Admiralty, and propose some method that we should be neither inattentive to the signals made, nor improperly annoyed by them; yesterday it had no effect upon me, (which I was sorry for,) as I knew from experience that it meant nonsense. I am afraid for dear Parker; but still, whilst there is life we may hope.

I beg my best respects to Mrs. Lutwidge, and believe me ever, my dear Admiral, your most obliged and affectionate,

NELSON AND BRONTE.

I wish you would order some Caulkers from the Overyssel, to assist in caulking the Vixen.

TO LADY HAMILTON.

[Extract from " the Letters of Lord Nelson to Lady Hamilton," vol. i. p. 60.]

Amazon, September 26th, 1801. Eight o'clock.

Our accounts of dear Parker, I fear, preclude all hopes of his recovery. It was my intention to have gone ashore this morning, to have called on Admiral Lutwidge; but, the wind's coming fresh from the S. W., I have declined it; for, I doubt, if I could get off again. At ten o'clock, with your letters, came off Dr. Baird's note, to say every hope was gone! I have desired, that his death should be sent, by telegraph, to the Admiralty. They will, surely, honour his memory, although they would not promote him.

NELSON AND BRONTE.

I send you the last report. Who knows!

TO DR. BAIRD.

[From " The Athenæum."]

Amazon, September 26th, 1801.

My dear Sir,

Although the contents of your letter were not unexpected, yet I am sure you will judge of my feelings—I feel all has been done which was possible : God's will be done. I beg that his hair may be cut off and given to me; it shall remain and be buried with me. What must the poor father feel when he is gone! I shall request Captain Sutton and Bedford to arrange the funeral, and I wish you to ask Admiral Lutwidge to announce it by telegraph to the Admiralty; the Board ought to direct every honour to be paid to the memory of such an excellent gallant Officer. Say every kind thing to the poor father, and believe me your obliged and affectionate,

NELSON AND BRONTE.

TO ALEXANDER DAVISON, ESQ.

[Autograph, in the possession of Colonel Davison.]

Amazon, September 27th, 1801.

My dear Davison,

My dear Parker left this world for a better at 9 o'clock this morning. It was, they tell me, a happy release ; but I cannot bring myself to say I am glad he is gone; it would be a lie, for I am grieved almost to death. May God bless you and yours. Amen.

NELSON AND BRONTE.

TO ADMIRAL THE EARL OF ST. VINCENT, K.B.

[From Clarke and M'Arthur, vol. ii. p. 303.]

[About 27th September, 1801.]

The scene, my Lord, with our dear Parker is closed for ever; and I am sure your good heart will participate in our grief, both as a public and private loss; not a creature living was ever more deserving of our affections. Every action of

his life, from Sir John Orde to the moment of his death,
showed innocence, joined to a firm mind in keeping the road
of honour, however it might appear incompatible with his
interest: his conduct in Orde's business [1] won my regard.
When he was abandoned by the world, your heart had begun
to yearn towards him—how well he has deserved my love
and affection his actions have shown. His father, in his
advanced age, looked forward for assistance to this good son.
Pensions I know have sometimes been granted to the parents
of those who have lost their lives in the service of their King
and Country. All will agree, none fell more nobly than
dear Parker; and none ever resigned their life into the
hands of their Creator with more resignation to the Divine
Will than our Parker. I trust much to your friendship to
recommend his father's case to the kind consideration of the
King. I fear his loss has made a wound in my heart which
time will scarcely heal. But God is good, and we must all
die. I am, &c.,

NELSON AND BRONTE.

TO DR. BAIRD.

[From " The Athenæum."]

Amazon, September 27th, 1801.

My dear Sir,
I should be a wretch if I did not feel sensible of all your
kindness to my dear Parker; we have the melancholy consolation to think that everything was done which professional
skill and the kindest friendship could dictate. God's will be
done; but if I was to say I was content, I should lie—but I
shall endeavour to submit with all the fortitude I am able.
Poor Mr. Parker! What a son has he lost! My pen fails to
express my feelings, except that I shall for life consider myself your obliged,

NELSON AND BRONTE.

[1] Vide vol. iii. p. 25.

TO EVAN NEPEAN, ESQ., ADMIRALTY.

[Original, in the Admiralty.]

Amazon, September 28th, 1801.

Sir,

Captain E. T. Parker having died in consequence of the wounds he received on the 16th of last month, I have given directions for his being buried this day with all the honours and respect due to so meritorious and gallant an Officer;[5] and I have to request that their Lordships will be pleased to direct the Sick and Hurt Board to defray all the expenses of his lodgings, &c. on shore, and also of his funeral. I am, Sir, &c.,   NELSON AND BRONTE.

TO ADMIRAL THE EARL OF ST. VINCENT, K.B.

[From Clarke and M'Arthur, vol. ii. p. 303.]

Amazon, September [about the 29th], 1801.

My dear Lord,

I send Nepean another Pilot's letter. I have experienced in the Sound the misery of having the honour of our Country intrusted to Pilots, who have no other thought than to keep the Ship clear of danger, and their own silly heads clear of shot. At eight in the morning of the 2nd of April, not one Pilot would take charge of a Ship. Brierly, who was Davidge Gould's Master in the Audacious, placed Boats for me, and fixed my order, saying, ' My Lord, if you will command each Ship to steer with the small red house open with a mill, until such a Church is on with a wood, the King's Channel will be open.' Everybody knows what I must have suffered; and if any merit attaches itself to me, it was in combating the dangers of the shallows in defiance of the Pilots. The business of Pilots brings all this fresh to my memory, and I long to have the Medal[6] which I would not give up to be made

----

[5] An account of Captain Parker's funeral is given in the Naval Chronicle, vol. vi. p. 341. Lord Nelson, who was one of the mourners, was visibly affected during the ceremony. Admiral Lutwidge, Lord George Cavendish, Colonel of the Derbyshire Militia, and Captains Poulden, Brodie, Rowley, Warren, Sarradine, Clay, Bazeley, and Sutton, and many other Officers of both Services attended.

[6] For the Battle of Copenhagen. Vide *post*.

an English Duke. You know, my dear Lord, with what
cheerfulness I came here, and the Country, as your Lordship
and Mr. Addington thought, attached a confidence to my
name which I submitted to, although I was conscious that
many more able Officers could be found every day in London;
but my zeal I will never give up to any man breathing.

This Boat-business must be over: it may be a part of a great
plan of Invasion, but can never be the only one ; therefore, as
our Ships cannot act any more in lying off the French Coast,
I own I do not think it is now a command for a Vice-Admiral.
Turn it in your mind. It is not that I want to get a more
lucrative situation—far from it : I do not know, if the Mediterranean were vacant to-morrow, that I am equal to undertake
it. You will forgive me if I have said too much; they are my
feelings, which for several years you have allowed me to
throw before you, not in an impertinent manner, but with all
the respect due to your great character and exalted situation.
I have answered Hawkins about the Pilots exactly as you see
it, that he was to go where he was ordered, without consulting
Pilots, and that when the Ship was standing into danger, they
were to point it out; but that it was not allowable for them
to dictate where it was proper for a Ship to be stationed in
the Channel. From my heart I wish the Enemy would try
and come over, and finish the war; although, without great
care, I see the misery of Peace. I am, &c.,

NELSON AND BRONTE.

TO CAPTAINS ROSE AND SOMERVILLE, HIS MAJESTY'S SHIPS
JAMAICA AND EUGENIE.

[From a Copy in the possession of the Right Hon. John Wilson Croker.]

Most Secret.

Sir,   Amazon, off Dover, 1st October, 1801.

It is my intention to send the Nancy Fire-Brig to attempt the
destruction of the Enemy in Boulogne. You are to take
particular care that she is not boarded, or in any way approached, so as to give the Enemy suspicion of her being an
English Vessel. You will know her by wearing the Admiral's
assenting Flag (red with white cross), and her fore-top-gallant
mast is cut close to the rigging. I am, &c.,

NELSON AND BRONTE.

P.S.—When you caution the Vessels under your orders not to molest a Brig of the above description, you are not to acquaint them what she is, but keep it a profound secret. If the wind is fresh, probably it may be to-morrow morning, at daylight. The King George Cutter will attend her, at a proper distance.   N. & B.

TO LIEUTENANT OWEN,[7] COMMANDING THE NANCY FIRE-VESSEL.

[Autograph draught, in the possession of the Right Hon. John Wilson Croker.]

Secret.

[Apparently about 1st October, 1801.]

Whereas I think it necessary for his Majesty's Service, that an attempt should be made to burn the Enemy's Flotilla in Boulogne Harbour, and repose entire confidence in your bravery and zeal, You are, therefore, hereby required and directed to take under your command his Majesty's Hired Cutter the King George, whose Commander has my directions to follow your orders; and whereas the greatest secrecy is necessary towards the success of this service, it is my positive directions that you hold no communication whatever with any Ship, or Vessel, or with the shore.

Whenever the wind comes between the West-North-West and North, and blowing so fresh as to force all the Enemy's Vessels from the Road of Boulogne into the harbour, you are to sail from this anchorage, and, directing the Cutter to keep upon you, approach within four leagues of the French Coast, at a distance of six or seven miles from you, to carry all the sail which the Nancy can bear, and run into the harbour of Boulogne, and there set her on fire, taking care that you enter the harbour half an hour, or three quarters of an hour, before high water, in order that the Nancy may drift up the harbour with the flood. And on your approaching the French Coast, finding that the wind blows into the harbour, you are to hoist the Admiral's assenting flag, red with a white cross, at your main top-gallant mast-head; and you are not to

---

[7] Apparently the present Captain William Fitzwilliam Owen, brother of Vice-Admiral Sir Edward W. C. R. Owen, G.C.B.

approach the Coast, unless you are pretty certain that the wind does blow into the harbour; and as this most honourable, and very important service is entrusted, from your character, to your conduct, I trust that I shall not be disappointed in the execution of it.   NELSON AND BRONTE.

TO CAPTAIN HARVEY, H. M. SHIP UNITE.

[Letter-Book.]

Sir,   Amazon, Downs, 1st October, 1801.

The signal to recall the Haughty was flying yesterday morning a considerable time on board the Amazon, and her Commander did not think proper to pay any attention to it. You will order him to return to the Downs immediately; and if my Flag is not flying there, to proceed under Dungeness; and you are to reprimand him severely for his inattention.

The moment the Gallant rejoins you, send her likewise to me, wherever I may happen to be. I am, Sir, &c.

NELSON AND BRONTE.

TO EVAN NEPEAN, ESQ., ADMIRALTY.

[Original, in the Admiralty.]

Amazon, Dungeness, 3rd October, 1801.

Sir,

I beg leave to acknowledge the receipt of your letter of the 1st instant, signifying their Lordships' direction to me to prevent any Vessels or Boats of any description from proceeding to France, except such Vessels or Boats as Mr. Otto may have occasion to send from Dover with his dispatches for the French Government, and I have to request you will assure their Lordships that strict attention shall be paid to these instructions. I have the honour to be, Sir, &c.

NELSON AND BRONTE.

TO EVAN NEPEAN, ESQ., ADMIRALTY.

[Original, in the Admiralty.]

Amazon, Dungeness, October 3rd, 1801.

Most Private,

My dear Nepean,

I have received your Public letter, dated the 1st, directing me to prevent all Vessels and Boats from going to France, except Mr. Otto's.[8] I take for granted it means to prevent all neutral Vessels from any part of the world from going to France—*am I right?* for in our narrow seas, the only means of prevention is bringing them to England. Under the circumstances which have given rise to this order, am I right in attempting anything which may be feasible against any of the French Ports? I have a little plan against Boulogne. Except to Lord St. Vincent, pray do not mention it; for everything I almost think on is known. I am almost done up, but I hope there will be but little more occasion for war. Cannot you announce by telegraph to-morrow to Lutwidge, *assent* for Lord Nelson, (to the attempt,) or, for Lord Nelson, *dissent*. I shall understand the words; but Admiral Lutwidge knows nothing of my plan. Ever, my dear Nepean, your obliged,

NELSON AND BRONTE.

Pray send my letter.

TO ADMIRAL LUTWIDGE.

[Autograph, in the possession of Major Lutwidge.]

Amazon, Dungeness, October 3rd, 1801.

My dear Admiral,

What can this order from the Admiralty mean? Is it a sign of Peace? I think, yes; for we cannot, at this time of the war, go to war with all Europe, and America, which must be the case, if we allow no trade to France; therefore I think and hope from my heart it is, to prevent stock-jobbing, and that the Preliminary Articles are on the very eve of being signed, if not already done. Our weather is very fine, but I cannot get

[8] The French Minister in London, to negotiate a Peace.

up my spirits. Captain Wodehouse[6] does not like his change : he thinks it is from *bad to worse*. The Lively Cutter will stay for my letters to-morrow. Will you direct that the Gun-brigs and Cutters which come into the Downs, may be turned out as soon as possible? *they* like Deal. With my best respects to Dr. Lutwidge, believe me ever your obliged and affectionate,

NELSON AND BRONTE.

TO ADMIRAL THE EARL OF ST. VINCENT, K.B.

[From Clarke and M'Arthur, vol. ii. p. 304.]

Dungeness, 3rd October, 1801.

Nepean's public letter has a little staggered me, whether it would be right, under our present circumstance with France, to do a violent thing? I am prepared to run a Fire-Brig into Boulogne harbour the first fresh wind, at from W.N.W. to N. But I shall stop until the *assent* or *dissent* comes by telegraph to-morrow. I intended not to have mentioned this matter to any one, even to you, until the trial had been made. However, if we are on the eve of Peace, which is Dungeness news, it would be a bad reconciliation. If I fail in this plan, I purpose to make an Infernal of one of the Bombs, and to have Fire-Boats, &c. &c., to keep them for ever in hot water. My mind is always at work; but I assure you I am seriously indisposed and low spirited from private considerations. My public duty is nothing; I could get over five times as much, were I in good health ; and I find every creature kind, good, and affectionate towards me, and you amongst the first. I am, &c.

NELSON AND BRONTE.

---

[9] Apparently Captain the Honourable Philip Wodehouse, second son of John, first Lord Wodehouse : he commanded in succession the Brilliant, Iris, and Resistance Frigates, and died a Vice-Admiral of the White, in January 1838.

TO ADMIRAL THE EARL OF ST. VINCENT, K.B.

[From Clarke and M'Arthur, vol. ii. p. 305.]

[October, 1801,]

Most heartily do I congratulate you on being a Member of that Administration, which has been able to comply with the almost unanimous wishes of the Country. All hands must now try to keep French men and French principles out of our happy Country. I am, &c.

NELSON AND BRONTE.

TO CAPTAIN OWEN, H.M. SHIP NEMESIS, AND THE COMMANDERS OF THE SEVERAL SQUADRONS UNDER LORD NELSON.

[Letter Book.]

Amazon, Dungeness, 4th October, 1801.

Sir,

Notwithstanding the Preliminaries of Peace are signed, you are to be very vigilant in watching the Enemy, and, on no account to suffer them to put into the Channel, as hostilities have not yet ceased. I am, &c.

NELSON AND BRONTE.

TO DOCTOR BAIRD.

[From " The Athenæum."]

Amazon, October 6th, 1801.

My dear Doctor,

I am truly sorry that my little remembrance[1] of your goodness to a set of brave men, should have deprived me of the pleasure of your company ; I beg I may see you at dinner to-morrow : and I hope to see you, where your humane disposition will be of the greatest service, at the Sick and Hurt Board, to effect which, nothing shall be wanting on the part of your truly obliged,

NELSON AND BRONTE.

---

[1] " The 'little remembrance' alluded to above, was a silver Vase, with the following inscription :—' Presented to Andrew Baird, Esq., M.D., as a mark of esteem for his humane attention to the gallant Officers and Men who were wounded off Boulogne on the 16th of August, 1801. From their Commander-in-Chief, Lord Viscount Nelson, Duke of Bronte.' "—*Athenæum.*

TO CAPTAIN FERRIER, H.M. SHIP YORK.

[Letter Book.]

Amazon, Downs, 7th October, 1801.

Sir,

Having reason to believe that the French will take every opportunity, especially in foggy weather, to put out of their Ports in Small craft and Rowing-boats, for the purpose of seizing our trade passing up and down Channel, I therefore desire you will keep all the Cutters cruizing in fine weather, more particularly in fogs, between Dungeness and the Coast of France; and that you keep the Launches equipped with their carronades mounted, masts stepped, and sails in them, ready to put off the moment any firing is heard; but in thick fogs, they are to row off the Ness Point. The Flat-boats are to be hoisted out, whenever firing may be heard, and sent with all expedition to the quarter it proceeded from. I am, &c.

NELSON AND BRONTE.

TO ALEXANDER DAVISON, ESQ.

[Autograph, in the possession of Colonel Davison.]

Amazon, October 9th, 1801.

My dear Davison,

Your kind letter has truly affected me. Can your offer be real? Can Davison be uncorrupted by the depravity of the world? I almost doubt what I read; I will answer, my dear friend, you are the only person living who would make such an offer. When you come to Town you shall know all my pecuniary affairs, and if in arranging them I should want your kind assistance, I will accept it with many thanks. In my present purchase I have managed tolerably well. I am trying to get rid of my Command, but I am to be forced to hold it, to keep the Merchants easy till hostilities cease in the Channel. I must submit; for I do not wish to quarrel with the *very great* folks at the Admiralty, the last moment. I have had hitherto one happiness under my Command, that not one English boat has been captured by the Enemy during the time of my command, within the limits of my Station; this is a comfort, and I hope none will be captured during the short time we have to stay. I see you did not know of the Peace when you wrote ; England called loudly for it, and now I see it is to be abused; but Englishmen never are satisfied, full nor fasting. We shall meet next month in Town. I beg my best respects to Mrs. Davison and all your family, and believe me ever your obliged and affectionate,

NELSON AND BRONTE.

TO ADMIRAL LUTWIDGE.

[Autograph, in the possession of Major Lutwidge.]

My dear Admiral,   Amazon, October 9th, 1801.

I have to thank you for your good news of the Ratification of the Peace, and I beg to thank Mrs. Lutwidge for her kind present of game and fruit. I cannot get the Admiralty to set me free. They wish to put some pounds into my pocket, I suppose, by keeping me on full pay ; but I am so ungrateful as not to thank them. But we shall all soon be adrift, and I shall ever feel myself your obliged and affectionate,

NELSON AND BRONTE.

TO THE RIGHT HON. HENRY ADDINGTON.[2]

[Autograph, in the Sidmouth Papers.]

My dear Sir,   Amazon, October 10th, 1801.

Every wish of yours I shall always be happy in complying with, and was there a probable chance that even a Boat of the

---

[2] In reply to the following letter :—

" Downing Street, October 8th, 1801.

" My dear Lord,

" Many thanks for your letter, every part of which gave me pleasure, that only excepted which refers to the state of your health. Captain Sutton has, I trust, relieved you, in a great degree, from the pressure of some of the most laborious parts of your duty ; and if you wish to remain chiefly on shore, or even to remove to London or elsewhere for a few days, you may, I know, rely on the acquiescence of the Board of Admiralty; but I owe it to my regard to your Lordship, and to my Public duty, to declare it to be my opinion, that it is of the utmost importance to your own high character, and to the interests of the Country, that your Flag should be flying till the Definitive Treaty has been signed. You will then have seen the

Enemy's could get into the Channel, I should stay with pleasure till hostilities cease; but we are so covered that they
cannot, if we all do our duty. After hostilities cease, the
thing for me is over; but if you cannot get a definitive Peace,
I shall be getting health to again take up the cudgels; and in
the good cause I hope to be able to be as fortunate as I have
been the whole war, and am ever your most obliged,

NELSON AND BRONTE.

TO ADMIRAL THE EARL OF ST. VINCENT, K.B.

[Autograph, in the possession of Vice-Admiral Sir William Parker, Bart., G.C.B.]

My dear Lord,   Amazon, October 10th, 1801.
Your letter of the 5th has only this moment reached me.
Every attention is paid to cover our Channel, and I do not
think that the French can with impunity send anything into
the Channel. Sutton sails in the morning for the Ness. As
Troubridge knows all my wishes, I shall only say in addition,
that whenever I am released, that I shall always be ready to
come forth again, when my health will allow, *barring* a winter
in the North Seas. Hoping very soon to see you I shall only
assure you that I am, with real regard and respect, your most
affectionate,   NELSON AND BRONTE.

TO DOCTOR BAIRD.

[From " The Athenæum."]

My dear Doctor,   Amazon, October 11th, 1801.
I will send to the Gannet for Smart Tickets. Will you dine
here? Can you can cure madness? for I am mad to read
that our d——d scoundrels² dragged a Frenchman's carriage.
I am ashamed for my Country. The Letter-boat can bring
you off at half-past two. Ever your obliged,

NELSON AND BRONTE.

Ship safe into Port, and may close with honour a career of unexampled success and
glory. With true regard, I am ever, my dear Lord, your sincere friend and faithful
servant, HENRY ADDINGTON.

" P.S.—The letters from Dumourier are at Wimbledon, but shall be returned
to-morrow. I beg your pardon for having kept them in my possession so long."—
Autograph, in the Nelson Papers.

² Alluding to the mob having drawn the carriage of General Lauriston, who
arrived in London on the 10th of October, with the Ratification of the Preliminaries
of Peace.

TO EVAN NEPEAN, ESQ., ADMIRALTY.

[Original, in the Admiralty.]

Sir,   Amazon, October 12th, 1801.

I send a parcel of letters from Captain Owen, giving me an account of two French Privateers being at sea, and his opinion, which I perfectly coincide in, that they will go to the northward, and their Prizes to Neutral Ports, till the Peace takes place. I keep the Defender till to-morrow after post, as probably I shall receive some directions from their Lordships, relative to the duration of hostilities. I am, Sir, &c.

NELSON AND BRONTE.

TO LADY HAMILTON.

[Extract from "Lord Nelson's Letters to Lady Hamilton," vol. i. p. 69.]

Amazon, Ten o'Clock, October 12, 1801.

My dearest Friend,

This being a very fine morning, and smooth beach, at eight o'clock, I went with Sutton and Bedford, and landed at Walmer, but found Billy[3] fast asleep, so left my card; walked the same road that we came, when the carriage could not come with us that night; and all rushed into my mind, and brought tears into my eyes. Ah, how different to walking with such a friend as you, Sir William, and Mrs. Nelson! Called at the barracks, on Lord George;[4] but he is gone to London. From thence to the Admiral's, found him up; and, waiting half an hour to see Mrs. Lutwidge, who entreated me to stay dinner—came directly on board. I did not even call to see poor Langford, who has been worse these few days past, and God knows when he will be well. I am afraid it will be a long time; for several pieces of bone are lately come away, and more to come. But Troubridge has so completely prevented my ever mentioning any body's service, that I am become a cipher, and he has gained a victory over Nelson's spirit. I am kept here; for what, he may be able to tell—I cannot; but long it cannot—shall not be.

³ Mr. Pitt.
⁴ Lord George Cavendish, Colonel of the Derbyshire Militia.

Sutton and Bedford are gone a tour till dinner time; but nothing shall make me, but almost force, go out of the Ship again, till I have done, and the Admiralty in charity, will be pleased to release me. I am, in truth, not over well. I have a complaint in my stomach and bowels, but it will go off. I thank you for the King's[5] letters. I shall write a kind line to Castelcicala, and answer the King's, very soon, and write to Acton, for he can make Bronté everything to me, if he pleases. I dare say I did wrong never to write him; but as he treated Sir William unkindly, I never could bring myself to do it.

NELSON AND BRONTE.

TO THE RIGHT HON. HENRY ADDINGTON.

[Autograph, in the Sidmouth Papers.]

Amazon, Downs, October 13th, 1801.

My dear Sir,

I send you a letter which I have just received from Germany. What the Order of Knighthood is,[6] I am totally ignorant of; but I can accept of nothing without his Majesty's approbation. I have therefore to request that you will have the goodness to obtain the King's opinion relative to accepting or refusing an honour from such a respectable Society in the Germanic Body, that I may conduct myself accordingly. I can, my dear Sir, have no vain desires, but I wish on this occasion to do what is right to such a Body, who have wished in my person to do honour to one of his Majesty's most faithful subjects, and, my dear Sir, your most obliged,

NELSON AND BRONTE.

I have just received a most affectionate letter from the King of Naples.

---

[5] The King of Naples.

[6] The Order of St. Joachim. If Lord Nelson had known the history of this apocryphal Order, he would scarcely have deigned to accept or wear it.

TO ADMIRAL LUTWIDGE.

[Autograph, in the possession of Major Lutwidge.]

Amazon, October 14th, 1801.

My dear Admiral,

I shall never get from the Downs. If I wished to stay, I dare say I should not have interest. I am quite angry; but who cares for that. I am desired to keep all my Cruizers at Sea, to guard the trade. I send a letter for Mrs. Lutwidge, from our excellent friend Lady Hamilton. With every good wish, believe me ever, your most obliged,

NELSON AND BRONTE.

TO EVAN NEPEAN, ESQ., ADMIRALTY.

[Original, in the Admiralty.]

Amazon, Downs, October 14th, 1801.

Sir,

Their Lordships' appointment for my Particular Service being now done away by the Preliminary Articles of Peace— viz., to prevent the Invasion of this Country, which service I have not only, by their Lordships appointing so large a force to serve under my command, been enabled effectually to perform, but also to be able to acquaint you that not even a Boat has been captured by the Enemy during the term of my command; and as my state of health requires repose on shore, I have to request their Lordships will, when they think the Service will admit of it, allow me permission to go on shore. I have the honour to be, &c.

NELSON AND BRONTE.

TO EVAN NEPEAN, ESQ., ADMIRALTY.

[Original, in the Admiralty.]

Amazon, Downs, October 15th, 1801.

Sir,

I am to acknowledge the receipt of their Lordships' order for the cessation of hostilities against the French Republic; likewise a copy of the Preliminary Articles of Peace between his Majesty and the said Republic.

I beg leave to know whether their Lordships approve of
my directing the Ships and Vessels under my command to
rendezvous in the Downs after the 22nd instant? I have the
honour to be, &c.

NELSON AND BRONTE.

P.S.—Orders are sent from the Navy Board, for some of
the Hired Cutters to be discharged, although the same has
not been signified to me by their Lordships, or the Navy
Board. I have not detained them.

TO LADY HAMILTON.

[Extract from " Lord Nelson's Letters to Lady Hamilton," &c., vol. i. p. 84.]

Amazon, October 17th, 1801.

My dearest Friend,

Although my complaint has no danger attending it, yet it
resists the medicines which Dr. Baird has prescribed; and, I
fancy, it has pulled me down very much. The cold has settled
in my bowels. I wish the Admiralty had my complaint:
but, they have no bowels—at least, for me. I had a very
indifferent night; but your and Sir William's kind letters have
made me feel better.

I send you a letter from Lord Pelham.[5] I shall certainly
attend; and let them see, that I may be useful in Council as I
have been in the Field. We must submit; and, perhaps, these
Admiralty do this by me to prevent another application.
. . . . I pray that I may not be annoyed on my arrival:
it is retirement with my friends that I wish for. Thank Sir
William, kindly, for his letter, and the inclosure, which I
return. Sutton is much pleased with your letter; and, with
Bedford, will certainly make you a visit. They are both truly
good and kind to me. Our weather has been cold these two
days, but not bad. I have got a fire in the cabin, and I hope
my complaint will go off.

NELSON AND BRONTE.

Amazon, 2 P.M.—Yawkins is in great distress: his Cutter[6]

[5] Thomas Lord Pelham, Secretary of State for the Home Department.
[6] Vide pp. 472, 473, ante.

is paid off, and he, like many others, very little to live upon. He begs his best respects to Sir William. He breakfasted here this morning. Many very long faces at Peace!"

TO LIEUTENANT . . . . . . , H.M. SLOOP . . . . . .

[Letter-Book.]

Amazon, Downs, 19th October, 1801.

Sir,

Notwithstanding your very improper conduct to your Captain, the Lords Commissioners of the Admiralty have been pleased to show their lenity to you, by cancelling their order for the Court-Martial, which I trust will prove a sufficient warning to you to behave, in future, with becoming respect to your superiors, and be a lesson to you not to listen to *bad* advice, for in the event of your erring again, you will inevitably meet with punishment. I am, &c.

NELSON AND BRONTE.

TO ADMIRAL LUTWIDGE.

[Autograph, in the possession of Major Lutwidge.]

Amazon, 4 P.M. [Apparently 19th October, 1801.]

My dear Admiral,

The Admiralty will not let me go. You are going to Portsmouth. I suppose you have your orders. The Express shall carry Medusa's men, and bring back the others. I will order a Vessel to attend the Convoy. Lady Hamilton's letter I have enclosed. When you write to Kingsmill,[9] remember me kindly to him. I am at dinner; but ever your obliged,

NELSON AND BRONTE.

Best compliments to Mrs. Lutwidge.

[9] Admiral Sir Robert Kingsmill, Bart. Vide vol. i. p. 40.

TO LADY HAMILTON.

[Extract from "Lord Nelson's Letters to Lady Hamilton," vol. i. p. 91.]

Amazon, October 19th, 1801.

My dearest Friend,

What a gale we have had! But Admiral Lutwidge's Boat came off; and, as your letter was wrote, it got on shore: at least, I hope so; for the Boat seemed absolutely swallowed up in the sea. None of our boats could have kept above water a moment; therefore, I could not answer all the truly friendly things you told me in your letters, for they were not opened before the Boat was gone.

They dine with Billy Pitt to-day; or, rather, with Mr. Long; for Pitt does not keep house, in appearance, although he asked me to come and see him: and that I shall do, out of respect to a great man, although he never did anything for me or my relations. . . . . . .

Poor Oliver! what can be the matter with him? I must leave my cot here till my discharge, when it shall come to the farm, as cots are the best things in the world for our Sea friends. Why not have the pictures from Davison's, and those from Dodd's; especially, my father's and Davison's? *Apropos!* Sir William has not sat, I fear, to Beechy.[7] I want a half-length, the size of my father's and Davison's. . . . . The weather to-day is tolerable; but I do not think I could well get on shore: but Thursday, I hope, will be a fine day.

---

[7] Sir William Beechey, R.A. The following pleasing anecdote of this eminent Painter occurs in a letter from Lady Nelson to her husband, dated 4th March 1800: " I think you will be surprised when I tell you our good father is sitting for his picture. Sir W. Beechey is the fortunate man. You must know it is a profound secret. I went to Sir W. B. to ask his price, look at his pictures, and then inquire whether he would go to an invalid? The answer, ' No,' puzzled me : however I said, ' sometimes general rules were broken through.' Sir W. finding I was rather anxious about this picture, said that really he never went to any person excepting the King and Royal Family. The Duke and Duchess of York had that instant left the house. I knew that. ' But, Madam, may I ask who is the gentleman?' ' Yes, Sir; my Lord Nelson's father.' ' My God, I would go to York to do it! Yes, Madam, directly.' He was as good as his word, and has been here twice. I think the likeness will be an exceeding good one. I don't know whether the picture is for you or me. . . . . The picture is for you, so I hear this morning."—*Autograph*, in the Nelson Papers.

I shall call on Mr. Pitt, make my visit at the Hospital, and get off very early on Friday morning. My cold is still very troublesome—I cannot get my bowels in order. In the night I had not a little fever. But never mind; the Admiralty will not always be there. Every one has their day. God bless you, my dear friend; and believe me ever yours most faithfully,

NELSON AND BRONTE.

TO LADY HAMILTON.

[From " Lord Nelson's Letters to Lady Hamilton," vol. i. p. 96.]

Amazon, October 20th, 1801.

My dearest Friend,

How could you think, for a moment, that I would be a time-server to any Minister on earth! And, if you had studied my letter a little closer, you would have seen that my intention was to show them that I could be as useful in the Cabinet as in the Field. My idea is, to let them see that my attendance is worth soliciting. For myself, I can have nothing; but, for my brother, something may be done. Living with Mr. Addington a good deal, never, in your sense of the word, shall I do it. What, leave my dearest friends to dine with a Minister? D—n me if I do, beyond what you yourself shall judge to be necessary! Perhaps it may be *once*, and *once* with the *Earl;* but that you shall judge for me. If I give up all intercourse, you know enough of Courts, that they will do nothing: make yourself of consequence to them, and they will do what you wish, in reason; and out of reason I never should ask them. It must be a great bore to me, to go to the House. I shall tell Mr. Addington, that I go on the 29th to please him, and not to please myself; but more of this subject when we meet. Dr. Baird is laid up with the rheumatism: he will now believe, that the cold may affect me. This is the coldest place in England, most assuredly. *Troubridge* writes me, that, as the weather is set in fine again, he hopes I shall get *walks* on shore. He is, I suppose, laughing at me; but, never mind. I agree with you in wishing Sir William had a horse. Why don't you send to the Duke for a pony for him? I am just parting with four of my Ships—

L L 2

Captains Conn, Rowley, Martin, and Whitter—who are proceeding to the Nore, in their way to be paid off. The surf is
still so great on the beach, that I could not land dry, if it was
necessary to-day; but, I hope, it will be smooth on Thursday :
if not, I must go in a Boat to Dover, and come from thence to
Deal. Sutton says, he will get the Amazon under sail, and
carry me down; for that I shall not take cold. Bedford goes
with a Squadron to Margate; so that all our party will be
broke up. I am sure, to many of them, I feel truly obliged.

Make my kindest respects to Sir William; and believe me
ever your most faithful and affectionate,

NELSON AND BRONTE.

I wish Banti was separated from Charles, for he is a
knowing one. I wish I could get him with a good Captain
who would keep him strict to his duty. Hardy cannot get paid
a hundred pounds he advanced for Mr. Williams's nephew.
Many thanks for Mrs. Nelson's letters. The Reverend Doctor likes going about. Only think of his wanting to come up
with an Address of Thanks! Why, [the] King will not receive
him, although he is a Doctor; and less for being my brother,
for they certainly do not like me.

TO LADY HAMILTON.

[From " Lord Nelson's Letters to Lady Hamilton," &c., vol. i. p. 101.]

Amazon, October 20th, 1801.

My dearest Friend,

Only two days more, the Admiralty could, with any conscience, keep me here; not that I think they have had any
conscience. I dare say, Master Troubridge is grown fat. I
know I am grown lean with my complaint; which, but for
their indifference about my health, would never have happened; or, at least, I should have got well long ago in a warm
room, with a good fire, and sincere friends.

I believe I leave this little Squadron with sincere regret,
and with the good wishes of every creature in it. I
did not think, tell Sir William, that impudence had got such
deep root in Wales. I send you the letter as a curiosity; and
to have the impudence to recommend a Midshipman! It is

not long ago, a person from Yorkshire desired me to lend him
three hundred pounds, as he was going to set up a school!
Are these people mad; or, do they take me for quite a
fool? However, I have wisdom enough to laugh at their
folly; and to be, myself, your most obliged and faithful
friend,

NELSON AND BRONTE.

TO ADMIRAL LUTWIDGE.

[Autograph, in the possession of Major Lutwidge.]

Amazon, 21st October, 1801.

My dear Admiral,

I have long since directed Captain Russel to deliver to Mr.
How, or yourself, all the unlanded packets, which I concluded
had been done : I now send your Boat to Captain Russel for
them. I think, after all this blowing weather, I stand some
chance for a fair beach. The Court-Martial[8] I wish may be
put off for ever. With my best respects to Mrs. Lutwidge,
believe me ever your obliged,

NELSON AND BRONTE.

TO EVAN NEPEAN, ESQ., ADMIRALTY.

[Original, in the Admiralty.]

Amazon, Downs, 22nd October, 1801.

Sir,

Agreeably to the direction of the Lords Commissioners of
the Admiralty, signified to me by your letter of the 20th
instant, I have ordered all the Ships named in the margin[1]
to proceed to the Nore ; and I have ordered the Gun-Vessels
named in the margin[2] to proceed to Sheerness, which, together
with those already there, and those named on the other side

---

[8] On Vice-Admiral Sir William Parker, for sending two Ships to the West Indies
contrary to his orders, and allowing them to cruize there. The Court assembled
on the 14th of November at Portsmouth : he was acquitted.

[1] Ardent, Glatton, Vlieter, Alliance, Beschermer, Redoubt, Batavier, Unité, Alceste, Daphne, Firm.

[2] GUN-VESSELS : Cracker, Boxer, Flamer, Haughty, Attack, Plumper, Bruiser,
Wolfe, Griper.

hereof, who are in a tolerable good state, make the whole number of the old Gun-Vessels under my command. I have the honour to be, Sir, your most obedient, humble servant,

NELSON AND BRONTE.

SHIPS AND VESSELS REMAINING UNDER THE COMMAND OF VICE-ADMIRAL LORD NELSON, K.B.

Isis, York, Leyden, Amazon, Medusa, Brilliant, Heldin, Nemesis, Jamaica, Arrow, Dart, Gier, Diligence, Hound, Alonzo, Galgo, Autumn, Eugenie, Savage, Gannett, Otter, Anacreon, Express.—NEW GUN-VESSELS: Conflict, Archer, Vixen, Minx, Bold, Locust, Jackall, Constant, Monkey, Mariner, Mallard, Snipe, Charger, Ferriter.—OLD GUN-BRIGS: Hasty, Biter, Eclipse, Defender, Bouncer.

TO EVAN NEPEAN, ESQ., ADMIRALTY.

[Original, in the Admiralty.]

Amazon, Downs, 22nd October, 1801.

Sir,

Be pleased to acquaint the Lords Commissioners of the Admiralty, that it is my intention to set off this evening for Merton,[1] agreeably to the leave of absence their Lordships have been pleased to grant me. I have the honour to be, &c.

NELSON AND BRONTE.

TO LADY COLLIER.

[Autograph, in the possession of Commodore Sir Francis Augustus Collier, K.C.H.]

Merton, October 24th, 1801:

Dear Madam,

If your son has served his time, I hope, if he is still in the Foudroyant, that he is promoted, as many will be made, by the capture of the French ships at Alexandria. If he has not served, he stands no chance, for it cannot be done, and if you will inquire of Lord St. Vincent or Sir Thomas Troubridge, they will tell you that I cannot get a Lieutenant made. If

---

[1] Lord Nelson had, shortly before, purchased a house with some land, at Merton in Surrey.

he has served his time and quitted a Flag-ship he is wrong, unless with the approbation of Lord Keith. With every good wish for your son, I have the honour to be, Madam, your most obedient Servant,

NELSON AND BRONTE.

TO CAPTAIN SUTTON, H.M. SHIP AMAZON, DEAL.

[Autograph, in the possession of Captain Ives Sutton.]

My dear Sutton,   October 25th, 1801.

The Committee at Lloyd's want to know the names and places of residence of the families of the killed. I send you Mr. Angerstein's letter. You will start at the smallness of the sum. The application should have been made before many of the Vessels are paid off; but we must get all we can. Send to Bedford, to get his Squadron's return; they should be directed to Mr. Angerstein, at Lloyd's. I am not yet got well; the cold of the Downs gave me a severe shake. The Commodore[2] will, I am sure, have the goodness to allow a Memorandum being given out. If you or Hardy will take the trouble of getting perfect Returns, I shall feel much obliged. Remember me kindly to the Commodore, Gore, Bedford, Hardy, and all friends; and believe me ever your much obliged,   NELSON AND BRONTE.

TO EVAN NEPEAN, ESQ., ADMIRALTY.

[Autograph, in the Admiralty.]

Sir,   Merton, October 28th, 1801.

I have to request you will be pleased to move the Lords Commissioners of the Admiralty to grant an order to the Navy Board, that the usual allowance may be paid to me for table-money, &c. from the 10th August, 1799, to the 17th of January, 1800, during which period I acted as Commanding Officer of His Majesty's Naval force in the Mediterranean.

My Secretary not having arrived from the Mediterranean,

---

[2] Commodore John Sutton, who has been frequently mentioned. He had a Broad Pendant flying in the Nemesis, Captain Owen, and died a Vice-Admiral, and a Knight Commander of the Bath.

I have just learnt from my Agents that the above has not yet
been paid to me. On your representation, however, I presume
their Lordships will issue the necessary orders for that purpose,
as the allowance was made to Lord Hood last war, and to Lord
Hotham, in 1795, under similar circumstances. I have the
honour to be, Sir,   NELSON AND BRONTE.

TO CAPTAIN SUTTON, AMAZON, DEAL.

[Autograph, in the possession of Captain Ives Sutton.]

Merton, October 31st, 1801.

My dear Sutton,

You will see my maiden Speech[3]—bad enough, but well
meant—anything better than ingratitude. I may be a coward,
and good for nothing, but never ungrateful for favours done
me. When you write to Bedford say everything which is
kind, and also to Gore. The latter will, I fancy, get relieved
—the Earl[2] talked to me about him yesterday. I come down

---

[3] On the 29th of October, Lord Nelson took his seat in the House of Lords as a
VISCOUNT, being introduced by Viscount Sydney and his old friend and patron,
Admiral Viscount Hood. On the 30th of that month, EARL ST. VINCENT moved,
" That the Thanks of this House be given to Rear-Admiral Sir James Saumarez,
K.B., for his gallant and distinguished conduct in the Action with the Combined
Fleet of the Enemy, off Algeziras, on the 12th and 13th of July last.

" LORD VISCOUNT NELSON seconded the motion. He said, he could not give his
silent vote to a motion that so cordially had his assent. He had the honour to be
the friend of Sir James Saumarez. The Noble Earl, at the head of the Admiralty,
had selected that great Officer to watch the French in that important quarter,
and the Noble Lord had not been deceived in his choice. He would assert, a
greater Action was never fought than that of Sir James Saumarez. The gallant
Admiral had, before that Action, undertaken an enterprise that none but the most
gallant Officer and the bravest seaman would have attempted. He had failed through
an accident—by the falling of the wind; for, he ventured to say, if that had not
failed him, Sir James Saumarez would have captured the French Fleet. The
promptness with which Sir James refitted, the spirit with which he attacked a
superior force after his recent disaster, and the masterly conduct of the Action, he
did not think were ever surpassed. His Lordship entered very much into the detail
of the Action. After which, he said, the merit of Sir James Saumarez would be less
wondered at, when the school in which he was educated was considered by their
Lordships. He was educated at first under Lord Hood, and afterwards under the
Noble Earl near him, (Earl St. Vincent.) Lord Nelson gave an account of some
of the memorable services of Sir James Saumarez while a Captain, and concluded
by apologising to the House for the trouble he had given their Lordships. (*A
general cry of hear, hear!*) The motion was then put and carried, *nem. dis.*"—
Naval Chronicle, vol. vi. p. 418.

[2] Earl St. Vincent.

here every evening—exactly one hour's drive from Hyde
Park or the Bridge. Remember me kindly to Langford and
Dr. Baird; and ever believe me your much obliged,

NELSON AND BRONTE.

I have wrote to Conn about the wine. Sir William and
Lady Hamilton desire their kind remembrances to you, Bedford, and all friends.

TO CAPTAIN SUTTON, H.M. SHIP AMAZON.

[Autograph, in the possession of Captain Ives Sutton. On the 3rd of November,
in the debate on the Preliminaries of Peace, Lord Nelson supported the opinion of
Lord St. Vincent, that the terms were equally honourable and advantageous to this
Country; and defended the Preliminaries against the imputation of too extensive
concessions.]

Merton, November 7th, 1801.

My dear Sutton,

I was in Town yesterday, which prevented my answering
your kind letter of the 4th. You must judge how far Mr.
Crannell can with propriety be allowed to go to Town. As
far as you think my name may be committed, you are heartily
at liberty to use it. Lord St. Vincent is very unwell: a most
violent cough. Mr. Emery, from the Active, is coming down
to join the Amazon: if you have room for him as Mid.,
he seems desirous of being rated. My Steward has not yet
arrived: the heavy gales have probably kept him in the river.
Remember me most kindly to Hardy, Bedford, and all friends,
and believe me ever your most affectionate,

NELSON AND BRONTE.

Sir William and Lady Hamilton desire their kindest regards
to you, Hardy, Bedford.

TO CAPTAIN SIR EDWARD BERRY.

[From a Copy in the Nelson Papers.]

Merton, November 10th, 1801.

My dear Sir Edward,

You have judged right to submit; for our *friends* at the
Admiralty have not much feeling for invalids. I spoke to
Troubridge about you: the result you know by experience.
I have not a scrap of interest, but believe me, I am ever your
much obliged and affectionate friend,

NELSON AND BRONTE.

TO GEORGE SMITH, ESQ., CAMER, KENT.

[Autograph, in the possession of William Masters Smith, Esq., of Camer.]

Merton, November 11th, 1801.

My dear Sir,

Your letter shall be given to Lord St. Vincent, with a note
from me on the back of it. I have very little interest. If I was
in Lord St. Vincent's place, he should have his Commission,
being ever your most sincere and faithful friend,

NELSON AND BRONTE.

TO SAMUEL BARKER, ESQ.

[Autograph, in the possession of his son, John Barker, Esq. of Norwich.]

Merton, Surrey, Nov. 11th, 1801.

My dear Sir,

Many, many thanks for your truly kind letter; I have no
thoughts of coming to Yarmouth, being at this moment only
absent from Deal on leave, for the benefit of my health;
I *never* shall forget all your goodness to me, and if ever I am
placed in a situation to show my gratitude, I trust I shall not
be found wanting. I beg my respects to Mr. Palgrave, and
beg you to believe me ever, my dear Sir, your most obliged,

NELSON AND BRONTE.

Sir William and Lady Hamilton charge me to present their
compliments.

I have wrote to Mr. Parker, and I have told Sir Thomas
Troubridge of your good wishes towards him.

TO CAPTAIN SUTTON.

[Autograph, in the possession of Captain Ives Sutton.]

Merton, November 12th, 1801.

My dear Sutton,

Yesterday was a fagging day: 150 dined at the London
Tavern, and I, being the Cock of the Company, was obliged
to drink more than I liked; but we got home to supper; and
a good breakfast at eight this morning has put all to rights

again. This day comes on the great Northern question.[3] Lords Spencer and Grenville, and all that party, are to be violent: Tierney and Grey are bought, which shows that all the disinterestedness of man is only like the Fox and the grapes—sour when they cannot be got at. I am quite sorry about Dr. Baird, and am fearful that these repeated attacks will destroy a very valuable member of society. When you see Langford, say everything that is kind. Although the Admiralty tells me nothing, yet every body says there will be a promotion; and if there is, both Somerville and him will certainly be made. I am glad the French Gun-boats are dished; for, although it is Peace, I wish all Frenchmen at the devil. I have wrote about your kind letter to the Admiralty. I wrote to good Bedford yesterday; but yesterday was a busy day, between gardening, attending the House, and eating, drinking, and hurraing. Sir William is gone this morning to see the King; but he and Lady Hamilton always bear in mind my worthy friends; and, with my kindest regards to all of them, believe me ever your much obliged and affectionate,

NELSON AND BRONTE.

How angry Foley and Fremantle will be, going to Jamaica!

TO WILLIAM PERRY, ESQ.[4] M.D., HILLINGDON, NEAR UXBRIDGE.

[From the " Gentleman's Magazine," vol. lxxvi. p. 218.]

Merton, Nov. 15th, 1801.

My dear Sir,

I do remember you very well; for early impressions of kindness are not easily eradicated. Your letter I have en-

---

[3] Lord Nelson spoke on the 12th of November, in support of a motion of Thanks to Lord Keith and the Officers under his command, for their services in Egypt. He said that " those services were of a double nature, yet of equal importance. It fell to the lot of the Army to fight, and of the Navy to labour. They had equally performed their duty, and were equally entitled to thanks."

[4] Dr. Perry was Surgeon of the Salisbury, bearing the Broad Pendant of Commodore Sir Edward Hughes, K.B., in the East Indies, in 1776, when Lord Nelson was a young Midshipman of the Seahorse, Captain Farmer. (Vide vol. i. pp. 3, 4.) In performance of his professional duties, Mr. Perry examined the boy, and finding him too delicate to remain in India, advised Sir Edward Hughes to send him to England in the Dolphin, Captain Pigot. In 1806, Dr. Perry published a whim-

closed to Lord St. Vincent, and I wish it may have the
desired effect; and I shall always consider myself, dear Sir, as
your much obliged,

NELSON AND BRONTE.

It was only last night that I received your letter.

TO THE RIGHT HON. THE LORD MAYOR.

[From a Copy in the Nelson Papers, on which Lord Nelson has written, "A copy
of my Letter to the Lord Mayor." He afterwards wrote to the Lord Mayor, desiring
to withdraw this Letter, because he was advised that it was not proper for him to point
out to the City of London what it ought to do. The subject was, however, renewed
in the following year.]

Merton, 20th November, 1801.

My Lord,

I have seen in this day's Paper, that the City of London
have voted their Thanks to the brave Army and Navy who
have so happily brought the Campaign in Egypt to a glorious conclusion, and no Thanks were certainly ever better
deserved. From my own experience, I have never seen, that
the smallest services rendered by either Navy or Army to the
Country, have missed being always noticed by the great City
of London, with one exception—I mean, my Lord, the glorious
Second of April—a day when the greatest dangers of navigation were overcome, and the Danish Force, which they thought
impregnable, totally taken or destroyed by the consummate
skill of the Commanders, and by the undaunted bravery of
as gallant a Band as ever defended the rights of this Country.

For myself, I can assure you, that if I were only personally
concerned, I should bear the stigma, now first attempted to be
placed upon my brow, with humility. But, my Lord, I am
the natural guardian of the characters of the Officers of the
Navy, Army, and Marines, who fought, and so profusely bled,
under my command on that day. In no Sea-action this war
has so much British blood flowed for their King and Country.

---

sical work, called "Dialogues in the Shades," and describing himself as "an old
man, but a young writer," said, "he little imagined that he should have more than
the common occasion of lamenting over the loss of a Nation's Hero, whom it was
his real and good fortune *once* to save." The object of his letter to Lord Nelson
was to recommend to him Lieutenant Richard Tooley, who will be again mentioned.

Again, my Lord, I beg leave to disclaim for myself more merit than naturally falls to the share of a successful Commander; but when I am called upon to speak of the merits of the Captains of His Majesty's Ships, and of the Officers and Men, whether Seamen, Marines, or Soldiers, I that day had the happiness to command, *then I say*, that never was the glory of this Country upheld with more determined bravery than upon that occasion ; and, if I may be allowed to give an opinion as a Briton, *then I say*, that more important service was never rendered to our King and Country.

It is my duty, my Lord, to prove to the brave fellows, my Companions in dangers, that *I* have not failed, at every proper place, to represent, as well as I am able, their bravery and meritorious services. When I am honoured with your Lordship's answer, I shall communicate it to all the Officers and Men who served under my command on the Second of April last. I cannot close my letter without bearing testimony to the extraordinary exertions of Rear-Admiral Sir Thomas Graves, and the Honourable Colonel Stewart. I am, &c.

NELSON AND BRONTE.[6]

TO THE RIGHT HON. HENRY ADDINGTON.

[Autograph, in the Sidmouth Papers.]

My dear Sir,   Merton, November 20th, 1801.

You will judge of my feelings by my letter to the Lord Mayor.[7] What has occasioned those who fought on the 2nd

[6] The Lord Mayor, Sir John Eamer, wrote Lord Nelson in reply—" I have only to assure your Lordship, that I shall give the subject a proper and early consideration."

[7] Mr. Addington did not answer this Letter until the 27th; (vide p. 533, *post*,) and Lord Nelson not having received a reply to it on the 23rd, he forwarded his letter to the Lord Mayor on that day. The following is a copy of Mr. Addington's letter :—

" Downing Street, November 27th, 1801.

" My dear Lord,—I reproach myself for having so long delayed my answer to your letter, but I can truly assure your Lordship that I have not had five minutes leisure since I received it. Having always expressed my opinions to you without reserve, I feel persuaded that no apology will be necessary for the freedom with which I acknowledge my anxiety that, on the subject in question, no letter, be the terms of it what they may, be written by your Lordship to the Lord Mayor. It

of April, when a great and most important Victory was obtained, from being noticed by the great City of London is beyond my comprehension; and I, their Commander, whatever may have been my demerits on that day, am forced to place in its true and proper point of view, the services and bravery of those under my command. I request your friendly opinion of my letter; for I should be glad to alter any word or sentence in it, to those more adapted to mark the great bravery and consummate skill shown by all under my command. Lord St. Vincent, in July, made me truly happy in the assurance that the King would grant Medals to those who fought on that day, as has been usual in other great Naval victories. With every sentiment of respect, believe me ever, my dear Sir, your most obliged,

NELSON AND BRONTE.

TO ADMIRAL THE EARL OF ST. VINCENT, K.B.

[From a Copy, in the Nelson Papers.]

Merton, 20th November, 1801.

My dear Lord,

I hope that you will approve of my letter to the Lord Mayor: I owe it as a debt of gratitude to the brave Officers and men under my command on the 2nd of April. You know, my dear Lord, the arduousness of the enterprise, and also the full effects of the glorious termination of it: your expanded mind must see the necessity of my stepping forth, or I should ill deserve to be *so* supported on any future occasion. Your Lordship's opinion of the services of that day induced you to hold [out] hopes amounting to certainty. I believed that the King would grant those who fought that day Medals, as had been done for other great Victories, and I have been, I own, expect-

---

could be productive of no good, and might, and (I firmly believe) would, lead to serious embarrassments. The grounds of this persuasion I shall be ready to state to you, whenever you will do me the favour of calling in Downing Street. They are not merely of a public nature, but are connected with the interest I shall ever take in your well-earned fame, and with the true regard with which I am, my dear Lord, your sincere friend, and faithful servant,—HENRY ADDINGTON."—*Autograph*, in the Nelson Papers.

ing them daily since the King's return from Weymouth. You
will judge of my feelings by my letter to the Lord Mayor; and
from my heart wishing you a speedy recovery, believe me
ever your affectionate,   NELSON AND BRONTE.[8]

[8] To this Letter Lord St. Vincent wrote two Letters in reply:—
                      " Admiralty, 21st November, 1801.
" My dear Lord,—I thank you for communicating the letter you have judged fit
to write to the Lord Mayor; and I have the honour to be, with the truest regard
and esteem, your Lordship's very affectionate and obedient servant,—ST. VINCENT."

                      " Admiralty, 21st November, 1801.
" My dear Lord,—In further reply to your Lordship's letter of yesterday, I must
beg leave to assure you that I have given no encouragement to the other subject
therein mentioned, but, on the contrary, have explained to your Lordship, and to
Mr. Addington, the impropriety of such a measure being recommended to the King.
With many thanks for the interest you take in the recovery of my health, believe
me to be, my dear Lord, very affectionately yours,—ST. VINCENT."—Autographs, in
the Nelson Papers.
     Greatly disappointed, and, as he conceived, unjustly treated by the Government,
in refusing to give Medals, and by the City of London, in withholding its Thanks,
for the Battle of Copenhagen, Lord Nelson showed his feelings in a very characteristic manner. To Captain Foley, (his Flag-Captain in the Elephant in that Battle,)
he declared he "would never wear his other Medals till that for Copenhagen was
granted," (Letter from Admiral Sir Thomas Foley, G.C.B., to Rear, now Vice-Admiral,
Sir Graham Eden Hamond, Bart., K.C.B., dated 23rd February, 1828;) and he
declined to accept its Thanks for any other services, or to dine with the Lord Mayor,
in his capacity of Chief Magistrate of the City of London, until the City had rendered
justice to his Companions at Copenhagen. (Vide subsequent Letters.) However
hopeless their claim, neither Lord Nelson, nor the Captains who fought on the 2nd
of April, ever abandoned their pretensions to Medals. In May 1804, the late Lord
Melville succeeded Lord St. Vincent as First Lord of the Admiralty, and in the
following month, Lord Nelson wrote to him on the subject. His Lordship's admirable reply shows the grounds upon which Government then considered it expedient
to refuse the request:
     " My dear Lord,   " Admiralty, 28th August, 1804.
     " Your letter of the 22nd of June, with the correspondence which passed between
your Lordship and Lord St. Vincent, has duly reached me. There seems to have
existed a most extraordinary misunderstanding between you on the subject, and I
am left perfectly in the dark what created the sudden change of sentiment you state
to have taken place. I am not likely soon to meet with Lord St. Vincent, nor am
I certain that he would feel disposed, or at liberty, to enter into any explanation
with me respecting it. I may probably, ere long, have an opportunity of mentioning
it to Mr. Addington.
     " Not knowing the reasons for resisting the wishes of the Officers who signalised
themselves at Copenhagen, it would be presumptuous in me to form any conjecture
respecting them. I am positive that any want of a just sense of the meritorious
services performed on that occasion neither did, nor could operate on the mind of any
of his Majesty's servants. But, whatever the reasons were, your Lordship must feel,
that in every view, the difficulties may have increased, but cannot have diminished by

TO ADMIRAL THE EARL OF ST. VINCENT, K.B.

[From a Copy in the Nelson Papers.]

Merton, November 22nd, 1801.

My dear Lord,

I was this morning thunder-struck by the reading your Lordship's Letter, telling me that you had never given encouragement to the expectation of receiving Medals for the

the delay. I will not, however, act so uncandidly with your Lordship, as to disguise from you that I feel a difficulty which, to my understanding, at present seems insurmountable. When Badges of Triumph are bestowed in the heat and conflict of War, they do not rankle in the minds even of the Enemy, at whose expense they are bestowed; but the feeling, I suspect, would be very different in Denmark, if the present moment was to be chosen for opening afresh wounds which are, I trust, now healed, or in the daily progress of being so. However much every gallant Officer wishes to bear about with him, and to transmit to his posterity, Badges of Military prowess and Distinction, I am confident the minds of our brave Officers, who signalised themselves at Copenhagen under their illustrious leader, are too generous and public-spirited to be solicitous of obtaining any Mark of Distinction which might tend to injure any of the substantial interests or alliances of their Country.

"If I am right in the view I have of the subject, and continue to think in that manner, I am sure your Lordship will not conceive I am less disposed than I know I am, to consult the nicest feelings of his Majesty's Naval Officers, if on the present occasion I do not concur with their wishes, in recommending to his Majesty the request which your Lordship has so forcibly conveyed to me. I have the honour to be, &c., MELVILLE."—*Autograph*, in the Nelson Papers.

On the extension of the Order of the Bath in 1815, additional mortification awaited such of the surviving Captains as had commanded Ships under Lord Nelson at Copenhagen, and who had not had a subsequent opportunity of gaining distinction, by not finding themselves included in the extensive Nominations then made to the Order. In February 1828, they presented a Memorial to the Duke of Clarence, the Lord High Admiral, praying his Royal Highness to obtain for them the Medals to which they conceived themselves entitled, and also, the rank of Knights Commanders of the Bath, to which rank, (or to the highest Class of the Order,) all the then surviving Captains who were in the great Naval Actions of the 1st of June 1794, 14th of February 1797, 11th of October 1797, and 1st of August 1798, had been admitted, except seven—namely, James Walker, John Lawford, Samuel Sutton, Graham Eden Hamond, all of whom were at Copenhagen, and Henry Digby, Edward Rotheram, and Charles Bullen, who were at Trafalgar, but of whom, however all, except Admirals Lawford and Sutton, had been made Companions of the Order.

On the 5th of March 1828, the Lord High Admiral wrote to Rear-Admiral Hamond, informing him that he had forwarded the Papers to the Duke of Wellington, " and this morning I had his Grace's answer, stating that his Majesty's Government were most perfectly sensible of the eminent services of yourself and your Companions in Arms under the great and immortal Nelson, but regretted they could not advise the King, at this late period, to issue Medals. Under the present circum-

Action of April 2nd. Had I so understood you, I never should, the same day, have told Mr. Addington how happy you had made me, by the assurance that the King would give us Medals; and I have never failed assuring the Captains, that I have seen and communicated with, that they might depend on receiving them. I own I considered the words your Lordship used as conveying that assurance. It was an apology for their not being given before, which, I understood you, they would have been, but for the difficulty of fixing who was to have them; and, I trust you will recollect that my reply was, that 'certainly they could not be given to any but those who fought;' and we entered into the difficulties of fixing whether they should be confined to the Ships of the Line, or extended to the Frigates, engaged. I could not, my dear Lord, have had any interest in misunderstanding you, and representing that as an intended Honour from the King, which you considered as so improper to be recommended to the King: therefore, I must beg that your Lordship will re-consider our conversation—to me of the very highest concern, and think that I could not but believe that we were to have Medals.

stances of the Order of the Bath, I know that any applications about K.C.B.'s would not be of any use, therefore, on that point, I did not touch."

After the accession of King William the Fourth, these gallant Officers renewed their application. His Majesty received their Memorial most favourably, and referred it to the Ministers; and on the 6th of October 1830, the Secretary to the Admiralty informed Sir Thomas Foley, (who had joined in that application,) that His Majesty had desired the Lords of the Admiralty "to cause you, and the other Officers in question, to be acquainted that, sensible as his Majesty is of your and their distinguished merit, there are general considerations connected with the sub-ject which prevent his Majesty from complying with the request contained in the Memorial."

Medals for Copenhagen were, consequently, never given; and only one of the Captains who were in that Battle lived to receive an Honorary reward specifically for his gallantry on that occasion—namely, Admiral John Lawford, who was made a Knight Commander of the Bath in August 1838, thirty-six years after the event, and twenty-three years after the Order had been enlarged, for the purpose of "marking, in an especial manner, the Prince Regent's sense of the valour, perseverance, and devotion manifested by the Officers of his Majesty's Forces by Sea and Land."

Of the other Memorialists, Rear-Admiral Sir Graham Hamond was made a Knight Commander of the Bath in September 1831; Rear-Admiral Walker died a Companion of the Order in July 1831; and Rear-Admiral Samuel Sutton, died in June 1832, and, like many of his gallant Companions in one of the most sanguinary of Naval Battles, without having received any mark of distinction whatever for his services.

The conduct of the City of London is to me incomprehensible; for Lord Keith, who has not been engaged, has been Thanked, &c., and Sir Hyde Parker for not fighting might, for what matters to me, have been Thanked, too; but surely, my dear Lord, those who fought ought not to have been neglected for any conduct of *others*.

I am truly made ill by your letter.[2] If any person had told me what you wrote, I would have staked my head against the assertion. With every kind wish, believe me, my dear Lord, your most affectionate,

NELSON AND BRONTE.

TO CAPTAIN SUTTON, H.M. SHIP AMAZON, DEAL.

[Autograph, in the possession of Captain Ives Sutton.]

Merton, November 22nd, 1801.

My dear Sutton,

I have been so much engaged and hurried about no notice being taken by the City of London of our April 2nd, and by Lord St. Vincent who, in contradiction to what I thought a most positive assurance that we were to have Medals, now tells me, that he has always thought it improper to recommend it to the King. You may judge my feelings: the result you shall know; but I am fixed never to abandon the fair fame of my Companions in dangers. I may offend and suffer; but I had rather suffer from that, than my own feelings. I am not well, and this thing has fretted me. Remember me kindly to all my friends with you, and believe me ever, your most obliged and affectionate,

NELSON AND BRONTE.

[2] Lord St. Vincent replied,—

"Admiralty, 23rd November, 1801.

" My dear Lord,—That you have perfectly mistaken all that passed between us in the conversation you allude to, is most certain; and I cannot possibly depart from the opinion I gave your Lordship in my last. At the same time I am extremely concerned that it should have had so material an effect upon your health, for the speedy re-establishment of which you have the fervent wishes of, my dear Lord, your very affectionate and obedient servant,—ST. VINCENT."—*Autograph*, in the Nelson Papers.

TO LIEUTENANT BAKER, R.N., DOVER-STREET.

[Autograph, in the possession of John Bullock, Esq.]

Merton, November 22nd, 1801.

Sir,

Every Officer who has lost a limb has certainly a right to a pension, and by application to the Admiralty you would certainly have one granted. I have, I can assure you, no power whatever to meet your wishes in getting you to the West Indies. With every good wish, I am, Sir, your most obedient Servant,

NELSON AND BRONTE.

ADMIRAL THE EARL OF ST. VINCENT, K.B.

[Autograph, in the possession of Vice-Admiral Sir William Parker, Bart., G.C.B.]

Merton, November 26th, 1801.

My dear Lord,

I have been much distressed at finding that Mr. Thomas Fellowes, who served with me as Purser during the whole time I commanded the Agamemnon, has not only lost his appointment of Purser to his Majesty's Ship Superb, owing to an arrest for a debt, but is involved, with a wife and family, in the most abject misery, without the slightest means of support for them, or for himself. The inquiries I have made of his Agents, and my own opportunity of observation, while he was under my command, leave not a shadow of doubt upon my mind but that the pecuniary embarrassments which are the source of this distress, are not the result of any extravagance or misconduct in the discharge of his duty; and indeed, speaking from my own knowledge, I can safely say that Mr. Fellowes is a man of strictly honest principles, and I believe his distresses to be chiefly owing to the want of integrity, or the negligence, of those who were intrusted with his concerns in the Ship, at those periods when he was absent on duty, as Commissary to the Troops and Seamen serving on shore in Corsica.

I should not preface the request I am about to make to your Lordship with this detail, but that I am anxious your compliance with it should proceed not less from attention to my recommendation, than from motives of justice and humanity towards an unfortunate sufferer in the Service, on the part of your Lordship.

A vacancy, I understand, is likely to occur very shortly in the Clerk of the Cheques' Office, at Chatham, by the resignation of Mr. Francis Smith, one of the Clerks. I shall feel sensibly obliged by your Lordship's appointing Mr. Fellowes to it; and I will pledge myself that his abilities will be found equal to the situation. The salary, though small, will be adequate to his support, and to a man wholly without pecuniary resources, it will be far preferable to another warrant as Purser. I shall only add, my dear Lord, that I feel much interested for Mr. Fellowes, and that I am ever your affectionate,

NELSON AND BRONTE.[3]

TO CAPTAIN SUTTON, H.M. SHIP AMAZON.

[Autograph, in the possession of Captain Ives Sutton.]

Merton, November 27th, 1801.

My dear Sutton,

I have discharged my Steward, James Bell, and also my servant Joseph White, who has behaved ill. You will, therefore, be so good as to discharge them from my retinue. I have had no answer about the Thanks, &c. from London, but I suppose they are ashamed and know not what to do: therefore, my letters are unnoticed. We have had a heavy fall of snow. Pray, make my kind remembrances to the Commodore, Gore, and all our friends, and believe me ever, my dear Sutton, your most obliged,

NELSON AND BRONTE.

[3] It appears, from an indorsement on this letter, that Lord Nelson's wishes could not be complied with, because "the Clerks in this Office rise according to seniority, and it is necessary that the First Clerk should know every branch of business transacted in the Office."

TO ALEXANDER DAVISON, ESQ., ST. JAMES'S SQUARE.

[Autograph, in the possession of Colonel Davison.]

Merton, November 28th, 1801.

My dear Davison,

My Father is going to call upon you this morning. I beg you will offer him the £500, for it is the same to me whether now, or on January 1st. We shall dine at home Sunday, Monday, and Tuesday next. I need not say how happy we shall always be to see as much of you as you please to give us. Mr. Addington has never deigned to answer my letter: the Lord Mayor did yesterday, and said the subject should have an early consideration. Either Lord St. Vincent or myself are liars;—so my affairs stand. Believe me ever, dear Davison, your most obliged and affectionate,

NELSON AND BRONTE.

My letter is withdrawn by advice from Mr. Addington. My Father leaves us on Tuesday morning.

ADMIRAL THE EARL OF ST. VINCENT, K.B.

[Autograph, in the possession of Vice-Admiral Sir William Parker, Bart., G.C.B.]

Merton, December 1st, 1801.

My dear Lord,

His Royal Highness the Duke of Kent has much at heart the welfare of Lieutenant Cowan,[4] and has desired me to state his merits to your notice, as he hopes it will be a means of getting some promotion for him.

I can assure your Lordship that Lieutenant Cowan was certainly the *most* active and zealous Officer of any serving in the Hired Vessels under my command, and is really deserving of your notice, and the friendship of the Duke. With every affectionate wish for your speedy recovery, believe me ever yours most truly,　　　　　NELSON AND BRONTE.

[4] Lieutenant Malcolm Cowan, was made a Commander in October 1802.

TO THE RIGHT HON. HENRY ADDINGTON.

[Autograph, in the Sidmouth Papers.]

Merton, December 2nd, 1801.

My dear Sir,

After the very friendly conversation I had the pleasure of holding with you the other day, on the subject of Medals for the Battle of Copenhagen, I own my vanity, but I trust a laudable one, in sending for your perusal a letter from General Waltersdorff; he at least must have formed a disinterested opinion of my whole conduct. If it is consistent with your station I wish you to see him, for with a true sense of honour, for his own Country, he is a real well-wisher to old England. For ever believe me, my dear Sir, your obliged,

NELSON AND BRONTE.

TO CAPTAIN SUTTON, H.M. SHIP AMAZON.

[Autograph, in the possession of Captain Ives Sutton.]

Merton, December 5th, 1801.

My dear Sutton,

Thanks for your letter, which I should have answered before, but I have not been very well. For what good purpose they can keep you thumping in the Downs, I cannot guess, but they seem determined not to pay Ships off till the Definitive Treaty is signed. Lord St. Vincent's conduct about the Medals for Copenhagen, appears to me extraordinary. I have had a meeting with Mr. Addington on the subject; I don't expect we shall get much by it, except having had a full opportunity of speaking my mind. I will show you, and tell you all when we meet, which I hope will be soon. I seldom go to London, and seldomer to the Admiralty, no longer necessary to keep all quiet. Remember me to all our friends, and believe me ever, your most obliged and affectionate,

NELSON AND BRONTE.

Sir William, Lady Hamilton, and Mrs. Nelson desire their regards.

TO SIR JOHN SINCLAIR, BART.

[From Sir John Sinclair's Correspondence, vol. i. p. 189, who says, "Having sent a Copy of my ' Thoughts on the Naval Strength of the British Empire' to Lord Nelson, I had the pleasure of receiving the following communication in return:"]

Merton, December 8, 1801.

Dear Sir,

I had the honour of receiving through the hands of Mr. Mollison, your very elegant present of a Book, to the subject of which too much attention cannot be paid: and without a compliment, no man in the Country is so able to place this important matter in its proper view before the public. I can hardly believe, however anxiously I have endeavoured to deserve it, the high compliment you are pleased to bestow upon me. But, dear Sir, I beg you to be assured that I am, with every sentiment of obligation, your most obedient servant,

NELSON AND BRONTE.

TO HERCULES ROSS, ESQ., ROSSIE CASTLE, N.B.[5]

[From a Copy in the Nelson Papers.]

Merton, Surrey, December 17th, 1801.

My dear Friend,

I shall certainly with much pleasure receive your friend Mr. M'Donald, whenever he pleases to make me a visit, and I assure you, for your friendship's sake, be very glad to be useful to his son, but I have the least interest of any man in my station of life—indeed, I do not believe I have any; but it may come in a future war, when I may again be wanted. In everything towards your friend's son, I will do what I can, and shall tell him so. It will always give me pleasure to hear of your happiness, and where the parents are good, there is every fair prospect that the children may give comfort to

---

[5] The following particulars of Mr. Ross, which ought to have been inserted in the first volume, have only lately been obligingly communicated by his son, Horatio Ross, Esq., late M.P. for Aberdeen and Montrose, and Lord Nelson's godson. Hercules Ross, Esq. of Rossie Castle, married Miss Parish, daughter of Mr. Parish, of Hamburgh, and died on the 24th of December 1816, leaving three daughters, all of whom are dead, and one son, Horatio Ross, Esq., above mentioned, who married, in 1833, Justina, daughter of Colin Macrae, Esq., and has five sons, "the eldest being, *fo course*, called *Horatio*."

them; and yours, with such examples, cannot fail to do well. I beg my respects to Mrs. Ross, and say that my loss must apologize for my not answering her very friendly and flattering letter, for writing is a very serious inconvenience to me, and I beg you to believe me as ever your much obliged and faithful friend,

NELSON AND BRONTE.

TO ALEXANDER DAVISON, ESQ., ST. JAMES'S SQUARE.

[Autograph, in the possession of Colonel Davison.]

Merton, Friday Morning. [Post-mark, December 18th, 1801.]

My dear Davison,

I am sorry to be disappointed at not coming to you this morning, but General Waltersdorff sent me word he should be here to breakfast to take leave; but I hope to be with you to-morrow, but do not wait for me. The valuation of the diamonds[4] is, as far as I have been told, shameful; therefore, although I am naturally very anxious not to obtrude more on your goodness than necessity obliges me, yet I wish to talk to you on the subject of being *even* a little longer in your debt, taking care, which I hope I shall be able, to secure the payment to you: but more of this to-morrow; and I am, as ever, your most obliged and affectionate,

NELSON AND BRONTE.

I would sooner beg, than *give* those fellows my diamonds.

TO J. HILEY ADDINGTON, ESQ.

[Autograph.]

My dear Sir,   Merton, December 21st, 1801.

Many thanks for your kind letter, and I shall call to thank you in person when I come to Town; but I was ignorant that you was fixed in the Treasury. I am fearful my poor fellow will be disappointed; for I think if he had a vote or interest, he would not have applied to me. Ever, my dear Sir, believe me your obliged,

NELSON AND BRONTE.

---

[4] It appears from this letter, that Lord Nelson was obliged to sell the diamonds with which he had been presented by Foreign Sovereigns.

TO CAPTAIN SUTTON, H.M. SHIP AMAZON.

[Autograph, in the possession of Captain Ives Sutton.]

Merton, December 20th, 1801.

My dear Sir,

I send you a £20 note, which will leave a little to go on with, and, if you please, to give the lads one guinea each[6] when there is a probability of your being paid off. If I can find out any good man commanding a Frigate, I should wish to place Connor with him: Banti must take his chance. I am not going abroad—that you may be assured of. Reports say, the Definitive Treaty will soon be finished, and then, I suppose, we shall all get our discharges; but I cannot obtain even mine. What a waste of Public money! But we hope soon to see you at Merton, where you shall have a hearty welcome; for believe me ever your much obliged,

NELSON AND BRONTE.

Sir William, Lady Hamilton, and Mr. Nelson, desire to wish you a merry Christmas.

---

[6] Mr. Charles Connor and Mr. Banti, Midshipmen of the Amazon.

APPENDIX.

Baron Nelson, Crea-⎱   GEORGE THE THIRD, by the Grace of God, &c., To all
tion of Viscount. ⎰ Archbishops, Dukes, Marquesses, Earls, Viscounts, Bishops,
Barons, Knights, Provosts, Freemen, and all other Our Officers, Ministers, and
Subjects whatsoever, to whom these Presents shall come, Greeting, Know ye that
We, of our especial grace, certain knowledge, and mere motion, have advanced,
preferred, and created Our right trusty and well-beloved HORATIO BARON NELSON,
Knight of the Most Honourable Order of the Bath, and Vice-Admiral of the Blue
Squadron of our Fleet, to the State, Degree, Dignity, and Honour of VISCOUNT
NELSON of the Nile, and of Burnham Thorpe, in our County of Norfolk; and him,
the said Horatio Baron Nelson, Viscount Nelson of the Nile, and of Burnham
Thorpe, aforesaid, do by these Presents create, advance, and prefer; and we have
appointed, given, and granted, and by these Presents, for Us, Our heirs, and successors,
do appoint, give, and grant unto him, the said Horatio Baron Nelson, the Name,
State, Degree, Style, Dignity, Title, and Honour of Viscount Nelson of the Nile,
and of Burnham Thorpe, aforesaid, to have and to hold the said Name, State,
Degree, Style, Dignity, Title, and Honour of Viscount Nelson of the Nile, and of
Burnham Thorpe, aforesaid, unto him the said Horatio Baron Nelson, and the
heirs male of his body, lawfully begotten, and to be begotten. Willing, and by
these presents, granting for Us, Our heirs, and successors, that he, the said Horatio
Baron Nelson, and his heirs male aforesaid, and every of them successively, may
bear and have the Name, State, Degree, Style, Dignity, Title, and Honour of Viscount
Nelson of the Nile, and of Burnham Thorpe aforesaid; and that they and every
of them successively, may be called and styled by the name of Viscount Nelson
of the Nile, and of Burnham Thorpe, in Our County of Norfolk; and that he, the
said Horatio Baron Nelson, and his heirs male aforesaid, and every of them suc
cessively, may in all things be held and deemed Viscounts Nelson of the Nile,
and of Burnham Thorpe aforesaid, and be held, treated, and reputed as Viscounts;
and that they, and every of them successively and respectively, may have, hold, and
possess a seat, place, and voice in the Parliaments and Public Assemblies and
Councils of Us, Our heirs and successors within our United Kingdom of Great
Britain and Ireland, amongst other Viscounts, as Viscounts of Parliament, and
Public Assemblies, and Councils. And also, that he, the said Horatio Baron
Nelson, and his heirs male aforesaid, may enjoy and use, and every of them suc-
cessively may enjoy and use, by the name of Viscount Nelson of the Nile, and of
Burnham Thorpe aforesaid, all and singular the rights, privileges, pre-eminences,
immunities, and advantages to the degree of a Viscount in all things duly and of
right belonging, which other Viscounts of this Our United Kingdom of Great
Britain and Ireland have heretofore honourably and quietly used and enjoyed, or as
they do at present use and enjoy. Lastly, we will, and by these presents for Us,
Our heirs, and successors, do grant to the said Horatio Baron Nelson, and his heirs
Male aforesaid, that these our Letters Patent, or the enrolment thereof, shall be
sufficient and effectual in the law for the dignifying, investing, and really ennobling
him, the said Horatio Baron Nelson, and his heirs male aforesaid, with the Name,
Title, Dignity, and Honour of Viscount Nelson of the Nile, and of Burnham
Thorpe aforesaid, and this without any investiture, rites, ornaments, or ceremonies

whatsoever, in this behalf due and accustomed, which, for some certain reasons best known to Us, We could not in due manner do and perform; any ordinance, use, custom, rite, ceremony, prescription, or provision due, or used or to be had, done, or performed, in conferring Honours of this kind, or any other matter or thing to the contrary thereof, notwithstanding. We will also, &c., without Fine in the Hanaper, &c. In witness, &c., witness, &c., the twenty-second day of May.

By Writ of Privy Seal.

No. II.

COPY OF THE PATENT CREATING THE BARONY OF NELSON OF THE NILE AND OF HILBOROUGH, DATED THE 18TH OF AUGUST, 1801.

Horatio, Viscount Nelson, Creation of a Baron, with Remainders. } GEORGE THE THIRD, by the grace of God, &c., to all Archbishops, Dukes, Marquesses, Earls, Viscounts, Bishops, Barons, Knights, Provosts, Freemen, and all other Our Officers, Ministers, and Subjects whatsoever to whom these Presents shall come, Greeting. Know ye that We, in our consideration of the great and important services that renowned man, HORATIO VISCOUNT NELSON, hath rendered to Us and to Our Realm, and in order to perpetuate to the latest posterity the remembrance of his glorious actions, and to incite others to imitate his examples, of Our especial grace, certain knowledge, and mere motion, have advanced, preferred, and created our right trusty and well-beloved cousin, the said Horatio Viscount Nelson, Knight of the Most Honourable Order of the Bath, and Vice-Admiral of the Blue Squadron of our Fleet, Duke of Bronté in Sicily, Knight of the Grand Cross of the Order of Saint Ferdinand and of Merit, and of the Imperial Order of the Crescent, to the State, Degree, Dignity, and Honour of BARON NELSON OF THE NILE AND OF HILBOROUGH, in Our county of Norfolk, and him, the said Horatio Viscount Nelson, Baron Nelson of the Nile and of Hilborough, aforesaid, do by these presents, create, advance, and prefer, and We have appointed, given, and granted, and by these Presents, for Us, Our heirs and successors, do appoint, give, and grant, unto him, the said Horatio, Viscount Nelson, the Name, State, Degree, Style, Dignity, Title, and Honour, of Baron Nelson of the Nile and of Hilborough aforesaid, to have, and to hold the said Name, State, Degree, Style, Dignity, Title, and Honour, of Baron Nelson of the Nile and of Hilborough aforesaid, unto him, the said Horatio Viscount Nelson, and the heirs male of his body, lawfully begotten, and to be begotten; and in default of such issue to our trusty and well-beloved Edmund Nelson, Clerk, Rector of Burnham Thorpe, in Our said County of Norfolk, father of the said Horatio Viscount Nelson, and the heirs male of his body lawfully begotten; and in default of such issue, to the heirs male of the body of Susanna, the wife of Thomas Bolton, Esquire, and sister of the said Horatio, Viscount Nelson, lawfully begotten, and to be begotten, severally and successively, one after another, as they shall be in seniority of age and priority of birth; and in default of such issue, to the heirs male of the body of Catherine, the wife of George Matcham, Esquire, another sister of the said Horatio Viscount Nelson, lawfully begotten and to be begotten, severally and successively, one after another, as they shall be in seniority of age and priority of birth; willing and by these presents granting for Us, our heirs and successors, that the said Horatio Viscount Nelson, and the heirs male of his body aforesaid; and in default of such issue, the said Edmund Nelson and the heirs male of his body aforesaid; and in default of such issue, the heirs male of the body of the said Susanna Bolton, severally and successively, as aforesaid; and in default of such issue, the heirs male of the body of the said Catherine Matcham, severally and successively as aforesaid; and every of them successively may bear and have the Name, State, Degree, Style, Dignity, Title, and Honour of Baron Nelson of the Nile and of Hilborough aforesaid, and that they and every of them successively, may be called and styled by the name of Baron Nelson of the Nile and of Hilborough, in Our County of Norfolk; and that he, the said Horatio Viscount Nelson, and the heirs male of his body aforesaid, and in default of such issue, the said Edmund Nelson, and the heirs male of his body aforesaid, and in default of such issue, the heirs male of the body of the said Susanna Bolton, severally and successively, as aforesaid, and in default of such issue, the heirs male of the body of the said Catherine Matcham, severally and successively, as aforesaid, and every of them successively, may in all things, be held and deemed Barons Nelson of the Nile and of Hilborough, aforesaid, and be created and reputed as Barons; and that they, and every of them, successively and respectively, may have, hold, and possess a seat, place, and voice in the Parliament and Public Assemblies and Councils of Us, Our heirs, and successors, within our United Kingdom of Great Britain and Ireland, amongst other Barons, as Barons of Parliament and Public Assemblies and Councils; and also, that the said Horatio Viscount Nelson, and the heirs male of his body, aforesaid, and in default of such issue, the said Edmund Nelson and the heirs male of his body, aforesaid, and in default of such issue, the heirs male of the body of the said Susanna Bolton, severally and successively, as aforesaid, and in default of such issue, the heirs male of the body of the said Catherine Matcham, severally and successively, as aforesaid, may enjoy and use, and every of them successively may enjoy and use, by the name of Baron Nelson of the Nile, and of Hilborough, aforesaid, all and singular, the rights, privileges, pre-eminences, immunities, and advantages to the degree of Baron in all things, duly and of right belonging, which other Barons of this our United Kingdom of Great Britain and Ireland have heretofore honourably and quietly used and enjoyed, or as they do at present use and enjoy. Lastly, We will, and by these Presents, for Us, Our heirs, and successors, do grant to the said Horatio Viscount Nelson, that these our Letters Patent, or the enrolment thereof, shall be sufficient and effectual in the law for the dignifying, investing, and really ennobling him, the said Horatio Viscount Nelson, and the heirs male of his body aforesaid, and in default of such issue, the said Edmund Nelson and the heirs male of his body aforesaid, and in default of such issue, the heirs male of the body of the said Susanna Bolton, severally and successively, as aforesaid, and in default of such issue, the heirs male of the body of the said Catherine Matcham, severally and successively, as aforesaid, with the Title, State, Dignity, and Honour of Baron Nelson of the Nile and of Hilborough, aforesaid, and this without any investiture, rites, ornaments, or cere- monies whatsoever, in this behalf due and accustomed, which for some certain reasons best known to Us, We could not in due manner do and perform, any ordinance, use, custom, rite, ceremony, prescription, or provision, due, or used, or to be had, done, or performed, in conferring Honours of this kind, or any other matter or thing to the contrary thereof, notwithstanding. And it is Our Royal will and pleasure, that the person and persons who shall hereafter from time to time succeed to the said Title and Dignity of Baron Nelson of the Nile and of Hilborough aforesaid, shall respectively take and use the Surname of Nelson only. We will also, &c., without Fine in the Hanaper, &c. In witness, &c., witness, &c., the eighteenth day of August. By Writ of Privy Seal.